THE NUCLEAR CLUB

THE NUCLEAR CLUB

HOW AMERICA AND THE WORLD POLICED
THE ATOM FROM HIROSHIMA TO VIETNAM

Jonathan R. Hunt

STANFORD UNIVERSITY PRESS
Stanford, California

STANFORD UNIVERSITY PRESS
Stanford, California

The views expressed in this book are those of the author alone and do not represent the views of the U.S. Government, the Department of Defense, or the U.S. Air Force.

Printed in the United States of America on acid-free, archival-quality paper

Library of Congress Cataloging-in-Publication Data

Names: Hunt, Jonathan R., author.
Title: The nuclear club : how America and the world policed the atom from Hiroshima to Vietnam / Jonathan R. Hunt.
Description: Stanford, California : Stanford University Press, 2022. | Includes bibliographical references and index.
Identifiers: LCCN 2021052384 (print) | LCCN 2021052385 (ebook) | ISBN 9781503630086 (cloth) | 9781503636309 (paper) | ISBN 9781503631724 (ebook)
Subjects: LCSH: Nuclear nonproliferation—History. | Nuclear arms control—Government policy—History. | Nuclear nonproliferation—Government policy—United States—History. | Nuclear arms control—Government policy—United States—History. | United States—Foreign relations—1945-1989.
Classification: LCC JZ5675 .H857 2022 (print) | LCC JZ5675 (ebook) | DDC 327.1/747—dc23/eng/20211122
LC record available at https://lccn.loc.gov/2021052384
LC ebook record available at https://lccn.loc.gov/2021052385

Cover Design: Zoe Norvell
Cover Photograph: Alamy, CWAP68

Typeset by Newgen in Adobe Garamond Pro 10/13.5

For my parents
&
for Terry and Carissa Chang

Contents

Acknowledgments

In Alexander Dumas's *The Count of Monte Cristo*, how Edmond Dantès recounts his flight from the island prison of Château d'If to avenge his honor and reclaim his lost love offers a parable for the thrill of writing the acknowledgments to one's own book: "How did I escape? With difficulty. How did I plan this moment? With pleasure." In contrast to Dantès, I had the good fortune of not one Abbé Faria in the cell next door but a host of companions who enriched my journey in ways that surpassed any hidden treasure. They have gilded me with laughter. They have showered me with wit. They have bejeweled my life with their generosity.

This book has had many homes and benefactors: the Department of Strategy at the U.S. Air War College, the History Department at the University of Southampton, Carnegie Corporation of New York, the Fox Center for Humanistic Inquiry at Emory University, the Stanton Nuclear Security Fellows Program at RAND Corporation, the Center for International Security and Cooperation (CISAC) at Stanford University, the Center on International Conflict and Negotiation at Stanford Law School, the Davis Center for Russian and Eurasian Studies at Harvard University, the Rothermere American Institute at the University of Oxford, the Kennan Institute at the Woodrow Wilson International Center for Scholars, the Eisenhower Institute at Gettysburg College, the George C. Marshall Foundation, the Society for Historians of American Foreign Relations (SHAFR), the U.S. Department of Education, and the Department of History at my alma mater, the University of Texas at Austin. Their support has funded visits to thirty archives in eleven countries, dedicated writing time, and an education in both history and the world.

If historians engage in arguments without end, they rely on their peers to temper their too-bold claims as well as archivists and librarians to leaven their intuitions with truth. This book would have been impossible without the assistance of a wealth of libraries, archives, and digital collections: in Paris—Les Archives d'histoire contemporaine, Centre d'histoire, Sciences Po; and Les Archives des affaires étrangères; La Bibliothèque nationale de France;—in London—the UK National Archives; the British Library of Political and Economic Science; and the British Library— in Dublin—the University College Dublin Archives and the National Archives of Ireland—in Ottawa—Library and Archives Canada—in Mexico City—lo Archivo de la Secretaría de Relaciones Exteriores—in Vienna—the International Atomic Energy Agency (IAEA) archives—in Brussels—NATO Archives—in Geneva—the International Committee of the Red Cross archives—in Moscow—Российский государственный архив новейшей истории—in Florence—the Historical Archives of the European Union—and across the United States—the Library of Congress; the George C. Marshall Library; the U.S. National Archives II; the Dwight D. Eisenhower Presidential Library; the John F. Kennedy Presidential Library; the Lyndon Baines Johnson Presidential Library; the Richard Nixon Presidential Library; the University of Pennsylvania's Kislak Center; Yale University's Beinecke Library, Providence College archives; NYU's Fales Library; the Julian Edison Department of Special Collections, Washington University; the Peace Collection at Swarthmore College; Princeton University's Public Policy papers; the United Nations archive in New York; and Harvard University's Project on Cold War Studies. I owe debts to Jayita Sarkar, Michelle Paranzino, Michael Morgan, Yogesh Joshi, Sergei Radchenko, and Joseph Torigian for sharing and even translating documents, and to Will and Marcie Foster and their family for sharing their memories and photographs. I was heartbroken to learn that Marcie passed away a few months before this book went to print. To those at the National Security Archive at George Washington University, especially Jim Hersberg and Bill Burr, and the Wilson Center, above all Christian Ostermann and Charles Kraus, this book would not have been possible without you.

The book has benefited from critical feedback at the University of Oxford's Department of Politics and International Relations and Rothermere American Institute, the University of Vienna, the University of Southampton, Science Po, the London School of Economics's Department of International History, the University of Stockholm, the Wilson Center, Tokyo's National Graduate Institute for Policy Studies, King's College London, the United Nations, ETH Zürich's Center for Security Studies, and London's Institute of Historical Research, in addition to meetings of the Historians of the Twentieth Century United States (HOTCUS), the History of Science Three-Society Meeting, Stanford CISAC's Social Science Seminar, the Pacific Coast Branch of the American Historical Association (AHA) and the annual AHA conference; the SHAFR Summer Institute, the Nuclear Studies Research Initiative, the Stanton Nuclear Security Fellows Seminar, the American Society for Environmental Historians, the European Summer School on Cold War History, and SHAFR.

My mentors and peers have left their fingerprints on every page of this book. Bill Brands and Mark Atwood Lawrence taught me how to write history and, most importantly, how to ask the right questions. They were the perfect advisors for a fresh-faced PhD student whose reach often exceeded his grasp. They were far from the only suppliers in Austin of good humor, faith, and advice. Christopher Dietrich, Renny Keller, Rachel Herrmann, Yana Skorobogatov, Cameron Strang, Christopher Heaney, Pablo Mijangos, Sarah Steinbock-Pratt, Tanvi Madan, Michelle Paranzino, Margaret Peacock, Eleanor Douglas, Brett Bennett, Joseph Parrott, Trevor Simmons, Peter Hamilton, Megan Reiss, Bob Whitaker, Storm Miller, Paul Rubinson, Marc Palen, and many others challenged and sustained me. Frank Gavin, Jeremi Suri, Charters Wynn, and Bruce Hunt read drafts of my dissertation. By then David Holloway, Scott Sagan, Lynn Eden, Norman Naimark, Sig Hecker, and Bart Bernstein had taken me under their wings at Stanford CISAC, where Malfrid Braut-Hegghammer, Vipin Narang, Benoît Pelopidas, Gil-li Vardi, Francesca Giovannini, Matt Daniels, Rob Rakove, Rebecca Slayton, Bertel Hansen, James Cameron, Emma Rosengren, Daniel Altman, Elaine Korzak, Neil Narang, Niccolo Petrelli, and Benjamin Wilson made my time in Silicon Valley rich and memorable. At RAND Corporation, Lynn Davis, Sarah Harting, Paula Thornhill, Sameer Lalwani, and Caroline Reilly Milne sharpened my analytical edge. At Emory, Johanna Winant and Rebecca Munson (who has left us far too soon) made Atlanta feel like home. I spent five rewarding years at the University of Southampton. Thanks are due to Kendrick Oliver, who hired and mentored me, and also to Chris Fuller, Eve Colpus, David Cox, Elisabeth Forster, George Gilbert, Pritipuspa Mishra, Christer Petley, Chris Prior, Charlotte Riley, Helen Spurling, Joan Tumblety, and Fiona Bowler, among so many others, who furnished intellectual ballast and taught a Texan how to be passably droll. Since I arrived at the U.S. Air War College, Patrick Budjenska, Carl Forsberg, Howard Hensel, Alex Lassner, David Palkki, Doug Peifer, Stephen Renner, Corbin Williamson, and Will Waddell have broadened my strategic horizons. Over the past decade, Or Rabinowitz, Hassan Elbahtimy, Malcolm Craig, Fintan Hoey, Thomas Jonter, Andreas Lutsch, J. Luis Rodriguez, Poldo Nuti, Carlo Patti, Elisabeth Röhrlich, Melvyn Leffler, David Painter, James Graham Wilson, Susie Colbourn, Mattias Haeussler, Stephanie Freeman, Sarah Snyder, Lauren Turek, Evan McCormick, Jennie Miller, Ryan Musto, Andrea Chiampan, Aiyaz Husain, Zach Fredman, Charlie Laderman, Jooeun Kim, David Fields, Henry Maar, Lydia Walker, Amanda Behm, Alexander Lanoszka, Simon Miles, Toshi Higuchi, Joseph Torigian, and Greg Brew have been collaborators as well as good company.

I could not have asked for a better team than the one I found at Stanford University Press. Alan Harvey steered the manuscript through reefs and shoals thrown up by authorial reticence and errant footnotes with timely assistance from Caroline McKusick and Cat Ng Pavel. The two anonymous reviewers markedly improved the manuscript by requesting clarifications and spotting where I had erred. What errors remain are my own.

I wish to acknowledge Routledge for granting me permission to adapt portions of my chapter, "Mexican Nuclear Diplomacy, the Latin American Nuclear-Weapon-Free Zone, & the NPT Grand Bargain, 1962–1968," in *Negotiating the Nuclear Non-Proliferation Treaty: The Making of a Nuclear Order*, edited by Andreas Wenger, Roland Popp, and Liviu Horovitz (New York: Routledge, 2017) and also Oxford University press for permission to adapt sections of my chapter "The Birth of an International Community: Negotiating the Treaty on the Non-Proliferation of Nuclear Weapons, in *Foreign Policy Breakthroughs: Cases in Successful Diplomacy*, edited by Robert L. Hutchings and Jeremi Suri (New York: Oxford University Press, 2015).

I count Elisabeth Leake, Harry Bullivant, James Cameron, Rob Rakove, Chris Dietrich, Veronica Jiménez Vega, Jeffrey Brideau, Estrella Bernal Amador, Bryan Gibson, Ashli Alberty Gibson, Daniel Blahut, Yasemin Ozcan, Brandon Hunter, Marc Palen, Rachel Herrmann, Brian McNeil, and José Cueto among my dear friends. They made this odyssey more enjoyable than it had any right to be. Todd Embleton, Shane Cleveland, Adam Carpenter, Philip Ilgenstein, and Jacob Kern have been with me since the beginning—they have never let me forget where I came from.

Without my family, I would never have become the person, let alone the scholar, I am today. My brother Tommy preceded me as a professor. His students at the University of Texas are lucky to have him, as are my nephews, Pierce and Bentsen, and my sister-in-law Hilary. On second thought, they're lucky to have one another. My father, Tom Hunt, has set Olympian standards for integrity, industry, and intelligence. He is my benchmark. My mother, Laurie Hunt, is a blessing and a force. She is my rock. My uncle, Paul "Pepper" Pierce, passed away this past summer—his laughter and his service live on with us, as do memories of my grandparents.

The greatest compensation this book has gifted me is the brilliant woman I met in San Diego in 2016 and the sparkling family—Terry, Carissa, and Hughie—that would accompany my wife. Since then Vivien Chang and I have been halfway around the world and back again, with Digby now riding herd over us. She is the smile on my face, our life together my greatest treasure.

THE NUCLEAR CLUB

Introduction

The Most Exclusive Club on Earth

It is most important, of course, that the [Nuclear Nonproliferation] Treaty is signed by those who are capable of making a bomb. I think that we will not be successful at avoiding small wars in the future, but allowing a large war with the use of nuclear weapons would be insane.

—U.S. senator George Aiken speaking to Pravda *reporter Yuri G. A. Zhukov on Capitol Hill, January 23, 1969.*[1]

THE RELATIONSHIP BETWEEN THE VIETNAM WAR and nuclear weapons was on Walt Rostow's mind as he addressed the National War College's Class of 1968 beneath a cloudless sky in Washington, D.C. While across the National Mall, President Lyndon Johnson's White House digested the headlines on the morning of May 8— Robert Kennedy's victory in Indiana's Democratic primary and National Liberation Front mortar attacks on Saigon—Rostow surveyed the horizon beyond the Anacostia River from Fort Lesley J. McNair.

How long, he asked the graduating officers in their dress uniforms, until "Germany, Japan, Italy, India, and others" built the atom bomb? The Treaty on the Non-Proliferation of Nuclear Weapons (NPT) that the United Nations (UN) was debating in New York would ask for higher sacrifices than the North Atlantic Treaty Organization (NATO) or the Alliance for Progress in Latin America, for which the United States had merely assumed a "due share in a communal effort." To the average American voter or to foreign leaders fearful of second- or third-class status, the U.S. State Department had billed the agreement as a natural successor to the 1963 Treaty Banning

Nuclear Weapon Tests in the Atmosphere, in Outer Space, and Under Water—"that is, an exercise in U.S.-Soviet *détente*, a good deed in a naughty world." In truth, U.S. leaders and their Soviet counterparts shared a compelling interest in halting "the potential diffusion of power at its most important point." This new world order would require, above all, a steady appetite for overseas adventures to enforce on the world's unruly masses a common law for the nuclear age. The treaty negotiations thus marked a subtle but momentous shift in how the world governed itself with the help of far-flung U.S. legionnaires, as Rostow and Johnson prepared to lock the country "into responsibility in the world—right around the periphery of Communist China and the Soviet Union, on the toughest of all issues."[2]

As Rostow linked victory in Vietnam to an endless crusade against the runaway atom, the UN First Committee was meeting in Manhattan's tony midtown neighborhood of Turtle Bay. Over the first eight plenary sessions clear divisions had revealed themselves in the sprawling complex, where representatives from developing countries faced off against those with commanding leads in world nuclear markets. On 16 May, Mexican deputy foreign minister Alfonso García Robles made the case for surgical revisions to the NPT that would help atomic newcomers catch up to more industrialized countries. To drive his points home, he compared the new accord with the Treaty for the Prohibition of Nuclear Weapons in Latin America, known as the Treaty of Tlatelolco after the Aztec square in Mexico City where it had been finalized the previous year, whose lack of discriminatory features made it "far superior to the draft before us."[3] For the NPT to earn a commanding majority in the UN General Assembly (UNGA), where Latin American and African delegations had enjoyed numerical dominance since 1965, García Robles challenged his audience to revise its preamble and articles so that they looked more like those in the Treaty of Tlatelolco.

After the Second World War, a cosmopolitan community of politicians, activists, bureaucrats, scientists, and diplomats constructed a near-universal regime to manage the most powerful technology ever devised—the power to split or fuse atomic nuclei to release wondrous new isotopes for medical cures and energy production or unprecedented explosive force for mass destruction and death. After numerous false starts, their campaign bore fruit in the 1960s, when multiplying regional crises and an emerging world market in fission reactors led an international society in the throes of decolonization to draw up a Magna Carta for the subatomic realm.

In combination with the Limited Test Ban Treaty (LTBT), referred to at the time as the Moscow Treaty, and the Treaty of Tlatelolco, the NPT enforced five rules for the nuclear realm.[4] First, nuclear experiments that states conduct cannot spread radioactive fallout beyond their borders or those of trustee territories, effectively sealing them underground. Second, in the event they agreed among themselves, regional blocs can banish atomic means of destruction from their neighborhoods. Third, the official nuclear club would close to new entrants on New Year's Day 1967, with the United States, the United Kingdom, France, the Soviet Union, and the People's Republic of China (PRC) prestigiously included as legacy members. Fourth, the international community recognized an inalienable right to peaceful science and technology. Finally, in exchange for legitimation under international law, the five legacy members, now authorized as nuclear-weapon states, would make concerted efforts to reduce and ultimately eliminate the world-threatening arsenals that distinguished them from the atomic unarmed.

Today the global nonproliferation regime that the NPT constituted is a centerpiece of world politics. The United States, the United Kingdom, and the Soviet Union moved all their nuclear testing underground after August 1963. France followed suit in 1974, and the PRC six years after that. More than fifty years later, the Treaty of Tlatelolco remains a template for existing and prospective zones free of nuclear weapons in the South Pacific, Southeast Asia, Africa, central Asia, and the Middle East. Since 1968, on net the unofficial nuclear club has grown by only four members. Four countries—South Africa, Kazakhstan, Belarus, and Ukraine—gave up their arsenals during that time, as the United States, at times authorized by the UN Security Council (UNSC) and at others abetted by willing partners, has intervened repeatedly to inhibit nuclear spread by means of financial sanctions, cyberattacks, cruise missiles, covert assassinations, and foreign expeditions. So far the global nuclear nonproliferation regime has for the most part achieved its headline goal—to ensure that the peaceful atom would not be diverted to violent ends. It has done so by perpetuating hierarchy among nations at the cost of displacing violence from the developed to the developing worlds—a marriage of convenience between humanitarian ideals and U.S. military supremacy.

The Nuclear Club recounts how what began as an attempt to build world government under law became a warrant for defying the UN Charter. If there is a central myth of the nuclear age, it is that nuclear arms rendered great-power war obsolete.[5] While scholars have taken pains to identify the exact conditions that ushered in this "Long Peace"—or disputed its scope or the necessity of nuclear weapons to it—most agree that the nuclear revolution has been a major determinant of patterns of war and peace since 1945.[6] What these narratives omit is the correlation between the stability that nuclear deterrence has enforced—the non-occurrence of shooting wars between nuclear-club members—and the frequency of civil wars, proxy conflicts, and territorial disputes for those outside its ranks.[7] The Long Peace has been real but far from universal. World War III has not happened (yet), but the scourge of war continues to afflict those denied membership in the world's most exclusive club.

The NPT's founding purpose was not peace but rather to nip the revolutionary potential of atomic physics in the bud. The global nuclear nonproliferation regime established more than a set of laws, rules, and norms to regulate atomic power worldwide—it sanctified UNSC permanent members' nuclear arsenals and also their right to intervene abroad to save humanity from the Promethean handiwork they themselves had wrought. Many features distinguished the geographic core in North America and western Eurasia, where the Long Peace prevailed, from what Paul Chamberlin styles the Cold War's "killing fields" in Asia and the Middle East.[8] Among them was a distinction between the members of the nuclear club—foremost among them the world's chief hegemon, the United States—and those whom they promised to protect from themselves, a dividing line that has outlived the Cold War. Weeks before Rostow's commencement speech on the banks of the Washington Channel, French foreign ministry lawyers had noticed that the UNSC resolution that would accompany the NPT hierarchized forms of aggression by elevating nuclear above non-nuclear forms of state violence while introducing into public international law an "ambiguous concept of 'menace.'" Theirs was a premonition of how nuclear nonproliferation would join humanitarian intervention as the chief caveats to the UN Charter's general ban on wars of aggression.[9] Thirty-three years after the NPT entered into force, their prophecy would be realized in the ruins of Iraq and the decades of upheaval that Operation Enduring Freedom would unleash in and around the Middle East.

I

The NPT concluded on 19 June 1968, where it had begun: in the UN General Assembly Hall, a cavernous, 1,898-seat circular room dominated by an Arctic map wreathed in olive branches—the emblem of the UN. It had been nearly ten years since the day in September 1958 when Irish foreign minister Frank Aiken brought home his motion at the thirteenth UNGA for a nuclear restriction with a plea to "preserve a *Pax Atomica* while we build a *Pax Mundi*."[10]

In the intervening years hundreds of plenary sessions convened in the Ten-Nation Committee on Disarmament (TNDC), the Eighteen Nation Committee on Disarmament (ENDC), the UN Disarmament Commission (UNDC), and the UN General Assembly, which passed eight resolutions on prevention of wider dissemination or on nonproliferation of nuclear weapons, and another twenty-three that addressed nuclear testing, weapon-free zones, or wholesale prohibitions.[11] Together the North Atlantic Council (NAC), the Warsaw Pact Political Consultative Committee, the International Meeting of Communist and Workers' Parties, the Conference of Non-Aligned Countries, the Afro-Asian People's Solidarity Organization (AAPSO), the European Economic Community (EEC), the Pugwash Conferences on Science and World Affairs, and the International Atomic Energy Agency (IAEA) devoted hundreds of hours to the subject. From March 1965 to February 1967, the Preparatory Commission for the Denuclearization of Latin America (COPREDAL) held fifty meetings to discuss the terms of regional denuclearization. From April to June 1968, the First Committee of the UN General Assembly met twenty-seven times to deliberate over a final draft nonproliferation treaty. A full accounting of all bilateral contacts in these years about these three agreements is beyond the grasp of any one scholar, while in recent years their direct descendants—the 1972 Strategic Arms Limitation (SALT) Treaty and Anti-Ballistic Missile (ABM) Treaty and the 1975 Helsinki Final Act—have themselves received book-length treatments.[12]

The NPT consummated a transition from basic anarchy to imperfect order in world nuclear affairs. Today its preamble and eleven articles enjoy more popularity than consensus. Interpretations diverged from the beginning. When the UN First Committee read the consensus text drafted by the ENDC on 26 April 1968, U.S. ambassador Arthur Goldberg credited "all nations, large and small," for inscribing into the accord three major purposes—to halt nuclear spread, to foster peaceful uses of atomic energy, and to spur disarmament, above all that of nuclear armaments. It was an early presentation of a grand bargain resting atop three pillars: nuclear nonproliferation, development, and disarmament. Later that afternoon, Soviet deputy foreign minister Vasily Kuznetsov told a different tale from the same dais, insisting that the compact had originated with a predominant motive—to close "all channels, both direct and indirect, leading to the possession of mass destruction weapons."[13]

These two readings—grand bargain and nonproliferation first—have set the terms of debates ever since. This dispute over original intent has unfolded in a world where nuclear threats remain a fact of life. For the lead U.S. negotiator in the 1960s, U.S. Arms Control and Disarmament Agency (ACDA) director William Foster, the treaty internationalized nuclear security through a combination of security assurances, regulated markets, and voice opportunities.[14] Soviet officials, by contrast, embraced a superpower condominium to restrain their historic assailant, the German nation, and marginalize their fraternal rival, the PRC.[15] The nuclear nonproliferation regime has consequently upheld two contradictory goals: to reduce the role that weaponized fission and fusion play in world politics and to confirm the importance of nuclear-backed security guarantees, above all between the United States and its Western European and East Asian allies. This paradox was visible as soon as the treaty opened for signature on 1 July 1968, when Johnson graciously announced that he and Soviet premier Alexei Kosygin would launch SALT and ABM talks "in the nearest future."[16] That summer, his administration reaffirmed standing commitments to respond with the full weight of U.S. armed might in the event that NATO members or Japan were to receive atomic threats while also underscoring the cast-iron link between allies' atomic forbearance and the presence of nuclear umbrellas over their heads.

This constitutional tension between disarmament and deterrence led many to conclude that the NPT resegregated international society in the 1960s by petrifying most states in positions of atomic inferiority. After all, the UNSC resolution that passed alongside the NPT obligated nuclear-armed, permanent members of the UNSC (whose veto rights embodied the original sin against sovereign equality in the UN Charter) to act immediately in response to acts or threats of nuclear violence.[17] The atomic triumvirate of the United States, the United Kingdom, and the Soviet Union issued identical vows. By the time the resolution passed on 19 June 1968, however, even such a stalwart of the nonaligned movement as the Republic of India had lost faith in collective security. The *Times of India*'s Washington correspondent, H. R. Vohra, observed how the NPT would cleave the world in three: the nuclear club, their sheltering allies, and those with "neither a treaty guarantee nor a promise of the security offered by the tripartite declaration and the tripartite resolution in the Security Council."[18]

In countries haunted by colonialism, the NPT resembled fetters set out to trap them before they ascended to international society's summit. The discrimination that postcolonial elites feared was neither primarily military nor geopolitical, but related to economic development and international status. Governments in Brazil, Mexico, and India worried that the treaty would perpetuate their dependence on wealthy, industrial nations. As New Delhi's delegate to the ENDC in Geneva, V. C. Trivedi, declared in 1967, his government could "tolerate a nuclear weapons apartheid, but not an atomic apartheid in their economic and peaceful development."[19] Chinese Communist Party (CCP) authorities were blunter. Even as the Cultural Revolution decimated its diplomatic corps, PRC premier Zhou Enlai accused the United States, the United Kingdom, and the Soviet Union of plotting to "turn non-nuclear countries into their protectorates and press forward with a new type of colonialism."[20]

Yet the global nuclear nonproliferation regime did more than divide the world into those who had been quick to manufacture nuclear arms and those now damned to survive without them. It re-legitimated a still-emergent order of alliances, clubs, markets, norms, and laws that would manage globalization and its discontents as the advanced and developing worlds debated the meaning of sovereign equality enshrined in the UN Charter since 1945. The regime confirmed the United States as first among equals, guardian of the "free world" from communist advances and of humanity from thermonuclear extinction. Its preeminence in the fields of finance, oceanic shipping, high technology, mass consumption, and industrial production had made it an architect of world order since the First World War.[21] Even before the achievements of the Manhattan Project were counted, no country held a candle to the North American colossus after the Second World War, when a U.S.-based power elite cemented their self-assigned roles as globalization's helmsmen, wielding arms and money in service of what Rostow would later characterize as an ersatz common law for the Cold War. Like other elements of the U.S.-led international order, the nuclear nonproliferation regime both empowered and constrained the leading state, whose supply of public, club, and private goods represented the going rate for the right to define global rules. Relative to the nuclear club, the cardinal rule was straightforward: those from states that had demonstrated atomic power before 1967 and henceforth upheld the NPT would be treated as the planet's nuclear guardians. Those who did so afterward would be branded volatile upstarts or dangerous rogues.[22]

For all its discriminatory thrust, the nonproliferation regime offered something to everybody. For the United Kingdom, the Soviet Union, France, and even the PRC, the benefits were clear: a freeze in the nuclear club's membership, which, after 1971 (when the PRC replaced the Republic of China in the UN) mirrored the UNSC's veto-wielding permanent members. For superpower allies, the novel arrangement would enhance their voice opportunities, guarantee their market access, and reaffirm their security relationships (albeit in the form of a protection racket for Warsaw Pact members).[23] Such aspirant regional powers as Israel, West Germany, South Africa, Brazil, Japan, and India could eye advanced nuclear infrastructures with few external restraints. If the NPT banned nuclear tests, it also implicitly authorized states to build world-class constellations (under safeguards) of breeder reactors accompanied by plutonium-reprocessing and uranium-enrichment facilities—closed fuel cycles that would mitigate or even forestall foreign dependence and strategically position them on the verge of the next great energy regime—or a latent nuclear-weapon capability.[24]

For lesser powers, the regime would keep a lid on regional arms races in which they had no business competing. India's neighbors were cases in point. Iran belonged to the Central Treaty Organization (CENTO), of which Pakistan was a member in addition to the Southeast Asia Treaty Organization (SEATO), both weak alliances designed to hold Moscow and Beijing—not New Delhi—at bay. Afghanistan, Nepal, Burma, Sri Lanka, Malaysia, and Indonesia lacked even those weak reeds. Small nonwhite nations dominated the UN General Assembly by the spring of 1968, by which time twenty-four Latin American and thirty-two African delegations sat alongside nine Middle Eastern and seventeen Asian counterparts. Altogether, Third World nations accounted for two-thirds of the member states. Most of the 124 countries represented in Turtle Bay had scant prospects of amassing large amounts of fissile material (enriched uranium or reprocessed plutonium), let alone the technical expertise to transmute it into explosives. They were receptive to arguments that only the superpowers, ideally moderated by the UN system, could keep their more formidable neighbors in check, and hopeful that peaceful atomic energy might one day turbocharge their economic development. Together they constituted a pivotal voting bloc on 12 June 1968, when the UN General Assembly roundly commended the NPT and requested that the depositary governments in Moscow, London, and Washington, D.C., open the accord for signature and ratification as soon as possible.

All told, fifty-five countries would sign one of the treaty copies on 1 July 1968. They did so for a variety of reasons. Most universal was a yearning for control over their atomic fates. When presented with a choice between nuclearizing local territorial disputes over Berlin, Palestine, Kashmir, Tibet, the Taiwan Strait, the Korean peninsula, or Cuba, or formalized superpower meddling in their backyards, a majority of states—if not necessarily of humanity—voted yes. The day before Rostow's speech at the National War College, Iranian ambassador Mehdi Vakil had dubbed the NPT a small step for which the less-powerful nations would have to take the lead. He reckoned that it would not be "a bad role in which to be cast."[25]

II

The Nuclear Club is a history of nuclear nonproliferation as an idea, a policy, and a regime. From 1945 to 1970 an increasingly postcolonial community of nation-states, as embodied in a cosmopolitan network of international diplomats, forged three multilateral accords (the Moscow Treaty, the Treaty of Tlatelolco, and the NPT), ushering in an era in which international rules and sanctions formally governed nuclear science, technology, and engineering, bringing a measure of law and order—if imperfect justice—to the atomic domain, with lasting consequences for international security and world politics.

This drama spanned the world's stage, bringing together the communist East and the capitalist West, what would become known as the Industrial North and the Global South. While no one can look out from every vista on proceedings that at one point engaged the entire membership of the UN—to say nothing of those outside the halls of power—scholars have widened our vantage dramatically since 1991 by declassifying and disseminating reams of relevant documents, revealing the coercion, resistance, dependence, cooperation, and accommodation at play in the making of our global nuclear order.[26] Our knowledge of nuclear war and peace has broadened thanks to this archival renaissance, paving the way for accounts of the creation and enforcement of nuclear law and order in which the parts are related to the whole, and the whole to grander patterns of change and continuity in global history.

This drama centered on Washington because it was the sole capital with sufficient reach. The United States had emerged from the Second World War in a position of spectacular privilege in every metric of national influence save brute land power: preeminence in industrial production, finance, and consumption, with dominant positions in manufacturing (above all the automobile, aeronautical, arms, and nuclear industries), oceanic shipping, capital investments, and gold reserves. It hosted the UN, the International Monetary Fund (IMF), the World Bank, Los Alamos National Laboratory, and the Electronic Numerical Integrator and Computer (ENIAC), the first digital data processor. The Manhattan Project epitomized the country's top billing, its military director, Army brigadier general Leslie Groves, having fused price-less global inputs—ranging from Hungarian mathematicians to Congolese ores—to North America's natural wealth, industrial might, and surplus labor to construct the world's first fission reactors and nuclear explosives.[27] The international settlements struck after Germany and Japan's surrenders institutionalized the dollar's role as a global reserve currency while according a veto over legitimate military action to five "policemen"—the United States, the United Kingdom, France, the Republic of China, and the Soviet Union—though, for the moment, only one possessed the atom bomb.[28]

The Cold War divided the wartime alliance between the United States, the United Kingdom, and the Soviet Union, as well as Europe's political map, with a divided Germany at its broken heart. The product of unresolved tensions over popular sovereignty, social organization, spheres of influence, and postcolonial nationalism, the gradual and then precipitous deterioration of U.S.-Soviet relations set in motion geo-ideological competition across Europe and the Middle East, then East Asia, and ultimately throughout the world. Postwar U.S. grand strategy aimed at sustaining the country's hegemonic authority, above all in Western Europe and East Asia.[29] As the wealthy and dynamic linchpin of two transoceanic military-alliances-cum-trading-blocs linking North American consumers, farmers, producers, and bankers to recovering industrial powerhouses in Western Europe and Japan—and commodity producers elsewhere in the world—U.S. political elites enjoyed an unmatched ability to dictate the thrust and timing of international nuclear diplomacy throughout the Cold War.

The global spread of nuclear science and technology led U.S. officials to centralize the means of atomic destruction to the greatest extent possible and to do so in humanity's name.[30] Investments in nuclear nonproliferation under John F. Kennedy and Lyndon Johnson happened as their administrations tragically escalated U.S. military involvement in Southeast Asia, transforming nuclear arms control from an exercise in bilateral stabilization to an instrument with which to absolve the sins of U.S. foreign policy, bolster U.S. hegemony, and empower the office of the president. Nuclear globalization prompted U.S. officials to reach out to their counterparts in Moscow, where Nikita Khrushchev, Alexei Kosygin, and Leonid Brezhnev also feared that events in the Third World were spiraling out of their control, as the forces of demography, self-determination, anti-imperialism, guerrilla warfare, and technology transfer threatened to loosen the superpowers' grip over client regimes.

After all, even a hegemon needed partners. The capitalist titan's head start had narrowed by the time the 1960s drew to a close, with Western Europe and Japan's recoveries proceeding apace and the Vietnam War deepening federal budget deficits amid Johnson's Great Society. Two other nuclear powers—one a close ally, the United Kingdom, another an archrival, the Soviet Union—made common cause in bringing order to the nuclear domain. With one eye on Europe's economic integration and another on its depleted coffers, British leaders conditioned their nuclear security on U.S. arms sales as the price of a high seat at the table, culminating in their support for a definition of nuclear nonproliferation that reduced both nuclear risks and the likelihood of declining status in Europe and around the world.[31] The Soviet Union embraced nuclear non-diffusion for more diverse reasons: to restrain West Germany, to marginalize revolutionary China, and to buoy socialist parties in Europe and Latin America. In time, the Communist Party of the Soviet Union (CPSU) proved such a reliable deputy that delegates to the ENDC, where the NPT was mostly drafted, voiced bewilderment at the extent of "Soviet-American collusion."[32] Moscow's role was central, yet secondary, as superintendent of the Warsaw Pact. Talks to shutter the nuclear club proceeded at Moscow's sufferance, but they relied on U.S. influence. The day after García Robles's speech, Kuznetsov asked Goldberg to "make good use of [U.S.] bargaining power" among Latin American, sub-Saharan African, and Western European countries, not to mention Israel and South Africa.[33] Save for the PRC, whose relationship with the Soviet Union was almost as stormy as its relationship with the United States, and which had gone nuclear in 1964, and India, whose leaders counted on both superpowers for help against communist China, the states most capable of building independent nuclear arsenals—West Germany, Italy, Israel, South Africa, Australia, Japan, and Brazil—were all U.S. allies or close partners.

Although efforts to internationalize the nuclear question had preceded the Kennedy and Johnson presidencies, their liberal instincts inclined them toward multilateral consensus, which in turn expanded the host of characters who would make significant contributions to the future global nuclear order.[34] For these efforts to bear fruit in the UN, superpower cooperation was necessary but insufficient. A diverse cast of actors accordingly left their mark on settlements whose form and content were sculpted by a complex interplay of forces: decolonization, competitive development, managed globalization, transnational science, international institutions, alliance politics, and ideology, above all the centrality of a kind, fruitful environment in both capitalist and communist imaginations.[35] Along the way, a community of diplomats hailing from the capitalist, communist, and nonaligned worlds met, deliberated, and socialized at intergovernmental venues in far-flung metropolises: Geneva, Mexico City, Vienna, Brussels, Cairo, Moscow, and New York.[36]

III

The golden age of global nuclear diplomacy has handed down durable myths. The first was that enlightened leaders from around the world joined hands to shut the nuclear genie back in her bottle.[37] The bombings of Hiroshima and Nagasaki, in this telling, drove scholars, scientists, and state officials to push international reforms equal in measure to the material challenges that nuclear fission and fusion posed. "The unleashed power of the atom has changed everything save our modes of thinking," Albert Einstein warned in 1946, "as we thus drift toward unparalleled catastrophe."[38]

Early efforts to place radioactive heavy metals under international oversight were inspired by Danish Nobel laureate Niels Bohr, elaborated by Los Alamos Laboratory Director J. Robert Oppenheimer, and certified by deputy secretary of state Dean Acheson and Tennessee Valley Authority director David Lilienthal. They failed in the summer of 1946, when the man President Harry S. Truman selected to make his case to the UN Atomic Energy Commission, New York financier Bernard Baruch, stiffened the conditions under which the Soviet Union would have to accept international ownership of fissile materials by insisting on territorial inspections and automatic, veto-proof collective military action in the event of noncompliance. A competing Soviet proposal to ban the use and possession of nuclear arms, which Soviet foreign minister Andrei Gromyko had modeled on the 1925 Geneva Protocol for the Prohibition of the Use in War of Asphyxiating, Poisonous or Other Gases, and of Bacteriological Methods of Warfare, fared no better. U.S. officials would not relinquish their nuclear monopoly without intrusive controls nor would the Soviets relinquish their UNSC veto. The preexistence of a breakneck Soviet nuclear-weapon program likely precluded either settlement at the dawn of the nuclear age.[39] A celebratory, progressive narrative of a global nuclear order based on technical best practice to reduce nuclear risks, what Johnson dubbed in June 1968 "a testament to reason," jars with the documentary record.[40] The nonproliferation talks would have disappointed Einstein. The tenor of negotiations was at times idealistic, even soaring, but the dictates of power politics were nevertheless omnipresent and decisive.

The second narrative holds that the nuclear order that coalesced in these years was the bitter fruit of unequal treaties akin to those that had been foisted in earlier centuries on Native American tribes, formal colonies like India, informal ones like Egypt, and prostrate powers like Qing China.[41] There is a seed of truth there, which fuels criticisms at NPT Review Conferences every five years. The LTBT omitted subterranean nuclear tests, whose expense and difficulty disqualified all but rich states with vast hinterlands, often the inheritance of settler colonialism or overseas colonies.[42] The Treaty of Tlatelolco was negotiated in the face of staunch Cuban dissent. The NPT was inherently discriminatory, elevating five nuclear-weapon states above the rest of the world and exempting from international regulation brutal uranium-mining operations in the postcolonial nations of Gabon, Madagascar, Namibia, Niger, and South Africa.[43]

Yet these treaties were never tantamount to Aesop's fable of a lion bargaining with the animal kingdom. However unequal the LTBT was in effect, countries were free not to join, unlike the 1842 Treaty of Nanking, the 1885 Treaty of Berlin, or the 1903 Platt Amendment.[44] The nuclear powers played marginal roles in negotiating the

Treaty of Tlatelolco. The first proposal to shutter the nuclear club came from Ireland, a small, neutral former British colony. During the drafting process, most of the NPT's preambular clauses and binding articles were either suggested by representatives from non-nuclear-weapon states or adapted from the Treaty of Tlatelolco. In the decades after the Second World War new technologies were also weakening existing global hierarchies. As the last high commissioner to the Philippines, Paul V. McNutt, observed when the country gained self-rule from the United States in 1946, even the great powers were losing some "of their absolute independence, to the airplane, the radio, and the atom bomb."[45]

Which nations would yield more or less of their sovereignty nevertheless remained an open question. *The Nuclear Club* argues that the international community then emerging from the Second World War and decolonization turned to global nuclear governance to redress the signature failure of the world after empire: the entanglement of territorial disputes and wars of national liberation in the Third World with the balance of terror established by NATO and the Warsaw Pact in Europe and the U.S. hub-and-spoke system of security alliances in East Asia. The prospects that countervailing U.S., Soviet, and communist Chinese interests at these flash points could precipitate all-out thermonuclear war was sobering and ever-present. Yet it was the concern voiced by Soviet ambassador Semyon Tsarapkin to Bill Foster in Geneva that the spread of nuclear science and technology would empower "all other countries . . . to obtain advantage from differences and contradictions between them" that led first Washington and Moscow, and then the wider community of nation-states, to internationalize regional nuclear competitions, first to firewall post-1945 territorial disputes from the balance of terror but later to perpetuate superpower influence over distant events by dint of their covert services, economic gravity, and expeditionary forces.[46] To ward off material and political challenges to their authority, Moscow and Washington—joined explicitly by London and tacitly by Paris— reconsolidated their respective hegemonies as the Sino-Soviet split and the Vietnam War triggered for each crises of confidence and legitimacy both domestically and internationally.[47]

How they made this new global nuclear order would prove as important as why. Johnson was right when he dubbed the NPT "the most important international agreement since the beginning of the nuclear age."[48] Andrei Gromyko, who had led the Soviet delegation to the San Francisco Conference in 1945 before serving as foreign minister from 1957 to 1985, listed only his signature on the UN Charter ahead of that on the NPT—"the single silk thread" binding the rivals together in the 1960s.[49] Not since the founding of the IMF, the World Bank, and the UN from the summer of 1944 to the spring of 1945 had world-makers fashioned regimes of comparable scale, though U.S. secretary of state George C. Marshall's 1947 European Recovery Program (the Marshall Plan) and Dwight D. Eisenhower's 1953 Atoms for Peace initiative had come close. Foster had spent the Second World War purchasing supplies for the

U.S. Army and the Truman administration as W. Averell Harriman's right-hand man at the U.S. Department of Commerce and the European Recovery Program. Both were card-carrying members of the American establishment who guided U.S. for- eign policy in the New Deal's heyday: Harriman, the scion of the Harriman railroad fortune and a senior partner at Brown Brothers Harriman, a Wall Street investment firm; and Foster, the founder of the Pressed & Welded Steel Products Company on Long Island, New York. Those in their circles commonly professed their faith that labor, consumers, and stockholders would all profit from scientific and technologi- cal advances, as long as a mixed-economy welfare state humanized market society at home and countries avoided the beggar-thy-neighbor trade wars that had followed the Great Depression and preceded the Second World War.[50] Harriman went on to finalize the Moscow Treaty with Soviet premier Nikita Khrushchev in August 1963. Five years later, his protégé, Foster, did more than any other U.S. official as ACDA director to bring the NPT into existence.

Like the Marshall Plan, the nonproliferation campaign aimed to deepen ties of knowledge, trade, and security between the United States and the rest of the world via private firms, public clubs, and international bodies such as the IAEA.[51] As act- ing chief of the Economic Cooperation Administration in 1950, Foster had defended before the U.S. Senate the sale of sixty Italian locomotives to the Soviet Union. First, he reminded the senators that in an age of total war there was no bright line between strategic and nonstrategic exports. Second, the country's leverage over its Western European allies' trade policies had never been absolute. To make his third and final point, he referred to scrap-iron shipments from the United States to Japan in the 1930s. Whereas the U.S. and Japanese economies had been functionally independent before the attacks on Pearl Harbor and the Philippines, the Iron Curtain had not so utterly riven the European market. Not to make allowances when Italy wished to trade locomotives for Russian or Eastern European iron ore, manganese, asbestos, pig iron, steel ingots, petroleum, copper, nickel, or high-grade wheat would handicap its industry and incite popular unrest that the Italian Communist Party would gladly fan. If members of the "free world" were to maximize their comparative advantages against their autarkic, communist foes, Washington would need to accept some level of consensual co-management.[52]

The nonproliferation regime applied similar precepts to a world nuclear market. U.S. officials could never impose unilateral controls on uranium ore or gas-graphite reactors, especially when importers and exporters hailed from the Global South as often as the Industrial North. Whereas the Marshall Plan had breathed life into "the West," Atoms for Peace and its regulatory corollary—nuclear nonproliferation—lent U.S. liberal hegemony a universal function beyond mere anticommunism.[53] Global nuclear governance was inspired by a vision of world politics based on breakneck modernization even as it prettified and perpetuated hierarchical forms of globalism that had survived the Great Depression and the Second World War.[54]

Ironically, this U.S. commitment to patrol the atomic black market along a global frontier came as it was courting disaster in the Third World. Just as nuclear-reactor technology was set to take off in the late 1960s, the Cold War stakes in Latin America, Africa, Asia, and the Middle East had never looked higher.[55] In the early 1960s, Europe looked like the Cold War's cockpit, with Germany's division figuring centrally for NATO nuclear defense as the alliance left behind fifteen years of imperial retreats.[56] It was nonetheless perceived threats in Latin America, Africa, Asia, and the Middle East that transformed nuclear globalization into a pressing challenge: crises in the Levant and the Taiwan Strait inspired Aiken's nuclear restriction in September 1958; the Cuban Missile Crisis in October 1962 drove Brazilian foreign minister Afonso Arinos de Melo Franco and García Robles to try to denuclearize Latin America; the concurrent Sino-Indian border war led Kennedy and Khrushchev to finalize a test ban in August 1963; burgeoning Israeli, South African, Brazilian, Indian, and Japanese nuclear capabilities prompted the ENDC and the UNGA to regulate the technology on a planetary basis beginning in July 1968.[57]

Who would have the necessary status to dictate matters of war and peace in a world after empire was the inescapable subtext of nonproliferation talks.[58] It was no coincidence that negotiations crested as Western European empires breathed their last. From 1945 to 1962, the United Kingdom and the Fifth French Republic compensated for lost colonies in part with newfound atomic radiance.[59] For London, this meant nuclearizing its special relationship with Washington lest British prime ministers find themselves at the mercy of Iraqi prime ministers.[60] It was a lonelier affair in Paris. The French military abandoned colonial wars in Indochina and Algeria for mechanized forces in central Europe and Charles de Gaulle leveraged a small nuclear arsenal to ensure French-led European integration.[61] Even communist China's nuclear breakthrough in 1964 carried postcolonial overtones. Beijing's replacement of Taipei as "the only legitimate representative of China to the United Nations" confirmed the equivalence between UN Security Council permanent members and nuclear-weapon states in 1971. Following Richard Nixon's pathbreaking visit to Beijing and North Vietnam's triumph at the Paris Peace Accords two years later, Mao Zedong's regime muffled its support for wars of national liberation. Even without its signature on a copy of the treaty until 1992, the fact that a crusade first launched to brand the PRC a rogue state now crowned it as a card-carrying member of the most exclusive club on Earth testified to nuclear nonproliferation's fundamentally conservative thrust.

IV

The idea of nonproliferation synthesized a quarter century of nuclear thinking. In the United States, the politics of atomic destruction was bound up in suburban anxiety and the imperial presidency. Ties between America's bustling commuter belt and the national-security state abounded during the Cold War. From Central Intelligence Agency (CIA) headquarters in Fairfax County, Virginia, to RAND Corporation (a U.S. Air Force think tank) offices next door to Douglas Aircraft in Santa Monica, California, military bases and industry speckled new interstate road maps.[62] After Hiroshima and Nagasaki, Truman recast his office as a paternal protector to the women and children in the United States and around the globe. Over the next decade, atomic culture forged a link between U.S. armed might, America's suburbs, and global order. When pursuing controversial policies or facing tough elections, a series of U.S. presidents defended their policies by asserting an executive duty to protect home-owning families and the larger human lineage from total destruction.

Others situated the nuclear question within larger debates about inequality, community, and self-determination. Two months after the bombings, George Orwell asked in the London *Tribune* whether the atom bomb could ever be a weapon of the weak. After deeming international control useless, he asked a preliminary question: "How difficult are these things to manufacture?" Prewar narratives had presented the invention of superweapons by scientific geniuses as revolutionary acts that would erode "the distinction between great states and small states" and "the power of the State over the individual." It struck him as inauspicious that the Manhattan Project had drawn on continental resources and global connections "such as only three or four countries in the world are capable of making . . . it may mean that the discovery of the atomic bomb, so far from reversing history, will simply intensify the trends which have been apparent for a dozen years past." To him the power to break atomic nuclei seemed "likelier to put an end to large-scale wars at the cost of indefinitely prolonging a 'peace that is no peace.'"[63]

Three years later, Orwell's bleak vision of monstrous super-states mobilized against each other and through their managerial elite against their toiling masses became the setting to *1984*. His belief in the atom bomb's counterrevolutionary significance—the implication of the phrase "cold war" he had so offhandedly coined, namely "an epoch as horribly stable as the slave empires of antiquity"—has been lost.

Orwell was no seer. He missed the problem of the color line, the plea of humanitarianism, or the advance of technology. In 1946, the African American scholar and activist W.E.B. Du Bois predicted that the Bomb would not long remain a "monopoly of white folk." What was more, he went on, imperial metropolises had more to fear from such prompt and utter destruction than the developing nations of India, China, or pan-Africa. Instead of a "peace that is no peace," insurgent forces in Vietnam, Cuba, Afghanistan, Colombia, and Mozambique, among others, would wage guerrilla campaigns with the millions of AK-47 Kalashnikov assault rifles that the PRC and Warsaw Pact member-states would manufacture.[64] The U.S. government for its part would hold back its nuclear might in Asia for fear of alienating local peoples, allied governments, and nonaligned nations, many of who questioned why nonwhite peoples appeared to be the only targets of atomic warfare.[65]

Nor would the technology stand still. The K-25 gaseous diffusion plant and Y-12 Alpha track at Oak Ridge National Laboratory in Tennessee were the largest, most expensive, energy-intensive structures in history. As the NPT talks entered their endgame, the British, West Germans, and Dutch moved to combine resources in the Urenco Group, a commercial uranium-enrichment enterprise; the light footprint of the group's new centrifuges made future detection of nuclear-weapon programs far more difficult. Just a few years later, a Urenco subcontractor employee, Dr. Abdul Qadeer Khan, would hand centrifuge blueprints to Pakistan's nuclear-weapon program.[66] Such "loopholes" for uranium enrichment and plutonium reprocessing were features, not bugs, of the nonproliferation regime. They were there because rich, powerful states with large ambitions in the world nuclear market rejected indefinite dependence on U.S.-sourced fissile material. As in the case of the Marshall Plan, the importance of "free world" prosperity on a basis of freer flows of commodities, manufactures, people, and knowledge had made sensitive technology transfers a near-certainty. That Washington would so readily disregard London's repeated warnings that the new centrifuges would lead to better-concealed nuclear-weapon programs demonstrated the secondary importance of inhibiting new nuclear powers to the nonproliferation regime.[67]

While Orwell's vision was imperfect, his core point continues to resonate. The nuclear nonproliferation regime achieved what the atom bomb alone never could: the conservation amid decolonization of the discretion and deference to which great powers had grown accustomed on grounds that nuclear anarchy risked universal destruction. Or, as a blue-ribbon committee that Lyndon Johnson assembled after Beijing tested its first atomic device explained to the president, "any major trend of nuclear capabilities among the populous, non-white nations of the earth would greatly strengthen their hand in attempting to obtain an ever greater share of the earth's wealth and opportunity."[68]

V

While scholars are unlikely to find conclusive answers to perennial debates about the causes of war and peace anytime soon, any discussion of the avoidance of total war since 1945 must take account of a parallel timeline of limited and civil wars, economic sanctions, and military interventions. These tensions were present at the creation. Chapter 1 divides thinking about nuclear war, peace, and order from the Manhattan Project to the Castle Bravo test into three general schools of thought: humanitarian universalism, existential deterrence, and technocratic development. The story starts with the first Westerners to visit Hiroshima after the bombing—Fritz Bilfinger and

Marcel Junod of the International Committee of the Red Cross (ICRC)—and then traces the lines of reasoning and action relative to the nuclear revolution against the backdrop of the Second World War, the Cold War, and decolonization.

Chapter 2 explains why Frank Aiken put forward his nuclear restriction proposal at the UNGA in September 1958 in the wake of two major crises in the Middle East and East Asia. The Irish Resolution was but one element of a larger proposal to foster areas of law to deal with the territorial squabbles that seemed endemic to postcolonial zones with arbitrary borders drawn by colonial authorities, and the concept of nuclear restraint would henceforth raise crucial questions related to international law, global governance, and popular sovereignty.

Chapter 3 explains why the atomic frontier became a source of unease and a target for what Rostow and Kennedy saw as a U.S. commitment to establishing a "common law for the Cold War." Eisenhower and Kennedy were reluctant to sacrifice a NATO multilateral nuclear force (MLF) so coveted by West German nationalists before the Cuban Missile Crisis and the Sino-Indian border disputes of October 1962 underscored the volatility of the Third World. Thereafter the United States would monitor nuclear programs in Israel and communist China and, with the Soviet Union, identify "important areas of common interest in the underdeveloped areas."[69]

Chapter 4 illustrates how Kennedy pursued a nuclear test ban to complement a military posture of flexible response around Eurasia, selling voters on a major agreement with the Soviet Union by underscoring how it would stop nuclear fallout from poisoning young children. In August 1963, Harriman and Khrushchev would finalize the LTBT in Moscow. Its silence on subterranean testing betrayed an ulterior motive—to turn aspirants to the nuclear club, namely Mao's China, into international pariahs.

Chapter 5 recounts how Foster's ACDA became first Kennedy's and then Johnson's "independent conscience," only for a nuclear nondiffusion treaty to remain just out of reach during the "long 1964" from Kennedy's assassination to the Americanization of the Vietnam War.[70] Johnson's unwillingness to choose between Europe-firsters and nuclear guardians yielded deadlock, and the window of condominium shut just as the PRC tested its first nuclear device on October 16, 1964.

Chapter 6 recounts how nonaligned politics and the Vietnam War circumscribed options for addressing Indian insecurity after China's test. It would take until the eve of midterm elections in the United States on 8 November 1966, for a breakthrough to occur as Johnson scrambled to burnish his credentials as a world peacemaker; in the meantime, neutral and nonaligned states passed UNGA Resolution 2028 (XX), outlining a prospective nonproliferation agreement that would "embody an acceptable balance of mutual responsibilities and obligations."

Chapter 7 turns to Latin America, where efforts to purge nuclear weapons from the neighborhood after the Cuban Missile Crisis offered an alternative vision for postcolonial nuclear politics.[71] The superpowers would make numerous concessions to Latin American demands in Geneva and New York, exemplifying the interactive relationship between regional and global regime-building in the 1960s; four articles and many preambular statements that the Treaty of Tlatelolco inspired or Mexican officials introduced were added to the nonproliferation treaty, with the effect that nuclear development and disarmament joined nonproliferation as its legal pillars.

Chapter 8 homes in on the personal diplomacy between Soviet and American officials in Geneva that added the final piece to the puzzle—a universal safeguard regime—as territorial disputes continued to cause upheaval in the Third World. U.S. and Soviet representatives ultimately bridged their differences by tapping the IAEA as a global watchdog thanks to their close social relations in Switzerland, but such a technocratic fix could not address the ensuing free-for-all among socialist, capitalist, and nonaligned states.[72]

Chapter 9 recounts the final phase of nonproliferation proceedings in 1968, when the two superpowers engineered a decisive majority in the UNGA by courting small powers, appeasing nuclear exporters, assuring close allies, and isolating aspiring regional powers such as West Germany, India, and Brazil by means of a handful of minor concessions proposed by Latin American delegations. The most sweeping covenant since the UN Charter failed to rescue from electoral defeat Johnson and his hopeful successor, Hubert Humphrey, whose promises to cultivate future generations were increasingly drowned out by White House picketers chanting, "Hey, hey, LBJ, how many kids did you kill today?"[73]

The international effort to coronate nuclear-weapon states as planetary guardians recast the U.S. presidency and international relations in lasting ways. Even U.S. president Richard Nixon and national security advisor Henry Kissinger, who had disparaged international nonproliferation efforts when they took power in 1969, changed their tune after India exploded a peaceful nuclear explosion (PNE) in 1974. Since then, U.S. political elites and the voters that elect them to office have considered it their duty—their right, even—to intervene wherever atomic power threatened the world they saw as theirs to lead. Fifty years later, it is clear that the destruction of Hiroshima sparked a rolling counterrevolution to preserve hierarchy in a world otherwise made level by the abolition of imperial prerogatives; the universalization of the nation-state; the ideal of inviolable borders; and the prodigious growth of international travel, migration, communication, as well as flows of capital and ideas. With luck the nuclear nonproliferation regime's greatest triumph—the continued non-use of nuclear weapons since Nagasaki—will grant us the time and wisdom necessary to judge its enduring legacy.

"Peace That Is No Peace"

Revolution and Reaction After Hiroshima, 1945–1955

Introduction—"You and the Atomic Bomb"

Neither his visits to the Kwangtung Army of Japan's internment camps in Manchuria nor the firebombing of Tokyo had prepared Fritz Bilfinger for the morning of August 30, 1945. Walking in the company of a Japanese captain named Shishido, the Swiss Red Cross delegate entered a no-man's-land that he would later describe as dotted with "carloads of dead bodies." An inner circle two kilometers in diameter had been totally destroyed. The rest of Hiroshima was "filled with the stench of corpses." Buildings were greatly damaged six kilometers from the hypocenter—the spot on the Earth's surface directly below the explosion—and slightly damaged four kilometers beyond that. The city's healers had suffered a terrible toll. Only two medical centers were left standing—the Horikawa Emergency Hospital, which the Prefectural Office had thrown together on August 16, and the blasted-out Red Cross Hospital, three-quarters of whose personnel were injured or dead. Only a few score doctors and nurses tended to survivors, among them Ken Takeuchi, the Japan Red Cross Society president. Sanitary conditions were medieval. Two months later medical supplies would remain in dire need.[1]

Bilfinger painted a grim picture the next day when he telegraphed Marcel Junod, the chief delegate of the International Committee of the Red Cross (ICRC) mission in Japan. He asked Junod to entreat the U.S. occupational authorities under General Douglas MacArthur to expedite medical relief and a fact-finding mission to investigate the strange effects that had afflicted survivors:

Visited Hiroshima . . . conditions appalling. City wiped out, eighty percent all hospitals destroyed or seriously damaged. Inspected two emergency hospitals, conditions beyond description. Effect of bomb mysteriously serious, many victims apparently recovering suddenly suffer fatal relapse due to decomposition to white blood cells and other internal injuries, now dying in great numbers. Estimated still over 100,000 wounded . . . sadly lacking bandaging materials or medicines. Please solemnly appeal to allied high command to consider immediate airdrop of relief action over center city.[2]

Bilfinger issued a more categorical judgment on October 24, when he counseled that ICRC leaders—for decades the custodians of international humanitarian law under the 1863 Geneva Conventions—"should participate in the international discussions concerning the control of nuclear energy and exercise its influence to have the use of atomic power as a destructive force outlawed."[3] The suffering to which he had borne witness ruled out halfway measures. He personally judged that their future use would amount to a crime against humanity.

Historians usually retell the bombings of Hiroshima and Nagasaki as the results of decisions made in Los Alamos, New Mexico; Washington, D.C.; Moscow, Russia; and Tokyo, Japan.[4] Just as consequential, however, was how influential voices described these mass killings in the following years. From the moment of their destruction, commentators like William Laurence, the *New York Times* journalist embedded within the Manhattan Project, held the bombings out as heralds of "the greatest age of all—the Age of Atomic Power, or Atomics."[5] His colleague, Sidney Shalett, announced the arrival of a revolution, whether as a "tremendous force for the advancement of civilization" or its destruction.[6] There were dissenters to this Promethean narrative. David Lilienthal, the inaugural chairman of the U.S. Atomic Energy Commission (AEC), described the atom bomb as "an exclamation point at the end of a continuous narrative of atrocity," as he lamented the ways in which total war had leveled fences between combatants and noncombatants.[7] In the pages of London's *Tribune*, George Orwell was even less optimistic: "the atomic bomb, so far from reversing history, will simply intensify the trends which have been apparent for a dozen years past" making more likely "the prospect of two or three monstrous super-states" of authoritarian character, locked in a state of permanent war of all against all.[8]

These contrasting threads—change and continuity, humanity and terror, revolution and counterrevolution—coexisted in the decade after Hiroshima, yielding a world poised between demobilization and bloodletting in which atomic terror staved off "large-scale wars at the cost of prolonging indefinitely a 'peace that is no peace.'"[9] Over the next quarter century, as the Cold War acquired an ideological significance, a worldwide cast of political leaders, international diplomats, rationalizing scientists, insurgent revolutionaries, and humanitarian actors would weave together these threads into a embryonic worldwide regime of nuclear law and order.

I

Long before August 1945, scientific and cultural authorities had held out atomic energy as a total rupture with the past which promised salvation and damnation in equal measure. Following Marie Curie's discovery of radium, nuclear pioneers represented radioactive substances and invisible rays as inescapably Janus-faced. In Frederick Soddy's *The Interpretation of Radium*, the English scientist, who with Ernest Rutherford had revealed that radioactivity emanated from elemental transmutations, rhapsodized about how scientific mastery of the atomic nucleus would hand nuclear engineers the power to "transform a desert continent, thaw the frozen poles, and make the whole world one smiling Garden of Eden."[10]

One year before the First World War began, fears that atomic power could imperil cities—even humanity itself—found expression in H. G. Wells's *The World Set Free*. Dedicated to Soddy, the book portrayed a near-future when aeronauts devastated metropolises with "atomic bombs" that released vast infernos and "puffs of luminous, radio-active vapor," an existential threat to Western civilization that only the foundation of a world government had averted, ushering in universal peace and prosperity, replete with terraformed wastelands, unbounded liberty, and flying cars.[11] Some scientists went so far as to worry that an artificial nuclear reaction could spread uncontrollably "like a train of gunpowder." The possibility was taken seriously enough that when the world's first fission device, code-named Trinity, exploded at Alamogordo, New Mexico, on the morning of July 16, 1945, Manhattan Project scientists speculated that it might ignite the nitrogen in the atmosphere and the hydrogen in the oceans, consummating the Second World War with a fiery apocalypse.[12]

For internationally minded scientists and world federalists, the nuclear revolution strengthened the case for the enlightened rule of experts. Niels Bohr, whose quantum model of atomic nuclei had provided the theoretical springboard for the Manhattan Project, wrote to President Franklin Roosevelt in July 1944 to warn how recent breakthroughs would "revolutionize industry and transport" and also "completely change all future conditions of warfare." To avert a world-threatening arms race, he promoted thoughtful schemes of international control.[13] In such a globe-spanning technocracy, international and supranational organizations would scale up expert-led solutions to save humanity from its own devices. There were those who went further, counseling that—as in *The World Set Free*—world government under universal law was the only solution of sufficient scale. And as the first test of fusion-based hydrogen explosives increased the potential power of nuclear weaponry by another order of magnitude in 1952, even those thinkers with well-thought-out reservations about world government proved open to schemes for a planet-bestriding leviathan.[14]

Atomic scientists enjoyed unexpected fame and esteem after 1945, notwithstanding the reservations some harbored about their creations. The largest scientific research and technological development project to date, the Manhattan Project had married North America's natural resources to foreign imports of world-class scientists and such rare commodities as Belgian Congolese uranium pitchblende and Norwegian-manufactured heavy water. By comparison, Nazi Germany and Shōwa Japan's wartime nuclear programs had languished in laboratory experiments and sputtering reactors. After the British equivalent, Tube Alloys, yielded the necessary proof of concept in the form of the MAUD Committee Report in March 1941, the U.S. Army's Manhattan District, located far beyond the Luftwaffe's range, would subsume the British Commonwealth venture.

The Manhattan Project drew on continental and transatlantic resources that even the British Empire could not muster. Military director and brigadier general Leslie Groves of the U.S. Army Corps of Engineers built massive new installations at Hanford, Washington, near the Columbia River, and Oak Ridge, Tennessee, near the Tennessee River. More than 560,000 workers labored at these facilities from 1941 to 1946, including Oak Ridge's K-25 Gaseous Diffusion Process Building, which outstripped the Department of War's new Pentagon building in northern Virginia as the world's largest structure. With metropolitan populations closer to 80 million in 1942, Nazi Germany and imperial Japan would have to resort to food rationing and slave labor to sustain their war industries, while the wealthier and more populous United States drew labor from a larger population of 135 million that managed to churn out both guns and butter. An additional 6 million women entered the labor force during the war to replace men who entered the service ranks.[15] The ethnic cleansing of Nazi science, which also afflicted conquered territories during the war, pushed some of Europe's best and brightest, including numerous future Nobel Prize winners, into exile in the United Kingdom and the United States, where many joined the Manhattan Project in the name of scientific progress and fascist defeat.[16]

Many of the most effective contributors were Jewish or had married into Jewish families. Italian physicist Enrico Fermi induced the first controlled fission reaction beneath the University of Chicago's football stadium. His wife, Laura Fermi, was a Jewish historian. Two German Jews, Otto Frisch and Rudolf Peierls, outlined the first technical case for a fission explosive after they took refuge in Australian professor Mark Oliphant's University of Birmingham laboratory. Hungarian physicist Leo Szilard dreamed up a neutron-induced atomic chain reaction while taking a bath in London. Three of his Jewish-Hungarian compatriots—Eugene Wigner, Johann von Neumann, and Edward Teller—would make equally signal contributions to the U.S. nuclear-weapon program: Wigner designed the plutonium reactors at the Hanford site; von Neumann calibrated the explosive lenses that initiated criticality in the uranium or plutonium pits; and Teller conceived a thermonuclear device with help from the Polish-Jewish mathematician Stanislaw Ulam that employed a fission bomb to trigger a secondary fusion reaction in which heavy hydrogen atoms bonded to one another, generating helium and enough stellar energy to swallow New York City.

Through the Manhattan Project, the U.S. government nationalized the republic of science that had birthed modern atomic physics, a monopoly that the ultimate demise of Anglo-American nuclear cooperation in 1946 would underscore.[17] This global flow of scientific talent was not without its hazards. The Soviet spy Klaus Fuchs infiltrated Los Alamos via the British mission there and passed on highly classified data that would expedite the Soviet nuclear-weapon program—the Ministry of Medium Machine-Building Industry. After Hiroshima, Soviet premier Josef Stalin placed the project under the supervision of NKVD director Lavrentiy Beria with an order that he and research director Igor Kurchatov supply "atomic weapons in the shortest possible time!"[18] The unprecedented concentration of scientific talent in North America had a time limit. After Berlin's downfall the United States and the Soviet Union ransacked occupied Germany for such first-rate talents as physicist Werner Heisenberg and rocketeer Werner von Braun. After the war, the United Kingdom, France, West Germany, and Japan would have to play catch-up with the superpowers' scientific bases and technological infrastructures, mimicking the state-funded big science that the United States had pioneered.[19] Promising students from new postcolonial states flocked to MIT, Berkeley, Oxford, the Sorbonne, and other blue-chip universities in North America and Western Europe for advanced degrees in physics, chemistry, and engineering. Once home, they would help build up nuclear programs across Latin America, Asia, Africa, and the Middle East.[20]

Hydropower was integral to the invention of nuclear power. The United States possessed prodigious hydroelectricity from the dam-building spree that Roosevelt's New Deal had accelerated. The Army Corps of Engineers had bottled the Columbia and Tennessee River systems earlier in the century, transforming these catchment basins into regional engines of electrification and industrialization.[21] Accompanied by two DuPont engineers, Colonel Franklin T. Matthias chose the 550-foot, mile-long Grand Coulee Dam in Washington, whose nine-generator Left Power Plant opened in 1941, to source 100,000 kilowatts of electric power for three plutonium-production reactors and two chemical-separation canyons at Hanford. The Columbia River easily supplied the 75,000 gallons per minute of water necessary to avert meltdowns in the uranium reactors at the new base.[22]

The Tennessee Valley Authority (TVA) held enough spare capacity to supply half of the electricity to the Aluminum Company of America (ALCOA) plant in Knoxville—the world's largest—amid a 600-percent production increase and a $300 million expansion and still fully electrify Oak Ridge: the X-10 graphite reactor, the Y-22 electromagnetic isotope-separation facility, and K-25's voracious gaseous-diffusion cascades. As an AEC official later recalled, the Manhattan Project "needed electric power, an enormous amount of electric power . . . in producing the atomic bomb. And the Tennessee Valley Authority (TVA)," which Lilienthal led as chairman, "gave us that."[23] Three-quarters of TVA electricity went to wartime industries from 1940 to 1945, even as the public corporation added seven dams and eleven hydroelectric generators to its empire of water.[24] Though North America's massive coal deposits could have powered the Manhattan Project, cheap hydroelectric power allowed Washington to avoid most trade-offs. Berlin or Tokyo would have required massive imports to generate sufficient weapons-grade fissile materials for atom bombs, while London recognized that the British Empire was too vulnerable to air raids and too energy-poor to succeed without Canadian and American help.

Massive dam projects would become staples of developmental campaigns in the 1950s, when superpower technocrats evangelized throughout the Third World on their behalf. The Soviet Union rebuilt and reinforced its own electrical grids partly through massive investments in hydroelectric power plants along the Volga River that bordered its industrial heartland in the Ural Mountains, including such closed cities as Sverdlovsk-44, Chelyabinsk-65, Tomsk-7, and Krasnoyarsk-26. Regional projects like the TVA and the Great Volga River Route project were testaments to the strategic dimensions of Cold War modernization, as were the formations of U.S. and Soviet "plutopias" along lines of race, class, and education.[25] If communism was "Soviet rule plus electrification of the whole country," as Stalin declared at the Eighth All-Russian Congress of Soviets in 1920, a Red Bomb promised to vindicate Marxist Leninism worldwide.[26] For its part the segregated U.S. nuclear-weapon complex reflected legacies of white supremacy that continued to deprive African Americans of equal opportunities under the law and color the perceptions of U.S. elites as they contemplated the place of increasingly populous and assertive nonwhite peoples in the world order after 1945.[27]

From its early years, the nuclear age therefore expanded and imperiled the industrial world over which the superpowers presided after the war. Two months after Nagasaki, Orwell envisioned an oligarchic rather than a democratic future after inferring that the financial and material prerequisites of the atom bomb outstripped the resources of all but three or four countries in the world. Yet as the United States and the Soviet Union sleepwalked into a global contest to shape a world upended by decolonization, both would prove surprisingly open to exporting the means of atomic destruction beyond their shores, as access to global markets replaced territorial resources as prerequisites of national wealth and power as well as hearts and minds in the developing world supplanted colonial outposts as the great prizes on the world's frontiers.[28]

II

The question of what would happen after the bombs dropped had loomed throughout the war. Bohr's arrival at Los Alamos in 1943 had brought a prophet of scientific global-ism into the weapons laboratory, where he influenced Robert Oppenheimer's thinking about world order. In describing atomic war as a "perpetual menace" and science as a transnational "brotherhood working in the service of common human ideals," he dismissed collective defense under the UN Charter as "entirely insufficient." That winter in the foreword to *One World or None*, a collection of essays published by the Federation of American Scientists—a pressure group of conscientious objectors that had formed at Oak Ridge, Los Alamos, Hanford, and the Metallurgical Laboratory (Met Lab) in Chicago—Bohr counseled that only ingenious regimes of international regulation could tame nuclear programs with dual-use (civilian and military) potential. His insistence that worldwide cooperation would be crucial lest atomic energy intensify international tensions rested on a hopeful premise: that nation-states might hold the common good as their highest calling.[29]

Bohr was not alone in preferring an open world and thus full transparency with Moscow. As the battle of Berlin loomed in the spring of 1945, many in the Manhattan Project had contemplated the enormity of atomic warfare. Once the Met Lab had made its breakthroughs in reactor design and plutonium separation, Szilard—who had first enlisted Albert Einstein in 1940 in his bid to have Washington race Berlin to an atom bomb—reached out to Roosevelt and, after the president's death on April 12, 1945, President Harry S. Truman and his incoming secretary of state, South Carolina senator James Byrnes. In his study in Columbia, South Carolina, Byrnes had disabused the Hungarian polymath of the notion that wartime cooperation would endure. He favored striking awe in—not sharing intelligence with—Josef Stalin.

This rejection notwithstanding, Szilard's trip breached the invisible wall between science and policy in the Manhattan Project. Soon after, Arthur Compton—the Nobel laureate who led the Met Lab—tasked James Franck with chairing the Committee on the Social and Political Implications of the Atomic Bomb, which in June called for a preliminary demonstration "on the desert or a barren island" before an international audience that would include Japanese and Soviet observers.[30] Its central justification was the impossibility of sustaining a monopoly on nuclear data or raw uranium and thorium.[31] In outlining the underlying mechanics of nuclear diffusion, the Franck report tackled the main challenge facing a nuclear-armed world: the future of Moscow and Washington's wartime partnership. Although the Franck Report never reached the desk of Henry Stimson, Truman's secretary of war, Szilard was undaunted. He followed up with a letter to Truman counseling restraint lest the United States surrender the high ground from which to bring "the unloosened forces of destruction under control."[32] Seventy scientists signed his petition, whose moral arguments rested not on saving lives but on nipping a U.S.-Soviet arms race in the bud. Oppenheimer advised the Interim Committee, which Stimson chaired and on which Byrnes served as Truman's personal representative, to bring Stalin more fully into the loop, only for Truman to limit himself in Potsdam, Germany, one week later to elliptical remarks to the Soviet dictator about "a new weapon of unusual destructive force."[33]

The detonation of Little Boy 1,800 feet above Hiroshima's Aioi Bridge publicized the most important fact about nuclear weapons—their manufacturability. The U.S. nuclear monopoly now had an expiry date, the Franck Report having already warned that it would not remain a secret weapon for long.[34] When Stimson urged Truman to avert a secret armament race by informing Stalin, he cited "feverish" Soviet efforts to match them—a veiled reference to Soviet espionage against the Manhattan Project. He deemed the duration of the U.S. monopoly of less consequence than that of U.S.-Soviet cooperation: "I consider the problem of our satisfactory relations with Russia," the outgoing secretary of war wrote, "as not merely connected with but as virtually dominated by the problem of the atomic bomb.[35]

Nuclear governance had domestic as well as international faces. The Federation of American Scientists achieved a victory when the 1946 Atomic Energy Act placed the AEC, an executive authority, atop the military services on the organization chart. Led by a five-person board whose chair served as first among equals, the AEC would helm the country's nuclear infrastructure for the next twenty-eight years. For technical advice, it could turn to a nine-person General Advisory Committee (GAC) composed of leading scientists while a new, bipartisan Joint Atomic Energy Committee on which eighteen senators and representatives held seats exerted oversight over federal efforts to control the spread of knowledge and the availability of uranium and thorium required for bomb work. Section 10 of the act deemed information related to designing, developing, or manufacturing nuclear weapons "born secret," laying out punishments for their mishandling amid mounting revelations that Manhattan Project scientists had funneled intelligence to Soviet handlers.[36]

Legislative action on Capitol Hill set the pace for diplomatic initiatives. The United Kingdom had operated as America's junior partner throughout the war, and while then British prime minister Winston Churchill had formalized the wartime partnership in his 1944 Hyde Park agreement with Roosevelt, Truman's meeting with Canadian prime minister William Lyon Mackenzie King and British prime minister Clement Attlee in November 1945 dashed what hopes remained that U.S.-UK collaboration would survive Roosevelt's recent death and Churchill's parliamentary ouster. The three-power trusteeship envisioned in Washington would multilateralize the emergent nuclear order and globalize peaceful uses of atomic energy, beginning with a UN Atomic Energy Commission (UNAEC). Byrnes journeyed to Moscow in December to discuss a multistage program of international control, only for the Senate Atomic Energy Committee to object to sharing data beyond those found in *Atomic Energy for Military Purposes*, the administrative history that Manhattan Project physicist Henry DeWolf Smyth had drawn up to justify its enormous costs to the American people.[37] Soviet physicists translated the book on a rush basis at Arzamas-16—the Soviet weapons laboratory near Moscow jestingly referred to as "Los Arzamas."[38]

After this rocky start, Byrnes tasked Under Secretary of State Dean Acheson with assembling a blue-ribbon committee to iron out a detailed U.S. proposal for international atomic control. James B. Conant, president of Harvard University and National Defense Research Committee (NDRC) member, presided alongside Vannevar Bush, wartime chair of the NDRC and the Office of Scientific Research and Development and champion of the National Science Foundation (NSF). Groves and former assistant secretary of war John J. McCloy rounded out the team with Bush, Conant, and Acheson, who designated a five-person board drawn from industry and government to consult on technical matters: Charles A. Thomas from Monsanto Chemical Corporation; Chester I. Barnard of New Jersey Bell Telephone; Harry Winne, vice president of engineering at General Electric; Lilienthal; and Oppenheimer.[39]

The former Los Alamos director quickly emerged as a driving force. Acheson later conceded that his was "the most stimulating and creative mind among us," and his technocratic inclinations resulted in a framework in which no party could be injured by another party's gain. The chain of reasoning stemmed from two interlocked assumptions: foreign societies would embrace peaceful atomic energy but struggle to weaponize it. The resulting Acheson-Lilienthal Report recommended the transfer of uranium and thorium mines, nuclear reactors, laboratories, and eventually national atomic arsenals to an International Atomic Development Authority answerable only to the UN Security Council (UNSC). Whereas fissile materials were ownable, basic science was self-liberating—a "wasting asset" whose only reliable use was to lock in advantages via international control.[40]

By the time the Acheson-Lilienthal Report was finalized on March 16, 1946, however, the world had already changed. At the Bolshoi Theatre on February 9, Stalin blamed the Second World War on capitalist competition for captive markets, prophesizing in the coming decades crises and conflicts among the moneymaking empires. The Bolshoi speech merely recapitulated Leninist articles of faith, but the U.S. deputy chief of mission in Moscow, George Frost Kennan, seized the moment to send a five-part, eight-thousand-word telegram to Washington in which he painted the Soviet Union as "impervious to the logic of reason" but "highly sensitive to the logic of force"—an unforgiving standpoint from which to judge the Acheson-Lilienthal plan. On March 5, Churchill described an Iron Curtain descending on a divided Europe (his own complicity in conceding Bulgaria, Hungary, and Romania to Soviet dominion went unmentioned). In Moscow, Andrei Zhdanov, Stalin's propaganda czar, enlisted Soviet citizens in a "democratic" battle against "imperialist" capitalism just as the House Committee on Un-American Activities (HUAC) in the U.S. Capitol launched congressional inquiries against subversive socialists in American society. The deterioration of the wartime alliance between the United States and the Soviet Union, including breaking news of Soviet atomic espionage during and after the war, had depleted the reservoirs of trust on which Oppenheimer's scheme would have drawn.[41]

That scheme was also predicated on a worldwide scarcity of uranium. The U.S. nuclear monopoly arose in part from an ephemeral Anglo-American-Canadian uranium monopoly—the Combined Development Trust. Respectable opinion on its time of death gradually hardened into a running five-year estimate with an indefinite start date and assorted benchmarks—fissile-material production, successful testing, weaponization, or an independent arsenal of indefinite scale and sophistication.[42] The deterioration of imperial preference zones during the war had undermined the trust, whose uranium sources descended from colonial land grabs: vanadium mines in the American West; uranium deposits near Great Bear Lake in Canada's Northwest Territories; superlative pits at Shinkolobwe in the Belgian Congo. Once Stalin placed the Soviet program on a crash course, geological surveys discovered massive Siberian repositories, to which the 1948 communist seizure of power in Czechoslovakia would add the Joachimsthal mine.[43]

The Acheson-Lilienthal plan therefore faced long odds in the UNAEC. Over the next two years, New York financier Bernard Baruch and Soviet diplomat Andrei Gromyko served as its gravediggers. Truman appointed Baruch, a Wall Street promoter and Democratic Party grandee who helped manage the country's finances during the First World War, to adjust Oppenheimer's plan to the political moment. While Bush would complain that Baruch "was the most unqualified man in the country," what the president wanted from the seventy-six-year-old philanthropist, whose beneficiaries included Truman's 1940 Senate campaign and whose assets included uranium mines, was to Americanize the initiative—to extend to the nuclear domain the hegemonic version of global governance on display at the World Bank, the International Monetary Fund (IMF), and the Global Agreement on Tariffs and Trade (GATT).[44] A bipartisan contingent was working to position U.S. foreign policy to back anticommunist forces in Western Europe and beyond. Ever one to read the political wind, Baruch understood that while the U.S. Congress had little interest in ceding authority to a stateless army of technocrats, the language of perpetual peace under world law would gleam just as brightly in defeat, throwing a flattering light on what would otherwise have been seen as a cynical power play.[45]

The hidden authors of the Baruch Plan were the U.S. military chiefs. Following the demobilization of 1.6 million men and women from wartime service in the one hundred days after Japan's surrender, wartime frontiers, especially in central Europe, where 2.5 million Red Army soldiers were garrisoned, had acquired an uneven character. When Baruch solicited their views, the U.S. Army and U.S. Navy chiefs touted forward operating bases and atom bombs as essential equalizers. Army Air Corps general Carl Spaatz's judgment was typical: the U.S. nuclear monopoly, however transitory, was "a critical factor in our efforts to achieve first a stabilized condition and eventually a lasting peace." In light of this fact, any negotiation that jeopardized that advantage "must follow, and not precede, assured methods of enforcing the agreements."[46]

What Baruch spelled out to the UNAEC on June 25, 1946, reflected Spaatz's advice. First, where Oppenheimer had intended an international authority to own "all intrinsically dangerous operations in the nuclear field," thus avoiding intrusive inspections or punitive measures, Baruch believed that both were critical to check malefactors, with the Soviet Union atop the list.[47] Second, whereas the physicist had envisioned a partial renunciation of nuclear sovereignty, Baruch wanted to nix veto rights held by UNSC permanent members under the San Francisco Charter.[48] The *Economist* had described Oppenheimer's Atomic Development Authority as supranational rather than international, an autonomous body of cosmopolitan technicians that would operate through the UN bureaucracy. The Baruch Plan went one step further. Economic and military sanction related to nuclear security would proceed via a majority vote in the UNSC, not the great-power unanimity on which Soviet negotiators had insisted when the charter was drafted in the summer of 1945.[49]

Gromyko emphatically rejected the U.S. proposal. His counteroffer would have reversed the Baruch Plan's sequence. Instead of waiting for sanctioned-enforced inspections, the upper chamber would first outlaw the use, manufacture, or possession of atomic weaponry following the ratification of half of the UN General Assembly (UNGA) and all permanent Security Council members, with the U.S. stockpile dismantled three months later.[50] Only then would inspections and verification proceed. Although the UNAEC continued to meet through the fall of 1948, it was clear that the two plans were born irreconcilable. Even U.S. secretary of commerce Henry Wallace, Roosevelt's first vice president and the most dovish member of Truman's cabinet, characterized the Gromyko Plan as "almost impossible to take seriously."[51] Once Beria established closed cities in conscious imitation of Oak Ridge and Hanford, Moscow would never have licensed an inspection regime of which they would have been in immediate violation. Distrust flowed both ways. Decades later, Gromyko revealed that Stalin had operated on the assumption that Truman would never give up his atomic weapons.[52]

The Soviet alternative nevertheless went beyond mere propaganda. The 1925 Geneva Protocol banning the use of chemical or bacteriological weapons, to which all European belligerents had formally adhered during the Second World War, offered precedent. Although the Gromyko Plan went further, barring even the possession of atomic arms, universal abolition squared more easily with humanitarian rejection of wanton, cruel instruments of war (a fact that Soviet peace offensives would exploit to the hilt as the Cold War took off). For all their rejection of a majoritarian UNSC,

Soviet foreign minister Vyacheslav Molotov's affirmation of "special inspections bodies" and Stalin's acknowledgment that safeguards would have to operate on a permanent basis attested that international obligations were acceptable if they preserved hard-won Soviet privileges. Molotov thus praised existing UNSC procedures and formal treaty adherence in the same breath. Either way Moscow would retain a veto.[53]

The debate in New York cast two contrasting visions of world order in sharp relief: one universal and progressive, the other regional and conservative. Hiroshima had revealed a lacuna in the armor of humanitarian law: weapons against which all imaginable defenses were impotent and whose interval from mobilization to detonation would be counted in terms of hours. The velocity with which strategic nuclear bombing could start and end a military conflict thus elided the rules governing when states went to war, *jus ad bellum* in the original Latin, and *jus in bello*, human rights in wartime. The only way out, it seemed, was to declare the Bomb evil in and of itself.

III

For all their differences, the Baruch and Gromyko Plans both classed Hiroshima and Nagasaki as revolutionary acts. For true-believing humanitarians, they were less technological marvels than industrial monsters, their chief significance arising from their troubling relationship to strategic bombing and the wartime failure to protect civilians from the scourge of total war.

Bilfinger's account of Hiroshima triggered immediate action in Japan and at ICRC headquarters in Geneva. Junod received his telegram in Tokyo's Marunouchi district on September 2—the same day that General Douglas MacArthur accepted Japan's surrender on board the USS *Missouri*—after which the ICRC's chief delegate rushed over to U.S. Supreme Allied Command's temporary headquarters at the Yokohama Chamber of Commerce. Within days, MacArthur dispatched twelve tons of supplies in care of the Red Cross, together with an expedition led by Brigadier General T. F. Farrell, who flew with a dozen scientists to investigate the effects of the atomic bomb.[54] Junod joined them on September 8 on Miyajima island, where they rendezvoused with two Japanese scientists, including Tsuzuki Masao, the country's leading authority on the biological effects of radiation as director of the Japanese Research Council and a lung surgeon at Tokyo Imperial University.[55] They embarked from there to assay the effects on human health and the environment, in what Junod later described as the "necropolis" of Hiroshima.[56] The ICRC had issued a public opinion on the strikes three days earlier, bundling the new weapon among various new tools of "totalitarian war" in calling on the victorious UN to revise the Geneva Conventions lest "destruction unlimited" forever subvert "the intrinsic worth and dignity of people."[57]

The ICRC were not alone in their unease. Though Truman's utterances on the atomic bomb varied with his audience, he clearly felt the moral weight of this new force. After meetings in Potsdam with Stalin and Attlee, whose Labour Party had defeated Churchill's Conservatives that summer, he set down in his diary that its employment should proceed "so that military objectives and soldiers and sailors are the target and not women and children." Paternal motifs would henceforth be staples of humanitarian criticisms of total air war.[58]

Truman's misimpression that Hiroshima was a purely military target had originated with Stimson, who contrasted it and Kyoto, Japan's ancient capital, too starkly when briefing the president.[59] The U.S. Army Air Corps' shift from precision to area bombing in late 1944, culminating when sixteen square miles of Tokyo went up in flame in March 1945, had blindsided the genteel statesman. A patrician New Yorker with degrees from Yale and Harvard Law School who rose to the rank of colonel as an artillery officer in the First World War, as Herbert Hoover's secretary of state Stimson had been the caretaker the 1929 Paris Peace Pact outlawing war, the 1930 London Naval Conference, and the 1932 World Disarmament Conference. Under Roosevelt and Truman, he continued to subscribe to the idea that prohibitions on unrestricted warfare against civilized nations in customary international law reflected virtuous statecraft. He was also attuned to how even a semblance of hypocrisy or inhumanity could diminish the majesty of distant governors, such as a president of the United States whose writ would soon run from Berlin to Tokyo. He had warned Truman in May 1945 that the "reputation of the United States for fair play and humanitarianism" would be instrumental for preserving a *pax Americana* after the war.[60] In Washington elite worldviews increasingly swallowed the globe. In his memoir, *On Active Service in Peace and War*, which he wrote with an amanuensis, McGeorge Bundy, Stimson set down that "no private program and no public policy" could succeed if it were "not framed with reference to the world."[61] The American colossus should stand as the vindicator of all humanity, a champion of peace, free trade, wealth preservation, Western tradition, and common decency, not a tyrant driven by lust for power, prestige, national glory, domination, or manifest destiny.

Stimson's calls for self-restraint were more aspirational than real. The U.S. Army Air Corps only began dropping propaganda leaflets warning Japanese civilians to flee target cities "in accordance with America's humanitarian policies" once victory in the Pacific was assured, and as chair of the Interim Committee, Stimson limited his conscientious objections to scratching Kyoto from nuclear target lists. After his retirement from public service in September 1945, Stimson labored to reconcile the decision to drop the atom bomb with his revulsion at the thought of nuclear warfare. His struggle emblematized the challenge of fusing armed might to moral right as Americans rechristened the Second World War as an antifascist crusade with reference to Japanese and Nazi enormities up to and including rape, ethnic cleansing, and genocide against Korean, Chinese, Jewish, and Slavic populations, elevating national security and defense spending as civic duties in a global campaign against communist totalitarianism.[62] With its own pressing interests in East Asia, Moscow would prove increasingly recalcitrant now that Japan had surrendered, making the drawing of bright lines between the region's new hegemons of utmost importance to leaders on both sides.

Truman's flinty pose hid serious qualms about utter destruction. Nagasaki's downfall on August 9 had taken him by surprise. Although he was commander in chief of the U.S. armed forces, as Groves later recalled, his role prior to the second attack had been "one of noninterference." Truman's reticence had stemmed from his belief that atomic destruction would be confined to military targets. In fact, he had been unaware that Hiroshima was a medium-sized city until August 8, when news reports of two hundred thousand dead—and a soul-searching meeting with Stimson in the Oval Office—forced a reappraisal. The fate of women and children became a recurrent motif for him (and his successors). When Georgia senator Richard Russell urged unrestricted warfare to bring the Japanese nation to its knees in an August 7 letter, the president demurred: "My object is to save as many American lives as possible but I also have a humane feeling for the women and children of Japan." He commanded U.S. major general Curtis LeMay that no further atomic bombings were to proceed without his express consent. In his own memoir, Secretary of Commerce Henry Wallace remembered the president's vocal regret at the death of "all those kids."[63]

Who commanded nuclear forces in a democratic republic carried weight. When Emperor Hirohito announced Japan's surrender on August 15, it was unclear whether military or civilian authorities in the United States were in charge of the small stockpile. Truman centralized nuclear decision making after Nagasaki, which the 1946 Atomic Energy Act later formalized, reasserting presidential war power just as the UN Charter entered into force. As with international law, the nuclear revolution blurred the line between war declaration, which the U.S. Constitution had vested in the legislative branch, and war waging, an executive duty. By enabling a surprise attack that could devastate the nation long before the U.S. Congress could convene, nuclear arsenals contributed powerfully to what historian Arthur M. Schlesinger Jr. would later style the "imperial presidency." While ensuring that an unhinged general or desperate pilot could not launch a nuclear war, presidential nondelegation opened nuclear-weapon policy to nonmilitary considerations.[64] In invoking women and children when expressing reservations about his new instrument of total violence, Truman not only hinted at to a taboo against their use, he set a new measure for their legitimacy: not just the security of his nation but the defense of all humankind.

This humanitarian reflux found a larger audience in August 1946, when the *New Yorker* devoted an entire issue to John Hersey's account of Hiroshima's destruction, weaving together the tales of six survivors of the bombing. The print run sold out within hours. New York City radio hosts read it verbatim over the airwaves. The Book of the Month Club distributed the paperback that Knopf rushed out for free. *Hiroshima* challenged the rightness of U.S. nuclear policy just two months after the Gromyko Plan. In doing so, it amplified key humanitarian concerns and tropes: medical relief, radiation sickness, innocent women, defenseless children. Hersey ended the story of his survivors' journeys to the beleaguered Red Cross hospital on a tragic, familial note, with Toshio Nakamura, an eleven-year-old schoolboy, recalling how two classmates, Kikuki and Murakami, had searched through the irradiated rubble for their mothers—one wounded, the other dead.[65] Hersey, who had reported on Red Cross relief operations in Japanese-occupied Manchuria throughout the war, donated proceeds from the standalone issue to the American Red Cross.[66]

Whereas early opinion polls had most Americans approving of Truman's boast that the air strike had repaid Japan's surprise attack on Pearl Harbor "many fold," *Hiroshima* led official explanations to shift ground. Stimson came out of retirement to author an apologia with Bundy in the February 1947 issue of *Harper's Magazine*—one month before Truman informed the U.S. Congress that Washington should replace London as Greece and Turkey's defender against the Soviet Union. The former secretary of war claimed that he and Truman had intended to deliver a "tremendous shock" to Hirohito and his court that, if effective, would induce their surrender, saving "many times the number of lives, both American and Japanese, than it would cost."[67] In lieu of military necessity or national vengeance, Stimson outlined a humanitarian calculus in which all lives would be weighed together, if not necessarily equally. Henceforth the arithmetic of human lives would be the benchmark of total nuclear war, at least rhetorically.

As Americans started to reappraise Hiroshima and Nagasaki, international councils worked to revise the laws of war. The nuclear revolution challenged just war tenets at a time of great flux, as global humanitarians wrestled with how to humanize air war. As with the Vatican, the ICRC's quiescence in the face of the war's many atrocities had blackened its name.[68] Meanwhile, the San Francisco Charter, the Nuremberg and Tokyo trials, and the 1948 Universal Declaration of Human Rights were clearing the way for a form of universal jurisdiction: introducing such terms and phrases as *genocide* and *crimes against humanity* into legal lexica; prosecuting individual conspirators for launching illegal wars of aggression or maltreating civilians, prisoners of war (POWs), and occupied populations; and recentering the legal person in international tribunals.[69] While the drafters of the UN Charter had placed their hopes in *jus ad bellum* to avert future monstrosities by effectively writing the Paris Peace Pact into the document, humanitarians remained focused on *jus in bello* in case all else failed.[70]

The Second World War's inventory of horrors made for grim reading. Around fifteen million men-in-arms had perished across all theaters, among whom were counted two million Soviet POWs and hundreds of thousands of Allied POWs. Approximately thirty-five million civilians had lost their lives, including six million Jews whom the shield of law had failed as the Nazis gassed them, burned them, or buried them in mass graves alongside communists, homosexuals, Romani, Slavs, and sundry "undesirables." The Axis powers held no monopoly on inhumanity. The commission and cover-up of the Katyn Forest massacre in Poland by the Soviet Red Army was but one example of allied misdeeds. Nanking, Coventry, Hamburg, Dresden, Berlin, Warsaw, Kiev, Minsk, Stalingrad, and Tokyo, among many others, lay in ruins. Millions of women had been subjected to sexual violence. After the shooting stopped, millions of refugees wandered across broken, ungoverned European and Asian landscapes.[71]

Most major belligerents had engaged in aerial bombardment. The International Military Tribunal to try Nazi leaders in Nuremberg was chartered on August 8, 1945, two days after the Hiroshima bombing and one day before Nagasaki. Together with the International Military Tribunal in the Far East, war crimes courts turned a blind eye to certain German and Japan transgressions lest they indirectly indict the UN.[72] All told, the U.S. Army Air Corps dropped around 335,000 tons of bombs over Europe from November 1943 to May 1945, and 170,000 tons over the Japanese islands from June 1944 to August 1945.[73] Little Boy and Fat Man were unique less for their scale or death toll than for their long-lasting effects.[74] Those in charge of Allied air campaigns already embraced tactics that were at best indifferent to civilian suffering.[75]

What separated atomic bombs from their conventional or incendiary cousins was their singular destructiveness and the insidiousness and persistence of their effects. When ICRC chief delegate Junod visited Hiroshima, his impressions largely mirrored Bilfinger's. His 1948 book, *Le Troisième Combattant*, which recounted his humanitarian work in the Second Italo-Abyssinian War, the Spanish Civil War, and the Second World War, foregrounded the new invention's superhuman power. He portrayed the blast as an act of God, whose absolute power Christian theology warned humanity against arrogating to itself: "Everything standing upright in the way of the blast, walls, houses, factories and other buildings, was annihilated and the debris spun round in a whirlwind and was carried up into the air. Trams were picked up and tossed aside as though they had neither weight nor solidity. Trains were flung off the rails as though they were toys."[76]

He highlighted how the sheer force of the blast had dehumanized Hiroshima's residents. "Horses, dogs and cattle suffered the same fate as human beings," his book reported. "Every living thing was petrified in an attitude of indescribable suffering: Even the vegetation did not escape. Trees went up in flames, the rice plants lost their greenness, the grass burned on the ground like dry straw."[77] Among humanitarians, the act of distinguishing between the treatment of people and that of animals was axiomatic, drawing on Christian theology and epistolary novels to assert humankind's claimed mastery over nature and singular capacity to suffer meaningfully. In the late eighteenth and nineteenth centuries, antislavery activists had adduced these sentiments to abolish the slave trade and chattel slavery.[78] In linking the fate of humans and nature, Junod implicitly condemned the *Enola Gay* for reducing humanity's lot to that of pets, livestock, or vermin. In his personal journal days after visiting Hiroshima he had made an explicit equivalence, noting how "thousands of human beings . . . died like flies."[79]

A rear admiral in the Japanese Navy Medical Corps, Tsuzuki was a first responder and an expert on radiation's biological effects. After accompanying Junod to Hiroshima, he related how after an impromptu experiment with an early X-ray machine in 1923, a rabbit had died within hours with hemorrhages throughout its body. He reran the experiment many times before presenting his findings in the *American Journal of Roentgenology*: "'Tomorrow when you go to Hiroshima you will see the upshot of my experiment,'" Junod wrote, reporting Tsuzuki's remarks. "80,000 dead and 100,000 wounded. . . . Yesterday it was rabbits, today it's Japanese.'"[80]

Over the next four years the ICRC would grapple with strategic nuclear bombing at a series of league and international conferences tasked with revising the Geneva Conventions. Both Junod and Bilfinger had called to have nuclear-weapon use declared verboten, as poison gas had been after the First World War.[81] True to form, medical zones and aerial bombardment were part of the agenda at the Preliminary Conference in Geneva from July 26 to August 3, 1946. Mere weeks after Baruch and Gromyko had unveiled their competing proposals, ICRC president Max Huber conceded that among those issues facing the Geneva Conventions, the "latest developments in physics" were "not only a moral one, but also a highly political one." When Basil O'Connor, since 1945 chairman of both the League of Red Cross and Red Crescent Societies and the American Red Cross, took the stage, he too praised "practical work" that "took note of the world as it is."[82] Unsurprisingly, the final conference report punted on issues related to aerial bombardment or even medical zones that might curtail its use in wartime.[83]

The international committee's juridical experts considered a more indirect approach. Although Jean Pictet, who led the ICRC's efforts to revamp the Geneva Conventions, conceded that Hiroshima "had changed the world," he classed atomic weapons with other weapons. The prolonged agony of atomic violence was "absolutely contrary to the law of nations," while, akin to rockets, their indiscriminate nature "imperiled the humane values for whose defense the Red Cross alone stood." He put forth two solutions. The first was a ban on the use of all "blind" weapons incapable of "precision against a discrete target," namely atomic, biological, or chemical warheads in addition to ballistic missiles.[84] His second recommendation was to formalize the demarcation of "security zones"—semi-elastic spaces near hospitals or shelters enjoying legal protection from military attack—with a view toward shielding innocent women, children, and the elderly. This pragmatic approach might help avert another Nagasaki—in a town or city, such zones, often in dense, central districts, would create a class of collateral damage whose targeting from the air, via conventional carpet or atomic bombing, would be effectively outlawed by the new and revised Geneva Conventions.[85]

The brewing Cold War, however, hampered efforts to humanize strategic bombing. Sixty-nine delegates from fifteen governments joined nongovernmental observers at the Conference of Government Experts for the Study of the Conventions for the Protection of War Victims in April 1947, at the Palais des Nations—the League of Nations' former headquarters in Geneva. No Soviet delegate attended, as Moscow had boycotted the ICRC since the Spanish Civil War. The conference discussed revisions to the Geneva Convention for the relief of the wounded and sick, the Tenth Hague Convention for the Adaptation to Maritime Warfare of the Principles of the Geneva Convention, and the 1929 Geneva Convention relative to the treatment of prisoners of war. It formalized Pictet's new draft convention for the protection of civilians—a far-reaching response to the victimization of occupied populations during the recent war.

Pictet's security zone concept was also on the agenda. It faced opposition, however, precisely because it would curtail indiscriminate attacks against population centers. The expert conference thus moderated antibombing efforts by limiting them to hospitals and shelters whose immunity would remain voluntary. Afterward, the ICRC's Presidency Council debated what position to take on two Yugoslavian resolutions on "the peace question" and "the humanization of war," both of which implicated the U.S. nuclear monopoly.[86] Director Claude Pilloud warned not to open Pandora's box lest proceedings "take a political turn" to the advantage of "the Eastern Red Cross societies." Frédéric Siordet backed Pictet in reminding the council that there were those in the United States who opposed the use of the atom bomb save in cases of last resort, but Pilloud nonetheless won the day.[87] The ICRC would err on the side of neutrality, which meant, in practice, upholding the status quo. To intervene when representatives of the world's governments and Red Cross and Red Crescent societies met in Stockholm to review the Geneva Conventions would force them to "stand up against a state that is armed, against a party that is judged likely to promote conflict," which could "spell the end of the Red Cross."[88]

O'Connor officially led the U.S. delegation of fourteen officials from the Pentagon and the State Department, in addition to his American Red Cross delegation. U.S. secretary of state George C. Marshall handed O'Connor detailed instructions to take a firm stand that the conference should "limit itself to purely humanitarian work." The UN rather than the Red Cross, the author of the European Recovery Act instructed," should handle international nuclear questions.[89] The ICRC directorate likewise instructed Pictet "to maintain the distinction between charity and peace." The Red Cross would absent itself from international politics. He and his team would consequently keep their own counsel on arms bans.[90]

Matters came to a head at the Geneva Diplomatic Conference from April 21 to August 12, 1949, when the new and revised Geneva Conventions were finalized. To the surprise of many, the Soviet Union sent a delegation to the Swiss city, where it and its socialist brethren proposed a resolution to ban the use of nuclear weapons altogether—a revealing qualification of the Gromyko proposal, which had promised wholesale abolition. Pictet took issue with the ensuing U.S.-UK move to have the conference declare itself "incompetent" on the matter, a maneuver he deemed "clearly abusive."[91] Security zones did not fare much better. During discussion on April 27 in committee deliberations over the new civilian convention, Monaco's delegate, Paul de la Pradelle, an international law professor based in Aix-en-Provence, importuned his fellow delegates that these zones "in the last resort were the only reply to the atomic bomb."[92] The Republic of China delegate's uncertainty about their "efficacity in an atomic war" registered the lost opportunity the next day.[93] British and U.S. objections ensured that states parties would have to conclude a model agreement annexed to the new convention, lessening prospects for erecting firewalls around areas of any size, as in wartime belligerents could refuse to recognize their adversaries' security zones. The 1949 Geneva Conventions consequently contained no real check on death from above, atomic or otherwise. In the next war, "wounded, sick and aged persons, children under fifteen, expectant mothers and mothers of children under seven" would find few shelters from the fate that had befallen kindred souls in Hiroshima and Nagasaki.[94]

Less than three weeks after the conference wrapped up, the Soviet Ministry of Medium Machine-Building Industry detonated Izdeliye 501, its first nuclear device. One week later, Truman's press secretary handed the White House press corps a presidential announcement that the federal government had obtained "evidence that within recent weeks an atomic explosion had occurred in the U.S.S.R." In early September, Air Weather Service flights out of Alaska carrying air-sampling, radiological systems had detected the blast, whose source acquired the nickname Joe-1.[95] One month later, the Chinese Communist Party (CCP) proclaimed the creation of a People's Republic of China. The U.S. nuclear monopoly had ended. The age of proliferation had begun.

IV

The arrival of a second member in the nuclear club forced a showdown between proponents of nuclear regulation and those who reckoned the technology would prove self-regulating. From 1949 to 1954, nuclear-weapon testing emerged as the focal point of that debate, pitting those who viewed grand questions of war and peace from standpoints of humanitarianism, technocracy, or deterrence against one another in a struggle to define the nuclear revolution. As testing gave birth to a transnational environmental crisis, the irradiation of the Earth motivated efforts both to halt the U.S.-Soviet nuclear arms race and to consolidate atomic privilege in existing hands.[96]

To Bernard Brodie, a student of naval warfare at Yale University's Institute for International Studies, what Oppenheimer characterized as "weapons of aggression, of surprise, and of terror" demanded a basic rethink of the military arts. In the six months after Hiroshima, he and his colleagues wrote *The Absolute Weapon*, with Brodie's keynote chapter ending on an iconoclastic note: the U.S. armed services should no longer aim to win wars but rather to avert them—they now served "no other useful purpose." This stunning departure from received wisdom flowed from a confluence of forecasts about air-atomic warfare: atom bombs were city-destroyers; there were no effective defenses against them—not even command of the air—and few prospects of inventing them soon; long-range bombers and ballistic missiles would shrink strategic spacetime, reducing windows for decision making; strategic nuclear superiority was unachievable through sheer numbers alone; world uranium resources were effectively unlimited; and it was only a matter of time before foreign powers acquired the "absolute weapon."[97] Arnold Wolfers, Brodie's colleague, went so far as to predict and praise a balance of terror once Stalin acquired a commensurate nuclear capability: "Soviet-American 'equality in deterring power,'" he reassured his readers, "would prove the best guarantee of peace."[98]

Nuclear statecraft was bound up in the deterioration of U.S.-Soviet relations after 1945 and Washington's implementation of a grand strategy to maintain the country's economic, technological, and military edge by containing Soviet geopolitical and ideological influence.[99] Brodie's "deterrence theory" offered a powerful justificatory logic and evaluative framework as the U.S. Congress drafted and passed the National Security Act of 1947 in consultation with the Truman administration. The act transformed the U.S. Department of War into the U.S. Department of Defense, now escorted by a wing of new national-security agencies: the Central Intelligence Agency (CIA), the Joint Chiefs of Staff (JCS), and the National Security Council (NSC). It also established the U.S. Air Force, whose senior leaders, Spaatz and Henry "Hap" Arnold, assigned LeMay, the mastermind of the aerial campaign against Japan, to lead a new Strategic Air Command (SAC). Like Oppenheimer and Brodie, LeMay believed the nuclear revolution had altered "the fundamental military concepts of the United States."[100] He accordingly set out to hone SAC into "a force so professional, so powerful that we would not have to fight. It would act as "a deterrent force."

Unlike Wolfers, LeMay rejected mutual vulnerability. Rather than accept that Soviet bombers might inflict a retaliatory blow on the U.S. mainland, he aimed to preempt them. His rhetoric exuded racialist thinking. When he addressed the National War College in April 1956, he pledged that SAC bombers would render the

Soviet Union "a nation infinitely poorer than China—less populated than the United States and condemned to an agrarian existence perhaps for generations to come."[101] His bombers would enforce humankind's division into capitalism's beneficiaries and those whom the U.S. Air Force would, if necessary, bomb "back into the Stone Age."[102]

First, however, the Truman and Eisenhower administrations needed to rebuild a nuclear enterprise that had entered the doldrums. When Lilienthal took over as AEC chair in October 1946, he was shocked at what had become of the Manhattan Project. When he visited Los Alamos in January 1947, "there really were no bombs in a military sense." The national laboratory had lost nearly its entire contingent of scientists and engineers; it took two days for an existing team of twenty-four to assemble just one of the few bombs on hand. Fissile-material production had also slowed to a crawl. Initial war plans that targeted twenty industrial centers in the Soviet Union for atomic strikes with a view to disrupting its oil infrastructure suffered from a lack of trained personnel, bombers, and bombs, with Spaatz counting about a dozen warheads and thirty-two nuclear-capable B-29 Superfortresses in the U.S. Air Force bomber fleet as late as April 1948.[103]

Worsening U.S.-Soviet relations tested Truman's reliance on the air-atomic offensive. Rapid demobilization fitted his austere financial instincts and unease with universal military training. A plummeting military budget, however, which Secretary of Defense James Forrestal initiated and his successor, Louis Johnson, deepened, stoked tensions among the newly unified armed services, with Spaatz pushing for a seventy-group U.S. Air Force and the U.S. Navy bristling at a reduced role in national strategy. The interservice rivalry exploded into public view when senior Navy leadership, including fleet admirals William Leahy, William Halsey, and Chester Nimitz testified alongside Chief of Naval Operations Louis Denfeld to the House Armed Services Committee. While criticisms of strategic bombing defined the admirals' revolt, their main grievance was the cancellation of a new generation of aircraft carrier outfitted for nuclear missions. Mounting tensions in central Europe—a communist coup in Czechoslovakia and Stalin's blockade of West Berlin after Western powers introduced a new deutschmark—did little to reverse the downward trend. For fifteen months, the United States, France, and British Commonwealth members airlifted supplies into the besieged city, while B-29s winged their way to the United Kingdom to signal resolve in case of Soviet military action. None were equipped for nuclear missions.[104]

The loss of the U.S. nuclear monopoly precipitated high-level reviews of the atomic stockpile and overall national-security strategy. Led by Oppenheimer, the AEC's GAC reviewed how best to bolster the stockpile after Joe-1: to pursue Teller's Super bomb, which would ignite various hydrogen-based fuels with a fission trigger, or to devote rare fissile materials to existing designs, including the new, more efficient, Mark 4 atom bomb tested in the AEC's Operation Sandstone in the summer of 1948. Oppenheimer joined a majority to advocate for an expanded arsenal of tried-and-true warheads on both strategic and humanitarian grounds, warning that thermonuclear arms "might become a weapon of genocide." In calling for Truman to back a universal ban on such armaments, physicists I. I. Rabi and Enrico Fermi evoked the 1948 Universal Declaration of Human Rights in their minority dissent. The two men, one Jewish and the other married to an Italian Jew, deemed the hydrogen bomb "necessarily an evil thing considered in any light" in calling for an international treaty to abolish them. Truman delegated the decision to Lilienthal, Johnson, and Acheson, who ultimately dismissed the GAC's reservations. At the behest of Lewis Strauss and Gordon Dean (who would replace Lilienthal as AEC commissioner), the AEC dismissed "moral considerations" as altogether irrelevant.[105]

Truman was easily persuaded. He had always viewed humanitarian considerations as the president's paternal responsibility. While the United States faced at worst a brief game of catch-up with the Soviets if it were to have forgone the thermonuclear route, the nationalist defeat in the Chinese Civil War was a major black eye for him and Acheson, who faced charges of "losing China" amid a gathering Red Scare in Washington. The arrest of British physicist and Manhattan Project veteran Klaus Fuchs on espionage charges that winter had turned unilateral restraint into political self-harm. On the heels of the Soviet nuclear test, the national-security bureaucracy pushed hard for a military force structure commensurate with the doctrine that Truman had sketched out in 1947 to bolster anticommunist forces in the eastern Mediterranean. A paper authored by Kennan's replacement at the Policy Planning Staff, Assistant Secretary of State Paul Nitze, NSC-68, "United States Objectives and Programs for National Security," called for a military buildup to counter Soviet support for communist insurrectionists worldwide, a massive expansion of U.S. national-security priorities.[106]

The outbreak of the Korean War on June 25, 1950, transformed NSC-68 into government policy. Nitze's blueprint for Cold War militarization leaned heavily on a strengthened nuclear deterrent by means of a crash thermonuclear program. When Kim Il Sung's forces poured across the 38th Parallel, where the occupying powers had divided the former Japanese colony between his communist forces and Syngman Rhee's U.S.-backed Republic of Korea (ROK), it looked like confirmatory evidence that Stalin was embarked on a globe-spanning effort to install communists in power across Europe and Asia. Whereas Kennan had tried to focus U.S. commitments on the industrial cores of Western Europe and Japan, Nitze identified even peripheral zones in Latin America or Africa as worthy of military intervention.

MacArthur's initial tactical brilliance with U.S. armed forces out of Japan masked the strategic deficits that Truman's decision to intervene under the flag of the UN had exposed. The general's subsequent insistence on reunifying the peninsula triggered a mammoth People's Liberation Army (PLA) counteroffensive in late November, and eventually a stalemate near the initial line of control. While U.S. military spending would quadruple over the next three years, the rapid change of fortune in Korea demonstrated the inadequacy of military strategy reliant on low-cost air-atomic power. Over the next three years the U.S. Air Force would drop more bombs on North Korea had it had on Japan from 1942 to 1945, yet Truman denied MacArthur's requests to go nuclear for fear of allied and Afro-Asian condemnation of the United States visiting atomic death on Asians once again.[107] His public rationales, however, focused on the humanitarian toll. The Korean War raised the specter of communist "slavery," but in his memoirs Truman justified his restraint on grounds that the Bomb should never again be used "on innocent men, women and children."[108]

The second nuclear age bloomed over Eniwetok Atoll in the Marshall Islands on November 1, 1952, when the United States tested a boosted hydrogen bomb—a fission primary surrounded by a rare hydrogen isotope called tritium—that exceeded Fat Man's destructiveness by a factor of 1,000. Code-named Ivy Mike, the blast replaced Elugelab island with a human-made caldera on the ocean floor. Led by the brilliant physicist Andrei Sakharov, the Soviets tested their own thermonuclear device based on a novel "layer-cake" design just nine months later, on August 12, 1953.

The thermonuclear revolution raised the Cold War's stakes immensely, as the testing of these superweapons came to overshadow and eventually subsume debates about nuclear war. Soviet premier Nikita Khrushchev's comment to Dwight Eisenhower in 1958, "we get your dust, you get our dust, the winds blow, and nobody's safe," typified a growing perception of humanity's ability to poison its planetary environment.[109] Fallout anxiety transcended borders, shifting elite and public opinion about arms control and U.S.-Soviet détente, while the shared knowledge that each side now held the key to the other's annihilation exerted a stabilizing influence on U.S.-Soviet competition.[110]

During his campaign against Democratic candidate Adlai Stevenson in 1952, Eisenhower had promised to "go to Korea." Long after the armistice that froze conflict near the 38th Parallel, the former five-star general and Supreme Allied Commander in Europe continued to use nuclear brinksmanship to ward off total thermonuclear war and a domestic garrison state. He had an eventful first term: Eisenhower backed coups in Guatemala and Iran; supported the French in Indochina and—after their defeat at Dien Bien Phu and the 1954 Geneva Conference—the Republic of Vietnam; accepted that Southern Jim Crow risked alienating Afro-Asian leaders following their inaugural meeting in Bandung, Indonesia, in April 1955; built the Interstate Highway System; and punished Paris, London, and Tel Aviv for their conspiracy to occupy the Suez Canal in 1956.[111] He saw the shattered atom as key to safeguarding U.S. democracy and capitalism without constructing a liberty-suffocating garrison state, justifying a nuclear buildup that would yield a "deterrent of massive retaliatory power," as his secretary of state, John Foster Dulles, described it to the Council on Foreign Relations in January 1954, even as he evangelized on behalf of its peaceful uses.[112] National Security Council report 162/2, on "Basic National Security Policy," intimated that brazen threats would terrify opponents into submission, or at least into restraining themselves near "free world" redoubts in South Korea, South Vietnam, the Republic of China, Japan, the Philippines, Australia, New Zealand, and West Germany.

Eisenhower sought to synergize the U.S. nuclear arsenal with covert and psychological operations to contain Soviet influence in Europe and in underdeveloped nations in the Third World while avoiding permanent military mobilization. His administration set out a New Look national-security doctrine in NSC 162/2, which called among other efforts for massive investments in nuclear forces.[113] "In the event of hostilities," the report affirmed, Eisenhower would "consider nuclear weapons to be as available for use as other munitions."[114] In lieu of combat troops, the AEC would enlarge the nuclear stockpile from 1,000 to 24,000 warheads, including city-busting thermonuclear warheads, over his eight years in office. Their means of delivery were diversified in the form of a triad held jointly by the U.S. Air Force, the U.S. Army, and the U.S. Navy: long-range B-52 Stratofortress bombers in the SAC; ground-launched, Jupiter medium-range ballistic missiles (MRBMs) and Thor intermediate-range ballistic missiles (IRBMs); and Polaris sub-launched ballistic missiles (SLBMs) aboard nuclear-powered, ballistic-missile submarines. If the *Enola Gay* had shown that a single bomb could replace an air division, the newest delivery systems compressed spacetime toward an event horizon—the destructive capacity of a world war in less than an hour, with at most thirty minutes' warning before the first staggering blow landed.

For Eisenhower, nuclear forces glued far-flung military outposts, deployments, and treaty arrangements together. Washington would wield atomic might on its allies' behalf in various ways. Extended nuclear deterrence amounted to formal or informal assurances to use nuclear weapons in retaliation when an ally faced armed aggression. There were a few downsides. Such commitments gave rise to perverse incentives for non-nuclear partners to act out, for example, in Republic of China president Chiang Kai-shek's repeated entreaties to retake the Chinese mainland with U.S. military assistance. And there was a credibility gap, as guarantees were less credible than self-centered threats: when the chips were down, would Eisenhower really sacrifice New York and Washington, D.C., for London and Paris? If positive assurances opened an umbrella over another country's territory, negative ones amounted to pledges not to use them in certain cases, signaling restraint and removing the need to respond in kind. In the final analysis, both forms of nuclear assurance had the added benefit of discouraging new states from acquiring arsenals.[115]

The New Look had two Achilles' heels. First, massive retaliation was unbelievable. Since a nuclear strike was so rarely proportionate to any military threat or objective, it suffered from a credibility gap in the eyes of adversaries and allies alike.[116] Yet Eisenhower was inclined by his study of military theory and his own wartime experience to doubt that commanders would holster their most powerful weapon amid the fog of war. He wagered instead that adversaries would fold when faced with the prospect of prompt escalation to all-out war. A wily strategist, he concluded that nuclear-weapon use was ill-suited to meaningful political ends and ran excessive risks—better to threaten all-out war than to sleepwalk into nuclear disaster. In the patois of the poker table, which he often frequented, Eisenhower would dare his opponents to call his bluff.[117]

While Eisenhower avoided a major war scare with the Soviet Union during his time in office, the nuclear card proved less availing in achieving battlefield success. Dulles claimed that a nuclear threat relayed through Jawaharlal Nehru, prime minister of India, helped end the Korean War in 1953, but it had been Georgy Malenkov's entreaties to Chinese foreign minister Zhou Enlai at Stalin's funeral that set those wheels in motion.[118] Nor had Viet Minh irregulars fled in 1954, when Dulles and Eisenhower flirted with furnishing two atom bombs to the beleaguered French garrison at Dien Bien Phu.[119] While one year later Mao would eventually cease bombarding the tiny offshore islands of Quemoy and Matsu that both he and Chiang claimed, Eisenhower and Dulles's ambiguity about their readiness to authorize nuclear retaliation bordered on reticence.[120] As the president would later concede, the costs were too high as decolonization transformed the international scene: the United States could not "use those awful things against Asians for the second time in less than ten years."[121] The risk of losing European or Japanese support for the U.S. overseas presence in Asia outweighed the tactical benefits in the theater.[122]

The second downside was that massive retaliation did little to discourage nuclear proliferation. To wield atomic forces so unapologetically had the effect of normalizing them, while the challenge of drawing clear redlines led allies to wonder whether their particular umbrella bore holes. Enemy missiles capable of hitting North America further undermined deterrence architectures that had been designed to offset conventional deficiencies in central Europe and East Asia. Soviet mastery of intercontinental ballistic missiles (ICBMs) following the successful orbit of *Sputnik 1* on October 4, 1957, hammered this point home. Once the United States faced preemptive or retaliatory strikes, allies would have to ask themselves how long elected U.S. officials would ensure their security using American lives as collateral.[123]

Conclusion

On the morning of March 1, 1954, the AEC exploded the world's first true thermonuclear device, Castle Bravo, on Bikini Atoll. Measuring 12 megatons, the blast was so colossal that observers witnessed it 176 miles away on Kwajalein Atoll. Good weather shifted unexpectedly into heavy winds above 10,000 feet that morning, and 28 American servicemen and 236 natives were evacuated as fallout swept through the Marshall Islands. Eighty-five miles away, radiation inundated the Japanese fishing ship *Fukuryu Maru*—the *Lucky Dragon*—while harvesting tuna outside a quarantine zone.

The Lucky Dragon incident inflamed Japanese and world opinion, jeopardizing the vital alliance established by the Security Treaty and the San Francisco Peace Treaty of 1951. The presence of American bases in the Philippines, Turkey, Great Britain, Cuba, and Okinawa now "brought home to nearby residents the possibility that they might be the targets of a nuclear attack."[124] Prime targets due to the presence of the U.S. Navy's Seventh Fleet, the Japanese were particularly uneasy with Eisenhower's New Look.[125] Their densely packed islands, so recently the target of widespread strategic bombing, made for a distinctly anxious target. When the *Lucky Dragon* returned home on March 14, panic struck the nation as the ship's twenty-three crewmen battled radiation poisoning. One eventually succumbed to what the Japanese dubbed the "ashes of death."[126] Local governments destroyed hundreds of tons of tuna while middle-class housewives from the Suginami ward of Tokyo circulated a petition against the hydrogen bomb. Over thirty-two million people—more than one third of Japan's population—signed it. The reaction was so vehement, demonstrative, and widespread that the U.S. ambassador to Japan, John Allison, concluded that the "government and people cracked."[127]

The global nuclear testing controversy placed a test ban atop the international agenda. Beginning with Nehru's call for a "standstill agreement" on April 2, 1954, a gathering sense that Asian people were "always nearer these occurrences and experiments" tied the U.S.-Soviet nuclear arms race to postcolonial grievances about international equity.[128] Over the course of his first term, Eisenhower offered various schemes in line with developmental or humanitarian narratives of nuclear science and technology: an Open Skies proposal to allow overflights of both superpowers' territory, an International Atomic Energy Agency to promote "Atoms for Peace" in a memorable speech to the UNGA in December 1953, and a two-year test moratorium in May 1957 in the service of general and complete disarmament. Yet nuclear globalization proceeded apace. By the time the United Kingdom became the third thermonuclear power after a successful test in the South Pacific on November 8, 1957, nuclear infrastructure had been seeded throughout North America, Europe, the Soviet camp, and the Third World. Hiroshima inspired a wave of new thinking about humanity, progress, security, and equality after the nuclear revolution. Over the next fifteen years, a growing society of nation-states would debate how far to let that revolution go.

2

"Uncontrollable Anarchy"
Founding the Nuclear Club, 1956–1961

Introduction—The Idea of Nuclear Restraint

"How can the course of history be turned away from death and towards life?" This was how Frank Aiken began his address to the UN General Assembly (UNGA) on September 19, 1958. Crowned by the UN emblem, he surveyed the circular hall that rectilinear banks of incandescent bulbs bathed in spectral light. An Irish Republican Army (IRA) commander in the country's civil war over the continuation of British rule, Aiken left Sinn Féin for the less militant Fianna Fáil in 1927. Now that he was Ireland's foreign minister, the notion that humanity's command over nature might spell "the destruction or mutilation of people everywhere" troubled his faith that the world's age-old conflicts would find resolution in the UN: "Today . . . the question for us all is how in the shadow of the Atom Bomb to build a world order in which our disputes will be resolved by an accepted common authority whose decisions are implemented by an international force—in short, how to preserve a *Pax Atomica* while we build a *Pax Mundi.*" With hopes for disarmament "vain" and the super-powers wielding "enormous destructive potentiality" in their nuclear stalemate, the international community assembled in New York faced a universal catastrophe, a challenge that grew more pressing and intractable "with every addition to the number of nuclear Powers." He called on those without such arms to forswear them and on "existing members of the so-called nuclear club—the United States, U.S.S.R., Great Britain and France . . . in God's name not to spread these weapons around the world."[1]

Even as Aiken put forward what would become known as the Irish Resolution in New York, Soviet deputy foreign minister Vasily Kuznetsov delivered a letter to the U.S. embassy in Moscow from Premier Nikita Khrushchev. Mao Zedong had welcomed the Soviet leader to Beijing that July for his first visit to the Soviet Union's premier communist ally. Mao was pushing buttons at home and abroad, as he protested his government's dispossession of its rightful seat on the UN Security Council (UNSC) by the Republic of China, led by his bitter rival Chiang Kai-Shek on the island of Taiwan; rebuffed Soviet advances for joint naval bases and submarine fleets; and steeled his countrymen for China's economy to vault past Great Britain's in the Great Leap Forward.[2] Khrushchev was correspondingly left in the dark when Mao ordered the People's Liberation Army (PLA) to shell Quemoy and Matsu—two island specks mere miles off the mainland's shore—on August 23.

Unbeknownst to both, the U.S. Joint Chiefs of Staff resolved that same day to meet an attack on Taiwan with "atomic strikes against the Chinese mainland."[3] President Dwight D. Eisenhower ordered two aircraft carrier groups redeployed from the Mediterranean and the Persian Gulf, where they had been supporting American and British landings in Lebanon and Jordan, to the Taiwan Strait, to form "the most powerful armada the world had ever seen."[4] The naval guardians of the Pacific Ocean would make a show of force to encourage the revolutionary to back down, just as Mao informed his fellow Chinese Communist Party (CCP) Politburo members that his intention had been to "prove that China supports the national liberation movements in the Middle East with not only words but also deeds."[5] The nuclear shield went with them. The Pentagon shifted Strategic Air Command (SAC) bombers and Nike Hercules surface-to-air missiles across the world ocean. Against the backdrop of an unforeseen crisis, Khrushchev wrote to warn Eisenhower that "atomic blackmail" would frighten neither him nor his Chinese allies. He reminded his American counterpart that he commanded a strategic nuclear arsenal as well, pledging that "if such an attack is made the aggressor will immediately receive a proper repulse with these very means."[6] He failed to mention that Soviet specialists were even then schooling their Chinese comrades in the modern arts of nuclear science and engineering.[7]

Aiken's remarks in New York therefore occurred as nuclear crises in the Middle East and East Asia threatened both the *pax Americana* and the *pax Sovietica*. Novelty lay in their substance rather than their form, as newborn nation-states emerged from colonialism with aspirations of rising wealth and newfound status. How to deal with international instability in an era when both radii and nations were undergoing fission had become an urgent matter.

This chapter recounts the history of nuclear restriction from the Irish Resolution to the nuclear powers' wary acceptance of it, as barring the door to the nuclear club went from concept to cause. The growing competitiveness of the global nuclear market and mounting evidence that some states with nuclear forces were lending material aid to those without prompted Aiken's proposal to internationalize nuclear restraint, its fate at four successive general assemblies hinging on superpower support at a time when Charles de Gaulle's France, David Ben-Gurion's Israel, and Mao Zedong's communist China all eyed independent nuclear-weapon programs and the North Atlantic Treaty Organization (NATO) debated how to share the burden of its nuclear defense after *Sputnik*. The Irish Resolution built on efforts to reorganize regional and global politics as the emergence of Latin America, Africa, Asia, and the Middle East from colonialism interacted with the Cold War's geo-ideological struggle. Advanced by a Northern postcolonial republic with an anticolonial tradition, the idea of restricting membership in the nuclear club was first presented as a means by which to achieve republican ends: a world order under the rule of universal law in which the atomic contagion would be quarantined en route to its eventual eradication.

I

Born in 1898, Aiken joined the IRA to free Ireland from British rule after leaving his family's home in Camlough, in what is today Northern Ireland, rising in time to serve as commandant of the IRA's Fourth Northern Division and eventually the guerrilla body's chief of staff. His revolutionary career came to an end in 1923, when he proclaimed the cease-fire that formally ended the uprising. During his second appointment as foreign minister following an unremarkable first stint from 1951 to 1954—and the Republic of Ireland's belated entry into the UN in 1955—Aiken made the UNGA, for him "the platform for the concentrated expression of the moral conscience of mankind," the focal point of Irish foreign relations. He did so in conscious homage to Ireland's small stature, anticolonial traditions, and liberal values.[8] Through the UN, Aiken remarked, small nations like Ireland "can compel a hearing for their opinions and their dreams."[9]

As a nation that had wrested partial independence from the United Kingdom, Ireland shared affinities with an expanding universe of postcolonial states as the 1950s gave way to the 1960s. As an Atlantic country, it knew its neighbors, many NATO members, and they knew it—Dublin had steered clear of the Atlantic Alliance "not based on neutrality or non-alliance as a principle" but in protest over the partition of Northern Ireland.[10] As for North America, the late-nineteenth-century Irish diaspora had forged links of kin and culture with its Eastern metropolises. Ireland accordingly joined the UN as a postcolonial republic unaffiliated with the nonaligned movement or the Atlantic Alliance, yet enjoying good relations with both. This singular identity—a small, neutral, liberal, colonial survivor in the North Atlantic—conditioned Irish elites to view the supranational organization with enthusiasm.[11] It also empowered Aiken to challenge Western powers as a friend, such as when he criticized them for kicking Beijing out of the UNSC, which he held had the deleterious effects of isolating the CCP from world opinion, disenfranchising six hundred million Chinese, and in these ways reinforcing "the darkest and most oppressive trends at work in China."[12]

For Aiken, the UN was "the embodiment of the principles which our patriots died to uphold." In a history lesson before a crowded room at the Chicago Rotary Club on October 31, 1960, he invoked Ireland's proud tradition as an insular nation that had "learned the value of civil, religious and national liberty the hard way" to explain his views on decolonization: "The Irish delegation feel bound to use our voice in the Assembly to defend national and individual rights wherever they may be attacked . . . and to help win self-determination for the peoples still under the yoke of the foreigner." His Irish nationalism disposed him kindly toward anticolonial movements in Africa and Asia; his backing of Algeria's freedom struggle in 1957 was an early sign that he was taking Irish foreign policy in a more independent direction. However, his republicanism, when applied to the supranational organization, his conservative Catholicism (which imbued his support of human rights with a religious fervor), and Taoiseach (Irish prime minster) Éamon de Valera's fear of alienating European trading partners, inclined Aiken against revolutionary violence. Algeria was a case in point. Although in 1960 Aiken called the cause of nationality "sacred, in Asia and Africa as in Ireland," de Valera's fear of trade restrictions and exclusion from the European Economic Community (EEC), founded by the French in March 1957, together with Aiken's personal respect for de Gaulle and affinity for Gaullism, led the Irish foreign minister to hold his fire.[13] Until his retirement from the foreign ministry in 1969, the importance of U.S. dollars and European markets in the development agenda of Seán Lemass, de Valera's successor as of 1961, would force Aiken to take U.S. and European views on Vietnam and NATO nuclear-sharing into stronger consideration.[14]

His revolutionary credentials lent credence to his pleas for restraint. He cited the UN as a new factor that had rendered otiose "armed struggle" such as that which soaked his native soil with blood, including by his own hands.[15] The UN would henceforth police the borders where conflicts between national sovereignty and human rights arose amid contests for national liberation. And as U.S.-Soviet relations languished, Aiken rallied neutral and nonaligned states, which with the addition of seventeen new African nations that year comprised half of the UNGA, to play a leading role "in the development of the United Nations in the nuclear age."[16] For its part, Ireland would serve as a peacemaker as the world community inched toward world government.[17]

While he would acknowledge that states would not lightly submit to its "charter of liberty" until its rule was "enforceable by an international police force," his interventions in New York had had a common theme since 1957: the UN's role in world affairs should grow continuously and organically.[18] He diagnosed the crises in the Levant and the Taiwan Strait as symptomatic of the tragedy of the Cold War in what was becoming known as the Third World: Moscow's and Washington's military reach had added the perils of nuclear brinkmanship to the harms of foreign intervention.[19] His guiding vision, "the rule of law based on justice," flowed from two judgments about the historical relationship among war, technology, and society. For him, the UN Charter marked the culmination of an epochal process in which the scale of the highest unit of political organization had grown to match the power of the preeminent engines of war. When called to defend his internationalist foreign policy before the Dáil Éireann, the lower house of the Oireachtas, Ireland's parliament, his remarks took a philosophical turn: When "a man could bar himself in his cave and be reasonably certain of defending himself and his family he could afford to be a law unto himself, but with the invention of the bow and arrow men had to combine into clans, and accept the law making and law enforcement authority of the head of the clan." These clans in time grew into "principalities" and "principalities into nations." Now faced with "monster alliances capable of mutual and total destruction," he envisioned a central authority that would resolve international disputes in line with the dictates of law and justice, with the power to enforce the collective will by force if necessary.[20]

This narrative arc informed his second point: the UN should grow methodically and holistically, beginning with regions whose political borders had been drawn by colonial authorities. When questioned in the Oireachtas about his preoccupation with the supranational organization in 1957, Aiken had likened it to "a seed or a plant . . . for I think we must depend upon organic growth and almost imperceptible growth for its perfection, rather than upon a mechanical process of building according to elaborately prepared plans."[21] Organicist conceptions had been present at the writing of the UN Charter (as with the League of Nations). Negotiators at Bretton Woods and San Francisco had justified such concessions to international hierarchy as veto powers for UNSC permanent members with claims that parliamentary features would eventually supplant those that had institutionalized the power of the victorious alliance.[22] His faith that representative consent would eventually triumph over arbitrary power led him to value expediency in UN campaigns. He cited the peacekeeping forces in Kashmir since 1949, the UN police action on the Korean peninsula from 1950 to 1953, and the first emergency force deployed to Suez in 1956 as signs of political maturation, foreseeing that the veto power would eventually "disappear like the Divine Right of Kings," that is, if the world were to avoid a third world war.[23] (The military forces that Ireland contributed to the UN peacekeeping mission to the Congo in 1960 would be held hostage by Katangese forces during the Siege of Jadotville). He omitted how the League of Nations and the UN had owed their existence to the first two world wars.

II

The nuclear restriction bore all the hallmarks of Aiken's republican internationalism. Whereas peace efforts had long fixated on grand solutions, most notably general and complete disarmament, Aiken insisted that it "follow, not precede, the reduction of the political tensions which cause wars to break out."[24] Arms races were after all "only the manifestations of a lack of mutual confidence," he stated: "the real problems are political in character."[25]

Fianna Fáil's victory in the 1957 election brought Aiken into office and Ireland's foreign policies into a more assertive configuration, as he charted more independent courses on Algeria, Berlin, Tibet, Hungary, and apartheid South Africa.[26] He endorsed careful steps toward a better tomorrow with a paternal admonition in a September address to the UNGA: "heir to many problems created by predatory ancestors in another age," his generation "must move swiftly, decisively and wisely if we are to save ourselves and our children." He cast a skeptical eye on nuclear terror. And his pessimism bled into outright cynicism when he spoke of general and complete disarmament, the subject of U.S.-Soviet dickering since 1953, which he compared to the failed disarmament campaigns that had preceded the Second World War. A letter to the U.S. State Department in 1961 would denounce "the shibboleths of 40 years of disarmament talks and conferences" as illusory, insincere, and counterproductive in the face of "two tremendous concentrations of power."[27] In his first speech to the UNGA as foreign minister in 1957, he warned that until "the political foundations of peace" were laid, "there can be no stable superstructure: only a flimsy and ephemeral façade."[28]

That superstructure had been teetering since autumn 1956, when Warsaw Pact tanks had rolled over the Hungarian revolt and France, Israel, and the United Kingdom's Suez adventure had incited nuclear threats from Moscow and economic retaliation from Washington. Aiken's criticisms of Middle Eastern interventions echoed those he had leveled at the East-West standoff in Europe in 1957. He had drawn inspiration from Korea's and Vietnam's longitudinal divisions and Soviet proposals to advance reciprocal disengagement: NATO and Warsaw Pact troops would pull back in symmetric phases, one inch west for every inch east. European NATO reactions were "cool to very negative"; the Warsaw Pact was "lukewarm."[29]

Mutual disengagement was less radical than it sounded. Various Eastern leaders and Western thinkers had already embraced its spirit. Polish foreign minister Adam Rapacki called to bar atomic forces from West and East Germany, Poland, and Czechoslovakia a few weeks later. In November, the strategist George Kennan pleaded for superpower withdrawal from central Europe in the BBC Reith Lecture; ten years of crisis and stalemate had discredited "sweeping and spectacular solutions."[30] Even sympathetic listeners dubbed his assault on Cold War nostrums "dangerous thoughts"; among other things, that the Soviets were neither implacably hostile nor clearly expansionist, that disarmament "put the cart before the horse" of military disengagement in central Europe, that nuclear threats heightened risks and eroded trust, and that Germany's division would not last forever.[31] After the NATO Council assembled in Paris the morning after Kennan's final broadcast on December 15, 1957, Republican and Democratic grandees lined up to reject his iconoclasm. Eisenhower's push to forward deploy tactical nuclear weapons in Western Europe in a stockpile that allied NATO militaries could access was formalized by NATO report MC 48/2, which endorsed "fully effective nuclear retaliatory forces of all services" with reliable availability "at the outset of hostilities."[32] After blaming the Soviet Union for recent setbacks in disarmament talks, the official communiqué from Paris publicized the alliance's decision to create a shared nuclear stockpile in addition to the placement of intermediate-range ballistic missiles (IRBMs) under Supreme Allied Commander Europe (SACEUR) control.[33]

Kennan's intervention was not without its admirers, however. One upstart young senator wrote to praise his intervention. Even as John Foster Dulles sent Dean Acheson a note thanking him for upbraiding his former director of policy planning publicly, a despondent Kennan received a letter from Senator John F. Kennedy of Massachusetts, who commended him for pushing those who managed U.S. national security "to test rigorously our current assumptions."[34] There were admirers abroad as well. Aiken cited Kennan's proposals to demilitarize and denuclearize central Europe when the Oireachtas attacked his own plans as "gratuitously hostile to the United States policy."[35]

Kennan and Aiken bridled at how nuclear brinksmanship had militarized the territorial disputes that decolonization had left behind. In this way they became unwitting allies of a cadre of strategic thinkers who sought to replace massive retaliation with a more flexible U.S. military posture. The CIA-backed Congress for Cultural Freedom had glimpsed in Kennan's Reith lectures the outline of a more *active* Western policy."[36] Whereas they believed that the Hungarian uprising had attested how social forces were chipping away at Soviet authority in Eastern Europe, Kennan's sympathy for German nationalism and nuclear abolitionism led him to reject the status quo. After NATO announced future deployments of Thor missiles to Britain late in 1958, he asked whether Cold War pathologies had become so ingrained as to be impervious to treatment by "any circle of human wills small enough to understand each other?"[37] For all his reservations about the UN, which he believed shortchanged traditional allies and dignified governments in Africa, Asia, and Latin America unworthy of the name, his fears of nuclear war were greater.[38]

Not unlike Kennan's reaction to a nuclearized Iron Curtain, the Irish Resolution derived from Aiken's response to the simultaneous crises in the Middle East and East Asia in the summer of 1958. When forces sympathetic to Moscow overthrew the Iraqi monarchy in July, Eisenhower sent fifteen thousand troops to Lebanon to fulfill his post-Suez pledge to back states facing "overt armed aggression from any nation controlled by international communism."[39] British prime minister Harold Macmillan followed his lead in dispatching British troops to neighboring Jordan. At an emergency session of the UNGA, Aiken proposed a ten-point plan to cure what he saw as the underlying disease—interventions that smacked of imperialism, "whether direct or indirect, Eastern or Western, diplomatic or military, capitalist or communist."[40]

Aiken called for the establishment of "areas of law" where the UN Charter would reign supreme and nuclear weapons would be banished. Together with Freddy Boland, Ireland's representative to the UNGA, Aiken warned that overlapping rivalries—East versus West, Arab versus Israeli—were transforming the Middle East into a Cold War tinderbox. If not for superpower meddling, he maintained, the Arab-Israeli dispute would never have amounted to "anything like the danger to world peace which exists at present."[41] He raised issues specific to the Levant (Arab unification, Palestinian reparations, the right to return) and also those relevant to the postcolonial world more generally: self-determination; human rights; freedom of trade, communication, and movement; and Cold War neutralization.[42] At Boland's behest he dropped his call for the recognition of Israel and its current borders (Iraqi and Israeli delegates flanked those of Ireland in the UNGA hall). As for the United States and the Soviet Union, he asked that they refrain from military or nuclear interventions in the region.

The areas-of-law resolution had shed its denuclearization provision when it passed on August 21, 1958, only for the Taiwan Strait Crisis to refocus attention on the matter. Mao's saber-rattling clarified how territorial bouts could spiral out of control. In response, Aiken universalized the denuclearization pillar of the "areas of law." Dubbing atomic armaments "the dominant factor of our time," he beseeched those assembled to halt their spread lest regional disputes assume cataclysmic proportions and the window for nuclear abolition close shut.[43] His impromptu proposal was so unexpected that most delegates, including those from the United States, had to request guidance from their capitals.[44] That a postcolonial country with neither nuclear ambitions nor military allies had issued the motion lent it moral force. Even if the U.S.-Soviet balance of terror were effective, he contended, recent events had demonstrated that the UN should play a more commanding role. And because the nuclear club neatly matched the "four effective permanent members of the Security Council" (France had been preapproved), their militaries could police collective actions.[45]

Beijing was the fly in the ointment. The second crisis in the Taiwan Strait had rung alarm bells, given how cavalierly Mao had previously talked about atomic warfare. The year before at the International Meeting of Communist and Workers' Parties in Moscow, he had foretold how communist China would rise phoenixlike from the ashes in a speech downplaying U.S. imperialism as a "paper tiger." His Soviet comrades were shaken. "I have asked Comrade Khrushchev for his view of this. He is much more pessimistic than I am. I told him that if half of mankind dies, the other half would remain while imperialism would be destroyed. Only socialism would remain in the world. In another half a century, the population would increase, maybe by more than half."[46] The next February, he assured the Soviet ambassador in Beijing that to win a nuclear war was in fact "inconceivable," only to ask Andrei Gromyko during the second Taiwan Strait Crisis six months later whether the Kremlin would launch a nuclear strike if the PLA were to lure the U.S. Marines into an amphibious assault on the mainland.[47] Gromyko later recounted how flabbergasted he had been that Mao would even entertain such an idea.[48]

Aiken's statement on September 19, that "if general war is brought upon the world for any motive . . . it will neither democratize nor communize it; it will annihilate it" implicitly rebuked Mao.[49] Aiken's guilty conscience for the blood (sometimes innocent) he had spilled during the Irish civil war had likely combined with his Catholic conservatism to sour him on violent means: "A revolutionary background," he later admitted, "puts a responsibility on you."[50] In a series of speeches that fall, he laid out four pillars of a "nuclear restriction." First, there was a meaningful distinction between the arrival of nuclear capabilities in new states and their increase in existing hands. Second, "steps towards the restriction of nuclear weapons . . . would be a step towards their abolition." Third, the likelihood of nuclear war would grow in geometric proportion to the expansion of the nuclear club. In contrast to George Orwell, he believed that history had proved that "weapons which are the monopoly of the Great Powers today become the weapons of smaller Powers and revolutionary groups tomorrow."[51] What would happen if communist guerrillas operating in Latin America, the Middle East, Africa, or Southeast Asia obtained such a violent instrument? His audience was implicated in his final assertion: nuclear globalization was beyond any one state's or alliance's ability to handle; to freeze the nuclear club would require the elaboration of public international law enforced by a combined authority.[52]

If the UN were key, Aiken needed to address popular associations of nuclear testing with neocolonialism, prominent since the *Lucky Dragon* incident.[53] India's minister of defense and chief UN representative V. K. Krishna Menon's response included recriminations directed against the "three hydrogen gentlemen." He might have possessed knowledge of Moscow's sensitive nuclear assistance to Beijing at the time.[54] While he expressed a strong preference for a total nuclear test ban, he nevertheless applauded the initiative in a handwritten note to the Irish foreign minister.[55] Other representatives from decolonized countries voiced displeasure at the idea of legitimating the nuclear arsenals of permanent UNSC members. Argentina's Mario Amadeo warned of "a judicial stamp of approval to this situation of inequality" with a reference to a Roman legal term, *capitis diminutio*, a "decrease of standing," which would codify a form of second-class international citizenship. Spanish delegate José Félix de Lequerica invoked the French Revolution in defense of sovereign equality, warning that a closed nuclear club would confer "an official seal to the clique of atomic aristocrats."[56]

European NATO delegations protective of the alliance's newly assembled atomic stockpile also expressed misgivings. Aiken's use of the word *supply* implied physical transfer, eliciting cheers from Eastern Europeans and jeers from their Western counterparts. Bonn's ambassador in Dublin had to intercede before the West German Foreign Ministry fired off a "formal démarche" informing Irish officials that the *Bundeswehr* viewed these weapons as vital to "their proper role in NATO."[57] That Paris found fault with a resolution that effectively nominated it for the nuclear club reflected how zealously de Gaulle guarded his privileges.[58] Officially, Henry Cabot Lodge, the U.S. ambassador in New York, took issue with a lack of verification language. Unofficially, Eisenhower's belief in the atomic stockpile had not wavered.[59] Uneasy with open security commitments, he wanted to move the continent toward self-sufficiency, envisioning a united Europe that could counterbalance the Soviet Union and the United States. Western and Eastern European fears of German rearmament nonetheless presented obstacles to a European "third force." Lord Hastings Ismay, NATO's inaugural secretary-general, had described the alliance's mission as to keep "the Americans in, the Russians out, and the Germans down." Nuclear-sharing helped meet those ends. That Eisenhower would countenance (or even assist) the British or French nuclear-weapon programs raised doubts about U.S. security guarantees, and any expansion of the nuclear stockpile into a joint force the specter of a nuclearized Germany. The Irish Resolution cast these contradictions in sharp relief. Only Soviet preoccupation with a summertime Conference of Experts and follow-on Conference on the Discontinuance of Nuclear Weapon Tests prevented a showdown.[60]

The crux of the issue was how to define membership in the nuclear club. Secretary of State Dulles had wondered aloud the year before about "how to prevent the promiscuous spread of nuclear weapons throughout the world." After the New Year, French scholar Raymond Aron followed up by asking whether "the so-called Atomic Club" could remain exclusive.[61] C. L. Sulzberger took on the subject of the nuclear club in the *New York Times* in February 1958, when he reckoned that Moscow might hold Beijing at bay if Washington and London were to do likewise with Paris and Bonn.[62] Yet where Sulzberger had eyed a "new European entente," for Aiken the nuclear dangers emanated from the areas where the Cold War and decolonization were interacting: "if only we can preserve peace for another few years, [the UN] will, with God's help, find ways of fostering our *esprit de corps* as a world community."[63] By contrast, nuclear dissemination, he warned, would worsen tensions between the two "governing currents of the mid twentieth century—the cold war and the widening of freedom," namely "the emergence into independent national life of vast areas, mainly in Asia and Africa, formerly subject to foreign states."[64]

Aiken made one last push before the moratorium went into effect on October 31. Quoting Amadeo that the proposal was "an attempt to localize the fire" before it could rage out of control, he disavowed any intention to stop states from stationing their own atomic forces abroad. Yet the presence of "shall not supply" in the draft resolution and disarmament amendments that Aiken had submitted was forbidding. His comparison of his resolution to "the great American initiatives of the Baruch proposal and the Marshall Plan" failed to win over Lodge. Faced with little support for a motion that called on states not to supply or acquire nuclear weapons while an ad hoc committee met to discuss the matter, he distilled the resolution down to its essence: "an increase in the number of States possessing nuclear weapons may occur, aggravating international tension and the difficulty of maintaining world peace and thus rendering more difficult the attainment of the general disarmament agreement."[65] Even that platitude proved too much for some. Canadian foreign minister Sidney Earle Smith lamented a choice between nuclear restriction and "uncontrollable anarchy." Ten days later, forty-four delegations abstained, including Canada, along with every other delegation from a NATO member state.[66] The Soviet Union and its allies, by contrast, voted yes on the resolution.

III

Despite the setback, Aiken left New York encouraged by his newfound public stature. Alastair Hetherington at the *Manchester Guardian*—then the British Labour Party's newspaper of record—reached out for an article in April 1959. The Irish Foreign Ministry repurposed the resulting encomium as a pamphlet, which U.S. representative Henry Reuss of Wisconsin would enter into the *Congressional Record*.[67] Irish officials reached out to Arthur Krock of the *New York Times*, Joseph Lash of the *New York Post*, and Walter Lippmann of the *New York Herald Tribune*.[68] Aiken published his own article, "Bomb Peril—Message from a Small Power," in *The Nation*, an influential voice on the American Left.[69] His office also exchanged letters with the Committee for a Sane Nuclear Policy (SANE) in New York, founded by *Saturday Evening Post* editor Norman Cousins the year before with a view to moralize U.S. nuclear policy. SANE vowed "to help in every possible way." The Campaign for Nuclear Disarmament (CND) that luminary British philosopher Bertrand Russell fronted, on the other hand, was warier, writing back with concerns about how the Irish Resolution might legitimate the atom bomb.[70] It was telling that the foremost antinuclear organizations on either side of the Atlantic were at odds on the relationship between restricting and abolishing nuclear weapons.

The Irish Foreign Ministry's next target following its breakthroughs in the United States and the United Kingdom were the national delegations of "Latin America and of the Afro-Asian Group" whose "support for our proposal at the next Assembly will

be of great importance."[71] Fifteen African nations were set to join the UN the following year. With dozens more on deck in the coming decade, the UNGA's central
axis was rapidly shifting from East-West to North-South. Irish diplomats went to
work on the leaders of the nonaligned movement, assuring Menon that their measure would neither sanctify nuclear testing nor derail test-ban proceedings.[72] They
reached out as well to Ghana, whose charismatic president, Kwame Nkrumah, was
railing against French nuclear testing in the northern Sahara and calling to declare
all of Africa a nuclear-free zone.[73] Boland outlined the strategy in late May 1959: "I
quite agree we should begin with Sweden. But I don't think we should stop there. If
we could get India or Burma, it would be well worth while. Both stand very high in
the Afro-Asian bloc and, indeed, in the U.N. generally." Among the Latin American
group, he viewed Mexico as key. As for the "Black Africans," Sudan stood out as "a
likely and effective supporter."[74] That December the *Economist* labeled the UNGA an
"Afro-Irish assembly" in recognition of Dublin's tireless outreach to the Third World.[75]

Aiken and his lieutenants worked hard to convince British and American officials.
Irish diplomats made the rounds in Washington, D.C., that summer. In a meeting
with U.S. State Department officials in July, J. F. Shields claimed the measure would
foster U.S.-Soviet détente. With relations between Moscow and Beijing coming un-
glued and a Eisenhower-Khrushchev summit in the works, he advised that a nuclear
restriction would allow the superpowers to focus on "the real danger"—the People's
Republic of China.[76] When Joseph Sisco of the department's Office of United Nations Political and Security Affairs asked about verification, Shields equivocated: a
"couple of experts at each nuclear energy plant" would suffice. Sisco's next protest
about Soviet grandstanding drew a more cutting retort: "it might be difficult to prevent the Devil from quoting Scripture . . . but that hardly constituted a cogent reason
for suppressing the Bible."[77]

That summer Soviet and U.S. experts in Geneva debated a test-ban "control
complex," most notably the placement of seismographs capable of detecting subterranean blasts and the mix of principals and neutrals to administer it all. It was unclear
whether American reservations hid ulterior motives or reflected longstanding shibboleths about the incompatibility of a closed Soviet society and international trust. It
was therefore fortuitous that opposition parties in the United States and the United
Kingdom had taken notice. In June Aiken nominated the item for the next UNGA's
agenda, in which "nuclear restriction" acquired a new, more distinct phrasing—the
"prevention of the wider dissemination of nuclear weapons." Kennan, who had followed "with great sympathy and admiration [Aiken's] valiant effort to combat the
spread of nuclear weapons," served as an eloquent ally in the United States, sharing
his "great misgivings" about the lack of attention paid to the problem with the U.S.
Senate Committee on Foreign Relations in May 1959.[78] As Kennan played Cassandra,

Irish envoy John Shamus climbed Capitol Hill to meet with Minnesota senator Hubert Humphrey, chairman of the Senate Select Committee on Disarmament and Democratic presidential hopeful, who promised that he would promote Aiken's "very fine Resolution!" with his friends in the U.S. State Department.[79]

On the eve of the fourteenth UNGA, the Irish resolution faced an international community that was receptive to nuclear governance yet of many minds about the makes and models on display. Despite concerns within the CND about normalization, the National Executive Committee had marginalized unilateral disarmers at the behest of British Labour Party leader Hugh Gaitskell by endorsing a "non-nuclear club" akin to the Irish Resolution in the likely event that general and complete disarmament talks were to falter. Although the party remained nominally committed to self-disarmament, moderates were placated by pro-NATO sentiment and a nonexistent deadline. Instead of neutralization and denuclearization, Labour's October 1959 manifesto embraced compromise: Britain would abide by its commitments, including hosting Thor missiles in East Anglia, whoever controlled Parliament.[80] Even French objections were softening. In an audience with Gaitskell, de Gaulle left the impression that he was not unalterably opposed to the idea. It was unclear whether the French president—whom even his prime minister, Michel Debré, found Delphic—meant before or after France's impending first nuclear explosion.[81]

Ahead of Khrushchev's visit to the United States in September, a new consensus had started to form among economists, humanists, and scientists that total nuclear war necessitated international action. The Joint Committee on Atomic Energy (JCAE) of the U.S. Congress discussed estimates that a nuclear Pearl Harbor would kill fifty million Americans and injure another twenty million.[82] In the *New York Times*, historian Arnold Toynbee wrote approvingly of the nuclear disarmament proposals in American moral philosopher Reinhold Niebuhr's new book, *The Structures of Empires and Nations*.[83] Harvard physicists counted up twenty-six countries economically capable of manufacturing atom bombs in *Daedalus*, the journal of the American Academy of Arts and Sciences, the nation's premier scientific organization. After a decade in which Winston Churchill's mutual balance of terror and Dulles's necessary art of brinksmanship had become conventional wisdom, searching reappraisals of nuclear anarchy were dwelling on the "Nth country problem."

Aiken made the case that nondissemination would promote world law and order when the UNGA reconvened on September 23, 1959.[84] As recent events underscored the dangers associated with the interaction of nuclear deterrence and territorial disputes, the attraction of his areas of law grew clearer. The right course, he maintained, was for states without nuclear arms in disputed regions to "undertake, firstly not to manufacture or acquire nuclear weapons or other weapons of *blitzkrieg* or mass destruction, and secondly to subject themselves to United Nations inspection to ensure that they are keeping to the agreement." The nuclear club in league with the entire UN would correspondingly "bind themselves in advance, by specific engagements, to defend the members of the area from attack, by means of a standing United Nations force." While the measure fell short of total nuclear disarmament, such a breakthrough seemed to him an unlikely preliminary to the monopolization of organized violence by the UN—only then would the nuclear powers disarm.[85] For him, world federation remained a necessary prerequisite to atomic abolition.

Aiken's deference to the status quo won over the nuclear club in New York. The language of *control* rather than *supply* conciliated the NATO alliance, as did the nomination of an ad hoc committee within the existing Geneva process to draft a treaty with "a reasonably practicable system of inspection and control."[86] U.S. officials openly fretted that it would still "give rise to misunderstandings" about Atlantic nuclear defense, with the Soviets only too "happy to confuse the issue."[87] When Aiken took the dais on November 13 to defend his proposal, he maintained that a nondissemination pact was necessary lest the world descend irretrievably into anarchy, as every enlargement of the nuclear club made "greater the possibility, mathematically and inexorably, of insane decisions and the further away the prospect of international agreement."[88] Although Moscow had reportedly regarded the measure "with great sympathy" that summer, it chose to abstain when the Irish Resolution was put to a vote.[89] He therefore won over the West without fully alienating the East (the Kremlin believed the devil was in the details). The First Committee thus passed Resolution 1380 on November 20, with seventy for, none against, and twelve—most notably France and Warsaw Pact members—abstaining. The new Ten-Nation Committee on Disarmament (TNDC) in Geneva was empowered to debate how "a wider dissemination of nuclear weapons might be averted."[90]

The Irish Resolution passed because it lacked many of the downsides associated with other proposals to govern nuclear technology amid decolonization. Resolutions for African or Central European nuclear-weapon-free zones (NWFZs) ran afoul of close U.S. allies in France and West Germany.[91] Aiken had effectively accommodated France, whose attitude softened from outright opposition to abstract misgivings about the indivisibility of nuclear non-dissemination and disarmament.[92] Communist China's absence in New York eased the passage of a resolution whose primary target was Beijing, one aimed not at preventing the spread of atomic weaponry per se but at managing the forces of the Cold War and decolonization, which Aiken had elsewhere called "to be diked and controlled, as our engineers have learned to control the great rivers of the world." The Irish Resolution therefore remained bound up in parallel efforts to limit the number of flash points for superpower quarrels in the Middle East, East Asia, and central Europe.[93]

The resolution nonetheless proved anticlimactic. Lacking agreements on general and complete disarmament or a nuclear test-ban treaty, U.S. and Soviet representatives would feud over procedure in Geneva. Moscow wanted an executive troika on which capitalist, communist, and nonaligned states would sit together on the presumption that its proposals would receive a more favorable hearing from the third grouping. Washington eventually came around, but the committee dissolved on June 27, 1960, without having discussed the Irish Resolution. Nearly two years would pass before the inaugural meeting of a new Eighteen-Nation Committee on Disarmament (ENDC), expanded to include four neutral delegations (Brazil, Mexico, Nigeria, and Sweden) and four nonaligned delegations (Burma, Ethiopia, India, and the United Arab Republic). Until then, nondissemination talks returned to New York, where Aiken continued to recruit co-sponsors in hopes of preventing the world's division into the quick and the damned.[94]

IV

Although Eisenhower had promoted civilian atomic energy from the beginning of his presidency, the Irish Resolution was not a natural fit for his administration. Before the UNGA on December 8, 1953, the former general had endeavored to shift the narrative about atomic energy away from existential deterrence toward themes of economic development. It was a masterclass of presidential rhetoric, harmonizing the discordant notes of Cold War competition into a hypermodern symbol of U.S. advancement and munificence—the peaceful atom.

Eisenhower had wanted to level with audiences at home and abroad about the hydrogen bomb, whose wholesale use would marry the urban ruin promised by strategic air power to the agricultural collapse of scorched-earth tactics.[95] The thermonuclear revolution jeopardized more than the United States or the interstate system. While Eisenhower and his cohort managed existential deterrence, scientific warnings from famous minds such as Albert Einstein and Russell drew attention to the fate of *Homo sapiens*, leading antinuclear activists to denounce nuclear armaments as antithetical to economic progress and nuclear-club statesmen to redeem them by sanitizing their effects.[96] The hydrogen bomb gradually became shorthand for a third world war—itself a metonym for global barbarism and human extinction.

Atoms for Peace was the brainchild of a Truman-era panel chaired by Robert Oppenheimer. The panel chose to address itself to a larger subject—the "Age of Thermonuclear Peril." The resulting Operation Candor marked Oppenheimer's final effort to shared his unease with the Super bomb beyond the U.S. national-security state, and his report was there when the new administration took office. For fear that a nuclear taboo would hamper U.S. defense plans, Eisenhower's assistant secretary of defense, Frank C. Nash, preferred to advertise a brighter tomorrow through atomic energy.[97] At a White House meeting on March 31, 1953, Eisenhower and Dulles expressed "complete agreement that somehow or other the taboos which surround the use of atomic weapons would have to be destroyed."[98] White House speechwriter C. D. Jackson worked throughout the summer on a speech that would not "scare the country to death."

Peace was a versatile symbol. Outgoing AEC chairman Gordon Dean had impressed on Eisenhower the advantages of redirecting fissile materials to civilian reactors with the aim of jump-starting research and power generation.[99] The president seized on the idea of an "atomic pool" to ease allied and neutral unease with the hydrogen bomb, pacify public opinion, legitimize U.S. nuclear technology, and divert precious Soviet materials, all in one blockbuster package. Only a last-minute intervention by Churchill removed Eisenhower's planned statement that in the event of aggression he would feel "free to use atomic weapons as military advantage dictates."[100] By describing the subject as "global, not merely national in character," he validated UN competence in the nuclear domain and showed willingness to frame the new language of atomic warfare as universal in both application and implication.

Eisenhower conveyed his fear of a third world war through a comparison to the second: "Today, the United States stockpile of atomic weapons . . . exceeds by many times the total [explosive] equivalent of the total of all bombs and all shells that came from every plane and every gun in every theater of war in all of the years of World War II." Famine would spread as large swaths of "an aggressor's land would be laid waste" by large-scale thermonuclear strikes, resulting in "the condemnation of mankind to begin all over again the age-old struggle upward from savagery towards decency, and right, and justice." In short, a thermonuclear war would reverse the developmental process that scientific and technological progress theoretically drove. If a third world war was modernization's antithesis, the antidote was heroic national leadership and affirmative global governance. He linked the atomic pool to his nation's claimed tradition of humanitarian aid, most recently to Western Europe under the Marshall Plan, offering to alleviate the "misery of Asia" by assisting "these people to develop their natural resources and to elevate their lives." Together the United States and willing partners would supply a new international agency "under the aegis of the United Nations" with enough yellowcake uranium and fissile material to yield agricultural plenty, medical breakthroughs, and "abundant electrical energy to the power-starved areas of the world."[101]

Little was promised by way of disarmament. Afterward Dulles cited distrust of communist parties in ruling out headway even if Khrushchev were to make every concession. The secretary of state's opposition was not categorical, but he dismissed the notion of ending the nuclear arms race "by a stroke of the pen."[102] On January 8, 1954, the National Security Council (NSC) authorized the use of nuclear arms if hostilities broke out with the Soviet Union or the People's Republic of China (PRC).[103] The concurrent pursuit of deterrence and development introduced a paradox to international nuclear politics. The official Soviet response spotted the dilemma. Because power reactors generated spent fuel that reprocessing plants could then transform into weaponizable plutonium, Eisenhower's Atoms for Peace "would in fact be giving direct sanction to the production of nuclear weapons."[104]

Atoms for Peace internationalized a secrecy regime that endeavored to seal restricted data related to nuclear-weapon production behind impenetrable walls of federal classification and security clearances while widely disseminating data that would facilitate commercial uses and foreign assistance.[105] By 1959 the U.S. nuclear posture rested on two foundation stones: the 1946 Atomic Energy Act, which the U.S. Congress had amended in 1954 and then again in 1958, and the Basic National Security Policy that NSC directive 5906/1 outlined that summer.[106] The Atomic Energy Act ensured that the president would act as the final arbiter of atomic war, with the executive and legislative branches together providing civilian oversight of the military atom. The act's ban on transfers of nuclear arms or data related to them, fissile-material production, or atomic-energy generation had legislated a passive national nuclear nondissemination policy. The 1954 amendment loosened the rules for data transfers to civilian enterprises and sensitive non-nuclear technology to allies who had made "substantial progress in the development of atomic weapons," provided that assistance did not significantly aid the acquisition of an independent arsenal.[107] The United Kingdom was the chief beneficiary, British armed forces having detonated a plutonium device in Operation Hurricane in the Monte Bello islands off Western Australia two years earlier. Across the channel, France's candidacy was supported by a planned nuclear test in the northern Sahara.

Dulles's replacement as secretary of state, Christian Herter, had NSC 5906/1 drafted to blunt the diplomatic blowback from the New Look. The Newer Look would shower more attention than previous versions on the interplay between the U.S. nuclear posture and those of European and Asian allies, affirming the importance of the NATO atomic stockpile while walking a tightrope on when tactical nuclear weapons might be unleashed. Right off the bat the document stated that the administration placed "main, but not sole, reliance on nuclear weapons," whose use was to be avoided "in those areas where main Communist power will not be brought to bear."[108] Whether this excluded the Chinese PLA was left up to the reader.

Eisenhower thus clarified that massive retaliation remained operative on the Cold War's central fronts of Germany and South Korea. The Newer Look signaled rather than dictated a meaningful shift toward better aligning deterrence with diplomacy; its nod toward limited wars outside the main anticommunist theaters would not yield major investments in conventional forces. The fact that Eisenhower had dismissed the State Department's more sweeping formulas—"a just peace or peace with justice"—as aims too idealistic to guide national strategic doctrine was revealing.[109] What NSC

5906/1 did reinforce was the value to NATO defense policy of nuclear forces, tactical arms as well as theater ballistic missiles, both to countering the Warsaw Pact's more numerous tanks divisions and infantry legions and to reassuring nervous Europeans that the United States would honor its commitments under Article 5 of the North Atlantic Treaty. As per the Atomic Energy Act, the warheads remained in U.S. military custody and required a presidential order to fire. Thor missiles in the United Kingdom and Jupiter missiles in Italy and Turkey in combination with Pershing 1 missiles, atom bombs loaded onto F-104G Starfighters by West German servicemen, and a welter of battlefield systems would defend the Fulda Gap no matter how many intercontinental ballistic missiles (ICBMs) the Soviet Union could launch. Even if a U.S. president were someday to recoil at the thought of trading New York for Paris, European member states would still have a nuclear umbrella ready nearby.

Nuclear weapons gave Eisenhower enhanced sway over Western Europe's nuclear affairs. Even before *Sputnik* illustrated North America's newfound vulnerability to a Soviet first strike in 1957, France, West Germany, and Italy had pooled their resources in nuclear science and technology. Given that these countries already collaborated with Belgium, Luxembourg, and the Netherlands on nonmilitary uses via the European Atomic Energy Community (Euratom), there were suspicions that their objectives were less than peaceful. The Newer Look advised against the multiplication of "national nuclear weapons capabilities" or "national control over nuclear weapons components"—for the moment. The key word in both clauses was *national.* The Newer Look remained open to alternative arrangements that would whet allies' appetite for nuclear autonomy up to and including hedging strategies without ejecting U.S. armed forces from the continent. The Pentagon would continue to study the benefits and risks of supplying chosen allies with "(1) information; (2) materials; or (3) nuclear weapons, under arrangement for control of weapons to be determined."[110]

One such arrangement would become known as the multilateral nuclear force (MLF). The idea originated in the Policy Planning Staff—the State Department think tank whose first two directors had been George Kennan and Paul Nitze—as a successor to SACEUR Lauris Norstad's plan for a force of IRBMs in Europe under NATO control. The current director, Gerard Smith, ordered a study after growing sympathetic to Kennan's judgment that the spread of nuclear weapons had not received the attention that it deserved.[111] What began as a rigorous look at a future world teeming with nuclear arsenals turned into a pitch for a NATO atomic armada when Smith's predecessor, Robert Bowie, submitted a competing report in which he claimed that U.S. allies should be able "to deter Soviet all-out attack on Western Europe by means under their own control." What was more, a NATO strategic nuclear arsenal, if done correctly, would have the bonus of halting the "proliferation of independent national deterrents [that] would be dangerous, inefficient, immensely costly, and have a major divisive effect on the Alliance."[112] Rather than France, Italy, or West Germany acquiring their own arsenal, or the United Kingdom maintaining its deterrent, an MLF would furnish a nuclear shield that the Atlantic Alliance would wield together.

This halfway measure marked a milestone at the crossroads of U.S. grand strategy, NATO defense, and international nuclear diplomacy, setting out proactive measures to stem the spread of atomic arsenals, including collective nuclear forces in Europe and elsewhere, to be overseen by the U.S. president. Norstad's more realistic yet destabilizing proposals for a land-based deterrent yielded in time to two general alternatives: Polaris-armed fleets whose vessels would be crewed by mixed nationals or a multinational fleet flying under the NATO flag. Washington's reticence on the issue of the presidential veto disquieted some European capitals while military officers and treasury departments warned over the comparative advantages of surface ships versus submarines.[113] Whatever their makeup, NATO defense arrangements clashed with an international nondissemination agreement because of the inherent contradiction between custody and control. The U.S. Atomic Energy Act continued to rule out unconditional transfers, yet a lonely U.S. soldier at German airfields guarded the Mark 7 bombs that Luftwaffe F-84Fs would carry. Even after electronic locks called permissive action links were added after October 1962, it was unclear what would stop German pilots from commandeering the ordnance in the event of war.

The project was also attractive to those who supported European union, including a group known as the "theologians" composed of Under Secretary of State George Ball and State Department officials working in the Bureau of European Affairs. This cadre feared that de Gaulle's return to power heralded the return of nationalism and its discontents across the continent. The United Kingdom had been a member of the nuclear club since 1952. Half the countries that a 1961 National Intelligence Estimate identified as nuclear-capable—France, Sweden, and West Germany—resided in Western Europe. Many belonged to the EEC and Euratom as well.[114] There was hope that a more robust, participatory, and credible nuclear umbrella could render new arsenals superfluous, but the prospect that the historically conflict-ridden European state system might soon feature many fingers on the button suggested that more active measures, and also closer observance of passive ones, were urgently needed.

The Newer Look therefore acknowledged that orderly co-management of the military atom was necessary lest the Atlantic Alliance crumble under its imbalances even as it struggled to reconcile the various tensions between alliance politics and atomic assurance. The uncertain fate of the British nuclear deterrent, which faced skyrocketing costs and technical hurdles as Macmillan's Conservatives worked to phase out long-range bombers and phase in ballistic missiles, was the proximate concern. In 1960 the cancellation of the homemade Blue Streak missile forced London to ask

Washington to buy the Skybolt air-launched ballistic missiles to extend the life of the British V bomber force, to which Eisenhower assented on the condition that U.S. Polaris submarines be able to dock at Holy Loch in Scotland. The Skybolt deal threw a lifeline to the British while laying bare the country's dependence on the United States amid massive antinuclear marches on British nuclear facilities. It also revealed Eisenhower's reluctance to bar ballistic-missile exports categorically, even when doing so would decrease the nuclear club's membership by one.

V

The likelihood that entrants from the Middle East or Asia might soon knock on the nuclear club's door was also growing more pressing. During Eisenhower's second term, intelligence poured in that Israel and communist China had made inroads on sufficient fissile materials to manufacture nuclear explosives. After fifteen years of benign neglect, U.S. political elites contemplated atomic upstarts on the Cold War's tumultuous frontier with an alarm that bordered on panic.

Beijing had been receiving strategic nuclear assistance from Moscow since 1954, when the communist giants embarked on a joint project to establish China's Second Ministry of Machine Building. Atomic self-sufficiency ran along parallel tracks to rapid industrialization: the Kremlin supplied technical advisors and the equipment necessary to prospect, mine, and enrich uranium and also the fissile material to fuel a large research reactor. Soviet academics trained their Chinese counterparts in both countries on textbooks translated into Mandarin.[115] The project got communist China's civilian and military programs off the ground, including a test facility near Lop Nur in the deserts of Xinjiang. In October 1957, Khrushchev rewarded Mao's support in his leadership contest with Georgy Malenkov with the New Defense Technology Agreement, which seeded mainland China with impressive technological bases for nuclear-weapon and ballistic-missile enterprises.[116]

The Second Taiwan Strait Crisis threw a wrench in those works. Mao's choice not to consult Khrushchev before provoking another confrontation with the United States infuriated the Soviet leader. As Aiken drafted his resolution in New York, Khrushchev rescinded his offer to furnish a teaching model based on the atom-bomb design that Soviet spies had secreted out from the Manhattan Project thirteen years earlier. According to Russian ambassador Roland Timerbaev, Khrushchev was driven by "fear that China's leadership would drag the Soviet Union into a conflict with the United States and the entire West," jeopardizing his visions of peaceful co-existence between the capitalist and socialist blocs.[117] His flirtations with a nuclear test ban further aggravated Mao, while Khrushchev's mounting misgivings about a nuclear-armed PRC brought about a common U.S.-Soviet interest in keeping the Middle Kingdom in check. The damage had nevertheless been done. As of 1958, the CIA lacked firm evidence that communist China had launched a weapons program.[118] By September 1960, the agency adduced scanty evidence of Sino-Soviet cooperation to support the claim that Beijing "almost certainty has started a weapons program."[119] One year later, intelligence and planning documents described a communist Chinese nuclear test as "expected" and estimated that it would possess a modest fleet of atom bombs and even thermonuclear-capable ICBMs by 1971.[120]

The Israel nuclear program began as a remora on a French shark. While the Weizmann Institute of Science was a fount of technical expertise in the young nation, Ernst Bergmann's Israel Atomic Energy Commission and Shimon Peres's Ministry of Defense cultivated the French connection, just as France's Commissariat á l'Énergie Atomique (CEA) and its government manager contemplated their own military options.[121] Peres earned his reputation as the "architect of the Franco-Israeli alliance," which took flight after socialist prime minister Guy Mollet won the Palais de l'Élysée in February 1956. Tel Aviv passed sensitive technology and intelligence along to Paris and received in return unique access to experimental data and state-of-the-art nuclear facilities at Chatillon, Saclay, and Marcoule.[122] The Jewish kinship of many scientists who had worked in France, most notably Bertrand Goldschmidt, the father of the French bomb, and Lev Kowarski, who had demonstrated that a nuclear chain reaction was attainable with Frédéric Joliot-Curie at the Sorbonne before joining the Israel Atomic Energy Commission. At the highest levels, Israeli prime minister Ben-Gurion's and Mollet's common identification with democratic socialism forged a personal bond between their two governments.[123] Then there was the shadow of the Final Solution.[124] According to Maurice Bourgès-Maunoury, who served as Mollet's defense minister and then as his successor, their partnership aimed "to prevent another Holocaust from befalling the Jewish people and so that Israel could face its enemies in the Middle East."[125] Ben-Gurion's motivations stemmed from the same catastrophe.

Israel's main rival was Egypt and its bold leader, Gamal Abdel Nasser. After more than eighty years of Anglo-French condominium over his nation, Nasser had helped depose Egypt's sybaritic monarch, King Farouk I, in 1952, turned his Free Officers organization into a ruling government, and then took the top job for himself. After a star turn at Bandung, Indonesia, where an assembly of Afro-Asian leaders espoused nonalignment in the Cold War's power blocs, an offer from the United States, the United Kingdom, and the World Bank to finance the Aswan High Dam on the Nile fell apart. Nasser's successful pursuit of economic aid and arms sales from the Warsaw Pact poured salt on the wound, but it was his expropriation of the navigation company that guided ships through the hemisphere's most valuable real estate—the Suez Canal—that triggered an armed intervention. He seized the Suez Canal Company (the top two shareholders were the British and French governments) on July 26, 1956, and with it "the flow of oil, trade, and troops" between Europe and the Indian Ocean on which depended the fortunes of two creaking empires.[126]

British, French, and Israeli retaliation was swift. London feared that the chokepoint's loss would hinder its strategic imperial retreat from the Middle East and Asia.[127] Paris resented Nasser's moral and material support for insurgencies in North Africa. Tel Aviv stated that their objective was to retaliate against Palestinian fedayeen raids, but Israeli leaders were also happy to see their most dangerous foe humbled and the Straits of Tiran reopened to their shipping—Nasser had closed it after striking a $320 million arms deal with Czechoslovakia the previous year. Peres and Mollet joined British foreign minister Selwyn Lloyd to conspire in the Paris suburbs that October. The Sèvres Protocol triggered an Israel Defense Forces (IDF) blitz of the Sinai before Britain and France issued ultimatums for both to withdraw from the canal zone. Thus, if Nasser refused to abandon Egyptian soil, the ensuing "police action" might earn a veneer of international respectability.[128]

The Suez adventure ended ignominiously for all involved, but its undoing would also hasten the quest for nuclear weapons by the two conspirators that lacked them at the time. Discussions between the French and Israelis had hitherto envisaged a research reactor like the Canada Deuterium Uranium (CANDU) model, which Canada had promised India the year before. In 1955, an agreement for technological and financial assistance from Washington under Atoms for Peace took care of that and more for Tel Aviv, but the bilateral safeguards and the reactor's 1-megawatt size ruled out reliable plutonium supply.[129] Only France was willing to overlook the dual-use problem. In September, Peres and Bergmann met with CEA high commissioner Francis Perrin together with Pierre Guillaumat and Goldschmidt to ask for a reactor from which Israel could harvest more sizable amounts of plutonium.[130] In fact, Peres had backed the Suez gambit in part "because he calculated that this could be the opportunity that would give Israel the reactor."[131] The two sides signed an interim agreement at Sèvres as the next step in a security partnership that already spanned major arms deals and a historic conspiracy.[132] The reactor type and possible inclusion of a plutonium reprocessing plant went unspecified, at least for now.

The Suez Crisis clarified what a nuclearized Levant might entail. Washington applied enormous political and financial pressure on Britain and France to stand down and on Israel to accept a cease-fire.[133] When Britain's reserves plummeted due to Eisenhower's refusal to lend either oil or gold to Macmillan's government, the conspiracy fell apart. While U.S. economic diplomacy was decisive, the impression left by Moscow's more coercive tactic was just as lasting. *Pravda* declared that Tel Aviv had jeopardized "the very existence of Israel as a State." Soviet premier Nikolai Bulganin reminded Ben-Gurion that Soviet missiles could easily reach Israel.[134]

The lesson for France and Israel was clear. Mollet's compunctions about atom bombs evaporated: "Only by developing [them] would the humiliation France had suffered in the Suez be avoided in the future."[135] As for Israel, French withdrawal elevated nuclear assistance to a matter of conscience: "I owe them the bomb," Mollet confessed.[136] He worried that an isotope-separation plant would amount to "a provocation since plutonium's only use is for military purposes." But as luck would have it, the staunchly pro-Israel Bourgès-Maunoury replaced him as prime minister in May 1957.[137] Before his government had even convened, he authorized the sale of a heavy-water reactor whose design permitted outputs as high as 40 megawatts (with 70–150 megawatts theoretically possible) and commensurate amounts of plutonium thanks to an included reprocessing facility. The only restriction that the French Foreign Ministry imposed was a signed statement of exclusively scientific intent.[138] The site chosen was about fifty miles south of Jerusalem, in the Negev desert, not far from the small city of Dimona.

Although Israeli officials worked to conceal Dimona's purpose, a showdown with Washington was brewing by 1960. Dimona had broken ground in late 1957. The following year French firms began work on the reactor and reprocessing plant. As work proceeded, France developed a case of buyer's remorse. After de Gaulle took power in June 1958, he reviewed the level of sensitive nuclear assistance his predecessors had accorded Israel. Ben-Gurion and Peres proved adept at the practice of putting off the hangman, delaying the suspension of cooperation until 1963 and bypassing French efforts to apply International Atomic Energy Agency (IAEA) safeguards altogether.[139] Although word reached the U.S. State Department that Israel, the United Kingdom, and Norway had agreed to transfer twenty tons of heavy water in June 1959, AEC and CIA analysts remained in the dark until a technician working onsite turned informer.[140] A special National Intelligence Estimate (NIE) concluded in late 1960 that Israel was building a complex of nuclear reactors and laboratories with "plutonium production for weapons . . . at least one major purpose of this effort."

Eisenhower and Herter asked Ben-Gurion and Israeli foreign minister Golda Meir tough questions on New Year's Eve: What was Dimona for? Where would the plutonium go? Was there a third reactor in the works? Would they accept safeguards? Even rumors of an Israeli program, they warned, would ignite the "particularly explosive tinder box" that existed in the Middle East.[141] The reactor's existence became public knowledge when the *Times* of London published a sweeping exposé, prompting CIA director John McCone to sit down with *Meet the Press* the following Sunday. Concerned that Israel had diverted U.S. aid for Dimona, Eisenhower pushed for foreign experts to confirm the facility's peaceful nature and that Israel planned neither to build weapons nor amass plutonium.[142]

With two months left in his term and McCone leaking information to the *New York Times* and the *Washington Post*, for the sake of continuity Eisenhower assigned the dossier to the State Department, which counseled "persistent but quiet diplomatic approaches" to lessen Arab alarm while the U.S. government downplayed concerns related to a reprocessing plant.[143] Herter felt that strongly worded communiqués did not go far enough and recommended blocking an upcoming loan to Israel. While the Development Loan Fund apparently mislaid his memorandum, his call for action was a hidden milestone. That U.S. national-security elites were willing to use coercion to inhibit another state's nuclear program was a sign of things to come.

Conclusion

The day before his inauguration on January 20, 1961, Kennedy and his cabinet joined their predecessors in the Oval Office for a survey of world affairs. When the president-elect asked which nuclear programs he should worry about most, Herter had an answer ready—"Israel and India."[144] The latter was striking, given that Menon seldom missed a chance to decry atomic weapons or nuclear fallout, but Chinese incursions into India's northern frontier and Mao's boasts about weathering a thermonuclear war had alarmed Indian prime minister Jawaharlal Nehru.[145] The CANDU reactor furnished New Delhi with a source of plutonium. Yet it was the gap between Tel Aviv's words and actions relative to Dimona—Israeli finance minister Addy Cohen had by then admitted to having lied to U.S. officials—that led Eisenhower's team to urge their replacements to hold Ben-Gurion to his word: Dimona's door should be thrown open to U.S. visitors.[146]

The Irish Resolution was neither preface nor proof of nondissemination's inherent virtues, but a guide to questions that the resolution had sought to answer: How to govern a postcolonial world in which the keys to the absolute weapon were being sold on the open market, if not given away? How to guarantee that the U.S.-Soviet balance of terror kept the Cold War frosty rather than fiery? How to ensure that nuclear weapons remained weapons of last resort rather than common instruments of war, of genocide, or of extinction? The new Kennedy administration would contemplate Aiken's proposal from a different standpoint: How to guard the frontiers of the "free world" from foreign threats, as the distribution of military, economic, and technological power continued to drift away from North America.

The Atomic Frontier

John F. Kennedy and Nuclear Containment, 1960–1962

Introduction—Barbarians at the Reactor

"I stand tonight facing west on what was once the last frontier," John F. Kennedy observed when he accepted the presidential nomination at the Democratic National Convention in Los Angeles on July 15, 1960. For Massachusetts's junior senator to invoke the American West—a mythic touchstone of national thinking about power, race, and progress—as a parable for his political platform was bold and revealing in equal measure. Before the Democratic Party delegates Kennedy heralded a brave new world from which want and war were to be banished, styling his candidacy a leap into a glittering future. In contrast to eight senescent years under President Dwight Eisenhower and Vice President Richard Nixon, he promised struggle and adventure: "we stand today on the edge of a New Frontier—the frontier of the 1960s—a frontier of unknown opportunities and perils—a frontier of unfulfilled hopes and threats." His speech dwelt on the current administration's failures in the Third World, where international communism had stolen a march on the "free world" in Southeast Asia, the Middle East, and the Caribbean, and covert operations and nuclear fallout had unsettled such key neutrals as India and allies as Japan, to which Eisenhower had recently canceled a visit amid student protests against a new U.S.-Japanese defense treaty. To redeem humanity, the country would need to prevail on the battlefields to which decolonization was giving rise: "More energy is released by the awakening of these new nations," Kennedy warned his fellow Democrats, "than by the fission of the atom itself."[1]

As president, Kennedy would find those two phenomena more intimately linked than he may have imagined when he flew back to Cape Cod the next day. As a young senator, he had expressed misgivings to George Kennan about the former diplomat's calls to halt the testing of nuclear weapons, resign their first use, and hasten their abolition, asking "if we could expect to check the sweep south of the Chinese with their endless armies with conventional forces?"[2] In the Oval Office, Kennedy's actions would determine whether Eisenhower's tentative steps toward nuclear arms control and nondissemination bore fruit. In his eyes the prime challenges that he and his country faced emanated from the edges of the globe-spanning U.S. alliance network—and from fissures within those alliances—as he worked to update U.S. foreign policy for a postcolonial era. Could the superpowers find common ground in Latin America, Africa, and Asia even as aspiring regional powers—France, communist China, and Israel—pursued the atomic bomb?

Kennedy's untimely death and the Americanization of the Vietnam War under his vice president and successor, Lyndon Johnson, would largely sanctify his legacy, with those in his inner circle lamenting the passing of an Arthurian leader who married courage to prudence in staving off crises and brokering peace.[3] Yet his counterrevolutionary impulses, his botched summitry, and his military build-up in Southeast Asia attested to his struggle to escape the constraints of the Cold War.[4] An idea of Kennedy emerges from these contradictions: a glamorous liberal and staunch anticommunist transfixed by the postcolonial world, whose presidential gambles—his willingness to negotiate and his unwillingness to yield—were often calculated to win elections in an increasingly suburban country.[5]

I

Though Kennedy mouthed the Cold War mantras in his inaugural address on January 20, 1961, his thrust was more ecumenical than Eisenhower's had been eight years earlier, when the retired general contended that the struggle against communism defined "the meaning of this day."[6] Kennedy's sweeping ambitions required new blueprints, ones that better reflected the shifting balance between Europe and zones from which its empires were receding. The forty-three-year-old described a post-imperial world that wintry morning, one in which "North and South, East and West" would band together in "a grand and global alliance" against "tyranny, poverty, disease and war itself," and also "the steady spread of the deadly atom."[7] With his country in the vanguard, the international community would thus bring order to the atomic frontier.

The containment of nuclear power supplemented that of communism for Kennedy's best and brightest. Weeks before inauguration, incoming deputy national security advisor Walt Rostow had sketched out a strategy of defending along two fronts—"the truce lines which emerged from the Second World War and its aftermath" and "the periphery of the Communist bloc and beyond," including Guatemala, the Congo, and Cuba. In place of the sledgehammer of massive retaliation, he held out a Swiss Army knife—"a country approach to the deterrence of military action" to squelch guerrilla uprisings with nation building and economic development while regulating arms flows to Latin America, Africa, Asia, and the Middle East. What he styled "a common law for the Cold War" would dictate a change of tack: whereas Eisenhower had not challenged "Communist arms shipments to the Free World since the 1955 Czech arms deal with the United Arab Republic," Kennedy would draw a red line. Disarmament, let alone détente, were dead on arrival as long as weapon imports destabilized U.S. allies and also nonaligned and neutral states.[8]

While Rostow's strategy struck some as farfetched, Kennedy had a weakness for bold, systematic solutions to matters as disparate as guerrilla operations and nuclear war. His new government wanted an answer to Nikita Khrushchev's endorsement of national liberation struggles earlier that month, when the Soviet premier had singled out Africa, Latin America, and Asia as "the most important centers of revolutionary struggle against imperialism."[9] According to Attorney General Robert "Bobby" Kennedy, his brother greeted the speech as "our clue to the Soviet Union."[10] In a special, first-year State of the Union address in May, President Kennedy designated "the whole southern half of the globe—Asia, Latin America, Africa and the Middle East—" as the "great battleground for the defense and expansion of freedom today."[11] And while the superpowers competed in many fields, Rostow wrote, there existed "important areas of common interest in the underdeveloped areas." If there was to be a linkage between U.S.-Soviet arms talks and transfers of MiG jets or Kalashnikov rifles, why not atom bombs as well?[12]

As Kennedy pledged to "pay any price, bear any burden," economic recoveries in Western Europe and Japan in combination with political decolonization were driving what Rostow liked to call a "diffusion of power."[13] The 1950s had been golden years in Western Europe—the *treinte glorieuse* in France and the *Wirtschaftswunder* in West Germany. French and Italian trade tripled; West Germany's quadrupled. The creation of the European Economic Community (EEC) knit the political economies of France, Italy, West Germany, Luxembourg, Belgium, and the Netherlands closer together after 1957 at the commanding heights of steel, coal, and atomic energy, integrating markets and driving intra-bloc trade volumes up 6 percent annually from 1953 to 1960.[14] Members of the European Atomic Energy Community (Euratom) would in time become competitors of the dominant U.S. nuclear industry. The story in Japan was no less miraculous, as its globally ascendant light industry rose from the ashes of the Greater East Asia Co-Prosperity Sphere. Its first commercial nuclear power plant was set to go critical in 1966.[15] Although far from eclipse, the United States in 1960 was losing its Jovian supremacy.

A wave of decolonization was transforming the international system more broadly, starting in the periphery and rebounding on the metropoles. As European empires regained their footing after the Second World War, anticolonial elites in their re-claimed colonies demanded independence with ink and blood. As London, Brussels, the Hague, and Paris lost their grip on possessions in Africa, the Middle East, and Southeast Asia, plans to establish new federations in portmanteau geographies like *Eurafrica* were coming to naught, and scores of untested regimes inherited ethno-national patchworks with deep-seated poverty and arbitrary borders.[16] Last-ditch efforts to preserve imperial polities engendered bitterness, rebellion, bloodshed, and re-armament. Charles de Gaulle's efforts to keep Algeria within Greater France, for instance, transformed Algiers into a "mecca of revolution" for anticolonial fighters in the Maghreb and beyond. With an insurgency to one side and truculent settlers and mutinous military officers to the other, de Gaulle turned to *radiance* in the form of world-class reactors and first-strike weapons to reform French strategic culture. French armed forces began to leave far-flung counterinsurgency campaigns behind in preference for mechanized warfare in a postnuclear European environment, whether with NATO allies or alone.[17]

The aftermath of decolonization had grown clearer. The world abounded with regional disputes in 1961: Indian versus Pakistani, Indian versus Chinese; Dominican versus Venezuelan; Cuban versus Bolivian; Indonesian versus Malaysian; Yemeni versus Yemeni; Arab versus Israeli.[18] Nor would Maoist rebels tend their own gardens. Laos, Vietnam, and Indonesia teemed with guerrilla fighters even as Castro lit a revolutionary beacon in Cuba, challenging the United States in its own backyard.[19] The dollar's status as the reserve currency to central bankers the world over had meanwhile become a drag on the U.S. domestic economy. The price of maintaining 275 military bases in thirty-one nations was staggering; American GIs spent too many dollars in Mannheim and Okinawa not to unsettle the balance of payments with security partners whose economies gushed exports onto U.S. main streets. A fiscal reckoning would imperil the gold-backed Bretton Woods system of monetary exchange that had greased the wheels of global commerce since 1945.[20]

Kennedy and his chief lieutenants thus faced challenges whose scale and com-plexity matched the world order they saw as theirs to lead.[21] Service in world wars and cold war informed their faith in U.S. hegemony. National Security Advisor Mc-George Bundy had taken to heart Dean Acheson's maxim: "the United States was the locomotive at the head of mankind, and the rest of the world the caboose."[22] These men—and they were all men—would scrutinize tactics rather than strategy. For them, it sufficed to diversify the tools and sources of authority necessary to fulfill a world-wide mission, adapting the country to a world that decolonization was fast upending. A national call for action resounded above all else. Young volunteers would join the

Peace Corps to alleviate the hunger and poverty that Kennedy's advisors deemed fertile soil for communism to take root. Or they could enlist in the U.S. Army's new Green Berets to combat insurgents where imperial retreats had left behind hapless nations with odd borders, dysfunctional politics, and underdeveloped, commodity-reliant economies. Kennedy had cast himself as the steelier, savvier commander in chief to defeat Nixon during the election. His next opponent was Khrushchev at the height of his powers, convinced that Soviet-led communism would best U.S.-style capitalism in the kitchen, in the fields, and on the rocket pad.[23] The Kremlin's increasingly bold moves together with rising civil and religious strife in Laos and Vietnam posed challenges to U.S. foreign relations in all four hemispheres.

The spread of nuclear science and technology via global markets and bilateral deals was the most disruptive result of the global economic recovery since 1945. Two interlocking factors conditioned governing views on the arrival of nuclear weapons in new lands and in new hands: their Cold War salience and the industrial capability of the state in question. The implicit nuclear guarantees that had accompanied the North Atlantic Treaty and the U.S.-Japanese Treaty of Mutual Cooperation and Security had cemented anticommunist bulwarks on the far sides of the world's two great oceans; to devolve atomic decision making to either region might crack that bedrock. Yet the sanctity of freer trade and modernization in postwar liberal discourse ruled out strong-arming allies. Complaints from EEC members that "if they do not have nuclear weapons, they, as a result, will have no nuclear industry" occurred amid a growing backlash against the coca-colonization of Western European culture.[24] The Japanese government and major utilities had launched their own ambitious Atoms for Peace program to resolve a perennial dependence on energy imports on account of their archipelago's dearth of coal, oil, or dammed rivers.[25]

By the same token, Kennedy's belief that history's cockpit had shifted to the developing world yielded a dilemma—should he continue Eisenhower's Atoms for Peace program or instead actively inhibit foreign nuclear programs? Nuclear assistance was subject to the same ideological crosscurrents and international forces as Cold War developmental work writ large. Nuclear assistance intrigued poorer nations. Leaving aside military motives, most governments welcomed free or subsidized research reactors with few strings attached, if simply to nurture their scientific bases. When Park Chung-hee of South Korea, badly trailing its coal-rich northern neighbor in electric-power generation, waved aside Kennedy's offer of reactors as prohibitively expensive, he added a grinning caveat: "if U.S. support were forthcoming, they would certainly consider it."[26] At one point in 1960, India's Homi Bhabha hosted Soviet and U.S. nuclear delegations at the same time in hopes of winning better terms so that his frugal government would agree to finance the long-term investments.[27] In time Canadian reactors and Commonwealth scientific ties would vault New Delhi into the Afro-Asian atomic vanguard. As London's influence waned in the Indian Ocean and the Persian Gulf, however, fledgling nuclear programs in the Middle East and South Asia would cause double takes in Washington. As Dimona surged toward criticality, U.S. policy makers wondered whether their longstanding policy of preserving strategic interests in the region, namely oil reserves, communication lines, and anticommunism, through a "position of impartiality between the Arabs and Israel," could survive an atomic accelerant.[28]

II

The Kennedy administration entered office radiating faith in liberal universalism. When Walt Rostow replaced Gerard Smith as Policy Planning Staff director in the November 1961 reshuffle that reassigned Under Secretary Chester Bowles as an ambassador-at-large and presidential advisor on African, Asian, and Latin American Affairs, and W. Averell Harriman as the assistant secretary of state for Far Eastern Affairs, the office's intellectual products took on its leader's commitment to the extension of market practices to underdeveloped territories.[29] Rostow was an industrial economist formerly of MIT's Center for International Studies, and his political influence drew level with his personal ambition when he became Kennedy's deputy national security advisor in January 1961. The author of a major primer on modernization theory, *The Stages of Economic Growth: A Non-Communist Manifesto*, he moved to expand containment doctrine once he was in the White House by reconceptualizing U.S. armed forces as "free world" shock troops tasked with spreading noncommunist forms of development, sometimes at the barrel of a rifle, with the aim of catalyzing "high-mass consumerism" in former colonies.[30] First, Washington would enforce Cold War common law.[31] Then, coercive and cooperative measures would build states and then nations where colonies had once been. Over time, this league of liberal nation-states would evolve naturally into an organized international community under a *pax Americana* and, when the U.S. president felt ready to lay down the burden, world law.

For this purpose, Rostow pushed a new Basic National Security Policy. The drafting process touched off wide-ranging interagency debates about the value of the ideas in foreign policy and whether and, if so, how Kennedy should promote liberal world order.[32] From the White House, Bundy announced his skepticism of grand designs that assumed "a kind of equal and adequate effort everywhere," discouraging any premature priority setting or taxing sources of national power.[33] He preferred to weigh cases on their individual merits with due attention to political circumstances at home. And he grumbled that Rostow had painted arms control and disarmament "with rather a thin brush."[34] UN ambassador Adlai Stevenson concurred, blasting the "dangerous under-emphasis" on nuclear threats whose multiplication were, in his eyes, eclipsing those of communist infiltration.[35] Later drafts duly tasked the Arms Control and Disarmament Agency (ACDA) with negotiating tightly safeguarded test-ban and fissile-material cutoff agreements and a nondissemination pact that would exempt current and future NATO nuclear arrangements. Even so, for Rostow multilateral settlements took a back seat to unilateral efforts in the developing world to stimulate capitalist growth and cauterize communist infection.[36] Carl Kaysen, Bundy's arms control expert in the White House, was the chief naysayer.[37] With Berlin, Laos, Cuba, and Vietnam all boiling over during Kennedy's first five hundred days in office, a doctrinal impulse to divide the world "neatly into two parts—a free world and a Communist world"—could lead U.S. policy makers, he warned, to mistake "social revolution internally generated" for Sino-Soviet meddling, with Kennedy's outreach efforts to Afro-Asian nations rendered collateral damage.[38]

The exercise nevertheless reflected Kennedy's longstanding interests in the Third World. Objections notwithstanding, the Basic National Security Policy anticipated the general line of U.S. foreign policy under both Kennedy and Johnson.[39] Although never formalized, the drafts made the case for preserving and enlarging a rule-based international order favorable to regulated free markets over which the U.S. president would serve as superintendent. Although Rostow's millenarian belief in societal development through industrial productivity, rapid urbanization, and rational management techniques would cause friction with nonaligned leaders, Kennedy found value in thinking about the conjoined subjects of national power and international purpose holistically. When leaks about a hypothetical U.S.-Soviet détente forced Rostow and Kennedy's secretary of state, Dean Rusk to submit testimony to the Senate Foreign Relations Committee, the president publicly backed them.[40] Although Bundy ultimately succeeded in shelving the doctrinal exercise, he never entirely purged its influence. Chairman of the Joint Chiefs of Staff (JCS) Maxwell Taylor was right when he likened the 285-page opus to the British Constitution, that is to say, "a living document."[41]

In Rostow's mind, liberal values could contribute to geo-ideological ends as well as Kennedy's reelection. The White House would address issues on a regional basis, leaning on alliance-based deterrence in Europe and East Asia, covert operations and military training in the Third World, and personal diplomacy and economic development everywhere else. Such an approach would preempt Republican red-baiting by cultivating Kennedy's reputation for toughness in the face of a communist offensive against the "free world." Years later he would describe the shift from Eisenhower to Kennedy as "not one of 180 degrees" but "from defensive reaction to initiative."[42] Because it would weaken U.S. deterrence architectures around the Soviet Union and the People's Republic of China (PRC) by reducing allied dependence, encouraging strategic decoupling, and fanning neutralism, nuclear diffusion could counteract that initiative. "There was a narrower American interest," Rostow recalled in 1972, that nuclear proliferation "could weaken the structure of collective security in the noncommunist world at critical points."[43] Assistant Secretary of State Phillips Talbot would put a finer point on it in 1963: the rise of new nuclear-weapon holders threatened to "reduce U.S. capability to act."[44]

European affairs were front and center when the new administration took charge of U.S. foreign policy. During the campaign, Kennedy had accused his predecessors of twin failures: of overseeing a "missile gap" with the Soviet Union and leaning too heavily on nuclear deterrence. While the gap was a mirage (force levels in fact favored the United States), massive retaliation was marked for burial, with divergent implications for Europe and East Asia. Kennedy and his team turned to a more diversified military posture of flexible response to defend U.S interests on a global basis. For now, Europe took precedence. To save Eisenhower's grand design of binding West Germany to Western Europe and North America through the Atlantic Alliance and regional union, Kennedy needed to square NATO nuclear integration, independent British and French arsenals, and U.S.-Soviet arms control.[45]

He walked a tightrope in Europe. To one side stood de Gaulle, busy selling Konrad Adenauer on a vision of a Europe from the Atlantic to the Urals led by Paris and Bonn, not Moscow and Washington. Nuclear aid to the United Kingdom had exacerbated Washington's issues with France, whose fledgling nuclear capability would accord it strategic capital and eventually serious financial debts. Eisenhower's reluctance to help the French had stemmed from political instability and data security: twenty-two leak-prone governments had passed through the French Senate and National Assembly between 1945 and 1959. Even after de Gaulle became prime minister and then president of a newly constituted Fifth Republic in 1958, his requests for Admiral Hyman Rickover's breakthrough naval reactor or advanced IBM computers to calculate high-energy equations of state were denied. In response Paris accelerated its nuclear-weapon program, with one eye on a potential deal with Washington.[46]

Misgivings had ebbed toward the end of Eisenhower's presidency. The French nuclear test on February 13, 1960, demonstrated substantial progress toward an independent capability as per the revised Atomic Energy Act. Views also softened after de Gaulle backed his U.S. allies when the Gary Powers incident wrecked the Paris Four Powers Summit in May 1960.[47] In an ensuing meeting with the French president, Rickover proposed naming the next class of Polaris SSBN submarines after the Marquis de Lafayette, the U.S. and French revolutionary hero. When the first-in-class *Lafayette* launched three days before Kennedy was sworn in, Rickover dubbed the christening "a symbol of the bonds that join our country to France—spiritually, intellectually, historically." French ambassador Hervé Alphand attributed the gesture to either Eisenhower or "a guilty conscience."[48] After an attempt by retired French Army generals in April 1961 to reverse de Gaulle's stunning about-face on Algerian self-determination failed, the colonial war that had divided the two NATO allies drew to a close. French diplomats' success in securing Sahara-based oil fields and atomic proving grounds in the Évian peace accords ensured that de Gaulle would retain key cards in his ongoing efforts to reinforce his position in Europe while boosting French national pride.

On Kennedy's other side stood German Gaullists such as Defense Minister Franz Josef Strauss clamoring for more say in NATO's nuclear defense.[49] The Federal Republic of Germany (FRG) had renounced atomic, biological, chemical, and radiological weapons at the time of the 1954 Brussels Pact, but the Bundeswehr had since committed to purchasing nuclear-capable aircraft and artillery, leading Strauss to express concerns about the availability of both atomic munitions for these expensive systems and U.S. tactical nuclear weapons.[50] More fundamental were concerns that if nuclear war were to erupt, Germany would occupy ground zero. West German officials warned that Warsaw Pact tanks would steamroll NATO conventional forces before the Supreme Allied Commander Europe (SACEUR) could let loose the atomic stockpile, turning central Europe into a radioactive wasteland as a result. When Washington sought approval from NATO's Military Committee to move forward with flexible response, Strauss insisted on "nuclear weapons in truly balanced forces."[51] It was an explosive request. President's Science Advisory Committee chairman Jerome Wiesner warned that to forward-station tactical nuclear weapons in central Europe was "like putting a stick of dynamite in one's house in order to be conscious of the danger of fire."[52]

Who controlled these nuclear forces went to NATO's heart. The White House feared that German interest in nuclear weapons, let alone its own independent force, would spell the end of the alliance, with dire consequences for a U.S. strategy that was based on a unified Atlantic defense.[53] De Gaulle exploited this tension, signaling his interest in greater military coordination among Western European powers and obliquely intimating the possibility of a future Franco-German nuclear force. If Bonn were to tilt toward Paris, Kennedy risked being marginalized on a continent whose political dysfunctions had twice in the past fifty years dragged his country into total wars. Flexible response had been devised for such challenges. Greater U.S. reliance on conventional forces would alleviate European fears that West Germany might bid for regional dominance or that the United States would abandon the continent for fear of Soviet atomic punishment while promises of a controlled, graduated escalation up the ladder from conventional to nuclear strikes pre-programmed to limit damage to military targets would enhance the credibility of deterrent threats.[54] Flexible response would update the necessary means for the 1960s, at least rhetorically, with West Germany integrated and re-armed and Western Europe recovered and integrating.[55] Dean Rusk warned U.S. ambassador to France James Gavin that the alternative—a German finger on a nuclear-launch button—"would shake NATO to its foundations."[56]

III

One of Kennedy's first decisions as president was to appoint Acheson to review U.S.-NATO relations in the context of adverse trends that included new nuclear-weapon programs. National Security Council (NSC) military expert Robert Komer had urged Kennedy to explore "a reasonable *modus vivendi*" for fear of "what a Franco-German combination might accomplish if they concluded they could no longer rely on us." The White House also deemed Italy's allegiances suspect after socialist inroads in recent elections raised the specter of a center-left government in Rome.[57] As for London—the U.S. bridgehead in Europe since 1941—its rudimentary, debt-ridden, operationally independent arsenal risked turning the English Channel into a moat. As Washington and London wrestled with Paris over British membership in the EEC, the nuclear question—who possessed atomic arms and at whose sufferance—threatened to disable the Atlantic Alliance.[58]

In acknowledgment of the need for a more robust nondiffusion policy, Acheson advised that proactive measures supplement existing negative safeguards on restricted data and dual-use exports. The United Kingdom would serve as the proof of concept. Referencing continental blowback against recent U.S.-UK atomic cooperation, he advised Kennedy to rescind the Skybolt offer and instead encourage "the British to drop their nuclear deterrent as painlessly as possible."[59] Bundy deemed this excessive for the moment.[60] National Security Action Memorandum (NSAM) 40 would note that British nuclear disarmament was desirable while condemning Skybolt with faint praise: The U.S. government should not purchase such a missile just to stave off the obsolescence of a foreign nuclear deterrent.[61] Meanwhile the AEC would restrict sales of compressors that might speed French uranium-enrichment centrifuges lest the West Germans follow suit.[62] U.S. officials would also downplay Bonn's nuclear potential. If trends in Europe "extended to Germany," NSAM 40 concluded, "it would strain NATO cohesion—possibly to the breaking point."[63]

This fear impelled administration soul-searching about a NATO atomic flotilla. Acheson's praise for the multilateral nuclear force (MLF) was faint compared to Robert Bowie's: he called it just one of the "positive steps to insure that nuclear weapons are a force for cohesion . . . in the alliance."[64] Arms control offered an alternative, but Komer was adamant that West German acceptance of flexible response come first, singling out nondissemination as one form of agreement "which might really undermine any new NATO deterrent posture."[65] When Rusk and Secretary of Defense Robert McNamara ran an interagency review of NATO defense policy and arms control in May, they found that enhanced nuclear sharing and integration might discourage France and West Germany from going nuclear—to consolidate Atlantic arsenals would centralize control in Washington.[66] For now, the MLF would have to await the completion of NATO's non-nuclear buildup around 1966.[67]

As Kennedy reviewed NATO policy, events in Berlin intervened. His first summit with Khrushchev in Vienna on June 4, 1961, had gone from promising to ominous when the Soviet premier resurrected his ultimatum to Eisenhower from three years before: on New Year's Eve, he would recognize the German Democratic Republic (GDR), placing in the hands of Walter Ulbricht—whose police state was then hemorrhaging around one million citizens per year—power over Western access via 100 miles of autobahn and railroad, three air corridors, and Berlin's streets.[68] Khrushchev's gambit hit at NATO's Achilles' heel: Bonn's nonrecognition of the GDR and Kennedy's equivocation in Vienna put Washington on the back foot. When the president stopped in Paris en route to Austria, he was forced to raise the credibility of U.S. security guarantees: as de Gaulle had put it, would any U.S. president "trade New York for Paris?"[69] Two months later, Kennedy announced on nationwide television that he would request an additional $3.25 billion from Congress to bolster the country's conventional forces: six new Army and two Marine divisions, plans to double or triple the draft and mobilize reserves, an increase in Army personnel from 875,000 to one million with another 29,000 for the Navy and 63,000 for the Air Force.[70] Flexible response went from concept to more boots on foreign soil overnight.

The yearlong Berlin crisis was at heart a nuclear crisis.[71] Disapproval of a German Bomb ran strong in both NATO and the Warsaw Pact. On his return to power in 1958, de Gaulle had terminated the French-Italian-German enrichment project that had been launched the year before.[72] Although he seemed to reverse course in 1960, when he assured Adenauer that "the day would come when there would be no discrimination as towards nuclear weapons for the two countries," he was notorious for speaking in the *longue durée*. As Euratom president Pierre Chatenet later recalled, de Gaulle's fears of German power "would never entirely diminish."[73] The French president also liked playing the nuclear card against the "Anglo-Saxons."[74] His warning to British prime minister Harold Macmillan about a Franco-German atomic partnership afforded leverage as he endeavored to win both nuclear aid from London and Washington and also entente with Bonn.[75]

Kennedy placed West German nuclear rights on the table long before Vienna, where the first item in his talking points had been the advantages of a test ban from the standpoint of nondissemination. Khrushchev would have understood that the FRG was among the "ten or even fifteen nuclear powers" Kennedy warned would exist without U.S.-Soviet cooperation.[76] When West German ambassador Wilhelm Grewe remonstrated with his U.S. counterparts for telling the Soviets that West Germany would have neither an independent nuclear arsenal nor national control over foreign atomic forces, Assistant Secretary of State for European Affairs Foy Kohler explained that it had been a "statement of fact."[77] When Kennedy contemplated International Court of Justice adjudication in Berlin, or a municipal plebiscite overseen by the UN, he included a nuclear-free zone in the two Germanys as part of a possible solution.[78]

Western European leaders resented their marginalization during the crisis, and Kennedy's praise for nonaligned involvement only poured salt in the wound. French foreign minister Maurice Couve de Murville groused that "India, Ghana or Indonesia" should not be "the decisive factor in the Berlin situation."[79] Ultimately, West European fears of U.S. withdrawal were less compelling than their discomfort at their bystander status. Beginning with Truman, Washington had committed to defend West Germany, not to reunify greater Germany. It was therefore unsurprising that Kennedy quietly welcomed the construction of the Berlin Wall in late October 1961, which defused the crisis by imprisoning East Germans in their own state. Even before NATO and Warsaw Pact tanks converged at Checkpoint Charlie, Rusk had admitted to Andrei Gromyko that avoiding a third world war was more important than closing the book on the Second World War. When the two men sat down in New York following Kennedy's September address to the UN General Assembly (UNGA), West Germany's non-nuclear status was treated as integral to any settlement.[80] In October Kennedy made explicit the restrictions on transfers of nuclear know-how or authority under the Atomic Energy Act.[81] One month later, Adenauer and Strauss conceded in an Oval Office meeting with Kennedy that a West German nuclear force was undesirable while insisting that Bonn hold a veto over an integrated NATO nuclear deterrent.[82] There was therefore little ambiguity when Kennedy informed Adenauer that West Germany would abide by its commitments made at the time of the Brussels Pact. When the chancellor retorted that it neither covered the receipt of atomic, biological, or chemical weapons nor included the Soviet Union as a contracting party, Kennedy made himself clear: as long as the United States stationed nuclear weapons in West Germany and NATO existed, "it was highly desirable for conditions to continue as stated in the Chancellor's declaration."[83] West Germany could have a transatlantic alliance, or it could have a fledgling nuclear arsenal, but it could not have both.

The Berlin Crisis ultimately gave nuclear test-ban talks, which had languished since 1960, a needed boost. Moscow and Washington had observed a moratorium since November 1958 on atmospheric blasts, but differences over onsite inspections to help identify underground tests had blocked a formal settlement. The control scheme at which technical experts had arrived after three years of exhaustive deliberations in Geneva amounted to a Rube Goldberg device: a troika of Western, Eastern, and nonaligned bureaucrats would determine when seismic events would trigger inspections.[84] That neutral Sweden, Nigeria, or India would mediate was an early sign of the internationalization of nuclear arms control and disarmament. For now, the Kremlin rejected all but symbolic verification while the White House demanded surefire solutions. When talks had resumed on March 21, 1961, they deadlocked almost immediately.

Khrushchev shattered the nuclear-test moratorium on September 1. By happenstance, the Non-Aligned Movement's inaugural conference was scheduled to meet in Belgrade that same day. Their failure to condemn the Soviet test undermined Indian, Egyptian, Indonesian, Yugoslavian, and Ghanaian claims to offer a principled check on superpower abuses. Their silence on Chinese repression in Tibet had similar implications for postcolonial regional disputes.[85] The test series peaked on October 30, 1961, when the largest human-made explosion in history, the 57-megaton Tsar Bomba, yielded a fireball more than nine kilometers in diameter above the northern Pacific island of Novaya Zemlya. By the time Stevenson rejected V. K. Krishna Menon's UNGA resolution on October 18 for omitting territorial inspections entirely, the initial wave of optimism that had attended Kennedy's election had petered out.[86] The U.S. president faced a dilemma. He could eschew tests despite stalled talks and cresting tensions, or resume testing and draw antinuclear and nonaligned ire. A new test series promised a grab bag of strategic game-changers: neutron bombs and sleeker warheads atop anti-ballistic-missile systems or intercontinental ballistic missiles (ICBMs) with multiple independent reentry vehicles (MIRVs).[87] Government scientists and Pentagon officers stressed their potential, but the White House was fixated on the politics. Moscow's "unpoliced arms controls" had precedence and simplicity on their side; for Komer, Tsar Bomba had placed them on "the hook of a self-imposed test ban on which [the] Soviets hope to keep us impaled."[88]

IV

As Kennedy reassured anxious Americans that their families would survive the rising nuclear tide, the Cold War imperative of winning Afro-Asian hearts and minds combined with the rhetoric of the African American freedom struggle in the United States made universal symbolism more appropriate than exclusionary nationalism.[89] Over the next two years Kennedy and his advisors would turn to tropes of parental guardianship in their promotion of nuclear restraint, drawing links between national security and executive action that would inaugurate a public association between humanity's salvation from nuclear catastrophe and the office of the U.S. president.

Renewed testing posed issues for the forthcoming midterm elections and Kennedy's own incumbent campaign two years later. Having won by the narrowest margin in fifty years, the youngest president ever elected could ill afford to disappoint any element of his fractious coalition. What was worse, the electoral optics of nuclear testing were tailor-made to divide the Democratic Party, with defense hawks and liberal anticommunists on one side and suburban parents and Catholic moralists on the other.[90] While scientists, philosophers, and ethicists such as Albert Einstein, Bertrand Russell, and Albert Schweitzer had called attention to atmospheric testing's many harms, Kennedy and his political advisors monitored the anxiety that women's peace activists and suburban housewives were expressing just as closely. While not fully persuaded by those such as Kennan who sought to wean the country off its atomic dependence, Kennedy was attuned to the shadow cast on New Frontier promises of suburban plenty by the nuclear arms race.

The U.S. antinuclear movement had split into two levels by 1959. Elite men like chemist Linus Pauling, pediatrician Benjamin Spock, and *Saturday Review of Books* editor Normal Cousins dominated newspaper headlines and evening newscasts, but at the grassroots suburban women who dressed their claims in the familiar garb of affluent white motherhood were the most active and affecting messengers. On November 1, 1961, 100,000 women marched "out of kitchens and jobs" to protest nuclear tests "which were poisoning the air and our children's food."[91] Women Strike for Peace embraced an inclusive feminism when its members insisted that mothers indeed knew best, marrying direct action at the nuclear proving grounds outside Las Vegas and at the Washington Monument to congressional letter-writing campaigns. In hijacking the postwar cult of domesticity against critics in the House Un-American Activities Committee (HUAC) they showed that women's traditional dominion over the domestic sphere afforded ramparts behind which to criticize the military-industrial complex.[92]

The vernacular of motherhood spellbound Americans in the early 1960s. The one million copies of Spock's *The Common Sense Book of Baby and Child Care* that sold every year did more than reassure parents that strict discipline was unnecessary. They affirmed seemingly commonsense views about women's roles in the home and in society. The postwar expansion of parenthood represented a landmark opportunity for ambitious politicians. The national census added twenty-nine million young children between 1950 and 1960—a nearly unprecedented rate of demographic growth. America's booming suburbs, whose size and segregation in the Sunbelt and elsewhere made them pivotal for any candidate for national office, cradled 83 percent of those babies.[93]

If Kennedy wanted to win over suburban mothers, the fallout issue required careful handling. The electoral prize of St. Louis was exemplary. Missouri's thirteen electoral votes had thrown Kennedy over the top against Nixon in 1960, and while African American voters had been crucial, he could not afford to alienate the St. Louis suburbs either. In 1957 such socialite reformers as Edna Gellhorn (mother of war correspondent Martha Gellhorn), worried parents as Dr. Louise Reiss and Dr. Eric Reiss, pacifist Quakers as Walter Bauer and John M. Fowler, and concerned scientists as Barry Commoner founded the Greater St. Louis Citizens' Committee for Nuclear Information (CNI). In a national climate that remained staunchly anticommunist, historian Kelly Moore observes, CNI presented a dispassionate face, "collecting and distributing in the 'widest possible manner' information concerning potential use of nuclear weapons in war, the testing of such weapons, and non-military uses of atomic energy."[94]

The CNI helped forge a bone-hard link between nuclear testing and the nuclear family in U.S. society. The Baby Tooth Survey was the committee's crowning

The Committee For Nuclear Information

The Baby Tooth Survey was initiated in December, 1958, as one of the activities of the Greater St. Louis Citizens' Committee for Nuclear Information (CNI). The Committee was organized in April, 1958, by a group of scientists and public-minded citizens who felt that the community should be given accurate information on the known effects of nuclear energy and radiation. Scientific facts are assembled and studied by the Committee and then made available to the public through regular bulletins and a speakers bureau.

The Idea

The initial impetus for the Baby Tooth Survey came from an article by Dr. Herman M. Kalckar, a Johns Hopkins University biochemist. In the article, which appeared in Nature, a British scientific publication (August 2, 1958), Dr. Kalckar proposed a worldwide survey of baby teeth for strontium-90 content and states "Such an International Milk Teeth Radiation Census would contribute important information concerning the amount and kind of radiation received by the most sensitive section of any population, namely, the children."

Because of the striking lack of scientific information on the human absorption of strontium-90, CNI responded to the challenge.

A Cooperative Program

To collect and catalogue the huge number of teeth needed to study the St. Louis area would be a difficult task for a professional research team. CNI, however, was in a position to enlist volunteer help and community-wide support for such a project, and could thus provide a research group with the teeth needed for study.

When the proposal was presented, an enthusiastic response came from the deans of both St. Louis and Washington University Schools of Dentistry. They joined with other scientists to form a Scientific Advisory Group

to guide the program. The Washington University School of Dentistry further aligned itself with the project by setting up a research team which immediately applied for a grant from the National Institute of Dental Research of the U.S. Public Health Service under which a laboratory could be established and maintained to carry out the strontium-90 studies. This grant for $197,454 has been approved and the laboratory is now set up.

The Collection

Under a physician director, and a Baby Tooth Survey Committee composed of women volunteers, the collection program was organized. Tooth forms describing the survey and listing necessary background information were prepared. All libraries and schools and later drugstores have become distribution centers. A mass distribution of these tooth survey forms to school children early in the program served to introduce the tooth survey into virtually every household with children in Greater St. Louis, and generous support by newspapers and radio and television stations has maintained a growing interest. Children's television programs have been especially influential in recruiting the support of the youngsters. Active participation in the program has come from church and social organizations, school teachers and school nurses, Boy Scout, Girl Scout and "Y" groups and a host of individuals. The 1960 spring drive began with a proclamation of Tooth Survey Week by the Mayor of St. Louis and was so widely supported by the entire community that 10,000 teeth were collected in a single month.

An Active Dental Community

The role of the dental community in this program has been one of major importance. In addition to the active support of both schools of dentistry, invaluable aid has

FIGURE 1 "Baby Tooth Survey" pamphlet, St. Louis Committee on Nuclear Information, undated.
Source: Harold Rosenthal Papers, Julian Edison Department of Special Collections, Washington University Libraries.

achievement. Dentists and parents sent extruded milk teeth to laboratories at Saint Louis University and Washington University to have annual levels of strontium-90 assayed. For all its efforts at neutrality, the symbolism of the Baby Tooth Survey nevertheless lent CNI activities a partisan hue and a gendered cast.[95] Donations were rewarded with buttons that read *I Gave My Tooth to Science*, featuring a cartoon of a smiling, gap-toothed boy: 14,500 donations had arrived by the end of 1959, and 27,000 by the end of 1960, with an additional 19,500 by June 1961.[96] The collision of domestic and political spheres in the figure of the postwar child held out a new object of presidential power in the age of atomic anxiety. When Louise Reiss published the initial findings in *Science* just weeks after the Women Strike for Peace march, President Kennedy called her at home himself to discuss the issue of strontium-90 levels in these children's bodies.[97]

Kennedy's misgivings about the effects of radioactivity on children must have hit close to home. The president was the father of four-year-old Caroline and one-year-old John Jr., and their births and the media attention lavished on his young family led him to heighten his fatherly affect after they moved into the White House. Kennedy's struggles with fatherhood in many ways mirrored his struggles with monogamy, and he and his political advisors sensed the dangers appearing aloof from his growing family. Whereas he had seemingly shrugged off the stillbirth of his first daughter, Arabella, remaining at sea rather than mourning at home with Jacqueline, their son Patrick's premature arrival on August 7, 1963, and death two days would bring on public displays of mourning.[98] The nuclear-testing dilemma in 1961 offered an early opportunity for Kennedy to expand this new role of dutiful young father to a national or even a global family in ways that accentuated rather than eclipsed his hardheaded stewardship of the national interest.

The Soviet moratorium violation proved useful fodder for the U.S. propaganda machine. Edward R. Murrow, whom Kennedy had plucked from CBS News to serve as U.S. Information Agency director, listed the many upsides of their newfound moral high ground when the UNGA reconvened in the fall of 1961: "isolate the Communist Bloc, frighten the satellites and the uncommitted, pretty well destroy the Ban the Bomb movement in Britain, and . . . induce sanity into the SANE nuclear policy group."[99] Proliferation hawks saw advantages as well. Komer, who himself distinguished between transfers like the MLF and "independent programs," felt increasingly isolated: most national-security officials believed that continued testing "would make it almost impossible to prevent a proliferation of nuclear capability."[100] According to CIA reports, even if left to their own devices, France, China, Israel, and others could build unsophisticated arsenals if given access to natural uranium in addition to plutonium separation or uranium enrichment, plus the weapons work itself.[101] Moreover, these prerequisites were growing more prevalent thanks to a burgeoning nuclear-export market and earlier sensitive nuclear aid.[102]

Khrushchev's action had sharpened the contrast between reckless Soviet testing and the safety-conscious U.S. series, offering Kennedy an opportunity to cast himself before a worldwide audience as a loving father to the planet. Stevenson had already urged him "to put the Soviets on the defensive" by endorsing a impressive slate of arms control measures. The result was a new three-stage general and complete disarmament program whose changes were nevertheless mainly superficial. While White House historian Arthur M. Schlesinger Jr. warned that the final stage might incite protests against "world government" from conservative quarters, the action plan neatly melded idealism and realism together without compromising flexible response: Assistant Secretary of State Harlan Cleveland touted "an attractive vision of Utopia" for neutrals that would not threaten "next year's Defense budget."[103]

The Kennedy administration hoped that the nuclear issue would help them turn the page in the the Afro-Asian world after early missteps. The fiasco that resulted when a CIA operation to land anticommunist warriors at a Cuban beach went badly awry in April 1961 had prompted soul-searching in Washington. Planned by Eisenhower but authorized by Kennedy, the Bay of Pigs operation, according to Schlesinger, had made "the New Frontier look like . . . stupid, ineffectual imperialists."[104] It had also raised the specter of Soviet nuclear intervention. The Cuban revolution had handed the Kremlin a launching pad for ideological warfare throughout Latin America and the Caribbean, and Soviet military and trade assistance to Havana had mounted in parallel to the deterioration of U.S.-Cuban relations, leading Khrushchev to announce on July 9, 1960, that "Soviet artillerymen can support the Cuban people with their rocket fire" at a range of 13,000 kilometers.[105] During the ill-fated invasion, Khrushchev went so far as to reaffirm that he would provide Cuba with "all necessary help."[106] Whether that included nuclear retaliation was left open to interpretation.

The haranguing that Stevenson had received at the UN after the Bay of Pigs fiasco had left an impression on Cleveland. As most new Afro-Asian states possessed few foreign consulates, they tended to invest their UN delegations with considerable authority. As a result, the UN had in Cleveland's eyes become "a world news center rivaling and, on some subjects, upstaging the traditional news centers of London and Washington." Lest they incur another black eye in the UNGA, he felt that Kennedy should invest more in parliamentary diplomacy.[107] The presidential requiem for global cooperation on September 25, 1961, thirteen days after UN secretary-general Dag Hammarskjöld's shocking death, reframed the U.S. commitment to arms control and disarmament. A eulogy for the world's foremost internationalist, killed in a plane crash while on a peace mission to the Democratic Republic of the Congo, carried an unmistakable subtext. Kennedy spoke of skies darkened by fallout "spread by wind and water and fear," ill omens of "the day when this planet may no longer be habitable," designating the UN system "the only true alternative to war": "Every man, woman and child lives under a nuclear sword of Damocles," he observed with a turn of phrase henceforth synonymous with mutual assured destruction, "hanging by the slenderest of threads, capable of being cut at any moment by accident or miscalculation or by madness."

Yet Kennedy was less interested in abolition than in formalizing nuclear containment. For him to state that these "weapons of war must be abolished before they abolish us" was more theater than testimony.[108] He did not seek a world freed from nuclear terror, but to consolidate U.S. nuclear-armed leadership amid the throes of decolonization, recasting his country as the international community's chosen guardian rather than as a mere anticommunist arsenal. When he elaborated on where the United Nation fit into a "peaceful world community" in his first State of the Union address fifteen weeks later, he grouped it with four other fields of action: NATO, the Organization of American States (OAS), U.S. development efforts, and—last but not least—U.S. global leadership.[109]

More prosaically, the disarmament scheme untied what had previously been indivisible. From it would spring limited measures whose implementation was meant to maintain deterrence, halt proliferation, and expand cooperation: a nuclear-test ban, a fissile-material cutoff, strategic-arms limits, and an agreement like the Irish Resolution, which Valerian Zorin, the Soviet representative in New York, had praised on September 27, two days after Kennedy's address.[110] Kennedy's presidency had already removed one U.S. reservation. Eisenhower's UN ambassador had cited the forthcoming "change-over period" between administrations when explaining his abstention the year before.[111] Frank Aiken's resolution nonetheless faced competition in the First Committee of the fourteenth UNGA that December. Swedish foreign minister Östen Undén's "non-nuclear club" would bar states from receiving nuclear weapons "on their territories on behalf of any other country," which threatened NATO's nuclear sharing. Atlantic unity was already shaky, with Canada, Denmark, Iceland, and Norway each brushing aside U.S. appeals to vote against the proposal. Stevenson advised against rejecting the Swedish resolution altogether. His delegation had already objected to resolutions from India for a test ban, from Ghana for an African nuclear-weapon-free zone (NWFZ), and from Ethiopia on wholesale abolition. How could Washington appear "second to none in its desire for disarmament" if it were to rebuff the Swedish as well?[112]

By late November the climate of opinion in New York had persuaded officials in the Bureau of European Affairs of the U.S. State Department that nondissemination was "the most satisfactory method of handling this complicated subject"; in short, the alternatives were even worse for NATO nuclear integration.[113] It helped that the Irish delegation was treating Western and Eastern requests with greater sympathy than those from nonaligned states. Consul Sean Ronan heeded U.S. requests, for instance, to revise the motion to "strengthen [the] U.S. hand as regards foreign bases."[114] The Soviets, for their part, got the better of the inspection battle even though Stevenson remained adamant that nuclear-club members would have to accept some form of international control. In the end, verification references were buried in the preamble. Aiken declined, by contrast, to co-sponsor Urdén's resolution with other prominent neutrals lest he "arouse strong antagonism" from NATO members who hosted U.S. nuclear weapons on their soil.[115] Ronan and Irish ambassador Fred Boland also rebuffed Arab entreaties to single out Dimona by stipulating punishments for those who refused International Atomic Energy Agency (IAEA) inspections on their facilities.[116]

After four years of promotion Aiken finally achieved his goal when the UNGA passed Resolution 1665, "On the Prevention of the Wider Dissemination of Nuclear Weapons," by acclamation on December 4, 1961. Among the nuclear powers, France was the lone holdout. He suspected the French had limited themselves to "admiring" remarks in deference to Bonn, but with African nations inveighing against French nuclear testing in the Sahara, Paris may simply have had enough of nuclear limitations.[117] Sweden's resolution earned majorities but little else. Lacking commitments from the Western powers, it would wither on the vine.

The meaning of nondissemination therefore remained up for grabs. Five days before the vote, Aiken had expressed his belief that the international community had a duty to manage global nuclear risks long enough "to evolve and strengthen a generally accepted system of world security based on international law and law enforcement."[118] Nondissemination was not to be an end in itself. Other UN delegates registered various reservations. Venezuela's ambassador warned that such an atomic binary obscured an important distinction: whether states "actually possessed the means or the potential to manufacture nuclear weapons."[119] The prominence of regional feuds in the plenaries had also been ominous. Iraq's representative accused Israel of pursuing weapons of mass destruction with French complicity, while Eastern and Western delegations clashed repeatedly over French and West German nuclear ambitions. The harshest criticism, according to Ronan, came from Menon, who had concluded that the resolution "did not go far enough."[120] Aiken's commitment was unshaken: "We in this generation, big nations and small, are the inheritors of entangled problems which have attached to many of them the detonators of local wars and civil strife and to some of them the detonators of nuclear war. . . . We must buy time."[121] It would be left to a new Eighteen Nation Committee on Disarmament (ENDC)—authorized by the same UNGA—where eight neutral and nonaligned states would join five Western and five Eastern powers in Geneva to debate nuclear questions in a world after empire.

V

Although Resolution 1665 marked a watershed for international diplomacy, it remained outside the dominant currents of the Cold War. The Soviets found Kennedy's disarmament schemes no more appealing than Eisenhower's had been. In the United States, Arizona senator Barry Goldwater lead a nationalist revolt in the Republican Party that regarded globalism as tantamount to communism. Calls to strengthen the UN inflamed his supporters. In a letter to the White House, former Texas lieutenant governor John Lee Smith labeled "Freedom from War"—the booklet that the U.S. State Department had printed to commemorate Kennedy's "Sword of Damocles" speech—"rank treason."[122]

The fate of nondissemination continued to run through Berlin in the winter of 1961. Kennedy's interest in the developing world notwithstanding, his national-security bureaucracy remained wedded to transatlantic solidarity as the linchpin of U.S. foreign policy, while Moscow continued to insist that West Germany's access to atomic weaponry was antithetical to any settlement over Berlin.[123] Neither Gromyko's proposal to denuclearize the region à la the Rapacki Plan nor Rusk's to have Berlin's four occupying powers certify the 1954 Paris agreements were acceptable to both sides.[124] When Stevenson advised that the ENDC should have a crack at a nondissemination treaty, Kennedy overruled him: the Berlin talks remained the only venue in which to discuss Europe's nuclear future.[125]

A new "nuclear weapons posture" that the U.S. State Department circulated on January 26, 1962, failed to resolve the issue.[126] A concerted effort to figure out how to halt the spread of nuclear weapons and of increasingly sophisticated delivery vehicles without impinging on U.S. strategic priorities, it joined the Atomic Energy Act and NSC 5906/1 as "the foundation stones" of U.S. nuclear policy. The new posture featured trade-offs, benefits, and contradictions. On the one hand, the Atomic Energy Act already barred Kennedy from relinquishing his veto over U.S.-made warheads, and, by couching nondissemination as a universal goal, it opened up space for him to side with Moscow against his own allies.[127] On the other hand, nondissemination hindered efforts to consolidate nuclear arsenals via nuclear-sharing arrangements. For instance, it ruled out transfers of enrichment technology or medium-range ballistic missiles (MRBMs), which the European bureau wanted to deal in exchange for the submission of the French nuclear deterrent to NATO control.[128] These plans were ultimately undone by congressional unease with communist influence in French society, which heartened the French architect of the European Coal and Steel Community, Jean Monnet, who hoped that "the special U.S.-U.K. relationship[s]" might one day become "a U.S.-European partnership" via NATO.[129] The unspoken mechanism was a joint NATO fleet bristling with state-of-the-art, nuclear-tipped Polaris missiles. Although Lauris Norstad and the Europeans had lobbied for the emplacement of third-generation, land-based MRBMs in Western Europe, McNamara and the Bureau of European Affairs argued that invulnerable submarines would project greater credibility via a posture of assured retaliation. When combined with Rickover's continuing opposition, considerations of money eventually won out—it was cheaper and simpler to host multilingual crews on surface ships than on cramped submersibles.[130] While keeping West Germany out of the nuclear club might convince Khrushchev to do likewise with communist China, the MLF remained the most promising means of consolidating U.S. nuclear hegemony.[131] As long as Kennedy's administration continued to prioritize European security, official directives such as the new posture would continue to temporize on multilateral nuclear restraint.

It was in East Asia and the Middle East, where Washington enjoyed less leverage, that a nondissemination accord or a test-ban treaty looked the most promising. Save for the Tripartite Declaration, which had frozen armistice lines around Palestine after the 1948 Arab-Israeli War, the United States had avoided formal security commitments to Israel, while the 1956 Suez Crisis had further impressed on Israeli leaders the folly of relying on U.S. goodwill. Kennedy confined himself to regulating arms traffic to the region.[132] With little room for error, David Ben-Gurion sought military forces sufficient to crush whatever his Arab neighbors could throw his way. He worried above all about Egyptian president Gamal Abdel Nasser's ability to achieve air superiority.[133] Desperate for U.S. Hawk surface-to-air missiles with which to counter Egyptian MiG-19s, he held a weak hand in 1961, but he had made a career out of winning with less. Kennedy had sought to distance himself from his father's well-known sympathies for the Nazi regime while U.S. ambassador to London from 1938 to 1940, going so far as to liken Zionism to Irish nationalism during the 1960 election campaign. Now he confronted an Israeli prime minister who had declared that if the Arab states were to defeat Israel "they would do to the Jews what Hitler did."[134]

If Dimona was life insurance for Israel, it was also a "time bomb" for U.S.–Middle East relations, endangering the balance at which the United States had aimed on the Arab-Israeli conflict since 1945.[135] On the one hand, U.S. society harbored Zionist sympathies after the Holocaust, and Jewish voters held sway in numerous cities. On the other hand, Arab rulers presided over greater wealth, more oil, and larger populations, with important implications for the Cold War struggle. Kennedy faced numerous challenges: how to guarantee Tel Aviv's survival without alienating Arab leaders; how to preserve flows of oil, communications, and shipping to Western Europe and East Asia; and how to avert a regional arms race in jet fighters, ballistic missiles, and atomic arsenals.[136] Arms transfers were a political tightrope: Tel Aviv was demanding enough to repulse Soviet-equipped neighbors even as U.S. allies in Saudi Arabia, Jordan, and Iran threatened to turn to the Eastern bloc if their requests went unmet. Komer fumed to an Israeli minister in 1963 that for decades Tel Aviv had seemed intent on forcing the United States off the "ostensibly middle position which permitted us to maintain reasonable relations with the Arabs and thereby combat Soviet penetration of the Middle East."[137]

Kennedy applied pressure on Tel Aviv straightaway. Kennedy worried that Nasser's United Arab Republic would ask Moscow for help manufacturing their own atomic weapons.[138] He had reminded Ben-Gurion as early as February 1961 about the invitation for U.S. scientists to visit Dimona. Tel Aviv stalled through Passover, leading Kennedy to insist before any discussion about the Hawks go forward. Israeli scientists showed two AEC officials around the installation on May 24, 1961. While they were permitted to visit the heavy-water reactor, six subterranean basements where Israeli

chemists separated plutonium from spent fuel rods were left off the tour. Heavy equipment hid the entrance to the reprocessing facility. The U.S. scouts consequently noted
"no present evidence that the Israelis have weapon production in mind." A follow-up
visit was recommended within the year.[139]

When Ben-Gurion pressed Kennedy on the Hawks the next week, Kennedy informed the Israeli prime minister that Dimona remained a stumbling block, inau-
gurating a clear link between conventional and nuclear hardware in the region. The
president related the Pentagon's reluctance to sell the Hawks lest "missiles come into
the Middle East" with the effect of driving an arms race with Cold War entanglements.
While Ben-Gurion made token concessions, he also played on Kennedy's fondness
for transformative infrastructure, making a case for the nuclear facility as indispensable if Israel were to irrigate the arid Levant with desalinated seawater. He insinuated
that insecurity, not inspections, would guide his policy: "we do not know what will
happen in the future; in three or four years we might have need for a plant to process
plutonium." He could have been staking out his freedom of initiative or hinting at
the existing facility, or both.[140] Top military brass urged Kennedy to head the issue off
via every available channel, "official, quasi-official and private."[141] In November 1961,
Rusk warned of "grave repercussions" if the reactor were to remain unsafeguarded; the
worst-case scenario featured Soviet nuclear weapons on Arab territories.[142]

No leader challenged John Kennedy on the world frontier quite like Mao Zedong.
Nuclear weapons in his hands would compromise U.S. containment efforts throughout Asia, threatening U.S. armed forces, raising Beijing's profile in the nonaligned
movement, and tilting the scales toward neutralism in Tokyo, Thailand, and Pakistan.
Kennedy's group was less dogmatic than that of Eisenhower, with the U.S. State Department and the White House both reviewing East Asia policy amid the Great Leap
Forward and the Sino-Soviet split.[143] When impoverished, landlocked Laos descended
into a three-way civil war, the president rejected military intervention, accepting
negotiations with Moscow to neutralize the country under a coalition government.
He was less restrained vis-à-vis the Democratic Republic of Vietnam (DRV), whose
anticolonial nationalism under Ho Chi Minh, Vo Nguyen Giap, Le Duc Tho, and
Le Duan's collective leadership seemed a more acute threat.[484] After Johnson returned
from Southeast Asia to warn that Kennedy faced a "fundamental decision"—beat back
"Communist expansion now" or "throw in the towel"—Kennedy expanded the U.S.
military presence in the Republic of Vietnam from six hundred to sixteen thousand
soldiers-at-arms, including U.S. Green Berets with U.S. Army counterinsurgency
manuals tucked in their chest pockets.[485] On the Policy Planning Staff, Rostow drew
an analogy with NATO's trials, characterizing the two communist titans as locked in
a "competition over the central issue of who gets nuclear weapons [and under] what
type of control."[144] His conclusion missed the force of Chinese nationalism and the
geo-ideological depth of the Sino-Soviet split.

Bundy launched a blue-sky review of China policy in January 1962. The Great Leap Forward had devastated grain harvests without the many-fold increase to industrial production that might have pulled the PRC abreast of the United Kingdom, as Mao had promised. Communist Chinese purchases of Soviet arms on a cash-and-carry basis had also come to an end. Rostow and Komer were nonetheless convinced not only that Chinese power was waxing but that its economic recovery would "coincide with . . . acquisition of their first home-grown nuclear weapons."[145] The CIA had estimated in early 1961 that Beijing would enter the nuclear club within two years.[146] The U.S. Air Force was even more pessimistic, while the Bureau of Far Eastern Affairs in the U.S. State Department treated it as a foregone conclusion.[147]

Kennedy and Rusk looked for ways to delay or at least mitigate the event. Chinese representation on world councils was a stumbling block. Eisenhower had taken an uncompromising stance, ostracizing the PRC and insisting that international bodies seat Chiang Kai Shek's nationalist regime instead. The new team was willing to take a fresh look. With the JCS warning that a Chinese nuclear test would have a "marked impact politically and militarily" on U.S. security interests in Asia, the desire to review "one China" policy won out over fear of the powerful congressional China lobby that remained invested in Chiang Kai-Shek. Roger Hilsman, director of the Bureau of Intelligence and Research, outlined a "two China" policy in July 1961.[148] Although the nuclear question was bound up in China's relationship to the UN, that linkage could cut either way. As Rusk informed the British ambassador to the United States early in Kennedy's term, "some sort of 'dialogue'" was unavoidable. Eventually Washington would have to invite the PRC to the table, and he hoped Mao might trade nuclear club membership for the credentials needed to rejoin the international community.[149] Komer likewise promoted an "attitude of reasonableness" in April 1961 with his eyes on two objectives: to allay allied and neutral misgivings about excluding the world's most populous nation from the UN and to justify a more flexible China policy to domestic audiences. "Instead of keeping Peiping out of the UN because it is evil," he maintained, "it is precisely for this reason that we must get Peiping involved in arms control; we can hardly do this if it isn't in the UN where we can get at it."[150] By October, he had reversed his line of reasoning. If they made nuclear forbearance a precondition of Beijing's admission to international society, it would no longer be "us trying to keep them out of the UN, but they refusing to come in."[151]

Conclusion

In the years ahead, Mao's "implacable hostility" would justify opposition to the PRC's international rehabilitation among U.S. elites. Rather than rethinking his Asia policy, in the end Kennedy preferred to "prolong [Beijing]'s time of troubles to allow Japanese and Indian strength to grow and to buy time to strengthen such peripheral areas" as Korea and Southeast Asia.[152] Rusk warned Japanese foreign minister Masayoshi Ōhira in December 1962 that a nuclear-armed PRC would destabilize the region "immeasurably." While increased Japanese military spending might help rebalance power in the Asia-Pacific region and ease the current account deficits driven by U.S. overseas deployments, only arms control could postpone communist China's entrance into the nuclear club. Rusk wondered whether PRC representatives might walk into the ENDC if some form of UN representation were offered in exchange.[153] Amid a growing Sino-Soviet split, Komer wrote from the White House observing that Khrushchev might not welcome help with his troublesome ally.[154]

Nuclear status was fast becoming a proxy not only for national greatness but also for whom the postcolonial community welcomed into its ranks. Would communist China trade membership in the nuclear club for that in an international system from which the United States and its allies had hitherto ostracised it? At the furtive sit-downs in Warsaw that were the sole point of contact between the two powers, Chinese emissaries equated such pacts to the unequal treaties of their "century of humiliation . . . No one would prevent China from exercising its legitimate rights," one foreign officer declared in April 1962.[155] Even if talks were to fail, however, the PRC would carry a scarlet letter. With luck, nuclear containment would preserve the peace long enough for a less problematic regime to arise. If not, Kennedy would enjoy solid grounds on which to exile Beijing from international organizations and marginalize it on the world stage. If the PRC were to become the first Afro-Asian nuclear power, the tools at Kennedy's disposal had advanced considerably since the days when European gunboats steamed up the Yangtze River. For the wider world to accept the U.S. president as humanity's nuclear guardian, however, required a better claim to the moral high ground in this global war of position.

Pax Nuclearis

Khrushchev, Kennedy, Mao, and the Moscow Treaty, 1962–1963

Introduction—Rogue One

Early in John F. Kennedy's only term in office, White House staffers reviewed the "basic philosophy" that should guide U.S. foreign policy. Newly ensconced in the Old Executive Office Building in February 1961, Robert Komer took a swing at what "basic philosophy" should inform the U.S. government's new foreign policy. If the Eisenhower administration had done its utmost to avert a garrison state at home and bolster anticommunist forces abroad, theirs should entertain grander notions: "evolution in the USSR," "common law" for the world, even the universal triumph of liberal democracy. Komer urged his officemates to "think big . . . with less pious twaddle about 'the genius, strength, and promise of America' . . . and more about doing what *must* be done over the next generation to realize this promise." To win the battles of the future, the new staff would need to "re-examine a lot of accepted shibboleths along the way."[1]

One such shibboleth would be nuclear testing. In the summer of 1963, Kennedy reached out to an old enemy, when Assistant Secretary of State W. Averell Harriman sat down in Moscow with Andrei Gromyko and British science advisor Lord Hailsham. Over the course of two weeks, the three men agreed to move their country's nuclear-testing regimes underground to preserve the Northern Hemisphere from long-lasting, gene-corrupting fallout. The real target, however, was the Chinese Communist Party (CCP) and its two-pronged campaign against alleged U.S. hegemony in Asia and Soviet dominion over international communism.[2] While Nikita Khrushchev played cat and mouse with Harriman, whose hunger for an anti-Beijing league was palpable, encouragement came from unexpected quarters. At a boozy reception at the Polish embassy halfway through the visit, Lydia Gromyko, Andrei's wife, cornered Foy Kohler to make the case for a limited test-ban treaty. "We have to have this," she confided to the U.S. ambassador, "so that when those Chinese have their first nuclear explosion, we will have a basis on which to call them to account."[3]

Back in Washington, Kennedy joked whether foreign operatives followed his wife Jacqueline's remarks as closely.[4] He was in high spirits. In the Limited Test Ban Treaty (LTBT), known also as the Moscow Treaty, the United States, the United Kingdom, and the Soviet Union offered themselves as planetary custodians at war with "the contamination of man's environment by radioactive substances."[5] It was more than the first visible sign of U.S.-Soviet détente. The treaty would redefine international status while elevating human rights and humanitarianism alongside development and deterrence as central tenets of enlightened global leadership. To achieve this fledgling condominium, Kennedy had had to recast the U.S. presidency. How eagerly would Americans "guard the boundaries" against threats ranging from AK-47-toting guerrillas to nuclear-tipped intercontinental ballistic missiles (ICBMs)?[6] George Kennan spoke for many affluent parents when he admitted that he "would rather see my children dead than to have them experience" total thermonuclear war.[7] To spare them such a fate, Kennedy vested in his office the responsibility to protect the health and prosperity of younger and future generations, whether through exploits of diplomacy, or feats of limited war.[8]

I

Kennedy would sustain U.S. hegemony amid the twin processes of decolonization and suburbanization. Republican claims that Harry S. Truman "lost China" had incapacitated the previous Democratic administration, while Adlai Stevenson never overcame a reputation for cerebral reticence in his two electoral contests with Eisenhower.[9] Kennedy, by contrast, opted for the offensive. In his debut speech to the U.S. Senate in 1958, the junior senator from Massachusetts had accused Eisenhower of tending to budgets rather than to the Soviet menace.[10] Against Richard Nixon two years later, he fended off insinuations of weakness by accentuating his masculine virtues—his military service, his sporting hobbies, his budding family. Once president, he sent Stevenson to New York as UN ambassador and appointed "action intellectuals" to the key national-security posts. If his strategic retreat from the Bay of Pigs had battered his tough-guy image, his game of chicken with Khrushchev over Berlin helped rehabilitate it.[11] As focus shifted to the Third World over the course of his first term, however, the White House worked to devise a new vernacular for executive leadership in an affluent, segregated democracy and an increasingly tumultuous world.

Kennedy's interest in the Third World was primarily ideological. He and many of his advisors believed that an admixture of structural poverty and exploding demography in Latin America, Africa, and Asia offered fertile terrain for nonwhite revolution. Their interest in these underdeveloped expanses was Janus-faced, rationalizing carrots in the form of the Alliance for Progress and the Peace Corps, and sticks ranging from Green Berets to forward-deployed nuclear systems. This preoccupation informed a gathering pivot in U.S. foreign policy. As Kennedy would summarize to Belgian prime minister Paul-Henri Spaak in May 1963, "today's struggle does not lie [in Europe] but rather in Asia, Latin America, and Africa."[12]

Kennedy's counterrevolutionary posture was part of a larger reckoning with an evolving U.S. role between Europe and Asia. Early in the twentieth century, international relations were synonymous with race development; by midcentury, stateside liberals had reasoned that the nuclear question would force them to take the mantle of world leadership in the name of a secular millenarianism.[13] The year that Kennedy won the presidency, in a presidential address to the American Historical Association, Sterling Professor of History at Yale University C. Vann Woodward, whose 1955 *The Strange Career of Jim Crow* had become a textbook of the civil rights movement, reflected on how to write history amid a "set of revolutions"—the nuclear arms race and decolonization. Atomic warheads atop long-range missiles had ended the country's mythical "free security," when two oceans and an impregnable Arctic had precluded the need for a leviathan fiscal-military state, bringing the curtain down on an "age of innocence" when elites had supposedly recoiled from responsibility in the world and "the guilt of wielding power." Blowing through histories of Indian violence and the Roosevelt Corollary to the Monroe Doctrine, he concluded that the nation should make itself accountable for the course of human events. For Woodward and other consensus historians, including Arthur M. Schlesinger Jr., Kennedy's court historian, the obsolescence of "America First," mass warfare, and European hegemony after 1945 called for a reinterpretation of world history, one in which a provincial United States mediated between an arrogant, modernizing Europe and a despotic, backward Asia.[14]

Woodward was not alone in rating the rise of the East as being more significant than the Cold War. Having patterned his address on Frederick Jackson Turner's 1893 "The Significance of the Frontier in American History," which submitted the advance of white settlement as the defining feature of national life, he foresaw a struggle for the New Frontier on the far side of the Pacific Ocean, quoting Indian historian K. M. Panikkar at length on the confrontation between East and West now that European forces had been ejected from India and China. He challenged his professional audience to recognize how witnessing two world wars and a global depression had equipped them "to interpret the old order to the new order." He left unsaid whether they should adjust U.S.-style liberalism to the nonwhite world, or the nonwhite world to U.S.-style liberalism.[15]

Woodward's views had a patrimony. The United States had a long, sordid history of anti-Asian prejudice in the name of countering "yellow peril": the 1882 Chinese

Exclusion Act, Japanese-American internment during the Second World War, the contested status of thirty thousand undocumented Chinese who sought asylum after the Chinese Civil War.[16] Eisenhower had warned his successor in January 1961 that the establishment of a Chinese communist bridgehead in Laos would finish "the West . . . in the whole southeast Asian area."[17] A year later, Kennedy explained to French minister of cultural affairs André Malraux that, in contrast to the Soviet Union, whose leaders knew that a thermonuclear war would have no winners, the Chinese "would be perfectly prepared, because of the lower value they attach to human life, to sacrifice hundreds of millions of their own lives."[18]

The CCP's self-promotion as a revolutionary Afro-Asian vanguard evoked three prime fears held by U.S. elites: nonwhite uprising, communist contagion, and nuclear spread.[19] Strategies of deterrence and development therefore shared core assumptions. Members of the Kennedy administration gamed out nuclear-use scenarios in Korea, Vietnam, and China at the same time that they debated economic development and family planning to control rising Third World birthrates as medium-term threats to the worldwide distribution of wealth and power.[20] When the National Security Council (NSC) met in the White House Cabinet Room on January 22, 1963, Kennedy singled the Chinese out as "our major antagonists of the late '60s and beyond."[21] Two months later in the briefing room of the U.S. State Department, he styled the arrival of atomic power in new hands "the greatest possible danger and hazard."[22] Little wonder he reportedly deemed a nuclear-armed People's Republic of China (PRC) "the great menace in the future to humanity, the free world, and freedom on earth."[23]

Khrushchev distrusted Mao Zedong for convergent reasons. The CCP competed with the Communist Party of the Soviet Union (CPSU) in Latin America, Africa, and Asia, trumpeting its nonwhite identity, breakneck industrialization, and agricultural communization in missions to those regions. Mao's brazen support for national liberation struggles discomfited both leaders.[24] Khrushchev relationship with the Chinese despot had started to deteriorate after he denounced his predecessor, Josef Stalin, and his cult of personality at CPSU's Twentieth Congress in February 1956. The repudiation stung Mao, whose autocratic rule emulated Stalin's as much as the heavenly Qing emperors. Regarding himself as the communist world's elder statesman after Stalin's death, Mao had no compunction about flouting the new Soviet premier even before Khrushchev canceled sensitive nuclear assistance to the PRC in October 1959. By the turn of the decade, the two communist giants were trading barbs at world congresses of communist and workers' parties, their widening split a frequent topic of conversation in Georgetown salons.[25]

For Kennedy, a nuclear-armed China represented a revolutionary beacon whose atomic shield might shelter communist insurgents across the region. In this, he differed little from Eisenhower, whose last secretary of defense, Neil McElroy, had warned

Gromyko about their common "yellow peril."[26] It was nonetheless unclear how best to handle the Sino-Soviet split. Rostow spied dangers: to lean toward Moscow would do Khrushchev no favors among fellow communists and might lead Mao to "take a more militant approach . . . especially in Southeast Asia."[27] While Khrushchev feared an impulsive nuclear-armed neighbor to his east, his public remarks also revealed his unease with Mao's growing sway among nonwhite nations. At the Twenty-Second CPSU Congress in October 1961, the CPSU renewed its attacks on Stalin at Khrushchev's behest. In response Mao coined a new aphorism: "whoever is against Stalin is against Mao." Khrushchev lambasted Mao in return for courting nuclear war with the United States and was labeled a revisionist and "Great Power chauvinist" for his trouble.[28] Neither Washington nor Moscow could afford to alienate Afro-Asian leaders in their respective tussles with Beijing. Khrushchev touted disarmament, development, and peace in opposition to Mao's puritanical anti-imperialism, while Kennedy applied a humanitarian polish to his atomic sword. From New Delhi, U.S. ambassador John Kenneth Galbraith cautioned that resuming nuclear testing would cause "the gravest difficulties in Asia, Africa and elsewhere." Although he warned that a proposed statement that praised clean hydrogen bombs for reducing the odds of large-scale extermination would stretch humanitarian rhetoric beyond the breaking point, U.S. nuclear diplomacy was nonetheless entering a new chapter.[29]

II

The Berlin crisis continued to take center stage in early 1962. In a conversation with Gromyko in March, Secretary of State Dean Rusk spelled out their common interest in nuclear nondissemination. To restrain Bonn together would corroborate accusations of treating Europeans high-handedly. A universal regime, by contrast, could embed regional protectorates in an impartial world order. For now, an interim accord would confirm the spread of nuclear arms as antithetical to "the cause of peace"; in the meantime, the United States and the Soviet Union could explore multilateral steps.[30] One potential deal came further into view in May when Khrushchev conditioned Sino-Soviet nuclear assistance on NATO's atomic fleet. However toothless, it hinted at a way forward: What if the superpowers were to check their respective allies in central Europe and East Asia?[31]

Such an arrangement could harmonize Kennedy's nuclear policies across the board. When confronted by Rostow's Basic National Security Strategy, McGeorge Bundy had raised "the problem of priority"—the centrality of Western Europe's wealth and, above all, its shared ideological heritage with North America. While developments in the underdeveloped areas were key, the NATO alliance and, most important, the "Western" character of the Atlantic community were fundamental. Later drafts prioritized "European" powers, including Canada, Australia, New Zealand, and Japan on such first-order issues as "military policy; arms control and disarmament policy; NATO; and Germany." The less-developed regions of Latin America, Asia, and Africa would enjoy preferential treatment on matters of foreign aid, international trade, and residual colonial issues, with anticommunist regimes receiving the benefit of the doubt in Southeast Asia and the Caribbean, where fear of ideological capitulation trumped all.[32]

It was unclear where nondissemination fit into Kennedy's grand strategy. France and West Germany had invested heavily in their nuclear sectors just as the main sources of U.S. capital in Europe had begun to depreciate. Overseas military deployments were siphoning gold from the U.S. Treasury, and both Eisenhower and Kennedy struggled to reduce balance-of-payments deficits with European allies, Japan, and South Korea.[33] U.S. security guarantees also looked less credible now that Soviet missiles could target U.S. cities. Full decoupling was unlikely: whereas Charles de Gaulle railed against the Anglo-Saxons in the same breath as Soviet hegemony, Konrad Adenauer continued to court the United States, his chief protector. Although Sweden joined West Germany as a threshold nuclear-weapon state in Western Europe, most problem states called other regions home: Israel and the United Arab Republic in the Middle East; Japan, India, and communist China on the other side of the Eurasian supercontinent.[34]

Many in Kennedy's cabinet expressed faith that a military posture of flexible response could bolster the containment of Cold War adversaries and nuclear spread in Europe and Asia. General Maxwell Taylor was the nearest it had to a patron saint. A vocal critic of the New Look as Eisenhower's army chief of staff, he had worked within the Pentagon late in Eisenhower's second term to equip the U.S. Army for limited nuclear conflicts and brushfire wars with a focus on Asia. After retiring in 1959, he published *The Uncertain Trumpet* to call for an expanded military draft, stronger conventional forces, and plans for conflict scenarios short of total thermonuclear war.[35] After Kennedy made him his military advisor after the Bay of Pigs, Taylor returned to military service as Joint Chiefs of Staff (JCS) chairman in late 1962. In his book he cited a string of civil wars, counterinsurgency campaigns, and crises since 1945—China, "Greece and Malaya, Vietnam, Taiwan, Hungary, the Middle East, Laos, to mention only a few"—to make the case that massive retaliation had averted "World War III" while falling short in peripheral conflicts whose stakes grew by the year.[36] Henry Kissinger and Herman Kahn also rejected massive retaliation as lacking in credibility, but Taylor was more explicit about his ultimate goal—to take the worldwide initiative. Deterrence was insufficient; the U.S. government should "prepare itself to respond anywhere, anytime, with weapons and forces appropriate to the situation," not only against the communist giants but "troublemaking powers like Cuba, Egypt, Indonesia, and North Vietnam."[37] While he did not reject diplomatic solutions altogether, he emphasized how the military arts could, if guided by the right hand, "create a better world."[38]

Flexible response would generalize U.S. reliance on extended nuclear deterrence while lowering the declared threshold for its use. As West German defense minister Franz Josef Strauss put it to Rusk in the summer of 1962, the U.S.-Soviet arms race and nuclear proliferation had raised doubts that Washington remained "in full control of the world."[39] Arms sales and military assistance drove demand for more of the same from the Persian Gulf around to Kamchatka. The year before, the NSC had drawn up plans for the prompt introduction of two troop divisions and nuclear striking power to the Central Treaty Organization (CENTO) for use against auxiliary airfields and troop movements through mountain passes in northwest Iran in the event of a Soviet incursion from the north.[40] Iranian shah Reza Pahlavi grew increasingly demanding of nuclear capabilities, pursuing both U.S. and Soviet missile bases in 1961, then complaining to Kennedy the next year that he had treated "Turkey as a wife, and Iran as a concubine." Although the U.S. government declined to supply him with U.S. Jupiter missiles like those in Turkey, Robert McNamara personally informed the shah of U.S. Air Force plans to launch nuclear strikes against Soviet armed forces that marched through the alpine crossings between the two countries.[41]

Flexible response promised to enable U.S. armed forces to engage revolutionary foes far from home under the cover of forward-deployed nuclear systems. While the transition from massive retaliation to flexible response was more rhetorical than real, the impulse among Kennedy's best and brightest to regain the initiative worldwide underlay their resistance to the spread of atomic weaponry.[42] The deterrence architecture in the Asia-Pacific region was even more expansive and multidomain than that in Europe, which posed issues for U.S. armed forces that patrolled the Korean demilitarized zone, taught counterinsurgency in Southeast Asia, backstopped the Republic of China on Taiwan, and operated bases from Okinawa to the Philippines. While Kennedy and Taylor resisted stationing combat troops in numbers approaching those in Europe, the rhetoric of flexible response encouraged mission creep. "If we are overrun in Korea, in Formosa, or in Western Europe," the president declaimed to his cabinet in May 1963, "we would obviously use nuclear weapons. If we are prepared to defend Korea and Thailand," he asked rhetorically, "why [should we] not be prepared to commit ourselves to defend India[?]"[43]

How then to make those commitments credible when nonalignment haunted U.S. diplomacy in Asia? The Bureau of Intelligence and Research and the Office of Far Eastern Affairs in the U.S. State Department had reached out to U.S. embassies in 1961 to gauge how a Chinese nuclear test would affect the region.[44] The general drift was troubling. In Hong Kong, the U.S. consul general emphasized how the political and psychological impact would stoke the fires of neutralism.[45] While South

Korea, South Vietnam, and Taiwan were trusted anticommunist stalwarts, neutralist opinion ran strong in Thailand and Japan. Many in the region would see a Chinese nuclear test as a shared accomplishment. From Jakarta, Ambassador Howard Jones highlighted how in places like Indonesia many "would see such achievement as dramatic evidence [that an] Asian (nation) can compete successfully with Occidentals in [a] technological race." What was worse, it could demonstrate how Chinese-style communism could modernize "formerly backward Asian society."[46] The aftershocks would extend well beyond East Asia. Embassy officials in Tehran worried that neutralist sentiment would spread among the Iranian people, while in Cairo they warned that Mao could offer to help Gamal Abdel Nasser counter Dimona. While Nasser, who resented Mao for egging on Egyptian communists, might instead join Jawaharlal Nehru in tacking westward, it was also possible that the two nonaligned luminaries would continue their drift toward Moscow. Regardless, Beijing's new-forged atomic shield would deprive Kennedy and Khrushchev of an important advantage in their rivalry with Mao, who—a follow-up exercise predicted—could accentuate to Southeast Asian neutralist countries the contrast between his peaceful and defensive actions and a hypocritical and aggressive United States.[47]

True enough, Mao outlined a broad anti-imperialist front at the tenth CCP plenum in September 1962. On the first day, the *People's Daily* complained that Washington's test-ban and nondissemination policies would bar Beijing from the nuclear club, insinuating that Moscow was in on the plot.[48] Mao now equated domestic revisionists with Josip Broz Tito and Khrushchev at the CCP's work conference in Beidaihe in the late summer, as he consolidated his grip on party leadership. On September 28, he publicly revised his theory of an "intermediate zone" of East-West struggle to lump the two superpowers together. PRC foreign policy would henceforth distinguish between two zones of conflict, one in the Third World, the other in Europe, to emphasize wars of national liberation in the former and scientific and economic ties with the latter, as Beijing promoted Mao Zedong Thought as the cure for "Great Power chauvinism" directed at the poorer nations.[49]

Flexible response promised to counter Mao's anti-hegemonic strategy. In the summer of 1961 the Pentagon had analyzed various escalation scenarios in Southeast Asia, ranging from a People's Liberation Army (PLA) intervention backed by Soviet atom bombs to a joint U.S.–Army of the Republic of Vietnam (ARVN) assault on Hainan and North Vietnam. The report figured that the issue would be decided by calibrated nuclear violence: against submarines and aircraft, atomic gravity bombs would avert defeat; against battlefield units or strategic assets, they would ensure victory.[50] Similar conclusions were drawn about the Korean Peninsula. On a fact-finding mission in the fall of 1962, Taylor advocated a clear distinction between deterring North Korean armed forces, for which two-plus U.S. Army and nineteen South Korean divisions would suffice, and a Chinese incursion across the demilitarized zone, which would necessitate atomic retaliation. Komer had summarized the state of play two days before Mao's "intermediate zone" speech: there was no real difference between Europe and East Asia; in both, U.S. armed forces would "resist conventionally unless and until confronted with an overwhelming attack."[51]

There was just one problem: nuclear strikes against Asians risked alienating allies around the world and neutrals across the region. The summer before, Pakistani president Ayub Khan had spelled out the dilemma to Kennedy: atomic actions would mean "forfeiting the support of peoples of Asia"; not to do so, however, would court defeat.[52] The communist powers were happy to aim a spotlight at U.S. race relations.[53] In a May 1962 discussion about how a Chinese atom bomb would affect relations with Taiwan, Harriman worried aloud about the cumulative effect of Mao's "propaganda theme that Americans used the atomic bomb only against Asians."[54]

In August 1962, an Arms Control and Disarmament Agency (ACDA) official disclosed to the press that the PRC was expected to test "within a matter of months."[55] Although the admission was quickly retracted, U.S. concerns were well known. The U.S. intelligence community had arrived at a tentative estimate that Beijing would explode "an all-plutonium device in early 1963."[56] The Institute for Defense Analyses, a Pentagon-affiliated think tank, predicted three years as the upper limit and attached a warning note that the hub-and-spokes system of U.S. alliances in the Asia-Pacific region could unravel without remedial action. While a Pacific Command force of Polaris submarines "plainly capable of devastating" mainland China might keep neutralism at bay in Thailand or Japan, a PLA rocket force would elevate the revolutionary power in Afro-Asian eyes and shield guerrilla forces operating near U.S. military outposts.[57] Before this could come to pass, Kennedy needed to realize flexible response's promise of freedom from the straitjacket of massive retaliation, so that victory in brushfire wars would not depend on the use of terror weapons.

III

The first step was to humanize U.S. atomic might. Kennedy's speech on March 2, 1962, announcing a new test series had ended on a discordant note as he cited his duty to humankind alongside his constitutional requirement "to uphold and defend the freedom of the American people."[58] While he offered reassurances that the Atomic Energy Commission (AEC) would take all necessary precautions, his claim that the health risks of increased radiation paled in comparison to those posed by nuclear parity did not cause antinuclear activism to abate. Women Strike for Peace had mounted a two-thousand-person picket outside the White House in January 1962. When the Student Peace Union and the Students for a Democratic Society rallied four thousand baby boomers for a second demonstration in February, Kennedy had

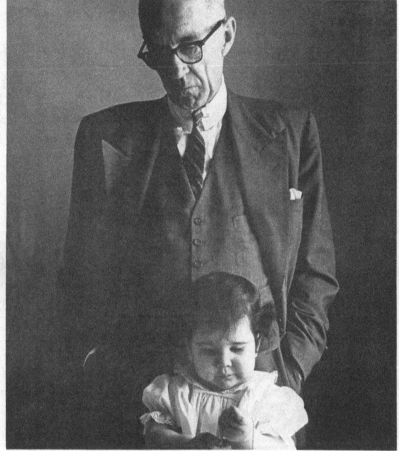

The New York Times.

LATE CITY EDITION

MONDAY, APRIL 16, 1962.

Dr. Spock is worried.

If you've been raising a family on Dr. Spock's book, you know that he doesn't get worried easily.

From the university in Ohio where he works, he sends you this message about the resumption of nuclear testing in the atmosphere:

"I am worried. Not so much about the effect of past tests but at the prospect of endless future ones. As the tests multiply, so will the damage to children—here and around the world.

"Who gives us this right?"

Some citizens would leave all the thinking to the government. They forget the catastrophic blunders that governments have made throughout history.

"There are others who think that superior armaments will solve the problem. They scorn those who believe in the strength of a just cause. They have forgotten that a frail idealist in a loin cloth compelled the British to back out of India.

"There are dangers in any course. I would rather we took small risks today if there is hope of lessening the enormous risks which lie ahead.

"And if I am to be destroyed through some miscalculation I would prefer to be destroyed while we are showing leadership in the search for a cooperative world than while sitting in an illusory fortress blaming our opponents for the lack of a solution.

"In a moral issue, I believe that every citizen has not only the right but the responsibility to make his own feelings known and felt."

—Benjamin Spock, M.D.

Dr. Spock has become a sponsor of The National Committee for a SANE Nuclear Policy.

Other sponsors are listed below, with a brief description of what SANE stands for.

If you are worried too about the present series of nuclear tests in the atmosphere, telegraph or write President Kennedy and your Congressman.

If you would like to do still more, send a contribution to help us run advertisements like this one all over the country. The National Committee for a SANE Nuclear Policy, 17 East 45th Street, New York 17, N.Y.

FIGURE 2 "Dr. Spock Is Worried." *New York Times*, 16 April 1962.

Source: Box 10, Series A, DG 58, SANE Papers, Peace Collection, Swarthmore College Libraries.

White House interns hand out coffee like an indulgent university dean. Two weeks later, U.S. and Soviet co-chairmen sat down with Women Strike for Peace's fifty-one emissaries in Geneva.[59]

Liberal tastemakers seized on suburban themes to promote a test ban. Founded by poet Lenore Marshall and *Saturday Review of Books* editor Norman Cousins, the National Committee for a Sane Nuclear Policy (SANE) garnered support from celebrities such as Harry Belafonte and Marilyn Monroe, prominent intellectuals like Albert Schweitzer and Bertrand Russell, socialists such as Norman Thomas, union leaders like A. Philip Randolph of the AFL-CIO and United Auto Workers (UAW) president Walter Reuther, and Democratic Party luminaries, most notably Eleanor Roosevelt. Civil rights activists like Martin Luther King Jr. and Bayard Rustin endorsed SANE's work, associating antinuclear protests with their own nonviolent actions. SANE furnished each delegation to the Eighteen Nation Committee on Disarmament (ENDC) with a small disarmament library and even dispatched a delegate to the 1961 Non-Aligned Conference in Belgrade. Nationally, it took out more than thirty full-page advertisements in the *New York Times* and other major newspapers to publicize its views, including one on April 16, 1962, featuring Dr. Benjamin Spock, in which the famous pediatrician towered over a brunette toddler, bridging the retail politics of domestic bliss with the universal ambitions of liberal modernity.[60] The heading read simply, "Dr. Spock is worried." The caption carried the rest of the message: "I am worried. Not so much about the effect of past tests but at the prospect of endless future ones. As the tests multiply, so will the damage to children—here and around the world. Who gives us this right?"[61]

The rhetoric of paternal guardianship would prove surprisingly tractable in Kennedy's hands, as his government contemplated how arms control could make the rhetoric of graduated response palatable to allies and neutrals alike. The uniformed services were skeptical. When Bill Foster had unveiled a more ambitious disarmament package in December 1961, JCS chairman General Lyman Lemnitzer had recoiled at trading off "our strategic nuclear superiority . . . for virtually no concession on the part of the Soviets."[62] The partial measure with the greatest domestic and international popularity—a comprehensive nuclear test ban—would not close off every route to the atom bomb, whether gas-centrifuge programs capable of enriching uranium clandestinely or stockpiling of proven, gun-type fission bombs that did not require testing. Two presidential task forces had yielded mixed results. That chaired by Bell Labs president James Fisk advised that a test ban exempting underground tests would never thwart a determined actor.[63] Physicist Wolfgang Panofsky's parallel effort in summer 1961 had noted a broader dilemma between nuclear superiority and mutual vulnerability, drawing the counterintuitive judgment that an effective test ban would freeze the former in place, while unrestricted testing would by contrast hasten U.S.-Soviet nuclear parity.[64]

As the president defended nuclear testing to neutral leaders, anxious parents, and antinuclear activists, his secretary of defense moved to humanize U.S. nuclear strategy. At a NATO ministerial meeting in Athens on May 5, 1962, McNamara sketched out a new deterrence strategy that would integrate conventional forces, graduated escalation, and ethical standards in a more restrained posture. Together with a claim that looming U.S.-Soviet nuclear parity would necessitate a more unified Atlantic defense, his address held implications for nuclear strategy. The force requirements of a declaratory policy that defined nonmilitary objectives as targets of last resort and lowered the threshold for nuclear escalation were beyond the capabilities of all but the superpowers. French sociologist Raymond Aron dubbed the proposed posture "graduated response," the moral virtues of which McNamara highlighted so as to shine an unflattering light on the more wanton, asymmetric postures toward which aspiring nuclear powers had by necessity gravitated.[65]

Humanitarian standards were dear to McNamara. While systems theory, management techniques, and accounting control had been his calling cards at Ford Motor Company and the Defense Department, his severe rationalism hid humanistic commitments.[66] The introduction of Single Integrated Operational Plan (SIOP)-62, which Lemnitzer believed would "permit the United States to prevail in the event of general nuclear war," had automated the release of more than 1,700 nuclear weapons against 725 targets throughout the communist bloc.[67] When confronted with this enormity, Kennedy had retorted, "and we call ourselves the human race." Graduated response operationalized his revulsion.[68] Borrowing RAND defense intellectual Herman Kahn's actuarial critique of massive retaliation to game out scenarios that predicted twenty-five million rather than seventy-five million U.S. deaths, McNamara wanted to reserve the lion's share of strategic nuclear forces to hold enemy cities hostage after a first strike had diminished their retaliatory assets. Whereas Lemnitzer had assured Kennedy that such a counterforce strategy had "little practical meaning as a humanitarian measure," McNamara drew a bright line between combatants and noncombatants in conformity with just-war tenets of discrimination and proportionality, reasoning that the smaller the warheads, the higher their accuracy, and the cleaner the airbursts, the lower the total sum of human suffering.[69]

McNamara also made clear the implications for nuclear proliferation in Athens. He rejected small, countervalue forces as "expensive, prone to obsolescence, and lacking in credibility." NATO would best address the Soviet nuclear arms buildup by placing its nuclear defense under indivisible command on a global basis. He elaborated further when he delivered the University of Michigan's commencement address two weeks later in Ann Arbor. For Britain or France to threaten massive retaliation against the

USSR "would be tantamount to suicide." A centralized nuclear arsenal, by contrast, offered a "chance of survival as nations."[70]

With the White House in search of a single political issue to harmonize its nuclear policies, Irish diplomats made the rounds in foreign capitals.[71] Since most Afro-Asian nations were on record in favor of test bans and nuclear-weapon-free zones (NWFZs), Frank Aiken and his diplomats pitched their idea as the best means to inoculate post-colonial states from U.S.-Soviet competition while winning "great prestige" in international councils, as one Irish envoy informed the deputy foreign minister of Nigeria, the sole sub-Saharan African member on the ENDC. Officials from Africa, Latin America, and Asia were becoming international lawmakers even as they remained its primary takers.[72] From his office overlooking UN headquarters, Stevenson noted the global consensus behind nuclear law and order: a lightly inspected comprehensive test ban, a partial test ban, and a nondissemination pact all enjoyed majority support in New York. Amid crises in the Congo, Southeast Asia, and the Caribbean, the U.S. delegation faced a groundswell of Afro-Asian criticism in the UN General Assembly (UNGA), while allies had grown impatient about U.S. intransigence on subterranean test-ban verification. Recalling how "resoundingly isolated and defeated" he had been the previous year, Stevenson begged for a more accommodating stance when the UNGA reconvened in August.[73]

Nuclear nondissemination could improve Kennedy's international standing without limiting his atomic authority. Foster advanced two test-ban options to the ENDC in August 1962: an inspected, total version and a three-environments ban that would permit underground blasts. While Lemnitzer saw malice aforethought when Foster circulated a draft nondissemination accord a few weeks later, reckoning that Khrushchev's real intention was to split NATO," McNamara took the opposite tack, citing the merits of a "greater degree of stability in the developing world" as President Ngô Đình Diệm's position deteriorated in South Vietnam.[74] For all their differences, Kennedy and Khrushchev shared an interest in guiding developments in present and future industrial regions. In McNamara's telling, nuclear proliferation would render them susceptible to "the undesirable aspirations of the smaller nations," which would exacerbate the "difficult problem of working out a stable political community." Khrushchev had assured Kennedy in March that Berlin did not preclude all cooperative ventures, "first of all, the question of the nuclear test ban."[75] In a letter to Foster on October 4 McNamara hinted at a larger objective: might the United States and the Soviet Union join hands to freeze the nuclear club at its current membership?[76]

IV

The Soviets dubbed the nerve-racking stretch from October 14 to November 22, 1962, the "Caribbean crisis." It certainly added a nuclear dimension to Latin American and Caribbean politics, inducing an Organization of American States (OAS) resolution to remove the missiles, inspiring regional NWFZ talks, and further polarizing the region.[77] But the causes and consequences went beyond the Western Hemisphere. Khrushchev hatched his plan to deploy Soviet medium-range ballistic missiles (MRBMs) and intermediate-range ballistic missiles (IRBMs) to Cuba while in Bulgaria, with one eye on U.S. Jupiter missiles in Turkey and another on U.S. troop movements in Southeast Asia.[78] When questioned by U.S. senators about Soviet military aid to Cuba, Rusk and Bundy had likened it to flexible response in Turkey and Iran and Warsaw Pact arms sales to Egypt, Indonesia, and Iraq.[79] Members of Kennedy's Executive Committee (ExComm) worried throughout the crisis that the Kremlin would broaden the conflict to Berlin.[80] Halfway around the world, hostilities broke out between the PRC and India, unsettling the subcontinent, widening the Sino-Soviet split, and sundering the Afro-Asian movement.[81]

To Algerian leader Ahmed Ben Bella, Kennedy characterized the Cuban Missile Crisis as "the outgrowth of a global problem between two camps in the international systems."[82] When the crisis threatened to boil over on October 26, Khrushchev warned Kennedy about "the knot of war" that bound their nuclear standoff to the insurrectionist forces emanating from the Third World.[83]

Khrushchev's main strategic goal was to shield Havana from counterrevolutionary action and give the Americans "a little of their own medicine."[84] Attorney General Robert Kennedy and the CIA executed Operation Mongoose over the course of 1962 with the aim of neutralizing Fidel Castro as a U.S. trade embargo throttled the Cuban economy.[85] The U.S. Navy practiced landings that spring in North Carolina and Puerto Rico, less than 600 miles from Guantánamo Bay—the epicenter of U.S. military operations in Latin America and the Caribbean, which Kennedy would later rate "the most dangerous area in the world."[86] Khrushchev informed the CPSU Central Committee Presidium that he wanted Kennedy to know "what it feels like to have enemy missiles pointing at you."[87] Soviet Strategic Rocket Forces were badly outgunned across delivery vehicles, while new Titan and Minutemen ICBMs in the U.S. interior handed the U.S. Strategic Air Command (SAC) superior reaction time.[88] The shipment of nuclear forces to Cuba looked like a silver bullet: it would turn the strategic tables, safeguard a faraway revolutionary ally, dispel Beijing's recriminations, and seize the initiative worldwide.[89] Robert Kennedy's military advisor had warned that summer that a Soviet military base in Cuba would take "a page from our book."[90] Unbeknownst to him and his boss, Operation Anadyr had already been authorized to land forty-two medium-range R-12s; thirty-two intermediate-range R-14s, which remained in transit when the crisis began; 42 Ilyushin-28 light bombers; and ninety-two tactical warheads, in the company of atomic cruise missiles, MiG-21s, helicopters, patrol boats, four submarines, a naval squadron, S-75 surface-to-air missiles, 43,000 Soviet troops and military advisors, and a naval base not far from Guantánamo Bay.[91]

The bolt did not arrive from the blue. After the Bay of Pigs, Bobby Kennedy had exhorted Moscow not to send atomic forces to Cuba and initiated contingency planning in the event that his red line was ignored.[92] CIA director John McCone also foresaw the move, criticizing a national intelligence estimate that discounted the threat even after noting the "considerable military advantage" that a Soviet military base in Cuba would confer.[93] Just weeks before U-2 surveillance planes spotted the installations, Kennedy publicly stated that Soviet missiles on Cuban soil or in Cuban hands would give rise to "the gravest issue."[94]

His reasoning was mainly political. When the JCS pushed for air strikes and invasion during the crisis, civilian advisors expressed skepticism about their necessity. When Bundy asked how gravely the missiles altered the status quo, Kennedy sounded dismissive: "You may say it doesn't make any difference if you get blown up by an ICBM flying from the Soviet Union or one from [Cuba]." McNamara was more categorical: "Not at all."[95] Kennedy later recalled viewing the missiles as "less a military threat than a major political act."[96] Bundy candidly advised him that congressional Republicans would attack any hint of weakness, harming his party in the November midterms.[97] Kennedy admitted to his mistake early on: "Last month I should have said we don't care." Once issued, however, the red line took on a life of its own: to drop it would undermine his word and his country's reputation.[98] He went on television on October to declare a "quarantine of all offensive military equipment" that the OAS and the UN Security Council (UNSC) would enforce.[99] While he called "to end the perilous arms race," the klieg lights cast his unblinking resolve in sharp relief. The next day he and his brother speculated that had they not taken such a hard, uncompromising line, Republicans would have moved for impeachment.[100]

The ExComm had worked through four options: outreach to Khrushchev or Castro, a naval blockade, surgical strikes, or limited war.[101] Stevenson marked off one end of the spectrum, recommending a swap of U.S. missiles in Turkey and Italy for those in Cuba, while the JCS pushed for air strikes against the missile installations preparatory to an amphibious assault. For all his tough talk, Kennedy inclined toward measured escalation from the onset, settling on a blockade for fear of uncontrolled escalation. Khrushchev ordered Soviet transports not to violate the quarantine for the same reason.

Kennedy and Khrushchev realized that revolutionary insurgency and assured retaliation were too combustible a mixture. On October 26, Khrushchev offered missile withdrawal for a promise not to invade Cuba. In a letter the next day, he demanded that U.S. efforts to reverse or neutralize Cuba's revolution come to an end: although Castro would lose his ace in the hole, the principle of sovereign inviolability would preserve his regime.[102] Even though Khrushchev added a demand to remove U.S. Jupiter missiles from Turkey, the dominant theme remained the denuclearization of U.S.-Soviet competition in the Third World. He would later contrast circumstances in Cuba with even those in Korea or Vietnam, let alone "the European socialist countries." In the Caribbean the correlation of forces, both conventional and nuclear, had been too unfavorable—what mattered was for the revolutionary island to survive and thrive. However Mao or Castro romanticized permanent war, anti-imperial resistance had to be firewalled from the balance of terror.[103] A string of mishaps had made a mockery of his and Kennedy's crisis management, including secret talks between Bobby Kennedy and Soviet ambassador Anatoly Dobrynin, culminating with the downing of a U.S. spy plane over Cuba on October 27. The next day Radio Moscow announced that the missile bases would be dismantled under UN supervision in exchange for a non-invasion pledge.[104]

Castro was blindsided. He had resented limits on Soviet military aid to Cuba following pro-Soviet Anibal Escalante's expulsion from the Popular Socialist Party in March had caused Khrushchev to worry that the Cuban firebrand would follow Mao's lead.[105] At the height of the crisis, Castro had excoriated U.S. imperialism and cited the inevitability of communist revolution in calling for unilateral escalation, even a Soviet first strike in case of a U.S. invasion.[106] "Only a person who has no idea what nuclear war means, or has been so blinded . . . by revolutionary passion," Khrushchev snapped three days later, "can talk like that."[107]

The crisis raised more questions than it answered, above all whether U.S. and Soviet atomic forces would be treated reciprocally. Castro issued five demands of his own on October 28: no more U.S. economic warfare, covert operations, surveillance overflights, or naval blockade, plus Guantánamo's repatriation.[108] He expressed contempt for Kennedy's non-intervention pledge and physical inspections after the U.S. president conditioned the blockade on the verified removal of all offensive weapons. It was unclear whether this included jet bombers or heretofore-concealed tactical nuclear weapons.[109] Khrushchev's chief lieutenant, Anastas Mikoyan, was sent to Havana to work out the details of his boss's settlement with Kennedy. He promised Castro that everything but the R-12s would stay in the name of revolutionary solidarity only to renege on his promise piece by piece.[110] First, at Kennedy's insistence the Ilyushin-28 bombers were slated for dismantlement. Then when Castro asked to keep the short-range rockets, Mikoyan fabricated a Soviet law that barred nuclear-arms transfers to foreign parties abroad, which Khrushchev promptly ratified in Moscow.[111] Small arms, tanks, armored vehicles, patrol boats, cruise missiles, and anti-aircraft systems would stay, but the risks of placing atomic forces and their delivery vehicles in foreign hands, even under Soviet control, was unacceptable. As Mikoyan put it, nuclear dissemination was "a line we cannot cross."[112]

Mao's opportunistic border war with India drove home the limits of the superpower's control. As soon as Mikoyan had informed Zhou Enlai of the Soviet missiles in Cuba on October 15, PLA troops had moved on disputed border territories.[113] The monthlong dustup divided revolutionary China from reformist India, loosened Afro-Asian solidarity, and worsened the Sino-Soviet rift.[114] Chinese attacks on Indian Army positions in Aksai Chin and across the Namka Chu River exposed the vulnerability of India's forward strategy in the Himalayas. It was a national scandal for Nehru's government. V. K. Krishna Menon lost his job as defense minister. The war also placed Khrushchev's relationship with Nehru at direct odds with his tempestuous alliance with Mao. When Khrushchev suspended MiG-21 sales to New Delhi at the start of hostilities, Kennedy leapt into the opening. His decision to supply New Delhi with arms and ammunition added a new military dimension to a U.S. relationship with India that Kennedy's personal engagement had already warmed.

These concurrent crises illustrated for the Kennedy administration the merits of restraints on Third World arms races. When Kennedy praised Khrushchev's contributions to peace on October 28, he distinguished between NATO-Warsaw Pact tensions and those in parts of the world where military spending was bankrupting development ventures.[115] Two days later, Foster wrote Rusk a memorandum in praise of gradual arms control to bring order to the world's troublesome frontiers, recommending that U.S. diplomats press neutrals to eschew military buildups and arms smuggling in preference for "greater economic progress and political stability."[116] Presidential rhetoric also shifted after the crises. Friendly White House reporters lauded Kennedy's resolve and paternal care under stress. Stewart Alsop and Charles Bartlett's account in the *Saturday Evening Post* highlighted Rusk's self-confident remark from October 24—"we're eyeball to eyeball, and I think the other fellow just blinked"—and attributed the missile-swap idea (which an unnamed source associated with Munich) to Stevenson. They credited Kennedy, by contrast, with arriving "coldly and decisively" at a position that was neither hawk nor dove. They also played up his fatherhood, relating how closely he had tended to his wife and children throughout the crisis.[117] Kennedy was painted as a father protector to the nation and even to the world, an image with which he would guard his right flank against such cold warriors as Curtis LeMay, Richard Nixon, and Barry Goldwater.

V

Averell Harriman had a knack for making himself indispensable. During the Second World War, Franklin Roosevelt had recruited the workhorse son of a railroad magnate to broker Lend-Lease agreements with Winston Churchill and Stalin, according Harriman a reputation as a capitalist who could work with parliamentarians and communists alike. Roosevelt made him U.S. ambassador to Moscow from 1943 to 1946—the terminal phase of the wartime partnership. Once back in Washington, D.C., Harriman had helped define the emerging Cold War, promoting Kennan's pleas from Moscow for Soviet containment, serving as Truman's secretary of commerce before taking a more direct role in managing the Marshall Plan as the U.S. special representative to the Economic Cooperation Administration in Paris. He then held the New York governorship in Albany from 1955 to 1958.

By the winter of 1963, Kennedy had come to rely on the septuagenarian for his instincts and his industry.[118] Harriman emerged as a valued fixer after the Bay of Pigs, leading the U.S. delegation that negotiated the International Agreement on the Neutrality of Laos, which took effect on July 23, 1962, signed by fifteen capitalist, communist, and nonaligned powers, including the Soviet Union, the PRC, and North and South Vietnam, buoying hopes that Third World ideological conflicts were indeed tractable.[119] From November 1961 to April 1963, revolutionary Cuba and communist China morphed from nuisances to nemeses, and a test ban from an arms-race offramp to a nondissemination measure; meanwhile Harriman rose from ambassador-at-large, to assistant secretary of state for Far Eastern Affairs, and finally to undersecretary of state for political affairs.[120]

Although a nondissemination pact had now joined a test ban among measures that he backed with conditions, Kennedy's flirtations with multilateral forces continued to hamper progress. On October 30, 1962, Foster reflected in a memorandum for Rusk on arms control's "two principal objectives"—to prevent another Third World nuclear crisis and reduce East-West tensions. The exclamation point that Carl Kaysen left on the White House copy next to Foster's defense of the multilateral nuclear force (MLF) flagged the contradiction.[121] In Geneva a few days later, Polish delegate Manfred Lachs related that Mao's border war and Castro's "hard stand" had vexed Khrushchev. The Soviet premier might "become more adventuresome" in order to outflank Central Committee rivals who had challenged his recent domestic reforms and also international communists who waxed revolutionary in Latin America, Africa, and Asia. Feelers were nonetheless likely on nuclear tests and West Berlin.[122]

As antinuclear activists picketed the White House from Lafayette Park, scientific advisors underscored the health and environmental effects of global fallout to both Kennedy and Khrushchev. Andrei Sakharov, the father of the Soviet thermonuclear program, petitioned the Central Committee to end testing, presenting the hydrogen bomb as a crime against humanity and nature alike.[123] Decades later he would cite the memory of "burned birds who are writhing on the scorched steppe" to explain his conversion from bomb designer to antinuclear activist.[124]

Jerome Wiesner served a similar function in the White House. Before he became Kennedy's science advisor, he had been a fixture at the Pugwash Conferences on Science and World Affairs organized by Leo Szilard, the Hungarian polymath with whom Albert Einstein had warned Roosevelt about militarized atomic energy in 1939 and who had gone on to found the Council for a Livable World in 1962. Soviet and U.S. scientists rubbed elbows at these annual meetings. At the height of the missile crisis, Szilard had written Khrushchev and—via Wiesner—Kennedy to promote an "Angels" project to enhance superpower goodwill in coordination with Norman Cousins's shuttle diplomacy for a test ban.[125] Years later Wiesner recalled the pathos with which Kennedy had absorbed news about the environmental hazards of atmospheric testing: "I told him that it [fallout] was washed out of the clouds by the rain, that it would be brought to earth by rain, and he said, looking out the window, 'You mean, it's in the rain out there?'—and I said, 'Yes'; and he looked out the window, looked very sad, and didn't say a word for several minutes."[126] After a tête-à-tête with Cousins led Khrushchev to concede to a token number of inspections in a letter to Kennedy on December 19, hopes that there might be a magic number between three and eight flickered briefly, although many in Washington harbored doubts that a communist regime would ever fully comply. Whether a treaty could move forward without France or communist China was not discussed.[127]

Britain's waning power was causing trouble for U.S. defense planning in Europe and along the anticommunist arc from Iran to the Sea of Japan.[128] British financial troubles had also overtaken Harold Macmillan and Duncan Sandys's campaign after the Sino-Indian border war to bring India and Pakistan into the Baghdad Pact in all but name to shelter under Britain's nuclear umbrella.[129] Its aging V bombers and canceled Blue Streak missile program had left the United Kingdom too reliant on U.S. technology to proceed alone. Hemmed in by Macmillan's efforts to join the European Economic Community (EEC) in the face of de Gaulle's veto, McNamara's decision to terminate Skybolt late in 1962 precipitated the lowest point in U.S.-UK relations since the Suez crisis and an opportunity to reduce the nuclear club by one. A summit in the Bahamas was arranged for the week before Christmas.[130]

Kennedy's conversations with Macmillan in Nassau called attention to the lure of nuclear status in international politics amid decolonization. In Europe, the U.S. delegation wanted to assuage Bonn's inferiority complex while retrenching in the region via its British beachhead, all without alienating Rome or Paris. Kennedy accordingly offered Macmillan the Polaris system on the sole condition that Britain commit its arsenal "to a multilateral or multinational force in NATO."[131] Given that the offer aimed at "discrediting national nuclear deterrents," Polaris would amount to golden handcuffs.[132] Macmillan was fighting for Britain's stature in a changing world, its security if the United States or NATO were to abandon his country, and his own political survival.[133] The United Kingdom was a legacy great power whose assets fell short of its former glory, and he feared that it would become "just a clown . . . a satellite." Although he agreed with McNamara that a small independent arsenal was "ridiculous," he nonetheless coveted "the valuation given by other countries to the UK's advice." Although it would be indecent for the Royal Navy to serve anyone save Her Majesty, his request for an opt-out clause from NATO command in cases of supreme national interests stemmed not from constitutional desiderata but the feared indignity of an Iraqi leader dictating terms or the United States or NATO leaving Britain to hold the bag.[134] Macmillan was invoking de Gaulle's syllogism—"a great country must have nuclear weapons"—to press home his request; the United Kingdom was a great country, "therefore it must have nuclear weapons."[135]

The special Anglo-American relationship assumed a new dimension after Nassau. U.S. nuclear abundance would henceforth undergird Britain's atomic façade and backstop a defense perimeter whose strategic linchpin would be the port of Singapore. While British armed forces would not withdraw from "East of Suez" until the mid-1970s, the Nassau agreement committed the U.S. government to pursue Western European atomic integration in parallel with Southeast Asian defense.[136] At an NSC meeting on January 22, 1963, Kennedy reviewed the state of the world, covering topics from income taxes to the MLF before assigning Livingston Merchant, the former NATO ambassador, to bring clarity to the nuclear question before April. He was preoccupied by Beijing, with McCone identifying Cuban subversion and PRC nuclearization as the paramount challenges ahead of the meeting.[137] Kennedy instructed his NSC to work out a test ban whose chief function would be "to halt or delay the development of an atomic capability by the Chinese Communists." Without it, the United States would "have a difficult time protecting the free areas of Asia." Executive branch unity was vital lest congressional opposition rule out new treaties.[138]

Harriman followed up the next day by letter, relating how Russian sources—most likely *Pravda* foreign editor Yuri Zhukov—had expressed interest in containing Bonn's and Beijing's respective nuclear advances. Years earlier a battle-weary Khrushchev had confided to Harriman his fear of the "rebirth of German militarism," thundering against "future German leaders" like Strauss. With this conversation in mind, Harriman endorsed a test ban of maximal scope. The Soviets were convinced that world opinion would follow their lead. Failing that, he warned, the U.S. Air Force might have to level the PRC's nuclear installations.[139]

NATO nuclear-sharing was also entering a critical stage by the summer of 1963, with implications for nondissemination efforts around the world. Kennedy worried that it was a losing proposition in the face of European indifference and French hostility, handing Rusk a three-week deadline on March 14 to force the issue to a conclusion.[140] Merchant had been making inquiries in Western European capitals about further centralization, but U.S. diplomats were clear about the extent of headwinds. From Moscow, Kohler conveyed that Kremlin opposition was "deadly earnest"; only a foolproof scheme *might* avoid the "very sensitive Soviet nerve."[141] On the other side, there was unease in Rome, London, and Bonn that a U.S. military monopoly would perpetuate a civilian one even as an "air of death" surrounded the elected governments in each capital.[142] For want of alternatives, Kennedy and other agnostics were loath to jettison the MLF, however devilish the details, though the president's dismissal in a meeting with NATO secretary general Dirk Stikker of "arguments in a rich man's club" showed where his mind was—"while we discussed nuclear sharing," he reminded Stikker, "the rest of the world stood around hungry and waiting."[143]

Having suffered a string of reversals, Khrushchev had grown uneasy about his own position in the Third World. The Kremlin's struggles had mounted following the Caribbean crisis and the Sino-India war. Mali and Guinea, two showcases for Soviet aid in West Africa alongside Ghana, were tilting toward China. Guinean leaders even refused requests to refuel Soviet planes flying to Cuba at a Soviet-built airfield at Conakry. In Iraq, the failed ar-Rashid revolt in March 1963 sounded a death knell for Iraqi communism and a triumph for a Ba'ath Party that no longer trusted the Kremlin.[144] On the Indonesian archipelago, the arrest of left-wing leaders in Singapore and the impending unification of Malaya, Singapore, North Borneo, and Sarawak had led Indonesian dictator Sukarno to intensify his anti-Malaysian campaign. The influence of the CPSU was under siege throughout Southeast Asia, where powerful Politburo members of the North Vietnam Workers' Party pitched a "South First" policy of armed resistance at the CCP's urging rather than the "North First" policy of nation-building that Khrushchev sponsored.[145] That May, Kennedy briefed Maurice Couve de Murville that Khrushchev's problems "lay in the direction of Communist China rather than Europe."[146]

Kennedy must have been sympathetic. Castro and Che Guevara continued to trouble noncommunist regimes throughout the Caribbean. In South Vietnam, President Ngô Đình Diệm and his brother Ngô Đình Nhu passed Decree Number 10 in May, touching off a crisis with the country's Buddhist majority, climaxing with a monk's self-immolation on June 11 and a U.S.-sanctioned coup against the Ngô brothers in November. The globalization of nuclear science and technology made matters worse. As advanced weaponry continued to flow into the Middle East, the CIA warned that Dimona could cement Arab estrangement from "the West" and ACDA officials that an Egyptian Bomb would inflame friends of Israel in the United States who might "force an ironclad security guarantee of Israel."[147] Kennedy pressed hard that spring, ordering an urgent, all-out effort to monitor Israeli and United Arab Republic (UAR) activities, pressing Israeli deputy defense minister Shimon Peres to expedite a second Dimona visit, and musing aloud about his "hole card"—a U.S. security guarantee in exchange for Israeli nuclear restraint.[148] Meanwhile, numerous Indian officials informed U.S. officials that their scientists could detonate a nuclear device before the decade was over. At a press conference on March 21, Kennedy shared his belief that without a test-ban treaty a future president could confront a world with ten nuclear powers by 1970.[149]

The White House acted as if India were the key. At an NSC meeting on April 27, Kennedy warned his cabinet members not to be "penny wise." Macmillan had pledged to match a U.S. contribution to any military assistance package for New Delhi, but the president's advisors were told to think bigger. McNamara took the occasion to assert that defending India against Chinese predation would "involve the use of nuclear weapons." Taylor issued a concurrence: "to counter its "hordes . . . any military contest with Communist China should be nuclear." The twin legacies of race and imperialism that suffused the U.S. presence in Asia inhered in flexible response's legitimation of atomic strikes. While Kennedy observed that his military commanders would resort to atomic force rather than court defeat in Europe or in the Pacific, many in Washington suspected the cure would be worse than the disease. Asians continued to cite Hiroshima and Nagasaki as proof that U.S. leaders assigned lower value to their lives. When Kennedy agreed with McNamara about offsetting U.S. ground troops in Asia with nuclear options, Under Secretary of State George Ball warned about the potential backlash if they proved themselves "prepared to use nuclear weapons against yellow people but . . . [not] against white people in Europe."[150] Later that summer Rusk exhorted McNamara to maintain enough conventional forces in the region to assure Asian allies that U.S.-PRC hostilities would not spark nuclear war.[151]

McNamara believed that his humanitarian posture of graduated response could encircle Eurasia in a forward-deployed deterrent without exacerbating the U.S.-Soviet arms race or expanding the atomic franchise. The administration therefore plunged into a major review of arms control in the late spring, beginning with the circulation of National Security Action Memorandum (NSAM) 239 on May 6.[152] An internal Pentagon study began with a sweeping rejection of Cold War geopolitical verities: "The world is no longer bilateral." Given this new reality, the U.S. government would need to combat the spread of nuclear forces worldwide; the debate between nuclear superiority and strategic stability had now become secondary:

> The acquisition of even a small number of atomic weapons by China, Israel, or the UAR decreases the power, influence and security of both the U.S. and the Soviet Union. Chinese development of 5 fifty kiloton weapons decreases the security of the U.S. more than the addition of 5 one megaton weapons to the current Soviet inventory.

While carrots and sticks might bring smaller nations to heel, to contain communist China's nuclear potential would require a full-spectrum approach: export restrictions on petroleum, oil, and lubricants; chemical fertilizers; foodstuffs; and even preventive action. For the last point, Khrushchev's tacit consent was deemed essential; without it, the risks of escalation were too great.[153]

To this end, Bundy sat down with Dobrynin on May 17, but Soviet approval was not forthcoming. The ambassador waved him off. As far as the Kremlin was concerned,

West Germany's participation in a multilateral force negated any "common interest" in Asia. As the president's national security advisor left the Soviet embassy, he must have wondered whether it was time for a higher intervention.

VI

Until the end of his life, Kennedy would relate his strategy of nuclear containment as a compelling story of global leadership. Harriman remained his point man, flying to Moscow in late April for "quiet negotiations" about a test ban and the German question. He met Khrushchev and Gromyko on April 26, days after the ENDC neutrals backed the U.S. position on inspections. After he underscored his desire to formalize Germany's division, Khrushchev shot down multiple trial balloons about the Sino-Soviet split.[154] When en route home Harriman swung through London on April 29, he paid a visit to Macmillan, who expressed his belief that the CPSU was reeling from a series of setbacks in Cuba, Iraq, Egypt, Congo, Guinea, Mali, and Indonesia, all made worse by Mao's vocal campaign of Afro-Asian solidarity.[155] The two aging scions agreed that they should work to bring the Soviets closer to Europe by inflaming fears of communist China, expanding de Gaulle's Europe "from the Urals to the Atlantic" to the Pacific and, in the process, remapping Russia as a Western power rather than a multiethnic Eurasian federation or a communist empire. As nonwhite anti-imperialists stressed the racial determinants of prevailing patterns of wealth and power, the British prime minister and the U.S. ambassador-at-large looked to welcome the Soviet Russians back as fellow Europeans.[156]

When Rusk met Dobrynin the next day, the Soviet ambassador confirmed that his bosses were reexamining matters with CCP emissaries set to arrive in Moscow on July 5. With the fate of Sino-Soviet relations in flux, Rusk referenced previous Soviet nuclear assistance to the PRC to underscore the difference between centralizing and diffusing atomic power.[157] When Rusk joined the North Atlantic Council to discuss East-West détente in Ottawa a few days later, he mused that the international communist movement was experiencing a "great crisis" amid a public choice "between pressing, or abandoning, world revolution." Following the backdown from Cuba, Soviet leaders were desperate to validate their peaceful coexistence and disarmament platforms that leftist Western European parties favored but Third World anti-imperialists found wanting—a foreign-policy orientation that U.S. officials were keen to encourage.[158]

Kennedy made the case for governing the atomic frontier in league with the Kremlin in a commencement address at American University on June 10, 1963. Drafted with the help of Norman Cousins and NSC experts, Kennedy and his chief speechwriter, Ted Sorensen, drew on antinuclear rhetoric to present nuclear restraint as a humanitarian imperative.[159] Since Bertrand Russell and Albert Einstein's joint manifesto in

1955, the transnational antinuclear movement had often reframed the planetary threat of thermonuclear war in terms that would resonate with an imagined public of two-parent households. The two had lectured, "People scarcely realize in imagination that the danger is to themselves and their children and their grandchildren, and not only to a dimly apprehended humanity."[160] In Washington, D.C., Kennedy delivered kindred messages: that a mutual understanding with the Soviet Union and presidential stewardship were both necessary for managing a globalizing nuclear world. His acknowledgement of Soviet sacrifices against the Nazi war machine would have been music to Khrushchev's ears, while his vision of a peace "that enables men and nations to grow and to hope and to build a better life for their children" summoned a future in which U.S. statecraft would have as its measure not endless competitions in arms or technology but the security and flourishing of generations present and future. In place of a cold warrior, he volunteered himself as humanity's guardian, finding in a bountiful, benevolent Earth a symbol capacious enough to bind America's nuclear families to those in the Soviet Union and also the Third World: "We all breathe the same air. We all cherish our children's future. And we are all mortal."[161] *Pravda* and *Izvestiya* reprinted the speech the next day, without deletions. When the Moscow Treaty faced hostility in Senate debates over ratification in September, Kennedy recorded his basic public relations playbook on a scratch sheet of paper: "Diminish danger, war by other means . . . fallout—radiation. Children."[162]

Nuclear guardianship represented a seamless alloy of Kennedy's "Third Worldism" and liberal universalism that would have the added benefit of not costing him elections. Three days after the American University speech, Foster's ACDA counseled a region-by-region approach to the destabilizing politico-military effects of nuclear diffusion for U.S. global interests.[163] Denuclearized zones merited consideration in Latin America and Africa but not in central Europe or the Middle East, where U.S. interests ran too deep. In Asia, there was a tension between communist and nuclear containment, with Soviet Red Army Rocket Forces and the Chinese PLA both continuing threats.[164] Kennedy should instead take the moral high ground. Although a test ban treaty was no panacea for Mao's China, whose "aggressive attitude, revolutionary zeal, antipathy toward the United States, and eagerness to challenge the position of leadership of the Soviet Union" made it "the premier 'Nth country,'" Mao might stop at a "demonstration of an initial capability" if the international community were to treat fallout emitters as international pariahs.[165] A novel international coalition—the United States, the Soviet Union, major U.S. allies, and large nonaligned states—would administer this badge of infamy. Together, they could enforce a common law to blunt the impact of a PRC nuclear test, expected within eighteen months by U.S. intelligence agencies, with major consequences for the U.S. position across the Pacific Rim.

Kennedy's public commitment to nuclear containment did not resolve the deadlocks in U.S. arms control policy. While nuclear guardians had the momentum, they faced concerted opposition from Maxwell Taylor and Lawrence Livermore National Laboratory director Edward Teller. The Principals Committee concluded at a meeting on June 14 that the Moscow talks should focus on a three-environment ban, with Kennedy described as dead set against "a larger and more difficult arms race."[166] Pentagon officials styled a test ban "the Flanders Field of disarmament policy," but Deputy Assistant Secretary of Defense Arthur Barber urged Assistant Secretary Paul Nitze to back it as the first of many steps: if it led to "measures limiting diffusion, and controlling nuclear weapons, there is no question that it would be in the national interest."[167] When Nitze claimed that nondissemination was a limited test ban's chief virtue, no one dissented. Afterward, Kennedy ordered ACDA deputy director Adrian "Butch" Fisher to draw up "a view of the world in 10 years, no treaty, worst assumptions, on rate of diffusion."[168]

The basic outline of a settlement was visible by late June, with Harriman now chosen as Kennedy's emissary to Moscow. In Moscow Harriman was to dispense with pleasantries; communist China was the benchmark. Neither a nondissemination nor a comprehensive test ban agreement should spoil a tacit understanding between the superpowers. A partial ban's limited enforcement machinery even held some advantages. Adherence would not require a signature, so Beijing could comply even though the PRC and U.S. government did not recognize each other.[169]

How to balance European and Asian security affairs nonetheless remained contested within the administration. The State Department continued to prioritize the Atlantic Alliance. Rusk subordinated a nondissemination accord to NATO solidarity and cast doubt on the supreme importance of Sino-Soviet competition for Khrushchev, while Ball viewed the MLF as the sole antidote to European nationalism. Erring on the side of superiority, Rostow warned that test ban and nondissemination treaties risked "a cheap sell-out of the MLF" whose influence on Soviet arms control thinking he believed exceeded that of "the possibility of a Chinese Communist nuclear capability."[170] He was right that Khrushchev's interest was mainly in embarrassing his Maoist antagonists, but Khrushchev would not have halted his quest for nuclear parity to scuttle a NATO atomic fleet that British foreign minister Lord Alec Douglas-Home had sworn at Nassau lacked "a single ally in Europe."[171] From the Pentagon, Nitze pushed for a more ambitious package: a nondiffusion pact that would shore up either test ban.[172] Frustrated at the maneuvering and confident of Kennedy's esteem, Harriman warned that if Rusk were to circumscribe his mandate in Moscow, he "might as well stay home."[173]

The final nail in a comprehensive treaty was hammered on July 2, when Khrushchev answered the American University speech with one his own in East Berlin, where he singled out a test ban that would exempt subterranean blasts and petitioned to add a NATO–Warsaw Pact non-aggression pact to Harriman's agenda. Kennedy's opportune visit to Macmillan's home at Birch Grove in Sussex had afforded an occasion for the allies to coordinate, with the prime minister eager to secure Britain's spot at the top table and Kennedy hoping that a limited ban would thread the needle between the Soviet Union and his own military.[174] The British prime minister reckoned that a partial test ban would allow the two sides to consolidate their positions in the face of allied recalcitrance—France, Germany, and others in Europe, and China in the communist world. While he rated it the second prize, a three-environments ban, he concluded, "would certainly be fatal to lose." Before the meeting, Macmillan's private secretary had remarked that "great men think alike."[175]

When Harriman arrived in Moscow on July 15, his instructions were therefore clear: pursue a limited test ban as "a significant first step toward the halting of the arms race," and "more important . . . [as] an indispensable first step toward the limitation of the further diffusion of nuclear weapons."[176] Harriman was accompanied by Kohler, Kaysen, Fisher, interpreter Alexander Akalovsky, Assistant Secretary of State for European Affairs William Tyler, and Dr. Franklin Long, ACDA's assistant director of science and technology, as well as Lord Hailsham, Macmillan's science advisor, whose flirtation with Khrushchev's non-aggression pact had led the Americans to sideline him.[177] Talks dragged on for eleven days as the three sides briefly dissented on underground verification before hammering out a limited test-ban treaty, roughing out a mutually acceptable nondiffusion pact, and tiptoeing around the topic of revolutionary China.

Harriman's meeting with Khrushchev on the first day illustrated how differently the two sides viewed a test ban. The Soviet leader made his lack of interest in a total ban clear from the outset, retracting even his token offer on inspections. He confined his grievances about Mao to a brief lecture on the advantages of peaceful coexistence versus permanent revolution, describing the modern world not as one of continuing imperialism but one where robbers and the robbed faced annihilation together. He was reticent on the PRC's bid for the nuclear club. When Harriman pressed him on a nondiffusion accord to internationalize efforts to sanction Beijing, Khrushchev challenged him to visit Mao in Beijing and agreed not to require a French signature on the treaty, which signaled that a one-for-one deal was not in the cards. The Soviet premier reminded his visitors that a test did not equal a threat: in his eyes the PRC lacked the economic heft to amass an arsenal large enough to threaten the United States or the Soviet Union. When Hailsham inquired whether Mao shared his views, Khrushchev teased that he and Harriman were model capitalists keen to sow division among the workers of the world.[178]

For Kennedy, even relatively small forces in revolutionary hands was intolerable. He instructed Harriman to press forward on a partial ban to limit diffusion while gauging whether Khrushchev would work more directly at "limiting or preventing Chinese nuclear development."[179] His envoy replied that his Soviet interlocutors were more interested in winning the battle of global opinion than in preventive strikes. Khrushchev wanted to appear above the fray when he drove a wedge between non-aligned powers and the PRC and mended fences with Castro, whom he had lavished with gifts that May. Zhukov expounded on the merits of marshalling UNGA and African opinion against a Chinese test to Harriman on July 18. Circumspection would be the name of the game. When Harriman put forward draft treaty language stating that a nuclear test would amount to an "extraordinary event" justifying withdrawal, Gromyko would have nothing of it. To do so would be tantamount to an open admission that the United States had forced them "to do something about [the] Chinese nuclear threat."[180] When the Moscow Treaty opened for signature in Moscow, Washington, and London on August 5, 1963, Beijing's angry denunciations would have to speak for themselves.

Conclusion

Kennedy's focus on China disconcerted West German foreign minister Gerhard Schröder, who warned that to base East-West détente "on peripheral issues" risked freezing the "status quo on central issues."[181] He had missed the point. Facing an atomic renegade in East Asia and revolutionary turmoil throughout the Third World, the United States and the Soviet Union turned to arms treaties to harness Afro-Asian opinion in defense of their nuclear condominium. "No Soviet leader would be insane enough . . . to launch an attack on Europe," Kennedy informed Italian deputy prime minister and foreign minister Attilio Piccioni on September 19, 1963, "just as we would not launch an attack on the Communist Bloc." "The problems that we would be facing in the 60's," he went on, "would consist of trouble in Latin America and Algeria. These were the trouble spots."[182]

Rusk spoke to this state of affairs when he met with Rostow's Policy Planning Staff on October 15. The Kremlin's statement in September that its security alliance with Beijing would not obtain in cases of PRC aggression against India or Taiwan had intimated that "the Soviet nuclear umbrella over the 'Socialist camp' does not mean unqualified support for Chicom aggression." Although Mao's entry into the nuclear club might lift Asian hearts, as long as the United States abstained from brute force they would eventually push back against Beijing's growing power. For similar reasons Bundy demurred when Republic of China defense minister Chiang Ching-kuo requested U.S. logistical support for a preventive action against PRC nuclear facilities. As Rusk had noted, the most promising circumstance in world affairs was that averting a communist Chinese Bomb had emerged as the "one important goal that we share in common with the Soviets." The Moscow Treaty was a testament to this common front. Better to enforce world peace together by criminalizing atmospheric nuclear testing than to face that same might wielded by those intent on remaking international society in their revolutionary image.[183]

An "Impossible Possibility"
Lyndon B. Johnson and the Nonproliferation Treaty That Failed, 1963–1965

Introduction—"An Approximation of Peace"

Before the World Council of Churches on June 15, 1964, William Foster quoted a 1939 lecture by Protestant theologian Reinhold Niebuhr whose thrust had been that the "task of creating community and avoiding anarchy is constantly pitched on broader and broader levels." Niebuhr's idea of an "impossible possibility"—the endless pursuit of "a tolerable approximation of this ethic in the form of justice," remained true "to an ever-increasing degree." This parable of a quixotic yet necessary quest informed his views on general and complete disarmament: "a difficult—yet—possible possibility," whose attainment might not arrive in the lifetimes of those present. Smaller steps—a fissile-material cutoff, a comprehensive test ban, a nondissemination treaty—would therefore have to "pave the way."[1]

This chapter addresses how from August 1963 to the summer of 1965 Foster and his lieutenants at the U.S. Arms Control and Disarmament Agency (ACDA) tried to avert anarchy and "turn the world back from what could be a fatal arms race."[2] Was a nonproliferation treaty achievable during the "long 1964" from Kennedy's assassination to the Americanization of the Vietnam War?[3] In a 1965 article for *Foreign Affairs*, "New Directions in Arms Control and Disarmament," Foster contrasted the continuing impasse over nuclear nondissemination with "real progress" in international efforts to govern outer space, fissile materials, and nuclear testing. As the likelihood of either nuclear disarmament or brinksmanship decreased after the Cuban Missile Crisis, the time factor for consolidating of nuclear power grew more urgent, as new atomic actors arose in Latin America, Africa, Asia, and the Middle East. Foster endorsed a seamless approach. Even after the People's Republic of China (PRC) tested on October 16, 1964, the country's worldwide commitments would rule out turning a blind eye toward limited proliferation to nonaligned powers like India or U.S. allies like Japan.[4]

His assertion that a regional conflict would invariably risk all-out thermonuclear war exaggerated matters—would U.S. armed forces really have waded onto radioactive battlefields in South America? The blue-ribbon panel that Lyndon Johnson assembled in November 1964 under former deputy secretary of defense Roswell Gilpatric to evaluate the relative importance of nonproliferation efforts after communist China entered the nuclear club feared that such weapons in postcolonial hands would upset relations between industrial and postcolonial nations. Yet when copies of *Foreign Affairs* hit newsstands in July 1965, the White House had yet to make any hard decisions over how the United States should police its atomic frontier. Should it arm and deputize local partners in Europe and East Asia? Or should it instead appeal to a higher authority?

I

President John F. Kennedy institutionalized arms control and disarmament in the U.S. government when he established ACDA. He had lifted the idea from his Democratic rival for the presidential nomination, Hubert Humphrey, a senator from Minnesota, who had himself poached it from Eisenhower's secretary of state, Christian Herter.[5]

Where would such a new agency fit into executive branch organization charts? To whom should it report: the secretary of state or directly to the president? Acting deputy director Edward Gullion of Eisenhower's ACDA had charted out two possibilities.[6] An executive agency would be in the best position to attract talent and resolve disputes among bureaus whose parochialism often hindered consensus. To remain within the U.S. State Department would make available its resources, including the secretary's customary seniority among the president's cabinet.[7] For these reasons, Gullion had wanted it to remain within State for fear it would otherwise fall under the Pentagon's sway.[8] Kennedy turned to John J. McCloy, Wall Street power broker, former assistant secretary of war, and chairman of the prestigious Council on Foreign Relations, for counsel. He preferred the first option, warning in U.S. Senate testimony that arms control was too important to be "buried in the State Department," advising that the agency should have statutory authority and a direct line to the U.S. Congress, which helped bring the Senate Foreign Relations Committee's powerful chairman, J. William Fulbright, around to his point of view.[9]

Kennedy would split the difference by means of a "two-hat arrangement." Congress would establish ACDA as a semiautonomous agency reporting to Dean Rusk but with independent statutory authority, its own budget, and direct access to the Oval Office. It would report to the U.S. Congress semiannually, subjecting it to partisanship, but also legislative patrons in case the executive branch proved recalcitrant. Elite opinion was split. Rusk prayed that the ACDA would be able to address matters that transcended the department's balkanized regional bureaus. Former secretary of defense Robert Lovett predicted it would become "a mecca for a wide variety of screwballs."[10]

Those "screwballs" would need an enterprising leader. Bill Foster was a businessman with experience in transatlantic diplomacy, a sense of civic duty, and an eye for public relations. He had earned his reputation as a tireless operator and an organization man whose insistence on clear lines of communication would disenchant some.[11] Born on April 27, 1897, in New Jersey, Foster studied at the Massachusetts Institute of Technology (MIT) and served in the U.S. Air Corps during the First World War before finding employment at Packard Motor Company as an engineer. As a registered Republican who mainly served in Democratic administrations, he brought an elite Rolodex with him. During the Second World War, he had consulted for the War Production Board, where he oversaw aircraft procurement for Secretary of War Henry Stimson. From 1946 to 1948, he was undersecretary of commerce before Secretary of State George C. Marshall selected him to support W. Averell Harriman, whom he eventually replaced as the European Recovery Program's chief administrator. He finished the Truman years as deputy secretary of defense. Kennedy's reasons for picking him were both cynical and shrewd. Foster was an effective manager with the savvy and experience to grapple with the Pentagon or the military chiefs, and whose party affiliation would screen the fledgling agency from partisan attack.[12]

His deputy director, Adrian "Butch" Fisher, helped turn ACDA into what a future director Fred Iklé labeled a "bureaucratically independent conscience."[13] Fisher launched his government career as McCloy's wartime deputy and then headed the U.S. Atomic Energy Commission (AEC), after which Dean Acheson had made him State's top lawyer.[14] He was a smart choice to build another atomic bureau from the ground up. Fisher and Foster meshed quickly and well, swapping roles so that "one mind[ed] the store" in Washington while the other attended plenaries in Geneva or toured foreign capitals.[15] They walked a tightrope in a fledgling arms control community that was riven between disciples of deterrence and apostles of disarmament, all under the watchful gaze of national security officials reluctant to lose any technological advantage to the Soviets (let alone a bureaucratic turf war).[16]

Foster's readiness to justify arms control according to military criteria drew disarmers' ire. In a letter written in November 1965 to Harvard professor of international law Louis Sohn, who had attended an MIT Summer Study on Arms Control at the American Academy of Arts and Sciences (AAAS) five years before, Foster equated the reduction of enemy forces via negotiated agreement with those destroyed via military action.[17] While such an equivalence resonated with Secretary of Defense Robert McNamara, it fared less well with others. After just one year on the job, the

Federation of American Scientists complained that Foster did not consult regularly with academic experts of the Boston-Cambridge Arms Control Seminar, casting aspersions on his fitness for the job.[18]

II

The major obstacle to U.S.-Soviet nonproliferation cooperation was the multilateral nuclear force (MLF), with few friends on either side of the Iron Curtain. In the UN Disarmament Commission (UNDC) and the Eighteen Nation Committee on Disarmament (ENDC), Warsaw Pact members demanded a prohibition on access to nuclear arms under any military scheme. The United States and NATO countered that the line should be drawn at transfers of control—meaning by extension the authority to fire.

There were two distinct constituencies for the MLF in the U.S. State Department. Policy Planning Staff members, namely Henry Owen, Robert Bowie, and Walt Rostow, patronized by Under Secretary of State George Ball, saw the European federation movement as the shape of things to come across the Atlantic. These "theologians" worried that the continental United States' growing vulnerability to Soviet intercontinental forces was undermining the U.S. nuclear umbrella and, by extension, their leadership position in Europe. Charles de Gaulle was their biggest conundrum. His attacks on NATO, his signature on the 1963 Franco-German Treaty of Friendship, and his hard line in European Economic Community (EEC) talks with the United Kingdom all substantiated fears that the U.S. position in Europe was slipping. Most of all these theologians worried that West Germany would align with nuclear-armed France. By bolstering their involvement in NATO nuclear defense and encouraging continental integration, they hoped to allay West German insecurity and inferiority so as to temper Gaullist tendencies there, solidifying their fealty at the heart of a unified, credible Atlantic community.[19]

Liberal internationalists feared that nuclear forces would spread in Europe, with West Germany, Sweden, Switzerland, and Italy more than capable of following Britain and France's lead, and then on from there. National security adviser McGeorge Bundy, Attorney General Robert Kennedy, McNamara, and Rusk saw NATO nuclear-sharing via a combined fleet as the least bad option for halting the spread of atomic forces in Europe and reconsolidating Britain and France's arsenals under U.S. sway. The price of Kennedy's rescue of the UK nuclear deterrent at Nassau was the integration of Atlantic nuclear defense "in the closest consultation with other NATO allies."[20] Nikita Khrushchev had taken a two-pronged approach to West Germany in the 1950s, seeking to freeze the territorial status quo in central Europe while keeping nuclear weapons out of German hands. After the Moscow Treaty, he persisted in mending ties with the West and working to stigmatize communist China, expressing his support for a nondissemination treaty on one condition: Kennedy would have to declare that West Germany would never be "in charge of nuclear weapons."[21]

This unsettled allies in Warsaw and East Berlin. Polish communist leader Wladyslaw Gomulka was flummoxed. Next to the part of Khrushchev's communiqué emphasizing an exit clause akin to that of the Limited Test Ban Treaty (LTBT) in case NATO nuclear-sharing went too far, he furiously scribbled, "prohibit the creation of multilateral nuclear forces now, and you will not [need to] reserve yourself the right to tear up the treaty!"[22] Believing the breakdown of Sino-Soviet relations responsible for Khrushchev's haste, he shared four admonitions. First, not to forbid a NATO nuclear force outright would amount to "silent consent." Second, disarmament efforts would suffer from Atlantic nuclear integration. Third, a carefree attitude toward West Germany's nuclear status within the socialist camp would alienate Poland and the German Democratic Republic (GDR). Lastly, East-West rapprochement could facilitate West German chancellor Konrad Adenauer's efforts to reunify the German nation through "atomic blackmail against the Warsaw Pact states."[23]

Alliance cohesion was uppermost in Gomulka's thoughts. The Politburo of the Polish United Workers' Party issued a unanimous directive questioning Khrushchev's reasoning, pointing out that West Germany was the only NATO member state strongly in favor of a seaborne Polaris force. Neither the United Kingdom nor France wanted another atomic power "among [the] imperialist states." Adenauer was on the verge of cementing a U.S.–Federal Republic of Germany (FRG) transatlantic axis. A united front might not halt the MLF, but it might heal the rifts within the socialist world that the LTBT had widened. The Warsaw Pact should reverse that polarity: nuclear nondissemination was a wedge to pry the Atlantic Alliance apart, not a knife to slit the throats of one's comrades.[24]

The window for a global nonproliferation treaty was closing quickly. In response to allied misgivings, Khrushchev had Soviet deputy foreign minister Vasily Kuznetsov present a revised position to the East German Politburo on October 14, 1963. While he acknowledged that the MLF's central purpose was to centralize atomic authority with the U.S. president, Moscow would reject any treaty that licensed it. The "positive outweighs the negative," he admitted, but under no circumstances would West Germany be allowed to benefit geopolitically. Not only were direct or indirect transfers of atomic forces through military alliances impermissible, but existing nuclear-sharing arrangements in NATO were also problematic. The Western nuclear powers would be forced to choose between multilateral forces and a nuclear nondissemination treaty.[25]

Back in Washington, the Johnson administration had launched a review of NATO nuclear policy after Kennedy's death on November 22. Two weeks later, Johnson, Rusk, McNamara, Bundy, Ball, and Rostow resolved that MLF supporters in the State Department should brief the U.S. Congress and a forthcoming North Atlantic

Council meeting in Paris.[26] Longing for a mandate free of Kennedy's election in 1961 and facing a flurry of matters relating to civil rights, foreign aid, social welfare, balance of payments, and Southeast Asia, Johnson had little appetite for a protracted battle with his European allies. With an election less than a year away, the battle lines had been drawn—the fate of a nonproliferation treaty was bound up in that of the MLF.

The forthcoming ENDC session threatened to reveal the paralysis in Washington. In early 1964, East Germany proposed that it and West Germany both renounce nuclear arms and multilateral forces. Washington and Bonn dismissed the overture as propaganda; after all, nuclear abstention was a bitter pill for Ludwig Erhard, who had succeeded Adenauer as chancellor on October 17, 1963, given the Warsaw Pact's conventional superiority. Rusk was hopeful nonetheless. Even the French, who continued to abstain from deliberations in Geneva on grounds that such matters should not be discussed outside the nuclear club, showed heightened interest in happenings there, where the West was primed to take the initiative on such measures as fissile materials.[27] Foster was more cautious. With Washington focused on Beijing, and Moscow on Bonn, they were likely to discuss nonproliferation "in a narrow fashion."[28]

Seven weeks into his presidency, Johnson moved to co-opt Kennedy's arms control legacy without making major concessions. In his first State of the Union address on January 8, 1964, he promised new arms control and disarmament proposals in Geneva and to cut stateside production of enriched uranium by one quarter as a goodwill gesture.[29] The National Security Council (NSC) staff was instructed to examine "whether we had anything in the Geneva kit" with which to follow up the speech.[30] Officials from the State Department, the Pentagon, the AEC, the CIA, and ACDA met one week later at Camp David to review their options. Peering from the outside, the World Council of Churches captured the mood: "The Test Ban and Next Steps: From Co-Existence to Co-operation."[31]

Johnson went back on nationwide television and radio two weeks later to lay out a package of "collateral measures." In highlighting safeguards, he failed to differentiate between a global regime that the IAEA would administer, as AEC commissioner Glenn Seaborg had endorsed, and an ad hoc system that would preserve European Atomic Energy Community (Euratom) safeguards, as Europeanists preferred.[32] He laid out his priorities in a letter to Khrushchev that same day: nuclear nontransfer, a fissile-material cutoff, a comprehensive test ban, and strategic arms limitations, plus boilerplate references to general and complete disarmament.[33] Johnson, Rusk, McNamara, Seaborg, Maxwell Taylor, CIA deputy director Marshall Carter, White House political aides Bill Moyers and Jack Valenti, and Butch Fisher had finalized this list at an extraordinary meeting a few days earlier. The only item they cut was unconditional support for nuclear-weapon-free zones (NWFZs) in Latin America and Africa, where—despite Fisher's exhortations—military objections had carried the day.[34]

Peaceful atomic energy promised to prettify Johnson's leadership at home and abroad. Arms control was not "the government's business," he told the nation; it was "everyone's business."[35] Decades later, Seaborg would fault the Vietnam War for having derailed Johnson's commitment to U.S.-Soviet détente via arms control. The conflict "consume[d] him."[36] Yet the relationship between nuclear diplomacy and military escalation was more intimate than Seaborg had appreciated in the mid-1960s. As the president made the decisions that would send hundreds of thousands of U.S. troops across the Pacific Ocean, his arms control policies advanced a powerful counternarrative. Even as antiwar protesters labeled him a warmonger and a child-killer, like Kennedy before him Johnson cultivated an image as a nuclear peacemaker and a kindly father.

Foster made the case in Geneva for Johnson's package on January 21. Foster deemed the LTBT the first "collateral" measure, "a modest step perhaps, but one which was achievable in today's world."[37] He worked hard to convince nonaligned representatives that his government was sincere in building trust with Moscow—what Khrushchev had dubbed "a policy of reciprocal example." Small steps would build confidence and goodwill at marginal risk. One week later, the Soviets submitted their own proposals. Their lead negotiator, Semyon Tsarapkin, called for an end to foreign military bases, across-the-board-military cuts, an East-West nonaggression pact, NWFZs—most notably the Rapacki Plan—a bomber jubilee, a nondissemination treaty, and an all-environments test ban. Foster observed that the Soviet and U.S. packages overlapped on two issues—nonproliferation and bombers—though both were for now nonstart-ers.[38] "Non-dissemination is nice," Tsarapkin informed the *Agence France-Presse* the next day, "but the chief obstacle is the American push for a multilateral force."[39]

Nuclear nondissemination raised troubling questions of hierarchy and fairness. On its face the LTBT regulated states with nuclear weapons. To shut the nuclear club formally, on the other hand, would seem to protect an oligarchy. When Foster cited "both moral sense and national self-interest" in defense of the concept, he likened how nations lacking nuclear arms feared that the superpowers would turn the planet into a irradiated wasteland to illustrate how their security would also "be decreased as among themselves by the wider dissemination of national nuclear weapons capa-bilities."[40] Questions of agency aside, he offered a solution: they should socialize the nuclear risks. Rather than bolster a techno-military hierarchy whose ranks included two colonial empires and two rival superpowers, a closed nuclear club would benefit all members of the world community. Not only did Eastern and Western bloc in-terests overlap; those of the atomic unarmed "overlap with each other and with the existing nuclear powers."[41] At the next day's plenary, Tsarapkin castigated the United States for nuclearizing the Bundeswehr, swearing that his government would never do likewise for East Germany or China. He belittled a nondissemination treaty's merits

FIGURE 3 Soviet ambassador Semyon Tsarapkin (left), U.S. Arms Control and Disarmament Agency director William Foster (right), and a Soviet translator (center) pose for a photograph in the Palais des Nations in Geneva, Switzerland, in 1964.
Source: William C. Foster Collection, Central Texas Historical Archive, Texas A&M University-Central Texas.

on the grounds that nuclear suppliers would never heedlessly transfer dual-use technology. In his response Foster lamented the "return of the Cold War" to the council chambers and dismissed the GDR's non-nuclear Germany proposal "as originating in a nongovernmental organization."[42]

Notwithstanding the theater, outside the plenaries the two men explored an interest in global nuclear governance. The frustrations of hegemony were a recurrent theme. Foster sensed a subtext in Tsarapkin's tirade against mounting U.S. military involvement in Vietnam. Rather than score points with neutral and nonaligned listeners, the Soviet plenipotentiary had underscored that "if U.S. as world's gigantic power and also [the] large Soviet Union were to reach agreements all troubles in [the] world could be readily controlled by us."[43] The fact that he ranked Moscow second in international echelons was revealing. In a private one-on-one, Tsarapkin warned that neutral and nonaligned countries and also non-nuclear allies were carving out a middle ground to accord themselves more room for maneuver. According to Foster, the Soviet ambassador made the case that "France, China, India, UAR [the United Arab Republic], . . . even [the] G.D.R.," were playing both ends against the middle; "they could do it in present circumstances but if U.S. and U.S.S.R. were to agree with each other everybody else would have no choice but to fall in line."[44] Kremlin envoys seldom exceeded their briefs. Andrei Gromyko and Khrushchev saw benefits to partnering with their U.S. counterparts in the nuclear realm, starting with a treaty to consolidate nuclear power in Europe and the wider world. At a staff meeting on February 27, Foster downplayed the need to work with other delegations if the Soviets were ready to make common cause.[45]

III

India was a focal point of superpower competition in the context of the Sino-Soviet split, the Vietnam War, and nuclear globalization. Communist China's impending entry into the nuclear club imperiled peaceful coexistence, nonalignment, and anti-nuclearism, which Prime Minister Jawaharlal Nehru had fashioned into mainstays of India's foreign policy. Nehru's record was not without ambiguities. On the one hand, his test ban advocacy had swung the Afro-Asian movement behind nuclear arms control in the 1950s. On the other hand, he diverged from his teacher Mahatma Gandhi, who had associated Hiroshima and Nagasaki with the innate brutality of modern industrial society.[46] Nehru, by contrast, viewed scientific discovery and technological innovation as bridges between the nation's agrarian past and its industrial future.[47] His line of reasoning possessed an anticolonial edge. He wedded the narrative of so-cietal progress and kindred faith in technocratic governance that he had imbibed at the University of Cambridge to a material theory of imperialism—faster ships, better machines, and deadlier guns had powered Westerners' colonial drive across India and the rest of the nonwhite world. When critics took issue with his 1948 Atomic Energy Act, Nehru had implored them to remember the steam engine and the industrial age, when India had first become "a backward country." The atomic age sprang from "something infinitely more powerful than either steam or electricity." Not to master it would be to turn one's back on history. And if threatened with nuclear destruction, "no pious sentiments" would deliver them from subjugation.[48]

This technological determinism informed Nehru's and the Congress Party's con-sistent support for civilian nuclear infrastructure. As prime minister he pursued im-port substitution, collective agriculture, industrial champions, and a bespoke mix of state planning and private enterprise in search of pathways to sustainable self-determination.[49] He found an able steward in Homi Bhabha, director of the Tata Institute of Fundamental Research, chair of the Indian Atomic Energy Commission, and the leader of the Indian Department of Atomic Energy. Both Cambridge-educated nationalists reared in great wealth and besotted with Western lifeways, Nehru and

Bhabha would oversee India's transformation into the foremost civilian nuclear power in the Third World.[50]

Whether the country would tilt toward military uses depended on various factors: among others, electoral politics, regional threats, and the scientific enclave that Bhabha led.[51] Bhabha's decisions to promote a breeder reactor, with its attendant requirement for a plutonium-reprocessing facility, for instance, promised to shorten the route to a military arsenal. There were international dimensions as well. In 1956 Bhabha had prevented International Atomic Energy Agency (IAEA) safeguards from applying to plutonium reprocessing, introducing to global discourse the terms *nuclear haves* and *have-nots* in making his argument.[52] India's development was nonetheless conditioned by economic geography and political economy. The subcontinent lacked natural uranium sources but possessed a wealth of thorium-232, whose chemical similarity to plutonium warranted a breeder program to transmute this element *en masse*. When the Indian government broke ground on a plutonium reprocessing plant at Trombay in April 1961, Pakistan and others rang the alarm bell. Nehru could now hedge his nuclear bets.[53] Subcritical testing for a fission device would require prime-ministerial authorization, but the groundwork had nonetheless been laid at little cost.[54]

Indian attitudes toward nuclear arms hardened after the 1962 Sino-Indian War. Nehru was among the first signers of the LTBT and rated the ENDC highly enough to send his cousin to represent him in Geneva.[55] Although B. K. Nehru chastised communist China for not signing the test-ban treaty and characterized a non-dissemination agreement as "vitally important," he refrained from committing his country to join even though UN Secretary General U Thant had recently lent his endorsement to "concrete measures" that would improve East-West relations.[56]

For all McNamara's efforts to normalize graduated response, cheaper, asymmetric options held an appeal to post-imperial and postcolonial powers both. Colonel Pierre Gallois, a French military theorist, published *Stratégie de l'âge nucléaire* in 1960, asserting that nuclear terror would obtain even in cases where regional powers wielded small arsenals vulnerable to first strikes.[57] Meanwhile, the basis of Western authority—U.S. nuclear superiority—looked ever more brittle. McNamara briefed the North Atlantic Council in February 1964, assuring allies that the advent of U.S.-Soviet mutual vulnerability around 1970 would not negate U.S. nuclear guarantees and leading even Canadian authorities to speculate about the merits of self-armament.[58] Indian officials spoke in similar terms. On October 30, 1963, Vijaya Lakshmi Pandit, Jawaharlal's sister, had praised Soviet leaders for conceding that nuclear forces would survive until the final stage of disarmament.[59] At a New Delhi–based Pugwash conference in early 1964, Bhabha channeled Gallois in asserting that nuclear deterrence was possible "even against another having a many times greater destructive power under its control," particularly versus "a country with a huge population," such as communist

China. Only guarantees from both superpowers, he added, could preclude the need for a national nuclear-weapon capability. In the audience that day were future Indian Atomic Energy Commission chairman Vikram Sarabhai, chief nuclear diplomat V. C. Trivedi, and Nehru's daughter and future prime minister, Indira Gandhi.[60] B. K. Nehru expanded on Bhabha a few days later in Geneva, where he declared it foolhardy to rely for protection on "the two great Powers."[61] Tsarapkin acknowledged one week later "an intimate link" between nuclear nondissemination and global peacekeeping.[62]

While the ENDC debated, the Johnson administration reassessed its South Asian policies. For a decade Pakistan had provided the United States with a geopolitical counter to Soviet influence and a base for which to monitor nuclear activities in the USSR and the PRC by means of seismic monitors and CIA airfields. With the U.S. military commitment escalating in Vietnam, India now beckoned as an anti-PRC bulwark.[63] A telegram from U.S. ambassador to India Chester Bowles on February 20, 1964, warned that if Southeast Asia capitulated, the nearly half a billion people in India would become a "political, economic and military front in conflict with China." In a classic statement of the domino theory, he gauged India's salience not to the Nonaligned Movement (NAM) arising from the 1961 Belgrade Conference but to "US security interests between [the] Sea of Japan and [the] Mediterranean."[64]

India's nuclear program illustrated the dilemmas of Cold War competition. Successive governments in Washington, D.C., had worked to keep the world's most populous democracy out of Soviet and communist Chinese orbits without diverting funds from Western-led economic development or spurring an arms race between India and Pakistan. There was a kind of hydraulic relationship between conventional arms dealings and nuclear nondiffusion efforts emerging in postcolonial hot spots, which at times justified advanced-weapon sales to volatile regions, exacerbating regional-security dilemmas in turn. As Pakistan and India, Ethiopia and Somalia, and Israel and Egypt amassed jet fighters, ballistic missiles, and atom bombs, Rusk hypothesized that "a coincidence of policy in Moscow, London, Washington and Paris" had arisen "to achieve nuclear arms control."[65]

From New Delhi, Bowles endorsed "reasonable limits" on Indian military power in preference for developmental programs that would foster "an economically viable, politically stable, Western-oriented India." JCS chairman Taylor was more interested in the military relationship after touring the subcontinent in December 1963, sponsoring a multiyear military assistance program to include high-performance aircraft lest the Indians purchase Soviet MiG-21s instead.[66] In New Delhi, former finance minister Morarji Desai had explained to Taylor that a PRC nuclear test would heighten pressure to go next, a feat that India could manage in "a couple of years."[67] Bowles's suggestion that a U.S. Navy task force patrol the Indian Ocean for part of the year evolved in time into proposals for an Asian MLF.[68] For now, however, Rusk's and

McNamara's fears that India and Pakistan's rivalry would acquire a nuclear dimension led to the cancellation of a F-104 fighter-bomber sale. After Nehru suffered a fatal heart attack in May 1964, Prime Minister Lal Bahadur Shastri reached an agreement with Moscow to supply MiG-21s and also a factory to build more.[69]

Three days later, a memorandum arrived on Rusk's desk warning that India could produce a crude nuclear device in as little as one year once its plutonium reprocessing facility went online.[70] One month after that the U.S. AEC circulated a report that atomic upstarts would soon no longer need such colossal, expensive pieces of infrastructure now that Union Carbide's nuclear division had demonstrated at Oak Ridge National Laboratory that efficient gas centrifuges could enrich uranium to weaponizable levels just as easily as energy-intensive gaseous-diffusion cascades.[71]

IV

When the ENDC reconvened in March, Foster called the atmosphere "good."[72] Despite the defection of a KGB agent attached to the Soviet delegation in Geneva named Yuri Nosenko, he believed that progress was possible ahead of the U.S. presidential election in November 1964. Foy Kohler had nonetheless preached patience from Moscow earlier that year, noting how Kremlin officials filtered "all foreign policy moves through the litmus of their quarrel with the Chinese."[73] The White House was sending mixed signals while it monitored European developments. Erhard's offer to bankroll agriculture and finance in East Germany and the Soviet Union had been repaid with an invitation to Moscow from Khrushchev. Meanwhile Supreme Allied Commander Europe (SACEUR) trials aboard an experimental mixed-manned destroyer had revealed numerous operations kinks. While Johnson personally assured Erhard in a March 4 letter that he championed "a free and reunified Germany," his silence on the future of the MLF was deafening.[74]

Johnson's cabinet worked to uncross their wires on April 10, when Ball assured the Principals Committee that the MLF should go forward before the year ended. Ever the skeptic, Bundy interjected that Foster, the JCS, and McNamara retained "serious reservations." Thomas Finletter, who had the best vantage as U.S. ambassador to NATO, stressed the need for resolve—London and Rome were not balking because they opposed the scheme on the merits, but because Kennedy and now Johnson had waffled. Foster felt isolated. He pressed home Moscow's "strongly negative view" of the NATO flotilla, referring to his conversations with Tsarapkin in gainsaying Kohler's conflicting advice: the unpopular scheme should not tie their hands "in future disarmament and non-dissemination discussions."[75]

Johnson's mind was surely elsewhere. He was busy steering landmark civil rights legislation through the U.S. Congress and absorbing the findings of McNamara and Taylor's recent, monthlong fact-finding mission to South Vietnam. Rusk would set out for Saigon one week later. The White House lacked the time and the focus to defy top diplomats or displease dear allies. Foster could have hammered his points home. The MLF was clearly obstructing nondissemination talks. During Rusk's absence from the Principals Committee, Ball ran the show, emphasizing the positives and repackaging the negatives of revitalizing NATO through atomic integration. Foster's entreaty to let an Atlantic nuclear deterrent sink or swim at "all deliberate speed" fell on deaf ears. Johnson resolved to split the difference, instructing Ball and Foster to promote the MLF without "trying to shove the project down the throats of the potential participants."[76]

With nuclear nondissemination talks at an impasse, more limited measures took the spotlight that summer. First the U.S. State Department refused West German requests for fast-burst reactors. Then Johnson and Khrushchev announced a joint cutback in fissile-material production. The Soviet premier advocated greater personal engagement in the Geneva process, proposing that Rusk and Gromyko, or even he and Johnson, meet on the sidelines of the UN General Assembly (UNGA) in New York to build on the Moscow Treaty.[77] It appeared that only high-level summitry could untangle the knot. West German intransigence played a role. To Deputy Under Secretary of State Llewellyn Thompson in August, Ambassador Karl Knappstein decried Foster's work in Geneva, where he believed the Soviets were working "to discredit [them] in the eyes of the world."[78] When the ENDC recessed on September 17, 1964, it was no closer to a draft nonproliferation treaty than when the year began.

Elections battles in the United States and the United Kingdom had contributed to that gridlock. After Barry Goldwater dispatched Nelson Rockefeller at that summer's Republican convention, Johnson faced a challenger whose conservative nationalism matched his social libertarianism in their nonconformity with New Deal–style liberalism.[79] His statements that tactical nuclear-weapon should be treated as "merely another weapon" in support of predelegating launch authority to SACEUR offered a dose of candor and a return to "massive retaliation." Eisenhower had after all acknowledged in 1955 that "against strictly military targets" tactical nukes were like "a bullet or anything else" and quietly empowered theater commanders in 1959 to go nuclear under set conditions. Foreign observers nonetheless wondered how multilateral diplomacy would fare under a presidential nominee who had opposed ACDA and the Moscow Treaty and also floated the use of "low-yield atomic weapons" to defoliate Vietnamese forests.[80] The Soviets foresaw little progress before Americans elected their new president, and talks in Geneva ground to a halt.[81]

The Kennedy and Johnson administrations had contemplated extreme measures to avert communist China's nuclear breakthrough. For the eighteen months before the test, the White House and the Pentagon had weighed the ramifications of reconnoitering installations deep in Chinese territory with U-2 overflights and deploying

Nationalist Chinese commandos or long-range bombers to level them.[82] The JCS had drawn up an action plan for "aborting the ChiCom nuclear capability" in April 1963: multilateral measures such as a test ban or nondissemination accord, or both, and unilateral sanctions in the form of an embargo or full-scale blockade. If all else failed, a "fourth level of action" would entail "jointly conducted U.S.-Soviet air strikes, using conventional rather than nuclear weapons."[83] The recommendation was unprecedented: U.S. armed forces had never before engaged in preventive strikes, nor had U.S. and Soviet armed forces fought together since the end of the Second World War.

The JCS study had abounded with qualifications.[84] It ruled out "invasion or land combat" altogether: U.S. armed forces would not have the opportunity to capitalize on long-range air strikes with low odds of success. Even acting JCS chairman Curtis LeMay deemed it "unrealistic to use overt military force" on account of the operational challenges, the likelihood that Moscow and Beijing would close ranks afterward, the UN Charter violations, and possible PRC retaliation in Taiwan, Korea, Vietnam, or elsewhere in Asia. The notion that Soviet and U.S. air forces would coordinate sorties on Chinese targets was even more fanciful. On May 17, 1963, Bundy had floated this idea to Anatoly Dobrynin only for the Soviet ambassador to prevaricate: the MLF continued to hamper Moscow's ability to address "Chinese nuclear ambitions."[85]

The feared backlash from the Third World was the final nail. Preventive discussions resumed when Johnson took over from Kennedy. The Policy Planning Staff contrasted the mature U.S. arsenal and a fledging Chinese one in downplaying the immediate threat, much as Khrushchev had reassured Harriman in Moscow. Incapable of threatening targets in the United States for years, Beijing would nonetheless enhance its Afro-Asian profile and "weaken the will of Asian countries" with the long-term aim of curbing the U.S. military presence in its backyard. Judging "explicit" Soviet support unlikely for measures that might incur "great political costs" and "high military risks" for a short reprieve, Rostow's analyst expressed preferences for covert operations and East-West multilateralism to marginalize Beijing. With tensions rising fast in Southeast Asia, only PLA provocation offered a sufficient pretext for preventive strikes.[86]

When Robert Kennedy met Dobrynin for lunch on July 7, 1964, the Soviet ambassador voiced unease about nuclear diffusion and Mao Zedong's adventurism while reaffirming Soviet support for a nondissemination treaty that forbade the MLF. He conceded that communist China would in time acquire "a real delivery system," but then pointed out that Beijing's severe economic problems militated against a survivable deterrent. The attorney general possessed secondhand information that Yugoslavian president Josip Tito believed that "the Soviets were determined not to permit the development of a Chinese nuclear weapon."[87] While such contradictory information kindled hopes of coordinated action, given their long history of bad blood, it was unclear whether Kennedy (who would resign the next month to run for the free

Senate seat in Massachusetts) acted on Johnson's behalf.[88] In the meantime, intelligence poured in from U.S. Pacific Command that communist China's test was so imminent that covert interceptions or sabotage were futile. The psychological impact in Asia would be "very large," with the PRC set to "acquire overnight the stature of a nuclear power in [Asian] minds."[89] John McCone informed Johnson that five Chinese Atomic Energy Authority facilities were either in progress or operational.[90] One month later, a national intelligence estimate gauged from U-2 reconnaissance out of Pakistan that the test would happen "in the next few months."[91]

With the presidential election three months away, Johnson contemplated U.S. foreign policy with suburban voters in mind. With 23,300 military advisors under U.S. Army general William Westmoreland's command unable to improve a deteriorating security environment in South Vietnam, Johnson seized on false alarms from the USS *Maddox* and the USS *Turner Joy* about North Vietnamese torpedo boats in early August to push through a joint congressional resolution that authorized him to render assistance to Southeast Asia Treaty Organization (SEATO) members, with "armed force" if necessary. The Gulf of Tonkin Resolution inoculated Johnson, hungry nine months into his accidental presidency for an electoral mandate, from Goldwater's attacks from his right, forming the decisive political context in which the White House would handle China.[92] Bundy, McCone, McNamara, and Rusk decided against preventive strikes on September 15 in the absence of a Chinese provocation. Bundy related high-level interest in "private and serious talks" to Dobrynin, but the ambassador once again referenced the MLF to gently remind Johnson's national security adviser that Khrushchev would not turn on his Chinese comrades.[93]

V

Whether Johnson would have approved a bombing raid with Soviet acquiescence or military assistance is unknowable. He had tacked strongly toward the middle in the months after the Gulf of Tonkin Resolution with a view to firming up his support among moderate suburban voters. Three weeks before the 1964 election, he disclaimed any intention "to send American boys nine or ten thousand miles away from home to do what Asian boys ought to be doing for themselves."[94] Four days later, a mushroom cloud rose high above the Lop Nur desert in Xinjiang province.

U.S. seismic and electromagnetic stations in Asia and radioisotope readers aboard Air Weather Service flights out of Japan quickly confirmed China's feat on October 16. With the Soviets opposed to military action and Johnson waxing pacific, for the moment, the U.S. State Department could only move to cushion the impact. As U.S. officials absorbed the news, reports of political upheavals in two of the other three nuclear capitals arrived. Harold Wilson's Labour Party would take power in London, and Khrushchev was out as Soviet general secretary in Moscow. Chinese state media bragged that Beijing had "broken the superpower monopoly," pledged not to fire first, and gamely called for wholesale abolition. When the NSC met the next day, Rusk underscored that the significant aftermaths were short-term fears of nuclear fallout throughout Asia and "serious, long-run effect[s] . . . in Japan and India."[95]

For now the White House focused on public relations with the U.S. presidential election two weeks away. In a national televised address on October 18, Johnson assured Americans that U.S. authorities were monitoring developments closely and that communist China would need years to build an arsenal formidable enough to threaten them directly. He then challenged the new Soviet leadership to join him in fighting the rise of new nuclear powers. Bundy had a reference to the Moscow Treaty added so that the president could blame Mao for enlarging "the danger of atmospheric contamination and of nuclear war," but Khrushchev's ouster just two days prior for, among other matters, alienating the PRC, ruled out a common-superpower refrain.[96] Fifteen months after the LTBT had opened for signature, the joint U.S.-Soviet effort to seized the moral high ground was relegated to one short sentence that White House speechwriters had added at the last moment.

Johnson took the more dramatic step of making the first nuclear guarantee unrestricted by treaty, pledging support for the atomic unarmed worldwide: if they needed his "strong support against some threat of nuclear blackmail, then they will have it."[97] The pledge was less binding than it sounded. What did "strong support" mean? What would count as "nuclear blackmail"— explicit threats, violent intents, new armaments, uranium enrichment, plutonium reprocessing? These were pressing questions, with U.S. intelligence agencies warning that India, Israel, and Sweden might follow communist China's lead in a matter of years or even months. In the event, an unbounded duty to provide world nuclear security was momentous, adding military teeth to Kennedy and Johnson's paternal rhetoric on the nuclear question.

With a strong lead in the polls, Johnson could afford a measured response. That same day, he pledged a blue-ribbon committee to reappraise U.S. nonproliferation policy in view of a fifth, hostile member joining the nuclear club.[98] On November 1, two days before ballots were cast in the United States, he announced a Special Task Force on Nuclear Proliferation, as well as its chairman, Roswell Gilpatric.[99] The fact that three more weeks passed before National Security Action Memorandum (NSAM) 320 formally commissioned the task force betrayed his ulterior motive, however much the country's growing isolation in international councils was the avowed reason.[100] Ambassador Llewellyn Thompson had been heading up a U.S. State Department committee on the subject of nuclear nonproliferation since August; his unwavering support for a multilateral force had provoked clashes with ACDA, the Pentagon, and the White House. The president's expressed desire for "a higher-level, harder look at the problem" than had been provided by the "interhouse machinery" was a tacit admission of his own failure to manage his national-security bureaucracy.[101]

Nuclear responsibility was a major theme in the contest between Goldwater and Johnson, who had dipped into Kennedy's playbook to paint the Arizona senator as radical and reckless. Goldwater's public remarks called into question a core tenet of U.S. declaratory nuclear policy since Nagasaki—the only legitimate use was to avert great-power conflict. Johnson's campaign exploited this heresy in a devastating national television commercial, "Peace, Little Girl"—more commonly known as the "Daisy ad." In the sixty-second spot (which was so controversial that it only aired once) a blond kindergartner picked petals amid a field of daisies—one presumes not far from her white-picket-fenced ranch-style home—struggling to count down from ten, before an ominous adult male voice cut in, intoning down to zero (skipping six), when the bucolic scene segued to a fiery mushroom cloud: "These are the stakes, to make a world in which all of God's children can live, or to go into the dark. We must either love each other, or we must die. Vote for President Johnson on November 3rd. The stakes are too high for you to stay home."[102] The Daisy ad marked the advent of the televised attack ad and consolidated Johnson's electoral lead. Featuring a collage of images, tropes, and symbols with which two decades of antinuclear discourse had acquainted domestic and world audiences—the death of the next generation, the annihilation of nature, the association of world peace with Christian love, a paternal president à la Kennedy at American University the year before—it attested to the political dividends of executive action in defense of suburban affluence and domestic innocence.

Branding Goldwater an extremist in contrast to Johnson's vigilant restraint proved devastating: "It's dangerous enough to have the Chinese Communists with the atomic bomb," Humphrey, now Johnson's running mate, emphasized one week before election day. "But it's unbelievably dangerous to have the Chinese Communists with an atomic bomb and have Senator Goldwater with his finger on the nuclear trigger. This we can't take." Suburban women were pivotal. In Georgia, the *Atlanta Constitution* had reported on October 26 in an article titled "Goldwater and the A-Bomb Scaring Off Women" that throughout the South "women have been convinced, in many cases, that the bomb and strontium 90 and fallout are what this campaign is all about." On November 3, 1964, the Johnson-Humphrey ticket received more than 60 percent of the popular vote and 486 out of 538 electoral votes.[103]

As Johnson's nuclear guardianship clinched a landslide victory, Harold Wilson and the Labour Party's own success in the October 16 general election ushered in a new British ambivalence toward its nuclear arsenal. Labour had embraced elements of unilateral nuclear disarmament before Wilson and northern union leaders outflanked George Brown and the Campaign for Nuclear Disarmament (CND) in the drafting of Labour's 1963 electoral manifesto.[104] While Shadow Secretary for Defence Denis Healey had railed against the MLF, international nuclear diplomacy accentuated the former empire's reputation as a responsible steward.[105] The Tories therefore turned to multilateral nuclear diplomacy to hold off Labour's surge. When Foreign Minister R. A. Butler backed a nondissemination treaty at the ENDC in February 1964, the French observer in Geneva surmised that it was so as not "to allow the opposition to outstrip [the Conservative Party] in the disarmament field."[106] It all came to naught. As prime minister, Wilson was inclined to do away with the costly Polaris flotilla, but when China tested a nuclear device on the same day as Labour's parliamentary victory, the increased likelihood of a nuclear-armed India was added to his worries.[107] Shortly thereafter, he brought Lord Chalfont, a defense editor at the London *Times* who was well respected within the British establishment, into his government as the country's first minister of disarmament.[108]

Weeks earlier Erhard had called for the formation of a joint nuclear force with the United States, reasoning that "a beginning had to be made" and then vowing days later that German soldiers would never face superior weaponry on the battle front.[109] His solo flight amped up criticism from both sides of the Iron Curtain. The Soviets took the firm line that NATO nuclear integration would bring arms control talks to a halt. In a major speech to the UNGA on December 7, Gromyko characterized the beleaguered fleet as a hindrance to U.S.-Soviet détente and German reunification.[110]

That same day, Harold Wilson arrived in Washington amid a monetary crisis in London. To appease Labour's antinuclear constituents, lessen the fiscal drag on Her Majesty's Treasury, and put an end to further talk of a nuclear *Bundeswehr*, Wilson had dreamed up what he dubbed the Atlantic Nuclear Force (ANF), an alternative of the MLF under which London would commit to NATO its full nuclear might— four V bomber wings and four Polaris submarines—in an artful disavowal of both British nuclear independence (already compromised by the Nassau agreement) and the Labour Party's flirtation with unilateral disarmament.[111] The new scheme would internationalize the British nuclear deterrent without abandoning control: the United States, the United Kingdom, and (if willing) France would retain vetoes over their participating forces. Wilson argued that this joint force would better consolidate Atlantic defenses by integrating portions of the U.S. arsenal with those of Britain and even France. It would hand Bonn its own veto but never "a finger on the trigger," which strengthened Wilson's claims to back a nuclear nondissemination treaty. The White House was intrigued though noncommittal. While Wilson's visit prompted the Johnson administration to set down its views on collective nuclear strategic defense in NSAM 322 on December 17, the president's failure to build consensus within his government left him no choice but "to put the ball in the court of the Europeans."[112]

Johnson's nondiffusion policy wrestled with a gap between rhetoric and reality that winter. In a Principals Committee meeting to discuss the UNGA, Rusk raised "the basic question" of whether select countries "obtaining nuclear weapons over the next ten years" might not benefit U.S. national security. Following China's test, might it not serve their interests if Japan or India were to go nuclear? It was a heretical view for the nation's chief diplomat to voice. Considering the impasse at which the government had arrived in the battle between Atlantic integration and global governance, his remarks laid bare why the U.S. State Department had stood its ground so doggedly against the combined forces of the U.S. Defense Department, the AEC, the Joint Committee on Atomic Energy (JCAE), the U.S. Mission to the UN, and ACDA: a deep-seated faith that a transatlantic liberal community remained the true lodestar of U.S. foreign relations.[113]

Whereas Rusk remained wedded to a Europe-first strategy, McNamara was mindful of the burgeoning U.S. military presence in Southeast Asia. Even as he expressed doubt in Japan's or India's ability to build "a suitable nuclear deterrent" by 1974, he took pains to affirm that not assisting new nuclear powers remained standing policy. His claims betrayed a blind spot. As a model posture, graduated response assumed that regional powers would covet the survivable, second-strike capabilities that the superpower possessed. Yet as de Gaulle had shown and Gallois popularized, limited nuclear arsenals whose postures eschewed assured retaliation incurred few costs and conferred real benefits. Seaborg showed more sensitivity to the strategic bets and political motives at play for regional powers in insisting that there was "no other pattern than non-proliferation" for a country whose interests spanned the entire globe; "anything else," he warned the rest of the high-level committee, "would involve a loss of U.S. control."[114]

On December 3 Foster unveiled a five-plank arms control platform that might maintain that control. Its centerpiece was a nondissemination treaty barring transfers of atomic forces to foreign authorities, which entailed, at a minimum, an inalienable veto over the use of U.S.-made atomic armaments by the Office of the President. It amounted to an end run around the U.S. State Department in the form of a pact that might sway Khrushchev's usurpers—Alexei Kosygin and Leonid Brezhnev—as they weighed "the competing pulls from [Beijing] and Washington."[115] The effort had the implied support of JCAE chairman Chester Holifield, a Democrat from California, who warned at that year's Atomic Industrial Forum that the Senate would balk at any arrangement that circumvented a presidential veto.[116] When Thompson raised objections, White House staffer Spurgeon M. Keeny Jr. defended Foster, calling the ambassador's memorandum a "remarkable document that essentially calls into question our entire arms control and non-proliferation policy," seeing as Foster's package reflected Johnson's preferences.[117]

VI

The Gilpatric Committee would push the Johnson administration to take a more global approach.[118] The committee met three times from December 1, 1964, to Johnson's inauguration on January 20, 1965. Its mandate was to resolve "competing goals and conflicting objectives in nuclear programs." Failing that, it would try to set priorities.[119] The initial agenda featured thirteen major issues and sixteen minor ones: nuclear nondiffusion and test-ban talks, nuclear assurances, ballistic-missile and fissile-material limits, technology transfers, anti-ballistic-missile (ABM) systems, the superpower arms race, and the U.S. nuclear image. Once deliberations were under way, the participants bore down on four problem sets. Two were explicit: Would it ever be in the national interest for a foreign country to acquire nuclear weaponry? If so, how should Washington manage it?[120] Two were more implicit: Was Europe more important than the rest of the globe? Was the primary significance of managed nuclear globalization political or military?

The meetings recapitulated established positions within the government, pitting the original architects of Roosevelt and Truman's Europe-first grand strategy against those who viewed events in the postcolonial world as epoch-making. Although the committee took cues from major federal stakeholders, it was not a blank slate. Gilpatric's remarks often begged the question that proliferation anywhere begat proliferation everywhere, leading him to treat the problem on a universal basis. He considered Soviet help "essential" lest French and Chinese exemptions spoil global governance.[121] Because of their advanced civilian programs, India and Japan were the chief trouble makers, all the more so because Indonesia, Australia, South Korea, and Taiwan looked capable of following suit.[122] In the Middle East, U.S. intelligence assets monitored Israel's Dimona reactor and Egypt's posture toward it. Sweden, Switzerland, West Germany, and Italy had the means and perhaps the motives in Europe. In Latin America, Argentina, Brazil, and Mexico were the main suspects, while in sub-Saharan Africa, recent orders for enriched uranium by yellowcake-producing South African authorities had raised eyebrows.[123]

The committee brought remarkable theoretical diversity and analytical rigor to the subject matter. Its members and consultants came from various institutional, academic, and professional backgrounds.[124] There were those who thought international laws and norms would best counter proliferation and those who stressed military disincentives. Harvard Law professor Roger Fisher elaborated on the "rules of the game," bringing humanitarian concerns about nuclear posture into the committee's analytical framework. The Hudson Institute's Max Singer seconded Fisher's appeal for a broad-spectrum "anti-nuclear-weapons policy," which he described as a "tradition of nuclear non-use" that would seek to delegitimize everything save the deterrence of other weapons of mass destruction.[125] Both were broadly in accord with McNamara's techno-humanist approach.

Rostow's microeconomic methods aimed to calibrate policies to "the calculus in each capital" with an understanding that each case was distinct and therefore discrete.[126] His two-sided framework encompassed both military and institutional means to strengthen dynamics against acquisition in foreign capitals and weaken those for. The Baruch Plan's failure was uncritically cited as proof that "pacific negative factors" had "clearly proved insufficient."[127] For him, a reputation for effective coercion was more important. The acquisition of advanced nuclear capabilities by allies, for instance, should trigger threats to "circumscribe the U.S. commitment to their defense." By the same token, he deemed victory in Vietnam the primary factor for "the calculus in New Delhi and Tokyo."[128]

Theoretical debates about what drove states to seek independent nuclear power interacted with those related to geopolitical priorities. Rostow's attention to how power, prestige, and security motivated states led him to back nuclear-sharing in both Europe and Asia. NSC staffer Robert Komer, by contrast, held that a presidential directive against evangelizing to Asian allies about nuclear-sharing was long overdue.[129] The U.S. State Department employee on the task force, Raymond Garthoff, took the company line in pushing hard for "country-to-country" solutions that would consequently favor West Germany.[130] Arthur Dean and McCloy, who had both served under five presidents, worried most about preserving momentum toward "a Europe united and in partnership with the United States." McCloy rated the risks of abandoning the MLF as "at least equal [to], if they do not exceed, those that we risk with the proliferation of nuclear weapons." For him, Western Europe remained "the keystone of our post-war policy."[131]

Cabinet members were equally divided. While neither was dogmatic, Rusk dwelt on the short-term diplomatic hazards while McNamara took a long-range, macro view. The defense secretary laid out a basic binary: in Model A, the United States would refuse new countries admission to the nuclear club; in Model B, it would accommodate them. He preferred to hold the club "to an absolute minimum" even if it came at a "a substantial price." Nonproliferation and comprehensive test-ban agreements, plus nuclear-tipped guarantees to states such as India, looked to him to be "the most effective means."[132] Rusk highlighted the difficulty of reassuring New Delhi in light of nonalignment and favored an Asian MLF that the United States or the British Commonwealth would outfit with nukes. As for West Germany, without greater say in NATO's defense planning, it was only a matter of time before they turned to France or went it alone. McNamara put the MLF's odds at four-to-one against, while Ball contended that a West German signature on a nonproliferation treaty was unthinkable without it. As Bonn viewed the issue from the standpoint of reunification, Rusk claimed, the MLF question evoked powerful strains of German nationalism.[133] Warring views over why Germans had become Nazis in the interwar years quietly haunted the deliberations.

After the interviews were complete, the committee outlined four strategies along a continuum from "selective relaxation" to the elevation of nonproliferation into a central pillar of U.S. foreign policy. The first option expanded on Rusk's and McNamara's flirtations with selective proliferation. At the other extreme, the long-term benefits were found to warrant the high short-term costs of opposing new nuclear powers and rolling back existing ones. The real choice was between the second option—the current "prudent" course—and the third—"hold the line."[134] Positions on European and Third World proliferation, security guarantees, nuclear-sharing, international treaties, U.S.-Soviet détente, fissile materials, technology transfers, and international safeguards were plotted according to these matrixes. Competing theories yielded inconsistency. Would recalling nuclear weapons to the continental United States lessen their worth? Or would it engender insecurity among allies who would then seek their own?[135]

With Rusk, Gilpatric hit on the matter's crux: "How [can we] approach the problem on a case-by-case basis when each case has so much impact on others[?]" His sweeping judgment irked the secretary of state, whose rebuttal was succinct—"Each case is different." Thompson echoed his boss, noting how indifferent the Soviets were to nuclear spread outside West Germany. Even though Rusk allowed that the prospect of nuclear capabilities in Israel, Japan, or India was more alarming, he believed that European security affairs nonetheless still merited first priority.[136]

The final report, drafted by Keeny, called for buttressing existing restraints with a bundle of new measures—better cooperation with foreign powers, tighter controls on nuclear exports and technology transfers, stiffer sanctions against offenders, and renewed investment in U.S.-Soviet arms control—all with a view to "hold the line" on nuclear globalization. An "energetic and comprehensive" mixture of international cooperation and targeted pressure would minimize "direct military threats" that might undermine U.S. influence abroad, spread the disease of neutralism, and fan the flames of isolationism at home.[137] The report commended efforts to finalize a Comprehensive Test Ban Treaty (CTBT) or NWFZ treaties in Latin America or Africa, and challenged Washington to contrast in its words and actions the downsides of military nuclear technology relative to civilian alternatives. NATO's nuclear integration survived, for now, with the U.S. veto retained and the European clause stripped. As a result the admonition that a nonproliferation treaty should "not wait, or be dependent upon" Europe's future deterrent architecture sounded like wishful thinking.

Deeper currents ran through these debates. Because Asia's nuclear dynamics were more chaotic and its median country, the Republic of China on Taiwan, less prosperous, international options looked more promising there. References to diffusion cascades—the "impossibility" that nuclear self-determination could be "compartmentalized, quarantined, or regionalized"—were couched so that new Asian nuclear powers (with or without U.S. assistance) would prompt European powers like West Germany to follow suit—never the other way around.[138] Differing orientations toward time were on display in the committee's deliberations. Those who sought fuller U.S. military integration in Europe referenced the interwar years. McCloy made an analogy between current affairs and French efforts to incapacitate Germany after the First World War: "Poincaré was wrong in 1919 and so is de Gaulle in 1965. The Germans must be given a position of equality with the other Western powers if they are not, in due course, to go off on another nationalist adventure. Twice such an adventure brought the nations to a world war in my lifetime. I do not think we should risk the same course to a third world war."[139] By McCloy's reckoning, nuclear developments in India, Israel, the United Arab Republic, and Pakistan were "less ominous." European proliferation was "more dangerous than proliferation in Asia, considering the past history of Europe."[140]

Most in the room, however, feared Asian nuclear power more. India was singled out as the most critical factor.[141] After Rusk and McNamara debated selective proliferation, Dean retorted that demographic growth might make this "a dangerous proposition."[142] A draft explained why the hazards of further nuclear spread would increase now that communist China "had proven that a poor, backward non-white power can make a bomb": Above all, the assembled grandees worried that elites from rapidly growing Third World countries would usurp them.

> The bargaining power of backward nations would be increased . . . since they would no longer feel the restraints of great power influence in local disputes. It would also be increased if in an effort to acquire nuclear weapons they were able to play off the United States, the USSR, China and other nuclear powers against each other. And any major trend of nuclear capabilities among the populous, non-white nations of the earth would greatly strengthen their hand in attempting to obtain an ever greater share of the earth's wealth and opportunity.

"Some or all of this may be desirable or inevitable," the report acknowledged; however, nuclear proliferation "would bring it about much more quickly and in a more disruptive fashion."[143]

The committee's reasoning went beyond geopolitics—this representative selection of U.S. technocratic elites preferred to hold the world's nonwhite masses at a material disadvantage on the assumption that Afro-Asian nations, however democratic or communist, would eventually train their sights on those holding title to a lion's share of the world's power and wealth. There was palpable anxiety among those present about the long-term sustainability of nuclear peace when leaders so seldom lived up to ideals of rationality. "For our own lifetime we might prefer to live in a 'Model B'" world," noted MIT's George Kistiakowsky, a Manhattan Project veteran and Eisenhower's science advisor, but "thoughts about his grandchildren" inclined him toward Model A. He blamed human nature rather than Afro-Asian political immaturity per se, judging the rest of the world as "at least as important as Europe in the light of growth in population and technological innovations."[144] As the country's power elite came to associate the future with developments in Latin America, Africa, Asia, and the Middle East, nuclear globalization in these regions appeared to jeopardize their self-appointed position at the helm of world affairs.

VII

For all its virtues, the White House buried the Gilpatric report. Bundy faulted it for "coming down hard on one side of this tough question." Although its recommendations had certified positions with which many, including Bundy, sympathized, Rusk had refused to give way, likening the report, about which he voiced "real doubts," "to an atom bomb."[145] Whatever his sympathies, Johnson's attention lay elsewhere. Two months later, Gilpatric blamed "the crisis over South Vietnam" for consigning nuclear non-diffusion to "second priority, and rightly so."[146]

Arms control was fast becoming a political football within the Democratic Party. The disparity in Kennedy's and Johnson's achievements was a sore point for a man who feared the Massachusetts dynasty as much as mounting hostilities in Southeast Asia. When Rusk testified to the Senate Foreign Relations Committee on April 28, Senator Joe Clark, a Democrat from Pennsylvania, scolded him for the "backsliding" on arms control since Kennedy's assassination. Where should the country draw the line between national sovereignty and international cooperation? While Rusk saw nuclear arms, like epidemic disease, as best handled under a "common law of mankind" that rose above "political borders," he questioned the UN's effectiveness in such matters. In Clark's cross-examination, the senator inquired why "the words general and complete disarmament" had become less popular "since President Johnson went into the White House." His allegation struck a nerve.[147] Johnson called his remarks "a great injustice" and in private demanded an apology.[148] After the White House drafted a summary of their efforts to date and the U.S. State Department entered an aide-mémoire into the congressional record, Bundy promised Johnson that he would "fold both of these documents around a stick and beat Joe Clark over the head with it tomorrow at breakfast."[149]

As the White House played politics, a global corps of arms controllers was joining the fray. On May 12, Frank Aiken warned that time for a nondissemination treaty was short, backing the Western line on control versus access and the need for inspections outside the nuclear club. He sided with the nonaligned on security guarantees and disarmament linkages, whose salience he believed had grown since 1961.[150] Foster took to the pages of *Foreign Affairs* in July to argue for a "most serious and urgent effort" to stem the nuclear tide, most of all that the U.S. government do its utmost to achieve a global nonproliferation treaty. Before publishing he took notes from those inside and outside government—Tsarapkin reportedly reviewed the article "word by word."[151] He accepted most of Rusk's edits but demurred at excising sections addressing the credibility of security assurances to countries threatened by Soviet or Chinese nuclear weapons, quoting French foreign minister Maurice Couve de Murville to the effect that NATO allies increasingly lacked confidence in the U.S. nuclear umbrella. On the other hand, he softened his claim that U.S. nuclear credibility would wane as that of the PRC waxed.[152] He also pushed back when Rusk questioned whether U.S.-Soviet arms control would strengthen nondiffusion efforts after McNamara admitted to the House Armed Services Committee that both arsenals were large and diverse enough to survive counterforce strikes. Whereas the nation's chief diplomat raised doubts that mutual vulnerability promised an end to the nuclear arms race, Foster maintained that only superpower restraint could yield "a world order in which the role of nuclear weapons would be diminished." Without it, he went on, "it is hard to see how . . . we can hope to put any limits of the membership in the nuclear club."[153]

The nondissemination treaty had a prominent champion in Robert Kennedy. The Democratic powerbroker Fred Dutton urged Kennedy, New York's new junior senator, to embrace the issue in his debut speech to the U.S. Senate on June 23, 1965, the second anniversary of the LTBT's opening for signature. Gilpatric, a close family friend, spent an afternoon at Kennedy's Georgetown residence briefing him and his speechwriter, Adam Walinsky, on his committee's work, whose classified report members of Congress had not yet read.[154] In the Senate chambers, Kennedy asserted that difficulties in "Vietnam, or the Dominican Republic, or Berlin" paled in comparison to those posed by "the question of nuclear proliferation," calling on the White House to give the matter "central priority" by reaching out to Beijing and adopting the Gilpatric Report in full.[155] The *New York Times* speculated that Kennedy had sided with Foster and Fisher with a view to end internal dissension over the report.[156]

Kennedy was now competing with Johnson for his brother's mantle, citing the planetary scale of atomic warfare fourteen times and a common duty to children five times.[157] The alarmist title that *Frontier* affixed to an excerpt from his speech was evocative: "Will There Be Any World Left for Our Children?"[158] The content and the timing of the speech infuriated Johnson. To the press corps, Press Secretary George Reedy quipped that the White House was "glad Senator Kennedy is also interested in this field." White House speechwriter Dick Goodwin had just finished a presidential address that would have highlighted nuclear arms control for events in San Francisco commemorating the UN's twentieth anniversary in two days' time. Johnson commanded him to delete "anything about the atom" to avoid any impression that he was following Kennedy's lead.[159] The *New York Times* publicized the Gilpatric Report's main recommendations two weeks later, most notably that the importance of a nondissemination treaty outweighed that of an Atlantic nuclear force.[160]

Signs of convergence in U.S.-Soviet views had reappeared in back-channel talks. Paul Doty, a Harvard biochemist, and Franklin Long, landed in Moscow on the invitation of Soviet Academy of Sciences vice president Mikhail Millionshchikov, an "old acquaintance" from Pugwash meetings. Millionshchikov and Vladimir Pavlichenko welcomed them to the Presidium of the Soviet Academy on June 9, where they spoke about détente, Vietnam, and nuclear issues. Doty conveyed a strong desire for détente in the United States, relating that even though no one in Washington wanted the MLF "with any degree of seriousness," the Soviets should not demand a "public burial." Millionshchikov sketched out a compromise "somewhere between the Irish resolution and the more recent Indian proposals." Détente remained on the table, even if the USSR accorded the visit little visibility.[161]

While competing joint nuclear forces consumed oxygen in NATO, McNamara and others mooted the idea of making more information—not hardware—available to allies. During the Kennedy years, NATO's Defense Data Program and McNamara's Athens speech had disseminated previously restricted data on U.S. nuclear capabilities, targeting, and plans to NATO national authorities. Now the Pentagon and ACDA moved to elaborate an alternative to an Atlantic or multilateral nuclear force through trilateral cooperation among the United States, the United Kingdom, and West Germany within an enhanced consultative framework for member states that remained invested in integrated military command. In May 1965, McNamara had proposed a select committee where he would sit down with a select group of fellow defense ministers to discuss communications, intelligence, and nuclear planning. When the Special Committee of Defense Ministers convened in December, it added a concrete link between U.S. nuclear strategy and alliance management. It also granted the FRG quasi-nuclear status by virtue of software rather than hardware, which the U.S. ambassador in Bonn described as "a hedge in our efforts to solve the nuclear problem which originally inspired the MLF."[162]

Foster's ACDA was gaining sway. On June 28, Bundy circulated NSAM 335—a new look at arms control and nondissemination that Foster and Fisher took the lead in drafting.[163] Two weeks later, Tsarapkin notified Foster that Moscow was ready to return to Geneva. To the NSC staff, resumed ENDC meetings were a stroke of good fortune, and Bundy encouraged Johnson to seize the opportunity, with the Soviets primed to make concessions amid their fraternal battles with their Chinese comrades. He reminded the president that "no one would have predicted a test ban treaty" in

April 1963.[164] Although he couched Geneva as a way to beat the Kennedys at their own game, his real motivation was to quell allied and nonaligned reservations as Johnson dramatically increased the U.S. combat presence in Vietnam. Komer had recited a "catalogue of horrors" to him the previous week: "Let's face the fact that the things we have to do in Vietnam and elsewhere are a heavy burden for us to bear in the Afro-Asian world as well as Europe . . . the tougher the line we feel compelled to take in Vietnam and similar crunches, the more we ought to offset their impact by positive and constructive initiatives in other fields like disarmament."[165]

Conclusion

Soviet and U.S. leaders looked to nuclear arms control to reduce Cold War tensions and cement their topmost positions in the international order after the LTBT entered into force. A nuclear nondiffusion treaty looked like the logical next step. Khrushchev and Kennedy's early momentum floundered, however, as allies and nonaligned states established middle grounds from which to thwart the superpowers. Poland and East Germany vetoed Khrushchev's move to bar Mao's China from the nuclear club in exchange for looking the other way on NATO's nuclear integration. Instinctual support for Bonn among Europe-firsters in the Johnson administration combined to yield deadlock, even though most domestic and international stakeholders backed nondiffusion in principle. One such nation was India, whose leadership had started to retreat from nonaligned solidarity and peaceful coexistence after the 1962 Sino-Indian conflict. China's test killed such Nehruvian hopes and prompted Bhabha to announce that India had the necessary art.

After Johnson chose not to abandon an Atlantic nuclear squadron as a necessary price to lock the nuclear club's door, a well-connected network of liberal internationalists seized the torch. Foreign development programs and a growing number of nuclear exporters had brought the absolute weapon within the reach of postcolonial nation-states with developing economies. Whether intentional or not, their calls to prevent nuclear war by restricting the size of the nuclear club would offer useful grounds on which to reestablish the virtues of U.S. global hegemony as its armed forces waded further into Vietnam.

"This Side of the Angels"
LBJ, Vietnam, and Nuclear Peace, 1964–1966

Introduction: "And Hell followed after"

Semyon Tsarapkin and Bill Foster addressed the Eighteen Nation Committee on Disarmament (ENDC) when it reconvened in the Council Chambers of the Palais des Nations on July 27, 1965. Framed by Josep Maria Sert's murals of humanity's progress from darkness to enlightenment, Tsarapkin blamed imperial U.S. adventures in "Viet-Nam, in the Congo, and in Latin America" for the regression since the last meeting.[1] When Foster spoke next, he lamented the Cold War climate in the room. He then read President Lyndon Johnson's message to the congregation: "The Bible describes 'death' as the fourth horseman of the Apocalypse saying: 'And hell followed after him.' Our genius has changed this from a parable to a possibility. For the wasting power of our weapons is beyond the reach of imagination and language alike. Hell alone can describe the consequences that await their full use."[2]

The apocalyptic rhetoric belied continuing, deep divisions in Washington that were taxing Johnson's and his advisors' patience. One year later, Hayes Redmon, a U.S. Air Force intelligence officer working under White House Press Secretary Bill Moyers, would complain that Cabinet officials had missed "the forest for the trees." With time running short to finalize a treaty "the Indians, Israelis, etc." might accept and "virtually everyone" in the United States, most of all suburban voters whose support could spell the difference in the midterm elections, favorably inclined, Johnson needed to position the Democratic Party "on the side of the angels."[3]

From October 1964 to December 1966 the superpowers resolved their differences over how to define nuclear proliferation. Together the Gaullist challenge in Europe, nuclear-armed China, and the Vietnam War exposed fault lines in the capitalist, communist, and nonaligned worlds, complicating the search for common ground in Geneva and New York. Into this vacuum stepped a transnational network of globalists, including an arms control cabal in Washington to whom stood opposed Europeanists fearful of a "frustrated and neurotic West Germany."[4] In the end, however, domestic politics moved Johnson to act. The Civil Rights Act, the Voting Rights Act, the Immigration and Nationality Act, and the Gulf of Tonkin Resolution collectively drove wedges between the suburban liberals, the white segregations, and the unionized workers that composed the Democratic coalition. As he Americanized the Vietnam War Johnson would wait until the eve of the midterm elections to throw his lot in with a nonproliferation treaty in an eleventh-hour bid to preserve his Great Society, laying claim to John F. Kennedy's heroic mantle of nuclear guardianship and, in doing so, issuing new warrants for U.S. military intervention abroad.

I

The Gilpatric Report had warned that nuclear diffusion in the Third World could upend world order. India looked increasingly like ground zero for this challenge.[5] Its forbearance had never been ironclad. Jawaharlal Nehru and Homi Bhabha often noted that they could build atom bombs quickly when boasting about their country's technological prowess. Though Nehru preferred moral capital and social development to military armament, he faced mounting ambivalence from the rest of the political universe.[6] In December 1963, Indian foreign secretary M. J. Desai—unrelated to then finance minister Morarji Desai—had acknowledged to U.S. ambassador Chester Bowles political pressure to match China.[7] With spent fuel from Canada India Reactor Utility Services (CIRUS) arriving at reprocessing plants elsewhere on the subcontinent, "only a major political decision" now separated New Delhi from the nuclear club.[8]

Lal Bahadur Shastri, a loyalist who followed Nehru as prime minister on May 27, 1964, was to retain Nehru's basic policy: atomic energy would be "for peaceful purposes," not the "manufacture, use, or possession of nuclear weapons."[9] U.S. officials worried nonetheless. India featured as a laboratory of noncommunist development, a vulnerable domino in need of defense, and as a counterbalance to communist China.[10] India's prominence in the nonaligned movement promised to exert a restraining force, but U.S. officials needed to tread carefully. When B. K. Nehru endorsed an Ethiopian proposal to outlaw nuclear-weapon use in September 1964, U.S. State Department officials sensed an opportunity to commit India to its basic policy.[11] When Foster acclaimed the speech too fulsomely, however, his Italian counterpart preached restraint: "no western power should [raise joint sponsorship] . . . Let the Indians lead."[12]

The near simultaneity of communist China's test and power transfers in London and Moscow had unsettled Indian nuclear policy, with a clamorous yet inconclusive debate erupting in New Delhi that pitted Shastri and Congress Party doves against Hindu nationalists and Congress Party hawks. Bowles grew more strident in his calls to bolster the U.S. position on the subcontinent, beginning with intelligence sharing about the People's Republic of China (PRC) nuclear-weapon program. Shastri beheld three options: issue an ultimatum akin to Kennedy's during the Cuban Missile Crisis; double down on nonalignment and development; or enter a regional arms race with China and Pakistan.[13] In the end, Shastri found a fourth one: he would hedge his bets.[14] States have strong incentives to hedge in the atomic energy field. The know-how, facilities, materiel, and personnel that enable peaceful uses—scientists and technicians, uranium and thorium, enrichment facilities and power plants—also shorten pathways to military hardware. Johnson's promise to repel "nuclear blackmail" had buoyed hopes that atomic shields could be extended to neutral parties, but Shastri still pressed Bhabha to demonstrate India's atomic skills without crossing the military threshold.[15] The chief of India's nuclear program was happy to oblige, endorsing peaceful nuclear explosives (PNEs) whose technology differed from military variants mainly in its size and stated purpose.

Indian officials keyed their nuclear diplomacy to nonaligned politics. With the Conference of Non-Aligned Countries meeting that year, B. K. Nehru implored Rusk to commend India's non-nuclear status when forty-seven delegations assembled in Cairo.[16] In a speech rife with Gandhian notions of agrarianism and nonviolence, Shastri enjoined those present to divert the PRC from its belligerent course, publicizing his recent command to Indian scientists not to undertake a "single experiment" or "single device" whose express purpose was not peaceful.[17] His intervention succeeded: nuclear non-diffusion and a total test moratorium joined nonaligned nostrums such as self-determination, peaceful coexistence, and anticolonialism in the joint statement on October 10, 1964. Although most of their countries fielded little besides research reactors and cyclotrons, the delegates in Cairo nevertheless pledged "not to produce, acquire, or test any nuclear weapons."[18] Back in New Delhi, nationalist views were gaining currency in the national media, with *The Statesman*, the *Indian Express*, and Gujarati- and Marathi-language papers all counseling readers to view the costs of a nuclear-weapon program from the standpoint of "national interest" rather than "world opinion." Now foreign minister, V. K. Krishna Menon remained unalterably opposed to the military option, styling it "the height of folly" given the likelihood of Soviet assistance in the event of a regional war.[19]

Policy makers in Washington redoubled their efforts to confirm India among the atomic unarmed. At Rusk's instruction, Bowles reminded Shastri that the Limited Test Ban Treaty (LTBT) barred transnational fallout while small arsenals like that of France increased the "danger of world nuclear war." The White House paid loud tribute to New Delhi's "high road."[20] Yet U.S. intelligence agencies worried about the low road's accessibility. While New Delhi should not initiate a military program in the near future, India's reprocessing plant could yield enough plutonium to arm a dozen Hiroshima-type bombs by 1970, with two National Intelligence Estimates (NIEs) figuring the odds at "better than even" based on China's advances, Sino-Soviet relations, security assurances, and acquisition costs.[21] Defense Minister Yashwantrao Chavan dubbed China's blast a "new factor," questioning the basic policy's wisdom in a rapidly changing strategic environment.[22] On October 24, Bhabha declared that nuclear explosives would afford cheap means to bolster security and development, claiming it would take at most three years to manufacture one. By omitting expenditures related to facilities, human resources, reprocessing, or infrastructure (much of which had already been committed), he estimated that fifty atom bombs would cost $21 million and the same number of hydrogen bombs $31.5 million. Despite various efforts to correct these "grossly misleading" figures, they were cited often.[23] When B. K. Nehru told Foster on November 3 that Shastri had reconfirmed Nehru's basic policy—omitting the PNE program—he admitted that pressure existed "to offset the genuine psychological advantages" that the Chinese Communist Party (CCP) had obtained, with Vice Chairman Zhou Enlai proposing a five-power conference on nuclear disarmament. He asked whether Washington would keep its promises if Moscow were to back Beijing in a nuclear showdown with New Delhi.[24]

The controversy intensified after Minister Mehr Chand Khanna called for India to join the nuclear club before the All India Congress Committee on November 7, when more than 100 delegates requested that a closed session consider an independent nuclear deterrent.[25] In defense of atomic restraint, M. J. Desai invoked "the Mahatama's teaching and Nehru's legacy" and warned that the costs would be "crushing."[26] When they carried a resolution reaffirming the basic policy, the *Hindustan Times* dubbed the outcome "nothing short of a miracle," but Shastri had been forced to admit that continued forbearance was contingent on real progress on international disarmament, leaving the door open to future reappraisal. Menon chastised the prime minister for equivocating, but Shastri refused to speak for his successors.[27] "So long as we are here," he reaffirmed ten days later, "we won't make the Bomb."[28] He would be dead one year later.

II

Washington turned to science and technology diplomacy including peaceful nuclear assistance to solidify New Delhi's self-restraint.[29] Flexible response had stopped short of the Indian subcontinent for reasons of geography and of nonalignment. Air Force chief Curtis LeMay recoiled at firmer pledges, praising Johnson's soft guarantee of October 1964 for omitting "any specific military course of action."[30] Llewellyn Thompson and Walt Rostow presumed that continuing U.S. military preponderance in Asia was key to moderating India's nuclear behavior, treating U.S. "military fortunes" in Southeast Asia as the chief barometer.[31] The alliance with Pakistan was secondary. Even as the U.S. ambassador in Karachi worked to allay President Ayub Khan's fears about the CIRUS reactor in India, he cautioned Washington that it could topple the region's "delicate balance of strategic forces." A nuclear-armed "colossus" next door would tempt Pakistan to pivot toward the PRC, to launch strikes against Indian nuclear facilities or military positions in Kashmir, or even to eye its own atomic breakout. If more binding guarantees for India were indeed on the table, Khan's goodwill would be tested.[32]

Against these headwinds the Johnson administration fell back on its stock-in-trade in the Third World—investments in modernization. Bowles made the case for a public relations blitz valorizing India's peaceful development while senior Atomic Energy Commission (AEC) officials toured the country for wide-ranging discussions on technology transfers and scientific collaboration. From embassies around the world U.S. diplomats barnstormed in support of an Indian resolution against nuclear testing in the UN General Assembly (UNGA) and behind the scenes to have Afro-Asian abstainers awarded the Nobel Peace Prize.[33] Voice of America touted India's scientific and technological accomplishments as unrivaled in the postcolonial world.[34] Nuclear reactors and space rockets would capture "the imaginations of Indians and Afro-Asians" and demonstrate India's technological genius even as titanic civil engineering under Project Plowshare solved "basic development problems" by rerouting great rivers, liberating natural gas, and blasting coastal harbors.[35] Presidential science advisor Jerome Wiesner jetted to New Delhi to explore joint ventures in aerospace, rocketry, satellites, plutonium and thorium recycling, breeder reactors, and PNEs. With Bhabha winging his way to Washington, D.C., in February and Afro-Asian Islamic and Non-Aligned Movement meetings in Bandung, Indonesia, set for March and April, respectively, Rusk was eager "to tout Indian scientific prowess and avert proliferation."[36]

Washington proved less willing to make substantive concessions.[37] Shastri had unveiled his version of a nondiffusion treaty on December 4, 1964, calling on the UN to expedite nuclear arms control and the United States, the United Kingdom, and the Soviet Union to "guarantee nonnuclear nations safety from atomic attack."[38] As Bowles temporized in New Delhi, the U.S. State Department reviewed the potential costs, benefits, and risks.[39] It was one thing to warn malefactors of the "heavy price" incurred by nuclear threats, but "freedom of action" remained paramount.[40] Spurgeon Keeny Jr. described the U.S. position as "disturbingly thin" on account of Rusk's and Thompson's reluctance to issue binding guarantees while Shastri dismissed London's proposed Commonwealth nuclear force as quasi-colonial, personally telling British prime minister Harold Wilson that Indian nonalignment necessitated a global solution.[41]

Shastri outlined an ambitious package for internationalizing nuclear security at the Trombay reprocessing plant on January 22, 1965: universal security guarantees, a comprehensive test ban, and accelerated disarmament.[42] Behind the scenes, however, Bowles had received word from a cabinet member that Bhabha had been authorized "to proceed with first stages of producing [an] atomic bomb." Bowles was flummoxed that Washington would continue to hold "at arm's length" a populous, nonaligned, nonwhite champion of global nonproliferation when presented with even odds of cementing India's nuclear forbearance.[43] After the remaining neutrals in the ENDC endorsed India's resolution, Wiesner saw a golden opportunity to institutionalize the status quo.[44] Yet Rusk preferred the Irish Resolution's permissiveness toward NATO nuclear integration, only agreeing to announce China's next test jointly with Shastri.[45] It was against a backdrop of U.S. intransigence that Bhabha coyly explained when he sat with AEC officials in Washington, D.C., on February 22 that an Indian PNE test would take eighteen months—or six months with their help.[46] Indian representatives said likewise in Geneva.[47]

Nonproliferation was therefore atop the agenda when W. Averell Harriman landed in New Delhi on March 4.[48] Shastri contended that any nuclear nondiffusion pact or multilateral assurances would need to cohere with nonaligned principles, claiming that it was unwise for him to accept bilateral assurances when communist China threatened "all non-nuclear states."[49] Harriman poured cold water on the notion that Moscow would make a public choice between the two most populous Asian nations and offered to have U.S. generals and admirals brief Shastri and his military chiefs on U.S. capabilities—conventional and nuclear—in the Asia-Pacific region.[50] Bowles kept pleading to internationalize the issue, recommending in late April that India or Ireland propose a resolution in the UN First Committee linking nuclear restraint to collective security. He wondered whether the Kremlin might go along if it were "optically directed against China as little as possible."[51] The rest of the Johnson administration appeared happy for New Delhi to remain Moscow's problem. After Johnson canceled back-to-back Indian and Pakistani state visits to Washington ahead of a contentious foreign aid vote on Capitol Hill, Rusk advised Shastri to raise the matter when Soviet premier Alexei Kosygin visited India in May. Although Kosygin dismissed Mao Zedong's Bomb as "a small toy" when he landed in New Delhi, he eventually consented to give the matter a second look back in Moscow.[52]

Moscow's reply had not arrived yet when the second Indo-Pakistani War erupted in June. Pakistani incursions precipitated full-scale mobilization followed by Pakistani thrusts into Kashmir in August and general warfare shortly afterward, bringing U.S. efforts to conciliate New Delhi after Beijing's atomic coming-out party to a close. Bowles depicted an Indian elite in an "angry, unreasonable, and indeed irrational mood" on account of Washington's neglect.[53] Johnson was even more exasperated after watching the summer war as a bystander, with Moscow ultimately brokering a cease-fire.[54] It had been unrealistic to expect the United States or the United Kingdom to contemplate security assurances while the Kashmir fuse on the subcontinent remained lit. The United States was reluctant to play the other cards—a total test ban or universal assurances—that it had left in the deck.

III

Tensions had mounted in Europe after China's test and Nikita Khrushchev's fall. In France, Pierre Gallois's concept of "asymmetric deterrence" legitimated France's limited deterrent (and found a sympathetic audience elsewhere) even if French authorities worried that the Germans would follow in their footsteps.[55] Even opponents of the *force de frappe* such as Raymond Aron stressed the limits of multilateralism where matters of state survival were concerned.[56] The French Ministry of Foreign Affairs was keeping its options open, dismissing a nondiffusion treaty on grounds that great powers would always work to arm themselves with the best weapons and to deny others the same while intimating that a change of heart might occur once the French arsenal was "credible and secure."[57]

British ambivalence, by contrast, inclined Whitehall toward a leading role in nuclear talks. After visiting New York and Washington in February 1965, Lord Chalfont and Defense Minister Michael Stewart journeyed to Moscow to ask Foreign Minister Andrei Gromyko to reengage with the ENDC.[58] Chalfont attributed his frosty reception there to Johnson's escalation in Southeast Asia, relaying that Soviet officials now wanted negotiations to take place in the 114-nation UN Disarmament Commission (UNDC) in New York in lieu of the more sedate ENDC.[59] The United States had launched Operation Rolling Thunder against North Vietnam that March along with the expanded use of napalm against the Vietnamese countryside.[60] By the end of the year, U.S. troop numbers there would reach 184,300. Although Beijing was Hanoi's main supplier, Moscow shipped advanced weaponry and technical advisors as Soviet mouthpieces denounced U.S. imperial aggression. According to historian Lien-Hang Nguyen, the "war effort became a central battleground in Beijing and Moscow's rivalry for leadership of the communist world."[61] Atomic coexistence risked becoming another casualty of this family feud.

The UNDC opened for business on April 26 with Egyptian diplomat Mohamed El Kony in the chair. The French ambassador to the UN noted how small nations had taken on active roles that they now "felt entitled to play" in New York.[62] Proceedings started well, as Soviet and U.S. officials agreed that limited nuclear deterrents could remain throughout the stages of general and complete disarmament. When discussions turned to nuclear nondiffusion and testing, however, cracks appeared in the Western front.[63] Italy wanted savings to finance Third World development while

Canadian general E.L.M. Burns called to make a nondiffusion pact "more palatable to the nonnuclear states" by means of security assurances, arms reductions, a limited duration, blanket inspections, and entry into force only after Canada, West Germany, India, Israel, Japan, Pakistan, and Sweden had signed and ratified.[64] Japan, Sweden, and Algeria, among others, called for communist China and republican France to send delegates to the ENDC, while Swedish disarmament minister Alva Myrdal lobbied for a fissile-material cut-off and a four-environment test ban. Adlai Stevenson had little to offer by comparison, recapping the previous year's package and Johnson's nonbinding assurances. Assistant Secretary of State Harlan Cleveland could only hint that more might be forthcoming in Geneva.[65]

Regional security dynamics competed with national sovereignty as the neutrals' polestar. Indian diplomats labored to place nondiffusion "within the framework of collective security" and censure China's atomic feat. B. N. Chakravarty had reformatted the Indian resolution, suggesting that nuclear club members pledge not to proliferate or enact nuclear threats against the atomic unarmed, who would all receive a UN guarantee against atomic blackmail.[66] Only after the international community had finalized a comprehensive test ban and a nuclear freeze would his country categorically renounce the atom bomb.[67]

China's nuclear testing divided the nonaligned camp. The second blast was timed to precede the Afro-Asian Summit in Algiers that July, but political fallout was already registering in New York, where India, Japan, the Republic of China, and a smattering of Western and Pacific delegations issued condemnations. V. C. Trivedi dubbed it "an attack not only on all that we stand for and all the efforts that we are making" but also "an attack on all of humanity."[68] While many Afro-Asian delegates expressed an urgent desire for a nondiffusion pact, others basked in the reflected glow of a nonwhite nation entering the most exclusive club on Earth.[69] Thirty-three delegations backed Yugoslavia's proposal of a world disarmament conference to which the PRC would be invited. The competing Indian resolution, which singled out Beijing in calling for a total test ban, fared less well. The Soviet permanent representative to the UN, Nikolai Fedorenko, had worked to tone down anti-PRC measures and offer "an honest defense for an absent party," leading some to guess that the Kremlin preferred to wait until after Algiers to greenlight the ENDC, lest the gathering turn into "a tribunal for China to denounce a vain dialogue or worse yet a Russo-American collusion."[70] Meanwhile, behind the scenes, nonaligned Cairo inquired whether Beijing might help build up its nuclear infrastructure.[71]

The UNDC wrapped up work on June 16, 1965. The Yugoslavian resolution had passed, but a world disarmament conference remained far-fetched as long as the PRC shunned multilateral forums. The Indian proposal was referred to Geneva, where it would meet longstanding U.S. opposition to a total test ban. Back in Moscow,

Tsarapkin was "gloomy" about a nondiffusion accord.[72] In Beijing, Zhou construed events in New York as bestowing a stamp of Afro-Asian approval on the CCP's atomic doings, informing the Politburo that notwithstanding misgivings there about atmospheric experiments, "the people of the world, including the Japanese . . . acclaim and congratulate us, and are happy." Although the Japanese and their American allies, he went on, channeling W.E.B. Du Bois, "must realize that if atomic bombs fall on their heads, their losses will be greater than ours." He worried nonetheless that the superpowers might try to neutralize communist China's Los Alamos one day soon.[73]

When the ENDC reconvened on July 27, there were as many positions as delegations among the Western Four—the United States, the United Kingdom, Canada, and Italy (Charles de Gaulle's France continued to abstain). The U.S. government was not the only one divided. Although the British Labour government had promised multilateral moves toward nuclear disarmament in its election manifesto, the British defense establishment was watching Israel, Egypt, Indonesia, and India carefully.[74] Whitehall had misread the tea leaves in Washington, where its ambassador mistook Foster's article in *Foreign Affairs* as an expression of official policy.[75] As a result British proposals to bar nuclear transfers to alliances or to a future majority-ruled, pan-European force failed to impress Rusk. The prospect of a united European community wielding its own arsenal would continue to haunt proceedings. Although Chalfont agreed to soften the language at Foster's request, reporting by *Frankfurter Allgemeine Zeitung* that Ludwig Erhard and Gerhard Schröder were seeking a bigger stake in NATO's nuclear defense gave Wilson second thoughts. Ambitions for a compromise package combining multilateral forces, security assurances, and International Atomic Energy Agency (IAEA) inspections akin to those recently proposed at the Latin American denuclearization talks in Mexico City accordingly withered on the vine.[76]

The Canadian delegate lamented that his U.S. counterparts had not done more to meet nonaligned and neutral requests.[77] The Italians were sharper, joking that the U.S. offer had not changed since early 1963 and was "no longer (if ever) acceptable to [the] Third World."[78] Foster could only plead for sympathy and recite bromides about the inadvisability of allowing communist or nonaligned governments to serve de facto on NATO's board of directors.[79] Foster deemed the intermural differences "more theoretical than real"—Western European political union remained a distant dream—yet Ottawa, Rome, and London all refused to co-sponsor. True to form, Tsarapkin blasted "West German revanchists and militarists" in subsequent remarks.[80] Foster's pleas had fallen on deaf ears back in Washington. French onlookers spotted a silver lining: for all the bloodshed in Vietnam, superpower diplomacy in Geneva had not yet become a victim.[81]

The nonaligned and neutrals left Switzerland feeling emboldened. The finer details of nuclear-sharing mattered little to India, Trivedi reminded Foster; it was the discriminatory nature of nondiffusion that concerned them. The Comprehensive Test Ban Treaty (CTBT) that he had set forth in New York remained their "best hope."[82] Myrdal, a trusted leader among the neutrals, was like-minded. Swedish newspapers questioned whether a nondiffusion treaty could work without French and Chinese support. Italian foreign minister Amintore Fanfani proposed another alternative—unilateral declarations for the atomic unarmed to remain so for as long as the nuclear club stabilized and decreased its collective stockpiles—but no one was pleased. Fanfani was most likely playing for time.[83] Neither the United States nor West Germany accepted nuclear disarmament as a basic premise, Foster retorted, while Trivedi pointed out that countries like India would not remain without atomic weapons indefinitely without meaningful nuclear-club arms cuts.[84]

Neutral delegations filled the vacuum at the UNGA on November 27. UNGA Resolution 2028 (XX) laid out five cardinal principles for the nonproliferation of nuclear weapons: an agreement would have to be "void of any loop-holes"; "embody an acceptable balance of mutual responsibilities and obligations of the nuclear and non-nuclear Powers"; assure general and complete and, "more particularly, nuclear disarmament"; usher in "acceptable and workable" implementation; and complement nuclear-weapon-free zones (NWFZs). The resolution's easy passage on November 19 attested to the growing assertiveness of nonaligned and neutral states, who were now threatening superpower prerogatives by asserting their anticolonial and national preferences.[85] It also introduced the term *nonproliferation* into the UN record, establishing an enduring link between the nuclear armament of existing possessors and their spread to new countries.

Four days earlier, Glenn Seaborg had passed along to the White House another special Union Carbide report on advanced centrifuges. Its conclusion was unsettling enough that the U.S. government classified the new designs in the face of strong resistance from West Germany. Even without access to restricted data, such blue-chip industrial powers would need about eight years to manufacture enough gas centrifuges to enrich a critical mass of uranium-235 above the 90 percent purity that warheads required. The devil was in the details. The smaller footprint of the new designs would do more than decrease energy consumption. It would render clandestine uranium enrichment virtually undetectable by surveillance satellites.[86]

IV

With nonaligned and neutral states taking the wheel in New York, McGeorge Bundy met Anatoly Dobrynin on November 24 for their "most candid and cordial conversation" to date. They first set about clearing the underbrush. Soviet and Warsaw Pact statements had been erratic and escalatory, first denouncing collective forces, then consultations, and finally existing arrangements. For their part the United States and

NATO had vacillated between collective forces and closer consultations by means of a formalized version of the Special Committee of Defense Ministers, the Nuclear Planning Group, which Bundy had pitched Johnson back in September as offering Germans a "more modest and more practical" role in NATO nuclear defense.[87] Dobrynin vowed that Kosygin and Leonid Brezhnev wanted to halt diffusion across the breadth of Eurasia, not just West Germany. The tsunami of criticism from Beijing, he insisted, should attest to their sincerity. Bundy wrote Johnson to encourage him to accept half the loaf: in the absence of European support, they should "make some money with Moscow if we tell them privately before we sink it publicly."[88]

That same day George Ball cabled Western European embassies to warn that de Gaulle was maneuvering to kill a NATO nuclear force with concessions on European Economic Community (EEC) negotiations, hypothesizing that Erhard and Schröder might opt to confront the French president with a multilateral nuclear force (MLF) as a "fait accompli."[89] Memories of the interwar years haunted Ball. Evoking the Treaty of Versailles, he had warned in October that young Germans, bursting with "a sense of isolation and discrimination, would "turn—as their fathers did—toward a revived German nationalism," whose reappearance would tilt Europeans toward "De Gaulle's vision of a Europe from the Atlantic to the Urals."[90] De Gaulle had invoked the world wars in remarks to Ball ten months earlier, but since then French resistance to an Atlantic armada had toughened.[91] In July, Foreign Minister Maurice Couve de Murville had insisted to Dean Rusk that the West Germans needed to come to terms with their junior role.[92] Henry Kissinger made similar representations to the White House after a European summer tour: he claimed there was little support for the MLF anywhere save Bonn; even there it was "the subject of acrimonious partisan debate." Robert McNamara's Special Committee, by contrast, had been well received.[93]

The West German leadership sensed the winds shifting against them. When he sat down with Johnson in December, Erhard cautioned that Germans would not accept living "forever without a nuclear deterrent." Although Johnson immediately changed the subject to Vietnam, Kissinger had informed Bundy that the German chancellor found Schröder's fixation on the MLF (and Rusk's and Ball's indulgence of it) increasingly tiresome.[94] Sensing this, later that afternoon the German foreign minister took a softer line, confessing that Wilson's Atlantic Nuclear Force (ANF) might suffice after all. New forces were unnecessary, he bartered; what mattered was to have a hand in those that existed already.[95] Just as Schröder came to terms with the ANF, however, the tide in London was turning. Wilson had offered measured praise for the joint air-sea force when he took Erhard's place in the Oval Office the next day only to reverse himself in the face of domestic headwinds and French trouble-making in European Common Market talks.[96] Johnson made one last push, instructing his London ambassador to hold Wilson's "feet to the fire," but the decision had been made—the United Kingdom would not relinquish its veto, whoever the recipient might be.[97] When Wilson wrote Johnson the next month to praise McNamara's committee, collective forces went entirely unmentioned.[98]

Powerful forces in the U.S. Congress shared Wilson's opinion. That summer, Arms Control and Disarmament Agency (ACDA) deputy director and former Capitol Hill staffer Butch Fisher enlisted to the cause Democratic senator John Pastore, a longstanding ally of Johnson's who oversaw U.S. nuclear law and policy as the rotating chair of the Joint Committee on Atomic Energy (JCAE).[99] A few days after the Vietnam War dominated the president's State of the Union address on January 12, 1966—nuclear arms control was mentioned once—Pastore introduced a U.S. Senate resolution on the nonproliferation of nuclear and thermonuclear weapons.[100] In likening the U.S.-Soviet arms race to nonproliferation, he drew an equivalence between arms cuts and nondiffusion. In recalling the 1959 JCAE hearings on the biological and environmental effects of thermonuclear war, he referenced the global commons and generational justice. In aligning the U.S. Senate's treaty prerogative with the ultimate goal of world law, he threw his lot in with the internationalists in the administration. The bill won broad, bipartisan support, with fifty-five co-sponsors sending a clear message: ACDA positions on issues including security assurances and IAEA safeguards now enjoyed a congressional seal of approval.[101] Pastore's closing remarks rang like a shot across the bow: "If peace were to settle on Vietnam with today's sunset, the night would be filled with an even greater danger."[102]

With the U.S. Senate declaiming on "the expansion of the nuclear club," Bundy told Rusk and Ball to get "in line with the President's thinking."[103] Even then, however, it took an eleventh-hour compromise between the White House and the Bureau of European Affairs to confirm that the U.S. president would not relinquish a veto over U.S.-built weapons of mass destruction.[104] While the revised nonacquisition and nondissemination articles had become "a shade more binding," the effect was largely symbolic.[105] According to the French observer, with the British, Italians, and Canadians now also on the same page, West German disarmament minister Swidbert Schnippenkoetter faced "a frightful dilemma": he could go along without concessions on reunification or refuse and find himself isolated.[106] The commercial downsides alone were staggering. After the AEC terminated a cooperation agreement covering fast-breeder reactors and plutonium reprocessing, West Germany's growing nuclear industry faced a huge loss of future global market share, with U.S. manufacturing giants alone set to sign contracts for fifty-eight plants over the next two years.[107]

Expectations were nonetheless tempered with the ENDC set to resume on January 27. Although CIA officials downplayed the odds of a major breakthrough, with U.S. troops flooding into Southeast Asia they deemed "even the agreement to resume talks an accomplishment."[108]

V

The ENDC resumed with a recited dedication from Pope Paul VI inspired by his predecessor Pope John XXIII's *Pacem in Terris* in 1963.[109] In harmonizing human rights, economic development, arms control, and global governance, the encyclical had imagined a world freed from the sins of colonialism. What remained was for those present to appreciate "that true and lasting peace among nations cannot consist in the possession of an equal supply of armaments but only in mutual trust."[110] Trust remained in short supply in Geneva, however, even as plenaries and tête-à-têtes kept lines of communication open. The neutrals looked to sustain what the French styled their "more significant and influential role" since the passage of UN Resolution 2028, while Tsarapkin assured Foster that forward strides were possible despite their differences in Southeast Asia.[111] Foster interpreted his brief liberally, informing the former French ambassador and fresh-minted secretary general of the French Foreign Ministry, Hervé Alphand, that Washington's new flexibility on collective forces was a game-changer.[112]

It was nonetheless Kosygin who seized the initiative in Geneva, where he pledged that the Soviet Union would not use "nuclear weapons against non-nuclear powers, signatories to the treaty, which have no nuclear weapons on their territory," cleverly disqualifying U.S. allies who hosted U.S. atomic forces.[113] The CCP's mouthpiece, the *People's Daily*, railed against breaking bread with Washington while multiple wars of national liberation raged.[114] Nonaligned and neutral delegations, on the other hand, were for the most part enthusiastic. Mexican delegate Juan Manuel Gómez Robledo deemed Kosygin's contribution in "complete concordance" with Nigeria's earlier proposal that the atomic unarmed enjoy immunity "in any circumstances whatever" from atomic means of destruction.[115]

Sensing weakness, the Kremlin instructed Tsarapkin to press the advantage.[116] When he claimed at the Soviet villa on February 14 that there had been "no change in U.S. position," Foster protested that control touched the heart of the matter: the independent power to launch the weapons. No "ingenious definition," the Soviet plenipotentiary shot back, would resolve the issue: consultative bodies and existing arrangements "all amounted to [the] same thing."[117] The plenaries featured moments of levity. When Tsarapkin claimed that within five years German reactors would generate enough plutonium to equip 170 atomic bombs per year, Foster scribbled to ACDA counselor George Bunn that for him to call the presentation a "'Red Herring' would be undiplomatic, although it would be fun. Everyone in this room . . . knows this is ridiculous."[118]

As Foster and Tsarapkin sparred in Geneva, a series of fatal events in South Asia refocused attention on New Delhi. Betty Lall, an American nuclear expert married to India's former representative to the UN, had passed along in October that the Indian government aimed, above all, at "Soviet movement toward the U.S. and away from China."[119] This intelligence was tested by the untimely deaths of India's prime minister and chief scientist. The Treaty of Tashkent formally ended the second Indo-Pakistani War on January 10, 1966, but it exacted a heavy toll. The following night Shastri collapsed and died of an apparent heart attack hours after the farewell reception. Two weeks later, Bhabha perished along with 117 fellow passengers when Air India Flight 101 slammed into Switzerland's Mont Blanc. Among the classified documents discovered years later at the crash site were a military estimate that the PRC nuclear stockpile would grow by twenty-four "heavy atomic bombs" per year and a dispatch from the Indian embassy in Beijing that attributed "a new freedom and flexibility" in Mao's foreign policy to his new-forged atomic shield.[120] The fact that the Indian ambassador to the PRC believed that "national ambitions" rather than ideological dogmatism guided the CCP's hands corroborated Lall.[121]

What did the decapitation of India's nuclear leadership portend? The British assumed that Bhabha's death would quiet the hawks in New Delhi, but his had been a voice of moderation.[122] Lacking "precise instructions," Trivedi, whom the British Foreign and Commonwealth Office considered a "partisan" of the atom bomb, postured in Geneva, castigating Beijing for twice irradiating the Earth's atmosphere while calling to treat "the disease instead of dealing merely with the symptoms."[123] He ended his lecture in the Palais des Nations, the former headquarters of the League of Nations, with a reference to Nehru's speech to the 1933 World Disarmament Conference, when the future Indian prime minister had likened the assembly to "a Moghul emperor . . . who was a drunkard himself but who prohibited drinking throughout his empire."[124] While the Italian representative read the remarks as typifying nonaligned and neutral dissatisfaction, there were in fact fault lines among them.[125] Mexican delegate Manuel Tello Macias had warned Bunn beforehand not to attack Trivedi lest the neutrals "join ranks," promising to "take him on" the following week.[126]

Congressional testimony in the United States from February 23 to March 7 to discuss the Pastore resolution explored the virtues of adding nuclear law enforcement to presidential war-making authorities without fully appraising its costs.[127] Although Rusk granted that further atomic spread would dent U.S. preponderance worldwide or catalyze U.S.-Soviet thermonuclear war, he insisted that the biggest challenges were in "the free world."[128] Foster flew back from Geneva to relate the serious intent that the Soviets had exhibited to finalize a nondiffusion treaty, with Seaborg effectively backing him up that afternoon when he extolled international regulation in comparison to "the marketplace," which tended to yield "the lowest common denominator—no safeguards at all."[129] McNamara's testimony the next week was pivotal. The secretary of defense presented atomic diffusion as the premier global challenge over the next decade or more. The U.S. government needed to dissuade states such as India, West

Germany, and Israel from associating an independent nuclear arsenal with national security or international status. Although he expressed approval for the MLF's original purpose—to bolster the nuclear umbrella over Europe post-*Sputnik*—he maintained that formalized consultations had a higher ceiling if they were to unlock a nonproliferation treaty: "As a nation we sometimes fail to accept small penalties in order to achieve large gains," McNamara cautioned the congresspeople, namely a world in which U.S. armed might remained for the most part undeterred.[130]

The hearings endorsed a presidential duty to contain the nonpeaceful atom worldwide. The Federation of American Scientists, the United World Federalists, the Unitarian Universalist Association, the Friends Committee on National Legislation, and the Council for a Livable World all sang the ensuing congressional resolution's praises. Representative Craig Hosmer, a Democrat from California, encapsulated the paternalistic, moralizing thrust of U.S. nuclear guardianship when he joked that any opponent must be "for sin and against motherhood." Others worried about a boundless commitment to contain atomic threats anywhere. During the hearings Pastore had asked more than once whether a nonproliferation treaty would "place the United States in the role of policing the world."[131] Notwithstanding these misgivings, the vote was nearly unanimous in support, clarifying the potential rewards of a U.S. president assuming responsibility for keeping the nuclear peace around the globe.

VI

The Pastore resolution arrived as the American people settled in for a long war in Vietnam. McNamara's consultative-committee proposal had gained traction in NATO, but Johnson was hesitant to issue the MLF's death warrant. French military withdrawal from NATO integrated command in March 1966 meanwhile unsettled the Atlantic Community, granting multilateral nuclear forces a stay of execution. Johnson remained fixated on the risks. Bundy had the impression that the president was loath to let Robert Kennedy "get out ahead of him." When Rostow replaced Bundy as national security advisor in April, Johnson's distaste at "wringing the German necks" stood out—best not to alienate a keystone ally as EEC talks marched ahead and U.S. troop redeployments drained U.S. diplomatic currency on the continent and gold reserves in Fort Knox, triggering a slow-burning transatlantic crisis.[132]

West Germany was increasingly isolated. During a visit to Moscow that spring, Wilson and Chalfont had failed to persuade Kosygin and Brezhnev to accept enhanced consultations or existing nuclear-sharing arrangements in NATO. When Chalfont briefed the North Atlantic Council (NAC) afterward, he pushed to nix hardware altogether: if West Germany "didn't like it . . . it was just too bad." In Geneva, Italian ambassador Francesco Cavalletti went so far as to accuse the Federal Republic of Germany (FRG) of undermining NATO.[133] With his position evaporating,

Schnippenkoetter inquired whether the French foreign ministry's aloofness hid a readiness to back their West German neighbors.[134] He received a cryptic reply for his trouble. Even Rusk was now asking whether NATO "must finally solve the Alliance nuclear problem before there can be a treaty."[135]

Gathering storm clouds in the Middle East and South Asia combined that summer with superpower rapprochement in global commons to improve the climate for nonproliferation talks. Exploratory meetings at the UN in May to demilitarize outer space and more promising remarks from Moscow on the McNamara Committee intimated that better U.S.-Soviet relations were possible.[136] Afro-Asian matters were prominent when the ENDC resumed in June. At the first plenary, Chalfont underscored how the spread of nuclear weapons was superseding Berlin in international importance while also predicting that over the next twenty-five years the greatest global challenges would emanate not from central Europe but "from the turbulent and seething world of Africa and Asia."[137] An NIE on West Germany reckoned that NATO and the European Communities, which were set to absorb the EEC, the European Coal and Steel Community (ECSC), and Euratom on July 1, 1967, would discourage Bonn from going nuclear lest it play "a lone hand against the world." According to the analysts, only a decision in Tokyo to go nuclear would have the potential impact to shift Bonn's calculus.[138] That May, Gamal Abdel Nasser had promised that the United Arab Republic (UAR) would match Israel reactor for reactor, bomb for bomb, leading Israeli prime minister Levi Eshkol to again pledge to "not be the first to introduce [nuclear weapons] into our region."[139] While State Department intelligence officers believed Washington had substantial leverage over Tel Aviv, it had far less over New Delhi.[140] McNamara intervened with Rusk to stress how indispensable a nonproliferation treaty would be for managing nuclear affairs in these regions.[141]

For all the urgency in the Third World, however, concerns about the U.S. position in Western Europe continued to dictate U.S. positions in Geneva.[142] The White House ordered a fresh look at the Indian nuclear question after China tested a deliverable atomic bomb on May 9.[143] The interagency review that National Security Action Memorandum (NSAM) 351 inaugurated did not finish in time for Foster to make new offers in Geneva or endorse the "dramatic steps" favored by his agency.[144] Yet Rusk was optimistic when the Principals Committee sat down on June 17. Now that the MLF looked dead, Soviet officials walked back their opposition to the Special Committee.[145] Fisher suggested that language barring nuclear-weapon transfers to "any group of states" might paper over the remaining differences save those related to the European option.

The impasse was finally broken by the Vietnam War. U.S. involvement in Southeast Asia had originated in Harry S. Truman's decision to lend support to French colonial authorities rather than the Viet Minh after Paris moved to retake its colonies in the wake of Japan's wartime occupation and eventual takeover.[146] If Truman and Dwight Eisenhower had assumed the burden of anticommunist defense in Southeast Asia, however, it was Kennedy, Johnson, and the liberal anticommunists in their administrations who turned the divided country into a laboratory for how to modernize Asian societies.[147] As military assistance gave way to counterinsurgency, culminating in the Gulf of Tonkin Resolution and the largest U.S. military intervention since the Korean War, the signature U.S. project to halt communism in Asia ushered in a bloody stalemate and a domestic revolt against "Johnson's War."[148]

As antiwar sentiment mounted, White House politicos imagined how a major peace deal would shift the narrative and buoy Johnson's electoral fortunes.[149] National surveys showed that most Americans wanted to sustain or expand the war effort, but Press Secretary Bill Moyers and his assistant, Hayes Redmon, worried that images of military bloodshed and civilian suffering would erode electoral support in Northern and Midwestern suburbs, leading the Democratic Party to hemorrhage seats in forthcoming congressional elections and imperiling Johnson's coveted Great Society. The 1964 Civil Rights Act, the 1965 Voting Rights Act, and the 1965 Immigration and Nationality Act had alienated segregationists and conservatives nationwide—Johnson would need liberals, workers, suburban women, and African Americans to make up the difference in November.

White House officials believed that themes of nuclear guardianship could offer a compelling counternarrative. Moyers's enthusiasm for liberal internationalism sprang from a set of judgments about presidential legacies that he had shared with Johnson ahead of his speech commemorating the twentieth anniversary of the UN in June 1965. First, the supranational organization evoked the New Deal with its legacies for modern liberalism and U.S. leadership in the world. For Johnson to throw in his lot with the UN also associated him with Franklin Roosevelt—his political hero and a popular icon. By the same token, acts of statesmanship weighed more heavily than legislation in presidential legacy-building: "history has a peculiar ability to forget what a President does at home and judges him on the size of his impact on the world beyond his shores." The Second World War had crowned Roosevelt's legacy. Truman was remembered most for "Point IV, the Marshall Plan, the Berlin Blockade, Greece and Turkey, and the Charter at San Francisco. Eisenhower was timid at home and abroad and already history has been harsh on him. Kennedy's legend rests on the pillars of the Cuban missile crisis—turning point in the Cold War—and his identifying America with the poor, colored nations of the world through the Alliance for Progress, the Peace Corps, and his speeches." By this "same irony of judgment," memories of the Great Society would fade over time; for this reason, Johnson ought "to do for the cause of peace in the world" what he had already done "for the cause of civil rights."[150]

Although the Americanization of the Vietnam War had proceeded without UN sanction, the Johnson administration nonetheless defended its military intervention in the language of collective security and international law. After Johnson had deployed 3,500 Marines to Vietnam in March, Moyers handed him a Policy Planning Staff memorandum that explained how to link post-1945 international institutions and the latest ground war in Asia.[151] In San Francisco, Johnson duly made "tackling the hard problems in the developing areas," rather than détente or disarmament, his central touchstone.[152] If peacekeeping was the most urgent problem that the world faced in 1965, his segue to the "clear and present dangers in southeast Asia" implied that U.S. armed forces were the legitimate enforcers of the UN spirit in the Third World.[153]

Moyers had counselled Johnson to ride "the affirmative side of the peace issue" to victory in the 1964 presidential contest. For the young politico, nuclear treaty-making had a magnetic spell on "women and younger voters"—all the more important with baby boomers starting to cast ballots in meaningful numbers. He found support for his thesis in flash polls that Gallup confidentially conducted for the White House. The fact that "American pride in the United Nations" drew support from 59 percent of Alabamans and 78 percent of residents of Jersey City evidenced how a globalist foreign policy could win hearts and minds at home.[154] Volatile support for the Vietnam War, by contrast, illustrated the electoral dangers of a protracted expeditionary war. By the summer of 1966, those Americans polled ranked Vietnam first among issues facing the nation—higher than inflation, tax rates, or racial integration. When Johnson's favorable numbers dipped in June, the slippage was immediately attributed to "the Vietnam situation."[155]

Thwarted bureaucratically by the State Department, nuclear guardians appealed to Johnson's political instincts. Foster hammered the political upsides of "measures contributing to international security and curbing the arms race" when news from Vietnam dominated headlines and newscasts, urging Johnson to make a "clear choice" for a nonproliferation treaty.[156] The Joint Chiefs of Staff (JCS) had also come around, conceding that there was "no current military necessity for additional nuclear-sharing arrangement with NATO allies."[157] The popularity of McNamara's Special Committee also compensated for the lack of a joint or unified NATO nuclear deterrent. Moyers and Redmon repeatedly invoked the Moscow Treaty in their attempts to force the issue. The advice that Fred Dutton gave them (which he also shared with Robert Kennedy) cited similar circumstances in 1963, when declining polls and legislative stasis had occasioned a "serious need for new initiatives." Redmon pointed out to Moyers that "the Non-Proliferation Treaty . . . would precisely fill the bill."[158]

Moyers wrote Johnson on July 17 in hopes of finally achieving a breakthrough. Almost the entire government, including the Pentagon and the U.S. Senate, he pointed out, favored a nonproliferation treaty. Superpower cooperation could postpone nuclear

arsenals in "India, Israel, Japan," or at least "buy time for . . . other political solutions."
From the standpoint of domestic politics, "large and magnanimous Presidential actions that leave a real imprint on the public mood" were priceless, with nonproliferation trailing only peace, anticommunism, and military strength when U.S. citizens
ranked their foreign policy priorities. "Every major poll shows the American people
wanting us to be firm in dealing with the Soviet Union, but that we should continue
to cooperate with them in achieving peace." A treaty would demonstrate Johnson's
"statesmanship," prove he was "not preoccupied with Vietnam," and offer "compelling reasons" to vote for Democrats in November.[159]

The memorandum did the trick. Two days later, Johnson told Rusk "to take another look at our non-proliferation treaty to see if a basis for a compromise with the
Soviets can be found" and Foster to "send him any ideas on this and similar matters
through [Moyers]." The guardians had not vanquished the Europeanists, whose resistance Moyers likened to that of Japanese soldiers holding out in Guam long after
Emperor Hirohito had surrendered.[160] Yet his advice that Johnson treat the European
clause "as a matter for future interpretation or amendment to the Treaty" represented
progress, as did his reminder that "the MLF Club at State and the German Government are not the President of the United States."[161]

VII

The U.S. position evolved rapidly on the eve of the midterms. Ball's resignation in
protest against the Vietnam War in September deprived the "German nuklites" of
their most ardent champion.[162] After Russian ambassador Alexei Roshchin reminded
Foster that alliance transfers were "the heart of the matter," ACDA drew up new language that would bar a NATO collective force.[163] On August 4, a Soviet official in
Geneva mentioned that Gromyko hoped for a breakthrough when he visited New
York once the UNGA resumed in October.[164] A European Union arsenal was so
speculative that it could bear considerable equivocation, to which Bunn's proposal of
a "constructive misunderstanding" to Soviet consul Yuli Vorontsov in early September attested: by issuing separate interpretive statements about the nondissemination
and nonacquisition articles, the two sides could kick the can until Western Europe
federated down the road.[165]

Erhard and Schröder were to confer with Johnson and Rusk in late September
about U.S. troop offsets from central Europe to Vietnam, France's withdrawal from
NATO integrated command, and nuclear matters. Beforehand the U.S. ambassador
in Bonn leveled with FRG foreign secretary Karl Carstens, blaming British coolness
when he revealed that multilateral forces were now fully on the chopping block.[166]
The message had been received: during his White House visit Erhard conceded that
his government was not "expecting a 'hardware solution' any longer."[167]

Erhard's days were numbered anyway. His parliamentary coalition was cracking under the weight of a sputtering economy and his defense of the Americanization of the Vietnam War. A new grand coalition of Kurt Georg Kiesinger's Christian Democrats and Christian Social Unions and Willy Brandt's Social Democrats would emerge victorious on December 1. Kiesinger took the chancellorship. For his part Vice Chancellor Brandt replaced Schröder—who nonetheless survived as defense minister—at the foreign ministry, where Brandt would make cautious steps toward what would become a new policy of *Ostpolitik* once he entered the chancellorship in 1969, when he would look to mend ties with East Germany and Eastern Europe more generally. Although Brandt assured Rusk in December that he was "ready to forget 'hardware' and . . . the European clause," powerful voices in West Germany still railed against a discriminatory settlement.[168] Konrad Adenauer styled it a "death sentence" and a "Morgenthau Plan"—the post-1945 proposal to deindustrialize and dismember Germany—"raised to the power of two." Franz Josef Strauss catastrophized about a "new Versailles of cosmic dimensions."[169] A potential loss of global market share if U.S. nuclear cooperation agreements were to come to an end also loomed as a consideration.

One reason Adenauer and Strauss were uneasy was the greater warmth that high-level U.S.-Soviet talks were exuding that autumn. Three days after UN secretary general U Thant lamented "a new low" in superpower relations at the first plenary on September 19, Rusk, Gromyko, and their respective contingents of arms control advisors and UN ambassadors sat down together a few blocks away at the Waldorf Astoria for the first in a series of conferences.[170] As "the initiative of the meeting," which started late in the evening, had come "from the American side," Gromyko let the U.S. secretary of state speak first. The thrust of Rusk's remarks were that although the increasing viability and intractability of nuclear-weapon programs in the Middle East and Asia demanded expeditious U.S.-Soviet agreement on the nonproliferation language, he and his government were unwilling to alienate West Germany as the price of doing business. His Soviet counterpart was nevertheless adamant that a treaty prohibit them from receiving "nuclear weapons via military blocs and groups of countries" irrespective of "which side has made concessions that allegedly damaged its prestige." The initial face-to-face ended without a breakthrough, although the Soviet party left the conference room satisfied that "the Americans were showing a more lively interest" in a settlement. Rusk and Gromyko tasked Foster and Roshchin with exploring "mutually acceptable language" before they sat down again.[171]

Two days later Rusk's effort not to "rub salt in the wound" of his chief European ally picked up where it had left off. The Soviet memorandum of conversation would record his claim that "firm pushback inside NATO" existed against a nuclear-armed FRG. Although he added that "all bets were off" in the event of a shooting war, "grave memories of the Second World War" that "the British, the French, the Belgians, the Dutch, the Greeks, and other people" shared with Warsaw Pact societies ruled out "the transfer of nuclear weapons to West Germany." He reiterated the illegality of a U.S. president ceding nuclear command and control under the U.S. Atomic Energy Act and their shared interest in preempting atomic challengers in the Middle East and Asia: "It was important and urgent to act now, before the horse escaped the stable; then it would be too late to close the door."[172]

Full agreement remained out of reach, for the moment, as the foreign ministers of the world's two superpowers commiserated at the increasingly numerous and onerous conditions that nonaligned and Indian officials in particular had listed as the price of their acquiescence over the previous year: assurances against nuclear attack, concrete disarmament steps, a fissile-material cutoff. Even though Foster's novel suggestion to ban transfers to "any recipient whatsoever" failed to move Gromyko off his preference, "directly, indirectly, to military alliances or groups of states," which would telegraph the sacrifice of NATO's long-suffering nuclear force, the Soviet foreign minister had demonstrated his reasonableness when he conceded that "the treaty should state that which is to be prohibited rather than that which is to be allowed." When the two sides left the hotel, their positions on the nondissemination and nonacquisition wording were "somewhat narrower." According to Roshchin, his group "had not gotten all it wanted and was not really satisfied," which he attributed to Erhard's impending visit to Washington, D.C., but he was pleased by the sympathy that Foster and U.S. ambassador to the UN Arthur Goldberg had shown for the Soviet position.[173]

The White House pushed for treaty language that might satisfy Soviet officials and the average voter. Although Rusk, Foster, and Rostow agreed at a high-level retreat at Camp David on October 1 that the time had come to lay the "Atlantic solution" to rest, Rusk refused to soften his objections to language that appeared to single out NATO. In the White House, Moyers received word from Spurgeon Keeny Jr. that "morale at ACDA is at an all-time low," with Foster eyeing resignation and Bobby Kennedy positioned to "pick up the issue as a 'club to beat the President with.'"[174] Rusk personally informed Gromyko on October 2 that the United States would cosponsor a Soviet resolution entreating UN members not to hinder nonproliferation treaty talks. The next day Goldberg assured Gromyko that with his visit to the Oval Office approaching, President Johnson was anxious to finish a treaty covering transfers "through the structure of an alliance" even as the Kremlin announced that it would furnish Hanoi with economic and military assistance.[175] On October 4 the *New York Times* reported that former president Eisenhower would not "automatically preclude anything" in waging the Vietnam War.[176] Moyers must have relished the opportunity to contrast Republican brinksmanship with Democratic statesmanship.

With weeks left before the midterm elections, the White House worked to project steely moderation, intensifying combat operations in the unlikely scenario that Hanoi cut off the National Liberation Front (NLF) while intimating troop withdrawals at a meeting with Asian allies in Manila. With McNamara pessimistic about pacifying the Vietnamese countryside or chastening North Vietnam, U.S.-Soviet nuclear talks offered a means of isolating Hanoi and accentuating U.S. global leadership. Johnson took the occasion of an address to the Carnegie Endowment for International Peace on October 8 to underscore the supreme importance of trust, dialogue, and peace-making with the Soviet archrival. His call to build bridges through cultural exchanges, consular facilities, and commerce was low-hanging fruit ripe for domestic consumption while his declaration that nonproliferation should not compromise "effective Western deterrence" lent him flexibility ahead of his meeting with the Soviet foreign minister.[177] Eastern bloc leaders read the speech with curiosity, with Wladyslaw Gomulka and Brezhnev of the opinion that PRC troublemaking in Vietnam had been its chief motivation. Gomulka believed that Johnson was bending "rapprochement" toward two cynical ends: to "show that despite the war in Vietnam, they are able to come to an understanding with the U.S.S.R." and "to all the more pit the Chinese against the U.S.S.R." To extend an open hand would only make strains within the international communist movement worse.[178] The Vietnamese Workers' Party rejection of Brezhnev's calls for "sensible negotiations" inclined him to hear Johnson out, however, and he faulted Gomulka for trivializing nonproliferation negotiations, as nuclear arms races in Asia and the Middle East would weaken Soviet influence by increasing their volatility and the perilousness of their local crises. A U.S.-Soviet-led nuclear condominium, on the other hand, might moderate these adverse trends.[179]

Johnson welcomed Gromyko to the White House on October 10 with a cheerful summons to "get our pencils out and work out an agreement."[180] That night Gromyko, Dobrynin, Rusk, Foster, Thompson, and Harriman tried to put pen to paper. Rusk was frank. Washington would not supply weapons of mass destruction to friend or foe, but NATO members had entrusted their nuclear security to the United States—any reference to alliances raised unwelcome doubts.[181] Final terms remained elusive. Although the White House had strengthened the president's public association with nuclear peacemaking, they chafed at the snail's pace of proceedings. Redmon claimed that the author of the article beneath the *Washington Post* banner headline the next morning, "Impasse on A-Weapons Spread Broken," had attempted "to make history not just report it." He nevertheless prayed that "such headlines may create an atmosphere in which it will be embarrassing not to achieve a treaty."[182] Fedorenko's declaration at the UN on October 20 that a treaty no longer faced "insurmountable difficulties" thanks to "changes for the better" on the U.S. side made the *New York Times* front page. On page three Goldberg was quoted praising a "new and promising situation".[183] Eighteen days later the Democratic Party retained majorities in the U.S. House of Representatives and the U.S. Senate in the face of a resurgent Republican Party, preserving Johnson's legislative agenda for another two years and buoying chances to ratify a nuclear nonproliferation treaty before January 20, 1969.

That December, the Central Committee of the Communist Party of the Soviet Union (CPSU) took stock of trends in Europe and the wider world amid a "struggle for cohesion in the world communist movement."[184] Though heavy on Marxist-Leninist bromides, the report's central thesis was that wars of maneuver in Latin America, Africa, and Asia could not be allowed to jeopardize a war of position in Europe. In recent years Soviet efforts to mold the populous, developing world into its image had suffered numerous reversals while Castro's intervention in Congo-Brazzaville to save President Alphonse Massamba-Débat had revealed a willingness of revolutionary parties to bypass Moscow en route to Latin American and African battlefields. With Mao's PRC ever more convulsed by the Cultural Revolution, Soviet emissaries worked with Italian and Polish counterparts to bring the North Vietnamese behind a negotiated settlement with the United States. They also looked to consolidate their historic gains in Europe since 1941, where de Gaulle's withdrawal from NATO command and warming relations with Italy, Turkey, and Bonn had yielded opportunities to modernize Eastern Europe's creaking industrial base.[185] In framing flexible dealings with Washington as its "great contribution to the preeminent question of keeping the nuclear peace," the Kremlin fused the international and ideological components of a renewed focus on Western Europe. "Start a war in Europe," Brezhnev rumbled, and "it can cover the whole world" in thermonuclear fire.[186] A nonproliferation treaty would internationalize West Germany's non-nuclear status, confirm the peace and antinuclear slogans of European workers' and communist mass parties, and encourage "more realistic positions" from the U.S. government on issues ranging from the Oder-Neisse line to East-West trade.[187]

Brezhnev consented to two minor concessions when the twenty-first UNGA session finished work later that month. Roshchin related that the Kremlin would accept "any recipient whatsoever," which would sink the MLF without rubbing "the Germans' nose in it."[188] On the European option, the two sides agreed to disagree. As a treaty would restrict nothing short of transferring "an ownership interest in nuclear weapons," a European nuclear force would hinge on the extent of political union.[189] This compromise brought the bilateral superpower phase of negotiations to a close. A consolidated deterrent based on limited nuclear-sharing, consultations, training, and transfers in the event of war would continue to shield Western Europe. While British and French arsenals offered insurance if the United States were to abandon the Atlantic community, a peacetime firewall would keep Germans far from the button.

Conclusion

Convinced that nuclear nonproliferation talks would redound to his party's electoral benefit as he increased the U.S. military commitment to Vietnam, Johnson embraced nuclear guardianship abroad with a view to preserving his Great Society at home. British disarmament minister Lord Chalfont declared the European Cold War "irrelevant" in June 1966.[190] Sure enough, the action was swinging to the postcolonial world. The UNGA credentialed four new delegations—Barbados, Lesotho, Botswana, and Guyana—that year, bringing the percentage of members hailing from outside Europe above 70 percent. Positive interactions between Soviet and U.S. officials had become an everyday occurrence. Matters between the nuclear club and the atomic unarmed were less promising. The nonaligned and neutral eight on the ENDC pushed the superpowers to amend their UNGA resolution to better reflect UN Resolution 2028.[191] UNGA Resolution 2153 (XXI) assigned a "high priority" to a nonproliferation treaty, but it failed to stave off a Pakistani amendment for a "conference of non-nuclear-weapon Powers" to happen within eighteen months. If the ENDC did not finish by then, the buck would pass to an international assembly to which no nuclear power would receive an invitation.

The next chapter concerns the Treaty of Tlatelolco, whose opening for signature on February 14, 1967, buoyed hopes that nuclear weapons could be banished from Latin America and the Caribbean. Orchestrated by Mexican undersecretary of foreign affairs Alfonso García Robles, the NWFZ talks illustrated that multilateral nuclear diplomacy was never the preserve of Northern great powers, embodying Latin America's faith in the transnational rule of law and the virtues of common security, affording an alternative model for regional nuclear governance, sustaining momentum in international nuclear diplomacy, and setting decisive precedents for a version of nuclear order that kept faith with the postcolonial world.

"Tall Oaks from Little Acorns"
Making the Treaty of Tlatelolco, 1963–1967

Introduction—A Purer Prohibition?

When Alfonso García Robles put the Treaty for the Prohibition of Nuclear Weapons in Latin America (the Treaty of Tlatelolco) to the Eighteen Nation Committee on Disarmament (ENDC) for approval on February 21, 1967, one week after it opened for signature in Mexico City, he expressed hopes that the treaty had lent "the necessary stimulus . . . to draft a universal treaty to prevent the dissemination of nuclear weapons in any form whatsoever." He took pains to point out that the provisions of the Latin American nuclear-weapon-free zones (NWFZs) were "even more ambitious than those of a non-proliferation treaty," as his region's exemplary negotiations had yielded "the first treaty ever concluded which will guarantee the complete absence of nuclear weapons in a region inhabited by man."[1]

García Robles had guided the Treaty of Tlatelolco through a series of obstacles arising from Latin America's Cold War—overweening U.S. power and John F. Kennedy and Lyndon Johnson's staunch anticommunism, Cuba's revolutionary isolation, and Brazil and Argentina's rising militarism.[2] An outgrowth of Latin American ideals of common security and sovereign equality, the treaty effectively added a new corollary to the Monroe Doctrine that would bar nuclear weapons and threats from most of the Western Hemisphere. It also altered the course of nuclear diplomacy elsewhere, inspiring amendments to a draft nuclear nonproliferation treaty as Cold War disputes about nuclear sharing gave way to sweeping debates about how to balance the scales of justice and technological equity in a new global nuclear order, with momentous bearing on balances of power and patterns of international commerce throughout Latin America, Africa, and Asia.

Mexico's role in the making of the global nuclear order revises narratives of Latin America's Cold War and international diplomacy in the 1960s. As the Western Hemisphere's hegemon, the United States often dictated terms to its southern neighbors.[3] Latin American elites were nonetheless savvy diplomatic operators, exploiting superpower interest in the region's ideological wars to solicit financial aid, arms sales, and counterinsurgency training to fight their own battles.[4] João Goulart's reformist government in Brazil originated the idea of a denuclearization treaty, praising its merits in its effort to mediate between the United States, the Soviet Union, and Cuba during the Cuban Missile Crisis.[5] Kennedy's and Johnson's subsequent benign neglect afforded García Robles leeway, while the region's worsening ideological polarization dogged his bid to spare it another nuclear crisis.[6] Latin Americans knew how to maximize their influence in international forums, influencing proceedings so as to ensure that the global nuclear regime better conformed to their circumstances, priorities, and worldviews.[7]

I

Regional and global nuclear diplomacy were from the start intertwined. In 1965, UN secretary general U Thant expressed hope that Latin American talks would have a "catalytic effect on other initiatives for denuclearization, for nonproliferation, and for other measures of disarmament," a view that those negotiating in Geneva shared.[8] The Cuban Missile Crisis galvanized efforts to govern nuclear science and technology at both levels.[9] There had been proposals for removing nuclear arms from Latin America before, but it was Brazilian foreign minister Afonso Arinos de Melo Franco who, in his role as UN General Assembly (UNGA) representative, raised the idea of freeing Latin America from their menace on September 20, 1962, one month before Kennedy announced that the Soviet Union had shipped atomic forces to Cuba.[10] As the United States, the Soviet Union, and Cuba, along with the rest of Latin America and the wider world, navigated the accelerating crisis, the wholesale denuclearization of the region garnered interest as a way to resolve the many-sided conflict in keeping with postcolonial presumptions of territorial inviolability and sovereign equality.

Latin American denuclearization was the culmination of Brazil's efforts to mediate between the parties to the conflict. Brazilian politics had tacked leftward in 1961 with the election of Goulart, who owed his rise to a coalition of leftists who admired Fidel Castro's revolutionary utterances, and nationalists, who distrusted the United States. Although U.S. suspicions of Goulart's leanings intensified after he sent observers to the 1961 Non-Aligned Conference in Yugoslavia, his flirtations with neutralism, and his refusal, with Mexico, to join the rest of the Organization of American States (OAS) in severing ties with Cuba, strengthened Brazil's regional clout. With its embassy in Havana and the second largest economy in the hemisphere, Rio de

Janeiro became a vital go-between when events in the Caribbean threatened to spiral calamitously out of control.

Pan-American unity was a central element of Kennedy's campaign to isolate and denuclearize Cuba. The OAS emergency resolution on October 23 calling on member states to "take all measures, individually and collectively, including the use of armed force" to deny Cuba threatening military equipment "from the Sino-Soviet powers" lent cover to Kennedy's quarantine while papering over the region's fractious politics.[11] Although Dean Rusk engineered the unanimous vote to present "an image of hemispheric solidarity," according to historian Renata Keller it masked a "variety of Latin American responses"—opportunistic anticommunism on the part of Argentina and Venezuela's military juntas as well as Brazil and Mexico's pleas for constructive dialogue and mediation.[12]

Faced with a close-in standoff that ran the risks of confrontations across the Cold War periphery, if not World War III, Kennedy identified three avenues for reaching out to Moscow and Havana: to Anatoly Dobrynin, via his brother Robert Kennedy; publicly, via U Thant; and to Castro, via Brazil's new military chief, General Albino Silva.[13] Brazilians' divided sympathies led Goulart to seek to internationalize the diplomacy, pitching UN inspections and regional denuclearization to, among others, the United States, the Soviet Union, and Cuba. He thereby aimed to solve many problems at once: to lessen tensions; to raise Brazil's profile with nonaligned states; to neutralize Cuba; and to inoculate Latin America against Cold War tumult. Above all, it would make it easier for Moscow and Havana to capitulate with their honor intact, bringing the crisis to a peaceful end.

The same day as the OAS meeting in Washington, D.C., the Brazilian ambassador there, Robert de Oliveira Campos, made a suggestion to turn Melo Franco's proposal into a formal UNGA resolution after his counterpart in Moscow relayed Soviet vice minister for foreign affairs Frol Kozlov's remark that it was important for the communist powers "to save face."[14] Over and above Brazilian chancellor Hermes Lima's suggestion to García Robles, then Mexico's ambassador in Rio, that Castro invite a UN investigating committee featuring neutral and nonaligned states, regional denuclearization offered a more conciliatory way to manage the crisis and also a prophylactic against future ones.[15] At a moment of extreme uncertainty, Brazil's plan would afford Moscow and Havana an escape hatch by emulating Polish foreign minister Adam Rapacki's 1957 proposal to rid central Europe of nuclear threats.[16]

Washington was at first cautiously supportive, in part to reward Rio's backing of the quarantine and in part because State Department officials saw it as a "bona fide Latin American initiative" and a "face-saver" for an embittered Castro.[17] The Arms Control and Disarmament Agency (ACDA) had already endorsed such zones in Africa and Latin America as long as they entailed regional consensus, international verification, nuclear-power assent, and transit rights, wagering they would go a long way toward nipping future crises in the bud.[18] The Pentagon had different ideas. The Joint Chiefs of Staff (JCS) complained that NWFZ talks could not guarantee the verified removal of the Soviet missiles and might even narrow their military options if push came to shove in the Caribbean.[19]

One day after Kennedy and Nikita Khrushchev's deal on October 28, Brazilian representatives made their denuclearization motion at the UNGA. Delegates went about debating how to turn words into deeds. The resolution enjoined Latin American states to "dispose forthwith of any nuclear weapons or nuclear delivery vehicles which may now be in territory under their jurisdiction" and (with language from the previous year's African NWFZ resolution) implored members "to refrain from using the territory, territorial waters, or air space of African or Latin-American countries for testing, storing, or transporting nuclear weapons or carrying devices."[20] From Brasília, Goulart laid out the merits of the resolution in letters to key neutral and Latin American states, in addition to Kennedy, Khrushchev, Castro, and Yugoslavian president Josip Broz Tito.[21]

Nonaligned attitudes were deemed vital. With Campos and Cuban president Osvaldo Dorticós convinced a U.S. military attack was imminent as early as October 26, Tito had consulted with Latin American and neutral states in hopes of averting bloodshed. That same day Dorticós maintained to Brazil's ambassador in Cuba that his government was "ready to negotiate any solution, including the disarmament, the denuclearization, and the neutralization" of Cuba rather than capitulate to the United States.[22] Dorticós was out of sync with Castro, whose telegram to Khrushchev that night hinted at preemptive nuclear strikes.[23] Venezuela, Chile, the United Arab Republic (UAR), and Ghana, as temporary UN Security Council (UNSC) members, had the standing to advance a resolution, but if a permanent member were to object, Brazil would captain an UNGA push to denuclearize Latin America and Africa, whose inclusion would rally African states resentful of French testing in the Sahara. The Middle East was left out lest suspected nuclear-weapon programs in Israel and the UAR hinder the resolution in support of which otherwise "all of Latin America and the neutral world would combine."[24]

True to form, Canada, Sweden, and Ghana spoke warmly of the proposal in New York, while the reserve of Mexico's representative raised questions about broader Latin American interest.[25] The Brazilian foreign ministry linked the measure with "progressive and controlled disarmament" that would funnel savings toward Third World development and the thesis that a neutral, non-interventionist Cuba could coexist with their noncommunist neighbors under conditions Goulart had enumerated at a OAS conference in Punta del Este that January.[26] These conditions were recapped when Silva outlined a settlement with Castro: in addition to the removal of offensive weapons, Goulart's envoy urged international verification of the missile removal and a halt to revolutionary incitement and subversive acts.[27] While Brazil's terms bore all the hallmarks of nonalignment and promised to handcuff the United States, they also ensured that Latin America's reformist and conservative governments would be shielded from communist sabotage.

The project came undone because of the long-running dispute over Guantánamo Bay's lease in perpetuity to the United States. From the start, Goulart's dual aims of preventing "the spreading of nuclear weapons and the installation of bases" had boded poorly for a negotiated settlement.[28] The reference to military bases implicated Guantánamo, which began life as a U.S. Navy refueling station established after Cuba became a quasi-colonial U.S. protectorate after the 1898 Spanish-American War, and the U.S. military presence worldwide, including atomic stockpiles in Western Europe and Asia—long a fixture of Warsaw Pact disarmament proposals. When Silva met with Castro at Rusk's behest on October 31, the Cuban leader demanded "the evacuation of Guantánamo."[29] Kennedy had steered a middle course on denuclearization once the crisis deescalated, standing firm on Cuban involvement while expressing sincere interest in the general idea.[30] As late as November 14, U.S. officials praised the UNGA resolution to a gathering of Latin American ambassadors at the White House as a "path towards a solution."[31] Yet many of Castro's conditions were nonstarters—the inclusion of Puerto Rico and the Panama Canal Zone, negative security guarantees from all nuclear powers, and an end to "all existing military bases in Latin American territory and Africa belonging to nuclear powers," which according to Cuban foreign minister Raúl Roa "obviously" included Guantánamo.[32] When Brazil's revised resolution excluded Africa and made a few concessions to the United States, Castro held his ground on the return of Guantánamo to Cuban sovereignty.[33]

Cuban threats to abstain eventually undid the draft resolution. Castro was not in a negotiating mood and the Soviet and Warsaw Pact officials were busy placating their frustrated ally.[34] Soviet delegates at the UN were told to coordinate with their Cuban counterparts, transforming the Cuban amendments into an East-West dispute rather than a regional matter.[35] Rusk tried to salvage the plan when Anastas Mikoyan visited Washington in late November, going so far as to concede that a zone might encompass the Panama Canal Zone and Guantánamo—as long as the U.S. Navy could continue to transit nuclear arms through the transoceanic passage. Without Guantánamo's repatriation, however, there was no deal.[36] With the superpowers at loggerheads, Melo Franco grudgingly retracted his resolution without a vote.

This failure notwithstanding, the Brazilian proposal illustrated the attraction and challenges of homegrown nuclear regimes. Moderate governments in Bolivia and Chile emerged as co-sponsors, while reactionary ones in the Dominican Republic, Guatemala, and Venezuela were more critical.[37] Mexican minister of external affairs

Manuel Tello remained noncommittal, despite the affinities at the time between Brazil and Mexico's left-liberal governments. The rise and fall of the Brazilian resolution revealed the tensions between regional security and global equality. Although Argentina's envoy would eventually vote for the resolution even after the Brazilians ditched limits on the transit or storage of nuclear weapons "as a result of strong U.S. objections," he spoke for many in the region when he warned "that a nuclear weapon-free zone could freeze Latin American states into a permanent state of nuclear inferiority."[38]

Nuclear arms control risked awakening long-dormant, non-ideological feuds in Latin America. Brazil and Argentina had been competing in peaceful nuclear science and technology since Brazil, so rich in sources of uranium and thorium, had assembled a national nuclear program in 1947. Argentina had followed suit four years later, when President Juan Perón established the National Nuclear Energy Commission. Although his claims of achieving thermonuclear fusion on Argentina soil proved fallacious, it led Brazilian president Getúlio Vargas and his successors to seek nuclear aid from West Germany and both countries to request Atoms for Peace assistance.[39] The Argentine delegate's broadsides perturbed Melo Franco, who caught "perhaps a glimpse of the intention of that country," which had opened the region's first research reactor four years earlier, "to develop a nuclear potential for non-pacific aims."[40] Brazilian interest in the scheme would ebb as the country drifted rightward following a U.S.-backed military coup in 1964, while many Latin American governments continued to worry more about communist subversion than nuclear diffusion, no matter whose finger ended up on the button.[41] Against this backdrop, leadership of the denuclearization campaign would fall to Mexico, whose Partido Revolucionario Institucional (PRI) was steering a course between leftist and reactionary forces in the region, and whose ambassador in Rio would shoulder the burden of eradicating atomic weaponry from a landmass that stretched from Cape Horn to Baja California and the Caribbean.

II

With his European degrees, his cosmopolitan outlook, and his Mexican identity, García Robles embodied the middle ground of international nuclear diplomacy as Latin American elites won newfound influence amid decolonization.[42] Later in life, he would look back on the Treaty of Tlatelolco as the "most transcendent event" in his six years as Mexico's undersecretary of external affairs, one for which he was awarded the Nobel Peace Prize in 1982.[43] Born in Zamora, Michoacán, in 1911, García Robles had earned a law degree at the Universidad Nacional Autónoma de México in 1934, then postgraduate law degrees from the University of Paris and the Academy of International Law in the Hague, where he was one of two laureates.[44] His first publication, "Pan-Americanism and the Good Neighbor Policy," introduced principles that would guide his life's work—hemispheric solidarity, raw-material sovereignty, the rule of law, and anticolonial internationalism.[45]

García Robles joined the Mexican Secretaría de Relaciones Exteriores (SRE) at its legation in Stockholm after witnessing the outbreak of the Second World War from Sweden. Once in the foreign service, he defended the expropriation of Mexican oil from foreign (mainly U.S.-based) firms in *La Question du Pétrole au Mexique et la Droit International*, souring opinion toward him in the U.S. government for decades.[46] During the war, he was involved in the creation of the UN, attending its founding conferences at Hot Springs, Dumbarton Oaks, and San Francisco as the subdirector of the SRE's General Directorate for Political Affairs, before joining the UN Secretariat as director of the Department of Political Affairs, where he oversaw the UN Special Committee on Palestine from 1946 to 1957, moderated territorial disputes in Indonesia and Kashmir, and directed the UN peacekeeping mission in Suez.

He returned to Mexico City and the foreign ministry in 1957. The NWFZ concept that he encountered after he became Mexico's ambassador to Brazil four years later accorded with his background and worldview in three ways. First, his fifteen years of experience at the nexus of multilateral and supranational diplomacy had prepared him to shepherd it through the new international landscape. Second, it harmonized with his legal training and his endorsement of a Bolivian myth of Latin America as a laboratory for social democracy, constitutional republicanism, and anti-imperialism.[47] He was fond of quoting a maxim popularized by Mexico's nineteenth-century reformer, Supreme Court president, and inaugural president under the 1857 Constitution, Benito Juárez—"among individuals, as among nations, respect for the rights of others is peace."[48] Lastly, to this constellation of ideals he added a familial duty of care to future generations, the preservation of the planetary environment, and a parental sense of responsibility for both. Warnings about the fallout of a thermonuclear war littered his writings, in which he would cite scientific warnings "that the whole Earth might eventually become uninhabitable."[49] He would write that it was the duty of Latin Americans living free of nuclear terror "to strive to make this situation a permanent and immutable one through a multilateral treaty . . . universally respected."[50]

The Second World War also haunted him, as it did many other international reformers of the era. He claimed that his lifelong commitment to nuclear arms control had had its genesis in the eighteen months in Sweden when he had witnessed its bloody course of mass violence: "the Second World War was at its apogee, or very close to its lethal apogee. And, perhaps constantly seeing, day after day, in the press and hearing over the radio, the scathing news of mankind's works in the world—the aerial bombings, the use of cannons and machine guns, the waves of soldiers invading one country or another and the concentration camps—perhaps all of that, gradually and by natural reaction, inspired me to try to contribute in whatever fashion was in

my power so that events such as these would never happen again."[51] He belonged
to a generation of thinkers and doers whose moral imagination had been forged in
the furnace of what Albert Camus called "more than twenty years of insane history,"
culminating in "a world threatened by nuclear destruction."[52]

After Brazil withdrew its UNGA resolution, Mexican officials resolved to breathe
new life into the initiative. Tello and his successor, José Gorostiza, heeded García
Robles's calls to show leadership in regional nuclear affairs, authorizing him to bring
a proposal for a joint declaration for regional denuclearization to the attention of
Goulart's government. He even recruited President Adolfo López Mateos to the cause,
handing Lima a letter in which the Mexican leader praised a "dramatic moment" when
members of the Latin American community of nations would pledge not to "manufacture, receive, store, or test nuclear weapons or devices for launching such weapons."[53]

In April, Mexico, Brazil, Bolivia, Chile, and Ecuador publicly endorsed the measure. Bolivian president Victor Paz Estenssoro dubbed it proof of "the peace-loving
tradition of the peoples of the hemisphere."[54] After Mexico and Brazil circulated the
five-nation declaration at the ENDC, the five Latin American states convened in-
formally to discuss next steps, with six more regional partners joining them months
later to petition the UN for technical assistance. Many issues that the regional talks
raised mirrored those of global schemes: security assurances, economic development,
peaceful nuclear explosives. Others were specific to Latin America: the Cuban question and whether to include dependent territories, foreign military bases, and global
shipping lanes.

In a speech to the UNGA in November, García Robles drew attention to the
advantages of a NWFZ—the "astronomical sums" saved for development, the "incal-
culable benefit" of peaceful nuclear technology, the avoidance of a regional arms race.
The unsettled questions were just as consequential: the zone's geographical scope; the
compliance of overseas nuclear powers; the distinction between peaceful and military
activities; the impact on colonial dependencies; and the best methods of control.[55]
Differences of opinion on these issues eventually gave rise to a diplomatic triangle in
the Western Hemisphere, with the United States, treaty promoters, and treaty spoil-
ers at odds over what form of prohibition would take root in the region and what
precedents it would set for others then being devised in Geneva.

III

In November 1963, Mexico invited all the Latin American states save Cuba and Venezuela to Mexico City, where García Robles identified three benchmarks: strategic
stability, self-determination, and international solidarity.[56] The new Johnson administration was "at best lukewarm." While a U.S. minister in Geneva confirmed that such
zones were welcome "under appropriate circumstances," the Pentagon continued to

worry about shipping atomic munitions through the Caribbean Sea and the Panama Canal.[57] Moreover, revolutionary Cuba remained a bogeyman for anticommunists in Washington and throughout the region. An internal U.S. State Department review would later recount multiple sources of pessimism: "the problems of Cuban participation, freedom of nuclear transit, and opposition by Latin American governments."[58] Rusk instructed U.S. diplomats in the region to point out how a global nonproliferation treaty "would attain the essential objective of a nuclear-free zone . . . and avoid the difficulties."[59]

García Robles's anticolonialism also raised eyebrows among U.S. officials. Embassy officers in Mexico City warned their superiors back in Washington about his "long record critical of U.S. motives," including his defense of oil expropriations and support for a UN resolution affirming non-intervention as a cardinal tenet of international affairs with its implicit censure of U.S. covert operations in Guatemala, Iran, Laos, and Cuba.[60] It was therefore richly ironic when another U.S.-backed military coup d'état, this time in Brazil, unseated Goulart, bringing Marshal Humberto de Alencar Castelo Branco to power and inducing García Robles to return to Mexico City, where he accepted the undersecretary post, the second most powerful job in the Mexican foreign ministry. Nuclear guardians in Washington held more favorable views, seeing the Latin American endeavor as complementary to their own labors. By granting new impetus at the UNGA for the Irish Resolution, ACDA officials believed the enterprise could help resolve deadlocks in Geneva. A November 1964 cable to the U.S. embassy in Mexico City asked that overtures to Latin American governments happen "on an informal basis," however, lest negotiations be compromised by "the impression of U.S. interference or pressure."[61]

The Kennedy and Johnson administrations were courting Mexico as a regional partner for multiple reasons. The PRI offered a successful counterexample to revolutionary Cuba. Mexican diplomats and operatives also maintained contacts with Castro's island that U.S. intelligence officers found useful. Top policy makers in Washington even appreciated Mexico's military restraint, with Rusk judging its government "sincere . . . about disarmament" because it was the only ENDC member then cutting its military budget.[62]

Statements from U.S. officials were therefore consistently accommodating. As early as November 1963, UN ambassador Adlai Stevenson commended a Latin American NWFZ proposal as a "constructive contribution," stressing that the necessary leadership should come from "Latin American states themselves."[63] That month the UNGA endorsed Resolution 1911 (XVIII), which commended the five-power resolution and passed without opposition. The United States and ninety other delegations voted affirmatively, while Cuba and its Warsaw Pact allies abstained on the same grounds as 1962. García Robles took the rostrum afterward to warn that "the very life of present and future generations of Latin Americans" demanded common sacrifice.[64]

The denuclearization push would occur as the Cold War deepened in that part of the world. Cuba's rejection of onsite inspection was a problem for U.S. policy makers. The five Latin American countries behind the joint statement were those that maintained the most contacts with the revolutionary island, yet, after repeated calls, Mexican inquiries about its interest and conditions for participating in negotiations went unheeded. Soviet officials encouraged their Cuban contacts to accept the offer, but Castro was charting a more independent course in foreign policy after the reversals of autumn 1962.[65] A preparatory study undertaken by ACDA delivered a mixed verdict, concluding that a Latin America free of nuclear weapons "without Cuban participation but with on-site inspection" would work assuming that surveillance overflights were to continue. Inclusion of Puerto Rico and the Panama Canal Zone would offer tokens of U.S. good faith. After García Robles invited Latin American UN Permanent Representatives (with the exceptions of Venezuela and Cuba again) to Mexico City for talks, U.S. officials asked how a NWFZ would address hidden weapon caches on the hostile island.[66]

Military coups and political violence were becoming rife in Latin America.[67] Inter-American relations had grown increasingly fraught due to U.S. meddling, beginning with Dwight D. Eisenhower's embrace of covert operations, anticommunist dictators, and foreign interventions such as that against Jacobo Árbenz's red-tinted regime in Guatemala in 1953.[68] In retaliation, leftist and worker's parties in the region forsook popular fronts and met state repression and violence in kind.[69] The Cuban Revolution, the Bay of Pigs, and the CIA operations against Castro in Cuba and Rafael Trujillo in the Dominican Republic sped the centrifuge while Kennedy's Alliance for Progress did little to halt a rising tide of anti-Americanism even as it facilitated military control of Latin American societies and economies.[70] Johnson's support for Goulart's overthrow, including the deployment of U.S. naval assets in a public show of support, brought a military government keen to build up Brazil's atomic infrastructure to power. Johnson's ensuing policy of benign neglect toward the denuclearization talks robbed U.S. diplomats of what leverage they might have had.

The United States and the Soviet Union expressed conditional support for the Latin American effort with one eye on their global ventures. Early in 1964 the Committee on Nuclear Proliferation had advised that whereas U.S. nuclear guarantees were central to U.S. security architectures in Western Europe and East Asia, NWFZs in Latin America or Africa would create a firewall against a U.S.-Soviet War nuclear arms race and, by association, Cold War proxy conflicts.[71] Soviet voices echoed these sentiments with fewer qualifications. Deputy foreign minister Nikolai Fedorenko declared to the UN First Committee his government's readiness to issue joint guarantees shortly after the Cuban Missile Crisis. Foreign minister Andrei Gromyko restated this position on December 7, 1964.[72] China's first nuclear test renewed the impetus for Latin America's denuclearization.[73] Although the Pentagon guarded its ability to transfer nuclear weapons around the world, the U.S. State Department and ACDA publicized a in November 1964 shared concern with Mexico "over the increased danger of proliferation . . . in view of the Chinese Communist test."[74] When the Gilpatric Committee finished its report a few months later, it endorsed NWFZs in Latin America, Africa, and the Levant, recommending for their benefit increased flexibility on transit rights, verification, and security assurances.[75] In his first Senate speech in June 1965, Robert Kennedy reminded his fellow lawmakers that "one of our greatest assets" was that neither Latin American nor Africa were home to nuclear arsenals; he enjoined them and Johnson to back the Mexico City talks "in every possible way."[76]

IV

García Robles associated the happenings in Mexico City with the region's rich tradition of enlightened jurisprudence. The original five-power declaration had appealed to legacies of interstate cooperation and dispute settlement in a region "which had so distinguished itself for its valuable contribution to the development of the great principles of law and justice."[77] While he stressed the global importance of the denuclearization bid, Latin America's exceptional contributions to progressive governance were a touchstone. When he opened the Preliminary Meeting on the Denuclearization of Latin America on November 27, 1964, he called attention to the universal stakes with a reference to John Kennedy's 1961 Sword of Damocles speech: "a nuclear disaster, spread by winds and water and fear, could well engulf the great and the small, the rich and the poor, the committed and the uncommitted alike."[78] Yet he closed the proceedings with Simón Bolívar's words to the Congress of Panama in 1826: "One hundred centuries from now, when posterity traces the origin of our public law back to the treaties that shaped its future . . . it will find the design of our future relations with the world." He ended where Bolívar had 138 years before: "What then will the Isthmus of Corinth be next to that of Panama?"[79]

As its final act the session tasked a preparatory commission to draft a treaty. La Comisión Preparatoria para la Desnuclearización de América Latina (Preparatory Commission for the Denuclearization of Latin America; COPREDAL) would convene in Mexico City four times between March 1965 and February 1967. The gravitational pull of the United States (despite its absence from official negotiations), territorial disputes with extraterritorial nations, and a rivalry between conservative and revolutionary powers in the region shaped the proceedings. Mexico's ambivalence toward its northern neighbor was clear and consequential. The commission picked García Robles as chair in part because the two countries enjoyed close relations; even so, he insisted on few formal ties to the OAS so as to neither ostracize nonmember Cuba nor advantage the North American superpower.[80]

Regional differences manifested themselves through committee assignments, with Brazil and Argentina teaming up against Mexico and its allies. Brazil's delegate, José

Sette Camara, divulged to U.S. listeners how García Robles had been forced to accept an Argentinian proposal to delegate the work to "small working groups located at U.N. headquarters."[81] After Brazil seconded the motion, the load was split among three working groups overseen by a coordinating committee: Group A would chart the zone's geographical boundaries; Group B would draft the verification, inspection, and control articles; and Group C would pressure nuclear club members to comply "in all aspects and consequences."[82] The distribution of labor had ulterior motives. Mexico was in Group B, whose purview was limited to matters in which Washington had less stake. Though Mexican-American relations were historically fraught, Mexico enjoyed a strong bilateral relationship with its northern neighbor in 1965, and Brazil and Argentina had taken note. The delegates took a few concrete steps. Jamaica, Trinidad, and Tobago (British Commonwealth members) received invitations to join them. Mexican foreign minister Antonio Carrillo Flores nevertheless felt obliged to inform the U.S. ambassador in Mexico City, Fulton Freeman, that Brazil and Argentina were conspiring to weaken North American influence.[83]

Rifts between the United States and the two South American heavyweights widened ahead of the second COPREDAL meeting in August 1965. Garcia Robles took advantage of Group B's technical focus to draft the verification and control articles before the other groups had finished work. Among its recommendations was for the International Atomic Energy Agency (IAEA) to manage inspections as a neutral party, which Bill Foster, Butch Fisher, and Glenn Seaborg welcomed as a useful precedent.[84] The commission also resolved the knotty questions of scope: in lieu of a subjective definition based on geography, language, or history, the zone would encompass the territory of any government that ratified the treaty.[85] The sleight-of-hand would deprive individual states of effective vetoes over the zone's entry into force. García Robles then turned his attention to a declaration of principles that would with minor amendments become the treaty's preamble. The fear among U.S. officials that he would endorse non-intervention proved accurate—formal ties to the U.S.-dominated OAS were omitted, while development and disarmament joined nuclear nonproliferation as fundamental principles, introducing a postcolonial balance of obligations that neutrals would inscribe on UNGA Resolution 2028 (XX) that December in New York.

U.S. possessions in the Caribbean were a sensitive issue. Citing the speed with which the British had withdrawn from the Caribbean, Foster relayed to García Robles that his government did not wish the zone to cover its unincorporated territories in the Caribbean—the Virgin Islands and Puerto Rico.[86] This effort to exclude U.S. possessions while demanding that other Latin American actors subject themselves to physical inspections prompted a rejoinder from Brazil's delegate, who refused to lend credence to U.S. claims that these exclusions resulted from constitutional rather than strategic considerations.[87]

The U.S. government eventually warmed to concessions to jump-start flagging global talks. There was also hope that Cuba could be persuaded to join. When Carrillo Flores confessed that his government had dispatched a mission to Havana in October 1965, Rusk was intrigued, confirming that the Panama Canal Zone and Guantánamo were on the table as long as nuclear transit rights remained.[88] More important, he abandoned Cuban participation as a "*sine qua non* condition" for his government.[89] The Pentagon was also coming around; the JCS had deemed such zones in the "overall security interest of the United States" the previous April.[90] An ACDA memorandum summed up the prevailing opinion ahead of the second COPREDAL: outside of Western Europe and East Asia, where NWFZs "might tip the balance to Soviet or Chinese Communist advantage . . . the advantages of these zones in restraining proliferation would outweigh any such disadvantage if we can maintain transit rights."[91] At the Second Special Inter-American Conference weeks later in Mexico City, Rusk praised the NWFZ enterprise as "constructive statesmanship in the best tradition of the hemisphere."[92] On December 10, Foster informed García Robles that his government would not block progress if their criteria for participation, verification, and security were met. The next week, the U.S. government endorsed a UNGA resolution commending Latin American efforts to denuclearize.

Brazilian and Argentinian obstruction were now the largest remaining impediments. Rusk had inquired about the two countries to Carrillo Flores, who characterized them as "unfriendly" following the military coups in both countries.[93] Based on conversations with Argentinian diplomats, he expanded in December 1965 on this thesis to Freeman, who informed Rusk that Mexico's foreign minister had "received clear impression Argentina expected [to] acquire its own nuclear capability within [a] "few years," and thus purchase its way into nuclear club as the "only way to exert its influence internationally on major discussion[s] [of] world affairs."[94] Foster's agency poured cold water on the idea that either South American power would go nuclear so soon.[95] Rusk was correspondingly hesitant to push Rio or Buenos Aires, fearing that overt pressure would backfire by fanning the flames of anti-Americanism in Brazil and "injecting matters in dispute among nuclear powers" in Mexico City. Even after Soviet officials complained that their U.S. counterparts had lost control of Brazil, Rusk held the line at "private and even discreet public support" so as "to avoid the impression of US interference or pressure."[96]

This policy left the United States with little clout in Mexico City, where debates about the legal distinction between "peaceful" and "non-peaceful" nuclear activities were having their first hearings. The COPREDAL assembled on April 19, when Brazil and Colombia advanced a raft of new conditions before a treaty could enter into force: ratification by all Latin American states plus extraterritorial powers, security assurances from all nuclear-weapon states, and full-scope IAEA safeguards on all parties.

Washington was caught flat-footed. A senior White House official marveled that "the Brazilians are pulling the rug out of the [talks] and it looks to me as if ACDA is just sitting there."[97] Spurgeon Keeny Jr. telephoned the State Department's Bureau of Latin American Affairs to lambaste the "hands-off" approach with Argentina, Brazil, and Venezuela threatening the talks "unless something happens—like us putting some pressure on these countries." The officer on duty acknowledged the inaction, leading Keeny to ask, "Do we just wait and say that is where the ball bounces or are we willing to take another look at it?"[98]

Fortunately for the Americans, García Robles averted the crisis with an ingenious workaround that took advantage of the zone's unique scope. The NWFZ would enter into force piecemeal. After each state party signed and ratified the treaty, their government could waive Brazil's conditions, after which point the zone would automatically cover their territories. Without the waiver under article 28, paragraph 2, their territories would remain outside the zone until these conditions were met. The denuclearization treaty would thus cover willing parties whether or not other states signed or ratified, granting potential members latitude to enroll on their own terms. Delegates adopted the resulting set of proposals when the session ended on May 4. With twenty-six articles and two protocols, the draft incorporated sovereign equality, economic development, and non-intervention as key tenets of postcolonial legal theory. Protocol I set out how nations with dependencies in the region could adhere, while Protocol II called on nuclear-weapon states not to defy the zone, abet violators, or "use or threaten to use nuclear weapons" against member states.[99]

Simmering U.S. discomfort with events in Mexico City peaked when the final session started on January 31, 1967, as tensions between the Johnson administration's support for reactionary governments in Latin America and its policy of benign neglect toward denuclearization came out into the open. The Argentinian coup that brought General Juan Carlos Onganía into office in August 1966 and Artur da Costa e Silva's assumption of the Brazilian presidency two months later heightened the collusion between the two military governments. The Brazilians in particular were vocal advocates of peaceful nuclear explosives, which raised questions about from what precisely the zone would be free. Would it prohibit all nuclear devices or only those made for war? Would the engines of nuclear-powered submarines count as weapons? Would there be a separate definition for Plowshare devices? If so, would members states be permitted to manufacture their own or would they have to rely on an international service?[100]

The answers to these questions could set troublesome precedents in Geneva, where Brazilian diplomats had become the main advocates for a sovereign right to manufacture PNEs. In Geneva on December 12, 1966, Brazilian ambassador Sergio Corrêa da Costa expressed his government's opposition to any limits on their development.[101] In Mexico City, Brazil was joined by Argentina, Colombia, and Venezuela in pushing for a narrow definition based on intent, while Chile, Ecuador, Mexico, and most Central American states insisted they were functionally equivalent.

The U.S. State Department could no longer avoid the crosswinds raised by the interplay of regional and global nuclear diplomacy, precipitating a rare dissent from a serving U.S. ambassador. Rusk and Foster wanted to avoid the appearance of interfering in a Latin American project, but they also wanted to nip in the bud any unwelcome precedents for a nonproliferation treaty. As delegates wrestled over the final text over two frenetic weeks in Mexico City, U.S. representatives intervened, circulating an aide-mémoire that affirmed the right to ship nuclear weapons through a future zone, discounted Protocol II, and characterized a treaty that sanctioned PNEs as "illusory."[102] While the U.S. position on transit rights carried the day, there remained misgivings in Washington, D.C., about nonmilitary explosives after references to a nuclear-weapon-state-supplied Plowshare service were nixed, on whose "grace and favor," the U.S. ambassador, Fulton Freeman, reported, the majority had refused to rely.[103]

Fearing that events were getting out of hand, Rusk sent an urgent telegram to Freeman instructing him to impart the message that the U.S. government would wash its hands of a treaty that permitted indigenous manufacture of nuclear explosives. Rather than execute the secretary's orders, however, Freeman logged a protest. Preoccupied by pressing matters in Vietnam and Europe, the United States risked losing what remained of its reputation as a good neighbor among Latin American political elites by raising objections in the eleventh hour: "We have been listened to sympathetically; a significant number of our points are reflected in the Treaty; and what has emerged represents the best possible compromise." To issue demands now that the Preparatory Commission had finalized the treaty "would not only be totally unproductive but deeply resented."[104] Rusk heeded his ambassador's dissenting counsel, averting a rupture with Latin American supporters of nuclear restraint. Although the tortured, compromise language of peaceful versus military technology that made its way into the text would henceforth cause headaches, U.S. diplomats could not afford to anger their counterparts from Brazil or Mexico—both of which seated delegations at the ENDC—let alone the twenty-four Latin American delegations to the UNGA in New York.

The U.S. government endorsed the Treaty for the Prohibition of Nuclear Weapons in Latin America (the Treaty of Tlatelolco) on February 14, 1967, when twenty-one Latin American nations, including Brazil and Argentina, signed the accord. A Cuban signature was conspicuous by its absence. The final text featured numerous preambular declarations, thirty-six articles, and two protocols for foreign powers. With talks in Geneva set to resume, nuclear guardians in Washington were eager to link the Latin American settlement to a nuclear nonproliferation treaty, which they saw as "the only

FIGURE 4 Mexican president Gustavo Díaz Ordáz (left), Ambassador Alfonso García Robles (center), and Mexican foreign minister Antonio Carrillo Flores attend the signing ceremony for the Treaty for the Prohibition of Nuclear Weapons in Latin America at the Secretaría de Relaciones Exteriores de Mexico in Tlatelolco, Mexico City.
Source: Secretaría de Relaciones Exteriores de Mexico, photographic archive, Mexico City, Mexico.

foreseeable chance to achieve comprehensive worldwide safeguards."[105] Following his change of heart, Rusk praised the Treaty of Tlatelolco as "a milestone on the road to general and complete disarmament and . . . the conclusion of a worldwide treaty prohibiting the proliferation of nuclear weapons."[106] Officials in ACDA nonetheless warned that Protocol II might prevent Mexican and, in turn, Latin American support from materializing in Geneva and New York.

V

The Latin American triumph rerouted the course of nuclear diplomacy worldwide. Mexican officials leaned on the nuclear powers to sign Protocol II in exchange for their support—and also that of their Latin American neighbors—in Geneva and New York. Mexico's seat on the ENDC allowed it to push for new language in a global nonproliferation treaty that would better reflect the interest of states in Latin America, Africa, Asia, and the Middle East. The presence of Brazilian officials in Geneva placed formidable sceptics athwart world nuclear law-making. Argentinian and Venezuelan diplomats would join them in New York to proselytize on behalf of writing into the global accord the narrow definition of nuclear weapons in the Treaty of Tlatelolco.

Because the Latin American vote in the UNGA was so sizable, the United States, the Soviet Union, and the United Kingdom could afford neither to ignore nor to deny altogether their requests.

The clash over PNEs exemplified the uneven line between peaceful and military activities. The U.S. Atomic Energy Commission (AEC) had promoted the economic benefits of nuclear earthmoving since Eisenhower's Atoms for Peace, establishing Project Plowshare in 1957 to explore the use of atomic energy for blasting harbors, liberating shale gas, and slicing a new canal through the Isthmus of Panama.[107] As Seaborg liked to point out, only the United States manufactured the "clean" thermonuclear explosives best suited for such monumental acts of civil engineering.[108] Since the Treaty of Tlatelolco outlawed "nuclear weapons" and not "nuclear explosives," many feared it had opened up a loophole through which a state could walk to the threshold of an independent atomic arsenal.[109] Whether a global nuclear charter would prohibit "nuclear devices of any kind," or only those expressly built for war, remained an open and momentous question.[110]

For a year after the Treaty of Tlatelolco opened for signature, Mexican and U.S. officials jockeyed over Protocol II. On their end, Fisher and Foster sponsored a broad definition of nuclear weapons in exchange for U.S. compliance with the zone.[111] García Robles countered that nuclear powers would need to sign on before Latin Americans would consider voting for a nuclear nonproliferation treaty.[112] When Foster and Fisher ordered an interagency analysis of the matter in the fall of 1967, it called for an interpretive statement to accompany any signature that would detail transit rights and affirm U.S. claims to the Virgin Islands and Puerto Rico.[113] Foster advised Rusk and Johnson to wait until more Latin American states had entered the legal zone before signing; that was, "unless other circumstances arise, such as the necessity of obtaining support for the NPT."[114] When Mexican president Gustavo Díaz Ordaz traveled to Washington in October 1967, Johnson informed him that a signature would be forthcoming after his team consulted with the U.S. Senate. With nonproliferation talks soon to move from Geneva to New York, his negotiators needed the Latin American vote in their pocket.

The Treaty of Tlatelolco emerged in Geneva as a template for reconciling nuclear development and disarmament with nondiffusion. U.S.-Soviet agreement on the critical nondissemination and nonacquisition articles shifted focus from atomic alliances to more all-encompassing matters: peaceful atomic energy, security guarantees, and arms control. The superpowers had saluted references to the IAEA in the Treaty of Tlatelolco. While Soviet representatives had ridiculed verification before the conclusion of the Moscow Treaty, they sounded "more Catholic than the Pope" now that West Germany and Japan were on the hook.[115] When Alexei Roshchin and Foster had jointly presented the first two articles to the ENDC on February 21, Roshchin stalked the corridors calling for each non-nuclear-weapon state to "accept IAEA safeguards on all its peaceful nuclear activities as soon as practicable."[116]

The atomic unarmed were increasingly vocal about exactly which form of treaty they would abide. In August 1967, Rostow briefed Johnson that "the game" would now "move to the non-nuclear powers" in Geneva, most significantly the Latin American, Asian, African, and Middle Eastern delegations—Brazil, Burma, Ethiopia, India, Mexico, Nigeria, Sweden, and the UAR—which the French observer described as the nonaligned and neutral camps' "first responders."[117] A process that had survived the Germans and the Italians now faced a "free-for-all."[118] The superpowers reviewed the Latin American example to find their way through the scrum. Their co-chairmen proposed a joint draft treaty on August 24. While for the moment they left Article III covering safeguards intentionally blank, a new Article IV spelled out signatories' "inalienable right" to develop "research, production and use of nuclear energy for peaceful purposes" as well as international exchanges of relevant information, research, and technology. The information sent to U.S. embassies explained that the language "was originally derived from the Treaty of Tlatelolco," which recognized an international right to "nuclear energy for peaceful purposes, in particular for their economic development and social progress."[119] Nuclear technology's association with societal revolution and the notion that its blessings should redound to the benefit of all hinted at a sovereign right to the fruits of technological advancement. It would become a bone of contention in ensuing decades as signatories would demand access to such sensitive technologies as uranium enrichment or plutonium reprocessing that could dramatically shorten their route to atomic weaponry.[120]

Emboldened by their achievement at home, Mexico's representative outlined three more articles that collectively aimed to level the playing field further. With U.S.-Soviet differences mostly resolved by the fall of 1967, neutral and nonaligned delegates had started to push for various amendments related to safeguards, technical assistance, peaceful explosives, treaty loopholes, security assurances, and disarmament progress. Jorge Castañeda's presentation on September 19 would have the biggest impact, resulting in major revisions to the peaceful uses of atomic energy language in Article IV along with three new articles. Castañeda advanced two revisions to Article IV. First, above and beyond a basic recognition of an "inalienable right," advanced nuclear powers were to accept a positive duty to supply the atomic unarmed with technical assistance. If some were to renounce certain scientific and technological activities, it was incumbent on privileged states to make up the difference. This extended to peaceful nuclear explosives. Although "nothing other than nuclear bombs," these devices held "enormous economic potential . . . in the execution of vast engineering projects." A new Article V should call for the expeditious establishment of an international service to provide them cheaply and reliably.[121] Next, a statement in the preamble that the nonproliferation treaty would not hinder the formation of NWFZs would become part of the operative body, namely Article VII of the draft Treaty for the Non-Proliferation of Nuclear Weapons.

Last, Castañeda sought stronger arms control and disarmament obligations for the nuclear club in line with the emergent consensus among nonaligned and neutral members of the ENDC. While he admitted that without sanctions "it would be an imperfect obligation," he maintained that "it would be more than a statement of intention." A preambular sentence enjoining nuclear-weapon states party "to pursue negotiations in good faith for nuclear arms control and disarmament as well as general and complete disarmament" would also move down to the body, transforming an expression of principle into a legal requirement.[122] The phrase "with all speed and perseverance" elaborated on the meaning of "good faith." Alva Myrdal likened the formula to a "promissory note"—a liability whose breach could void a contract.[123]

Egypt, India, Burma, Sweden, Brazil, and Romania all threw their support behind the Mexican amendments. The Indian and Brazilian representatives went further, demanding measures to combat "vertical proliferation"—the increase and perfection of existing arsenals—such as a comprehensive test ban or a fissile-material cutoff treaty.[124] Foster and Roshchin's failure to reach consensus on Article III had also allowed Myrdal to submit a Swedish version that would impose IAEA safeguards on nuclear-material transfers whether or not importers or exporters joined the treaty. She even envisioned their eventual extension to the nonmilitary nuclear activities of the nuclear club. The superpowers consequently faced a broad-based effort to embed technical assistance, universal safeguards, and disarmament duties in a treaty. Even Japan, which had so far kept its distance, weighed in, with Foreign Minister Takeo Miki stating on September 22 that conferences of states parties should convene to review the treaty's founding bargain every five years.[125]

The fact that the most popular amendments had originated with a Latin American state was significant. While U.S. officials looked askance at arms control obligations, they viewed the regional bloc as a vital ally in the UNGA, where delegations from developing nations now numerically dominated. Just one month earlier, Latin American delegates had exerted a moderating influence on an UNGA resolution bearing on the aftermath of the Six-Day War between Syria, Egypt, Jordan, Palestinian groups, and Israel in June, moving Arthur Goldberg to tell Johnson and his cabinet that "the more Latin Americans countries can be involved in world affairs, the better."[126] This was all the more true after every Arab country save Jordan severed relations with Washington after Johnson leaned toward Israel after the shooting stopped.[127] The Treaty of Tlatelolco's two protocols would be key. Latin American states "will be observing US action on these protocols closely," Rusk reminded Johnson, "as an indication of support" for the NWFZ "and arms control measures generally."[128]

Mexican representatives were sensitive to U.S. reservations about Protocol I, which bore on U.S. legal claims to the Virgin Islands and Puerto Rico, but Protocol II was another matter: the Soviet Union and France had made it known that they would adhere once the United States had. Back in May the Latin American Bureau of the CPSU's Central Committee's International Department had criticized the Treaty of Tlatelolco's failure to "address the demands put forward by the USSR and Cuba," namely the inclusion of all U.S. dependencies in the Caribbean and central America, the "liquidation of US naval base on Guantánamo . . . and other US military bases in [Latin America]."[129] Soviet and French reticence notwithstanding, Rusk warned Johnson that Mexico would resist signing the treaty unless the nuclear club played ball. After the United Kingdom broke the deadlock by signing Protocol II in 1967, García Robles redoubled his efforts, informing Fisher that Soviet officials had told him that they would follow Johnson's lead and that Cuba might even make a late entry into the zone. He emphasized "the salutary effect" that a U.S. signature would have on Latin America support when it came time to finalize a nuclear nonproliferation treaty.[130]

Conclusion

Thanks to the Treaty of Tlatelolco and the UNGA's tilt from the Industrial North to the Global South, Latin American delegations emerged as leading nuclear diplomats in 1967. Mexico in particular would leave lasting marks on global nuclear law. Its interventions in Geneva and New York, both during and after its campaign to create a Latin American NWFZ, transformed the international nonproliferation regime from a superpower compact into a postcolonial settlement by, however partially, accommodating the interests of those dreaming of sovereign equality in the Global South.[131] After the Treaty of Tlatelolco had opened for signature, the superpowers acquiesced to new articles and preambular statements in the NPT that offset the rights lost by non-nuclear-weapon states with compensatory licenses and duties. Nuclear exporters were asked to facilitate transfers of peaceful nuclear information, materials, and equipment; supply peaceful nuclear explosives (PNEs); respect NWFZs; and commit to curbing the arms race and making strides toward disarmament. The Treaty of Tlatelolco's pivotal influence revealed how middle and small powers contributed to ordering the nuclear world in the 1960s. It also confirmed that the addition of technical assistance and disarmament pledges to the treaty's "grand bargain" was pivotal.[132] Although U.S.-Soviet cooperation would be vital for the NPT to open for signature, not just the legitimacy but the viability of a global nuclear regime would rise or fall on a basis of political support that only the UN system could provide.

"A Citadel of Learning"
Building an International Community, 1966–1968

Introduction—We'll Always Have Geneva

It was a hallmark moment. Lawyers from the United States and the Soviet Union put the finishing touches on a joint nuclear nonproliferation treaty. Its submission to the Eighteen Nation Committee on Disarmament (ENDC) now awaited Moscow's final say-so, which arrived late during the night of January 17, 1968, six hours ahead of Eastern Standard Time. Butch Fisher leapt into action in Geneva. With President Lyndon Johnson set to deliver the State of the Union address in Washington, D.C., that evening, Fisher rushed to the U.S. embassy to send a cable about the break-through before the joint session in the U.S. House of Representatives got under way. On the way there, his car broke down in the snow, delaying his wire. Years later he would recall how a Russian deputy in a car trailing his had exited the Soviet govern-ment vehicle, walked over, and offered him a lift: "Now, look, you fellows got to get a telegram out. You can't afford to waste your time pushing a car."[1]

The international community was on the brink of a final nonproliferation treaty on January 18, 1968. With the question of NATO nuclear-sharing resolved, the fate of East-West atomic coexistence hung on a safeguard controversy, while North-South differences ran along lines of security, development, and disarmament. The central task in Geneva was to forge consensus around a fair and effective agreement. Superpower delegates nevertheless struggled to harmonize European Atomic Energy Community (Euratom) safeguards with those of the International Atomic Energy Agency (IAEA). West Germany and Italy resisted Euratom's integration into the IAEA inspectorate on commercial and political grounds, giving rise in central Europe to charges of

U.S.-Soviet complicity.[2] Among Afro-Asian nation-states, New Delhi asked nuclear club members to extend atomic guarantees to the nonaligned world, only for the United States to decline lest it overextend itself militarily as U.S. armed forces waged war in Vietnam. In the Middle East, the Six-Day War underscored how an atomic spark could set the region alight, occasioning a summit between Lyndon Johnson and Soviet premier Alexei Kosygin in Glassboro, New Jersey, to improve their relations and press forward on nuclear arms control and nonproliferation.

It would fall to the community of negotiators in Geneva to resolve the safeguards dispute. Goodwill in the Swiss Alps made possible searching midlevel explorations whose results would include a practical solution to the safeguards controversy, prying open a window for U.S.-Soviet détente through the global regulation of atomic energy. Thanks to their efforts, Soviet and U.S. delegations would propose identical treaty drafts—with the safeguards language in Article III studiously left blank—on August 24, 1967. After six years, a new act began in the search for a global nuclear nonproliferation treaty, with nonaligned and neutral views now center stage.

I

The Treaty of Tlatelolco strengthened Latin American hands in Geneva and New York. Brazil and Argentina waited to sign the Treaty of Tlatelolco until May and September 1967, respectively, as an implicit defense of peaceful nuclear explosives.[3] (Brazil would ratify the treaty in January 1968, but without waiving the requirements for national entry into force under article 28, paragraph 2, while Argentina and Chile would defer until 1994.) The complete zone, including Brazil and Cuba, would achieve the universal membership of all thirty-three states and thus full entry into force when Fidel Castro's government ratified it on October 23, 2002.

The meaning of peaceful atomic energy differed from place to place. Net technology importers such as Mexico, Brazil, South Africa, and India, many with sizable uranium or thorium deposits, held out for maximum rights and foreign aid to reduce their dependence on northern exporters. For them, the issue of peaceful nuclear explosives and the expansion of Atoms for Peace were of utmost importance. Exporters such as West Germany, Canada, Switzerland, and Japan, on the other hand, worked to protect their atomic-energy sectors from unfair competition or burdensome regulation. To complicate matters further, the Netherlands, Belgium, Luxembourg, Italy, West Germany, and France belonged to Euratom, which already administered safeguards on their interdependent nuclear industries. Warsaw Pact powers were loath to let Western European countries inspect themselves, while France's inclusion gave rise to unique issues: How could Euratom safeguard its nonmilitary nuclear enterprises, according to European officials, so that Paris did not "enjoy an export advantage" over its neighbors and dominate the field "in sales to countries not signatory to the NPT."[4]

Superpower relations were marked by both public vitriol and private inroads in 1967. Although Kosygin took the opportunity of the Outer Space Treaty's signing ceremony on January 26 to berate the returning U.S. ambassador to the Soviet Union, Llewellyn Thompson, who had previously served in Moscow from 1957 to 1962, the demise of the multilateral nuclear force (MLF) afforded grounds for optimism even as the Vietnam War raged.[5] Walt Rostow nevertheless related his doubts to Anatoly Dobrynin the next day that lesser nations would "sign a non-proliferation agreement if they saw the United States and the Soviet Union entering another major round in the arms race."[6] By the time Dobrynin met Robert McNamara in April to discuss arms control and European affairs, the defense secretary assured him that U.S. allies in Western Europe, excluding France, would back a treaty once a few clarifications were issued about NATO's nuclear defense.[7]

When Butch Fisher spoke to the Notre Dame American Assembly on March 16, 1967, he asked rhetorically whether the status quo would "continue to prevent the Federal Republic of Germany (FRG)," Europe's most populous nation and a major exporter of advance technology, "from seeking its own national nuclear defense." However unlikely, he warned that German weapons of mass nuclear destruction would trigger "an international crisis which would make the ten days preceding October 27, 1962, look like ten relaxed days indeed."[8]

German nationalism and the Cuban Missile Crisis were a compelling combination to bring sympathetic, internationalist audiences around to the idea of global nuclear governance. Bonn's priorities were in the process of shifting. While fears of an atomic Fourth Reich were shared across the Iron Curtain, continental integration shaped elite European attitudes on global nuclear governance to an increasing degree. Two questions stood out. How would Euratom safeguards synchronize with those of the IAEA? Would a treaty recognize a European federation as a *de jure* nuclear power—an atomic confederacy—if the United Kingdom or France were to bequeath its nuclear arsenal to a unified European state?[9] The joint U.S.-Soviet draft treaty barred nuclear-weapon states from transferring "an ownership interest in nuclear weapons." If Western European countries were to federalize, the resulting superstate could inherit the British and French arsenals, although the Warsaw Pact had made its opposition to this scenario abundantly clear. Bill Foster clarified for West German officials—the Soviets had "agreed that those things which were not prohibited were permitted," but if the European options were "written in large neon lights, there would be no treaty."[10]

The West German coalition government was less interested in becoming an atomic deputy than in the balance sheets of Siemens and Allgemeine Elektricitäts-Gesse-llschaft AG (AEG), the industrial conglomerates that would merge their atomic-energy divisions into a joint subsidiary—Die Kraftwerk AG—in April 1969. After two decades of unfulfilled promises, worldwide reactor sales were booming in 1967. That year the IAEA reported reactor orders that could generate 23,000 megawatts of electricity per day—triple the fleet of nuclear power plants then in operation worldwide.[11] Representatives of the nuclear industry claimed that these would cost less than coal-fired competitors, leaving aside accident liability, capital subsidies, research and development, mining and enrichment, and waste management, whose bills national governments often footed. In February Willy Brandt informed the Bundestag that protecting domestic businesses in the face of new global regulations was for him "a decisive question."[12]

The IAEA was the most logical regulator. Although the Vienna-based agency would suffer from a dual identity as both the promoter and watchdog of atomic energy worldwide, it had proved a fruitful forum for dialogue and cooperation among Western, Eastern, and neutral and nonaligned states.[13] In Washington, D.C., Glenn Seaborg was such a vocal champion of the international agency that Dean Rusk took to calling the nonproliferation pact "Seaborg's treaty" after the Atomic Energy Commission (AEC) chairman nixed State Department language that would have had the IAEA and Euratom treated as equals.[14] Seaborg was in good company—most states preferred a centralized, universal system rather than a patchwork of jurisdictions. And while the Soviets supported peaceful technologies aside from peaceful nuclear explosions (PNEs)—a major concession in light of the advanced research and development in uranium enrichment and plutonium reprocessing in Western Europe—they insisted that the IAEA handle safeguards.[15] As ways of softening the blow, Foster advocated an early transition period and a focus on the flow of fissile materials rather than forensic investigations of nuclear facilities.[16]

Japanese commercial interests resembled West Germany's. West German nuclear investments doubled in 1967; as West European and Japanese industrialists looked to capture market share, the Bretton Woods system buoyed the dollar's exchange value, making U.S. exports expensive compared to foreign firms. Even so, West Germany was not alone in relying on U.S.-sourced enriched uranium.[17] In separate conversations, Brandt and a low-level German diplomat passed along that General Electric was raising doubts in the minds of Spanish industrialists that Siemens or AEG could guarantee future supplies of enriched uranium, raising "the specter of potential unfair competition."[18] International inspections also raised questions of industrial espionage. West German officials told Fisher that they feared spying from an "inspector named Ivanovich" or "a fellow named Johnson." Foster and Seaborg's solution was to open civilian nuclear facilities in the United States to the IAEA. Neither Westinghouse nor General Electric was adamantly opposed, while London and Ottawa were both supportive.[19] The White House authorized Rusk and Foster to broach the subject at North Atlantic Council meetings that April.[20]

The nonproliferation treaty was deepening rifts in Bonn, leading U.S. diplomats to warn that the treaty could blow up Kurt Georg Kiesinger's coalition.[21] The joint superpower draft treaty had left Franz Josef Strauss apoplectic, and the arrival of a critical aide-mémoire from Bonn on February 4, 1967, weeks after Kiesinger's cabinet had agreed "in principle" to back a treaty and days before Brandt arrived in Washington, D.C., had been greeted as a conservative end run.[22] According to London newspapers, the West German financial minister had cornered Harold Wilson and George Brown in the German capital, where he lambasted the treaty as a "rape," a "diktat," and "a new Versailles."[23] Kiesinger himself lamented superpower "complicity" at a press conference on February 27, railing against a treaty that would have his government "enter into a binding agreement with its major adversary, limiting even further its capabilities in the nuclear field." Kiesinger claimed to John McCloy that his remarks had been made "smilingly," but it was unclear whether West German diplomats took their cues from him or from the foreign minister.[24] Just ten days earlier in the Bundestag, Brandt had decried treaty opponents for "exaggerated polemics."[25] Yet rumors swirled that Swidbert Schnippenkoetter was being sent to Washington "to prevent the NPT."[26] Johnson could only reassure Kiesinger in a letter on March 11 that he would "work out formulas which the Federal Republic and our other Allies will find acceptable."[27] The inaugural meeting of the NATO Nuclear Planning Group in early April at least offered a release valve for German resentments about their lack of nuclear prerogatives.

The transatlantic controversy paralleled a European one that Britain's second application to the EEC had set off.[28] When Canadian officials asked Maurice Couve de Murville in February to reengage in Geneva, the French foreign minister had defended anew the French "attitude of abstention."[29] While his diplomats remained aloof, Charles de Gaulle positioned French industry and agriculture to profit from European integration without losing clout in European or international councils. Wilson's decision to reapply to the EEC had sprung from the economic and political shocks of the previous year: the sterling crisis and French withdrawal from unified NATO command. To join the common market would boost the British economy and bridge the Atlantic Alliance and the future European Communities by way of the special relationship. The issue divided the six members of what would shortly become the European Communities on July 1, when the European Merger Treaty would enter into force, combining the EEC, the European Coal and Steel Community, and Euratom into one administrative body with a single commission and council. The melding of Euratom and IAEA safeguards also required France's signoff, effectively handing de Gaulle a wrench to throw in the works of nonproliferation diplomacy in addition to European integration, where he would once more veto new members on September 13.[30] He had already sacked Euratom president Étienne Hirsch in 1962 for circumventing the French veto to expand research and development related to advanced centrifuges and breeder reactors.[31] Bonn and Rome were happy for Paris to play the foil, while Brussels, Luxembourg, and Amsterdam viewed IAEA primacy as a price worth paying to keep their bigger neighbors out of the nuclear club, especially if Euratom retained freedom of maneuver as one institutional element in a worldwide regime.[32]

France was less eager for U.S.-Soviet détente than the rest of Western Europe. The previous November, de Gaulle had enlightened Couve de Murville as to why he "thought it unwise to be dragged into joining" any kind of nonproliferation treaty. Not only was it superfluous, in common with the Moscow Treaty it had "no other real purpose and can have no other result than to uphold the unacceptable Russian and American monopoly." In any event, it would "stand in the way of real nuclear disarmament. Why get caught up with this," the French president sermonized, "who thinks that we would 'give' the atomic bomb to anyone?"[33]

It was nonetheless an open question whether de Gaulle's personal reservations would override his country's national interest. After all, the treaty would internationalize West Germany's commitment under the 1954 Paris Accords not to produce atomic, biological, or chemical weapons. And while de Gaulle held a dismal opinion of the UN General Assembly (UNGA), the UN Security Council (UNSC) was another matter. By sanctifying the atomic forces of current and future members the NPT would ensure that the nuclear club remained exclusive, crowning de Gaulle's quest to return France to the highest ranks of international society.

Senior French policy makers pleaded with the Élysée Palace to, at a minimum, not actively sabotage the treaty. Commissariat á l'Énergie Atomique (CEA) high commissioner Francis Perrin warned Couve de Murville in February 1967 that "India, Israel, Japan, Sweden, and West Germany, despite the Paris Accords and EURATOM," would soon be able to fabricate nuclear weapons, and invoked the threat of a "giant, hostile China" to rebut the claim that proliferation would hasten abolition. The U.S. monopoly on free-world fissile materials and the opportunity to handicap West German industry constituted the main sticks and carrots. "It is important for French nuclear development that there is no organized, public hostility to the treaty, that the government avoid denigrating it, and above all that it encourage countries, such as Germany, who hesitate to sign." It was not just economically that West Germany worried Perrin. The specter of German militarism loomed large enough that he had gamed out why Kosygin's proposal to spare non-nuclear states party from nuclear threats would not necessarily stop France from beating back a conventional future German blitzkrieg with nuclear strikes, even in the event that the United States were to threaten atomic retaliation on West Germany's behalf.[34]

European integration also drew attention to the likelihood of a nuclear-armed United States of Europe. The Soviet Union strongly opposed a future European Union over which West Germany would potentially tower. U.S. officials denied that a non-proliferation treaty had any bearing on European federation; legally, they claimed, it "would not bar succession by a new federated European state to the nuclear status of one of its former components." It was a long-held tenet of international law that sovereigns seamlessly inherited the rights, duties, and properties of their predecessors. If Western Europe were ever to establish a central government responsible for foreign and defense policy, that succession doctrine would theoretically apply.[35] Eastern Europeans were unimpressed, as were West Germans and Italians, whose officials complained that they "had been sold down the river on this point." Even though the European option was "left open," they pointed out, "all possible way stations" had been "effectively boarded up."[36] Rusk therefore drew the line at publicizing this legal opinion lest he embolden opponents, leaving the European clause hanging over proceedings that summer—a final relic of the impasse over nuclear sharing.[37]

II

That spring U.S. NATO allies pressed their U.S. partners in Geneva to meet halfway neutral members hungry for developmental aid and suspicious of legal discrimination. Lord Chalfont underlined the "need for means of redress" if the nuclear powers were to fail at arms control.[38] His Italian colleague maintained that effectiveness and equity were interdependent: a nonproliferation treaty should never establish "a perpetual discrimination between two classes of countries." He referred to Frank Aiken's recent remarks that the treaty should be a starting point for moderating and reversing the nuclear arms race en route to total abolition.[39] Canadian lieutenant general Tommy Burns acknowledged that it was natural and reasonable for the atomic unarmed to condition their adherence on "a clear and compelling declaration" that the treaty would not eternalize the international community's division into the quick and the damned.[40]

Senior U.S. officials worried less about European sentiments than about instability in Latin America, Africa, the Middle East, and, above all, Asia, as U.S. armed forces poured into South Vietnam. McNamara was clear on this point, while Fisher explained to Georg von Lilienfeld, the director of the U.S. division of the West German foreign office, that they were "not concerned that the dam holding back proliferation would break in Europe but that it would happen elsewhere in the world."[41] The United States lacked data about the nuclear intentions of India and other non-European powers.[42] Even as Johnson continued to woo Pakistan, the Senior Interdepartmental Group that Under Secretary of State Nicholas Katzenbach had chaired since March 1966 identified "a broader Asian interest in an India better able, than it was in 1962, to deal with a future Chinese venture . . . without unleashing a regional arms race."[43]

The tension between these objectives was undeniable. Just as communist China had rationalized an escalatory ladder in Indochina that went from easy finance and police training to counterinsurgency and search-and-destroy, it had hindered efforts to limit arms sales in South Asia as dollars and gold drained out of treasuries in the United States and the Third World. The teetering Bretton Woods system made U.S. Agency for International Development loans less saleable on Capitol Hill than cash-yielding military assistance programs that the Pentagon doled out.[44] With debt crises empowering generals, nationalists, and revanchists across Latin America, Asia, and Africa, where sundry territorial disputes continued to simmer, the appeal of nuclear arms mounted for hawks, who refused to rate second militarily, and also for doves, who hoped investments in atomic infrastructure would appease the military and placate the masses, showcasing development, and, if all else failed, furnishing an atomic shield without bankrupting their country.[45]

In India, Indira Gandhi prevailed over Morarji Desai, a staunch nationalist, in the National Congress leadership contest after Lal Bahadur Shastri's death. Desai's ensuing assignment to the Finance Ministry kept a gifted and tight-fisted adversary close to Gandhi, but the young prime minister could no longer afford to commit indefinitely and without qualification to the basic policy.[46] Indian officials in New Delhi and Geneva bemoaned the lack of "even a gesture of equality of sacrifice" in the draft nonproliferation compact, not to mention safeguards that would not apply to the nuclear club, underlining as well the need for a "real assurance" to defend against "their main enemy" in Beijing. The fact that Japanese and West German authorities were reportedly passing intelligence to their Indian counterparts indicated that affinities among nuclear-capable regional powers were growing apace.[47]

India's redlines were shifting. To date New Delhi had upheld sovereign equality as paramount. Just the previous July, V. C. Trivedi had demanded that global nuclear diplomacy should not "freeze [the] present status quo and must represent costs to the nuclear powers," adding that "the only essential clause would be a cut-off in the production of fissile materials."[48] Mindful of these sensitivities, White House staffers warned Rostow in March 1967 that military assistance programs to India and Pakistan would require deft handling so as not "to hit the Indians with this in such a way as to jeopardize the NPT."[49] Now Indira Gandhi desired clarifications about how the nuclear powers planned to counter a nuclear-armed China and make their own "sacrifices on behalf of the NPT."[50] In early March, the new Soviet co-chair, Alexei Roshchin, asked Foster to consider a joint approach to New Delhi, which the White House interpreted as "substantial progress."[51] Not long after, Gandhi sent her personal secretary, L. K. Jha, to London, Paris, Moscow, and Washington, to discuss security provisions in relation to the nonproliferation treaty. His country's priority, he informed Couve de Murville, was "to benefit indirectly from the deterrent power of existing nuclear forces."[52] In the Kremlin, Andrei Gromyko handed Jha a draft declaration that would commit these guardians to "act quickly through the Security Council" if a third party were to face an "unprovoked nuclear . . . attack." Jha suggested adding the word *threat* to cover atomic blackmail. The Soviets revised their offer as the Indian envoy winged his way from Moscow to Washington, D.C.[53]

In the U.S. capital Johnson and Rostow assured Jha that they would study "separate but similar declarations" with Soviet leaders, whose readiness to distance themselves from Beijing amid the Vietnam War delighted Walt Rostow and others on the NSC staff, who wrote Johnson to applaud this "major change in the Soviet position."[54] From the U.S. State Department, Foy Kohler counseled a wait-and-see approach. Rusk remained hypercautious about security commitments, and the Soviet offer was no more than notional.[55] Rusk and McNamara also recommended that the declaration take executive privilege into account by mandating a UNGA resolution subsequent to UNSC proceedings in lieu of consent from the U.S. Senate.[56] And even though the Soviet text did not strike Rostow as "too onerous, at first glance," it could have the effect of fettering U.S. military might in East Asia, leading Rusk to warn Johnson via Rostow that such a declaration would "clearly preclude us from first use of nuclear weapons in either North Korea or Vietnam."[57]

As Jha crisscrossed the Atlantic Ocean, other neutral and nonaligned delegates in Geneva worked to cement nuclear development and disarmament alongside nonproliferation as the treaty's core tenets. After the ENDC had adjourned in March, Soviet ambassador to the UN Nikolai Fedorenko sent word to French ambassador Roger Seydoux that the superpowers were "very close" in Geneva, where the biggest obstacle was no longer "the adherence of the Federal Republic of Germany but the treaty's acceptance by the Indian Government." The extension of blanket guarantees to neutral states was the most promising route to winning New Delhi over. It was also the costliest: Warsaw Pact forces would never rule out atomic threats against West Germany and the U.S. military retained contingency plans for nuclear use on the Korean peninsula and in Southeast Asia. The issues were most acute in East Asia, where "Chinese political developments and their effects on neighboring countries" cast a long shadow. India had surged against the treaty, with Brazil and West Germany potentially in tow.[58]

The safeguard issue nonetheless continued to resist resolution. In the break between ENDC sessions, Senator John Pastore had suggested in a congressional speech that Euratom "develop equivalent technical safeguards" to those of the IAEA that the international agency would then certify.[59] Johnson's arms control cabal was paying attention. U.S.-Euratom talks ended on May 14 having made little headway. While Brandt had bent on procedural issues, Bonn placed two conditions on a joint proposal of draft treaties that would omit Article III.[60] First, the consultations would need to proceed privately, and, second, Foster would need to commend the current draft article in plenary. These concessions opened the door for back-channel talks that would demonstrate Geneva's value as a middle ground of Cold War diplomacy.

The Soviet and U.S. co-chairs settled one key point in the seven weeks between sessions—New Year's Day 1967 would henceforth mark the deadline for member-ship in the nuclear club on the basis of a successful test. Foster and Fisher also added a preambular statement enjoining the nuclear-armed to "end the nuclear arms race" and a new article endorsing non-explosive research and development. A West German campaign to limit the treaty's duration and general calls to permit amendments of, or withdrawal from, the treaty free from nuclear-club vetoes went unheeded.[61] When the ENDC resumed on May 18, Brazilian and Indian delegates associated the PNE question with the relative lack of industrialization in the Third World on account of the region's colonial and neocolonial dependence on Northern metropoles. Brazilian delegate Sergio Corrêa da Costa had requested on March 14 that disarmament savings finance development programs.[62] Two months later he read a spirited defense of Rio's plans to hasten Brazil's "peaceful nuclearization" as one element of a national drive "to eliminate poverty and underdevelopment" through an active industrial policy, championing PNEs for "great civil engineering projects" and "an ever-increasing variety of applications." He attacked a ban on them as tantamount to "an irreparable relationship of dependence."[63]

Brazil's military government feared that atomic regulation would lessen their status and autonomy. In a meeting of his national security council in October 1967, President Artur da Costa e Silva would frame PNEs as a "sovereign right" and an es-sential element of "international power." And while his generals portrayed an atomic arsenal as a "last resort," they also cited the imperfect record during the Second World War of the 1925 Geneva Protocol banning chemical weapons to qualify their sup-port of a nuclear nonproliferation treaty. Foreign Minister José de Magalhães Pinto reported that he and his diplomats had encountered "great pressure from the big powers," who were unlikely to cede ground in Geneva or Brazil. The Costa e Silva administration was nonetheless loath to sign away their rights "on the threshold of a great revolution."[64] Indian senior officials shared their fear. Five days after Corrêa da Costa's address, Trivedi sharpened Gandhi's recent admonition that a treaty should not embargo tools capable of narrowing the gap between industrial powerhouses and commodity exporters. He did so with an analogy to South Africa's *de jure* white supremacy: "The civil nuclear Powers can tolerate a nuclear weapons apartheid, but not an atomic apartheid in their economic and peaceful development."[65] His thrust was not that a closed nuclear club would systematize racial prejudice in international relations, but that discriminatory restrictions on dual-use technology should err on the side of national sovereignty and technological self-determination.

As Brazilian and Indian officials worried about an atomic-energy hierarchy, the superpowers embarked on the first top-level talks since Nikita Khrushchev's Vienna summit with Kennedy in June 1961 and the first visit of a head of government to the rival's territory since Khrushchev's trip the United States two years before that. With the Vietnam War weighing down his domestic agenda, Johnson wagered that progress on the Arab-Israeli conflict, nuclear arms control, and Southeast Asia presupposed a stronger rapport with the Kremlin. That spring, Israel and its Arab neighbors engaged in an escalating cycle of covert operations, mobilizations, and tit-for-tat incursions. In response to unfounded Soviet warnings of an imminent Israeli attack against Syria in May, Gamal Abdel Nasser expelled UN peacekeepers and sent more than 100,000 troops into the Sinai Peninsula. A preemptive Israeli strike on the Egyptian Air Force initiated full-blown hostilities on June 5, which ended on June 10 with a jubilant Israel in control of East Jerusalem, the Sinai, the West Bank, the Golan Heights, and the Gaza Strip.[66] The Six-Day War threw the Middle East into turmoil and led Johnson to invite Kosygin (who had plans to address the United Nations in New York) to Glassboro, New Jersey, in late June to discuss the region and the wider world. "I think I can get on with him all right," the president assured Senate Foreign Relations Committee chairman William Fulbright: "I got along with Khrushchev all right."[67]

The Glassboro summit revealed that the superpowers had more in common in suppressing foreign nuclear forces than in curbing their own. Kosygin dismissed McNamara's attempt to interest him in strategic arms limitations or an agreement not to develop anti-ballistic-missile (ABM) defenses, rejecting the secretary of defense's assertions that strategic missile defenses were a technical fantasy and a fiscal black hole with the exclamation, "Defense is moral, and aggression is immoral!"[68] Nuclear nonproliferation was a lonely bright spot. In discussions with Gromyko, Rusk singled out three obstacles in addition to the elusive safeguards language: assurances for India, treaty duration, and arms control linkages. On the first, he intimated that a UNSC resolution would allow the executive branch to circumvent the U.S. Senate while meeting Indian preferences for universality. Both men believed that the ENDC could finish a "common text" by October. Because the Soviet Union remained opposed to European "family control" via Euratom, however, Gromyko proposed that U.S. and Soviet delegates table identical draft treaties jointly in Geneva with the safeguards article for now left blank.[69]

The summit illustrated a central irony of nuclear nonproliferation efforts during the Cold War. Even as the United States and the Soviet Union sparred over Latin America, Asia, Africa, and the Middle East, their common desire to maintain sway over regions whose national elites feared economic dependence and international second-class status led them to cooperate at the global level.

III

Explosive developments in the Third World shadowed nonproliferation talks. In Latin America, a death spiral of revolution and counterrevolution held up completion of the nuclear-weapon-free zone (NWFZ), as the military juntas in Brasília and Buenos Aires beholden to nationalists nursed grievances related to nuclear self-denial. In the Middle East, the rise of risk-keen military actors in Cairo, Damascus, and Tel Aviv yielded low-level violence just as Israeli scientists fabricated from plutonium generated in Dimona's reactors the pits for primitive atom bombs. In South Asia, the wobbly power balance between the United States, the Soviet Union, and the People's Republic of China (PRC) had heightened elite Indian interest in U.S.-Soviet détente but also lessened Gandhi's willingness to sacrifice her country's independence.

In February 1967, Rusk had implored Brandt that "the primary adherence problems should not lie in an East-West context but rather with countries such as India."[70] Jha's tour of friendly nuclear club capitals had triggered a review process in New Delhi, raising basic issues of India's foreign and domestic policy at a touchy moment in its relations with both superpowers. As Washington weighed different assurance models, it announced that it would resume sales of military spare parts to India and Pakistan on April 13, fifteen months after the Treaty of Tashkent. Although this restrictive approach vexed officials in Pakistan, their Indian counterparts were even more frustrated. Rawalpindi was reliant on U.S. military purchases while a worsening dollar shortage in the Indian treasury would restrict their military industry in the absence of International Monetary Fund (IMF) funds, World Bank loans, or increased foreign aid.[71]

On his return to New Delhi in May, Jha filed two memoranda about his meeting and the larger nuclear question. He was pleased that the revised draft covered nuclear blackmail and envisaged action before the UNSC met, but there were nonetheless three major weaknesses: explicit links to the treaty, weak operative clauses, and a vague rather than binding reference to Article 51 of the UN Charter authorizing individual and collective self-defense.[72] While security assurances through the UN would harmonize with nonalignment, they needed to be "categorical," "convincing," and "prompt," and issue from "as many nuclear weapon States as possible and from the U.S.A. and the U.S.S.R. as the very minimum." The superpowers would never accept blanket, legally binding obligations "beyond the U.N. Charter" that would shield the atomic unarmed indefinitely. Rather, what India might expect would, "in political terms . . . amount to a promise of full support in the eventuality of a nuclear attack on a non-nuclear country," placing the United States and the Soviet Union on the record that Chinese nuclear threats would never go unpunished.[73]

There was a lack of consensus in New Delhi over the treaty. Jha reported that in contrast to those in London, Paris, and Washington, officials in Moscow had used "very strong words" to imply that continued economic and military assistance would depend on an Indian signature.[74] For this reason, the Indian government needed to resolve its "considerable difference of opinion" on the matter. Nuclear arms would come at a high cost. Neither China nor Pakistan was an existential threat, while a nuclear-weapon program would steal funds from the economy as well as moral capital in the "ideological battle against China." It would also divert funds from conventional forces needed to combat pressing threats of "subversive activities and guerilla warfare" via China, Pakistan, and domestic communist insurgencies in Nagas and Mizos. "To put it briefly," he concluded, "we cannot, with our limited resources, follow China's foot-steps in the nuclear field without also adopting the Chinese way of life politically and economically."[75]

The dilemma went to the heart of India's place in the world. No commitment between states was ever "water-tight." In Paris, Couve de Murville had reminded Jha that even Article 5 of the NATO Treaty was merely promissory. Neither the United States nor the Soviet Union, he continued, "can afford to let India go under Chinese domination." Superpower assurances had political value nonetheless, as they would demonstrate that Moscow and Washington could put aside their differences in the nuclear realm. "On the whole," Jha finished, "I would remain non-nuclear for the present, though it does mean living dangerously."[76] Soviet ministers inferred that Indian nuclear policy was undergoing "gradual radicalization" after Foreign Minister Mohamed Ali Currim Chagla rejected the draft treaty in the Lok Sabha—the lower house of India's parliament—in June. They blamed nonaligned politics rather than nuclear ambitions, but the case for superpower security assurances was becoming more compelling by the month. Chagla's replacement in September by the more cosmopolitan Rajeshwar Dayal (Dag Hammarskjöld's former deputy during UN peacekeeping missions to Lebanon and the Congo) looked like a positive development. Even so, the conspicuousness and potential consequences of Indian unease with the treaty grew in proportion to the degree of superpower consensus.[77]

The nonproliferation talks also progressed against a backdrop of escalating tensions in the Middle East. The Six-Day War had transformed the regional strategic environment in four ways. First, the Israeli victory had enhanced Tel Aviv's position in Washington. Israel had taken the Golan Heights, the West Bank, the Gaza Strip, and the Sinai Peninsula, embarrassing two Soviet allies—Egypt and Syria—and closing the Suez Canal to Soviet shipments heading to Southeast Asia. Their triumph led Johnson, long considered a friend to Israel, to furnish strategic dialogue and arms sales.[78] Second, the war revived interest in using atomic energy to solve the region's development issues. Back in February 1964, Johnson had proposed nuclear desalination to alleviate the water shortages that plagued irrigation projects throughout the Levant. In the weeks after the Israeli victory, Dwight D. Eisenhower emerged from retirement to elaborate on a Water for Peace plan: three nuclear plants would sit on the Mediterranean and the Gulf of Aqaba, pacifying the desert and the Arab-Israeli conflict, as Israel, Lebanon, Syria, and Jordan all drew water from the Jordan River system.[79]

Third, the war refocused attention on Dimona while simultaneously rekindling efforts to have it inspected. The Johnson administration had at first linked the two, as the unspoken task of Water for Peace had been "to see whether we can tie nuclear safeguards to these desalting plans, both in Israel and Egypt," which Washington included for fear that otherwise Moscow might supply Cairo instead.[80] Rusk warned that Levi Eshkol's lack of transparency could prompt Nasser to invite Soviet nuclear forces into the Arab world.[81] The White House was nonetheless pessimistic. Rostow advised Johnson that, even with their trump card, it was "probably unrealistic to expect Israel to accept safeguards on all its reactors." By November 1967 "joint Jordanian-Israeli management of the Jordan valley" had replaced IAEA safeguards as the principal "quid pro quo."[82] The Six-Day War had dramatized the limits of superpower influence in the region. The conflict had featured a hidden nuclear dimension, with Egyptian jets reconnoitering Dimona in May, by which point Israel likely possessed a few makeshift atom bombs.[83] When NATO foreign ministers met one week later, Rusk asked whether if faced with defeat Tel Aviv could unleash a nuclear strike, a point to which British foreign minister Brown returned at the ensuing press conference. Harlan Cleveland, now the U.S. ambassador to the North Atlantic Council, spoke for many when he noted that the war had "forced everybody to think hard about non-European reasons for [the] NPT."[84]

Amid an escalating regional arms race, desalination was a throwback to a time when Washington approached Middle Eastern affairs from the standpoint of big-ticket development initiatives. Water for Peace featured a battle between "desalters" and "disarmers" in Washington, D.C., intersecting with a Middle Eastern arms race after Johnson authorized the sale of M48 tanks and 48 A-4 Skyhawk jet bombers to Israel on the condition that the latter never carry atom bombs.[85] The use of atomic energy for desalination would make it easier for Eshkol to break this promise, leading Rostow to warn Johnson about the inherent conflict between "nuclear desalting" and keeping "Israel off the nuclear track."[86]

The nuclear desalination debate occasioned doubts about atomic assistance more generally. Albert Wohlstetter, a consultant from the University of Chicago, itemized the risks for the White House: plutonium by-products, imperfect verification, crisis-time reversibility, and human and intellectual spin-offs that would necessarily facilitate weapons work. "Dimona could produce enough plutonium to build one bomb a year," he calculated, and "this plant is at least [eight] times larger." The claim that "good" and "bad" atoms were a fallacy departed from the technocratic approach that had prevailed since the 1954 Atomic Energy Act.[87] In Wohlstetter's eyes, the hazards of managed nuclear globalization were so extreme that only foolproof, irrevocable safeguards could pass muster.[88] Although his views were—for now—in the minority as nonproliferation talks proceeded in Geneva and New York, they made a deep impression on a PhD student at the University of Chicago, Paul Wolfowitz, who would write his dissertation, "Nuclear Proliferation in the Middle East: The Politics and Economics of Proposals for Nuclear Desalting," under Wohlstetter.

On June 17, 1967, communist China became the fourth thermonuclear power, refuting claims that its nuclear-weapon program was unsophisticated. U.S.-Soviet atomic coexistence had consistently aimed at closing the nuclear club and containing new entrants from challenging their hegemonies. It was an awkward moment in communist Chinese politics, as Mao Zedong had unleashed the Cultural Revolution the year before. Not only was the PRC's diplomatic presence severely curtailed around the world (most Chinese embassies were kept vacant), the political upheavals unleashed by Red Guards petrified Chinese foreign policy. Despite the advantages of formally joining the nuclear club, the Chinese Communist Party (CCP) leadership denounced the draft nonproliferation treaty as the product of U.S.-Soviet collusion. The Joint Committee on Atomic Energy (JCAE) under Pastore's leadership forecasted a PRC ballistic-missile capability within five years.[89] Rusk had been courting Beijing as part of a larger bridge-building campaign amid the Vietnam War; however, the returns to date had been meager.[90]

The superpowers were less and less inclined to help allies with nonmilitary atomic development. After North Korean premier Kim Il Sung's furtive visit late in 1966, Kosygin and Leonid Brezhnev had welcomed Vice Premier Kim Il to Moscow on February 13, 1967, only to rebuff Pyongyang's request for an atomic-energy reactor. They had received practically no information from a research reactor that Soviet engineers had built in North Korea eighteen months earlier.[91] The Kremlin had previously offered reactors without safeguards on the condition that spent fuel was returned, but now its denizens had lost faith that recipients would honor the terms. The White House was also eyeing allies more skeptically. The AEC had scrutinized South Africa's uranium exports and enriched-uranium imports late in 1966 in preparation for a bilateral renegotiation of their nuclear assistance agreement the following summer. The JCAE and the AEC wanted firmer nonproliferation pledges from Pretoria. They were especially concerned that South African mines were shipping uranium ore to France without conditions, and threatened to embargo the enriched uranium that fueled the Pelindaba research reactor if Pretoria did not apply safeguards. Chastened, South African diplomats promised to follow closely "the outcome of the deliberations . . . in Geneva," where the battle between IAEA and Euratom safeguard jurisdiction continued.[92]

IV

The international community in Geneva would prove instrumental in resolving the safeguards deadlock. As the *New York Times* reported that nonaligned and neutral delegates anxiously awaited a draft treaty on which to "put their stamp," Foster offered an encomium to Geneva in an interview for ABC News.[93] The former home of the League of Nations, in addition to the ENDC the lakeside conurbation hosted the International Labour Organization, the UN Commission on Human Rights, the World Health Organization, and since 1964 the UN Conference on Trade and Development (UNCTAD). The International Committee of the Red Cross headquarters had looked down on the Palais des Nations from across Avenue de la Paix since 1863. A patchwork of highland French-, German-, and Italian-speaking communities, Switzerland had exemplified European cosmopolitanism since its founding over a century before. Geneva became a social microcosm of the international system when the League of Nations was formed in 1921, with anticolonial Egyptian nationalists breathing the same air as mandatory-power delegations from the United Kingdom, France, Belgium, Australia, New Zealand, South Africa, and Japan.

Whereas interwar Geneva was renowned for the pageantry and festivities of the European haut monde that gathered for assembly sessions every year, the ongoing decolonization of the UN system since 1947 had yielded a more diverse if not necessarily less elite diplomatic gathering place when the ENDC first met in 1962.[94]

This postcolonial community eased communication between the East and the West and between the North and the South. It was "the only place," Foster noted to ABC, "where we have a continuing contact with the Soviet Union outside of normal diplomat channels"; "the only place, too, where we can take broad soundings on opinions and ideas of the non-aligned nations." Inside and outside the formal plenaries and in the co-chair meetings, the committee served "as a university . . . a citadel of learning for representatives in the ENDC—indeed for all."[95] When he had applauded the committee's invaluable worth to the UN Society of Berlin the previous July, he had commended the egalitarian milieu in Geneva, "co-chairmen [meetings], social gatherings, working lunches, etc.," whose totality "permits all voices [to] be heard—large [and] small." He believed that ENDC deliberations carried the torch that the Moscow Treaty had first lit, reassuring global publics who felt anxious about nuclear testing and warfare. The challenge was nonetheless formidable: Could the seventeen delegations find a "balance of responsibilities and obligations" when the "lion's share" would fall on the atomic unarmed even as the nuclear club shouldered its own burden to "limit and reduce nuclear armaments?"[96]

What the nuclear club would owe the world would bear out how a postcolonial world order differed from imperial antecedents. Multiple UNGA resolutions had already noted the relationship between nuclear proliferation, the U.S.-Soviet arms race, and wholesale abolition. While the breakthrough on the nonacquisition and nondissemination articles had raised hopes about U.S.-Soviet relations generally, Beijing's accusations that Moscow preferred peaceful coexistence to wars of national liberation, combined with Soviet efforts to match the United States missile-for-missile, had blocked forward movement on concrete arms control commitments. In contrast to the years after the Second World War, however, Soviet and U.S. delegates built personal relationships in Geneva. The generation of Soviet apparatchiks who had come to power under Stalin had feared foreign associations. The Soviet member of the International Military Tribunal at Nuremberg, Iola Nikitchenko, had presided over the show trials and formed no lasting connections with his fellow judges, disappearing behind the Iron Curtain as soon as the verdicts had been rendered.[97] The cohort that worked under Brezhnev and Kosygin had witnessed the Secret Speech of 1956, when Khrushchev denounced Stalin's cult of personality and endorsed "peaceful coexistence" with the capitalist world. Those whom the Kremlin sent to Geneva grew comfortable rubbing shoulders with their rivals. Decades later Arms Control and Disarmament Agency (ACDA) general counsel George Bunn would recall the Soviets' combative style in 1962, when "even in a cocktail party . . . they seemed to be trying to make points against you.[98] In the intervening five years, however, the climate had thawed thanks to shared labors and leisure. The interminable plenaries, hallway chatter, consulate parties, boozy lunches, about-town jaunts, outdoor recreation, and yacht cruises on Lake Geneva had helped foster an esprit de corps among the delegations.[99] By the end of his assignment in Switzerland, Bunn "had learned how to drive a Volga automobile, and drunk a good deal of vodka with . . . [my] fellow Soviet negotiators." By the summer of 1967, there was "just a complete change in the attitudes and relationships between the two delegations."[100]

His Soviet counterparts shared his newfound sense of rapport. Roland Timerbaev had joined the Soviet Ministry of Foreign Affairs out of the Moscow State Institute of International Studies in 1949. Nearly fifty years later he too would look back fondly on his growing affinity for Bunn: "Fortunately, we did not turn into 'opposite numbers' representing two rival 'superpowers' of the Cold War era, which was typical for that time. Very soon, we realized we were like-minded people. We deeply believed in the vital need to stop the proliferation of nuclear weapons, and we did our utmost to achieve that goal. This was the inherent basis of our close personal friendship that lasted for more than [fifty] years."[101] Their working relationship would help them navigate the final roadblock to a joint U.S.-Soviet draft treaty—the issue of universal safeguards.

Foster and Bunn believed that the U.S. State Department was too solicitous of West German and Italian demands about Euratom in light of Japanese demands for a fair shake in a future reactor emporium.[102] Foster took advantage of the ENDC's postponement to fly to Tokyo in April, where his hosts made clear their position that nuclear-club civilian facilities fall under the IAEA's watch.[103] It was unclear whether the White House would follow through. Bunn would later characterize Johnson at this point in time as "totally preoccupied with the war in Vietnam."[104] Unbeknownst to Rusk or Rostow, Foster resolved to proceed "at the lower level." The assignment fell to junior members of the delegations—Bunn and Culver Gleysteen for the United States and Timerbaev and Vladimir Shustov for the Soviet Union—so as to shield their bosses from any blowback. According to Timerbaev, it was "the first time in Soviet-American arms control that we were able to discuss *ad referendum*."[105] Bunn would characterize the discussions as "what if . . . exploratory negotiation[s]" that had proceeded in the face of Rusk's orders to conciliate Euratom members.[106]

The Swiss Alps made for a picturesque backdrop for the meetings. "We had gotten to know each other through originally just working on the two delegations," Bunn would reminisce, "but times had gotten better, relations had gotten better, at least at the delegation level, and we often hiked in the mountains—went together on the weekends—and talked." He and Timerbaev took a cable car up Aiguille du Midi near Mont Blanc in June, where the latter suggested "an agreement to agree"—the two sides would work out a solution after the treaty was signed. If it were possible for member states to sign as groups, Euratom could negotiate "for all the countries together with the IAEA," which would apply forensic materials accounting methods to certify Euratom's work. As officials back in Moscow and Washington still needed to authorize the move, the two delegations engaged in a bit of collective subterfuge, presenting the formula as the other side's offer back home. Fisher telephoned Rusk on June 23 to fill him in ahead of the Glassboro summit, alluding in an ensuing cable to an informal Soviet proposal to allow bilateral or multilateral agreements as per the Treaty of Tlatelolco, citing the example of "certified public accountants and corporation bookkeepers."[107] He took the opportunity to push for the United States and the Soviet Union to bring the IAEA into their own civilian nuclear installations.[108]

The ploy was effective. When later that summer Thompson mentioned the new "Soviet proposal" to Gromyko, the Soviet foreign minister was flummoxed: "What do you mean, Soviet delegation proposal? I thought that was a American delegation proposal[!]"[109] Despite the ruse, Gromyko gave his go-ahead to submit identical U.S.-Soviet draft treaties with Article III left blank. Rostow underscored the act's momentousness in a memorandum to Johnson on August 10: "Now the game will move to the non-nuclear powers; and some months of negotiations lie ahead. But it is something of an event."[110]

V

On August 24, 1967, the Soviet and American governments announced the existence of identical draft treaties in Geneva, Washington, and Moscow. Fisher admitted this "might cause the FRG some pain," but it was more important how the United States and the Soviet Union would handle allies and the neutrals. Were they "now in for a free-for-all?" Thus far he and Foster had weathered attacks from the Germans and the Italians. With Soviet help, "the dangers of objecting to [the NPT] are also greater."[111] Among the neutrals and nonaligned, Mexico, Sweden, and Nigeria sounded genuine in their desire to improve the treaty, while Brazil and India dug in their heels on everything from peaceful uses to nuclear assurances. Among the allies, West Germany and Japan worked from the outside and Italy from within for better terms on matters related to markets, security, and procedure, while the French continued to keep their distance. De Gaulle's dismissal of the ENDC as a superpower creature raised fears of a last-minute intervention, as did the CCP's *People's Daily* when it branded the treaty "an outright hoax" on September 3.[112]

The acquiescence of presumptive nuclear club members was vital to winning over the larger mass of small and middle powers. Barring that, the superpowers needed to discourage their outright hostility. Fortunately, nearly all of the advanced industrial powers were U.S. allies, positioning Washington as the primary broker, whose leaders worked through bilateral and multilateral channels to homogenize markets, buttress security, and expand choice. For legitimacy, a supermajority of the UNGA, its numbers swollen by decolonization, needed to vote yes. The United States, or the Soviet Union, or both, would recruit them with pledges of security goods through universal assurances or arms sales, or both, while guaranteeing them market access and political input through international and multilateral institutions. These two related goals would demand an elegant mixture of persuasion, consultation, horse trading, pressure, and compromise.[113] The first phase of negotiations would take place at the ENDC in Geneva that fall and the following spring, before a final push to occur at a special UNGA session in New York from April to June 1968.

Neutral and nonaligned states in Latin America, Africa, Asia, and the Middle East were key recruits. The Cuban Missile Crisis, the Sino-Indian border conflict, the Vietnam War, Indo-Pakistan hostilities, and the Six-Day War had all attested to the instability and violence of these regions, where the cocktail of local conflicts and Cold War rivalries was most explosive.[114] The inclusion of four neutral and four nonaligned states on the ENDC had institutionalized their involvement in global nuclear diplomacy. Leading the charge were Brazil, India, Egypt, Mexico, Nigeria, and Sweden, whose delegations used the committee to pursue their socioeconomic wants, political preferences, and security needs. UNGA Resolution 2028's mandate to avoid loopholes and strike a fair contract cast them in leading roles in Geneva and New York.[115]

Washington asked neutral and nonaligned powers to shoulder this burden, encouraging those supportive of global nuclear governance to mediate while fending off Soviet impulses to railroad the treaty.[116] The UNGA's majoritarianism empowered Latin American and African delegations, who comprised nearly half the delegations and often voted *en masse*. The Treaty of Tlatelolco had strengthened the hands of Mexican diplomats, who campaigned for technical assistance in the forms of international aid and loan subsidies for developing nations.[117] Alfonso García Robles and his co-nationals aimed not to alter the treaty's spirit but to prevent the recurrence of the conditions that had allowed foreign control of Mexico's oil industry earlier that century: the scarcity of native experts, uncompetitive licenses on vital machinery, and educational and financial disparities. Rather than push a redistributive approach that would channel disarmament savings to developmental ends as Brazilian diplomats had requested, Mexico preferred to protect local energy markets from foreign ownership.

The Mexican amendments had added new articles chartering an international PNE service, internationalizing great-power arms control and disarmament, and carving out special dispensations for NWFZs. U.S. negotiators welcomed them. They would counter accusations that Washington and Moscow intended to force the treaty on nonaligned and neutral states.[118] Demands for concrete concessions from the nuclear club fared less well. Alva Myrdal moved to rein in the superpower arms race, characterizing comprehensive test-ban, fissile-material cutoff, and nonproliferation treaties "as parts of one comprehensive pattern."[119] Foster had previously called the move to supplement a nonproliferation treaty with a total test ban "the most significant step we could take" to conciliate opposition to nuclear law and order.[120] The Pentagon and the AEC continued to approach the issues from the standpoint of the U.S.-Soviet arms race, however, as McNamara and Seaborg made preparations for a "new generation" of strategic and defensive nuclear systems. The White House was willing to contemplate offering more than words to India and Japan, with Harold Saunders and Walt Rostow promoting a Policy Planning Staff recommendation to grant the two Asian powers access to U.S. atom bombs in the event of a regional nuclear crisis or future ABM systems to relieve mounting insecurity vis-à-vis China's growing arsenal.[121]

Indian attitudes were hardening by the week. Canadian officials in New Delhi met a frosty reception in December 1967, when High Commissioner James George insinuated that India's intransigence would jeopardize foreign aid. Foreign Minister Dayal accused him of acting as a U.S. pawn and waved aside his threats, vowing that "India would never give up an iota of its hard-fought independence by signing the NPT." Gandhi was equally blunt in their meeting, belittling security guarantees as useless when Washington would arrive at a decision to intervene in cold blood: "If they don't want to come to our aid, they won't even if we do sign the treaty." George blamed AEC chairman Vikram Sarabhai, who enjoyed a warm personal relationship with Gandhi. His characterization of the Cambridge-educated nuclear physicist as "emotional and somewhat irrational" dripped with condescension. Sarabhai would likely have agreed with Dayal that Indian leaders "held in sacred patrimony the free-dom of future generations."[122]

The safeguards controversy still impeded progress across the nonproliferation agenda. Bunn and Timerbaev had loosened the knot without untangling it; the atomic unarmed could exploit any further delay at the UNGA in November 1967 and were now bolstered by five conditions listed by the European Communities with a view to preserving Euratom's independence, integrity, and competitiveness.[123] Foster tried to break the stalemate on November 2 by handing a revised article to Dobrynin in which the IAEA was made the final arbiter, but the Soviet ambassador would not budge—the Kremlin wanted a clear reference in the NPT to "IAEA safeguards." Ros-tow set out the dilemma for Johnson a few days later: to acquiesce would hand "the Germans an excuse for rejecting the Treaty . . . [and] seriously damage our relations with them." Meanwhile, continued deadlock imperiled the treaty.[124] From Geneva, Foster advised that Johnson was "being asked to fight mainly for the interests of only one of our allies, as against our own national interests and those of most of the rest of our allies and most of the rest of the world." Although in memoranda Rusk agreed that a fragmented regulatory environment carried significant downsides, in person the secretary of state raised doubts to Johnson about the wisdom of imposing the treaty on Bonn, from where the U.S. ambassador cited the fragility of the Kiesinger-Brandt coalition in warning the president that he faced a choice "between the NPT and keeping Germany as an ally."[125]

Johnson eventually opted to appease West Germany once more. First, he offered to place civilian nuclear facilities in the United States under IAEA safeguards on December 2, which Brandt lauded as a "significant step." That same day, he urged Kiesinger to accept the November 2 formulation that the Soviets had accepted with the lone exception of a reference to "IAEA safeguards." While Kiesinger chose not to send a "a stiff letter," he nonetheless rejected the Soviet proposal on December 8.[126] Johnson had left the ball in Kosygin and Brezhnev's court.

As the UNGA deliberated that winter, Soviet and U.S. diplomats whipped votes in anticipation of a return to Geneva.[127] Soviet Ambassador Vasily Kuznetsov leaned on the Indians and the Egyptians to co-sponsor a resolution for a final draft treaty, leaving Arab and socialist delegates puzzled at how harmoniously the superpowers were now working together.[128] Their protracted disputes had taken a toll, however, leading Soviet negotiators to warn their U.S. counterparts that there were now "more opponents than supporters of the treaty." The postponement of the Conference of Non-Nuclear-Weapon States until August 1968 afforded breathing space, but only after Kuznetsov and his U.S. counterpart, Arthur Goldberg, beat back a neutral "gang-up" in the UN First Committee to pass Resolution 2346, which would have had the ENDC issue a report by March 15. If they were not on the same page when the disarmament committee recommenced on January 18, Kuznetsov warned, "it might be too late."[129]

Kuznetsov's warning reflected the Kremlin's concerns that key regional powers and neutral states would mount a concerted defense of nuclear anarchy. Fearing a loss of control in the Middle East and Asia, observers in ACDA observed an evolution in Soviet attitudes from "parochial concern" with West Germany to "a broader view." Soviet willingness to accept a "NPT text largely on our terms" was a clear indication that the Third World took precedence.[130] French attitudes, on the other hand, remained Delphic. De Gaulle was deemed willing to "prevent German adherence" or even "wreck the NPT." French defense minister Pierre Messmer had already publicly dismissed the treaty as a tool of U.S.-Soviet dominance. In late January de Gaulle mused that wealthy Japan would inevitably seek "commensurate military power."[131] The French Foreign Ministry informed its NATO partners one week later that a nuclear nonproliferation accord would consolidate superpower rule, reaffirming the Gaullist maxim that states should freely organize their defense as well as their intention to abstain scrupulously from the ENDC. French officials were more forthcoming in person, however, reassuring Soviet contacts that they had no intention of sabotaging the treaty and were in fact working hard "behind the scenes to get Germany to sign."[132]

When Foster and Roshchin at long last submitted identical draft treaties on January 18, 1968, there was vocal astonishment from neutral and allied delegates alike in Geneva, incredulous at the extent of superpower cooperation even as an all-out proxy war raged in Southeast Asia.[133] Twelve days later, North Vietnamese troops and Viet Cong guerrillas mounted a surprise offensive on the holiday of Tet—the Vietnamese New Year.

Conclusion

With the resolution of the safeguards controversy, the outlines of a global nuclear regime were coming into view. For all the attention paid to the Vietnam War, U.S.-Soviet relations were improving thanks in part to midlevel fraternization in Geneva. The Six-Day War revealed that postcolonial battlegrounds could draw the superpowers into regional disputes whose escalation might trigger a third world war. Eastern and Western policy makers struggled to allay India's anxieties as China's nuclear capabilities grew. In the absence of superpower accord on Article III, the neutral members of the ENDC introduced new amendments to nudge the compact toward a more equitable bargain reflective of postcolonial conceptions of sovereign equality. The Mexican amendments would prove instrumental in winning broad support for the NPT in the UN First Committee the following year.

The next chapter concludes the history of the negotiation of the nuclear nonproliferation treaty. When the Soviet and U.S. delegations proposed a comprehensive draft together on January 18, 1968, they kicked off a conclusive period of negotiations in Geneva and then in New York. The nonproliferation campaign had become a barometer of U.S.-Soviet relations. In a January 26 letter to Foster, then at Walter

Reed medical center recovering from a minor heart attack, a Soviet official praised "the greatest achievement between the Soviet Union and the United States which had taken place since World War II."[134] The world indeed looked much different than the one the two rivals had encountered in 1945, transformed as it had been by the spread of industrial production, science and technology, and armed might, with the end of formal imperial rule near at hand. The views of potential irreconcilables—Brazil, Israel, South Africa, and India—stood in stark contrast to the superpowers' self-imposed constraints on security assurances and their unwillingness to permit indigenous development of any nuclear explosive. The campaign for the UNGA to endorse the draft treaty and the UNSC to punish atomic threats faced resistance from African and Latin American states. France's veto on the Security Council made de Gaulle's attitude toward the treaty and the assurances resolution that would accompany it potentially decisive. The fate of a new global nuclear order now hinged on French, nonaligned, and neutral misgivings about a legal regime that would empower the nuclear club to close its doors forcefully in humanity's name.

"A Decent Level of International Law and Order"
Final Negotiations for the NPT, 1967–1970

Introduction—"A Good Deed in a Naughty World"

The NPT's opening for signature on July 1, 1968, furnished the keystone of international nuclear law—a watershed for the Cold War and world order after empire. In 1968 the universe of nation-states featured a variety of generic types: the superpowers and their client states; nuclear-armed France, the People's Republic of China (PRC), and the United Kingdom; industrial exporters such as West Germany and Japan; commodity producers such as South Africa and Australia; developing importers such as Mexico and Nigeria; nuclear-capable regional powers such as India, Brazil, and Israel; and small powers incapable of amassing atom-splitting arsenals. Most countries belonged to multiple classes. West Germany and Japan, for instance, were simultaneously U.S. allies hungry for allied reassurance, advanced exporters covetous of Third World markets, and aspirants to the nuclear club. Latin American, African, Asian, and the Middle Eastern nonaligned and neutral countries coveted a place in the sun, just as territorial rivalries, resurgent nationalism, and emboldened militaries increased demand for advanced weaponry across the Third World. The superpowers confronted a world where their armed superiority and unrivaled status were under threat from crises of political legitimacy at home and challenges to their hegemonic leadership abroad.[1]

This chapter recounts the decisive phase of international nonproliferation diplomacy from the superpowers' introduction of a consensus draft treaty in late 1967 to the NPT's entry into force in March 1970. As the Vietnam War escalated, the United States, the Soviet Union, and an increasingly postcolonial community of nation-states finalized a nuclear constitution for all signatories. The treaty extended to the nuclear realm a liberal world order to which U.S. hegemony had been inextricably bound since 1945. It was enacted with U.S. leadership, Soviet and British backing, and French and Chinese acquiescence, and at small and middle powers' invitation. With nonproliferation, technological equity, and arms control now its foundational pillars, the NPT required a winning majority in the UN General Assembly (UNGA), where Latin American and African countries held the numerical balance. To achieve enduring legitimacy, the superpowers needed to bring these delegations around to their theory of the case: that the resulting global nuclear order would feature an inviting fusion of markets, security, and voices for members in good standing.

I

The Central Committee of the Communist Party of the Soviet Union (CPSU) waited until the last moment to approve the draft treaty. The reasoning was political—the Soviet Union had more to gain from global détente than to lose from West German vice chancellor Willy Brandt's European variant. NATO and Warsaw Pact allies were clearly discombobulated. At the North Atlantic Treaty meeting in Paris on January 18, 1968, West Germany's envoy called for neutral views to "be weighted and not counted," as Bonn continued to draw closer to Rio and New Delhi. His response was "upbeat" when compared to that of Italy's ambassador, who related that Rome had received the news in a "state of shock."[2] Later that spring, the Italian Foreign Ministry would inquire whether the Ukrainian and Belarusian republics would count as nuclear-weapon states: if not, the Soviet Union would have to welcome International Atomic Energy Agency (IAEA) inspectors on its territory; if so, communist nuclear powers would outnumber those in NATO. It was "a question with ingenious subtext," Leonid Brezhnev joked later that spring. "They must have invented it at a Jesuit gathering somewhere in the Vatican."[3]

Bill Foster and Butch Fisher worked to dispel these reservations with promises of market access and political input in the future regime. Thanks to the Soviet Union's capitulation on safeguards, Euratom members and Japan had agreed to globalize a nuclear regime supportive of research, development, and exports. Together with the promotion of automated systems in nuclear facilities, advanced exporters could look forward to a world market in which commerce rather than controls determined regulation.[4] The fact that civilian facilities in the United Kingdom and the United States would apply IAEA safeguards strengthened arguments about fair play. Even so, Italian, Japanese, and West German officials continued to plead for greater "flexibility"—a quarter-century sunset, five-yearly review conferences, and a permissive exit clause—to enhance the regime's accountability and correspondingly their future sway as nuclear order-makers.[5]

U.S. armed forces stood ready to patrol insecure neighborhoods. Foster had worked so hard to mend fences with West Germany that when the Eighteen Nation Committee on Disarmament (ENDC) adjourned, he joked that Bonn had "written half the treaty."[6] U.S.-Soviet détente suited Brandt's Ostpolitik, which would have the Federal Republic of Germany (FRG) strengthen ties with the German Democratic Republic (GDR) and Eastern Europe more generally.[7] NATO's Nuclear Defense Affairs Committee (NDAC) and the Nuclear Planning Group (NPG) handed Western Europe the trappings of atomic might; they also enhanced their input in nuclear posturing and their appreciation of its worst consequences.[8] The European contingent in NATO could veto nuclear-weapon use on their home territories—a major concession to fears of escalation in the name of flexible response. Whereas once they had begged for reassurance that the U.S. nuclear umbrella remained credible, now Robert McNamara noted that European powers were "scared to death of the use of nuclear weapons."[9]

Above all, Amsterdam, Brussels, Copenhagen, London, Luxembourg, Oslo, and Paris were determined not to let West Germany or Italy sidestep the treaty—they could have allies without nukes, or nukes without allies, but not both. Walt Rostow was therefore stating the obvious when he warned a high member of Kurt Georg Kiesinger's Christian Democratic Union Party that for them to hedge their atomic bets would "tear apart the Alliance."[10] Although the draft treaty had given rise to a "heavy and despondent" mood in Bonn, where Franz Josef Strauss continued to attack the treaty, Kiesinger and Brandt understood that alliance solidarity would require the country not only to show "support for non-proliferation but that it is a good ally."[11]

Lacking an East Asian treaty organization of comparable scale, Washington defaulted to bilateral assurances and strategic coordination vis-à-vis Tokyo and Seoul. Communist China's nuclear breakthrough had prompted Prime Minister Eisaku Satō to entertain an independent arsenal, leading Johnson to confirm that the U.S.-Japanese Treaty of Mutual Cooperation and Security covered nuclear threats: "If Japan needs our nuclear deterrent for its defense," he affirmed on January 12, 1965, "the United States would stand by its commitments and provide that defense."[12] The transpacific partners also deepened strategic consultations by means of a new subcommittee reporting to a biannual Security Consultative Committee in emulation of NATO's Nuclear Planning Group, with a view to educate Japanese military officers and policy makers about "overwhelming [U.S.] strategic superiority" and "overall ballistic missile defense problems."[13] McNamara reframed the Sentinel anti-ballistic-missile (ABM) system to this same end: as a buttress for the U.S. nuclear umbrella in East Asia, which also helped justify a big-ticket item whose political value exceeded its likely efficacy against Soviet intercontinental ballistic missiles (ICBMs).[14]

True to form, these new forums aimed to discourage neutralism rather than nuclear proliferation per se.[15] What Satō dubbed Japan's "nuclear allergy" had yielded a paradoxical policy: while a sovereign arsenal, a multilateral force, or ABM systems were dead on arrival, the U.S. nuclear umbrella could remain out of sight and out of mind. Public protests against U.S. military bases in Japan or the nuclear-powered USS *Enterprise*, whose port call near Nagasaki in January 1968 occasioned mass demonstrations, attested to the limits to its invisibility. Satō had acknowledged reality the month before, when he pledged that he and his administration would neither possess, manufacture, nor introduce atomic arms into Japan, with unclear meaning for the "impressive infrastructure" of decoupled nuclear systems and naval delivery vehicles that the U.S. Navy based on the Ogasawara and Okinawa island chains.[16] Satō would later dismiss these pledges as "nonsense" to the U.S. ambassador in Tokyo. Against the backdrop of Diet debates over Okinawa's reversion, however, they remained bound up in evolving U.S.-Japanese security relations, rather than a prerequisite for Japan's signature on a nuclear nonproliferation compact.[17]

Across the world in Geneva on February 13, Ethiopia's delegate to the ENDC observed that there were "as many ways of looking at this treaty as there are member nations."[18] From a hospital bed in Maryland, Foster noted that the draft treaty had galvanized "skeptics amongst our 'principal' partners" and "'friends' to the south," deeming the Brazilians "one of the great puzzles and disappointments." Once back in Switzerland, he found them cagey and the Romanians locked in a "fraternal battle" with their Warsaw Pact allies.[19] Romanian foreign policy continued to exhibit a "maverick" streak under Communist Party general secretary Nicolae Ceaușescu, whose willingness to mediate between Washington and Hanoi, support for Alexander Dubček's "socialism with a human face" in Czechoslovakia, and pursuit of Western nuclear exports marked Romania out as the most independent-minded Eastern bloc country in Geneva.[20] He and his chief nuclear advisor, Ion Gheorghe Maurer, had informed Leonid Brezhnev, Alexei Kosygin, Yuri Andropov, and Andrei Gromyko the previous March of their reluctance to forswear nuclear arms formally.[21] When the Romanians proposed eleven burdensome new amendments in Geneva, including a blanket non-use pledge that would have removed NATO nuclear hosts from Soviet nuclear targeting, few observers were surprised.[22]

Neutral and nonaligned differences came into sharper relief as talks entered the home stretch. Mexico and Sweden led the moderates, who stressed international fairness, while Brazil and India vented their individual frustrations in increasingly unequivocal terms. Alva Myrdal laid out the basic dilemma when she took her turn at the rostrum on February 8: "How can we—the non-nuclear-weapon States—be expected to enter into an interminable obligation to remain non-nuclear if the nuclear-weapon States are engaged in an interminable nuclear escalation?" Johnson and Kosygin's failure to make headway on Strategic Arms Limitations Talks (SALT) in Glassboro looked like a poor omen for Article VI's arms control and disarmament requirements. Of more immediate concern, Foster and Alexei Roshchin had deleted key clauses from Mexico's draft: "with all speed and perseverance," "arrive at further agreements," and "the prohibition of all nuclear-weapon tests." Short of clear benchmarks, Myrdal feared that the "nuclear-weapon states" would never concede their privileges. Would the treaty foster the conditions necessary to bring the U.S.-Soviet arms race to an end? Rather than "any *quid pro quo*," she insisted it was a question of "the whole atmosphere."[23]

The neutrals met in late February to discuss how to "clear out the remaining underbrush."[24] For all their "irritation at Soviet-American collusion," consensus continued to elude them.[25] Indian diplomats had tried to marshal a nonsigning bloc in Geneva, only for Brazilian foreign minister José de Magalhães Pinto to dub it "a losing game" at a UN Conference on Trade and Development (UNCTAD) meeting in New Delhi earlier that month.[26] There Indian officials had expressed praise for Pierre Gallois's concept of asymmetric deterrence and raised questions about the readiness of the U.S. government to "retaliate against anyone that dropped a nuclear explosive on New Delhi."[27] Lyndon Johnson had little room for maneuver in the aftermath of the Tet Offensive. On February 27, Indian delegate M. A. Husain made an impassioned plea for major revisions—the "urge to seek greater security," he asserted, "cannot be curbed by a prohibition applied only to those that do not already possess them."[28] Yet his call for non-use guarantees troubled the Pentagon, whose contingency plans for major land operations in Korea and Vietnam entailed tactical nuclear-weapon use.[29] He was actually holding back. The Hungarian ambassador in New Delhi cabled his superiors in Budapest that Indira Gandhi had ordered Husain "not to take a stand on the draft treaty for the time being."[30]

Brazil's and India's tactical caution allowed Foster and Roshchin to present a draft on March 11 with only a handful of minor revisions—a nonbinding reference to a comprehensive test ban and requirements for periodic review conferences and also "negotiations in good faith on effective measures relating to cessation of the nuclear arms race at an early date and to nuclear disarmament."[31] Consensus was nevertheless unforthcoming. In the end the committee would refer the draft treaty to the UNGA without endorsement and as a matter of form.

The fact that Romania joined Brazil and India in abstaining was a source of vexation for the Kremlin at a time of mounting disunity in the international communist movement. Moscow faced challenges to its standing as the architect of socialist development from more militant parties in Havana and Beijing as well as reformist regimes in Prague and Bucharest more open to liberal practices and Western investment.[32] Moscow intended the treaty to bolster its control over the Warsaw Pact, its promotion of peaceful development among European socialists, and its conditional support for Third World revolutionaries. The Warsaw Pact's Political Consultative

Committee met in Sofia in March to discuss the Vietnam War, unified military command, and the nonproliferation treaty—the final item at Romanian general secretary Ceauşescu's request. In Bulgaria, Brezhnev warned that a failed treaty risked "unfavorable consequences . . . both in Europe and throughout the world." His fellow committee members concurred that "the Federal Republic of Germany's nuclear armament" required urgent action. Ceauşescu was the lone holdout and, as a result, there were six rather than seven signatures on the committee's joint declaration supporting the treaty. Broadsides in *Ivestiya* and *Pravda* aimed at Bucharest heralded more family quarrels to come.[33]

The Plenum of the CPSU Central Committee's Presidium assembled for two days of meetings on April 9 and 10. Inside the Kremlin, Brezhnev explained how a new nuclear order would benefit the Soviet Union, European comrades, and international socialism. January's Tet Offensive had confirmed Moscow as an indispensable power. Johnson's war in Vietnam therefore offered opportunities in Southeast Asia and also within the United States. If they could parlay talks between Washington and Hanoi in Paris and nuclear peacemaking in Geneva and New York into a more equal relationship with the capitalist superpower, it would create space for European détente and a buffer against Maoism in the Third World. If nuclear nonproliferation were to become synonymous with world peace, Brezhnev could portray permanent and unbounded revolution as a dangerous heresy within Marxism-Leninism.[34]

Brezhnev and Johnson thus conspired to revolutionize world law and order. The proposed UN Security Council (UNSC) resolution was of special significance. The security assurance part of the nonproliferation package would shift the legal criteria for lawful military intervention, obliging permanent members of both the nuclear club and the Security Council to take "immediate action" whenever nuclear strikes or threats thereof materialized. Foster expounded on this momentous wrinkle at a press conference when the ENDC adjourned on March 7: while "procedural debate" might be necessary, the UN Charter already authorized individual or collective action to fend off a "threat of aggression."[35] Washington and Moscow would thus avoid a public choice between New Delhi and Beijing by opting for supranational coverage—implications for the laws of war were secondary.[36]

French Foreign Ministry lawyers had a different take. In a report that Foreign Minister Maurice Couve de Murville received on March 18, they warned that equating acts and threats of military aggression could have the perverse effect of authorizing nuclear club members to wage "preventive war." For this reason, they counselled that a reference to Article 51 of the UN Charter recognizing an "inherent right of individual or collective self-defense," be removed from the legal apparatus. They also questioned the value of introducing a new class of state—"permanent members of the Security Council possessing nuclear armaments"— that so clearly singled out communist China. In sum, their report concluded, the resolution would afford the atomic unarmed little peace of mind, as the "Anglo-Saxons and Soviets" would retain "freedom of action as far as what measures they choose to adopt."[37] While equivocating on the matter of a French Security Council veto, a second memorandum delivered the next day spelled out their reservations in more detail:

> The juridical reasons are there to fight against a project that, in its letter if not its spirit, constitutes a revision of the Charter: it discriminates among non-nuclears to the advantage of treaty signatories; it hierarchizes forms of aggression and introduces the ambiguous concept of "threat of aggression;" it distinguishes among the permanent members those which possess nuclear arms and invests thereby the present situation with an anti-Chinese character that Beijing does not fail to note. Finally, it departs from the established jurisdiction of the Security Council, whose decisions have always applied to specific problems.

With near-nuclear powers increasingly "unable to hide their disillusionment with a treaty whose discriminatory character is ever more apparent," the French found themselves between a rock and a hard place. Romania and Japan were urging them to intervene directly in New York.[38] Theoretical reservations aside, the use of a UNSC veto was never trivial. The fate of a global nuclear order hung in the balance, with the great-power unanimity principle now in play at UN headquarters in Manhattan.

II

The special UNGA session was essential to the treaty's legitimacy. Only a UN resolution could endow lasting authority, yet humanity's parliament had changed dramatically from its first incarnation as a debating club for European empires, American republics, and a smattering of Afro-Asian states.[39] In historian Ryan Irwin's reckoning, for a moment in the late 1960s "the United Nations and the vision of internationalism embodied therein seemed to function as an inclusive intellectual and political umbrella of this world."[40] Postcolonial members from Africa and Asia represented a strong plurality of the cacophonous 124-nation assembly, vaulting Portuguese colonialism in southwest Africa; South African apartheid; and Israeli control of the West Bank, the Gaza Strip, the Golan Heights, and the Sinai Peninsula atop the General Assembly's agenda. With delegations from Latin America, whose societies retained a cultural identification with anticolonialism and whose elites feared U.S. economic hegemony, the Third World bloc could dictate outcomes in the UNGA. Nuclear restrictions had garnered general nonaligned and neutral approval since the Irish Resolution in 1958. Although U.S. Arms Control and Disarmament Agency (ACDA) officials doubted they would "repudiate the approval they had always given in principal to the quest," each delegation would render a final judgment in light of its distinct interests and worldview. U.S. ambassador Arthur Goldberg and Soviet ambassador Vasily Kuznetsov faced skepticism, if not outright hostility, from nuclear aspirants.[41] With the Conference of Non-Nuclear-Weapon States set for August and a U.S. presidential election for November, the window for a global nuclear nonproliferation treaty was narrowing by the day.

Most delegations lacked the infrastructure or the resources to build atom bombs. The superpowers would try to isolate them from those with the wherewithal.[42] There was nonetheless variation within this "overwhelming majority." Many had been early champions of nuclear restrictions in the belief that multilateral measures would check the arrival of atomic arsenals in their backyards.[43] Others saw a worldwide nuclear regime as a launching pad for U.S.-Soviet détente and collective security in keeping with the principles of nonalignment and the imperatives of development, if not necessarily economic independence or sovereign equality. While ACDA analysts reckoned that laggards would eventually come around, Latin American and African states knew their parliamentary worth.[44] The Treaty of Tlatelolco had made global rules in the Western Hemisphere redundant, even if the region's elites retained faith in collective security. Alfonso García Robles rallied his fellow Latin Americans to demand more concessions—by early May, U.S. observers had come to view their reticence in New York as the "most troubling recent development."[45] Black Africans, on the other hand, cared most about long-running disputes with Pretoria's apartheid regime, its defense of Portuguese colonialism in Angola and Mozambique and white rule in South West Africa (modern-day Namibia), its regionally dominant economy, and its bountiful uranium mines where black South Africans labored in appalling conditions. These long-running objects of condemnation were readily channeled into expression of concern about South Africa's military nuclear potential.[46]

While U.S. and Soviet officials worked hand-in-glove in New York, a successful outcome would ultimately hinge on U.S. global influence. The superpower delegations drew the benchmark for success at more than one hundred yes votes in the UN First Committee and in the UN General Assembly. While coordination between them was peaking, with Foster speaking highly of the "maximum cooperation" offered by his Soviet counterparts, Moscow remained the junior partner.[47] Anatoly Dobrynin implored Foster to "make a special effort" with Brazil, Israel, South Africa, and others "where the Soviet Union had little or no influence."[48] Behind the scenes, Goldberg coached Kuznetsov to avoid "steam-rolling" tactics. They should instead intimate that delegates should endorse the treaty with "possible minor changes."[49]

The nuclear club's newest members—France and the PRC—were targets as much as beneficiaries. To observers in Washington, Moscow sounded eager "to underscore Communist China's isolation from the mainstream of international relations" amid the Cultural Revolution.[50] If the treaty were to enter into force, the PRC could choose to become an authorized nuclear-weapon state by becoming a signatory, even though the rival nationalist government on Taiwan continued to represent the Chinese nation in New York. For now, however, the NPT remained a political football in the international communist movement. The New China News Agency had denounced it in February for preemptively disarming those "subjected to aggression and threats by U.S. imperialism and its accomplices" while leaving the superpowers "to practice nuclear blackmail freely."[51] While the PRC was unwelcome in New York, Albania served as its proxy. Nor could France remain aloof much longer, making Charles de Gaulle's attitude a source of considerable interest and speculation. The superpowers also could not afford to ignore Romania or Yugoslavia, whose representatives privately characterized the agreement as unsound, referencing "numerous and well-founded objections" within the nonaligned camp.[52] Since Romanian foreign minister Corneliu Mănescu's would serve as UNGA president through September, the U.S. State Department judged his support "key." And because Yugoslavia was a founding member of the nonaligned movement, its diplomats drew attention to the draft treaty's lack of concrete arms control commitments on April 15, when its government issued a "plea to nuclear powers to initiate nuclear disarmament negotiations at [the] earliest possible date as a mean[s] of attracting non-aligned support to [the] NPT."[53]

Moscow and Washington held new nuclear assurances back as last resorts. The issue had garnered renewed attention after Japan affirmed that the UN Charter's ban on wars of aggression applied to nuclear weapons as well, and Foster and Goldberg wanted to set out a non-use formula in case the Soviets were to invoke the Kosygin proposal. Before the UNGA convened, Foster, Goldberg, and Secretary of Defense Clark Clifford requested presidential authorization to note the country's intent to spare those who lacked both atomic arms and nuclear-armed allies from any "threat or use of nuclear weapons," but the U.S. Joint Chiefs feared that this would dilute U.S. military credibility, limit options in Southeast Asia and the Korean peninsula, and lend impetus to appeals for more categorical bans. It was not an abstract debate. As the battle for Khe Sanh raged throughout February, General William Westmoreland, the commander of U.S. military forces in Vietnam, had requested the transfer of atom bombs into the theater. Johnson had overruled the request, which would have invited Chinese intervention and the nonproliferation treaty's demise; even so, it was another matter to renounce tactical nuclear-weapon use in perpetuity. For the time being Dean Rusk held back on spelling out additional pledges.[54]

Preponderant U.S. military power in the Atlantic and the Pacific would after all serve as critical buttresses of a post-treaty nuclear order. Yet the North Atlantic Treaty's twenty-year duration raised a troubling question: Would the NPT outlast NATO? John McCloy had warned his West German contacts in March that after France's disengagement the treaty organization might not survive another quarter century.[55] And as NATO's charter allowed members to withdraw as early as 1969, if Bonn were to enter into an open-ended obligation not to arm itself with nuclear weaponry, its leaders would want the alliance "extended on a long term basis." The Atlantic Alliance would need to square this circle before the UNSC voted on security assurances, even as Johnson pressured his West German allies to foot more of the bill for U.S. troops stationed on its soil.[56] U.S. under secretary of state Eugene Rostow proposed a solution to the FRG's top diplomat, Georg Duckwitz, on March 30: West Germany's allies would clarify that their adherence to the NPT would be contingent on "the confidence of members in the North Atlantic Treaty."[57] The two allies nevertheless remained at odds over the state of affairs. The minutes of a National Security Council (NSC) meeting in the White House on May 22 minced few words: "The Non-Proliferation Treaty—the Germans don't like it."[58]

The treaty also occasioned "profound soul searching" in Japan, whose actions were closely watched from Australia to Korea.[59] Tokyo had a world-class civilian atomic energy industry and a fledgling space program. The sophisticated nuclear infrastructures of the Republic of China and the Republic of Korea (ROK) raised eyebrows as well. In the absence of a regional security alliance, client states relied more on the United States. When they were promoting the nonproliferation treaty, U.S. ambassadors in Taipei, Manila, Wellington, and Canberra were instructed to echo Ambassador William Porter's tributes to the U.S.-ROK mutual defense treaty in Seoul.[60] The hub-and-spoke alliance network imposed few neighborly commitments on Tokyo. For this reason, Satō toured Southeast Asia in November 1967 to reassure his hosts that he harbored no secret atomic ambitions. Officials in Tokyo and Washington believed that the U.S.-Japanese mutual defense treaty, with its hidden atomic underpinnings, anchored the Asia-Pacific region. As Satō had acknowledged in a meeting with McNamara the previous November, "not only Japan, but Korea, Taiwan, and the Philippines . . . relied on the U.S. presence and arrangements in Okinawa." That U.S. nuclear forces underwrote the region's security convinced Satō to face down public pressure to denuclearize the Japanese archipelago that spring. In the event of emergency, Okinawa would remain available as a staging ground for nuclear-armed U.S. B-52s and Iwo Jima for U.S. Navy Polaris SSBNs.[61]

An afterthought to this point, Australia posed unique challenges as a major U.S. ally and a uranium exporter. Prime Minister John Gorton's Liberal cabinet had to consider how the treaty would affect both their country's security and its commerce. Following the British announcement that its military forces would withdraw from east of Suez by 1971, the Australia, New Zealand and United States Security (ANZUS) Treaty emerged as the mainstay of their security strategy, with the effect that supranational assurances raised doubts over whether—if push came to shove—the United States would repulse conventional onslaughts from Indonesia or China with nuclear means. Australian Atomic Energy Commission (AAEC) chairman Sir Philip Baxter had assembled a formidable nuclear infrastructure even as the country's intelligence services kept a close eye on Indian, Japanese, and Pakistani nuclear developments.[62] ACDA officials were in close correspondence with Gorton's foreign ministry, which was at loggerheads with the AAEC over the treaty. At an ANZUS meeting in April, Rusk was taken aback how "like de Gaulle" Gorton sounded in his questioning of U.S. nuclear credibility.[63] He accordingly dispatched a delegation led by George Bunn and Peter Scoville of the U.S. AEC to answer his queries. Would the NPT forbid enrichment or reprocessing? Would it mandate safeguards on uranium mines? How close could states party venture toward manufacture without a violation?[64] Australian officials made a point of underscoring their need "to be in a position to manufacture nuclear weapons if India and Japan were to go nuclear."[65]

Nuclear aspirants in Latin America, Asia, Africa, and the Middle East represented the hardest cases. Gandhi waited only a handful of days after the ENDC had finished its work to declare her nonsupport. After a note arrived the next day from the Canadian embassy stating that Ottawa would henceforth insist on the inclusion of IAEA safeguards in all future atomic assistance agreements, Indian officials informed the U.S. embassy that Gandhi "does not view NPT as a step toward peace. She sees no advantage accruing to India in signing the treaty. In her view the tripartite . . . security assurances resolution is not credible."[66] Faced with the prospect of crossing both the superpowers and also nuclear exporters, Gandhi nonetheless instructed her representative in New York to tread lightly.[67] Brazil sounded even more intransigent. João Augusto de Araújo Castro, the Latin American power's chief nuclear diplomat, characterized the treatment of peaceful nuclear explosives in the NPT as "*leonine*"—an unequal treaty imposed by a stronger party—and "an instrument of North American imperialism in the atomic domain."[68] Argentinian and Peruvian representatives spoke as kindred spirits. On April 17, Magalhães Pinto explained to U.S. ambassador John Tuthill that his government had made a "firm" decision not to sign—only his willingness to come to Washington to sit down with Rusk softened the blow.[69] U.S. State Department officials gathered from nationalist sentiment in Brazil that the ambitious foreign minister might try to thwart the treaty in New York, or, barring that, shrink the majority to the vanishing point.[70]

In the Middle East, Gamal Abdel Nasser's lieutenants explained to Soviet and U.S. visitors that Egypt's attitude rested on Israel and South Africa's behavior. ACDA assistant director Samuel De Palma had been either misleading or misinformed when he assured Egyptian officials in February there was "reason to believe" Israel would sign.[71] In fact, U.S. officials had hit a wall in their campaign to satisfy themselves that Dimona was not a front for plutonium reprocessing. CIA director Richard Helms had informed Johnson by May that Israel had crossed the nuclear threshold based on observations made by Lawrence Livermore National Laboratory director Edward Teller during visits to Israel, along with other intelligence.[72] While Johnson withheld the news from Rusk and McNamara, senior officials were growing wise to Israel's games. Whether France would retrieve the spent fuel from Dimona was, by early 1968, a secondary cause for concern.[73] U.S. ambassador Wally Barbour requested another tour of the reactor building on April 30 to show that Washington was "serious" following intelligence that Israel was refining unsafeguarded ore from Argentina.[74]

In the face of these headwinds, Johnson's government turned to commercial and technological carrots and sticks. Miners were a special case. Canadian officials had served as effective representatives for commodity producers in Geneva, but the South African government, which had ambitions to reduce foreign dependence and ascend the value chain through uranium enrichment and plutonium reprocessing, raised issues about the effect of IAEA safeguards on sales of uranium and thorium ore. They were reassured that the treaty would permit fissile-material production under safeguards and that only uranium concentrate, or yellowcake, would count as safeguard-worthy "source material."[75] While the South Africans remained noncommittal, U.S. ambassador William Rountree, with one eye on Black African opinion, begged them to keep their reservations to themselves in New York.[76]

For advanced exporters, the U.S. government counted on its free-world monopoly on reactor-grade uranium and plutonium. Euratom had contracted with the U.S. Atomic Energy Commission (AEC) for 35,000 kilograms of fissile uranium in 1963, and, thanks to the boom in reactor construction the previous two years, eyed multi-decade contracts for another 145,000 kilograms. Washington was bound to honor its existing commitments, but the draft treaty required that future cooperative agreements mandate IAEA safeguards. The resulting jeopardy offered an unimpeachable pretext to strong-arm countries reliant on U.S.-sourced fissile materials.[77] A *New York Times* article by John Finney asserting that Washington would sever enriched-uranium supplies to noncompliant states elicited a strong denial from the U.S. State Department.[78] For all Rusk's protests that such an eventuality was "remote," the dilemma was clear. Euratom could finance uranium-enrichment and plutonium-reprocessing facilities, whose construction would take at least five years, or abandon their plans for nuclear development.[79] Or they could adhere to the NPT and accept international regulation.

The Soviets took the lead with India and Egypt, with mixed results. Soviet and U.S. diplomats had regular high-level dialogue with Indian officials, whom they implored to play ball. They were careful not to alienate Gandhi, so, rather than twist her arm, they stressed the political importance of UN-based security assurances and sold assistance to India's cash-strapped atomic-energy program. Outside Europe, the Kremlin accorded nonproliferation secondary priority. The Soviets preferred not to risk India as a counterweight to Mao Zedong's China. Within weeks of personally exhorting Gandhi to adhere in March, Kosygin signed a modest nuclear agreement with her government. Although Indian nuclear experts likened it to "seventeen pages of crap," the signal had been sent: Soviet investments in India were not on the table.[80]

The Soviet Foreign Ministry and the International Department of the CPSU nevertheless embarked on a full-court press of friendly governments and leftist partisans that spring. Ahead of the special UNGA session, the CPSU's Central Committee had directed the Foreign Ministry to telegraph Soviet ambassadors in seventy countries and the UN, with special instructions to those in the Warsaw Pact (where Mongolia was an observer) and France, Italy, Mexico, Japan, and India, to relate the "exceptionally great importance" that the Soviet government assigned "to the question of the non-proliferation of nuclear weapons" on which they expected the government in question "take a favorable position."[81] While the Soviet ambassador in New Delhi exhorted Gandhi's government not to make its support of the nonproliferation accord conditional on arms control or disarmament, additional correspondence with the pro-Soviet faction of the Communist Party of India (CPI), whose members had split in 1964 with more radical, pro-PRC comrades, bore witness to Soviet anxieties about the limits of ideological solidarity.[82] That spring in a closed session, the Central Executive Committee of the CPI's National Council reportedly rejected the NPT on the grounds that it "infringe[d]" upon Indian sovereignty, commanding its twenty-three representatives in the Lok Sabha to join the Indian National Congress in opposition to the pact. In his remarks to the lower house, the CPI's deputy leader, Hirendranath Mukherjee, acquitted himself as a patriot: "India is a country that doesn't put its signature when someone orders it to do so. It doesn't have any need to sign a non-proliferation treaty."[83]

Johnson faced his own dilemma relative to Israel: Should he try to buy Tel Aviv's compliance by threatening planned sales of F-4 Phantoms? Rusk and Foster made a last-ditch effort to win Prime Minister Levi Eshkol's agreement on April 28, two days after the UNGA special session launched. The White House had rejected requests for a presidential communiqué, however, and their mission came to naught.[84] Johnson's affinity for Israel and the importance of Jewish voters to the Democratic Party had won out. Rusk, Foster, Anatoly Dobrynin, and Kuznetsov meanwhile went to work on other nuclear-capable regional powers. In early April, Foster had described Brazil as "leading the opposition" with West Germany, Italy, and India in tow, and even Japan sympathetic.[85] So it was therefore something of a coup when Rusk convinced Magalhães Pinto not to "proselytize against the NPT" when he sat down with the Brazilian foreign minister on May 6. A letter sent three weeks earlier, in which Rusk had implicitly threatened the long tradition of U.S.-Brazilian cooperation, may have done the trick.[86] That same day, Kuznetsov scored his own coup when the UN First Committee's Egyptian president, Ismail Fahmy, announced that Cairo would co-sponsor a resolution endorsing the draft treaty. The anti-treaty coalition had been nipped in the bud. Egyptian ambassador Mohamed Awad El Kony confided to French ambassador Armand Bérard that Nasser had made the decision "under strong pressure from Moscow," to whom the Romanians also shared that a Israeli signature had been promised as part of the deal.[87]

III

Superpower cooperation was necessary but insufficient to send the treaty over the finish line. According to Foster, the Latin American and African blocs, with twenty-four and thirty-two members apiece, held the balance in New York, where they amounted to nearly half of the UNGA delegations.[88] With the West and the East, they represented two-thirds of the plenary vote. The African bloc was both the largest and the least directly preoccupied with nuclear issues. The fact that the UN ambassador from Ghana hammered the draft treaty for its failure to address the U.S.-Soviet arms race unsettled the Western and Eastern contingents, but most sub-Saharan African countries were more interested in a supplementary motion to censure South African interference in South West Africa.[89] To pacify them without encouraging further demands to ostracize the apartheid regime, U.S. diplomats implored Pretoria to speak out in support of the treaty.

Discussion began in the UN on April 26, when Goldberg and Kuznetsov elaborated their governments' positions before the First Committee. Although their speeches were similar enough that one listener joked, "The only thing they didn't do was hold hands," there remained notes of discord in the hall.[90] Goldberg enumerated three major purposes for the treaty: to lessen the odds of nuclear proliferation and war, to promote a regulated and equitable distribution of the atom's "peaceful blessings," and to compel serious disarmament strides. He singled out periodic review conferences as the primary means of enforcement and arms control headway as the chief barometer of success: "The permanent viability of this treaty," he continued, "will depend in large measure on our success in the further negotiations contemplated by Article VI."[91] His government, he pledged, would hold up its side of the bargain. While Goldberg presented the NPT as resting on three pillars, Kuznetsov struck a different note, insisting that the "uppermost and in our opinion the predominant feature of the draft" was to shut off "all channels, both direct and indirect, leading to the possession of mass destruction weapons." While his presentation reflected Soviet obsessions with NATO nuclear-sharing and West Germany, Goldberg's formula framed the treaty as a global achievement—"the creation of all nations, large and small."[92]

The superpowers were not alone in mythologizing about the treaty's origins. Latin America, and, above all, Mexico, whose delegation García Robles led, worked hard to accentuate the treaty's anticolonial features. The breakdown of Latin American views in New York mirrored those in the nuclear-weapon-free talks in Mexico City the year before. Brazil had made clear that neither it, nor Argentina, nor Chile, would back the resolution. As for the rest of the regional grouping, García Robles led a group emboldened by the Treaty of Tlatelolco, which he likened to a "gadfly and inspiration" for the nonproliferation agreement now under debate.[93] At UN headquarters, he pushed his government's line to its limits, distributing a working paper to the Latin American group on May 8, which prompted Rusk to urge Mexican foreign minister Antonio Carrillo Flores to rein in his special representative, who, he quipped, sounded "more Mexican than the Mexicans."[94] Undaunted, García Robles and his Latin American confederates drew up a list of desired revisions, occasioning the most acute crisis of the special session.

García Robles unveiled his recommendations to the UN First Committee on May 16. His address led off with praise for Irish foreign minister Frank Aiken, "who ten years ago, in the autumn of 1958, first introduced the proposal" that had become UNGA Resolution 1665 (XVI). He commended Foster, Fisher, Roshchin, Lord Chalfont, and Fred Mulley (British minister for disarmament since 1967) for their contributions before listing his demands: a preambular reference to the prohibition on wars of aggression in the UN Charter; a "right of access to scientific and technological information . . . and to participate in the fullest possible exchange of such information" in the Atoms for Peace language of Article IV; and the creation of the international PNE service that Article V promised "as soon as possible." Most dramatically, he petitioned for the arms control and disarmament language in Article VI to reference the "manufacture and perfection" of existing arsenals. He contrasted his own handiwork with the draft NPT in a forceful criticism of the two-tier nuclear order on offer: Latin America's "special conditions" had brought into existence "a multilateral instrument which, from the standpoint of disarmament and treaty law is undeniably far superior to the draft before us." When compared to the NPT, he maintained, the Treaty of Tlatelolco was "much more complete."[95]

Rusk ordered Goldberg and Foster to hold a "common front" with Kuznetsov and Roshchin lest García Robles "open the floodgates."[96] Yet the superpowers now found themselves on the defensive in the UN First Committee, with industrial states demanding clarity on the letter, and developing nations on the spirit, of a treaty that would sanctify a nuclear club whose members would tower above the rest of the world. A late intervention by Australia was also forcing Washington to detail its vision of a regulated world market for nuclear commodities and technology. Foreign Minister Paul Hasluck viewed Australia as a blue-ribbon member of the "free world." When he had addressed the Australian parliament that spring, he defended the role that "middle and small powers" like theirs played in "great world issues of power and their interaction with issues of regional security."[97] After Bunn reported that

Australian policy makers feared falling "behind India and Japan," officers in ACDA and the State Department specified exactly what the treaty would entail with three aide-mémoire that, among other matters, noted the exemption of uranium exports from IAEA safeguards and the permissibility of all dual-use activities save explosive work.[98] When word of the documents leaked in New York, the aide-mémoire was circulated to all Euratom and NATO members, as well as the Japanese, Israeli, and South African delegations.[99]

In the days after García Robles's speech, Rusk and Kuznetsov weighed their options. Their resistance toward amendments was slipping, with Rusk convinced they were losing the high ground in New York and Kuznetsov that Mexico's revisions "would not only bring along virtually all L[atin] A[mericans] but also be very helpful with [the] Africans and Asians."[100] Goldberg counted eighty reliable votes. Kuznetsov countered with sixty.[101] Minor edits might achieve "significantly wider adherence." Since the African, Latin American, and French delegations were the greatest sources of apprehension, Kuznetsov urged Rusk to "make good use of [U.S.] bargaining power" while he went to work on the Romanians and the Yugoslavs. Among the Africans, Ghana, Tanzania, and Kenya were critical, and the Soviet deputy foreign minister saw two ways to win them over. First, African ministers had resolved at a recent Afro-Asian meeting that their support of the nonproliferation accord would depend on a concurrent resolution on the political situation in Southern Rhodesia, where the white-settler regime continued to marginalize native Africans. Although the support of Francophone African countries was suspect, Kuznetsov reckoned that the French might help sway their ex-colonies. As for Latin America, he asked for "U.S. help." He concluded that Pretoria's and Tel Aviv's attitudes would be pivotal "in swinging the entire African vote."[102]

Latin America's common front ultimately compelled Washington and Moscow to accept a handful of revisions as well as a less binding resolution. When Goldberg and Kuznetsov sat down with the Latin American working group on May 28, García Robles disclaimed any desire to open "Pandora's box." On the contrary, he believed that his alterations would drive favorable votes above the one-hundred mark.[103] In addition the UNGA should commend—rather than endorse—the revised treaty so that capitals would not feel as if their UN vote would box them into signing the NPT.[104] The preamble would affirm the UN Charter's ban on wars of aggression and effective arms control measures "as soon as possible," while an international organization such as the IAEA would stand up a Plowshare service expeditiously. These revisions were never meant to be transformative. García Robles himself had characterized them as "minor and harmless," however necessary they were to win a commanding majority.[105] Rusk and Kuznetsov had prevailed on the Mexican diplomat to remove the freeze proposal—the most consequential—because its verification would mean "standing guard over every weapon."[106] Although he tolerated his deputy foreign minister's negotiating prowess, President Gustavo Díaz Ordaz was more interested in peaceful nuclear assistance for national development than in curbing the U.S.-Soviet arms race. As Bérard reported back to the Quai d'Orsay, these last-minute adjustments "dispelled the reservations of the majority and, at least, those of the Latin American countries."[107]

IV

Israel's ambassador pledged his support for the Treaty on the Non-Proliferation of Nuclear Weapons on May 29. One week later, Foreign Minister Abba Eban confirmed that Israel "would sign an acceptable NPT." Their assurances were a façade. The new Israeli ambassador in Washington, Yitzhak Rabin, made known on June 4 that a decision to sign would not happen lightly—nuclear ambiguity remained vital to keeping the Arabs off balance.[108] South Africa's kindred declaration the day before proved no more binding.[109] Even so, the success of the United States in riding herd over its proxies had mollified the African and Middle Eastern caucuses. For their part European allies were reassured that NATO would not only survive; they would receive expanded roles in future arms control negotiations. In East Asia, Rusk extracted a promise from Japanese vice minister of foreign affairs Nobuhiko Ushiba to back the resolution, though co-sponsorship proved a bridge too far for Tokyo.[110]

Although collectively the handful of concessions were more symbolic than real, they unlocked an impressive majority in New York. The UN First Committee commended the NPT on June 10. The treaty sponsors picked up two more votes in the UNGA on June 12. The final tally was ninety-four in favor, four against. There were twenty-one abstentions. Twelve Latin American delegations served as co-sponsors. Bérard was first to address the plenary after the vote, promising that although France would not sign the NPT, it would "behave . . . exactly as the States which decide to."[111] The Brazilian abstention was pro forma, with President Artur da Costa e Silva trivializing the treaty in Rio the next day.[112] That the United States, the United Kingdom, and the Soviet Union had failed to whip more than one hundred delegations seemed to vindicate Garcia Robles's eleventh-hour intervention.

Happy to escape antiwar protests outside the White House, Johnson accepted Goldberg's offer to make a surprise visit to UN headquarters. Before the UNGA, he called on the nuclear club, with the international community's help in Geneva, to advance "the limitation of strategic offensive and defensive nuclear weapons."[113] Kuznetsov's mention of the desirability of SALT negotiations in late April had been taken as a good omen.[114] While Foster had lost a critical ally when McNamara resigned in late November 1967 citing military stalemate in Vietnam, Rusk's evolution was a source of consolation.[115] Johnson spoke at greater length when the treaty opened for signature in London, Moscow, and Washington, D.C., on July 1, 1968, lauding the atomic charter for keeping the nuclear peace. His concluding announcement that the United States and the Soviet Union had agreed to launch SALT and ABM negotiations "in the nearest future" (Soviet and U.S. officials had been discussing a second Kosygin-Johnson summit for weeks) telegraphed who would act as the chief arbiters of "sanity and security" in the new nuclear order.[116]

Johnson once more had his eye on the electoral calendar. His announcement on March 31 that he would not seek another term had turned Vice President Hubert Humphrey and Robert Kennedy, both longstanding champions of nuclear arms control, into the front-runners for the Democratic nomination. After Kennedy fell to an assassin's bullet on June 5, Humphrey and his interim boss became the sole inheritors of John Kennedy's legacy of nuclear guardianship. Johnson had not ruled out elbowing Humphrey aside if his political fortunes were to improve. Nor had he turned over U.S. foreign policy amid his increasingly desperate quest to wrest victory from the ashes in Vietnam. Whoever was on the ballot, the momentum that the NPT had created in U.S.-Soviet relations offered an opportunity to present Johnson and Humphrey as peacemakers as the Vietnam War and the backlash against civil rights continued to wrack American society.[117]

The UNSC resolution was the final puzzle piece. While the UNGA resolution had lowered the temperature in New York, there remained numerous critics of the nonproliferation concept on the Security Council that summer. That the Republic of China and not the PRC would cast a vote in the high council illustrated the resolution's ulterior motive even as the PRC's informal accreditation as a nuclear-weapon state weakened the U.S. case not to seat Mao's delegation in New York. The U.S. State Department believed it could count on eight delegations—the Republic of China, Canada, Denmark, Hungary, and Paraguay, in addition to the three sponsoring nuclear powers. France, Algeria, and India were likely to abstain. A pivotal ninth vote would have to come from one of Brazil, Ethiopia, Pakistan, and Senegal. Algiers was closely aligned with communist China, about whose absence it was expected to raise a fuss. Pakistan would be reluctant to preempt the forthcoming Conference of Non-Nuclear-Weapon States, which it had originally sponsored.[118]

The French attitude toward the treaty was cryptic, with the Security Council meeting bringing a long-simmering debate in Paris to a head. With his great-power veto, de Gaulle could throw a wrench in the works, if he were so inclined. He had long thought that the drive to integrate NATO's conventional and nuclear defense mainly benefited the "American strategic monopoly."[119] He was likewise convinced that the NPT would consolidate an "unacceptable American and Russian monopoly."[120] In the first draft of his speech, Bérard was set to remind the council that nuclear nonproliferation would never be equivalent to nuclear and general disarmament.

There were nonetheless significant benefits if France were to tolerate the NPT, which the high commissioner of the *Commissariat à l'Énergie Atomique* (CEA), Francis Perrin, had outlined the year before. Geopolitically, no potential development imperiled French security more than a nuclear-armed West Germany—the NPT offered another layer of insurance against this scenario. Technologically, the costs of rejecting the treaty outstripped the benefits. Like the rest of Euratom, French commercial reactors relied on U.S.-sourced enriched uranium and plutonium; unlike them, that reliance stemmed in part from the allocation of fissile materials to warhead production. Perrin expressed confidence in existing U.S.-Euratom supply agreements—U.S.-sourced plutonium to fuel a prototype Phénix breeder reactor as early as 1970 was another matter. Reputationally, the UN security assurances cast an unflattering light on France's asymmetric posture, whose *tous azimuts* formula targeted the population centers of friends and foes alike for indiscriminate strikes. Even without its veto, the UNSC resolution would not weaken the national deterrent. Leaving aside the possibility of a future German blitzkrieg, Paris would balk at threatening Bonn for fear that Washington would retaliate against Paris.[121] Perrin had advised that the French Foreign Ministry should neither belabor nor sharpen its criticisms of the NPT, nor humor requests to intervene from recalcitrant regional powers such as West Germany or Japan.[122] The Quai d'Orsay duly appended an affirmation of the *force de frappe*'s defensive function and a more accommodating conclusion to Bérard's speech, which declared France "ready for all initiatives that the other Powers would be disposed to accept."[123] The next day Kuznetsov thanked Bérard for "having done nothing to thwart Moscow and Washington's policies."[124]

The Security Council debate nevertheless featured a raft of profound criticisms of the treaty regime. Representatives from Canada, Denmark, Paraguay, Hungary, and Senegal endorsed the measure on June 17, with Paraguay's plenipotentiary underscoring the importance that Latin American states ascribed to peaceful atomic energy for economic development.[125] The next day was livelier. New Delhi told its permanent UN representative, Gandhi's close advisor Gopalaswami Parthasarathi, to demand a vote on each paragraph and then object to every reference to the NPT itself. When Bérard informed him he would not support such a motion, Parthasarathi overruled New Delhi for fear of "dividing the abstentionists."[126]

The debate was nevertheless heated. Algeria's delegate railed against the treaty as an affront to the PRC while Brazil's lambasted the Soviet Union for not adhering to the Treaty of Tlatelolco's Protocol II. Pakistan's envoy made it clear that Islamabad preferred to vote after the Conference of Non-Nuclear-Weapon States had convened in August. He raised two more concerns—the security assurances were not surefire and the formula "aggression with nuclear weapons or the threat of such aggression" could become a perverse justification of atomic coercion from UNSC permanent members.

India's objections extended those of its rival next door. Parthasarathi maintained that a formal link between UNSC assurances and the NPT would condemn noncompliant nation-states to a state of perpetual insecurity by imposing second-class status on them: "The basis for any action by the Security Council for the maintenance of international peace and security," he reminded those in the chamber, was the UN Charter, which did not "discriminate between those who might adhere to a particular treaty and those who might not do so." The new language in the preamble introduced by García Robles had not eased his mind. He found it maddening that an unequal treaty would add conditions to collective security, dividing the world into two castes "which were not found in the UN Charter, and whose application could lead to abuses" by sanctioning the arbitrary use of coercive power by members of the nuclear club.[127]

These reservations notwithstanding, UNSC Resolution 255 passed on June 18. Ten voted in favor. France, India, Brazil, Algeria, and Pakistan abstained. Afterward Goldberg and Kuznetsov celebrated a burgeoning U.S.-Soviet détente, but the debates in New York had further alienated rising regional powers, raising questions about how the NPT would alter the international system's operation.[128] From Beijing, Chinese premier Zhou Enlai summed up the radical postcolonial critique of the NPT when he described it as a smokescreen behind which the United States, the United Kingdom, and the Soviet Union worked to "turn non-nuclear countries into their protectorates and press forward with a new type of colonialism—nuclear colonialism."[129]

V

The treaty's survival would turn on whether the nuclear club could foster a broadly accepted distribution of nuclear security, market equity, and political choice. The preponderant influence of the United States remained key. Its concentration in Western Europe and East Asia—and its diminution elsewhere—would set enduring patterns for the successes and failures of the new regime.

To enhance their nuclear security and political rights under the new regime, West European allies had extracted two concessions from the Johnson administration. The Federal Republic's observer status at the UN had not stopped the West Germans from "mischief-making" in New York.[130] Their most pressing demand related to NATO. With the alliance's withdrawal clause set to take effect the following year, they asked their treaty partners to reaffirm their Article V commitments.[131] NATO issued a joint statement ahead of a special ministerial session in Reykjavik declaring their confidence in the alliance "an essential factor" in any future approach to the NPT.[132] Washington also promised closer consultations with NATO once SALT got under way. Following the UNSC vote, Foster and Cleveland stressed to Rusk how the NPT had "copper-bottomed" the nuclear umbrella over Europe. The secretary of state must have caught their drift from the title of their memorandum—"NATO's

Going to Want a Role in Arms Control Talks."[133] Tokyo was more ambivalent. The treaty package had reportedly emboldened "Japanese advocates of keeping nuclear options open." Nevertheless, as Foreign Minister Takeo Miki confided, there was "no one else to whom Japan could turn," raising hopes within the Johnson administration that Japan would sign within the year.[134] That August the two sides discussed a joint communiqué that would reaffirm their mutual defense treaty when Satō visited Washington, D.C., but with a U.S. presidential election on the horizon such a high-level meeting was for the moment ruled out.[135]

Among the developing nations, circumstances were most promising in Latin America. Rusk came away from their meetings convinced that political opportunism had accounted for Magalhães Pinto's troublemaking, while Mexico's intervention had proved instrumental in New York. In Mexico, Comision Nacional de Energia Nuclear director José Gorostiza joined García Robles in assuring President Díaz Ordaz that the nonproliferation treaty would boost the country's atomic-energy efforts, which as the country's oil reserves depleted would become "a paramount factor in the country's economic life."[136] Industry would face no additional burdens because both the NPT and the Treaty of Tlatelolco required IAEA safeguards.[137] To adhere would also expand on Atoms for Peace programs, fostering knowledge and technology transfers via research centers, educational institutions, international organizations, and nuclear imports. Like the leaders of other underdeveloped oil-producing countries whose reliance on Western expertise and capital chafed, Mexican officials feared technological dependence. It was essential, Gorostiza therefore counseled, that industrial powers provide "the equipment and materials without which scientific and technical information alone would be meaningless and lacking in real utility."[138]

Whether Israel, South Africa, or India adhered would have far-reaching ramifications throughout their neighborhoods. In August, Soviet and U.S. observers to the Conference of Non-Nuclear-Weapon States were disabused of the idea that India would eventually warm to the NPT regime. South African officials likewise claimed that they could not accede until Black African states stopped trying to eject Pretoria from the IAEA. Johnson tiptoed around the issue of Israel's signature until after the F-4 Phantom sale was finalized on the sole condition that the fighter-bombers never carry atom bombs. His advisors had failed to convince him to bring personal pressure to bear until he was a lame duck as the White House grew resigned to Eshkol and Rabin's intransigence.[139] In December 1968, Walt Rostow would surmise that the Israelis had made the bet that promises not to introduce nuclear weaponry into the region would suffice "so long as they had neither tested it nor made its existence public." With Tel Aviv running out the clock on the administration, Walt Rostow ended on a dour note: "Needless to say, that view leaves a lot to be desired."[140] Their

FIGURE 5 Soviet ambassador Anatoli Dobrynin signs the NPT in the East Room of the White House on July 1, 1968, as British ambassador Sir Patrick Dean and ambassadors from nonaligned states look on.
Source: Lyndon B. Johnson Presidential Library.

successors, President Richard Nixon and National Security Advisor Henry Kissinger, would prove even more open to Israeli arguments that theirs was a special case.

In the summer of 1968 White House interest in nuclear diplomacy fully revolved around the November elections. For Johnson, the treaty offered a rebuttal to an ever more vocal antiwar movement. When he had seen the president in the spring, Goldberg played up this theme, styling the NPT "the most momentous achievement for peace since the Limited Test Ban Treaty" despite having "not yet fully sunk in with the public."[141] When Johnson sent the treaty to Capitol Hill in June, he had assumed that sixty-four Democratic senators would expedite its ratification, handing him and Vice President Humphrey favorable headlines and pushing Vietnam off the front pages. Secretary of Defense Clifford's growing unease about a potential Soviet intervention in Czechoslovakia went unheeded in the White House, which moved to jointly announce strategic arms talks with the Kremlin within the month, with a U.S.-Soviet summit in Russia set to follow in October, weeks before the election.[142] A press conference was scheduled for August 29, when it would preempt the Conference of Non-Nuclear-Weapon States and also highlight Johnson's record of nuclear statecraft on the final day of the Democratic National Convention.

Brezhnev's crackdown on the Prague Spring was the plan's undoing. The night before the White House press conference to announce SALT negotiations, Dobrynin broke the news to Johnson in the Oval Office that Warsaw Pact tanks had rolled into Czechoslovakia, dropping a curtain on the theater of détente. Brezhnev's assertion of the CPSU and its Eastern European comrades' right to impose ideological conformity on Eastern Europe brought Dubček's "socialism with a human race" to a bloody end, revived anti-Soviet sentiment in the United States, and killed whatever chances Johnson had had that nuclear arms control could deliver a cease-fire in Vietnam, a Democratic dynasty at home, and his own political rehabilitation.[143]

With U.S.-Soviet relations now a third rail (and Nixon and Kissinger engaged in undermining peace talks with representatives of the North Vietnamese regime in Paris), Johnson's team turned to the tried-and-tested rhetoric of nuclear guardianship to make the case for a third consecutive Democratic presidential term. Harry McPherson, the chief White House speechwriter, tried to summon anew the magic Bill Moyers had used to such devastating effect in 1964 and 1966. Nixon's public opposition to NPT ratification after the Warsaw Pact crackdown on Czechoslovakia inspired a draft statement impugning the Republican candidate's motives and casting Johnson once more as a concerned father to all humankind.[144] Across Pennsylvania Avenue, the U.S. Senate recoiled at ratifying U.S.-Soviet détente. Although the Senate Foreign Relations Committee eventually backed the NPT on September 17, Majority Leader Mike Mansfield, a Democrat from Montana, succeeded in blocking a motion in the full Senate. In a public address on October 11, Johnson took both Nixon and the U.S. Senate to task. In comparing withdrawal from Southeast Asia to the likelihood of nuclear war without a nonproliferation treaty, he mounted an extended defense of executive action to prosecute expeditionary wars on behalf of anxious families lest "other nations trigger a nuclear conflict which could involve us." "As President," he warned, "I can tell you that our chance of doing so will be greatly reduced . . . and the world our children will inhabit made far more perilous, if we fail to act soon."[145] In an earlier draft Rusk and Walt Rostow had laid the paternalistic tropes on even more thickly, referring to "children and grandchildren" and "generations unborn" in asking U.S. citizens "to act now with the highest interests of the nation and of the human family in mind."[146]

Unfortunately for Johnson, by the fall of 1968 international nuclear diplomacy had become a sideshow when compared to the Vietnam War. McPherson promised Johnson that a special U.S. Senate session to debate the NPT would "set the Republicans to hollering, and make it a hell of an issue in the campaign." Neither senators nor presidential candidates, he assured the president, wanted to appear to be "on the side of nuclear war."[147] More to the point, Humphrey had been "on the right side" of the issue since his days on the Senate Subcommittee on Disarmament, when he had first proposed an arms control and disarmament agency.[148] He recommended a televised address from the Cabinet Room, where Johnson would hold the NPT up alongside the 1964 Civil Rights Act, the 1965 Voting Rights Act, and other Great Society legislation in a "vivid story of the past 5 years of achievement," before making "a hard pitch for Humphrey." (Johnson scribbled "Excellent!" next to his initials when he approved the idea).[149]

Then, one week before the election, Johnson changed tack, making a last-ditch effort at a cease-fire agreement with North Vietnam the centerpiece of his proxy campaign. The Humphrey-touting spectacle in the White House was pared down to a restrained radio address on October 27, when Johnson compared his vice president's record to those of Nixon and Alabama governor George Wallace, the segregationist American Independent Party candidate. Executive branch responsibility for nuclear security was a secondary theme: "When John Kennedy turned to him at the signing of the Nuclear Test Ban Treaty and said, 'Hubert, here is this pen; that is your treaty,' that was the culmination of years of working and planning for a world without nuclear fallout. . . . [He] is fighting now for a new treaty to halt the spread of nuclear weapons, though his opponent counsels delay in adopting this most urgent of international agreements, this vital step in protecting America and the world from nuclear war."

Echoing the Daisy ad from four years earlier, Johnson went on to warn that "none of us know how dangerous it is to counsel delay or what results may flow from it." His coda had been drafted to hit close to home: "You and your children in the next generation, and my grandson and new granddaughter will be mighty glad you did."[150] No advice was offered to childless voters or those deploying to Vietnam about how to cast their vote.

Johnson must have intuited that the charms of nuclear guardianship had passed their prime. Those who supported the war were less enamored of the United Nations, multilateral endeavors, or U.S.-Soviet détente. College-age, antiwar protesters and their sympathizers were for their part less interested in atom bombs than in Agent Orange and more invested in direct action than in presidential statecraft. Paternal safeguards were losing their appeal as thousands of young Americans died each year in a distant land, antiwar protestors and anti-establishment activists marched through main streets and occupied college quads, and newsstands and television screens filled up with images of Vietnamese children seared by napalm. The notion that presidents could keep existential threats to an affluent society indefinitely at bay without lasting damage to the nation's social fabric or its moral compass had grown fanciful.[151] The same day as his radio address, Johnson's ninth-inning push to engineer a bombing halt in exchange for Hanoi's commitment to respect a demilitarized zone pushed over a run. He announced over the air on October 31 that he had ordered "that all air, naval, and artillery bombardment of North Vietnam cease," promising further "progress toward a peaceful settlement of the Vietnamese war."[152] Five days ahead of the election, Johnson and Humphrey's records as nuclear peacemakers were afterthoughts.

Nixon's victory on November 5, 1968, marked a changing of the guard. Walt Rostow had long predicted an irreversible "diffusion of power," with advancing Western European and Japanese economies, a military stalemate in Southeast Asia, and a Soviet nuclear buildup imperiling U.S. global hegemony. It was means rather than ends that would change. If Kennedy, Johnson, and Nixon shared the same paramount goal—to preserve U.S. influence amid tectonic changes at home and abroad—the new administration homed in on different methods. When Nixon took the oath of office on January 20, 1969, the presidency was transferred from a Democratic mini-dynasty, whose crusade for a "common law" for humankind had yielded conflict in Southeast Asia and two globe-spanning nuclear treaties negotiated with the Soviet Union, to a Republican regime that relied on regional proxies, police forces, financial markets, and great-power summitry to insulate U.S. hegemony from dissent at home and multiplying external challenges emanating from friends as well as foes.[153]

Although Nixon and Kissinger never disavowed the NPT, their neglect of it proved benign only because elements of the national-security bureaucracy and the international community remained strongly invested in the nascent nonproliferation regime.[154] Nixon saw the treaty as the handiwork of the "loyal" opposition—for good reason—he and Kissinger were adamant that their approach to arms control represented a departure from past practice. When Gerald C. Smith, Foster's successor as ACDA director, portrayed the SALT treaty as building on "twenty-five years of consistent American policy to bring nuclear weapons under control," Nixon cursed him for "trying to give credit to the Democrats."[155] In public the president associated the NPT with his détente strategy. In private, he dismissed it entirely. Even after a NSC Review Group found few cons to the NPT (the benefits of selective proliferation to Japan or India were crossed out), Nixon did "the absolute minimum" to bring it into force. At a White House meeting on January 29, 1969, he implied it was not worth the paper on which it had been printed and rejected "arm twisting" to gain adherents, above all West Germany.[156] In the face of an internal consensus that high-level pressure should be brought to bear on uncooperative, bellwether states, the White House demurred.[157]

Political philosophy informed Nixon's and Kissinger's "ambivalence" toward the NPT.[158] Their emphasis on power politics resulted in a corresponding disinterest in economics, democracy, and ethics. For them multilateralism should run through Moscow and Beijing rather than London, Paris, Bonn, or Tokyo. Rather than viewing the Third World as history's cockpit, they treated all save a select group in Latin America, Asia, Africa, and the Middle East as peripheral, even contemptible. Under the doctrine that Nixon outlined in Guam on July 25, 1969, his administration would keep the United States at the helm of world affairs by devolving responsibility for anticommunist containment to authoritarian partners in Tehran, Riyadh, Brasília, Pretoria, Taipei, and Seoul, even after U.S. military forces withdrew from Vietnam following a "decent interval." While they would make good on treaty commitments and atomic assurances, U.S. troop numbers plummeted in Asia and Europe under Nixon. Whereas Kennedy and Johnson had catastrophized about proliferation in an effort to institutionalize U.S. hegemony, Nixon and Kissinger sought medium-term goals by means of a linkage policy that conditioned arms cuts or trading relations on matters as disparate as the Paris Peace Talks or Soviet covert aid for Third World revolutionaries.[159]

The result was a risk-averse nonproliferation policy as U.S. strategic retrenchment weakened the collective security environment on which the NPT had been based. While U.S. Senate ratification dictated bureaucratic buy-in for the NPT, the White House avoided hard choices. In East Asia, where Taipei and Seoul were militarizing their nuclear programs in response to Nixon's opening to China and U.S. troop drawdowns in South Vietnam and South Korea, Nixon and Kissinger remained passive.[160] Nor would they shy away from atomic diplomacy with Beijing and Moscow as Tokyo and Washington discussed gaseous-diffusion technology for uranium enrichment and the disposition of U.S. atomic assets in the Ryukyu islands following Okinawa's reversion to Japanese administration. When Kissinger landed in Beijing for his first meeting with Premier Zhou on July 9, 1971, he speculated that without U.S. superintendence the Japanese "military machine" might acquire "nuclear weapons". Six months later, Nixon intimated to Satō that Japanese adherence to the NPT was less important than the geopolitical leverage its nuclear latency provided against the PRC and the USSR: "In fact," he added meaningfully, "Japan might take its time and thus keep any potential enemy concerned." The president's statement was enough of a bombshell that he asked the prime minister to "forget the preceding remarks."[161]

In the Middle East, Nixon mirrored Johnson's reluctance to hold Israeli officials' feet to the fire. After an interagency study called in April for a major push for an Israeli signature on the NPT, up to threatening F-4 Phantom sales, Nixon's nonproliferation policy faced its first major test. After Golda Meir succeeded Eshkol as prime minister following his death in February, she continued to insist that her country would "not be the first to introduce nuclear weapons onto the Arab-Israel area."[162] Citing the limits of U.S. influence over matters of war and peace, Kissinger advised Nixon to cushion the inevitable blow. "In this case," he wrote, "public knowledge is almost as dangerous as possession itself." If Israel nonacquisition was a lost cause, they could still curb regional proliferation or Arab reliance on Soviet arms sales; the key was "to keep Israeli possession from becoming an established international fact.[163] By the time Nixon sat down with Meir for a White House meeting on September 26, 1969, he had decided that discretion was the better part of valor. By all accounts the two lead-ers came to an tacit understanding: Israel's nuclear arsenal would remain plausibly deniable. Most important, Tel Aviv would neither conduct a nuclear test nor allow public disclosure of its weapons work.[164] The United States and Israel would abide by the letter rather than the spirit of the NPT, which recognized nuclear status based on when a state "manufactured *and* exploded a nuclear weapon or other nuclear explosive device."[165] The termination of U.S. courtesy visits to Dimona confirmed that Nixon preferred not to know what was happening at the facility. On February 23, 1970, Rabin informed Kissinger that "Israel has no intention to sign the NPT."[166]

Nixon's White House could barely bring itself to formalize the NPT. Only six countries had ratified by the time he had taken office, prompting Spurgeon Keeny Jr. to warn of a vital loss of "momentum."[167] The heavy centralization of foreign policy making in Kissinger's NSC marginalized the State Department, ACDA, and the Pentagon, all of whose senior officials championed the treaty. Those working below Secretary of State William Rogers, a foreign policy neophyte, were instructed in no uncertain terms to underscore how NPT ratification would tee up "an era of negotiations."[168] Ahead of the West German elections, the new NSC staff urged Nixon to accommodate Bonn's attempts to tie NPT ratification to Soviet waivers of intervention rights until a formal peace deal was inked. After Brandt's election as chancellor paved the way for a West German signature on November 28, 1969—and joint U.S-Soviet ratification four days earlier—the president at first refused even to attend the deposit ceremony. He only relented in deference to London and Moscow, where Wilson and Kosygin respectively marked the occasion on March 5, 1970. Still he refused to deliver any remarks, leading Rogers and U.S. under secretary of state Elliott Richardson to vow that unless Nixon spoke "at least one sentence he had best not go at all." The one lawyerly sentence that he finally agreed to deliver at the cer-emony distanced himself from his predecessors (a few more were eventually added after a copy of Kosygin's lengthier and more auspicious remarks in Moscow earlier that day reached Washington).[169] Rusk, Foster, Fisher and Seaborg received invitations to the festivities, as did Johnson, albeit with only three days' notice. Nixon person-ally ensured that Humphrey was not invited. A tribute to Johnson's achievements in the field of nuclear arms control was nixed at the last minute, with a laconic Nixon instead delivering a homage to bipartisanship in the making of U.S. foreign policy.

Conclusion

The superpowers had won a commanding majority in the UN for a two-tier nuclear order with an abundance of persuasion and a smattering of coercion.[170] With Soviet and British encouragement, the United States had convinced allies and smaller powers that its armed forces would continue to police their neighborhoods against atomic threats. Washington had brought industrial titans and commodity producers around to the idea that a global regulatory regime would ensure competitive markets for their wares even as its near-monopoly on critical supplies of fissile materials left an implicit threat hanging over their heads. Johnson had assured key partners that although they would deny themselves the ultimate weapon, their voices would matter more in future chapters of global nuclear diplomacy.

From the beginning, the bargain embodied by the NPT carried within it the seeds of its own destruction. Its footing was less secure in South Asia, which was lightly patrolled by U.S. armed forces, and the Middle East, where Johnson and Nixon resisted scenarios in which Israel incurred punishment for spurning the treaty. Eight years after Eisenhower had brought Israel's nuclear program to Kennedy's attention, his vice president, Nixon, swept it under the rug. However long the Soviet Union had insisted that the NPT was aimed first and foremost at averting a nuclear-armed Fourth Reich, the formalization of the nuclear club coincided with Brezhnev's decision to send Warsaw Pact forces into Czechoslovakia and his resort to nuclear threats amid a border war with Beijing in the summer of 1969. The United States would keep on fighting in and dropping bombs on Vietnam and, after March 1969, Cambodia, until the Paris Peace Accords were signed in January 1973. Nixon and Kissinger were never natural spokesmen for global nuclear governance. In a private conversation in 1972 recorded on the tape system that Nixon had had installed in the Oval Office, the two men minced few words. "Let me say, the State [Department] always puts that Nonproliferation Treaty in there," Nixon complained. "You know what the reason is? The State Department bureaucracy considers that to be theirs. . . . [T]he Nonproliferation Treaty has nothing to do with the security of the United States of America. You know very well." Kissinger's concurrence put a finer point on it: "It's made at the expense of other countries."[171]

Conclusion
Saving Humanity from Itself

TWENTY-THREE YEARS AFTER THE U.S. ARMY Air Corps dropped two atom bombs on Japanese cities, the United States, the Soviet Union, and a large majority of the world's states—though representing a bare majority of its people—acclaimed the international community's division into two classes: a select club of nuclear powers and a general mass of atomic unarmed.[1] Since the Treaty on the Non-Proliferation of Nuclear Weapons (NPT) entered into force in March 1970, the mosaic of treaties, norms, and institutions that constitute the global nuclear nonproliferation regime has expanded and deepened, remaining a constant influence on the distribution of nuclear science and technology and also the red lines of territory and organized violence that lend predictability and significance to world politics. By the first quinquennial Review Conference in 1975, ninety-nine nation-states had signed and ratified the NPT. Today that number stands at 190. India, Israel, Pakistan, and South Sudan are the only countries still outside the regime, while the Democratic People's Republic of Korea (DPRK) claims to have left its ranks voluntarily—a defection that the other 189 for now reject.

In regarding the NPT as the crowning achievement of the search for nuclear order after the Second World War, the conservative arc of global nuclear politics comes into higher focus. From this standpoint the well-worn tale of a nuclear revolution turning total war into a relic of the past acquires a compelling subplot: the dawning recognition by the superpowers that the rampant spread of the art and science of fission and fusion—and the economic potentialities that make possible their transformation in tools of warfare—necessitated a spirited counterrevolution to consolidate brute force and moral capital in existing hands, and by doing so prolong their moment in the sun.

The nuclear club's formalization was an acknowledgment of the technological oligopoly and political oligarchy that were replacing the collapsing imperial order as the world proceeded to decolonize after 1945. The dual-use nature of advanced nuclear technology, most of all uranium enrichment, plutonium reprocessing, and nuclear explosives of all types, complicated the enterprise from the beginning. The presidential administrations of Richard Nixon, Gerald Ford, and Jimmy Carter revitalized American power by harnessing the energies of transnational exchange via market mechanisms that international clubs of rich-world actors would superintend as much as, if not more than, international institutions.[2] As in the realms of trade and finance, the United States turned to associations outside the United Nations (UN) system to manage the dilemmas of nuclear globalization. Less than four months after India detonated a peaceful nuclear explosion (PNE) on May 18, 1974, cheekily code-named "Smiling Buddha," the IAEA published a "trigger list" of sensitive items that the Zangger Committee had identified with a view "to harmonize the interpretation of nuclear export control policies for NPT Parties."[3] The fourteen members of the committee were all North American or Western European, with the sole exception of Japan.[4] Around the same time Henry Kissinger and British foreign secretary James Callaghan launched an initiative to revive a defunct Western Suppliers Group on an East-West basis. The group was commonly referred to as "the London Club," after the city where its headquarters was located, and Canada, France, Japan, the United Kingdom, the United States, the Soviet Union, and West Germany were its founding members. In 1976, the group expanded to include Belgium, Italy, the Netherlands, Sweden, East Germany, Poland, and Czechoslovakia.[5]

Proponents styled the two organizations as necessary sources of "multilateral nuclear export control policy." For those reliant on imports of advanced nuclear equipment or fissionable materials, on the other hand, they formed a "secret cartel forcing up uranium prices," as M. V. Kamath of the *Times of India* wrote in 1976.[6] After the Organization of Arab Petroleum Exporting Countries (OAPEC) had embargoed Canada, Japan, the Netherlands, the United Kingdom, and the United States in retaliation for their support of Israel during the 1973 Yom Kippur War, Kissinger must have relished the chance to turn the tables. The U.S. monopoly on uranium-enrichment, plutonium-reprocessing, and other dual-use items gave way to an oligopoly, a world market for nuclear commodities and technology with "few firms . . . on the supply side and a very large number of buyers on the demand side."[7] In 1978 the renamed Nuclear Suppliers Group publicized its guidelines in order to fend off accusations of secrecy and collusion, but the cumulative effect was one of perceived export coordination. Glenn Seaborg had warned the U.S. Joint Committee on Atomic Energy (JCAE) in March 1966 that without treaty-making "the marketplace" would yield "the lowest common denominator—no safeguards at all."[8] With the NPT in force, the atomic oligopoly found the means and the will to cooperate, with global security rather than market price as its governing mandate.

With the admission of the People's Republic of China (PRC) into the UN in 1971, the nuclear club became synonymous with the veto-wielding permanent members of the UN Security Council (UNSC). When the PRC joined the Nuclear Suppliers Group in 2005, the overlap between the nuclear-market oligopoly and the self-anointed oligarchy was complete—though in the interim communist China had substantially assisted the Pakistani nuclear-weapon program.[9] To the greatest extent possible NATO and the Warsaw Pact had concentrated the power to make nuclear war: the first through consultation and cooperation, as demonstrated by the survival of an independent French nuclear deterrent and a dependent British one; the second through coercion, as the invasion of Czechoslovakia in 1968 made clear. The United States inhibited the atomic aspirants of its allies unapologetically, quelling Japanese, South Korean, Brazilian, and Taiwanese weapon programs at various stages of development over the course of the 1970s and 1980s, as well as former adversaries, such as when the George H. W. Bush and Bill Clinton administrations cajoled the new nation-states of Ukraine, Belarus, and Kazakhstan to return Soviet nuclear forces to the Russian Federation.[10] Against non-allies, sticks were wielded more often than carrots: diplomatic ostracism, economic sanctions, cruise-missile strikes, cyberattacks, preventive war, regime change, and territorial occupation. Meanwhile, the canon of nonproliferation—the prioritization of nuclear over non-nuclear ("conventional") violence—has led even those who remained outside the NPT regime to justify the destruction of disagreeable nuclear facilities in its name.[11]

For what benefits the nuclear nonproliferation regime has granted the world—and they are many and momentous—this reactionary campaign has featured darker aspects: the perpetuation of the international social order, the criminalization of a species of advanced technology and engineering, the hierarchization of nuclear and non-nuclear violence, and the legitimation of five world-threatening arsenals. The price of saving humanity from itself was clear to George Orwell just months after two U.S. B-29s put Hiroshima and Nagasaki to the torch: "an end to large-scale wars at the cost of indefinitely prolonging a 'peace that is no peace.'"[12]

I

The NPT remains a Rosetta Stone of the second nuclear age, when the world transitioned from organized anarchy to provisional order. Together with the 1963 Moscow Treaty and the 1967 Treaty of Tlatelolco, the NPT inaugurated a regime of global governance—however spotty and imperfect—institutionalizing a status quo that had emerged from the interaction of the Cold War, nuclear globalization, and decolonization from 1945 to 1970. Those who drafted it hailed from North and South America,

Europe and Asia, the Middle East and Africa. They inscribed in it the ambitions and the anxieties of a moment when nation-states and global markets were replacing transoceanic empires as the chief regulators of transnational flows of capital, goods, peoples, commodities, and ideas, yet they did not do so equally—the gravitational pull of military power and diplomatic influence mattered much for whose voice carried weight and when.

Atop the regime sat the UN General Assembly (UNGA) and the UNSC. To win international consensus, the architects of the nonproliferation regime had had to identify common interests, manage unequal power, and mediate difference.[13] In other words, global nuclear governance needed to attain near-universality, credible effectiveness, and procedural justice or legitimacy. For the regime to offer public goods on a worldwide basis, its regulating authorities would need to be open to all recognized nation-states. For credibility's sake, a critical mass of those with world-class nuclear infrastructures would have to be inside the regime. Since most were U.S. allies, the United States guaranteed their nuclear security, their market access, and their political voice by means of bilateral or alliance-based assurances, targeted reciprocity, and institutionalized dialogue. A supermajority of the UNGA—whose ranks the processes of decolonization had decisively diversified—provided accreditation on the condition that states formally consent and that review conferences every five years review the NPT's present and future amid changing circumstances.

The achievement of these three related ends demanded a virtuosic ballet of consultation, persuasion, trade-offs, and concessions between the superpowers, their allies, and nonaligned and neutral states, whose governments were increasingly defining their national interests according to regional challenges and comparative advantages rather than international conventions or postcolonial utopias.[14] Thanks to an open drafting process and preexisting structures of reassurance, diplomacy, and institutionalization, the superpowers and their partners built a global nonproliferation regime while rarely resorting to outright coercion.

In the preambulatory phrases and binding articles of the NPT was inscribed the collective wisdom (albeit its lowest common denominator) of the world after empire. Although the fingerprints of power politics were there in invisible ink, the NPT was nevertheless that rare artifact—a universal security pact forged in peacetime. The 1921 Washington Naval Conference had met in the shadow of the Great War, excluding from the table at which warship tonnage and battleship numbers were settled all but envoys from the era's foremost naval powers—the United Kingdom, Japan, France, Italy, and the United States. The Belgian, Chinese, Portuguese, and Dutch plenipotentiaries had had to limit themselves to the China question: the integrity of its territorial sovereignty and the openness of trade across its borders.[15] When U.S. secretary of state Frank B. Kellogg and French foreign minister Aristide Briand opened the 1928

Paris Peace Conference, culminating in the General Treaty for Renunciation of War as an Instrument of National Policy (the Kellogg-Briand Pact), they had summoned the ghosts of the Great War to sanctify proceedings. Unlike the Washington Naval Treaty, all recognized nation-states were welcome to sign and ratify the Moscow Treaty or the NPT. Unlike the Kellogg-Briand Pact, the NPT illegalized not war itself but a certain tool of war, empowering the UNSC (and implicitly unilateral or multilateral action) to preserve a five-member nuclear club.

The treaty's text was a snapshot of a global society in flux, its content contested, its meaning in dispute. The NPT regime exists in a world that has undergone radical changes over the past half century, and continues to experience them today, as the enforcement of the treaty's letter repeatedly runs up against differing interpretations of its spirit. For the five authorized nuclear-weapon states, the first and second articles spelled out the treaty's cardinal virtue—the neologism in the treaty's title. From Irish foreign minister Frank Aiken's first proposal in 1958 to the NPT's opening for signature ten years later, various terms had risen and fallen in the discourse: *restraint, restriction, nondiffusion, nondissemination.* The word *nonproliferation* was not uttered at the Eighteen Nation Committee on Disarmament (ENDC) until February 18, 1963; it was ensuing negotiations in Geneva that imbued it with lasting meaning.[16] The U.S. lawmakers who drafted the Nuclear Non-Proliferation Act of 1978 never defined the term. The nearest it came was to cite activities which might "further any military or nuclear explosive purpose," the incorporation of "the Treaty" in the U.S. Legal Code having rendered it superfluous.[17]

Terminological battles reflected proxy wars over nuclear order. When Aiken begged "the so-called nuclear club . . . in God's name not to spread these weapons around the world," he did not mention whether that would include when the superpowers stationed their atomic forces on foreign soil, such as the United States in NATO's nuclear stockpile or the Soviet Union when Nikita Khrushchev precipitated the Cuban Missile Crisis. U.S. and Soviet negotiators summarized this as the difference between "possession" and "control." If the former, tactical nuclear weapons stationed in Western Europe would have faced the chopping block. If the latter, then the U.S. government could not transfer homemade atomic forces to another entity, whether a foreign nation or a multinational treaty organization. The irony of the five years after 1961 during which talks marked time was that the chief obstacle—a NATO multilateral nuclear force (MLF)—had started life as a way to keep West Germany out of the nuclear business or even roll back the British and French arsenals by consolidating the Atlantic Alliance's nuclear deterrent.

President Lyndon Johnson's reasons for pursuing Defense Secretary Robert Mc-Namara's consultative committee in lieu of the MLF in 1966 went beyond NATO defense policy. The diffusion of atomic power posed challenges to U.S. influence and grand strategy worldwide. As Assistant Secretary of State Phillips Talbot had noted three years earlier, the "unchecked" spread of atomic weapons threatened to "reduce U.S. capability to act."[18] Nor had National Security Council (NSC) staffer Robert Komer's exhortation from 1965 lost its force. The fact that covert and military interventions in Vietnam and beyond were a "heavy burden" for the United States "to bear in the Afro-Asian world as well as Europe" commended a search for positive measures elsewhere, most notably in the field of "disarmament."[19] When faced with nuclear nonproliferation talks with the Soviet Union that had languished for five years and a midterm election fraught with perils for his domestic agenda, Johnson embraced his politicos' advice to place himself "on the side of the angels."[20]

If, as U.S. president John F. Kennedy had stated in 1963, the question was "how to divide the power of the atom" within the communist and noncommunist worlds, the NPT ensured that U.S. and Soviet hands remained at the helm.[21] Nuclear status would be consolidated, the authority to use atomic force centralized in the hands of the superpowers. As the U.S. political counselor in the Moscow embassy explained in a November 1966 letter to the U.S. expert in the Soviet Foreign Ministry, U.S. Arms Control and Disarmament Agency (ACDA) Director William Foster had chosen "whatsoever" as "the clearest and firmest statement . . . that none of us will ever give another the right to bring our own nuclear weapons into operation."[22]

U.S. secretary of state Dean Rusk and Soviet foreign minister Andrei Gromyko thus came to an agreement to outlaw the MLF but not NATO's tactical nuclear stockpile. Under the treaty, they would vow not "to encourage, assist, or induce" any party "whatsoever" to manufacture or otherwise acquire nuclear explosives or control over them, let alone direct or indirect transfers. Non-nuclear-weapon states would accept the obverse. Restrictions on nuclear-armed ballistic missiles stationed abroad, on the other hand, remained tacit. As Gromyko informed Rusk in Manhattan's Waldorf Astoria on September 24, 1966, a treaty would only "provide for things that are prohibited, specifically prohibited."[23] The secret deal that had ended the Cuban Missile Crisis had brought an end to overseas ballistic-missile deployments, but the Euromissile Crisis from 1977 to 1987, when Soviet RSD-10 Pioneer intermediate-range ballistic missile (IRBM) deployments would induce NATO's "dual-track" decision to negotiate while counterdeploying U.S. Pershing IIs and cruise missiles to Western Europe illustrated that "nonproliferation" stipulated "non-acquisition" and "non-transfer," never "non-deployment."[24]

The 1963 Moscow Treaty had been the nonproliferation regime's first cornerstone. The nuclear test-ban campaign had arisen out of the irradiated ashes of Bikini Atoll that blanketed the Japanese vessel, *Lucky Dragon*; the effects of the fallout on the thirteen fishermen and the planet's ecosphere highlighted the apocalyptic threat of all-out thermonuclear war. As global nucleonics transformed territorial disputes and revolutionary movements into what Aiken had styled Cold War "flash points," a test ban morphed from a solution to transnational pollution and the U.S.-Soviet arms race into a form of atomic containment. As McNamara had mused two weeks before the Cuban Missile Crisis, Soviet premier Nikita Khrushchev's "anxiety" about a German Bomb might help bring about superpower solidarity on "the disarmament problem," most of all its relationship to revolutionary China.[25]

European détente thus promised to unlock a counterrevolutionary consensus in the Third World. McNamara had deemed the likelihood of Chinese Communist Party (CCP) leader Mao Zedong obtaining a handful of atom bombs more fearsome than five more hydrogen bombs in those of Khrushchev. He overestimated Khrushchev's sway over Mao, but there was a reason that the U.S. Defense Department and ACDA had advocated for U.S.-Soviet strategic arms limitations and a nonproliferation pact to complement the Moscow Treaty, whose omission of subterranean explosions was more than a loophole; since a three-environment ban would not require intrusive verification, Bonn and Beijing could comply without officially signing. Seeing as Washington did not recognize the former nor Moscow the latter, this was no small matter.[26] In league with key allies and nonaligned states, the superpowers would moderate communist China's achievement by treating it and all other radioactive polluters as uncivil, threatening "rogue states." The criminalization of nuclear testing helps justify UN and unilateral sanctions against the DPRK even now. The Moscow Treaty's imprint remains visible not only in the NPT preamble's call to finalize a comprehensive test ban treaty (CTBT). The nonproliferation treaty defines an authorized "nuclear-weapon state" as "one which has manufactured *and* exploded a nuclear weapon or other nuclear explosives device prior to 1 January 1967."[27]

The NPT's third and longest article set out requirements for International Atomic Energy Agency (IAEA)–standardized safeguards on "source or special fissionable material" and their general principles. The safeguards article took more than one year to hash out not only because it was difficult to conceptualize, design, and implement a foolproof system (in fact, the IAEA was a bystander throughout the proceedings) but because nuclear science and technology possess an inherent dualism: from them engineers can forge tools of war as well as peace. The existing inspection regime that Euratom administered for Belgium, Italy, Luxembourg, the Netherlands, Germany, and France, combined with French president Charles de Gaulle's resistance to the NPT, required U.S. and Soviet negotiators to harmonize a future iteration of IAEA safeguards with those in Euratom without according rich Western European nations an unfair advantage. While Soviet officials had ridiculed verification relative to a CTBT, they sounded "more Catholic than the Pope" once West Germany and Japan were the ones facing inspections.[28] While Soviet negotiator Roland Timerbaev and his U.S. counterpart, George Bunn, massaged the issue by allowing groups of states to negotiate with the IAEA to have their systems certified by international inspectors, this interpolation of regional and global regimes eventually yielded a safeguard blueprint that in deference to national commercial interests maximized use of instruments such as seals and cameras in preference to human inspectors.[29] Commercial fairness, not nuclear inhibition, would be the IAEA's watchword.

II

If the first three articles of the NPT were largely East-West affairs, with their finalization in the summer of 1967, "the game," as Walt Rostow dubbed it, "move[d] to the non-nuclear powers" in the ENDC, most of which resided in Latin America, Africa, Asia, or the Middle East. Among the neutral and nonaligned delegations, the opinions of those from Sweden, Egypt, Brazil and India carried weight for the advanced status of their nuclear infrastructure or their proximity to hostile neighbors with such endowments. Mexican diplomats earned clout, by contrast, from their leadership of nuclear-weapon-free negotiations in Latin America, the outlook of whose twenty-three participants (Cuba absented itself throughout) would be crucial if the UNGA were to approve a nuclear nonproliferation agreement. Mexican officials approached matters of world order from both liberal and anticolonial standpoints, prioritizing sovereign control over natural resources but also subsidized transfers of foreign technology and know-how.[30] The successful conclusion of the Treaty of Tlatelolco on 14 February 1967, therefore, represented more than a source of regional pride. When Mexican deputy foreign minister Alfonso García Robles quoted Simón Bolívar's appeal at the 1826 Congress of Panama for a Latin American confederation, "What then will be the Isthmus of Corinth next to that of Panama?," his message was clear.[31] Like the "little acorns" in his proverb, which would one day grow into "tall oaks," Latin America's nuclear-weapon-free zone (NWF) offered "an example for the denuclearization of other areas of the world" and also "a transcendental contribution to hastening the day when general and complete disarmament under effective control may become the reality aspired to by all the peoples of the world."[32]

The Treaty of Tlatelolco was accordingly, in García Robles's words, "both gadfly and inspiration for [the] NPT."[33] Brazil and Mexico's seats on the ENDC and Latin American numbers in the UNGA helped extract two types of concessions from the nuclear club. First, the superpowers were asked to ratify Protocol II of the Treaty of Tlatelolco, which would bind them to respect its terms—the United Kingdom and the United States did so in 1969 and 1971, respectively; France in 1974; the USSR in 1979. Second, the superpowers acquiesced to new articles and preambular statements in the NPT, most introduced at the ENDC in September 1967 by Jorge Castañeda, who would go on to serve as the director general of the Mexican Foreign Ministry's International Organizations office four years later. What came to be known as the

"Mexican amendments" offset the privileges that non-nuclear-weapon states stood to lose with compensatory responsibilities and rights. Nuclear exporters were asked to facilitate transfers of relevant information, materials, and equipment; make speedy provisions to supply PNEs; condone the free creation of NWFZs; and consent to institutionalized accountability for nuclear arms control and disarmament. These concessions paved the way for the NPT's commendation in the summer of 1968 on the basis of what future jurists would term the treaty's "grand bargain" of nuclear nonproliferation, peaceful atomic development, and arms control and disarmament progress.[34]

Those who resisted the superpower nonproliferation consensus sought related ends—to promote a free and nonprejudicial nuclear market and to condition and one day abolish the treaty's signal defect: the world's formal division between the nuclear club and the atomic unarmed. For both reasons the NPT's fourth article stipulated an "inalienable right . . . to develop research, production and use of nuclear energy for peaceful purposes without discrimination." However limited it was by the non-acquisition article, its origins in Article 17 of the Treaty of Tlatelolco, which upheld a sovereign prerogative "to use nuclear energy for peaceful purposes, in particular for their economic development and social progress," broached larger debates about the role of the UN in not just the affirmation but also, as Castañeda had contended at the UNGA's International Law Commission eight years earlier, "the creation of international law." Like Frank Aiken and other reformers of the imperial rules, Castañeda and García Robles championed "permanent sovereign" rights to nuclear data, material, and machinery, and by association science, commodities, and technology more generally, as integral to decolonizing a world order whose framework had been erected "not only behind the backs of the small states, but also against them."[35]

The conflict between an "inalienable right" to modern science and technology and the idea of nonproliferation was most apparent in the NPT's treatment of PNEs and nuclear arms control and disarmament in Articles V and VI, respectively. The first issue cut across ideological and geographical lines by implicating questions of trust, security, and nationalism between rising regional powers and their less-capable neighbors. That atomic energy inescapably facilitated military uses had informed Vyacheslav Molotov's cautious response to Dwight D. Eisenhower's Atoms for Peace proposal in December 1953, when the Soviet foreign minister had warned that "the very application of atomic energy for peaceful purposes" would open a gate to "increasing the production of atomic weapons" by making "harmless atomic materials . . . explosive and fissionable."[36] What Eisenhower had styled the "atomic dilemma" arose from the innate ambiguity of all technology: His entreaty to the UNGA that atomic armaments should "be put into the hands of those who know how to strip its military casing and adapt it to the arts of peace" omitted that the Manhattan Project's initial feat was to build a nuclear research reactor on the campus of the University of Chicago.[37]

PNEs encapsulated this ambivalence. While gas-centrifuge enrichment and plutonium reprocessing have stimulated continuing debates over proliferation risks and nuclear-fuel cycles, like Alfred Nobel's invention of trinitrotoluene (TNT), atomic explosives remain the most "sensitive" dual-use technology. Brazil's position in Mexico City was that PNEs were distinct from nuclear weapons and therefore covered by the "inalienable right." To rebut Soviet and U.S. officials, among others, who remained adamant that they were "no different from the devices used in nuclear bombs," Brazilian delegate Sergio Corrêa da Costa had countered that a PNE ban would give rise to "an irreparable relationship of dependence."[38] As was his habit, Castañeda charted the middle path: "Nothing other than nuclear bombs," their "enormous economic potential" nevertheless merited an international PNE service that would reliably and cheaply provide them for such "vast engineering projects" as trans-isthmus canals, fossil-fuel exploitation, and human-made harbors.[39]

Before the first conference of states party to review the NPT could convene on May 30, 1975, Smiling Buddha exposed the deficiencies of a regime that lacked a comprehensive test-ban treaty. For its part, Israel's undeclared arsenal revealed how measuring nuclear status on the basis of both possessing and testing atomic charges had given rise to a political loophole. Built on the intellectual foundation of the Moscow Treaty, the NPT had only forbidden "nuclear explosive devices." The assurances of Israeli representatives not to "introduce" nuclear weapons into the Middle East, as Walt Rostow would gather in December 1968, was a promise not to forswear the absolute weapon but never to publicize it through either declaration or detonation. Although both India and Israel declined to join the regime, in the absence of a test violation, a country possessing atomic arms could conceivably remain in good standing indefinitely, a means of evasion that would motivate a series of efforts to reinforce IAEA inspections and enforcement to regulate and punish not the intention but rather the capability to manufacture the world's most powerful weapon.

The simple injustice at its heart has haunted nuclear nonproliferation since the Irish Resolution. The nonaligned and neutral members of the ENDC repeatedly asked why a growing nuclear club and the U.S.-Soviet arms race were incommensurable, drawing an equivalence between "horizontal" and "vertical" proliferation. Military industry was a moving target. Warheads and delivery vehicles developed qualitatively through technical sophistication such as miniaturization and also quantitatively through the sheer accumulation of stockpiles and arsenals. The discriminatory purpose of the nonproliferation regime fell afoul of central tenets of postcolonial visions of world order: universality, nondiscrimination, and equality. Even a nuclear freeze would leave the atomic unarmed at a disadvantage. Italy's delegate in Geneva observed in February 1967 that "effectiveness" and "equity" were "closely interdependent": "There could be no universal approbation for a non-proliferation treaty that established a perpetual discrimination between two classes of countries." He approvingly quoted Frank Aiken's contention that nuclear restraint should be the starting point for the control and gradual elimination of nuclear arms, not the perpetuation of a *"pax Atomica."*[40]

Yet the record over the past fifty years has been mixed. Lyndon Johnson and Soviet premier Alexei Kosygin announced strategic arms and anti-ballistic-missile (ABM) limitation at the ceremony celebrating the NPT's opening for signature on July 1, 1968. The Strategic Arms Limitation Treaty (SALT) that the governments of Richard Nixon and Leonid Brezhnev finalized in 1972 capped arsenals without dismantling a single warhead, leading Swedish disarmament minister Alva Myrdal to denounce the Soviet Union and the United States for defaulting on Article VI and thus playing "the game of disarmament."[41] It was not until 1987 that the superpowers liquidated any portion of their arsenals when Ronald Reagan and Mikhail Gorbachev signed the Intermediate-Range Nuclear Forces (INF) Treaty, which eliminated all ballistic and cruise missiles whose ranges fell between 500 and 5,500 kilometers. Successive U.S.-Soviet and U.S.-Russian agreements—the 1991 Strategic Arms Reduction Treaty (START), the 2002 Strategic Offensive Reductions Treaty (SORT), and the 2011 New START—have cut deployed warhead numbers on both sides to 1,550, a more-than-tenfold decrease. Notwithstanding these forward leaps, however, the position of the non-nuclear-weapon states never changed. With a numerator of zero, the ratio of their atomic inferiority remains unbounded. Their grievances are categorical, all the more so as all nine legal and extralegal members of the nuclear club are now modernizing their arsenals.

In the interim, the indefinite extension of the NPT in 1995 in exchange for U.S. and Russian pledges to bring the CTBT into force has sapped the atomic unarmed of their institutional power—the carrying power of their voice—to effect further arms control steps. Since January 2021, when the Treaty on the Prohibition of Nuclear Weapons came into effect, consummating the Gromyko proposal of 1946 and the International Committee of the Red Cross's 1950 endorsement of "the prohibition of atomic weapons," the NPT regime faces competition.[42] The remarks of the Argentinian ambassador to the UN in 1968 still resonate more than a half century later: above all, the treaty exists to enforce the "disarmament of the disarmed."[43]

III

The nuclear club's foundation from 1945 to 1970 refashioned the Cold War and U.S. global power, or what others less enamored of their reach would style Soviet and U.S. hegemonies. Though the Soviet Union left its marks on the new nuclear order, as did

U.S. and Soviet allies in addition to neutral and nonaligned nations in Geneva and New York, the nuclear club relied on the structural power of the United States. The NPT accordingly renewed a liberal world order that senior U.S. government officials viewed as providential in a bid to absolve U.S. armed might amid its greatest crisis—the Vietnam War. Powerful forces in the executive and legislative branches adopted the cause of nuclear nonproliferation for reasons both high-minded and self-serving: to lower the odds of an ecocidal war and to secure their self-appointed right to shape the world as they pleased, even as a diffusion of power made international politics ever more unbiddable to Washington's best and brightest.

The NPT extended to nuclear science and technology a world order based on the imperial presidency. Efforts to reduce the number of fingers on the button were in many ways extensions of efforts to concentrate nuclear decision making in the Office of the President that went back to Harry S. Truman's shock at Nagasaki's destruction and debates about pre-delegation and nuclear sharing in the Eisenhower, Kennedy, and Johnson years.[44] Nixon's and Kissinger's ambivalence toward nonproliferation was not atypical. For all the credit they deserved for negotiating the Moscow Treaty and the NPT, and for acquiescing to the Treaty of Tlatelolco, Kennedy and Johnson had stopped short of punishing Israel, meeting India halfway, or twisting the arm of the West German chancellor or the Japanese prime minister.

Nixon's Democratic rivals had cast themselves as nuclear guardians to help win numerous elections. Nuclear testing and the atom bomb's prevalence in popular culture served as connective tissue between U.S. armed forces and America's baby boom, and U.S. presidents found it expedient to defend their policies by vowing to protect home-owning families from nuclear annihilation. The social origins of détente reached deep into the country's growing suburbs, as the White House pledged to defend innocent children to sell voters on a major arms control agreement with the Soviet Union, couching a nuclear-test-ban treaty as the best way to stop atmospheric testing from poisoning innocent young girls and boys.[45] At American University in June 1963, Kennedy had asked whether fallout was not "a matter of human rights—the right to live out our lives without fear of devastation—the right to breathe air as nature provided it—the right of future generations to a healthy existence."[46] Under Johnson the White House upheld its authority over nuclear war and peace by recasting the president as humanity's paternal protector. The real contrast between Johnson and Nixon was that the NPT had already internationalized nuclear politics by the time the latter entered office. Where presidential indecision would have previously spelled deadlock, Nixon's indifference merely yielded inertia, even as Nixon and Kissinger also found themselves catering to the anxieties of suburban voters for law, order, and security.[47]

For Moscow, the nuclear nonproliferation regime eased the chief terror of recent memory—the forward thrust of German industry, nationalism, and militarism—while securing Soviet leadership over the international communist movement in the face of the Maoist challenge. The Kremlin's message to the Indian communist party offered an inventory of the advantages that Soviet statesmen believed would accrue from the NPT: "West Germany, Japan, Israel, Italy, Canada, the Republic of South Africa, Sweden, Brazil, and a number of other countries, including India, are prepared in their scientific and technical level or almost prepared to begin the production of nuclear weapons." With the exception of India, every country on the list was "capitalist" and correspondingly a U.S. ally or partner whose nuclearization would diminish the relative power of the Warsaw Pact. Even in a letter to comrades living thousands of miles from Berlin, the Central Committee felt the need to reiterate that the nonproliferation treaty "ought to also be viewed as a means to protect against West Germany having access to nuclear weapons."[48]

Most consequential of all was the redemption of superpower military intervention in the name of nuclear nonproliferation. Walt Rostow entered the White House in 1961 seeking a "common law for the Cold War." As Johnson's national security advisor during the standoff between Europe-first champions of the MLF and globalists supportive of an nonproliferation accord, he viewed the question as "how the West and Asia may decide, with us, to organize nuclear arrangements in the future."[49] Well after Johnson had sunk the MLF in deference to French and Soviet objections, Rostow pushed an Asian MLF that would have made atom bombs available to Indian air forces in the event of a communist Chinese incursion or atomic blackmail. He exited the White House convinced that nuclear nonproliferation and the Vietnam War were two sides of the same coin: the delicate credibility of U.S. military commitments. He warned the National War College graduates in May 1968 that if the country failed in Vietnam, it would not be long before "India and Japan produced their own nuclear weapons." "If we mean it," he concluded, "the NPT would ask them to take "a position, as a nation, which does not permit us to back away much from the world."[50]

The father of the neoconservative movement, Irving Kristol spoke much the same language in the *New York Times* that week—though his Manichean worldview yielded more dire predictions. In a magazine article that came out the Sunday before Rostow's speech, Kristol had argued that the United States could never "resign as 'policeman of the world'"—U.S. leadership was too critical to "the preservation of a decent level of international law and order." As antiwar sentiment portended a nation less willing to fight limited wars abroad, insecure nations around the globe would have no choice but to arm themselves with the most powerful weapons. "It may yet turn out to be one of the great ironies of world history that the United States and the Soviet Union," he alerted his readers, "should have succeeded in negotiating a nonproliferation agreement at the very moment when such an agreement could only be another scrap of paper."[51] Rostow underlined this claim when he forwarded the article to President

Johnson, though neither man needed convincing that to abandon South Vietnam would wreck harm on the worldwide credibility of the United States and the liberal world order over which they thought themselves privileged to preside.

A treaty that Frank Aiken had prayed would preserve world peace until "the rule of law replace[d] brute force in the settlement of international disputes" had yielded a two-tier postcolonial hierarchy in which ambiguous nuclear "threats" could supersede the UN Charter's ban on wars of choice.[52] Many attributes have distinguished the long peace in North America and Europe since 1945 from the "killing fields" of Africa, Asia, Latin America, and the Middle East, though Russia's invasion of Ukraine in February 2022 now stands as evidence that that geographical exemption may no longer hold.[53] One has been an enduring distinction between the nuclear club and the rest of humanity, in whose name its members and above all the United States have recurrently intervened to stop any hands save their own from wielding weapons of mass destruction. For decades, this counterrevolution has averted a world teeming with nuclear powers. Even so, as long as a justice of equals eludes any community, a revolution can never be fully ruled out.

Notes

INTRODUCTION

1. "Yuri Zhukov conversation with George Aiken of the Senate Foreign Relations Committee," 23 January 1969, fond 5, opis 61, delo 557, listi 33–36, Российский государственный архив новейшей истории [RGANI]. Translated by Joseph Torigian.

2. Walt Rostow, "Remarks at the National War College: The United States and the Changing World: Problems and Opportunities Arising from the Diffusion of Power," Washington, DC, 8 May 1968, box 7, Name file, National Security Files [NSF], Lyndon Baines Johnson Library [LBJL], 15–17. Emphasis in the original.

3. UN General Assembly (UNGA), 22nd Session, First Committee, Verbatim Record, 1569th Meeting, 16 May 1968, A/C.1/PV.1569, Official Record, 11, UN Audio-visual Library of International Law, http://legal.un.org/avl/ha/tnpt/tnpt.html.

4. Steven E. Miller, *Nuclear Collisions: Discord, Reform and the Nuclear Nonproliferation Regime* (Cambridge, MA: American Academy of Arts and Sciences, 2012); William Walker, "Nuclear Enlightenment and Counter-Enlightenment," *International Affairs* 83, no. 3 (May 2007): 431–453.

5. Keir A. Lieber and Daryl Grayson Press, *The Myth of the Nuclear Revolution: Power Politics in the Atomic Age* (Ithaca, NY: Cornell University Press, 2020).

6. John Lewis Gaddis, "The Long Peace: Elements of Stability in the Postwar International System," *International Security* 10, no. 4 (Spring 1986): 99–142.

7. Robert Jervis observed that the stability that nuclear deterrence affords may well yield instability at lower levels of violence, a phenomenon commonly referred to as "the stability-instability paradox." *The Illogic of American Nuclear Strategy* (Ithaca: Cornell University Press, 1984), 31.

8. Paul Thomas Chamberlin, *The Cold War's Killing Fields: Rethinking the Long Peace* (New York: Harper, 2018).

9. "Traité de Non-proliferation," note, 18 March 1968, box 769, cote 517INVA, Centre des Archives Diplomatiques de La Courneuve [CADLC], 41–42, 7–8.

10. Frank Aiken, *Ireland at the United Nations, 1958* (Dublin: Brún agus Ó Nualláin Teo, 1958), 15–18.

11. "Treaty on the Non-Proliferation of Nuclear Weapons," UN Audiovisual Library of International Law, http://legal.un.org/avl/ha/tnpt/tnpt.html (accessed 23 December 2019).

12. The most comprehensive history of the treaty negotiations remains Mohamed Ibrahim Shaker's three-volume *The Nuclear Non-Proliferation Treaty: Origin and Implementation, 1959–1979* (London: Oceana, 1980); see also Edwin Brown Firmage, "The Treaty on the Non-Proliferation of Nuclear Weapons," *American Journal of International Law* 63, no. 4 (October 1969): 711–746; James Cameron, *The Double Game: The Demise of America's First Missile Defense System and the Rise of Strategic Arms Limitation* (New York: Oxford University Press, 2018); and Michael Cotey Morgan, *The Final Act: The Helsinki Accords and the Transformation of the Cold War* (Princeton, NJ: Princeton University Press, 2018).

13. "Excerpts from Speeches by Goldberg and Kuznetsov on Nuclear Pact," *New York Times*, 27 April 1968, 14.

14. William C. Foster, "New Directions in Arms Control and Disarmament," *Foreign Affairs* 43, no. 4 (July 1965): 594–605.

15. Roland M. Timerbaev, *Россия и ядерное нераспространение, 1945–1968* (Moscow: Nauka, 1999).

16. Lyndon Johnson, "Remarks on Signing the Nuclear Nonproliferation Treaty," 1 July 1968, Miller Center of Public Affairs, University of Virginia, https://millercenter.org/the-presidency/presidential-speeches/july-1-1968-remarks-signing-nuclear-nonproliferation-treaty (accessed 12 December 2018).

17. "Resolution on Security Assurances adopted by the United Nations Security Council," 19 June 1968, quoted in Firmage, "Treaty on the Non-Proliferation of Nuclear Weapons," 741.

18. H. R. Vohra, "India and Nuclear Security: The West Perplexed," *Times of India*, 12 July 1968, 8. ProQuest Historical Newspapers.

19. Final Verbatim Record of the 298th Meeting of the Conference of the Eighteen-Nation Committee on Disarmament (ENDC), 23 May 1967, Geneva, Switzerland, ENDC/PV.298, 10, quod.lib.umich.edu/e/endc/; *pace* Shane Maddock, *Nuclear Apartheid: The Quest for American Atomic Supremacy from World War II to the Present* (Chapel Hill: University of North Carolina Press, 2010), as Trivedi explicitly specified nonmilitary applications. For more on the roles that techno-politics and geopolitics played in India's nuclear program and U.S.-India-PRC relations, read Jayita Sarkar, *Ploughshares and Swords: India's Nuclear Program in the Global Cold War* (Ithaca, NY: Cornell University Press, 2022), and Tanvi Madan, *Fateful Triangle: How China Shaped U.S.-India Relations during the Cold War* (Washington, DC: Brookings Institution Press, 2020).

20. "Chou Flays U.S., Russia: 'Nuclear Colonialism,'" *Times of India*, 20 June 1968, 9. ProQuest Historical Newspapers.

21. Adam Tooze, *The Deluge: The Great War, America and the Remaking of the Global Order, 1916–1931* (New York: Penguin, 2015); Victoria De Grazia, *Irresistible Empire: America's Advance Through Twentieth-Century Europe* (Cambridge, MA: Belknap Press, 2005); Stefan J. Link, *Forging Global Fordism: Nazi Germany, Soviet Russia, and the Contest over the Industrial Order* (Princeton, NJ: Princeton University Press, 2020).

22. For a general survey of the literature on hegemonic orders and transitions, begin with G. John Ikenberry and Daniel H. Nexon, "Hegemony Studies 3.0: The Dynamics of Hegemonic Orders," *Security Studies* 28, no. 3 (27 May 2019): 395–421. For a discussion of the importance of interpersonal and interorganizational relationships, read Daniel H. Nexon and

Iver B. Neumann, "Hegemonic-Order Theory: A Field-Theoretic Account," *European Journal of International Relations* 24, no. 3 (September 2018): 662–686. I am indebted to the distinction that A. G. Hopkins draws between empires and hegemons in *American Empire: A Global History* (Princeton, NJ: Princeton University Press, 2018), 31–32.

23. Harlan Cleveland and William Foster, memorandum, "NATO's Going to Want a Role in Arms Control Talks," 14 July 1968, box 8, NPT, DOF, RG 383, NARA II, 1–2.

24. Ariel E. Levite, "Never Say Never Again: Nuclear Reversal Revisited," *International Security* 27, no. 3 (January 2003): 59–88.

25. UNGA, 22nd Session, First Committee, Verbatim Record, 1562nd Meeting, 7 May 1968, A/C.1/PV.1562, Official Record, 7.

26. Roland Popp, Liviu Horovitz, and Andreas Wenger, eds., *Negotiating the Nuclear Non-Proliferation Treaty: Origins of the Nuclear Order* (New York: Routledge, 2017).

27. Andrew Jon Rotter, *Hiroshima: The World's Bomb* (New York: Oxford University Press, 2008); Målfrid Braut-Hegghammer, *Unclear Physics: Why Iraq and Libya Failed to Build Nuclear Weapons* (Ithaca, NY: Cornell University Press, 2016).

28. Mark Mazower, *No Enchanted Palace: The End of Empire and the Ideological Origins of the United Nations* (Princeton, NJ: Princeton University Press, 2009); Stephen Wertheim, "Instrumental Internationalism: The American Origins of the United Nations, 1940–3," *Journal of Contemporary History* 54, no. 2 (April 2019): 265–283; Benn Steil, *The Battle of Bretton Woods: John Maynard Keynes, Harry Dexter White, and the Making of a New World Order* (Princeton, NJ: Princeton University Press, 2014).

29. Melvyn P. Leffler, *A Preponderance of Power: National Security, the Truman Administration, and the Cold War* (Stanford, CA: Stanford University Press, 1992); G. John Ikenberry, *Liberal Leviathan: The Origins, Crisis, and Transformation of the American World Order* (Princeton, NJ: Princeton University Press, 2011).

30. Francis J. Gavin, "Strategies of Inhibition: U.S. Grand Strategy, the Nuclear Revolution, and Nonproliferation," *International Security* 40, no. 1 (July 2015): 9–46; Francis J. Gavin, *Nuclear Weapons and American Grand Strategy* (Washington, DC: Brookings Institution Press, 2020).

31. Donette Murray, *Kennedy, Macmillan and Nuclear Weapons* (New York: St. Martin's Press, 2000); Matthew Jones, "Prelude to the Skybolt Crisis: The Kennedy Administration's Approach to British and French Strategic Nuclear Policies in 1962," *Journal of Cold War Studies* 21, no. 2 (May 2019): 58–109.

32. Bernard de Chalvron, telegram from Geneva to Paris, "Disarmament," 29 February 1968, box 768, cote 517INVA, CADLC. For a history of the U.S.-Russian nonproliferation partnership, read William C. Potter and Sarah Bidgood, eds., *Once and Future Partners: The United States, Russia, and Nuclear Non-Proliferation*, Adelphi Series 464–465 (Abingdon, UK: Routledge, 2018).

33. *Foreign Relations of the United States [FRUS], 1964–1968*, vol. XI, document 239.

34. Robert B. Rakove, *Kennedy, Johnson, and the Nonaligned World* (Cambridge, UK: Cambridge University Press, 2013).

35. Odd Arne Westad, *The Global Cold War: Third World Interventions and the Making of Our Times* (New York: Cambridge University Press, 2005), 8–72; James C. Scott, *Seeing Like a State: How Certain Schemes to Improve the Human Condition Have Failed* (New Haven, CT: Yale University Press, 2008).

36. Akira Iriye, *Global Community: The Role of International Organizations in the Making of the Contemporary World* (Berkeley: University of California Press, 2002); Jonathan Hunt, "The

Birth of an International Community: Negotiating the Treaty on the Non-Proliferation of Nuclear Weapons," in Robert L. Hutchings and Jeremi Suri, eds., *Foreign Policy Breakthroughs: Cases in Successful Diplomacy* (New York: Oxford University Press, 2015).

37. William Walker, *A Perpetual Menace: Nuclear Weapons and International Order* (New York: Routledge, 2012); Chalmers Roberts, *The Nuclear Years: The Arms Race and Arms Control, 1945–1970* (New York: Praeger, 1970); Joseph S. Nye Jr., "NPT: The Logic of Inequality," *Foreign Policy* 59 (Summer 1985): 123–131; Glenn T. Seaborg, *Stemming the Tide: Arms Control in the Johnson Years* (Lexington, MA: Lexington Books, 1987); McGeorge Bundy, *Danger and Survival: Choices About the Bomb in the First Fifty Years* (New York: Random House, 1988); Walker, *A Perpetual Menace*.

38. Quoted in Robert R. Holt, "Meeting Einstein's Challenge: New Thinking About Nuclear Weapons," *Bulletin of the Atomic Scientists*, 3 April 2015, https://thebulletin.org/2015/04/meeting-einsteins-challenge-new-thinking-about-nuclear-weapons/.

39. Campbell Craig and Sergey Radchenko, *The Atomic Bomb and the Origins of the Cold War* (New Haven, CT: Yale University Press, 2008).

40. "LBJ on Nuclear Pact: 'A Testament to Reason,'" *Washington Post*, 13 June 1968, A9. ProQuest Historical Newspapers.

41. Joseph Gerson, *Empire and the Bomb: How the U.S. Uses Nuclear Weapons to Dominate the World* (London: Pluto Press, 2007); Maddock, *Nuclear Apartheid*.

42. Daniel Immerwahr, *How to Hide an Empire: A History of the Greater United States* (New York: Farrar, Straus and Giroux, 2019), 348–354; Sarah Alisabeth Fox, *Downwind: A People's History of the Nuclear West* (Lincoln: University of Nebraska Press, 2014); Barbara Rose Johnston, ed., *Half-Lives and Half-Truths: Confronting the Radioactive Legacies of the Cold War* (Santa Fe, NM: School for Advanced Research Press, 2007).

43. Gabrielle Hecht, *Being Nuclear: Africans and the Global Uranium Trade* (Cambridge, MA: MIT Press, 2012).

44. Anthony Aust, *Modern Treaty Law and Practice* (Cambridge, UK: Cambridge University Press, 2013), 280–286.

45. Quoted in Immerwahr, *How to Hide an Empire*, 349.

46. William Foster to Dean Rusk, "Memorandum of Conversation with Tsarapkin [2 of 2]," 11 February 1964, box 11, SF-Disarmament, NSF, LBJL; Ikenberry and Nexon, "Hegemony Studies 3.0: The Dynamics of Hegemonic Orders."

47. Jeremi Suri, *Power and Protest: Global Revolution and the Rise of Detente* (Cambridge, MA: Harvard University Press, 2005).

48. Johnson, "Remarks on Signing the Nuclear Nonproliferation Treaty."

49. Roland M. Timerbaev, Рассказы о Былом: Воспоминания о Переговорах по Нераспространению и Разоружению и о Многом Другом (Moscow: ROSSPEN, 2007), 17, and "К Истории Разработки Контрольных Положений ДНИаО (Политические аспекты)," Ядерный Контроль 5 (октябрь 1998). Translated by Joseph Torigian.

50. Amy C. Offner, *Sorting Out the Mixed Economy: The Rise and Fall of Welfare and Developmental States in the Americas* (Princeton, NJ: Princeton University Press, 2019).

51. Michael J. Hogan, *The Marshall Plan: America, Britain, and the Reconstruction of Western Europe, 1947–1952* (Cambridge, UK: Cambridge University Press, 2002), 418; Nicolaus Mills, *Winning the Peace: The Marshall Plan and America's Coming of Age as a Superpower* (Hoboken, NJ: Wiley, 2008), 197.

52. Congressional Record: Proceedings and Debates of the 81st Congress, Second Session, 21 August–6 September 1950, vol. 96, part 10, 12968–12970.

53. William I. Hitchcock, "The Marshall Plan and the Creation of the West," in Melvyn P. Leffler and Odd Arne Westad, eds. *Origins*, vol. 1, 3 vols., *The Cambridge History of the Cold War* (Cambridge, UK: Cambridge University Press, 2010).

54. Or Rosenboim, *The Emergence of Globalism: Visions of World Order in Britain and the United States, 1939–1950* (Princeton, NJ: Princeton University Press, 2017); Stephen Wertheim, *Tomorrow, the World: The Birth of U.S. Global Supremacy* (Cambridge, MA: Belknap Press, 2020); Jacob Darwin Hamblin, *The Wretched Atom: America's Global Gamble with Peaceful Nuclear Technology* (New York: Oxford University Press, 2021).

55. Stephen Rabe, *The Most Dangerous Area in the World: John F. Kennedy Confronts Communist Revolution in Latin America* (Chapel Hill: University of North Carolina Press, 1999); Fredrik Logevall, *Choosing War: The Lost Chance for Peace and the Escalation of War in Vietnam* (Berkeley: University of California Press, 2001); Piero Gleijeses, *Conflicting Missions: Havana, Washington, and Africa, 1959–1976* (Chapel Hill: University of North Carolina Press, 2002); Guy Laron, *The Six-Day War: The Breaking of the Middle East* (New Haven, CT: Yale University Press, 2017); Sergey Radchenko, *Two Suns in the Heavens: The Sino-Soviet Struggle for Supremacy, 1962–1967* (Washington, DC: Woodrow Wilson Center Press, 2009); Lorenz M. Lüthi, *The Sino-Soviet Split: Cold War in the Communist World* (Princeton, NJ: Princeton University Press, 2008).

56. Marc Trachtenberg, *A Constructed Peace: The Making of the European Settlement, 1945–1963* (Princeton, NJ: Princeton University Press, 1999); Susanna Schrafstetter and Stephen Twigge, *Avoiding Armageddon: Europe, the United States, and the Struggle for Nuclear Nonproliferation, 1945–1970* (Westport, CT: Praeger, 2004); Andrew Priest, "The President, the 'Theologians' and the Europeans: The Johnson Administration and NATO Nuclear Sharing," *International History Review* 33, no. 2 (June 2011): 257–275; Hal Brands, "Non-Proliferation and the Dynamics of the Middle Cold War: The Superpowers, the MLF, and the NPT," *Cold War History* 7, no. 3 (August 2007): 389–423; Timothy A. Sayle, *Enduring Alliance: A History of NATO and the Postwar Global Order* (Ithaca, NY: Cornell University Press, 2019), 28–49.

57. Gordon H. Chang, "JFK, China, and the Bomb," *Journal of American History* 74, no. 4 (March 1998): 1287–1310; William Burr and Jeff Richelson, "Whether to 'Strangle the Baby in the Cradle': The United States and the Chinese Nuclear Program, 1960–64," *International Security* 25, no. 3 (Winter 2000): 54–99.

58. Scott Sagan points to security threats, politico-bureaucratic lobbying, and status-defining norms as three alternative explanations for proliferation decisions in "Why Do States Build Nuclear Weapons? Three Models in Search of a Bomb," *International Security* 21, no. 3 (Winter/97 1996): 54–86. While this study cites evidence for all three frameworks, the general narrative emphasizes the importance of international status in nuclear order-making from 1945 to 1970. Adom Getachew, *Worldmaking After Empire: The Rise and Fall of Self-Determination* (Princeton, NJ: Princeton University Press, 2019); Ryan M. Irwin, *Gordian Knot: Apartheid and the Unmaking of the Liberal World Order* (New York: Oxford University Press, 2012).

59. John Baylis, *British Nuclear Experience: The Roles of Beliefs, Culture and Identity* (New York: Oxford University Press, 2015); Gabrielle Hecht, *The Radiance of France: Nuclear Power and National Identity after World War II* (Cambridge, MA: MIT Press, 1998).

60. Ian Clark, *Nuclear Diplomacy and the Special Relationship: Britain's Deterrent and America, 1957–1962* (New York: Oxford University Press, 1994).

61. Douglas Smith, "The Broken Hexagon: French Nuclear Culture Between Empire and Cold War," *Modern and Contemporary France* 18, no. 2 (May 2010): 213–229.

62. Kenneth D. Rose, *One Nation Underground: The Fallout Shelter in American Culture* (New York: New York University Press, 2001); Andrew Friedman, *Covert Capital: Landscapes of*

Denial and the Making of U.S. Empire in the Suburbs of Northern Virginia (Berkeley: University of California Press, 2013); Lisa McGirr, *Suburban Warriors: The Origins of the New American Right* (Princeton, NJ: Princeton University Press, 2001); Fred M. Kaplan, *The Wizards of Armageddon* (New York: Simon and Schuster, 1983).

63. George Orwell, "You and the Atomic Bomb," 19 October 1945, *The Tribune,* in Sonia Orwell and Ian Angus, eds., *The Collected Essays, Journalism and Letters of George Orwell,* vol. 4 (London: Secker & Warburg, 1968), 6–10.

64. Larry Kahaner, *AK-47: The Weapon That Changed the Face of War* (Hoboken, NJ: Wiley, 2007); M. T. Kalashnikov and Elena Joly, *The Gun That Changed the World* (Cambridge, UK: Polity Press, 2006).

65. Quoted in Matthew Jones, *After Hiroshima: The United States, Race, and Nuclear Weapons in Asia, 1945–1965* (New York: Cambridge University Press, 2010), 461.

66. Gordon Corera, *Shopping for Bombs: Nuclear Proliferation, Global Insecurity, and the Rise and Fall of the A.Q. Khan Network* (New York: Oxford University Press, 2006).

67. William Burr, "To 'Keep the Genie Bottled Up': U.S. Diplomacy, Nuclear Proliferation, and Gas Centrifuge Technology, 1962–1972," *Journal of Cold War Studies* 19, no. 2 (Spring 2017): 115–157; John Krige, "The Proliferation Risks of Gas Centrifuge Enrichment at the Dawn of the NPT: Shedding Light on the Negotiating History," *Nonproliferation Review* 19, no. 2 (July 2012): 219–227.

68. Summary, President's Committee on Nuclear Proliferation—A Report to the President," draft, undated, box 10, Gilpatric papers, JFKL.

69. Walt Rostow to Dean Rusk, memorandum, "Nuclear Weapons: The Dilemma and Thoughts on Its Resolution," 6 January 1961, box 64A, staff memos, President's Office Files [POF], John F. Kennedy Presidential Library [JFKL], 5–6.

70. Fred Iklé, "Address to the Arms Limitation and Disarmament: Seventeenth Strategy for Peace Conference Report," 7–10 October 1976, Stanley Foundation, http://files.eric.ed.gov/fulltext/ED148666.pdf (accessed 4 May 2020).

71. Francesca Giovannini, "Cooperating to Compete: The Role of Regional Powers in Global Nuclear Governance," dissertation, University of Oxford, October 2012, 134.

72. ACDA, memorandum of conversation, Edward E. Tomkins, Adrian S. Fisher, et al., "Non-Proliferation Treaty," 23 August 1967, document 5a, NPT, NSA, http://nsarchive.gwu.edu/nukevault/ebb253/doc5a.pdf; Elisabeth Roehrlich, *Inspectors for Peace: A History of the International Atomic Energy Agency* (Baltimore: Johns Hopkins University Press, 2022).

73. Kyle Longley, *LBJ's 1968: Power, Politics, and the Presidency in America's Year of Upheaval* (New York: Cambridge University Press, 2017), 3–4.

CHAPTER 1

1. Fritz W. Bilfinger, "Report on the Effects of the Atomic Bomb at Hiroshima," 24 October 1945, Archives of the International Committee of the Red Cross (ICRC), Geneva, Switzerland, 9, provided via email by Fabrizio Bensi.

2. Fritz Bilfinger to Marcel Junod, telegram, "Hiroshima in Ruins," 30 August 1945, G 8/76, ICRC.

3. Bilfinger, "Report on the Effects of the Atomic Bomb at Hiroshima," 13.

4. Tsuyoshi Hasegawa, *Racing the Enemy: Stalin, Truman, and the Surrender of Japan* (Cambridge, MA: Belknap Press, 2005).

5. William Laurence, "Tentative Draft of Radio Address to Be Delivered After the Successful Use of the Atomic Bomb over Japan," August 1945, Harry S. Truman Presidential Library and

Archive, http://blog.nuclearsecrecy.com/wp-content/uploads/2015/10/ 1945-05-17-Laurence-draft-press-release-atomic-bomb.pdf (accessed 9 September 2019).

6. Sidney Shalett, "First Atomic Bomb Dropped on Japan; Missile Is Equal to 20000 Tons of T.N.T.; Truman Warns Foe of a 'Rain of Ruin,'" *New York Times*, 7 August 1945, http:// events.nytimes.com/learning/general/onthisday/big/0806.html#article.

7. Quoted in Andrew Jon Rotter, *Hiroshima: The World's Bomb* (New York: Oxford University Press, 2008), 27.

8. George Orwell, "You and the Atomic Bomb," 19 October 1945, *The Tribune*, in Sonia Orwell and Ian Angus, eds., *The Collected Essays, Journalism and Letters of George Orwell*, vol. 4 (London: Secker & Warburg, 1968), 7–8.

9. Orwell, "You and the Atomic Bomb," 10.

10. Spencer R. Weart, *Nuclear Fear: A History of Images* (Cambridge, MA: Harvard University Press, 1988), 6.

11. Spencer R. Weart, *The Rise of Nuclear Fear* (Cambridge, MA: Harvard University Press, 2012), 12.

12. Richard Rhodes, *The Making of the Atomic Bomb* (New York: Simon and Schuster, 2012), 418–420.

13. Niels Bohr to Franklin Roosevelt, memorandum, July 1944, http://www.atomicarchive .com/Docs/ManhattanProject/Bohrmemo.shtml (accessed December 3, 2018).

14. Fritz Bartel, "Surviving the Years of Grace: The Atomic Bomb and the Specter of World Government, 1945–1950," *Diplomatic History* 39, no. 2 (1 April 2015): 275–302; Campbell Craig, *Glimmer of a New Leviathan: Total War in the Realism of Niebuhr, Morgenthau, and Waltz* (New York: Columbia University Press, 2003); Alison McQueen, *Political Realism in Apocalyptic Times* (New York: Cambridge University Press, 2018).

15. David M. Kennedy, *Freedom from Fear: The American People in Depression and War, 1929–1945* (New York: Oxford University Press, 1999), 776–782.

16. The most comprehensive treatments of the Manhattan Projects are Richard G. Hewlett and Oscar E. Anderson, *The New World, 1939–1946*, vol. 1, 2 vols., *A History of the United States Atomic Energy Commission* (Berkeley: University of California Press, 1962), and Rhodes, *The Making of the Atomic Bomb*.

17. Rotter, *Hiroshima*, 7–58, 88–126.

18. David Holloway, *The Soviet Union and the Arms Race*, 2nd ed. (New Haven, CT: Yale University Press, 1984), 20.

19. Naomi Oreskes and John Krige, eds., *Science and Technology in the Global Cold War* (Cambridge, MA: MIT Press, 2014); Audra J. Wolfe, *Freedom's Laboratory: The Cold War Struggle for the Soul of Science* (Baltimore: Johns Hopkins University Press, 2018).

20. Gabrielle Hecht, ed., *Entangled Geographies: Empire and Technopolitics in the Global Cold War* (Cambridge, MA: MIT Press, 2011); George Perkovich, *India's Nuclear Bomb: The Impact on Global Proliferation* (Berkeley: University of California Press, 1999); Feroz Hassan Khan, *Eating Grass: The Making of the Pakistani Bomb* (Stanford, CA: Stanford University Press, 2012).

21. Richard White, *The Organic Machine: The Remaking of the Columbia River* (New York: Farrar, Straus and Giroux, 2013).

22. Hewlett and Anderson, *The New World, 1939–1946*, 189; "Hanford History," 19 April 2019, hanford.gov/page.cfm/HanfordHistory.

23. OMB No. 1024–0018, "National Register of Historic Places Multiple Property Documentation Form: Historic Resources of the Tennessee Valley Authority Hydroelectric System," 38, https://www.nps.gov/nr/feature/places/pdfs/64501263.pdf (accessed 28 July 2020).

24. William Wade Drumright, "A River for War, a Watershed to Change: The Tennessee Valley Authority During World War II," PhD dissertation, University of Tennessee, Knoxville, 2005, v.

25. Kate Brown, *Plutopia: Nuclear Families, Atomic Cities, and the Great Soviet and American Plutonium Disasters* (New York: Oxford University Press, 2015).

26. David E. Kromm, "Soviet Planning for Increases in Electric Power Production and Capacity," *Transactions of the Kansas Academy of Science* 73, no. 3 (1970): 281–291.

27. Ira Katznelson, *Fear Itself: The New Deal and the Origins of Our Time* (New York: Liveright, 2013), 433–466; Kiran Klaus Patel, *The New Deal: A Global History* (Princeton, NJ: Princeton University Press, 2016), 269, 282, 294–298.

28. Orwell, "You and the Atomic Bomb"; Odd Arne Westad, *The Global Cold War: Third World Interventions and the Making of Our Times* (New York: Cambridge University Press, 2005), 8–72.

29. Niels Bohr, "Foreword," in Dexter Masters and Katharine Way, eds., *One World or None: A Report to the Public on the Full Meaning of the Atomic Bomb* (Washington, DC: McGraw-Hill, 1946), xv–xx.

30. Rotter, *Hiroshima*, 146–152.

31. Quoted in Michael D. Gordin, *Red Cloud at Dawn: Truman, Stalin, and the End of the Atomic Monopoly* (New York: Farrar, Straus and Giroux, 2009), 76.

32. "A Petition to the President of the United States," 17 July 1945, https://www.atomicher itage.org/key-documents/szilard-petition.

33. Campbell Craig and Sergey Radchenko, *The Atomic Bomb and the Origins of the Cold War* (New Haven, CT: Yale University Press, 2008), 78.

34. "Report of the Committee on Political and Social Problems," University of Chicago, Manhattan Project Metallurgical Laboratory, 11 June 1945, https://www.atomicheritage.org/key-documents/franck-report.

35. Henry Stimson to Harry S. Truman, letter and memorandum, "Our Relations with Russia in Respect to the Atomic Bomb," September 11, 1945, Harry S. Truman Presidential Library and Archive, https://www.trumanlibrary.gov/library/research-files/henry -stimson-harry-s-truman-accompanied-memorandum.

36. Alex Wellerstein, *Restricted Data: The History of Nuclear Secrecy in the United States* (Chicago: University of Chicago Press, 2021).

37. Craig and Radchenko, *The Atomic Bomb and the Origins of the Cold War*, 117–120; Henry DeWolf Smyth, "Atomic Energy for Military Purposes: The Official Report on the Development of the Atomic Bomb Under the Auspices of the United States Government," 1 July 1945, https://www.atomicarchive.com/resources/documents/smyth-report/index.html.

38. Arnold Kramish to H. A. Fidler, "Russian Smyth Report," 18 September 1948, in Richard C. Tolman Papers, Caltech Institute Archives, Pasadena, California, box 5, folder 4, reproduced by Alex Wellerstein, *Restricted Data: The Nuclear Secrecy Blog*, http://blog.nuclearsecrecy.com/wp-content/uploads/2016/02/48-09-18-Kramish-to-Fidler-Russian-Smyth-Report-5.4.pdf (accessed 24 August 2020).

39. Barton Bernstein, "The Quest for Security: American Foreign Policy and International Control of Atomic Energy, 1942–1946," *Journal of American History* 60, no. 4 (March 1974): 1003–1044.

40. Quotes from Gordin, *Red Cloud at Dawn*, 46–48.

41. Craig and Radchenko, *The Atomic Bomb and the Origins of the Cold War*, 111–134.

42. Gordin, *Red Cloud at Dawn*, 72–86.

43. Robert S. Norris, *Racing for the Bomb: General Leslie R. Groves, the Manhattan Project's Indispensable Man* (South Royalton, VT: Steerforth Press, 2002), 325–327.

44. Quoted in Gordin, *Red Cloud at Dawn*, 51.

45. Stephen Wertheim, *Tomorrow, the World: The Birth of U.S. Global Supremacy* (Cambridge, MA: Belknap Press, 2020).

46. Bernstein, "The Quest for Security," 1036.

47. Acheson-Lilienthal Report on the International Control of Atomic Energy, 16 March 1964, http://www.learnworld.com/ZNW/LWText.Acheson-Lilienthal.html.

48. Quoted in Marco Borghi, "Political Authority or Atomic Celebrity? The Influence of J. Robert Oppenheimer on American Nuclear Policy after the Second World War," Nuclear Proliferation International History Project #14, August 2019.

49. "Atomic Progress Report," *The Economist* 150, no. 5358 (4 May 1946), 697–698.

50. "Russians Offer Pact on Atom," *Daily Mail*, 20 June 1946, 1. Gale Primary Sources.

51. Quoted in Gordin, *Red Cloud at Dawn*, 55.

52. Anatolii Gromyko, *Andrei Gromyko: Polet ego strely* (Moscow: Nauchnaia kniga, 2009), 115–116, quoted in David J. Holloway, "The Soviet Union and the Baruch Plan," *Sources and Methods*, 11 June 2020, History and Public Policy Program, Woodrow Wilson International Center for Scholars, https://www.wilsoncenter.org/blog-post/soviet-union-and-baruch-plan.

53. "Cable Nos. 512–515, Molotov to Druzhkov [Stalin]," 2 December 1946, History and Public Policy Program Digital Archive, RGASPI, f. 558, op. 11, d. 103, ll. 0082–0084, https://digitalarchive.wilsoncenter.org/document/209737, contributed by Sergey Radchenko and translated by Gary Goldberg.

54. "ICRC Report on the Effects of the Atomic Bomb at Hiroshima," *International Review of the Red Cross* 97, no. 899 (September 2015): 881, appendix 4.

55. M. Susan Lindee, *Suffering Made Real: American Science and the Survivors at Hiroshima* (Chicago: University of Chicago Press, 1997), 24–26.

56. Marcel Junod, *Warrior Without Weapons*, trans. Edward Fitzgerald (London: Jonathan Cape, 1951), 269.

57. "Circular Letter No. 370 to the Central Committees of the Red Cross Societies," 5 September 1945, *Report of the International Committee of the Red Cross on Its Activities During the Second World War*, May 1948, vol. I, ICRC, 688–690.

58. Harry S. Truman, diary, 25 June 1945, quoted in Barton J. Bernstein, "Truman at Potsdam: His Secret Diary," *Foreign Service Journal* (July/August 1980): 34, https://nsarchive2.gwu.edu/NSAEBB/NSAEBB162/38.pdf.

59. Alex Wellerstein, "The Kyoto Misconception: What Truman Knew, and Didn't Know, About Hiroshima," in Michael D. Gordin and G. John Ikenberry, eds., *The Age of Hiroshima* (Princeton, NJ: Princeton University Press, 2020), 34–55.

60. Sean L. Malloy, *Atomic Tragedy: Henry L. Stimson and the Decision to Use the Bomb Against Japan* (Ithaca, NY: Cornell University Press, 2008), 6, 106.

61. Henry L. Stimson, *On Active Service in Peace and War* (New York: Harper, 1948), 11–12.

62. Studs Terkel, ed., *The Good War: An Oral History of World War Two* (New York: New Press, 1997); Michael Brenes, *For Might and Right: Cold War Defense Spending and the Remaking of American Democracy* (Amherst: University of Massachusetts Press, 2020).

63. Wellerstein, "The Kyoto Misconception," 34–55.

64. Garry Wills, *Bomb Power: The Modern Presidency and the National Security State* (New York: Penguin, 2014); Arthur M. Schlesinger, *The Imperial Presidency* (Boston: Houghton Mifflin, 1973).

65. John Hersey, "Hiroshima," *New Yorker*, 31 August 1946, https://www.newyorker.com/magazine/1946/08/31/hiroshima.

66. John Hersey, Note, "The Red Cross," 1946, John Hersey papers, Beinecke Rare Books Library and Archive, Yale University.

67. Henry Stimson, "The Decision to Use the Bomb," *Harper's Magazine*, February 1947.

68. Gerald Steinacher, *Humanitarians at War: The Red Cross in the Shadow of the Holocaust* (New York: Oxford University Press, 2017), 1–5.

69. Ruti Teitel, *Humanity's Law* (Oxford, UK: Oxford University Press, 2014), 39–41; Elizabeth Borgwardt, *A New Deal for the World: America's Vision for Human Rights* (Cambridge, MA: Belknap Press, 2005).

70. Oona A. Hathaway and Scott J. Shapiro, *The Internationalists: How a Radical Plan to Outlaw War Remade the Modern World* (New York: Simon and Schuster, 2017).

71. Keith Lowe, *Savage Continent: Europe in the Aftermath of World War II* (London: Penguin, 2013), xiii–72; "World War II," in *A Dictionary of World History* (Oxford, UK: Oxford University Press, 2006); Diana Lary, *China's Civil War: A Social History, 1945–1949* (Cambridge, UK: Cambridge University Press, 2015); Ronald H. Spector, *In the Ruins of Empire: The Japanese Surrender and the Battle for Postwar Asia* (New York: Random House, 2007).

72. Elizabeth S. Borgwardt, "Ideology and International Law: The Dissent of the Indian Justice at the Tokyo War Crimes Trial," *NYU International Law and Politics*, no. 373 (1990): 373–444.

73. Ian Dear and M.R.D. Foot, eds., *The Oxford Companion to the Second World War* (New York: Oxford University Press, 1995), 1074, 1078.

74. Charles S. Maier, "Targeting the City: Debates and Silences About the Aerial Bombing of World War II," *International Review of the Red Cross* 87, no. 859 (September 2005): 430.

75. For a debate over doctrinal and operational approaches to civilian death during the Second World War, including Giulio Douhet's influence, see Alfred C. Mierzejewski, Kenneth P. Werrell, and Ronald Schaffer, "American Military Ethics in World War II: An Exchange," *Journal of American History* 68, no. 1 (June 1981): 85–92; Ronald Schaffer, "American Military Ethics in World War II: The Bombing of German Civilians," *Journal of American History* 67, no. 2 (September 1980): 318–334; A. C. Grayling, *Among the Dead Cities: Was the Allied Bombing of Civilians in WWII a Necessity or a Crime?* (London: Bloomsbury, 2006).

76. Junod, *Warrior Without Weapons*, 296.

77. Junod, *Warrior Without Weapons*, 296.

78. Brigitte Nicole Fielder, "Animal Humanism: Race, Species, and Affective Kinship in Nineteenth-Century Abolitionism," *American Quarterly* 65, no. 3 (2013): 487–514.

79. Marcel Junod, "The Hiroshima Disaster (II)," *International Review of the Red Cross* 22, no. 231 (December 1982): 330.

80. Junod, *Warrior Without Weapons*, 293–294, 299–300.

81. Junod, "The Hiroshima Disaster (II)," 344.

82. "Conférence préliminaire des Sociétés nationales de la Croix-Rouge pour l'étude des Conventions et de divers problems ayant trait à la Croix-Rouge," *Revue Internationale de la Croix-Rouge* 28, no. 332 (August 1946): 642–649.

83. "Rapport sur les travaux de la Conférence préliminaire des Sociétés nationales de la Croix-Rogue pour l'étude des Conventions et le divers problems ayant trait à la Croix-Rogue," *Revue Internationale de la Croix-Rogue* 28, no. 336 (December 1946): 999, 1013–1014; "Report of the Work of the Preliminary Conference of National Red Cross Societies for the Study of the Conventions and of Various Problems Relative to the Red Cross, July 26–August 3, 1946"

(Geneva: 1947), RC 1946, Series 1, #3, U.S. Army JAG School Library, https://www.loc.gov/rr/frd/Military_Law/pdf/RC_report-1946.pdf (accessed 3 July 2017).

84. "Report on the Work of the Conference of Government Experts for the Study of the Conventions for the Protection of War Victims," 1947, ICRC, 26, 300.

85. Jean-S. Pictet, "La défense de la personne humaine dans le droit future," *Revue Internationale de la Croix-Rouge* 29, no. 338 (February 1947): 124–125.

86. Compte-Rendu de la 1ème séance, 22 June 1948, CRI 25/7, ICRC, 10.

87. "Delegation du CICR à la Conference de Stockholm, Séance de preparation," Compte-Rendu de la 2ème séance, 29 June 1948, CRI 25/7, ICRC, 7–8.

88. Rapport interne No 5 pour la delegation du CICR à Stockholm, "Le Croix-Rouge et la Paix," undated, ICRC, CRI 25/7, ICRC, 5–6.

89. Steinacher, *Humanitarians at War*, 213.

90. Delegation du CICR à la Conference de Stockholm, Séance de preparation," Compte-Rendu de la 9ème séance (d'après le Rapport résumé), 12 August 1948, CRI 25/7, ICRC, 1–7. François Bugnion, "The International Committee of the Red Cross and Nuclear Weapons," 517; Letter, Jean Wilhelm to F. W. Dohany, 18 October 1948, CR 254/1, ICRC, 4.

91. Rapport Special Etabli par M. C. Pilloud, "VI. Procédure," CR 254, ICRC, f.

92. Summary Record of the Third Meeting held on Wednesday, 27 April 1949, at 3 p.m., CDG/CIV/CR.3/CORR. 18, in Committee III, "Convention on the Protection of Civilians" meeting notes, April–July 1949, Arthur E. Clattenburg Jr. Collection, Rare Books and Manuscripts, Kislak Center for Special Collections, University of Pennsylvania, 9.

93. Summary Record of the Fourth Meeting held on Thursday, 28 April 1949, at 3 p.m., CDG/CIV/CR.4, in Committee III, "Convention on the Protection of Civilians" meeting notes, April–July 1949, Arthur E. Clattenburg Jr. Collection, Rare Books and Manuscripts, Kislak Center for Special Collections, University of Pennsylvania, 6.

94. International Committee of the Red Cross, *Geneva Convention Relative to the Protection of Civilian Persons in Time of War (Fourth Geneva Convention)*, 12 August 1949, 75 UNTS 287, Part II, Article 14, https://www.refworld.org/docid/3ae6b36d2.html.

95. Gordin, *Red Cloud at Dawn*, 179–231.

96. Toshihiro Higuchi, *Political Fallout: Nuclear Weapons Testing and the Making of a Global Environmental Crisis* (Stanford, CA: Stanford University Press, 2020).

97. Bernard Brodie et al., eds., *The Absolute Weapon: Atomic Power and World Order* (New York: Harcourt, Brace, 1946); Fred M. Kaplan, *The Wizards of Armageddon* (New York: Simon and Schuster, 1983), 9–34.

98. Quoted in Gregg Herken, *The Winning Weapon: The Atomic Bomb in the Cold War, 1945–1950* (New York: Vintage Books, 1982), 22.

99. Melvyn P. Leffler, *A Preponderance of Power: National Security, the Truman Administration, and the Cold War* (Stanford, CA: Stanford University Press, 1992), 15–19.

100. Quoted in Herken, *The Winning Weapon*, 213.

101. Quoted in Richard Rhodes, "The General and World War III," *New Yorker*, 12 June 1995, https://www.newyorker.com/magazine/1995/06/19/the-general-and-world-war-iii.

102. Michael S. Sherry, *The Rise of American Air Power: The Creation of Armageddon* (New Haven, CT: Yale University Press, 1987), 180; Curtis Emerson LeMay and MacKinley Kantor, *Mission with LeMay: My Story* (New York: Doubleday, 1965), 565; Warren Kozak, *LeMay: The Life and Wars of General Curtis LeMay* (Washington, DC: Regnery, 2011), 341–342.

103. Herken, *The Winning Weapon*, 196–197; David Alan Rosenberg, "American Atomic Strategy and the Hydrogen Bomb Decision," *Journal of American History* 66, no. 1 (June 1979): 62–87.

104. Leffler, *A Preponderance of Power*, 267–272.

105. Appendix B, 30 October 1949, in Gregg Herken, *Cardinal Choices: Presidential Science Advising from the Atomic Bomb to SDI* (New York: Oxford University Press, 1992), 34–48.

106. Campbell Craig and Fredrik Logevall, *America's Cold War: The Politics of Insecurity* (Cambridge, MA: Belknap Press, 2012), 102–138; Curt Cardwell, *NSC 68 and the Political Economy of the Early Cold War* (Leiden, Netherlands: Cambridge University Press, 2011); Michael J. Hogan, *A Cross of Iron: Harry S. Truman and the Origins of the National Security State, 1945–1954* (New York: Cambridge University Press, 1998), 265–314.

107. H. W. Brands, *The General vs. the President: MacArthur and Truman at the Brink of Nuclear War* (New York: Doubleday, 2016).

108. Harry S. Truman, *Years of Trial and Hope* (New York: Doubleday, 1955).

109. Quoted in John Lewis Gaddis, *We Now Know: Rethinking Cold War History* (New York: Oxford University Press, 1998), 229.

110. David Holloway, "Nuclear Weapons and the Escalation of the Cold War, 1945–1962," in Melvyn P. Leffler and Odd Arne Westad, eds., *Origins*, vol. 1, 3 vols., *The Cambridge History of the Cold War* (Cambridge, UK: Cambridge University Press, 2010), 376–397.

111. Mary L. Dudziak, *Cold War Civil Rights: Race and the Image of American Democracy* (Princeton, NJ: Princeton University Press, 2002); Kenneth Alan Osgood, *Total Cold War: Eisenhower's Secret Propaganda Battle at Home and Abroad* (Lawrence: University of Kansas, 2006); William I. Hitchcock, *The Age of Eisenhower: America and the World in the 1950s* (New York: Simon and Schuster, 2018).

112. Robert R. Bowie and Richard H. Immerman, *Waging Peace: How Eisenhower Shaped an Enduring Cold War Strategy* (New York: Oxford University Press, 1998).

113. John Lewis Gaddis, *Strategies of Containment: A Critical Appraisal of American National Security Policy During the Cold War* (New York: Oxford University Press, 2005), 125–196.

114. *FRUS, 1952–1954*, vol. II, part 1, document 101.

115. Lawrence Freedman, *The Evolution of Nuclear Strategy*, 3rd ed. (New York: Palgrave Macmillan, 2003); Jeffrey W. Knopf, *Security Assurances and Nuclear Nonproliferation* (Stanford, CA: Stanford University Press, 2012).

116. Henry Kissinger, *Nuclear Weapons and Foreign Policy* (New York: Harper, 1957).

117. Campbell Craig, *Destroying the Village: Eisenhower and Thermonuclear War* (New York: Columbia University Press, 1998); Evan Thomas, *Ike's Bluff: President Eisenhower's Secret Battle to Save the World* (New York: Little, Brown, 2012).

118. Hitchcock, *The Age of Eisenhower*, 103–107.

119. Fredrick Logevall, "'We Might Give Them a Few.' Did the US Offer to Drop Atom Bombs at Dien Bien Phu?," *Bulletin of the Atomic Scientists*, 21 February 2016, http://thebulletin.org/we-might-give-them-few-did-us-offer-drop-atom-bombs-dien-bien-phu9175; Matthew Jones, *After Hiroshima: The United States, Race, and Nuclear Weapons in Asia, 1945–1965* (New York: Cambridge University Press, 2010), 206–216.

120. H. W. Brands, "Testing Massive Retaliation: Credibility and Crisis Management in the Taiwan Straits," *International Security* 12, no. 4 (Spring 1988): 124–151.

121. Jones, *After Hiroshima*, 215.

122. Matthew Jones, "Targeting China: U.S. Nuclear Planning and 'Massive Retaliation' in East Asia, 1953–1955," *Journal of Cold War Studies* 10, no. 4 (Fall 2008): 37–65.

123. Robert A. Divine, *The Sputnik Challenge* (New York: Oxford University Press, 1993).

124. Rotter, *Hiroshima*, 4.

125. Walter LaFeber, *The Clash: U.S.-Japanese Relations Throughout History* (New York: Norton, 1998), 296–324.

126. Lawrence S. Wittner, *Confronting the Bomb: A Short History of the World Nuclear Disarmament Movement* (Stanford, CA: Stanford University Press, 2009), 8.

127. *FRUS, 1952–1954*, vol. XIV, part 2, document 762.

128. Jones, *After Hiroshima*, 201–203.

CHAPTER 2

1. Frank Aiken, *Ireland at the United Nations, 1958* (Dublin: Brún agus Ó Nualláin Teo, 1958), 15–18.

2. Jian Chen, *Mao's China and the Cold War* (Chapel Hill: University of North Carolina Press, 2001), chap. 7.

3. Morton H. Halperin, "The 1958 Taiwan Straits Crisis: A Documented History," Memorandum RM-4900-ISA (December 1966: RAND Corporation), v–viii.

4. Gordon Chang, *Friends and Enemies: The United States, China, and the Soviet Union, 1948–1972* (Stanford, CA: Stanford University Press, 1992), 185.

5. Quoted in Gregg Andrew Brazinsky, *Winning the Third World: Sino-American Rivalry During the Cold War* (Chapel Hill: University of North Carolina Press, 2017), 168.

6. "Telegram from the Embassy in the Soviet Union to the Department of State," Moscow, September 19, 1958, *FRUS, 1958–1960*, vol. XIX, document 110.

7. John Wilson Lewis and Litai Xue, *China Builds the Bomb* (Stanford, CA: Stanford University Press, 1991); Austin Jersild, "Sharing the Bomb Among Friends: The Dilemmas of Sino-Soviet Strategic Cooperation," 8 October 2013, Cold War International History Project [CWIHP] e-Dossier No. 43, https://www.wilsoncenter.org/publication/sharing-the-bomb-among-friends-the-dilemmas-sino-soviet-strategic-cooperation.

8. John Hearne to Frank Aiken, letter, "Conversation with Archbishop Cushing," 20 September 1958, document 6052, Frank Aiken papers [FA], University College Dublin [UCD], 2–3; Joseph Morrison Skelly, *Irish Diplomacy at the United Nations, 1945–1965: National Interests and the International Order* (Dublin: Irish Academic Press, 1997), 15–24.

9. Skelly, *Irish Diplomacy at the United Nations, 1945–1965*, 13. For sketches of Frank Aiken's decades-long record in domestic politics and foreign policy, see Bryce Evans and Stephen Kelly, eds., *Frank Aiken: Nationalist and Internationalist* (Dublin: Original Writing, 2014).

10. Frank Aiken, draft, "Ireland's Decision Against NATO Membership," 9 January 1962, document 5858, FA, UCD.

11. Skelly, *Irish Diplomacy at the United Nations, 1945–1965*.

12. Frank Aiken, draft, "The United Nations as a Universal Organization," 1958, document 6047, FA, UCD, 2.

13. Christophe Gillissen, "Ireland, France and the Question of Algeria at the United Nations, 1955–62," *Irish Studies in International Affairs* 19 (2008): 151–167.

14. Evans and Kelly, *Frank Aiken*, 76–80.

15. Quoted in Evans and Kelly, *Frank Aiken*, 339.

16. Frank Aiken, speech at Rotary Club Luncheon, Chicago, "Ireland at the United Nations," 31 October 1960, document 6231, FA, UCD, 1.

17. Hearne to Aiken, letter, 20 September 1958, 2–3.

18. Frank Aiken, draft with handwritten edits, "Speech for Dáil Debate on UN foreign policy," October 1959," document 6121, FA, UCD, 2.

19. Frank Aiken, *Ireland at the United Nations, 1957* (Dublin: Brún agus Ó Nualláin Teo, 1957), 13.

20. Frank Aiken, amended typescript, "Response to Questions from Declan Costella on Irish Position at the UN," 26 November 1957, document 5871, FA, UCD, 3.

21. Aiken, amended typescript, 26 November 1957, 12–13.

22. Stephen Wertheim, "The League That Wasn't: American Designs for a Legalist-Sanctionist League of Nations and the Intellectual Origins of International Organization, 1914–1920," *Diplomatic History* 35, no. 5 (November 2011): 797–836.

23. Aiken, amended typescript, 26 November 1957, 12–13.

24. Frank Aiken, speech at Rotary Club Luncheon, Chicago, 31 October 1960, 4.

25. Memorandum of conversation, 22 July 1958, 305/173/III, Foreign Ministry Papers [FMP], National Archives of Ireland [NAI], quoted in Skelly, *Irish Diplomacy at the United Nations, 1945–1965*, 153. The memorandum of conversation was circulated to all Irish foreign missions.

26. Norman Macqueen, "Frank Aiken and Irish Activism at the United Nations, 1957–1961," *International History Review* 6, no. 2 (May 1984): 210–231.

27. Frank Aiken, statement, "Obtaining US State Department Support for Nuclear Restraint," 1961, document 6365, FA, UCD.

28. Aiken, *Ireland at the United Nations, 1957*, 15–21.

29. Noel Door, "Frank Aiken at the United Nations: Some Personal Reflections," in Evans and Kelly, *Frank Aiken*.

30. George Kennan, "Lecture 2: The Soviet Mind and World Realities," in *Reith Lectures 1957: Russia, the Atom and the West*, 17 November 1957, BBC, 5.

31. Kennan, "Lecture 2," 6; "Lecture 3: The Problem of Eastern and Central Europe," "Lecture 4: The Military Problem," in *Reith Lectures 1957: Russia, the Atom, and the West*, 17 November 1957, *BBC*, 5–6; BBC Symposium, transcript, "Russia, the Atom, and the West," 29 December 1957, box 138, Correspondence, George F. Kennan papers, PPP, Mudd Library, 5.

32. NATO Military Committee, Report 48/2, "Measures to Implement the Strategic Concept," https://www.nato.int/docu/stratdoc/eng/a570523b.pdf (accessed 14 September 2021).

33. NATO Council, final communiqué, https://www.nato.int/docu/comm/49-95/c571219a.htm (accessed 14 September 2021).

34. John Lewis Gaddis, *George F. Kennan: An American Life* (New York: Penguin, 2011), chap. 20, footnote 51; John F. Kennedy and Martin W. Sandler, *The Letters of John F. Kennedy* (London: Bloomsbury, 2015), 67.

35. Aiken, amended typescript, 26 November 1957, 14.

36. Round table discussion, transcript, "Russia, the Atom, and the West," 18 January 1958, Congress for Cultural Freedom, box 138, Series 1: Correspondence, GFK, PPP, Harvey Mudd Library, 38.

37. George F. Kennan, response to round table discussion, "Russia, the Atom, and the West," 18 January 1958, 4–5.

38. Campbell Craig, *Glimmer of a New Leviathan: Total War in the Realism of Niebuhr, Morgenthau, and Waltz* (New York: Columbia University Press, 2003); Alison McQueen, *Political Realism in Apocalyptic Times* (New York: Cambridge University Press, 2018).

39. *FRUS, 1955–1957*, vol. XII, document 183.

40. Aiken, *Ireland at the United Nations, 1957*, 21.

41. Quoted in Skelly, *Irish Diplomacy at the United Nations*, 154.

42. Aiken, *Ireland at the United Nations, 1958*, 3–14.

43. Aiken, speech at Rotary Club Luncheon, Chicago, 31 October 1960, 2.

44. Con Cremin to Fred Boland, confidential letter, "Nuclear Restriction Question,' 22 May 1959, 440/8/1, FMP, NAI.

45. J. F. Shields, "Meeting at the State Department," 10 July 1959, 440/8/4, DFA, NAI, 2.

46. Quoted in Shen Zhihua and Xia Yafeng, "Between Aid and Restriction: The Soviet Union's Changing Policies on China's Nuclear Weapons Program, 1954–1960," *Asian Perspective*

36 (2012): 103; "Statement of Chinese Government Spokesman—Commentary on the Soviet Government Statement of August 21," *Renmin ribao*, 1 September 1963, 1. Cited in Shen and Xia, *Mao and the Sino-Soviet Partnership, 1945–1959*, 268.

47. "Conversation of Mao Zedong with Soviet Ambassador Pavel Yudin (Excerpt)," 28 February 1958, Woodrow Wilson International Center for Scholars [WWICS], Digital Archive, http://digitalarchive.wilsoncenter.org/document/114342.

48. Andrei A. Gromyko, *Memoirs* (London: Arrow Books, 1989), 251–2.

49. Aiken, *Ireland at the United Nations, 1958*, 15.

50. Quoted in Evans and Kelly, *Frank Aiken*, 74.

51. Evans and Kelly, *Frank Aiken*, 31–33.

52. Aiken, amended typescript, 26 November 1957, 13.

53. Matthew Jones, *After Hiroshima: The United States, Race, and Nuclear Weapons in Asia, 1945–1965* (New York: Cambridge University Press, 2010).

54. "Copies of Statements Made by Foreign Delegates on the Restriction of the Dissemination of Nuclear Weapons," 10 October—4 November 1958, document 6073, FA, UCD, 35.

55. Handwritten note, V. K. Krishna Menon to Frank Aiken, 4 November 1958, document 6081, FA, UCD.

56. "Copies of Statements," 10 October—4 November 1958, 40.

57. Con Cremin to Frank Aiken, confidential note, "Brief Conversation with Felician Prill re Nuclear Restriction," undated, document 6069, FA, UCD.

58. "Copies of Statements," 10 October—4 November 1958, 7.

59. Con Cremin to Frank Aiken, note, "Brief Conversation with German Ambassador re Nuclear Restriction Speech," undated, document 6069, FA, UCD; "Lodge Comments at Thirteenth Session, UNGA, First Committee," 31 October 1958, 440/8/1, FMP, NAI.

60. F. Biggar, letter, "Lunch at Soviet Embassy with Alexei Roshchin," 13 May 1959, 440/8/1, FMP, NAI, 2; Benjamin P. Greene, *Eisenhower, Science Advice, and the Nuclear Test-Ban Debate, 1945—1963* (Stanford, CA: Stanford University Press, 2007).

61. Quoted in Howard Simons, "Worldwide Capabilities for Production and Control of Nuclear Weapons," *Daedalus*, vol. 88, no. 3 (Summer 1959): 385–409; round table discussion, transcript, "Russia, the Atom, and the West," 18 January 1958, 10.

62. C. L. Sulzberger, "The Prospects of a New European Entente," 10 February 1958, *New York Times*, 22. ProQuest Historical Newspapers.

63. Aiken, *Ireland at the United Nations, 1958*, 25.

64. Frank Aiken, speech before the UNGA, "The Cold War, Decolonization, and the United Nations," 6 October 1960, document 6269, FA, UCD archives, 2–4.

65. Aiken, *Ireland at the United Nations, 1958*, 29–40.

66. "Extract from Speech by Sidney Smith," undated, 440/8/1; "Ireland Supported by Canada in U.N.: Atomic Control Proposed," *Irish Times*, 21 October 1958, 440/8/1, FMP, NAI. The *Irish Times* reported that Smith said "uncontrolled anarchy."

67. Alastair Hetherington to Conor Cruise O'Brien, letter, 17 April 1959, 440/8/1, FMP, NAI; "Ireland's Frank Aiken Offers a Proposal for Nuclear Disarmament—Extension of Remarks of Hon. Henry S. Reuss of Wisconsin in the House of Representatives," *Congressional Record: Proceedings and Debates of the 86th Congress, First Session*, 440/8/1/, FMP, NAI.

68. Arthur Krock to J. F. Shields, 16 June 1959; Walter Lippmann to J. F. Shields, 19 June 1959; Fred Boland to Cornelius Cremin, 26 June 1959, 440/8/4, FMP, NAI.

69. "The Nation's Request for an Article," undated, document 6008, FA, UCD.

70. E. L. Kennedy to Fred Boland, letter, "SANE's Position on Irish Resolution," 3 July 1959, 440/8/4, FMP, NAI, 2.

71. Draft letter to Alastair Hetherington, "Article on Nuclear Restriction," May 1959, 440/8/1; E. L. Kennedy to Frank Aiken, "Nuclear Weapons Dissemination," 13 August 1959, 440/8/4, FMP, NAI, 2.

72. "Conversation with Mr. Husain, Minister in the Indian Mission in London and Dublin," 6 August 1959, 440/8/4, FMP, NAI.

73. Jean Allman, "Nuclear Imperialism and the Pan-African Struggle for Peace and Freedom: Ghana, 1959–1962," *Souls* 10, no. 2 (June 13, 2008): 83–102; Vincent J. Intondi, *African Americans Against the Bomb: Nuclear Weapons, Colonialism, and the Black Freedom Movement* (Stanford, CA: Stanford University Press, 2014), 57–59.

74. Fred Boland, "The Nuclear Restriction Question," 28 May 1959, 440/8/4, FMP, NAI, 4–5.

75. Quoted in Donald H. Akenson, *Conor: A Biography of Conor Cruise O'Brien* (Montreal: McGill-Queen's University Press, 2014), 159.

76. Frank Aiken, note, "Meeting re Nuclear Restriction Draft Resolution," 16 July 1959, document 6218, FA, UCD, 1.

77. Aiken, note, 16 July 1959, 2–3; J. F. Shields, "Meeting at the State Department," undated, 440/8/4, FMP, NAI, 3.

78. "Report of Proceeding United States Senate Committee on Foreign Relations General Discussion on Foreign Policy," 12 May 1959, and George F. Kennedy, letter to John J. Hearne, 15 June 1959, 440/8/4, FMP, NAI.

79. "Meeting with Senator Humphrey," 23 July 1959, 440/8/4, FMP, NAI.

80. "Nuclear Arms and Peace," *New York Times*, 27 June 1959; F. Biggar to Dr. C. O'Brien, "The Non-Nuclear Club and British Labour," 23 June 1959, [27–29]; F. Biggar to Dr. C. O'Brien, "Labour Party Executive Non-nuclear Club Resolution," 28 July 1959, 440/8/4, FMP, NAI; R.K.S. Taylor, *Against the Bomb: The British Peace Movement, 1958–1965* (New York: Oxford University Press, 1988).

81. Letter to Frank Aiken, "General de Gaulle and British Labour's Plan for Nuclear Weapons," Paris, 7 August 1959, 440/8/4, FMP, NAI.

82. "Biological and Environmental Effects of Nuclear War," 22–26 June 1959, *Hearings Before the Special Subcommittee on Radiation*, JCAE, 86th U.S. Congress (Washington, DC: U.S. Government Printing Office, 1969), 5.

83. Kennedy to Aiken, "Nuclear Weapons Dissemination," 31 August 1959; Reinhold Niebuhr, *The Structures of Empires and Nations: A Study of the Recurring Patterns and Problems of the Political Order in relation to the Unique Problems of the Nuclear Age* (London: Faber and Faber, 1959).

84. Frank Aiken, *Ireland at the United Nations, 1959* (Dublin: Brún agus Ó Nualláin Teo, 1959), 68.

85. Aiken, *Ireland at the United Nations, 1959*, 9–19.

86. E. MacW to Frank Aiken, letter, "Discussions with the Americans," 17 July 1959, 440/8/4, FMP, NAI; Aiken, *Ireland at the United Nations, 1959*, 13–14.

87. F. Biggar to Frank Aiken, "The Non-nuclear Club," 20 August 1959, 440/8/4, FMP, NAI.

88. Frank Aiken, speech before the First Committee, "Introducing Irish Resolution on the Prevention of the Dissemination of Nuclear Weapons," 1959, FA, UCD, 6.

89. Biggar to Aiken, 20 August 1959.

90. Department of External Affairs, memorandum for the government, "15th Session of UNGA," 9 September 1960, FA, UCD.

91. Melvyn O'Driscoll, "Explosive Challenge: Diplomatic Triangles, the United Nations, and the Problem of French Nuclear Testing, 1959–1960," *Journal of Cold War Studies* 11, no. 1 (Winter 2009): 28–56.

92. Monsieur Blanchard, French chargé d'affaires, to Frank Aiken, note, "French Position on Irish Resolution," 10 September 1959, FA, UCD.

93. Frank Aiken, speech before the UNGA, 6 October 1960, 2–4.

94. Frank Aiken, statement to the First Committee of the UNGA, "Prevention of the Wider Dissemination of Nuclear Weapons to Additional Nations," 29 November 1960, FA, UCD, 7.

95. McGeorge Bundy, *Danger and Survival: Choices About the Bomb in the First Fifty Years* (New York: Random House, 1988), 255.

96. Toshihiro Higuchi, "'Clean' Bombs: Nuclear Technology and Nuclear Strategy in the 1950s," *Journal of Strategic Studies* 29, no. 1 (February 1, 2006): 83–116.

97. Frank C. Nash to C. D. Jackson, memorandum, "DoD Comments on Fourth Draft Speech on Atomic Energy," White House Central Files, Subject Series, Candor and the United Nations Speech, box 13, Dwight D. Eisenhower Presidential Library [DDEPL]: 1–3.

98. Quoted in Ira Chernus, *Eisenhower's Atoms for Peace* (College Station: Texas A&M University Press, 2002), 33.

99. Chernus, *Eisenhower's Atoms for Peace*, 28.

100. Bundy, *Danger and Survival*, 244; Winston Churchill to Dwight D. Eisenhower, letter, 6 December 1953, Churchill Papers, CHUR 6/3A/80, Cambridge University.

101. "Dwight D. Eisenhower's 'Atoms for Peace' Speech," address to the 470th Plenary Meeting of the United Nations General Assembly, 8 December 1953, in Chernus, *Eisenhower's Atoms for Peace*, xi–xix.

102. "Summary of Meeting with the Secretary of State on Implementation of the President's December 8th Speech," 6 January 1954, White House Central Files, Subject Series, Candor and the United Nations Speech, DDEPL.

103. Bundy, *Danger and Survival*, 244.

104. "Statement by the Soviet Government on President Eisenhower's "Atoms for Peace" Address," 21 December 1953, in ACDA, *Documents on Disarmament, 1945–1959*, vol. 1 (Washington DC: U.S. Government Printing Office, 1960): 401–407, quoted in David Holloway, "The Soviet Union and the Creation of the International Atomic Energy Agency," *Cold War History* (6 January 2016), 1–17.

105. Alex Wellerstein, *Restricted Data: The History of Nuclear Secrecy in the United States* (Chicago: University of Chicago Press, 2021); Jacob Darwin Hamblin, *The Wretched Atom: America's Global Gamble with Peaceful Nuclear Technology* (New York: Oxford University Press, 2021).

106. "U.S. Department of State, CW-5966, U.S. Nuclear Weapons Posture," undated [cover letter 26 January 1962], Nuclear Weapons: Testing: U.S. Resumption: Announcement and Reactions, 2 March 1962, September 1961–January 1962, NSF, Presidential Papers [PP], JFKL, http://www.jfklibrary.org/Asset-Viewer/Archives/JFKNSF-302-002.aspx (accessed 15 July 2016).

107. Public Law 83–703, Atomic Energy Act of 1954, as amended, 30 August 1954, https://www.nrc.gov/docs/ML1327/ML13274A489.pdf.

108. *FRUS, 1958–1960*, vol. III, document 70, 5 August 1959; Jones, *After Hiroshima*, 382–384.

109. *FRUS, 1958–1960*, vol. III, document 61, 25 June 1959.

110. NSC 5906/1, *FRUS, 1958–1960*, vol. III, document 70, 5 August 1959; Grégoire Mallard, *Fallout: Nuclear Diplomacy in an Age of Global Fracture* (Chicago: University of Chicago Press, 2014).

111. "Multilateral Force," in Euud van Djik, William Gleen Gray, Svetlana Savranskaya, Jeremi Suri, and Qiang Zhai, eds., *Encyclopedia of the Cold War* (New York: Taylor and Francis, 2008), 602–603.

112. Extracts from the Bowie Report, "The North Atlantic Nations: Tasks for the 1960s," August 1960, http://www.sscnet.ucla.edu/polisci/faculty/trachtenberg/documents/bowie.html (accessed 4 August 2016).

113. Lawrence S. Kaplan, "The MLF Debate," in Douglas Brinkley and Richard T. Griffiths, eds., *John F. Kennedy and Europe* (Baton Rouge: Louisiana State University Press, 1999), 51–65.

114. National Intelligence Estimate 4-3-61, "Nuclear Weapons and Delivery Capabilities of Free World Countries Other Than the US and UK," 21 September 1961, http://nsarchive.gwu.edu/NSAEBB/NSAEBB155/prolif-6b.pdf.

115. Lewis and Litai, *China Builds the Bomb*.

116. Shen Zhihua and Xia Yafeng, "Between Aid and Restriction: The Soviet Union's Changing Policies on China's Nuclear Weapons Program, 1954–1960," *Asian Perspective* 36 (2012): 102.

117. Roland M. Timerbaev, *Россия и ядерное нераспространение, 1945–1968* (Moscow: Nauka, 1999), 48.

118. National Intelligence Estimate 100-6-57, "Nuclear Weapons Production in Fourth Countries: Likelihood and Consequences," 18 June 1957, http://nsarchive.gwu.edu/NSAEBB/NSAEBB155/prolif-2.pdf.

119. National Intelligence Estimate 100-4-60, "Likelihood and Consequences of the Development of Nuclear Capabilities by Additional Countries," 20 September 1960, http://nsarchive.gwu.edu/NSAEBB/NSAEBB155/prolif-5.pdf.

120. *FRUS, 1961–1963*, vol. XXII, document 62, 28 September 1961, and document 76, 26 October 1961.

121. Gabrielle Hecht, *The Radiance of France: Nuclear Power and National Identity after World War II* (Cambridge, MA: MIT Press, 1998).

122. Benjamin Pinkus, "Atomic Power to Israel's Rescue: French-Israeli Nuclear Cooperation, 1949–1957," *Israel Studies* 7, no. 1 (2002): 104–38, esp. 115–118.

123. Pierre Péan, *Les Deux Bombes* (Paris: Fayard, 1982).

124. Avner Cohen, *Israel and the Bomb* (New York: Columbia University Press, 1998), 10.

125. Pinkus, "Atomic Power to Israel's Rescue," 118.

126. Douglas Little, "The Cold War in the Middle East: Suez Crisis to Camp David Accords," in Melvyn P. Leffler and Odd Arne Westad, eds., *Crises and Détente*, vol. 2, 3 vols., *The Cambridge History of the Cold War* (Cambridge, UK: Cambridge University Press, 2010), 306.

127. Benjamin John Grob-Fitzgibbon, *Imperial Endgame: Britain's Dirty Wars and the End of Empire* (New York: Palgrave Macmillan, 2011); John Darwin, *The Empire Project: The Rise and Fall of the British World-System, 1830–1970* (New York: Cambridge University Press, 2009); Guy Laron, *Origins of the Suez Crisis: Postwar Development, Diplomacy, and the Struggle over Third World Industrialization, 1945–1956* (Washington, DC: Woodrow Wilson Center Press, 2013); William Roger Louis, *Ends of British Imperialism: The Scramble for Empire, Suez and Decolonization; Collected Essays* (London: Tauris, 2006).

128. Little, "The Cold War in the Middle East," 305–312.

129. An IAEC scheme to modify the small reactor to produce approximately eight grams of plutonium per month died for reasons of U.S. safeguards and internal dissent. Cohen, *Israel and the Bomb*, 41, 44–47.

130. Pinkus, "Atomic Power to Israel's Rescue," 119.

131. Cohen, *Israel and the Bomb*, 53.

132. Cohen, *Israel and the Bomb*, 49.

133. Diane B. Kunz, *The Economic Diplomacy of the Suez Crisis* (Chapel Hill: University of North Carolina Press, 1991); William Roger Louis and Roger Owen, eds., *Suez 1956: The Crisis and Its Consequences* (New York: Oxford University Press, 1989).

134. Cohen, *Israel and the Bomb*, 55.

135. Cohen, *Israel and the Bomb*, 57.

136. Pinkus, "Atomic Power to Israel's Rescue," 123.

137. Pinkus, "Atomic Power to Israel's Rescue," 124–127. Pinkus cites Matti Golan, *Shimon Peres: A Biography* (London: Weidenfeld and Nicolson, 1982), 72.

138. Cohen, *Israel and the Bomb*, 60.

139. Cohen, *Israel and the Bomb*, 73–75.

140. Memorandum of conversation, Norwegian Foreign Ministry, 5 June 1959, http://nsar chive.gwu.edu/nukevault/ebb510/docs/doc 2A.pdf; U.S. embassy in Tel Aviv to State Department, cable, "French Atomic Energy Project in Israel," 2 August 1960, https://nsarchive2.gwu .edu/nukevault/ebb510/docs/doc 3.pdf.

141. *FRUS, 1958–1960*, vol. XIII, document 181, 31 December 1960.

142. Memorandum of conversation, Dwight Eisenhower et al., 19 December 1960, http:// nsarchive.gwu.edu/nukevault/ebb510/docs/doc13A.pdf.

143. *FRUS, 1961–1963*, vol. XVII, document 3, 19 January 1961. Report here: https://nsar chive2.gwu.edu/nukevault/ebb510/docs/doc%2026.pdf.

144. Richard Reeves, *President Kennedy: Profile in Power* (New York: Simon and Schuster, 1994), 29–33, cited in http://nsarchive.gwu.edu/nukevault/ebb547-Kennedy-Dimona-and-the -Nuclear-Proliferation-Problem-1961-1962/#_edn1 (accessed 15 August 2016).

145. *FRUS, 1961–1963*, vol. XIX, document 35, 8–9 August 1961.

146. U.S. embassy in Tel Aviv to U.S. Department of State, cable, 23 December 1960, http:// nsarchive.gwu.edu/nukevault/ebb510/docs/doc%2015.pdf; Murat W. Williams to William L. Hamilton, "A Catalog of Replies Regarding the Reactor," 16 January 1961, http://nsarchive .gwu.edu/nukevault/ebb510/docs/doc%2025.pdf.

CHAPTER 3

1. John F. Kennedy, film, "Excerpt, 1960 Democratic National Convention," 15 July 1960," JFKL, https://www.jfklibrary.org/Asset-Viewer/AS08q50Yz0SFUZg9uOi4iw.aspx (accessed 25 November 2015).

2. George Kennan, oral history, JFKL, 14.

3. Robert F. Kennedy Jr., *Thirteen Days: A Memoir of the Cuban Missile Crisis* (New York: Norton, 1969); Arthur M. Schlesinger, *A Thousand Days: John F. Kennedy in the White House* (New York: Houghton Mifflin, 2002); Theodore C. Sorensen, *Kennedy* (New York: Harper and Row, 1965).

4. Seymour M. Hersh, *The Dark Side of Camelot* (New York: Back Bay Books, 1998); Thomas G. Paterson, *Kennedy's Quest for Victory: American Foreign Policy, 1961–1963* (New York: Oxford University Press, 1989); Stephen Rabe, *The Most Dangerous Area in the World: John F. Kennedy Confronts Communist Revolution in Latin America* (Chapel Hill: University of North Carolina Press, 1999); and Stephen Rabe, *John F. Kennedy: World Leader* (Washington, DC: Potomac Books, 2010).

5. James N. Giglio and Stephen G. Rabe, *Debating the Kennedy Presidency* (Lanham, MD: Rowman and Littlefield, 2003); Lawrence Freedman, *Kennedy's Wars: Berlin, Cuba, Laos, and Vietnam* (New York: Oxford University Press, 2000); Fredrik Logevall, *Choosing War: The Lost Chance for Peace and the Escalation of War in Vietnam* (Berkeley: University of California Press, 2001); Robert B. Rakove, *Kennedy, Johnson, and the Nonaligned World* (Cambridge, UK: Cambridge University Press, 2013).

6. "Inaugural Address of Dwight D. Eisenhower," 20 January 1953, Dwight D. Eisenhower Library and Archive, http://www.eisenhower.archives.gov/all_about_ike/speeches/1953_inau gural_address.pdf.

7. "Inaugural Address of John F. Kennedy," 20 January 1961, Avalon Project, Yale Law School, http://avalon.law.yale.edu/20th_century/kennedy.asp.

8. Walt Rostow to Dean Rusk, memorandum, "Nuclear Weapons: The Dilemma and Thoughts on Its Resolution," 6 January 1961, box 64A, staff memos, POF, JFKL, 5–6.

9. Quoted in Hal Brands, *Latin America's Cold War* (Cambridge, MA: Harvard University Press, 2010), 23.

10. Odd Arne Westad, *The Cold War: A World History* (New York: Basic Books, 2017), 281.

11. John F. Kennedy, "Special Message to the Congress on Urgent National Matters," 25 May 1961, JFKL, https://www.jfklibrary.org/archives/other-resources/john-f-kennedy-speeches/united-states-congress-special-message-19610525.

12. Walt Rostow to John Kennedy, memorandum, "Some Possible Messages to Moscow," 16 February 1961, box 64A, staff memos, POF, JFKL; Rostow to Rusk, memorandum, 6 January 1961.

13. Walt Whitman Rostow, *The Diffusion of Power: An Essay in Recent History* (New York: Macmillan, 1972).

14. William Hitchcock, *The Struggle for Europe: The Turbulent History of a Divided Continent 1945 to the Present* (New York: Anchor Books, 2013), 131–161.

15. David Reynolds, *One World Divisible: A Global History Since 1945* (New York: Norton, 2000).

16. Leslie James and Elisabeth Leake, eds., *Decolonization and the Cold War: Negotiating Independence* (London: Bloomsbury, 2015).

17. Jeffrey James Byrne, *Mecca of Revolution: Algeria, Decolonization, and the Third World Order* (New York: Oxford University Press, 2016); Douglas Smith, "The Broken Hexagon: French Nuclear Culture Between Empire and Cold War," *Modern and Contemporary France* 18, no. 2 (May 2010): 213–229; Gabrielle Hecht, *The Radiance of France: Nuclear Power and National Identity After World War II* (Cambridge, MA: MIT Press, 1998); Frédéric Bozo, *Two Strategies for Europe: De Gaulle, the United States, and the Atlantic Alliance* (Lanham, MD: Rowman and Littlefield, 2001).

18. Rakove, *Kennedy, Johnson, and the Nonaligned World*, 135–173.

19. Piero Gleijeses, *Conflicting Missions: Havana, Washington, and Africa, 1959–1976* (Chapel Hill: University of North Carolina Press, 2002); Renata Keller, *Mexico's Cold War: Cuba, the United States, and the Legacy of the Mexican Revolution* (New York: Cambridge University Press, 2015).

20. Paterson, *Kennedy's Quest for Victory*, 5; Francis J. Gavin, *Gold, Dollars, and Power: The Politics of International Monetary Relations, 1958–1971* (Chapel Hill: University of North Carolina Press, 2003).

21. Richard H. Immerman, *Empire for Liberty: A History of American Imperialism from Benjamin Franklin to Paul Wolfowitz* (Princeton, NJ: Princeton University Press, 2010).

22. Paterson, *Kennedy's Quest for Victory*, 11.

23. Alexander Fursenko, *Khrushchev's Cold War: The Inside Story of an American Adversary* (New York: Norton, 2006), 229, 255.

24. *FRUS, 1961–1963*, vol. XII, document 186, 2 April 1963; on coca-colonization, see Hitchcock, *The Struggle for Europe*, 159–160.

25. Laura Elizabeth Hein, *Fueling Growth: The Energy Revolution and Economic Policy in Postwar Japan* (Cambridge, MA: Harvard University Press, 1990).

26. *FRUS, 1961–1963*, vol. XXII, document 247, 14 November 1961.

27. David C. Engerman, "Development Politics and the Cold War," *Diplomatic History* 41, no. 1 (January 2017): 6–7; Sara Lorenzini, *Global Development: A Cold War History* (Princeton, NJ: Princeton University Press, 2019).

28. *FRUS, 1961–1963*, vol. XVII, document 314, 30 June 1962; *FRUS, 1961–1963*, vol. XVIII, document 368, 21 November 1963.

29. David Ekbladh, *The Great American Mission: Modernization and the Construction of an American World Order* (Princeton, NJ: Princeton University Press, 2005); Mark H. Haefele, "Walt Rostow's Stages of Economic Growth: Ideas and Action," in David C. Engerman, ed., *Staging Growth: Modernization, Development, and the Global Cold* (Amherst: University of Massachusetts Press, 2003); Nils Gilman, *Mandarins of the Future: Modernization Theory in Cold War America* (Baltimore: Johns Hopkins University Press, 2003).

30. Walt Rostow, *The Stages of Economic Growth: A Non-Communist Manifesto* (Cambridge, UK: Cambridge University Press, 1960); David Milne, *America's Rasputin: Walt Rostow and the Vietnam War* (New York: Hill and Wang, 2008); Bradley R. Simpson, *Economists with Guns: Authoritarian Development and U.S.-Indonesian Relations, 1960–1968* (Stanford, CA: Stanford University Press, 2008).

31. Rostow to Rusk, memorandum, 6 January 1961, 5–6.

32. Bruce Kuklick, *Blind Oracles: Intellectuals and War from Kennan to Kissinger* (Princeton, NJ: Princeton University Press, 2007), 1–2.

33. *FRUS, 1961–1963*, vol. VIII, document 77, 13 April 1962.

34. *FRUS, 1961–1963*, vol. VIII, documents 70 and 148, 4 December 1963.

35. *FRUS, 1961–1963*, vol. VIII, document 75, 9 April 1962.

36. *FRUS, 1961–1963*, vol. VIII, document 93, 22 June 1962.

37. *FRUS, 1961–1963*, vol. VIII, document 85, 15 May 1962, and document 94.

38. *FRUS, 1961–1963*, vol. VIII, document 79, 16 April 1962.

39. Kuklick, *Blind Oracles*, 1–2; John Lewis Gaddis, *Strategies of Containment: A Critical Appraisal of American National Security Policy during the Cold War* (New York: Oxford University Press, 2005), 197–200.

40. *FRUS, 1961–1963*, vol. VIII, document 95.

41. *FRUS, 1961–1963*, vol. VIII, document 94.

42. Quoted in Thomas G. Paterson, "Bearing the Burden: A Critical Look at JFK's Foreign Policy," *VQR: A National Journal of Literature and Discussion* 54, no. 2 (Spring 1978), 193–212.

43. Rostow, *The Diffusion of Power*, 379.

44. *FRUS, 1961–1963*, vol. XVIII, document 247, 14 May 1963.

45. Frank Costigliola, "The Pursuit of Atlantic Community: Nuclear Arms, Dollars, and Berlin," in Paterson, *Kennedy's Quest for Victory*, 24–56.

46. Susanna Schrafstetter and Stephen Twigge, *Avoiding Armageddon: Europe, the United States, and the Struggle for Nuclear Nonproliferation, 1945–1970* (Westport, CT: Praeger, 2004), 94.

47. Hervé Alphand to Mr. Rose, telegram, "JCAE Meeting re Holland & Submarine Assistance," 10 June 1960, 91QO/468, CADLC, 1–2.

48. Hervé Alphand to Maurice Couve de Murville, letter, "Voyage à Groton le 17 janvier 1961," 26 January 1961, 91QO/468, CADLC, 1–3.

49. Hitchcock, *The Struggle for Europe*, 221–241.

50. MAAG Germany to Dean Rusk, cable, "Tactical Nuclear Weapons," 16 November 1961, Series #1, Germany, Countries, NSF, PP, JFKL, http://www.jfklibrary.org/Asset-Viewer/Archives/JFKNSF-074-010.aspx; Henry Kissinger to McGeorge Bundy, letter, "Conversation with Strauss," 1 June 1961, box 31, Special Correspondence, POF, JFKL.

51. Maxwell Taylor to John Kennedy, memorandum, "27th meeting, NATO Military Committee in Chiefs of Staff Session, Summary Report (U)," NATO, 1961–1963, Komer, NSF, JFKL, 5, http://www.jfklibrary.org/Asset-Viewer/Archives/JFKNSF-439-001.aspx.

52. *FRUS, 1961–1963*, vol. VII, document 2, 21 February 1961, microfiche supplement.

53. Henry Owen, "A New Approach to France," 21 April 1961, box 70, NSF, JFKL, quoted in Costigliola, "The Pursuit of Atlantic Community," 31.

54. Francis J. Gavin, "The Myth of Flexible Response: United States Strategy in Europe During the 1960s," *International History Review* 23, no. 4 (December 2001): 847–875.

55. Quoted in Joseph S. Nye Jr., *The Paradox of American Power* (London: Oxford University Press, 2002), 33.

56. *FRUS, 1961–1963*, vol. XIII, document 227, 5 May 1961.

57. Komer to Acheson, memoranda, "Using Arms Control to Bolster the New NATO Posture," 28 February 1961, and Robert Komer, "First Things First—Accommodation with De Gaulle," 20 February 1961, NATO, 1961–1963, Robert Komer files, NSF, JFKL, http://www.jfklibrary.org/Asset-Viewer/Archives/JFKNSF-439-001.aspx.

58. Andrew Moravcsik, *De Gaulle and Europe: Historical Revision and Social Science Theory* (Cambridge, MA: Minda de Gunzburg Center for European Studies, Harvard University, 1998).

59. "A Review of North Atlantic Problems for the Future," report, March 1961, JFKNSF-439-001, NATO, 1961–1963, Robert Komer files, NSF, JFKL, 45–46, 61, http://www.jfklibrary.org/Asset-Viewer/Archives/JFKNSF-439-001.aspx (accessed 1 August 2016).

60. "Proposed Policy Directive for NSC Consideration regarding NATO and the Atlantic Nations," 3 April 1961, JFKNSF-329-015, NSAM 40, Meetings and Memoranda, PP, NSF, JFKL, 9, http://www.jfklibrary.org/Asset-Viewer/Archives/JFKNSF-329-015.aspx.

61. *FRUS, 1961–1963*, vol. XIII, document 100, 20 April 1961.

62. "A Review of North Atlantic Problems for the Future," March 1961, 45.

63. U.S. embassy in Paris to Dean Rusk, cable, "Copenhagen's 322 to Department," 19 November 1961, and U.S. embassy in Bonn, cable to Dean Rusk, "Copenhagen's 322 and Moscow's 1567 to Dept," 20 November 1961, Series #1, Germany, Countries, NSF, PP, JFKL, http://www.jfklibrary.org/Asset-Viewer/Archives/JFKNSF-074-010.aspx; "A Review of North Atlantic Problems for the Future," March 1961, 44.

64. "A Review of North Atlantic Problems for the Future," March 1961, 46. Underlining in the original. Robert Komer to the president, memorandum, "Your Meeting with Mr. Acheson on March 7," 6 March 1961, Series #12, NATO, 1961–1963, White House memoranda, Robert Komer files, PP, NSF, JFKL, http://www.jfklibrary.org/Asset-Viewer/Archives/JFKNSF-439-002.aspx.

65. Komer, "Using Arms Control to Bolster the New NATO Posture," 28 February 1961.

66. Dean Rusk to Copenhagen et al., cable, "Alleged German Demands for Nuclear Weapons," 28 May 1961, Series #1, Germany, Countries, NSF, PP, JFKL, 1, http://www.jfklibrary.org/Asset-Viewer/Archives/JFKNSF-074-010.aspx.

67. "Proposed Policy Directive for NSC Consideration regarding NATO and the Atlantic Nations," 20 April 1961.

68. *FRUS, 1961–1963*, vol. XIV, document 34, 5 June 1961.

69. *FRUS, 1961–1963*, vol. XIV, document 30, 31 May 1961, quoted in Erin Mahan, *Kennedy, de Gaulle and Western Europe* (New York: Palgrave Macmillan, 2014), 46–47.

70. John Kennedy, "Radio and Television Report to the American People on the Berlin Crisis," 25 July 1961, American Presidency Project, University of California, Santa Barbara, http://www.presidency.ucsb.edu/ws/?pid=8259.

71. *FRUS, 1961–1963*, vol. XIV, document 70, 15 July 1961; *FRUS, 1961–1963*, vol. XVII, document 221, 22 November 1961; Marc Trachtenberg, *History and Strategy* (Princeton, NJ: Princeton University Press, 1991), 169–234.

72. Gene Gerzhoy, "Alliance Coercion and Nuclear Restraint: How the United States Thwarted West Germany's Nuclear Ambitions," *International Security* 39, no. 4 (April 2015): 108–110. For the larger bilateral relationship, see Georges-Henri Soutou, *L'alliance Incertaine: Les Rapports Politico-Stratégiques Franco-Allemands, 1954–1996* (Paris: Fayard, 1996).

73. Pierre Chatenet, oral history, Institut Charles de Gaulle. For general French opposition to nuclear collaboration with West Germany, see "Coopération atomique franco-allemande," Direction politique, Service des Pactes, 16 May 1961, Pactes 1951–1970, Politique de l'OTAN, carton 409, dossier Atome/général, CADLC, cited in Mahan, *Kennedy, de Gaulle and Western Europe*.

74. Marc Trachtenberg, "The de Gaulle Problem," *Journal of Cold War Studies* 14, no. 1 (Winter 2012): 81–92.

75. Mahan, *Kennedy, de Gaulle and Western Europe*, 69–73.

76. *FRUS, 1961–1963*, vol. V, document 87, 4 June 1961; *FRUS, 1961–1963*, vol. XIV, document 32, 4 June 1961, 10:15 a.m.

77. *FRUS, 1961–1963*, vol. XIV, document 43, 17 June 1961.

78. *FRUS, 1961–1963*, vol. XIV, document 141, 5 September 1961.

79. *FRUS, 1961–1963*, vol. XIV, document 92, 5 August 1961.

80. *FRUS, 1961–1963*, vol. XIV, document 164, 2 October 1961, and document 168, 3 October 1961.

81. *FRUS, 1961–1963*, vol. XIV, document 176, 13 October 1961.

82. *FRUS, 1961–1963*, vol. XIV, document 222, 22 November 1961.

83. *FRUS, 1961–1963*, vol. XVI, document 219, 21 November 1961, and document 222, 22 November 1961.

84. Harold Karan Jacobson and Eric Stein, *Diplomats, Scientists, and Politicians: The United States and the Nuclear Test Ban Negotiations* (Ann Arbor: University of Michigan Press, 1966).

85. Jack Homer, *Belgrade: The Conference of Nonaligned States* (New York: National Committee for a SANE Nuclear Policy, 1961), 34–35; Vijay Prashad, *The Darker Nations: A People's History of the Third World* (New York: New Press, 2008), 95–101; Ivana Ancic, "Belgrade, The 1961 Non-Aligned Conference," *Global South Studies: A Collective Publication with the Global South*, 17 August 2017, https://globalsouthstudies.as.virginia.edu/articles/pdf/256.

86. *FRUS, 1961–1963*, vol. XXV, document 186, 18 October 1961; UNGA Resolution 1648 (XVI), 6 November 1961, https://undocs.org/en/A/RES/1648(XVI).

87. Harold Brown, report, "Questions Bearing upon the Resumption of Atomic Weapons Testing," 15 May 1961, box 299, Subject files—Nuclear Testing 5/61, NSF, JFKL.

88. Robert Komer, "The Case for Resumption of Nuclear Tests," 28 August 1961, box 299, Subject files—Nuclear Testing 5/61 NSF, PP, JFKL.

89. Ronald T. Takaki, *Double Victory: A Multicultural History of America in World War II* (Boston: Little, Brown, 2001); Thomas Borstelmann, *The Cold War and the Color Line: American Race Relations in the Global Arena* (Cambridge, MA: Harvard University Press, 2003); Brenda Gayle Plummer, ed., *Window on Freedom: Race, Civil Rights, and Foreign Affairs, 1945–1988* (Chapel Hill: University of North Carolina Press, 2003).

90. W. J. Rorabaugh, *The Real Making of the President: 1960* (Lawrence: University of Kansas Press, 2012); Theodore H. White, *The Making of the President, 1960* (New York: HarperPerennial Political Classics, 2009).

91. "Collection Information: Women Strike for Peace records, 1961–1996," Collection DG 115, Swarthmore College Peace Collection, http://www.swarthmore.edu/Library/peace/DG100-150/DG115/DG115WSP.html (accessed 15 November 2017).

92. Amy Swerdlow, *Women Strike for Peace: Traditional Motherhood and Radical Politics in the 1960s* (Chicago: University of Chicago Press, 1993).

93. James T. Patterson, *Grand Expectations: The United States, 1945–1974* (New York: Oxford University Press, 1996), 77, 80–81, 314, 333; Matthew D. Lassiter, *The Silent Majority: Suburban Politics in the Sunbelt South* (Princeton, NJ: Princeton University Press, 2006).

94. *St. Louis Post-Dispatch*, 22 April 1958, quoted in Kelly Moore, *Disrupting Science: Social Movements, American Scientists, and the Politics of the Military, 1945–1975* (Oxford, UK: Oxford University Press, 2013).

95. W. K. Wyant Jr., "50,000 Baby Teeth," *The Nation*, 13 June 1959, 535–537.

96. Ellen Gerl, "Scientist-Citizen Advocacy in the Atomic Age: A Case Study of the Baby Tooth Survey, 1958–1963," *PRism* 11, no. 1 (2014): 10.

97. Louise Zibold Reiss, "Strontium-90 Absorption by Deciduous Teeth," *Science* 134, no. 3491 (24 November 1961): 1669–1673; Gerl, "Scientist-Citizen Advocacy in the Atomic Age," 1.

98. Steven Levingston, *The Kennedy Baby: The Loss That Transformed JFK* (New York: Diversion Books, 2013).

99. *FRUS, 1961–1963*, vol. XXV, document 130, 31 August 1961.

100. Komer, "The Case for Resumption of Nuclear Tests," 28 August 1961.

101. National Intelligence Estimate 100-4-60, "Likelihood and Consequences of the Development of Nuclear Capabilities by Additional Countries," 20 September 1960, http://nsarchive2.gwu.edu//NSAEBB/NSAEBB155/prolif-5.pdf.

102. National Intelligence Estimate 4-3-61, "Nuclear Weapons and Delivery Capabilities of Free World Countries Other Than the US and UK," 21 September 1961, http://nsarchive2.gwu.edu//NSAEBB/NSAEBB155/prolif-6b.pdf.

103. *FRUS, 1961–1963*, vol. XXV, document 177, 5 August 1961.

104. Schlesinger, *A Thousand Days*, 291.

105. Nikita Khrushchev, speech to the RFSR Teacher's Congress, "On Cuba," 9 July 1960, https://sourcebooks.fordham.edu/mod/1960khrushchev-cuba1.asp.

106. Brands, *Latin America's Cold War*, 34.

107. *FRUS, 1961–1963*, vol. XXV, document 169, 2 May 1961.

108. John Kennedy, "UNGA Speech," 25 September 1961, box 35, Speech files, POF, JFKL.

109. John Kennedy, "Annual Message to the Congress of the State of the Union," 11 January 1962, American Presidency Project, http://www.presidency.ucsb.edu/ws/?pid=9082. John J. McCloy coined and Edward Murrow endorsed the phrase. *FRUS, 1961–1963*, vol. XXV, document 123, 8 June 1961.

110. Frank Aiken, "Prevention of the Wider Dissemination of Nuclear Weapons," 30 November 1961, 440/8/10, 16th UNGA session, NAI, 3–4.

111. John J. Hearne, confidential note, "Conversation with Charles Bohlen," 14 December 1960, FA, 2.

112. Alexis Johnson to Dean Rusk, memorandum, "Voting Instructions on the Swedish Resolution on Nuclear Weapons," 28 November 1961, and Alexis Johnson, "IO's Position on the Swedish Resolution," 28 November 1961, Series #2, NATO, Regional Security, NSF, PP, JFKL, http://www.jfklibrary.org/Asset-Viewer/Archives/JFKNSF-224-002.aspx; Adlai Stevenson to John Kennedy, letter, "UN Matters," 3 July 1961, Series #5, UN, Subject files, NSF, PP, JFKL, 3.

113. "EUR Position on Swedish Resolution," 28 November 1961, Series #2, NATO, Regional Security files, NSF, PP, JFKL, 2, http://www.jfklibrary.org/Asset-Viewer/Archives/JFKNSF-224-002.aspx.

114. New York to Dublin, cable, "Preliminary Draft Resolution," 4 October 1961; and "Preventing the Spread of Nuclear Weapons," 28 October 1961, 440/8/10, 16th UNGA session, NAI.

115. Draft telegram, "Aiken to UN Ambassador re Swedish Resolution," 10 November 1961, 440/8/10, 16th UNGA session, NAI.

116. Permanent Irish Mission to the UN to Dublin, "Preventing the Spread of Nuclear Weapons," 8 November 1961, 440/8/10, 16th UNGA session, NAI, 4–5.

117. Permanent Irish Mission to the UN to Dublin, "Preventing the Spread of Nuclear Weapons," 5 December 1961, 440/8/10, 16th UNGA session, NAI, 3.

118. Aiken, "Prevention of the Wider Dissemination of Nuclear Weapons," 30 November 1961, 2.

119. Permanent Irish Mission to the UN to Dublin, "Preventing the Spread of Nuclear Weapons," 11 November 1961, 440/8/10, 16th UNGA session, NAI, 2.

120. Permanent Irish Mission to the UN to Dublin, "Preventing the Spread of nuclear weapons," 5 December 1961, 5–8.

121. Aiken, "Prevention of the Wider Dissemination of Nuclear Weapons," 30 November 1961, 5.

122. John Lee Smith to John Kennedy, letter, "Department of State Publication No. 7277," 4 April 1962, box 367, Carl Kaysen files, NSF, JFKL.

123. McGeorge Bundy to the president, memorandum, "Your Meeting with the Secretary of State This Afternoon," 2 October 1961, Series #7, UN, Department and Agencies, POF, PP, JFKL, http://www.jfklibrary.org/Asset-Viewer/Archives/JFKPOF-088-005.aspx.

124. James Stocker, "Accepting Regional Zero: Nuclear Weapon Free Zones, U.S. Nonproliferation Policy and Global Security, 1957–1968," *Journal of Cold War Studies* 17, no. 2 (April 2015): 36–72; "Nuclear Weapons," undated, Series #2, NATO, Regional Security files, NSF, PP, JFKL, 2, http://www.jfklibrary.org/Asset-Viewer/Archives/JFKNSF-224-002.aspx.

125. John Kennedy to Adlai Stevenson, letter, "Your Letter of May 10 on Disarmament and Nuclear Testing," 23 May 1962, Series #5, UN, Subject files, NSF, PP, JFKL, http://www.jfklibrary.org/Asset-Viewer/Archives/JFKNSF-312-005.aspx.

126. U.S. Department of State, CW-5966, "U.S. Nuclear Weapons Posture," 26 January 1962, Nuclear Weapons; Testing; U.S. Resumption, September 1961–January 1962; Subject files, NSF, JFKL, 2–3.

127. *FRUS, 1961–1963*, vol. XV, document 44, 30 April 1962, and document 54, 17 May 1962.

128. Schrafstetter and Twigge, *Avoiding Armageddon*, 144.

129. Dean Rusk to the president, memorandum, "Nuclear Aid to France," 9 March 1962; memorandum for the record, "Luncheon with Monnet, Kohler, Tuthill, and Fessenden," 15 December 1961, NATO: Subjects: Nuclear Deployment, Carl Kaysen files, NSF, PP, JFKL, 1–2, http://www.jfklibrary.org/Asset-Viewer/Archives/JFKNSF-375-005.aspx.

130. *FRUS, 1961–1963*, vol. XIII, document 92, 1 February 1961.

131. U.S. Department of State, CW-5966, "U.S. Nuclear Weapons Posture," 26 January 1962, 7–12.

132. Peter L. Hahn, *Caught in the Middle East: U.S. Policy Toward the Arab-Israeli Conflict, 1945–1961* (Chapel Hill: University of North Carolina Press, 2004).

133. Avner Cohen, *Israel and the Bomb* (New York: Columbia University Press, 1998), 65.

134. *FRUS, 1961–1963*, vol. XVII, document 57, 30 May 1961.

135. *FRUS, 1961–1963*, vol. XVII, document 92, 3 April 1961.

136. Douglas Little, "From Even-Handed to Empty-Handed: Seeking Order in the Middle East," in Paterson, *Kennedy's Quest for Victory*, 156–177; *FRUS, 1961–1963*, vol. XVII, document 314, 30 June 1962.

137. *FRUS, 1961–1963*, vol. XVIII, document 368, 21 November 1963.

138. *FRUS, 1961–1963*, vol. XVII, document 57, 27 June 1961, and document 7, 3 February 1961.

139. *FRUS, 1961–1963*, vol. XVII, document 53, 26 May 1961.

140. *FRUS, 1961–1963*, vol. XVII, document 57, 30 May 1961.

141. *FRUS, 1961–1963*, vol. XVII, document 95, undated.

142. *FRUS, 1961–1963*, vol. XVII, document 143, 22 November 1961, and document 5, 30 January 1961.

143. Zach Fredman, "'The Specter of an Expansionist China': Kennedy Administration Assessments of Chinese Intentions in Vietnam," *Diplomatic History* 38, no. 1 (1 January 2014): 111–136; Michael J. Green, *By More Than Providence: Grand Strategy and American Power in the Asia Pacific Since 1783* (New York: Columbia University Press, 2017), 197–323.

144. *FRUS, 1961–1963*, vol. XXII, document 82, 12 January 1962.

145. *FRUS, 1961–1963*, vol. XXII, document 84, 29 January 1962.

146. *FRUS, 1958–1960*, vol. XIX, document 364, 13 December 1960.

147. Lt. General John K. Gerhart to Air Force Chief of Staff Thomas White, memorandum, "Long-Range Threat of Communist China," 8 February 1961, Secret, and John M. Steeves to Roger Hilsman, memorandum, "National Intelligence Estimate on Implications of Chinese Communist Nuclear Capability," 12 April 1961, Secret, in NSAEEB no. 38, http://nsarchive2 .gwu.edu/NSAEBB/NSAEBB38/.

148. Arleigh Burke, "U.S. Policy Toward Communist China," 16 June 1961; Robert Komer, draft, "Strategic Framework for Rethinking China Policy," 7 April 1961, box 410, Robert Komer files, NSF, PP, JFKL; Roswell Gilpatric, "U.S. Policy Toward Communist China," 3 July 1961; Bureau of Research and Intelligence, Report, "China Policy," 7 July 1961, box 410, Robert Komer files, NSF, PP, JFKL, 40.

149. *FRUS, 1961–1963*, vol. XXII, document 13, 14 March 1961.

150. Robert Komer, draft, "Strategic Framework for rethinking China policy," 7 April 1961, 29–32, 40.

151. Robert Komer to McGeorge Bundy, memorandum, "Our China's International Position," 19 October 1961, box 410, Robert Komer files, NSF, PP, JFKL, 1.

152. Quoted in James Fetzler, "Clinging to Containment: China Policy," in Paterson, *Kennedy's Quest for Victory*, 192; *FRUS, 1961–1963*, vol. XXII, document 157, 30 November 1962.

153. *FRUS, 1961–1963*, vol. XXII, document 36, 23 December 1962; Noam Kochavi, *A Conflict Perpetuated: China Policy during the Kennedy Years* (Westport, CT: Praeger, 2002).

154. Robert Komer, "Two Problems re China," 29 January 1962, and Robert Komer to Walt Rostow, memorandum, "On China," 11 April 1961, box 410, Robert Komer files, NSF, PP, JFKL.

155. *FRUS, 1961–1963*, vol. XXII, document 10, 12 April 1962.

CHAPTER 4

1. Robert Komer, "Review of Basic Policy," 28 February 1961, Basic National Security Policy, 22 June 1962 and undated [1 of 2], NSF, PP, JFK, JFKL. Digital identifier: JFKNSF-294–001.

2. Jeremy Friedman, *Shadow Cold War: The Sino-Soviet Competition for the Third World* (Chapel Hill: University of North Carolina Press, 2018); Gregg Andrew Brazinsky, *Winning the Third World: Sino-American Rivalry During the Cold War* (Chapel Hill: University of North Carolina Press, 2017).

3. Averell Harriman to Dean Rusk, telegram, "Mrs. Gromyko Spills the Beans," 24 July 1963, box 369, Carl Kaysen files, NSF, JFKL.

4. *FRUS, 1961–1963*, vol. VII, document 349, 24 July 1963.

5. "Treaty Banning Nuclear Weapon Tests in the Atmosphere, in Outer Space and Under Water," 5 August 1963, UN Office for Disarmament Affairs, https://disarmament.un.org/treaties/t/test_ban/text.

6. *FRUS, 1961–1963*, vol. VIII, document 79, 16 April 1962.

7. *FRUS, 1961–1963*, vol. VIII, document 85, 15 May 1962.

8. Alice L. George, *Awaiting Armageddon: How Americans Faced the Cuban Missile Crisis* (Chapel Hill: University of North Carolina Press, 2003); Mark Eastwood, "Anti-Nuclear Activism and Electoral Politics in the 1963 Test Ban Treaty," *Diplomatic History* 44, no. 1 (November 15, 2019): 133–156.

9. Campbell Craig and Fredrik Logevall, *America's Cold War: The Politics of Insecurity* (Cambridge, MA: Belknap Press, 2012), 109–138, 174, 221; Julian E. Zelizer, *Arsenal of Democracy: The Politics of National Security-from World War II to the War on Terrorism* (New York: Basic Books, 2012), 81–96, 178.

10. Odd Arne Westad, *The Cold War: A World History* (New York: Basic Books, 2017), 228.

11. David Halberstam, *The Best and the Brightest* (Bridgewater, NJ: Paw Prints/Baker & Taylor, 2008); Theodore White, "The Action Intellectuals," *Life* 62, no. 23 (9 June 1967): 43–76.

12. Bruce Kuklick, *Blind Oracles: Intellectuals and War from Kennan to Kissinger* (Princeton, NJ: Princeton University Press, 2007), 103; *FRUS, 1961–1963*, vol. XIII, document 198, 28 May 1963.

13. Robert Vitalis, *White World Order, Black Power Politics: The Birth of American International Relations* (Ithaca, NY: Cornell University Press, 2015).

14. C. Vann Woodward, "The Age of Reinterpretation," American Historical Association, Publication #35, 1961, 16.

15. Woodward, "The Age of Reinterpretation."

16. Mae M. Ngai, *Impossible Subjects: Illegal Aliens and the Making of Modern America* (Princeton, NJ: Princeton University Press, 2014), 167–224; Ronald T. Takaki, *Strangers from a Different Shore: A History of Asian Americans* (Boston: Little, Brown, 1998).

17. Quoted in Westad, *The Cold War*, 230; *FRUS, 1961–1963*, vol. XXIV, document 5, 3 January 1961.

18. William R. Tyler, oral history, 7 March 1964, quoted in Gordon Chang, *Friends and Enemies: The United States, China, and the Soviet Union, 1948–1972* (Stanford, CA: Stanford University Press, 1992).

19. Brazinsky, *Winning the Third World*, 3.

20. Matthew Connelly, "Taking Off the Cold War Lens: Visions of North-South Conflict During the Algerian War for Independence," *American Historical Review* 105, no. 3 (June 2000): 739–769; *Fatal Misconception: The Struggle to Control World Population* (Cambridge, MA: Belknap Press, 2010).

21. *FRUS, 1961–1963*, vol. XIII, document 462, 22 January 1963.

22. John Kennedy, "News Conference 52," 21 March 1963, State Department Auditorium, Washington, DC, http:// www.jfklibrary.org/Research/Research-Aids/Ready-Reference/Press-Conferences/News-Conference-52.aspx.

23. Tyler, oral history, 7 March 1964.

24. Friedman, *Shadow Cold War*.

25. Lorenz M. Lüthi, *The Sino-Soviet Split: Cold War in the Communist World* (Princeton, NJ: Princeton University Press, 2008), 148, 152, 246–272; Sergey Radchenko, *Two Suns in the Heavens: The Sino-Soviet Struggle for Supremacy, 1962–1967* (Washington, DC: Woodrow Wilson Center Press, 2009).

26. Andrei Andreevich Gromyko, *Memoirs* (New York: Doubleday, 1989), 174.

27. *FRUS, 1961–1963*, vol. VIII, document 70; Walt Rostow, "U.S. Policy Regarding the Sino-Soviet Split," April 1962, Declassified Document Reference Service [DDRS], quoted in Brazinsky, *Winning the Third World*, 183–184.

28. Luthi, *The Sino-Soviet Split*, 219; Brazinsky, *Winning the Third World*, 181–182; William Taubman, *Khrushchev: The Man and His Era* (New York: Norton, 2004), 540.

29. Stephen T. Possony to Walt Rostow, memorandum, "Statement If Tests Resumed," 8 May 1961, box 299, Subject File—Nuclear Weapons Testing 5/61, NSF, JFKL, 1–2.

30. *FRUS, 1961–1963*, vol. XV, document 8, 12 March 1962.

31. "World War III," 17 June 1962, 440/8/10, 16th UNGA session, NAI.

32. Walt Rostow to McGeorge Bundy, memorandum, "Western Europe in Our Strategy and in the BNSP," 18 April 1962, Basic National Security Policy, 22 June 1962 and undated [1 of 2 folders], NSF, presidential papers (PP), JFKL.

33. Francis J. Gavin, *Gold, Dollars, and Power: The Politics of International Monetary Relations, 1958–1971* (Chapel Hill: University of North Carolina Press, 2003).

34. Philip H. Gordon, "Charles de Gaulle and the Nuclear Revolution," in John Lewis Gaddis, *Cold War Statesmen Confront the Bomb: Nuclear Diplomacy Since 1945* (New York: Oxford University Press, 1999), 216–235.

35. Maxwell D. Taylor, *The Uncertain Trumpet* (New York: Harper, 1960).

36. Taylor, *The Uncertain Trumpet*, 506.

37. Taylor, *The Uncertain Trumpet*, 73, 104, 146.

38. Ingo Trauschweizer, *Maxwell Taylor's Cold War: From Berlin to Vietnam* (Lexington: University Press of Kentucky, 2019), 103.

39. *FRUS, 1961–1963*, vol. XIII, document 140, 9 June 1962.

40. *FRUS, 1961–1963*, vol. XVII, document 46, 10 May 1961; document 51, 19 May 1961; document 168, 18 January 1962; document 228, 29 March 1962; document 69, 28 June 1961; and document 121, 4 October 1961.

41. *FRUS, 1961–1963*, vol. XVII, document 228, 29 March 1962; documents 243 and 244, 12 April 1962; Roham Alvandi, "The Shah's Détente with Khrushchev: Iran's 1962 Missile Base Pledge to the Soviet Union," *Cold War History* 14, no. 3 (July 3, 2014): 423–444.

42. Francis J. Gavin, "The Myth of Flexible Response: United States Strategy in Europe During the 1960s," *International History Review* 23, no. 4 (December 2001): 847–875.

43. *FRUS, 1961–1963*, vol. XIX, document 293, 9 May 1963.

44. Dean Rusk, circular CG 238, "Implications of Communist China's Eventual Acquisition of an Independent Nuclear Capability," 22 May 1961, box 410, Robert Komer files, NSF, PP, JFKL.

45. Samuel Gilstrap, department airgram C-999, Hong Kong, "Main Impact CHICOM Detonation Atomic Device or Acquisition Limited Nuclear Capability," 9 June 1961; Leonard Unger, "Department Circular CG-999," 7 June 1961, box 410, Robert Komer files, NSF, PP, JFKL.

46. Howard P. Jones, "Indonesians and ChiCom Nuclear Achievement," 9 June 1961, box 410, Robert Komer files, NSF, PP, JFKL.

47. Stuart W. Rockwell, "Consequences in Iran of Communist China's Acquisition of Nuclear Capability," 20 June 1961, 4; "Department's CG 999," 14 June 1961; "Southeast Asian Neutralist Reactions," October 1962, box 410, Robert Komer files, NSF, PP, JFKL; U.S. Central Intelligence Agency, "Daily Log," 16 October 1962, CIA Freedom of Information Act Electronic Reading Room, RDP80B01676R001300090035-3.

48. "Peiping Opposes Non-diffusion of Nuclear Weapons," 16 January 1963, box 410, Robert Komer files, NSF, PP, JFKL.

49. Lüthi, *The Sino-Soviet Split*, 221–222.

50. Lyman Lemnitzer, "US Nuclear Weapons Policy and Communist China with Appendix," 15 June 1961, box 410, Robert Komer files, NSF, PP, JFKL.

51. *FRUS, 1961–1963*, vol. XXII, document 279, 26 September 1962.

52. *FRUS, 1961–1963*, vol. XIX, document 30, 11 July 1961.

53. Mary L. Dudziak, *Cold War Civil Rights: Race and the Image of American Democracy* (Princeton, NJ: Princeton University Press, 2002); Ryan M. Irwin, *Gordian Knot: Apartheid and the Unmaking of the Liberal World Order* (New York: Oxford University Press, 2012); Matthew Jones, *After Hiroshima: The United States, Race, and Nuclear Weapons in Asia, 1945–1965* (New York: Cambridge University Press, 2010).

54. *FRUS, 1961–1963*, vol. XXII, document 114, 29 May 1962.

55. Victor Zorza, "China May Explode Atomic Bomb," 28 August 1962, 440/8/10, 16th UNGA session, NAI.

56. National Intelligence Estimate 13-2-62, "Chinese Communist advanced Weapons Capabilities," 25 April 1962, 3, CIA FOIA Electronic Reading Room, https://www.cia.gov/library/readingroom/docs/DOC_0001097940.pdf.

57. Major General John B. Cary, study memorandum no. 14, "Military Implications of a Communist Chinese Nuclear Capability," 31 August 1962, Institute for Defense Analyses, xi, 1, 131–136, https://nsarchive2.gwu.edu/nukevault/ebb488/docs/Doc%204B%208-31-62%20pacifica%20military%20implications.pdf.

58. John Kennedy, radio and television address, "Nuclear Testing and Disarmament," 2 March 1962, JFKL, https://www.jfklibrary.org/asset-viewer/archives/TNC/TNC-307/TNC-307.

59. W. J. Rorabaugh, *Kennedy and the Promise of the Sixties* (Cambridge, UK: Cambridge University Press, 2004), 54–58.

60. Jack Homer, *Belgrade: The Conference of Nonaligned States* (New York: National Committee for a SANE Nuclear Policy, 1961); Lawrence S. Wittner and Glen Harold Stassen, *Peace Action: Past, Present, and Future* (New York: Routledge, 2016), 18–19.

61. "Dr. Spock Is Worried," *New York Times*, 16 April 1962, SANE records, Swarthmore College Peace Collection.

62. Lyman Lemnitzer, Foster panel draft, "Proposed Disarmament Program, Revision 9 (U)," 6 December 1961, box 367, Carl Kaysen papers, NSF, JFKL, 1–2.

63. *FRUS, 1961–1963*, vol. VII, document 3, supplement.

64. Sarah Bridger, *Scientists at War: The Ethics of Cold War Weapons Research* (Cambridge, MA: Harvard University Press, 2015), 40–42; Gregg Herken, *Cardinal Choices: Presidential Science Advising from the Atomic Bomb to SDI* (New York: Oxford University Press, 1992), 112, 132–133.

65. Raymond Aron, *The Great Debate: Theories of Nuclear Strategy* (New York: Doubleday, 1965).

66. Aurélie Basha i Novosejt, "Breaking Ranks: Robert McNamara, Adam Yarmolinsky, and the Montreal Speech," *Diplomatic History* 43, no. 3 (June 2019): 493–516.

67. Quoted in Scott D. Sagan, "SIOP-62: The Nuclear War Plan Briefing to President Kennedy," *International Security* 12, no. 1 (Summer 1987): 22; National Security Archive, Electronic Briefing Book no. 130, https://nsarchive2.gwu.edu/NSAEBB/NSAEBB130/press.html (accessed 9 April 2019).

68. Dean Rusk, *As I Saw It* (New York: Norton, 1990), 246–247.

69. Herman Kahn, *On Thermonuclear War* (Princeton, NJ: Princeton University Press, 1960); *FRUS, 1961–1963*, vol. VIII, document 82, 5 May 1962.

70. Robert McNamara, commencement address, University of Michigan, 9 July 1962, in Robert Chadwell Williams, Philip L. Cantelon, and Richard G. Hewlett, eds., *The American Atom: A Documentary History of Nuclear Policies from the Discovery of Fission to the Present* (Philadelphia: University of Pennsylvania Press, 1991), 207–209.

71. Irish embassy in Washington, DC, to Frank Aiken, "U.S. State Department Response to Irish Aide Memoire," 15 March 1962, 440/8/10, 16th UNGA session, NAI.

72. E. L. Kennedy to Frank Aiken, memorandum, "The Restriction of the Further Dissemination of Nuclear Weapons," 26 March 1962, 440/8/10, 16th UNGA session, NAI; Mark Mazower, *No Enchanted Palace: The End of Empire and the Ideological Origins of the United Nations* (Princeton, NJ: Princeton University Press, 2009).

73. Adlai Stevenson to John Kennedy, letter, "Disarmament Problems," 28 June 1962; Arthur Schlesinger Jr. to the president, memorandum, "UNGA Delegation," 2 July 1962, box 367, Carl Kaysen papers, NSF, JFKL.

74. Lyman Lemnitzer to Robert McNamara, memorandum, "Agreement on Non-diffusion of Nuclear Weapons," 18 September 1962, box 376; Robert McNamara to William Foster, letter, Carl Kaysen files, NSF, JFKL.

75. *FRUS, 1961–1963*, vol. XV, document 3, 10 March 1962.

76. McNamara to Foster, letter, 4 October 1962.

77. S. A. Mikoyan and Svetlana Savranskaya, *The Soviet Cuban Missile Crisis: Castro, Mikoyan, Kennedy, Khrushchev, and the Missiles of November* (Washington, DC: Woodrow Wilson Center Press, 2012), 1; Renata Keller, "The Latin American Missile Crisis," *Diplomatic History* 39, no. 2 (2015): 195–222.

78. Aleksandr Fursenko and Timothy J. Naftali, *One Hell of a Gamble: Khrushchev, Castro, and Kennedy, 1958–1964* (New York: Norton, 1997), 433, 513; Nikita Segeevich Khrushchev, *Khrushchev Remembers*, trans. Strobe Talbott (New York: Bantam Books, 1971), 492–494.

79. Michael R. Beschloss, *Presidents of War* (New York: Crown, 2018), 414, 428–429.

80. McGeorge Bundy and James G. Blight, "October 27, 1962: Transcripts of the Meetings of the ExComm," *International Security* 12, no. 3 (Winter 1987/1988): 50, 54–55, 58, 89; Robert F. Kennedy, *Thirteen Days: A Memoir of the Cuban Missile Crisis* (New York: Norton, 1969), 30; C. Douglas Dillon, "Scenario for Airstrike Against Offensive Missile Bases and Bombers in Cuba," 25 October 1962, National Security Archive, https://nsarchive2.gwu.edu/nsa/cuba_mis_cri/19621025dillon.pdf.

81. Amit Das Gupta and Lorenz M. Luthi, eds., *The Sino-Indian War of 1962: New Perspectives* (London: Routledge, 2017).

82. Quoted in Mikoyan and Savranskaya, *The Soviet Cuban Missile Crisis*, 189.

83. *FRUS, 1961–1963*, vol. VI, document 65, 26 October 1962.

84. Khrushchev, *Khrushchev Remembers*, 492–494.

85. Richard Helms, "Meeting with Robert Kennedy Concerning Cuba," 19 January 1962, National Security Archive, https://nsarchive2.gwu.edu/nsa/cuba_mis_cri/620119%20Meeting%20with%20the%20Attorney%20Gen.pdf; William M. LeoGrande and Peter Kornbluh, *Back Channel to Cuba: The Hidden History of Negotiations between Washington and Havana* (Chapel Hill: University of North Carolina Press, 2014).

86. *FRUS, 1961–1963*, vol. XII, document 295, 30 June 1963.

87. Quoted in Fursenko and Naftali, *One Hell of a Gamble*, 179–180.

88. Robert Norris, "The Cuban Missile Crisis: A Nuclear Order of Battle, October/November 1962," presentation, Wilson International Center for Scholars, 24 October 2012.

89. Taubman, *Khrushchev*, 529–534.

90. *FRUS 1961–1963*, vol. X, document 341, 31 May 1962.

91. Vladimir Zubok, *A Failed Empire: The Soviet Union from Stalin to Gorbachev* (Chapel Hill: University of North Carolina Press, 2009), 143–144.

92. *FRUS, 1961–1963*, vol. X, document 304, 19 April 1961.

93. *FRUS, 1961–1963*, vol. X, document 433, 19 September 1962; Beschloss, *Presidents of War*, 412–414.

94. John Kennedy, "Statement on Cuba," 4 September 1962, in U.S. Department of State, *Bulletin* 47, no. 1213 (July–September 1962), 450.

95. "White House Tapes and Minutes of the Cuban Missile Crisis: ExComm Meetings," October 1962, *International Security* 10, no. 1 (Summer 1985): 184–185.

96. *FRUS, 1961–1963*, vol. XIII, document 402, 19 December 1962, 9:45 a.m.

97. *FRUS, 1961–1963*, vol. X, document 401, 31 August 1962.

98. "White House Tapes: ExComm Meetings," October 1962, 184–187.

99. John Kennedy, "Radio and Television Report to the American People on the Soviet Arms Buildup in Cuba," 22 October 1962, JFKL, https://microsites.jfklibrary.org/cmc/oct22/doc5.html.

100. Michael Dobbs, *One Minute to Midnight: Kennedy, Khrushchev, and Castro on the Brink of Nuclear War* (New York: Knopf, 2008), 68; Thomas G. Paterson and William J. Brophy, "October Missiles and November Elections: The Cuban Missile Crisis and American Politics, 1962," *Journal of American History* 73, no. 1 (June 1986): 87–119.

101. LeoGrande and Kornbluh, *Back Channel to Cuba*, 53–54; Ted Sorensen, memorandum, "ExComm Views Summary," 18 October 1962, https://microsites.jfklibrary.org/cmc/oct18/doc2.html.

102. Melvyn P. Leffler, *For the Soul of Mankind: The United States, the Soviet Union, and the Cold War* (New York: Hill and Wang, 2007), 154–155.

103. Nikita Khrushchev, cable to Anastas Mikoyan, "Cuba and the Il-28s," 11 November 1962, Wilson Center Digital Archive, https://digitalarchive.wilsoncenter.org/document/115098.

104. Michael Dobbs and Scott Sagan both underscore how mobilization loosened leaders' grips on the course of events. Dobbs, *One Minute to Midnight*; Scott Douglas Sagan, *The Limits of Safety: Organizations, Accidents, and Nuclear Weapons* (Princeton, NJ: Princeton University Press, 1993).

105. Taubman, *Khrushchev*, 534; Odd Arne Westad, *The Global Cold War: Third World Interventions and the Making of Our Times* (New York: Cambridge University Press, 2005), 175.

106. Fidel Castro to Nikita Khrushchev, letter, 26 October 1962, JFKL, https://microsites.jfklibrary.org/cmc/oct26/doc2.html.

107. Nikita Khrushchev to Antonin Novotny, 30 October 1962, quoted in Hershberg, "The Cuban Missile Crisis," in Melvyn P. Leffler and Odd Arne Westad, eds., *Crises and Détente*, vol. 2, 3 vols., *The Cambridge History of the Cold War* (New York: Cambridge University Press, 2010), 65–87.

108. Fursenko and Naftali, *One Hell of a Gamble*, 291.

109. U Thant, remarks, 30 October 1962, https://cubanmissilecrisissla.weebly.com/resolution-to-the-cuban-missile-crisis.html; CNN *Cold War* series, episode 10. Alexander Alekseyev characterized Fidel Castro likewise, as quoted in Mikoyan and Savranskaya, *The Soviet Cuban Missile Crisis*, 179–180; Castro to Nikita Khrushchev, letter, "Your Letter," 28 October 1962.

110. Fidel Castro and Anatas Mikoyan, memorandum of conversation, 3 November 1962, quoted in "Mikoyan's Mission to Havana: Cuban-Soviet Negotiations," November 1962,"

CWIHP Bulletin 5, quoted in Westad, *The Global Cold War*, 175; Mikoyan and Savranskaya, *The Soviet Cuban Missile Crisis*, 195–234.

111. Mikoyan and Savranskaya, *The Soviet Cuban Missile Crisis*, 224.

112. Mikoyan and Savranskaya, *The Soviet Cuban Missile Crisis*, 228–229.

113. Lüthi, *The Sino-Soviet Split*, 224–225.

114. Brazinsky, *Winning the Third World*, 186.

115. Office of the White House Press Secretary, statement by the president, 28 October 1962, JFKL, https://microsites.jfklibrary.org/cmc/images/sub/oct28/cmc_jfk_statement_oct28.jpg.

116. William Foster to Dean Rusk, memorandum, "U.S. Arms Control and Disarmament Objectives [Post Cuba]," 30 October 1962, box 367, Carl Kaysen files, NSF, JFKL.

117. Stewart Alsop and Charles Bartlett, "In Time of Crisis," 18 December 1962, *Saturday Evening Post*, http://www.saturdayeveningpost.com/wp-content/uploads/satevepost/1962-12-08-missile-crisis.pdf.

118. Walter Isaacson and Evan Thomas, *The Wise Men: Six Friends and the World They Made: Acheson, Bohlen, Harriman, Kennan, Lovett, McCloy* (New York: Simon and Schuster, 1986); Halberstam, *The Best and the Brightest*.

119. Edmund F. Wehrle, "'A Good, Bad Deal': John F. Kennedy, W. Averell Harriman, and the Neutralization of Laos, 1961–1962," *Pacific Historical Review* 67, no. 3 (August 1998): 349–377.

120. Piero Gleijeses, *Conflicting Missions: Havana, Washington, and Africa, 1959–1976* (Chapel Hill: University of North Carolina Press, 2002); Brazinsky, *Winning the Third World*.

121. Foster to Rusk, memorandum, 30 October 1962.

122. Manfred Lachs and Robert E. Matteson, memorandum of conversation, "Disarmament, Cuba, China, Khrushchev," 2 November 1962, box 367, Carl Kaysen files, NSF, JFKL; Taubman, *Khrushchev*, 586–588.

123. Khrushchev, *Khrushchev Remembers*, 68–71.

124. David Holloway, *Stalin and the Bomb: The Soviet Union and Atomic Energy, 1939–1956* (New Haven, CT: Yale University Press, 1994), 307

125. Matthew Evangelista, *Unarmed Forces: The Transnational Movement to End the Cold War* (Ithaca, NY: Cornell University Press, 1999), 25–89.

126. Glenn T. Seaborg and Benjamin S. Loeb, *Kennedy, Khrushchev and the Test Ban* (Berkeley: University of California Press, 1983), xiv, 242, 293–299; Paul Rubinson, "'Crucified on a Cross of Atoms:' Scientists, Politics, and the Test Ban Treaty," *Diplomatic History* 35, no. 2 (April 2011): 284.

127. Robert Matteson and Victor Karpov, memorandum of conversation, "Disarmament," 15 February 1963, box 368, Carl Kaysen files, NSF, JFKL; Taubman, *Khrushchev*, 583–585.

128. This imaginary expands on Wen-Qing Ngoei, *Arc of Containment: Britain, the United States, and Anticommunism in Southeast Asia* (Ithaca, NY: Cornell University Press, 2019).

129. *FRUS, 1961–1963*, vol. XIX, document 224, 13 December 1962, document 230, 20 December 1962, and document 269, 25 March 1963.

130. Matthew Jones, "Prelude to the Skybolt Crisis: The Kennedy Administration's Approach to British and French Strategic Nuclear Policies in 1962," *Journal of Cold War Studies* 21, no. 2 (May 2019): 58–109.

131. *FRUS, 1961–1963*, vol. XIII, document 401, 16 December 1962.

132. *FRUS, 1961–1963*, vol. XIII, document 406, 20 December 1962, 10:00 a.m.

133. *FRUS, 1961–1963*, vol. XIII, document 403, 19 December 1962, 4:30 p.m.

134. *FRUS, 1961–1963*, vol. XIII, document 406, 20 December 1962, 10:00 a.m.

135. *FRUS, 1961–1963*, vol. XIII, document 198, 28 May 1963.

136. Lawrence S. Kaplan, Ronald D. Landa, and Edward J. Drea, *The McNamara Ascendancy, 1961–1965*, vol. 5, *History of the Office of the Secretary of Defense* (Washington, DC: Historical Office, Office of the Secretary of Defense, 2006), 405.

137. McGeorge Bundy to the president, memorandum, "Your Discussion Before the NSC Tomorrow," 21 January 1963, NSC meetings, 1963: no. 508, Meetings and Memoranda. NSF, PP, JFKL, JFKNSF-314–002; *FRUS, 1961–1963*, vol. XXII, document 162, 10 January 1963; *FRUS, 1961–1963*, vol. VIII, document 125, 22 January 1963.

138. "Notes on Remarks by President Kennedy Before the National Security Council, Tuesday, January 22, 1963," and "Remarks of President Kennedy to the National Security Council on January 22, 1963," undated, NSC meetings, 1963: no. 508, Meetings and Memoranda. NSF, PP, JFKL, JFKNSF-314–002.

139. Taubman, *Khrushchev*, 169, 465, 583–584; Averell Harriman to John Kennedy, letter, "Question of Attempting to Prevent Red China from Obtaining Nuclear Capability," 23 January 1963, Kennedy, John—General 1963, W. Averell Harriman Papers [AH], Library of Congress [LOC].

140. *FRUS, 1961–1963*, vol. XIII, document 174, 18 February 1963; *FRUS, 1961–1963*, vol. XV, document 181, 14 March 1963.

141. Foy Kohler to Ambassador Bruce, memorandum, "Soviet Reactions to Multilateral Force," 8 February 1963, box 540, AH, LOC.

142. *FRUS, 1961–1963*, vol. XII, document 186, 2 April 1963.

143. *FRUS, 1961–1963*, vol. XIII, document 179, 6 March 1963.

144. Paul Du Quenoy, "The Role of Foreign Affairs in the Fall of Nikita Khrushchev in October 1964," *International History Review* 25, no. 2 (June 2003): 348–349; Friedman, *Shadow Cold War*, 79.

145. Ngoei, *Arc of Containment*, 114–148; Lien-Hang T. Nguyen, "The War Politburo: North Vietnam's Diplomatic and Political Road to the Tết Offensive," *Journal of Vietnamese Studies* 1, no. 1–2 (February 2006): 4–58.

146. *FRUS, 1961–1963*, vol. XIII, document 271, 25 May 1963.

147. "Non-dissemination of Nuclear Weapons: Egypt," in ACDA, White Paper #4, "The Relationship Between a Test Ban Treaty and the Non-diffusion of Nuclear Weapons," 18 June 1963, box 369, Carl Kaysen files, JFKL; *FRUS, 1961–1963*, vol. XVIII, document 121, 6 March 1963.

148. *FRUS, 1961–1963*, vol. XVIII, document 222, 27 April 1963.

149. Robert Matteson and Arthur Lall, memorandum of conversation, "Disarmament, India, USSR," 29 March 1963, box 368a, Carl Kaysen files, JFKL, iii; *FRUS, 1961–1963*, vol. XIX, document 304, 3 June 1963.

150. *FRUS, 1961–1963*, vol. XIX, document 293, 9 May 1963; *FRUS, 1961–1963*, vol. XXII, document 177, 11 May 1963.

151. *FRUS, 1961–1963*, vol. XIX, document 345, 20 December 1963; *FRUS, 1961–1963*, vol. XXII, document 182, 1 August 1963.

152. ACDA, "Working Group on a Proposed Program for Gradual Arms Control and Disarmament," May 1963, box 367, Carl Kaysen files, NSF, JFKL.

153. NSAM 239, *FRUS, 1961–1963*, vol. VII, document 284; introduction to NSAM 239 review, "Can the Genie Be Put Back in the Bottle?," undated, box 369, Carl Kaysen files, NSF, JFKL, 1–4.

154. Memorandum of conversation, "Nuclear Test Ban and Germany," 26 April 1963, box 538, AH, LOC.

155. Averell Harriman, "Memorandum Concerning the Soviet Union," undated, box 538, AH, LOC.

156. Averell Harriman and Harold Macmillan, memorandum of conversation, 29 April 1963, box 538, AH, LOC; David S. Foglesong, *The American Mission and the "Evil Empire": The Crusade for a "Free Russia" Since 1881* (New York: Cambridge University Press, 2007), 120–121.

157. Dean Rusk and Anatoly Dobrynin, memorandum of conversation, 18 May 1963, box 1, Llewellyn E. Thompson papers, RG 59, NARA II, 4.

158. Memorandum of conversation, "31st Ministerial Meeting of the NAC," 21 May 1963, box 540, AH, LOC.

159. Allen Pietrobon, "The Role of Norman Cousins and Track II Diplomacy in the Breakthrough to the 1963 Limited Test Ban Treaty," *Journal of Cold War Studies* 18, no. 1 (January 2016): 60–79.

160. Bertrand Russell and Albert Einstein, "Manifesto," 9 July 1955, Jussi M. Hanhimäki and Odd Arne Westad, eds., *The Cold War: A History in Documents and Eyewitness Accounts* (Oxford, UK: Oxford University Press, 2004), 280–283.

161. John F. Kennedy, commencement address, American University, 10 June 1963, https://www.jfklibrary.org/archives/other-resources/john-f-kennedy-speeches/american-university-19630610.

162. John Kennedy, handwritten note, 9 September 1963, Disarmament: Nuclear Test Ban Negotiations, Office files, PP, JFKL.

163. Working Group IV, "Nuclear Containment and Non-proliferation," 13 June 1963, box 369; ACDA, White Paper No. 4, 18 June 1963, 1–2.

164. Working Group IV, 13 June 1963.

165. *FRUS, 1961–1963*, vol. VIII, document 138, 24 July 1963; ACDA, White Paper No. 4, 18 June 1963, 3, 5–6.

166. Memorandum of conversation, "Committee of Principals—Nuclear Test Ban Treaty," 14 June 1963, box 367, Carl Kaysen files, NSF, JFKL.

167. Memorandum of conversation, "Committee of Principals—Nuclear Test Ban Treaty," 14 June 1963; Arthur Barber to Paul Nitze, memorandum, "Thoughts on a Debate: Suggestions on a Disarmament Strategy," 17 June 1963, box 370, Carl Kaysen files, NSF, JFKL.

168. Memorandum of conversation, "Committee of Principals—Nuclear Test Ban Treaty," 14 June 1963; handwritten notes, "McNaughton," undated, box 370, Carl Kaysen files, NSF, JFKL.

169. ACDA Report, "Harriman Mission to Moscow," 20 June 1963, box 370, Carl Kaysen files, NSF, JFKL.

170. Walt Rostow to John Kennedy, memorandum, "The Harriman Probe," 9 July 1963, box 370, Carl Kaysen files, NSF, JFKL.

171. *FRUS, 1961–1963*, vol. XIII, document 402, 19 December 1962.

172. David Bruce, telegram, "SECTO 15: Mission to Moscow," 27 June 1963, box 370; Committee of Principals, memorandum of conversation, "Nuclear Test Ban Treaty," 14 June 1963, box 367, Carl Kaysen files, NSF, JFKL, 9; *FRUS, 1961–1963*, vol. XIII, document 79, 20 June 1963.

173. Carl Kaysen to McGeorge Bundy, memorandum, "Mission to Moscow," 28 June 1963, box 370, Carl Kaysen files, NSF, JFKL.

174. Kendrick Oliver, *Kennedy, Macmillan, and the Nuclear Test-Ban Debate, 1961–63* (New York: St. Martin's Press, 1998); memorandum of conversation, "President-Prime Minister test ban conversations," 30 June 1963, box 370, Carl Kaysen files, NSF, JFKL.

175. Harold Macmillan to John Kennedy, letter, "Khrushchev's Speech," 4 July 1963, box 370, Carl Kaysen files, NSF, JFKL.

176. Carl Kaysen, "Instructions for Averell Harriman," 8 July 1963, box 370, Carl Kaysen files, NSF, JFKL.

177. Benjamin H. Read, oral history, 22 February 1966 and 17 October 1969, JFKL, 17–19.

178. Averell Harriman to Dean Rusk, memorandum, "Meeting with Khrushchev," 16 July 1963, box 369, Carl Kaysen files, NSF, JFKL, 1–20.

179. *FRUS, 1961–1963*, vol. VII, document 326, 15 July 1963.

180. Averell Harriman to Dean Rusk, telegram, "Non-dissemination," 18 July 1963; Harriman to Rusk, telegram, "Soviet Objectives," 23 July 1963; Harriman to Rusk, telegram, "Withdrawal Clause," 19 July 1963, box 369, Carl Kaysen files, NSF, JFKL.

181. *FRUS, 1961–1963*, vol. XV, document 215, 24 September 1963.

182. *FRUS, 1961–1963*, vol. XIII, document 212, 23 September 1963.

183. *FRUS, 1961–1963*, vol. XXII, document 183, 15 October 1963, and document 185, 10 September 1963; McGeorge Bundy and Chiang Ching-kuo, memorandum of conversation, 19 September 1963, NSAEEB 38, document 9.

CHAPTER 5

1. William Foster, draft, "Possible Remarks for World Council," 15 June 1964, William Foster papers, George C. Marshall Library [GCML], 1–3.

2. Foster, draft, 15 June 1964, 1–3.

3. Fredrik Logevall, *Choosing War: The Lost Chance for Peace and the Escalation of War in Vietnam* (Berkeley: University of California Press, 2001), xii.

4. William C. Foster, "New Directions in Arms Control and Disarmament," *Foreign Affairs* 43, no. 4 (July 1965): 587–601.

5. Edmund A. Gullion to John Kennedy, memorandum, "U.S. Arms Control Administration," undated, ACDA, POF, JFKL, https://www.jfklibrary.org/Asset-Viewer/Archives/JFKPOF-069a-004.aspx.

6. Gullion to Kennedy, memorandum, undated 1.

7. Quoted in Thomas Graham Jr., "A Return to Arms Control and Non-proliferation Process," 15 May 2008, 110th United States Congress, Testimony to the Subcommittee on Oversight of Government Management, the Federal Workforce, and the District of Columbia, Committee on Homeland Security and Government Organization, United States Senate.

8. Gullion to Kennedy, memorandum, undated, 1.

9. John J. McCloy to Senator J. W. Fulbright, letter, 2 August 1961, ACDA, Departments of Agencies, POF, JFKL, https://www.jfklibrary.org/Asset-Viewer/Archives/JFKPOF-069a-004.aspx.

10. Duncan L. Clarke, *Politics of Arms Control: The Role and Effectiveness of the U.S. Arms Control and Disarmament Agency* (New York: Free Press, 1979), quoted in Michael Krepon, "Can This Agency Be Saved?," *Bulletin of the Atomic Scientists* 5, no. 10 (December 1988): 35–38.

11. Author's interview with Ambassador James E. Goodby, 18 March 2013, Hoover Institution, Stanford, California.

12. "Announcement of William Foster as Director of the ACDA," 26 September 1961, ACDA, Departments and Agencies, POF, JFKL, https://www.jfklibrary.org/Asset-Viewer/Archives/JFKPOF-069a-004.aspx.

13. Fred Iklé, "Address to the Arms Limitation and Disarmament: Seventeenth Strategy for Peace Conference Report," Stanley Foundation, 7–10 October 1976. http://files.eric.ed.gov/fulltext/ED148666.pdf (accessed 4 May 2020).

14. "Obituary; Adrian S. Fisher, 69, Arms Treaty Negotiator," *New York Times*, 19 March 1983, http://www.nytimes.com/1983/03/19/obituaries/obituary-adrian-s-fisher-69-arms-treaty-negotiator.html.

15. Adrian Fisher, oral history, part 2, 7 November 1968, LBJL, 8–9.

16. Benjamin Wilson, "Insiders and Outsiders: Nuclear Arms Control Experts in Cold War America," PhD dissertation, Massachusetts Institute of Technology, 2014.

17. William Foster to Louis Sohn, letter, "Critique of CSIS Memorandum with Letter to Admiral Arleigh Burke," 15 November 1965, folder 6, box 14, William Foster papers, GCML.

18. Federation of American Scientists, "Current State U.S. Arms Control and Disarmament Agency," summer 1962, box 367, Carl Kaysen papers, NSF, JFKL.

19. Andrew Priest, "The President, the 'Theologians' and the Europeans: The Johnson Administration and NATO Nuclear Sharing," *International History Review* 33, no. 2 (June 2011): 257–275.

20. Joint Statement, "The Nassau Agreement," 21 December 1962, http://www.presidency .ucsb.edu/ws/index.php?pid=9063.

21. Cited in Douglas Selvage, "The Warsaw Pact and Nuclear Proliferation, 1963–1965," Working Paper, Cold War International History Project (Washington, DC: Woodrow Wilson International Center for Scholars, April 2001).

22. Selvage, "The Warsaw Pact and Nuclear Proliferation, 1963–1965," 21.

23. Selvage, "The Warsaw Pact and Nuclear Proliferation, 1963–1965," 20–24.

24. Selvage, "The Warsaw Pact and Nuclear Proliferation, 1963–1965," 23–24.

25. Selvage, "The Warsaw Pact and Nuclear Proliferation, 1963–1965," 20–26.

26. Quoted in Shane Maddock, *Nuclear Apartheid: The Quest for American Atomic Supremacy from World War II to the Present* (Chapel Hill: University of North Carolina Press, 2010), 222 (footnote 11).

27. William Foster and Pierre Pelen, memorandum of conversation, French embassy, box 10, Subject file—Disarmament, NSF, LBJL.

28. P. O. Alphand, telegram from New York to Paris, "Foster's Views," 15 January 1964, box 768, cote 517INVA, CADLC.

29. Lyndon Baines Johnson, "State of the Union," 8 January 1964, Miller Center of Public Affairs, University of Virginia, http://millercenter.org/president/speeches/detail/3382.

30. Dean Rusk to McGeorge Bundy, note, "Possible More Dramatic Proposals in Geneva," box 10, Subject file—Disarmament, NSF, LBJL.

31. Elfan Rees and O. Frederick Nolde to William Foster, letter with attached report, "Test Ban and Next Steps: From Co-Existence to Co-operation," 20 January 1964, box 16, William Foster papers, GCML.

32. Lyndon Johnson, "Speech to the Nation on Arms Control," 21 January 1964, in *Public Papers of the Presidents of the United States: Lyndon B. Johnson* (Washington, DC: U.S. Government Printing Office, 1967), 172–175.

33. President Johnson to Nikita Khrushchev, letter, 18 January 1964, quoted in ACDA, *Documents on Disarmament, 1964* (Washington, DC: U.S. Government Printing Office, 1965), 5, quoted in Glenn T. Seaborg, *Stemming the Tide: Arms Control in the Johnson Years* (Lexington, MA: Lexington Books, 1987), 7.

34. Spurgeon M. Keeny Jr. to McGeorge Bundy, memorandum, "Summary of Arms Control Activities for Period 17 January—3 February, 1964," 3 February 1964, box 10, SF-Disarmament, NSF, LBJL.

35. Johnson, "Speech to the Nation on Arms Control," 21 January 1964.

36. Seaborg, *Stemming the Tide*, 16.

37. Prepared Statement, "157th ENDC Plenary," 24 January 1964, box 16, William Foster papers, GCML.

38. William Foster, "Co-Chairmen Talking Points," 29 January 1964, box 16, William Foster papers, GCML.

39. Bernard de Chalvron to M. Gastambide, telegram from Geneva to Paris, "Conference on Disarmament," 23 January 1964, box 768, cote 517INVA, CADLC.

40. William Foster, "164th ENDC Plenary," box 16, William Foster papers, GCML, 4. Underlining in the original.

41. Foster, "164th ENDC Plenary," 4.

42. Bernard de Chalvron to M. Gastambide, telegram from Geneva to Paris, "Conference sur le Désarmament," 7 February 1964; and Herve Alphand, telegram from New York to Paris, "ENDC," box 768, cote 517INVA, CADLC.

43. William Foster to Dean Rusk, telegram to Geneva, "Memorandum of Conversation Between Foster & Tsarapkin [1 of 2]," 11 February 1964, box 11, SF-Disarmament, NSF, LBJL.

44. William Foster to Dean Rusk, telegram to Geneva, "Memorandum of Conversation Between Foster & Tsarapkin [2 of 2]," 11 February 1964, box 11, SF-Disarmament, NSF, LBJL.

45. "Staff Meeting Talking Points," 27 February 1963, folder 18, box 16, William Foster papers, GCML.

46. Mahatma Gandhi, "The Atom Bomb," http://www.mkgandhi.org/momgandhi/chap94.htm.

47. Itty Abraham, *The Making of the Indian Atomic Bomb: Science, Secrecy and the Postcolonial State* (New York: St. Martin's Press, 1998), 1–47.

48. George Perkovich, *India's Nuclear Bomb: The Impact on Global Proliferation* (Berkeley: University of California Press, 1999), 20.

49. V. R. Krishna Iyer, *Nehru and Krishna Menon* (Delhi: Konark, 1993); Jawaharlal Nehru, *The Essential Writings of Jawaharlal Nehru* (New Delhi: Oxford University Press, 2003); Shashi Tharoor, *Nehru: The Invention of India* (New York: Arcade, 2003).

50. Perkovich, *India's Nuclear Bomb*, 21; Jayita Sarkar, *Ploughshares and Swords: India's Nuclear Program in the Global Cold War* (Ithaca, NY: Cornell University Press, 2022).

51. Itty Abraham, "The Ambivalence of Nuclear Histories," *Osiris* 21, no. 1 (2006): 49–65.

52. Perkovich, *India's Nuclear Bomb*, 28.

53. Ariel E. Levite, "Never Say Never Again: Nuclear Reversal Revisited," *International Security* 27, no. 3 (January 2003): 59–88.

54. Nehru left marginalia in a letter from Bhabha about the Indo-Canadian reactor deal: "Apart from building power stations and developing electricity there is always a built-in advantage of defence use if the need should arise." Quoted in Perkovich, *India's Nuclear Bomb*, 63.

55. ENDC/PV.164, 6 February 1964, 22–29.

56. ENDC/PV.162, 31 January 1964, 8–15; U Thant, "Statement by the Secretary-General at his Press Conference at United Nations Headquarters," 12 September 1963, S-0886–002, Secretary-General's Statement, UN Archives.

57. Pierre M. Gallois, *Stratégie de L'âge Nucléaire* (Paris: Calmann-Lévy, 1960).

58. Bernard de Chalvron to M. Gastambide, telegram from Geneva to Paris, "Conference sur le Désarmament," 19 February 1964, box 768, Cote 517INVA, CADLC, 1.

59. ACDA, *Documents on Disarmament, 1964*, 29–30.

60. Perkovich, *India's Nuclear Bomb*, 60–61.

61. ENDC/PV.165, 11 February 1964, 15.

62. ENDC/PV.167, 18 February 1964, 28.

63. Chester Bowles to Dean Rusk, telegram to New Delhi, "Politico-Military Balance in South Asia," undated, box 128, Country file [CF]—India, NSF, LBJL, 1.

64. Chester Bowles to Dean Rusk, telegram to New Delhi, "U.S. Politico-Military Assistance to India," 20 February 1964, box 128, CF—India, NSF, LBJL, 2.

65. Dean Rusk and Manuel Tello, memorandum of conversation, "Control of Nuclear Weapons & Disarmament," 21 February 1964, box 59, CF—Latin America-Honduras, NSF, LBJL.

66. Bowles to Rusk, telegram, 20 February 1964, 2; Chester Bowles to Dean Rusk, telegram, "Importance of Early Decision in Regard to South Asia Policy," 3 December 1963, box 128, CF—India, NSF, LBJL, 1–2.

67. Chester Bowles to Dean Rusk, telegram to New Delhi, "Summary of General Taylor's Discussion with Indian Officials," undated, box 128, CF—India, NSF, LBJL, 4.

68. Chester Bowles to the president, Dean Rusk, Robert McNamara, George Ball, Averell Harriman, Phillips Talbot, and McGeorge Bundy, telegram from New Delhi to Washington, cc Karachi, "South Asian policy," 6 December 1963, box 128, CF—India, NSF, LBJL, 1–2.

69. Perkovich, *India's Nuclear Bomb*, 45.

70. George C. Denny Jr., Intelligence and Research Division, to Dean Rusk, memorandum, "Possible Indian Nuclear Weapons Development," 24 February 1964, box 128, CF—India, NSF, LBJL.

71. S. A. Levin, L. R. Powers, and E. Von Halle, Union Carbide Corporation Nuclear Division, "Nth Power Evaluation," 4 March 1964, U.S. Atomic Energy Commission, 11.

72. State Department, memorandum for the record, "Gomulka Proposal," 2 April 1964, box 10, SF-Disarmament, NSF, LBJL; Hervé Alphand, telegram from Washington to Paris, "Interview with William Foster's ACDA Confidant," 13 March 1964, box 768, Cote 517INVA, CADLC, 1. On Nosenko, see T. H. Bagley, *Spy Wars: Moles, Mysteries, and Deadly Games* (New Haven, CT: Yale University Press, 2007).

73. Hervé Alphand, telegram from Washington to Paris, "Conversation with M. Beam of ACDA re ENDC," 1 April 1964, box 768, Cote 517/INVA, CADLC, 1–2; *FRUS, 1964–1968*, vol. XV, document 6, 24 January 1964.

74. *FRUS, 1964–1968*, vol. XV, document 15, 4 March 1964.

75. *FRUS, 1964–1968*, vol. XIII, document 16, 10 April 1964.

76. MemCon, "MLF," 10 April 1964.

77. *FRUS, 1964–1968*, vol. XI, document 26, 1 May 1964, and document 31, 5 June 1964.

78. *FRUS, 1964–1968*, vol. XI, document 46.

79. Rick Perlstein, *Before the Storm: Barry Goldwater and the Unmaking of the American Consensus* (New York: Hill and Wang, 2001).

80. Gordon M. Goldstein and Fredrik Logevall, "Compared to Trump, Goldwater Was a Sensible Moderate," *Daily Beast*, September 17, 2016.

81. Hervé Alphand, telegram from Washington to Paris, "Soviet Views on Potential for ENDC Progress," 5 May 1964, box 768, cote 517INVA, CADLC.

82. William Burr and Jeff Richelson, "Whether to 'Strangle the Baby in the Cradle: The United States and the Chinese Nuclear Program, 1960–64," *International Security* 25, no. 3 (Winter 2000): 54–99; Gordon H. Chang, "JFK, China, and the Bomb," *Journal of American History* 74, no. 4 (March 1998): 1287–1310.

83. ACDA, "Report on the Subject of Nuclear Containment and Non-proliferation," TAB E, "Aborting the Chicom Nuclear Capability"; TAB H, "JCS Study of Chinese Communist Vulnerability," 17 June 1963, Llewellyn Thompson Papers, NARA II, College Park, Maryland.

84. Francis J. Gavin, "Strategies of Inhibition: U.S. Grand Strategy, the Nuclear Revolution, and Nonproliferation," *International Security* 40, no. 1 (July 2015): 9–46.

85. Quoted in Burr and Richelson, "Whether to 'Strangle the Baby in the Cradle,'" 17.

86. Robert Johnson, "Implications of a Chinese Communist Nuclear Capability," 16 April 1964, 1, 9; "An Exploration of the Possible Bases for Action Against the Chinese Communist Nuclear Facilities," 14 April 1964, box 237, CF—Communist China, NSF, LBJL, 1–4.

87. Memorandum for the record, "Robert Kennedy's Luncheon with Dobrynin," 7 July 1964, box 3, McGeorge Bundy files, NSF, LBJL, 1–2.

88. Robert A. Caro, *The Passage of Power* (New York: Knopf, 2012).

89. U.S. Pacific Command to McGeorge Bundy et al., telegram, "Chicom Nuclear Program," 13 July 1964, 1–2; Memorandum to the Joint Chiefs of Staff, "Chicom Nuclear Testing Program," July 1964, box 237, CF—China, NSF, LBJL.

90. *FRUS, 1964–1968*, vol. XXX, document 38, 24 July 1964.

91. *FRUS, 1964–1968*, vol. XXX, document 43, 26 August 1964.

92. Mark Atwood Lawrence, *The Vietnam War: A Concise International History* (New York: Oxford University Press, 2008), 85–87.

93. McGeorge Bundy and Anatoly Dobrynin, memorandum of conversation,, 1 October 1964, box 4, McGeorge Bundy files, NSF, LBJL.

94. Lyndon Johnson speech, 12 October 1964, in *Public Papers of the Presidents: Lyndon B. Johnson, 1963–64* (Washington, DC: U.S. Government Printing Office, 1996), vol 2., 95–97, quoted in Lawrence, *The Vietnam War*, 87.

95. "Summary Notes of 543rd NSC meeting," 17 October 1964, box 18, McGeorge Bundy files, NSF, LBJL, 1.

96. "Outline for Possible Presidential Statement," 17 October 1964, box 4, McGeorge Bundy files, NSF, LBJL.

97. Seaborg, *Stemming the Tide*, 115–116.

98. Francis J. Gavin, "Blasts from the Past: Proliferation Lessons from the 1960s," *International Security* 29, no. 3 (Winter 2004): 100–135.

99. Maddock, *Nuclear Apartheid*, 238.

100. *FRUS, 1964–1968*, vol. XI, document 51, 25 November 1964.

101. *FRUS, 1964–1968*, vol. XI, document 49.

102. Robert Mann, *Daisy Petals and Mushroom Clouds: LBJ, Barry Goldwater, and the Ad That Changed American Politics* (Baton Rouge: Louisiana State University Press, 2011).

103. Peter J. Kuznick, "Scientists on the Stump," *Bulletin of the Atomic Scientists* 60, no. 6 (November 2004): 28–35.

104. Tony Southhall and Julian Atkinson, *CND 1958–1963: Lessons of the First Wave* (New York: Open Road, 1981).

105. J. Burkett, "Re-Defining British Morality: 'Britishness' and the Campaign for Nuclear Disarmament 1958–68," *Twentieth Century British History* 21, no. 2 (June 1, 2010): 184–205; Christopher Leslie Brown, *Moral Capital: Foundations of British Abolitionism* (Chapel Hill: University of North Carolina Press, 2006).

106. Geoffroy Chordon de Courcel, telegram from London to Paris, "Butler's Visit to Geneva," 26 February 1964, box 768, cote 517INVA, CADLC.

107. Susanna Schrafstetter, "Preventing the 'Smiling Buddha': British-Indian Nuclear Relations and the Commonwealth Nuclear Force, 1964–68," *Journal of Strategic Studies* 25, no. 3 (September 2002): 87–108.

108. Alun Jones Chalfont, *The Shadow of My Hand* (London: Weidenfeld and Nicolson, 2000).

109. Arthur J. Olsen, "Action with U.S. on Atomic Fleet Hinted by Erhard," 7 October 1964; "Erhard Sees Need for New Weapons," *New York Times*, 11 October 1964. ProQuest Historical Newspapers.

110. Selvage, "The Warsaw Pact and Nuclear Proliferation, 1963–1965," 14–15.

111. *FRUS, 1964–1968*, vol. XII, document 236.

112. Roswell Gilpatric to John H. Rubel, letter, "The Subject of Proliferation," box 10, Gilpatric papers, Personal papers, JFKL; John W. Young, "'Killing the MLF?': The Wilson Government and Nuclear Sharing in Europe, 1964–66," *Diplomacy and Statecraft* 14, no. 2 (June 2003): 295–324; Saki Dockrill, "Britain's Power and Influence: The Wilson Government's Defence Debate at Chequers in Nov. 1964," *Diplomacy and Statecraft* 11 (2000), 230.

113. *FRUS, 1964–1968*, vol. XI, document 50, 23 November 1964.

114. *FRUS, 1964–1968*, vol. XI, document 50, 23 November 1964.

115. William Foster to the Committee of Principals, memorandum, "Subjects to Be Discussed with the USSR," 3 December 1964, box 13, SF-Disarmament, NSF, LBJL, 1.

116. Glenn T. Seaborg, *Journal of Glenn T. Seaborg*, vol. 9, 17 vols. (Berkeley: University of California Press, 1989), 472, 529c.

117. *FRUS, 1964–1968*, vol. XI, document 57, 16 December 1964.

118. Recent studies of U.S. nonproliferation policy cast the Gilpatric Committee as transformative: Gavin, "Blasts from the Past"; Hal Brands, "Rethinking Nonproliferation: LBJ, the Gilpatric Committee, and U.S. National Security Policy," *Journal of Cold War Studies* 8, no. 2 (January 2006): 83–113; Dane E. Swango, "The Nuclear Nonproliferation Treaty: Constrainer, Screen, or Enabler?," dissertation, University of California, Los Angeles, 2009; Nicholas L. Miller, *Stopping the Bomb: The Sources and Effectiveness of US Nonproliferation Policy* (Ithaca, NY: Cornell University Press, 2018). For a more critical treatment, see Maddock, *Nuclear Apartheid*, 238–244.

119. "Outline of Roswell L. Gilpatric's Opening Remarks," 1 December 1964, box 10, Gilpatric papers, NSF, JFKL.

120. "Nonproliferation Committee's Major Issues," box 10, Gilpatric papers, NSF, JFKL.

121. "Tentative Thoughts on Certain Proliferation Problems," 4 December 1964, box 10, Gilpatric papers, NSF, JFKL.

122. Russell Murray, "Problems of Nuclear Proliferation Outside Europe (Problem 2)," 7 December 1964, box 5, Committee on Non-Proliferation, NSF, LBJL, 3. Cited in Gavin, "Blasts from the Past," 106.

123. Richard K. Betts, "A Diplomatic Bomb for South Africa?," *International Security* 4, no. 2 (Fall 1979): 91–115.

124. The committee included Arthur Dean, Allen Dulles, Alfred Gruenther, George Kistiaskowsky, John McCloy, James Perkins, Arthur Watson, William Webster, and Herbert York. Spurgeon M. Keeny Jr. was staff director and the principal author. Officials from the U.S. Department of State, the U.S. Department of Defense, the NSC, the AEC, and ACDA were consulted, with Raymond Garthoff, Russell Murray, George Rathjens, Henry Rowen, Roger Fisher, and Steven R. Rivkin making contributions as well.

125. Roger Fisher to Roswell Gilpatric, "A Proposed Decision on the General U.S. Policy Toward Nuclear Weapons," 17 December 1964; Roger Fisher, "Preventing the Spread of Nuclear Weapons: A Theoretical View of the Problem," 26 November 1964; and Max Singer, Hudson Institute, "United States Policy and Nuclear Spread," 20 December 1964, box 10, Gilpatric papers, Personal papers, JFKL.

126. W. W. Rostow, "A Way of Thinking About Nuclear Proliferation," 19 November 1964, box 10a, Gilpatric papers, Personal papers, JFKL, 14.

127. "Summary of Statement Made Before Gilpatric Committee," 17 December 1964, box 10, Gilpatric papers, JFKL, 2, 8.

128. Rostow, "A Way of Thinking About Nuclear Proliferation," 16–18.

129. Robert Komer to McGeorge Bundy, memorandum, "Nuclear Sharing in Asia," December 1965, box 6, Robert Komer papers, NSF, LBJL.

130. *FRUS, 1964–1968*, vol. XI, document 56, 13–14 December 1964.

131. John J. McCloy, memorandum for the chairman, 8 January 1965, box 10a, Gilpatric papers, JFKL, 3.

132. "Minutes of Briefing by Secretary McNamara on Issues Related to Proliferation," 7 January 1965, box 10, Gilpatric papers, JFKL; Robert McNamara, testimony, 7 March 1966, Joint Committee on Atomic Energy [JCAE], Hearings on Senate Resolution 179, "Nonproliferation of Nuclear Weapons," Eighty-Ninth Congress, Second Session (Washington, DC: U.S. Government Printing Office, 1966), 3.

133. *FRUS, 1964–1968*, vol. XI, document 59, 7 January 1965.

134. Gavin, "Blasts from the Past," 109.

135. Stephen R. Rivkin, "Problems Concerning Alternative Courses of Action," undated, box 10a, Gilpatric papers, JFKL, 3.

136. *FRUS, 1964–1968*, vol. XI, document 59, 7 January 1965.

137. *FRUS, 1964–1968*, vol. XI, document 64, 21 January 1965.

138. *FRUS, 1964–1968*, vol. XI, document 60, 7–8 January 1965; see Roswell Gilpatric, notes, "Discussion with Messrs. Dean and McCloy on Problems of Europe and NATO," 9 December 1964, box 10, Gilpatric papers, JFKL, 2.

139. John J. McCloy to Roswell Gilpatric, memorandum, 8 January 1965, box 10a, Gilpatric papers, JFKL, 3–5.

140. McCloy to Gilpatric, memorandum, 8 January 1965, 5.

141. "Course III—Actions," undated, box 10, Gilpatric papers, JFKL.

142. Arthur H. Dean, memorandum to the chairman, 18 January 1964, box 10, Gilpatric papers, JFKL.

143. "Summary, President's Committee on Nuclear Proliferation—A Report to the President," draft, undated, box 10, Gilpatric papers, JFKL. Underlining in the original.

144. *FRUS, 1964–1968*, vol. XI, document 60, 7–8 January 1965.

145. *FRUS, 1964–1968*, vol. XI, document 63.

146. Roswell Gilpatric to Isidor Shaffer, letter, "Halperin's book *China and the Bomb*," 28 April 1965, box 10, Gilpatric papers, JFKL.

147. Minutes, Senate Foreign Relations Committee discussion between Senator Clark and Secretary Rusk, 28 April 1965, box 10, SF—Disarmament, NSF, LBJL, 38–42.

148. Spurgeon M. Keeny Jr. to McGeorge Bundy, memorandum with attachments, "Senator Clark and Disarmament," 29 April 1965, box 10, SF—Disarmament, NSF, LBJL.

149. McGeorge Bundy to Lyndon Johnson, memorandum, 29 April 1965, box 10, SF—Disarmament, NSF, LBJL.

150. Roger Seydoux, telegram from New York to Paris, "M. Aiken's Views on Nonproliferation Proceedings," 13 May 1965, box 769, cote 517INVA, CADLC.

151. Arthur Krock, "In the Nation: Priority in the Quest for Peace," *New York Times*, 27 June 1965, E11. ProQuest Historical Newspapers.

152. Foster, "New Directions in Arms Control and Disarmament," *Foreign Affairs*. The final draft read, "With the passage of time a similar erosion of confidence might occur with respect to any assurances designed to counter the Chinese threat." William Foster to Dean Rusk, letter, "Suggested Changes to Forthcoming Article in *Foreign Affairs*," 11 May 1965, William Foster papers, GCML.

153. Foster to Rusk, letter, 11 May 1965.

154. Adam Walinsky, "RFK's Second Speech," 23 September 1965, box 10, Gilpatric papers, personal papers, JFKL; John R. Bohrer, *The Revolution of Robert Kennedy: From Power to Protest After JFK* (New York: Bloomsbury, 2017), 184–190; "Kennedy Proposes Treaty to Check Nuclear Spread," *New York Times*, 24 June 1965, box 6, 1968 presidential campaign national HQ files, press division, Robert F. Kennedy [RFK] papers, JFKL.

155. "Text of Senator Kennedy's Speech Urging Pact to Check Nuclear Weapons Spread," *New York Times*, 24 June 1965, 16. ProQuest Historical Newspapers.

156. E. W. Kenworthy, "Kennedy Proposes Treaty to Check Nuclear Spread: White House Is Cool to Plan to Assign 'Central Priority' to Pact that Would Include Chinese Communist Regime," *New York Times*, 24 June 1965, 1. ProQuest Historical Newspapers.

157. "Text of Senator Kennedy's Speech," 16.

158. Robert F. Kennedy, "Will There Be Any World Left for Our Children," *Frontier* 16, no. 10 (August 1965), 1968 presidential campaign national HQ files, Press division, RFK papers, JFKL.

159. Bohrer, *The Revolution of Robert Kennedy*, 188.

160. "Atom-Curb Panel Stirs U.S. Dispute: Report Said to Urge Putting Arms-Spread Halt Ahead of NATO Nuclear Force," *New York Times*, 1 July 1965, 1. ProQuest Historical Newspapers.

161. William Foster, draft, "Doty-Long Visit to USSR, June 10 and 11, 1965," 16 June 1965, box 14, William Foster papers, GCML, 3–13.

162. Quoted in Timothy Andrews Sayle, "A Nuclear Education: The Origins of NATO's Nuclear Planning Group," *Journal of Strategic Studies* 43, no. 6–7 (November 9, 2020): 949–950.

163. White House, National Security Action Memorandum (NSAM) 335, "Preparation of Arms Control Program," 28 June 1965, box 13, SF—Disarmament, NSF, LBJL.

164. McGeorge Bundy to Lyndon Johnson, memorandum, "Attached Draft Statement on Disarmament," 13 July 1965, box 13, SF—disarmament, NSF, LBJL.

165. Robert Komer to McGeorge Bundy, memorandum, "A Rounded Foreign Policy Stance," 7 July 1965, box 6, Robert Komer papers, NSF, LBJL.

CHAPTER 6

1. ENDC/PV.218, 27 July 1965, 7.

2. ENDC/PV.218, 27 July 1965, 10.

3. Hayes Redmon to Bill Moyers, memorandum, "Committee of Principals Meetings and Arms Control Agenda," 31 May 1966, box 12, Bill Moyers files, LBJL.

4. George Ball to Robert McNamara, "The Danger from a Psychotic Germany," appendix, 27 October 1965, https://nsarchive2.gwu.edu//dc.html?doc=4415103-Document-08-The-Danger-from-a-Psychotic-Germany.

5. Dane E. Swango, "The Nuclear Nonproliferation Treaty: Constrainer, Screen, or Enabler?," dissertation, University of California, Los Angeles, 2009.

6. George Perkovich, *India's Nuclear Bomb: The Impact on Global Proliferation* (Berkeley: University of California Press, 1999), 40; Jawaharlal Nehru, *The Discovery of India* (Oxford, UK: Oxford University Press, 1989).

7. U.S. embassy in New Delhi to Dean Rusk, telegram, "Political-Military Balance in South Asia," 10 December 1963, box 128, CF—India, NSF, LBJL, 3–4.

8. U.S. Department of State, Director of Intelligence & Research, to Dean Rusk, memorandum, "Indian Nuclear Weapons Development," 14 May 1964, box 128, CF—India, NSF, LBJL.

9. ENDC/PV.212, 1 September 1965, 5.

10. David C. Engerman, "South Asia and the Cold War," in Robert J. McMahon, ed., *The Cold War in the Third World* (New York: Oxford University Press, 2013), 67–84; Andrew Jon Rotter, *Comrades at Odds: The United States and India, 1947–1964* (Ithaca, NY: Cornell University Press, 2000).

11. U.S. Department of State, telegram, "Indian Resolution to Outlaw Use of Nuclear Weapons," 2 September 1964, box 11, SF—Disarmament, NSF, LBJL.

12. William Foster, telegram from Geneva to Washington, "Meeting with Italians," 25 November 1964, box 11, SF—Disarmament, NSF, LBJL.

13. Chester Bowles to McGeorge Bundy, letter, "Tactics of Handling Questions Involving Nuclear Power in India," 16 September 1964, box 129, CF—India, NSF, LBJL, 2–3.

14. Ariel E. Levite, "Never Say Never Again: Nuclear Reversal Revisited," *International Security* 27, no. 3 (January 2003): 59–88.

15. CIA Intelligence Information, cable, "Indian Government Reaction to Chicom Nuclear Explosion," 19 October 1964, box 128, CF—India, NSF, LBJL.

16. U.S. Department of State, telegram to New Delhi and Cairo, "Indian Response to ChiCom Nuclear Test," 7 October 1964, box 128, CF—India, NSF, LBJL, 1–2.

17. G. G. Mirchandani, *India's Nuclear Dilemma* (New Delhi: Popular Book Services, 1968); Perkovich, *India's Nuclear Bomb*, 65; Lorenzo Lüthi, "Non-Alignment, 1961–1974," in Sandra Bott et al., eds., *Neutrality and Neutralism in the Global Cold War: Between or within the Blocs?* (New York: Routledge, 2016), 95–96.

18. Lüthi, "Non-Alignment, 1961–1974," 95; Second Conference of Heads of State or Government of Non-aligned Countries in Cairo, "Programme for Peace and International Development Co-operation," 10 October 1964, enclosed in UNGA A/5763, 29 October 1964.

19. Perkovich, *India's Nuclear Bomb*, 65–66; U.S. consulate in Bombay to Dean Rusk, telegram, "Official and Press Reactions in India to China's Test," 27 October 1964, box 128, CF—India, NSF, LBJL, 2–3.

20. Department of State, telegram to New Delhi, "Interview with Shastri," 28 October 1964, box 128, CF—India, NSF, LBJL, 1, 5–6.

21. National Intelligence Estimate 4-2-64, "Prospects for a Proliferation of Nuclear Weapons over the Next Decade," 21 October 1964, Digital Archive, Cold War International History Project, http://digitalarchive.wilsoncenter.org/document/115994; *FRUS, 1964–1968*, vol. XXV, document 78, 10 December 1964.

22. U.S. consulate in Bombay to Rusk, telegram, 27 October 1964, 1.

23. Perkovich, *India's Nuclear Bomb*, 67–68; Itty Abraham, *The Making of the Indian Atomic Bomb: Science, Secrecy and the Postcolonial State* (New York: St. Martin's Press, 1998).

24. *FRUS, 1964–1968*, vol. XXV, document 74, 3 November 1964.

25. Perkovich, *India's Nuclear Bomb*, 74.

26. Inder Halhortra, "Shastri Gets His Way on Nuclear Policy," *Indian Express*, 15 October 2012, http://www.indianexpress.com/news/shastri-gets-his-way-on-nuclear-policy/1016715/0.

27. "Menon Scores Shastri on Atom Policy," *New York Times*, 11 January 1965, 2. ProQuest Historical Newspapers.

28. "Shastri Appeals on Arms," *New York Times*, 21 January 1965, 4. ProQuest Historical Newspapers.

29. David C. Engerman, *The Price of Aid: The Economic Cold War in India* (Cambridge, MA: Harvard University Press, 2018).

30. Memorandum for Robert McNamara, "The Indian Nuclear Problem: Proposed Course of Action," 23 October 1964, with letter to Dean Rusk, 28 October 1964, NSAEEB6, http://www.gwu.edu/~nsarchiv/NSAEBB/NSAEBB6/docs/doc02.pdf.

31. "Background Paper on Factors Which Could Influence National Decisions Concerning Acquisition of Nuclear Weapons," in Praveen K. Chaudhry and Marta Vanduzer-Snow, *The United States and India: A History Through Archives. The Later Years. Volume 2* (Thousand Oaks, CA: Sage, 2011), 338.

32. U.S. embassy in Karachi to Dean Rusk et al., telegram, "Indian Nuclear Program," 8 November 1964, box 128, CF—India, NSF, LBJL, 1–3.

33. Telegram from New Delhi to Washington, "India and Nuclear Proliferation Problem," 12 November 1964, box 128, CF—India, NSF, LBJL, 1–3.

34. *FRUS, 1964–1968*, vol. XXV, document 79, 12 December, 1964.

35. "Background Paper," in Chaudhry and Vanduzer-Snow, 335–339.

36. *FRUS, 1964–1968*, vol. XXV, document 85, 21 January 1965; Telegram from New Delhi to Washington, "Wiesner's Visit to India to Tout Indian Scientific Prowess and Avert Proliferation," 21 January 1965, box 129 [1 of 2], CF—India, NSF, LBJL.

37. Dean Rusk to Averell Harriman, telegram, 27 February 1965, NSAEEB6, http://www.gwu.edu/~nsarchiv/NSAEBB/NSAEBB6/docs/doc07.pdf.

38. "Nuclear Guarantee Is Urged by Shastri," *New York Times*, 5 December 1964, 9. ProQuest Historical Newspapers.

39. *FRUS, 1964–1968*, vol. XXV, document 90, 25 February 1965.

40. "Wiesner's Visit," 21 January 1965, footnote 7.

41. Spurgeon M. Keeny Jr. to McGeorge Bundy, memorandum, "Draft Statement of Assurances for India," 16 March 1965, box 129 [1 of 2], CF—India, NSF, LBJL; "Briton Urges Nuclear Power to Join in Guarantee to the World," *New York Times*, 18 December 1964, 8. ProQuest Historical Newspapers; Susanna Schrafstetter, "Preventing the 'Smiling Buddha': British-Indian Nuclear Relations and the Commonwealth Nuclear Force, 1964–68," *Journal of Strategic Studies* 25, no. 3 (September 2002): 87–108.

42. "Shastri Warns U.N. on Nuclear Menace," *New York Times*, 23 January 1965, 6. ProQuest Historical Newspapers.

43. *FRUS, 1964–1968*, vol. XXV, document 82, 31 December 1964, and document 83, 8 January 1965; Telegram to Washington, "USG Holding India at Arm's Length on Proliferation Resolution," 16 January 1965, box 129 [1 of 2], CF—India, NSF, LBJL, 1.

44. "Wiesner's Visit," 21 January 1965.

45. Telegram from New Delhi to Washington, "Indian Simultaneous Statement re Chicom Nuclear Explosion," 10 February 1965, box 129 [1 of 2], CF—India, NSF, LBJL.

46. Memorandum of conversation, "Indian Nuclear Energy Program," 22 February 1965, box 129 [1 of 2], CF—India, NSF, LBJL, 1–2.

47. ACDA, memorandum of conversation, William Foster and Avtar Kirshna Dar, "UNDC and Plowshare Initiative," 8 April 1965, box 129 [1 of 2], CF—India, NSF, LBJL, 3.

48. Rusk to Harriman, telegram, 27 February 1965.

49. *FRUS, 1964–1968*, vol. XXV, document 91, 5 March 1965, and document 92, 7 March 1965.

50. Rusk to Harriman, telegram, 27 February 1965.

51. Telegram from New Delhi to Washington, "Security Assurances to India," 5 May 1965, box 129 [1 of 2], CF—India, NSF, LBJL, 1–6.

52. Telegram from New Delhi to Washington, "Nuclear Assurances," 23 May 1965, box 129 [1 of 2], CF—India, NSF, LBJL; "Politburo Talk by Zhou Enlai on Receiving a Group of [Central] Military Commission Operational Meeting Comrades," 21 May 1965, Digital Archive, Cold War International History Project, http://digitalarchive.wilsoncenter.org/document/114363.

53. *FRUS, 1964–1968*, vol. XXV, document 119, 10 May 1965.

54. *FRUS, 1964–1968*, vol. XXV, document 178, 2 September 1965.

55. Marc Trachtenberg, "The de Gaulle Problem," *Journal of Cold War Studies* 14, no. 1 (Winter 2012): 81–92.

56. Raymond Aron, "The Spread of Nuclear Weapons," *Atlantic Monthly* 215 (1965): 44–50.

57. Direction des Affaires Politiques, report, "Désarmement re non dissémination des armes nucléaires," 3 February 1965, box 768, cote 517INVA, CADLC, 8.

58. Alun Jones Chalfont, *The Shadow of My Hand* (London: Weidenfeld and Nicolson, 2000), 112.

59. Pierre de Leusse, telegram from Paris (NATO) to other stations, "Lord Chalfont Visit to the NATO Council," 31 March 1965, box 768, cote 517INVA, CADLC, 3.

60. Robert M. Neer, *Napalm: An American Biography* (Cambridge, MA.: Harvard University Press, 2015), 109–125.

61. Lien-Hang Nguyen, *Hanoi's War: An International History of the War for Peace in Vietnam* (Chapel Hill: University of North Carolina Press, 2012), 119, 326 (note 49); Lorenz M. Lüthi, *The Sino-Soviet Split: Cold War in the Communist World* (Princeton, NJ: Princeton University Press, 2008), 71–119.

62. Direction des Affaires Politiques, note, "Sessions de la Commission du Désarmement (26 avril—16 juin 1965)," 27 July 1965, box 769, cote 517INVA, CADLC, 1–8.

63. Direction des Affaires Politiques, note, 27 July 1965, 8–9.

64. E.L.M. Burns, "The Nonproliferation Treaty: Its Negotiation and Prospects," *International Organization* 23, no. 4 (October 1969): 792.

65. "U.S. Weighs Plan for Atomic Curb," *New York Times*, 15 April 1965, 1. ProQuest Historical Newspapers.

66. Direction des Affaires Politiques, note, "Commission du Désarmement," 27 July 1965, 10.

67. Direction des Affaires Politiques, note, "Commission du Désarmement," 27 July 1965, 8–16.

68. "India and Japan Denounce China," *New York Times*, 15 May 1965, 2. ProQuest Historical Newspapers.

69. Roger Seydoux, telegram from New York to Paris, "Commission du Désarmement," 25 May 1965, box 769, cote 517INVA, CADLC, 2.

70. Roger Seydoux, telegram from New York to Paris, 25 May 1965, 2; "La Commission du Désarmement," 17 June 1965, box 769, cote 517INVA, CADLC, 3.

71. Lorenz M. Lüthi, *Cold Wars: Asia, the Middle East, Europe* (New York: Cambridge University Press, 2020), 299, 349.

72. Burns, "The Nonproliferation Treaty," 790.

73. "Politburo Talk by Zhou Enlai," 21 May 1965, 27–28.

74. Telegram from London to Paris, "UK Labour Reactions to News of Geneva Reset," 14 July 1965, 1; "UK Problems with U.S. draft," 20 August 1965, box 768, cote 517INVA, CADLC, 2.

75. U.S. Department of State, telegram to London, 13 July 1965, box 13, SF—Disarmament, NSF, LBJL; telegram from Geneva to Paris, "Soviets Come Out Against MLF at End of ENDC," 2 August 1965, box 768, cote 517INVA, CADLC.

76. "Proposed Formulations of a Non-proliferation Agreement," 3 August 1965; telegram from Washington to Geneva, "IAEA Safeguards and Non-proliferation," 2 September 1965, box 13, SF—Disarmament, NSF, LBJL, 3.

77. Telegram from Washington to Geneva, "Non-proliferation Treaty, IAEA Safeguards," 9 August 1965, 1–2; ACDA, memorandum of conversation, "ENDC and Related Matters," 10 August 1965, box 13, SF—Disarmament, NSF, LBJL, 3.

78. U.S. Mission to Geneva, telegram to Washington, "Non-proliferation Treaty," 27 July 1965; U.S. Department of State, telegram to Geneva, "Non-proliferation Treaty," 4 August 1965, box 13, SF—Disarmament, NSF, LBJL, 3–4.

79. Draft letter to UK foreign minister Michael Stewart, "Geneva," 4 August 1965, box 13, SF—Disarmament, NSF, LBJL, 2.

80. William Foster, telegram to Washington, "Soviet Rejection," 21 September 1965, box 13, NSF, SF—Disarmament, LBJL.

81. William Foster, "Answers We Propose to Give to Tsarapkin's Questions," 18 August 1965, folder 10, box 17, FP, GCML, 1–2; telegram from Geneva to Paris, "Soviets Come Out Against MLF at End of ENDC," 2 August 1965, box 768, cote 517INVA, CADLC.

82. William Foster, telegram to Washington, "Courtesy Call by Trivedi on Foster," 4 August 1965, box 13, NSF, SF—Disarmament, LBJL.

83. Leopoldo Nuti, "'Me Too, Please': Italy and the Politics of Nuclear Weapons, 1945–1975," *Diplomacy and Statecraft* 4, no. 1 (March 1993): 114–148.

84. "Draft Unilateral Non-acquisition Declaration, Fanfani Proposal, Cavalletti Draft," 25 August 1965, folder 13, box 17, FP, GCML; Telegram from Geneva to Paris, "Chalfont Questions Soviets," 3 September 1965, box 768, cote 517INVA, CADLC.

85. UNGA Resolution 2028 (XX), https://undocs.org/en/A/RES/2028(XX) (accessed 15 February 2020).

86. Glenn Seaborg to McGeorge Bundy, memorandum, "Summary of 'Nth Country Evaluation,'" 23 November 1965, box 22, Charles Johnson papers, NSF, LBJL, 4–5.

87. Quoted in Shane Maddock, *Nuclear Apartheid: The Quest for American Atomic Supremacy from World War II to the Present* (Chapel Hill: University of North Carolina Press, 2010), 255–256.

88. *FRUS, 1964–1968*, vol. XIII, document 111, 24 November 1965.

89. *FRUS, 1964–1968*, vol. XIII, document 112, 24 November 1965; Andrew Priest, "George W. Ball, the Multilateral Force and the Transatlantic Alliance," in Giles Scott-Smith and Valérie Aubourg, eds., *Atlantic, Euratlantic, or Europe-Atlantic? The Atlantic Community and Europe* (Paris: Soleb, 2011).

90. *FRUS, 1964–1968*, vol. XIII, document 112, 24 November 1965; Ball to McNamara, "The Danger from a Psychotic Germany," 2–3; Susanna Schrafstetter, "The Long Shadow of the Past: History, Memory and the Debate over West Germany's Nuclear Status, 1954–69," *History and Memory* 16, no. 1 (2004): 118–145.

91. *FRUS, 1964–1968*, vol. XIII, document 64, 15 December 1964.

92. *FRUS, 1964–1968*, vol. XIII, document 96, 12 July 1965.

93. Henry Kissinger to McGeorge Bundy, letter, "Observations from European Journey," 20 July 1965, box 20, Francis Bator papers, LBJL, 1.

94. *FRUS, 1964–1968*, vol. XIII, document 119, 20 December 1965; Maddock, *Nuclear Apartheid*, 259.

95. *FRUS, 1964–1968*, vol. XIII, document 120, 20 December 1965.

96. *FRUS, 1964–1968*, vol. XIII, document 121, 23 December 1965.

97. *FRUS, 1964–1968*, vol. XIII, document 124, 17 January 1966.

98. Andrew Priest, "From Hardware to Software: The End of the MLF/ANF Debate and the Rise of the NATO Nuclear Planning Group," in Andreas Wenger, Christian Nünlist, and Anna Locher, eds., *Transforming NATO in the Cold War: Challenges Beyond Deterrence in the 1960s* (London: Routledge, 2012), 153–154.

99. George Bunn, *Arms Control by Committee: Managing Negotiations with the Russians* (Stanford, CA: Stanford University Press, 1992), 73; Author's interview with Ambassador James E. Goodby, January 20, 2013, Hoover Institution, Stanford, CA.

100. "President's State of the Union Message to Joint Session of Congress," transcript, *New York Times*, 13 January 1966, 14. ProQuest Historical Newspapers.

101. "Text of the Pastore Resolution," 18 January 1966, box 13, SF—Disarmament, NSF, LBJL.

102. Senator John O. Pastore, "The Resolution of Non-proliferation of Nuclear and Thermonuclear Weapons," remarks, undated, box 13, SF—Disarmament, NSF, LBJL, 1.

103. *FRUS, 1964–1968*, vol. XIII, document 124, 17 January 1966.

104. Adrian Fisher and William Foster, memorandum of conversation, "Johnson's Letter to Khrushchev," 31 January 1966, folder 10, box 13, FP, GCML, 1–2.

105. McGeorge Bundy to Lyndon Johnson, "Kosygin's Letter on Nonproliferation Treaty," 23 January 1966, box 13, SF—Disarmament, NSF, LBJL.

106. Telegram from Bonn to Paris, "German Fears of an NPT," 29 January 1966, box 768, cote 517INVA, CADLC, 2.

107. Steve Cohn, *Too Cheap to Meter: An Economic and Philosophical Analysis of the Nuclear Dream* (Albany: State University of New York Press, 1997), 33.

108. CIA, "Disarmament Negotiations Resume in Geneva," report, 28 January 1966, box 13, SF—Disarmament, NSF, LBJL, 8.

109. ENDC/PV.242, 27 January 1966, 9–10.

110. *Pacem in Terris: Encyclical Letter of His Holiness Pope John XXIII* (Washington, DC: National Catholic Welfare Conference, 1963).

111. CIA, "Disarmament Negotiations Resume in Geneva," 8.

112. P. O. Alphand, telegram from Paris to Geneva, "Meeting with Foster," 26 January 1966, box 768, cote 517INVA, CADLC.

113. McGeorge Bundy to the president, memorandum, "Chairman Kosygin's Message of February 2 to ENDC," 2 February 1966, box 13, SF-Disarmament, NSF, LBJL.

114. Telegram from Beijing to Paris, "*The People's Daily* Attacks the Soviets," 31 January 1966, box 768, cote 517INVA, CADLC.

115. ENDC/PV.242, 22 February 1966, 6–7.

116. Adrian Fisher and William Foster, memorandum of conversation, 10 February 1966, folder 10, box 13, FP, GCML.

117. William Foster and Semyon Tsarapkin, memorandum of conversation, "New U.S. Draft Language," 14 February 1966, folder 10, box 13, FP, GCML, 2.

118. Handwritten notes, 17 February 1966, box 17, FP, GCML.

119. Betty Goetz Lall, memorandum of conversation, "Indian Attitudes Toward Nuclear Weapons," 14 October 1965, box 129, CF—India, NSF, LBJL.

120. "Excerpt of an Indian Document on Chinese Nuclear Delivery Capability," January 1966, History and Public Policy Program Digital Archive, Françoise Rey collection, http://digitalarchive.wilsoncenter.org/document/155181 (accessed 14 June 2018).

121. Indian embassy in Beijing to foreign secretary, secret letter PEK/104/66, "China and the West," 9 January 1966, Digital Archive, History and Public Policy Program, Françoise Rey collection, http://digitalarchive.wilsoncenter.org/document/155180.

122. Telegram from London to Paris, "Du probleme nucléaire Indien," 16 February 1966, box 768, cote 517INVA, CADLC.

123. Telegram from Geneva to Paris, "Indian Position," 16 February 1966, box 768, cote 517INVA, CADLC.

124. ENDC/PV.240, 15 February 1966, 13.

125. Geneva, telegram to Paris, "Cavalletti's Address to the North Atlantic Council," 16 February 1966, box 768, cote 517INVA, CADLC.

126. Handwritten notes, 17 February 1966.

127. Bunn, *Arms Control by Committee*, 73.

128. Dean Rusk, testimony, 23 February 1966, JCAE, Hearings on Senate Resolution 179, "Nonproliferation of Nuclear Weapons," Eighty-Ninth Congress, Second Session (Washington: U.S. Government Printing Office, 1966), 3–30.

129. Glenn Seaborg, testimony, 1 March 1966, JCAE, 53.

130. Robert McNamara, testimony, 7 March 1966, JCAE, 73–93.

131. William Foster, testimony, 1 March 1966, JCAE, 37.

132. Priest, "From Hardware to Software," 154–155; Maddock, *Nuclear Apartheid*, 259; Francis J. Gavin, *Gold, Dollars, and Power: The Politics of International Monetary Relations, 1958–1971* (Chapel Hill: University of North Carolina Press, 2003).

133. *FRUS, 1964–1968*, vol. XI, document 121, 2 March 1966; Telegram from Geneva to Washington, "ENDC Daily Summary and German Obstructionism," 17 March 1966, box 13, SF—Disarmament, NSF, LBJL, 1.

134. Matthias Küntzel, *Bonn and the Bomb: German Politics and the Nuclear Option* (London: Pluto Press, 1995); telegram from Bonn to Paris, "Lunch with German Rep to NATO, M. Schnippenkoetter," 3 March 1966, box 768, cote 517INVA, CADLC, 1.

135. *FRUS, 1964–1968*, vol. XI, document 119, 20 February 1966, 304; "Atom Pact Proviso Denied by Russians," *New York Times*, 22 June 1966, 6. ProQuest Historical Newspapers.

136. Ambassador Arthur J. Goldberg, statement before General Assembly Committee I (Political and Security), 17 December 1966, reprinted in *Department of State Bulletin* 56, (1967), 80, quoted in Francis Lyall and Paul B. Larsen, eds., *Space Law* (Burlington, VT: Ashgate, 2007), 151–188.

137. ENDC/PV.265, 16 June 1966, 9.

138. National Intelligence Estimate 23–66, "West German Capabilities and Intentions to Produce and Deploy Nuclear Weapons," 28 April 1966, Secret, excised copy, https://nsarchive2.gwu.edu//dc.html?doc=4415112-Document-11-National-Intelligence-Estimate-23-66.

139. "Nasser Cites Need for Nuclear Arms," *New York Times*, 9 May 1966, 8. ProQuest Historical Newspapers; Avner Cohen, *Israel and the Bomb* (New York: Columbia University Press, 1998), z233.

140. Jayita Sarkar, "The Making of a Non-aligned Nuclear Power: India's Proliferation Drift, 1964–8," *International History Review* 37, no. 5 (20 October 2015): 933–950.

141. *FRUS, 1964–1968*, vol. XI, document 135, 7 June 1966.

142. Adrian Fisher to Committee of Principals, memorandum, "Proposed Revisions of Draft Non-proliferation Treaty," 8 July 1966, box 56, NSC Histories—NPT, NSF, LBJL; Bunn, *Arms Control by Committee*, 75.

143. National Security Action Memorandum (NSAM) 351, "Indian Nuclear Weapons Problem," https://www.fas.org/irp/offdocs/nsam-lbj/nsam-351.htm (accessed 5 July 2018).

144. *FRUS, 1964–1968*, vol. XI, document 136, 9 June 1966; *FRUS, 1964–1968*, vol. XXV, document 359, 25 July 1966, and document 363, 1 August 1966.

145. ACDA records, Meeting of the Committee of Principals, 17 June 1966; telegram from Geneva to Washington, "Co-chairman Talks," 14 June 1966, box 56, NSC Histories—NPT, NSF, LBJL.

146. Fredrik Logevall, *Embers of War: The Fall of an Empire and the Making of America's Vietnam* (New York: Random House, 2012).

147. Mark Atwood Lawrence, *Assuming the Burden: Europe and the American Commitment to War in Vietnam* (Berkeley: University of California Press, 2005).

148. Michael E. Latham, *Modernization as Ideology: American Social Science and "Nation Building" in the Kennedy Era* (Chapel Hill: University of North Carolina Press, 2000); Michael

Hunt, *Lyndon Johnson's War: America's Cold War Crusade in Vietnam, 1945–1968* (New York: Hill and Wang, 2011).

149. Christian G. Appy, *Working-Class War: American Combat Soldiers and Vietnam* (Chapel Hill: University of North Carolina Press, 1993); Randall Woods, *J. William Fulbright: Vietnam, and the Search for a Cold War Foreign Policy* (New York: Cambridge University Press, 1998).

150. Bill Moyers to Lyndon Johnson, letter, "UN Speech in San Francisco," 21 June 1965, box 11, Bill Moyers files, LBJL.

151. Bill Moyers to the president, memorandum, "The Underdeveloped World and the U.N.," 24 June 1965, box 11, Bill Moyers files, LBJL.

152. Henry Owen to Bill Moyers and Richard Goodwin, memorandum, "President's San Francisco Speech," 22 June 1965, box 11, Bill Moyers files, LBJL.

153. Lyndon Johnson, "Address in San Francisco at the 20th Anniversary Commemorative Session of the United Nations," 25 June 1965, http://www.presidency.ucsb.edu/ws/index.php?pid=27054.

154. Bill Moyers to the president, memorandum, "Nuclear Test Ban Treaty," 23 September 1964, 2; memorandum to the president, 15 August 1964; memorandum to the president, "American Pride in the U.N.," 21 June 1965, box 11, Bill Moyers files, LBJL, 1.

155. Hayes Redmon to Bill Moyers, memorandum, "President in Bad Shape," 9 June 1966, box 12, Bill Moyers files, LBJL, 1.

156. *FRUS, 1964–1968*, vol. XI, document 131, 25 May 1966; William Foster to the president, memorandum, "New Language for Non-proliferation Treaty," undated, box 8, RG 383-ACDA, NARA II, [169].

157. JCS to the secretary of defense, memorandum, "Nonproliferation Treaty," 29 June 1966, box 8, RG 383-ACDA, NARA II.

158. Hayes Redmon to Bill Moyers, memorandum, "Fred Dutton and Peace Issue," 9 June 1966, box 12, Bill Moyers files, LBJL.

159. Bill Moyers to the president, memorandum, "Non-proliferation Treaty," 17 July 1966, box 16, Handwriting file, June 1966—August 1966, LBJL.

160. Bill Moyers to the president, memorandum, "MLF Club at State," 29 July 1966, box 12, Bill Moyers files, LBJL, 2; William Foster to Bill Moyers, memorandum, "Cover Sheet for Memorandum: Achievement of a Non-proliferation Agreement," 20 July 1966, box 8, NPT, DOF, RG 383, NARA II.

161. Moyers to the president, memorandum, 17 July 1966.

162. On George Ball's skepticism toward Vietnam, see Fredrik Logevall, *Choosing War: The Lost Chance for Peace and the Escalation of War in Vietnam* (Berkeley: University of California Press, 2001), 173–175; Moyers to the president, memorandum, 29 July 1966.

163. Telegram from Geneva to Washington, "Soviets on New Language and the Permissibility of Alliance Nuclear Consultations," undated; and "Impressions of a Non-proliferation Treaty That Might Be Negotiable with the Soviet Union," 25 August 1966, box 56, Histories—NPT, NSF, LBJL.

164. Roger Tubby, cable, "Weiler and Cheprov Discuss Article I," 4 August 1966, box 8, RG 383-ACDA, NARA.

165. J. M. Vorontsov and George Bunn, memorandum of conversation, "MLF and NPT," 9 September 1966, box 13, SF—Disarmament, NSF, LBJL.

166. Küntzel, *Bonn and the Bomb*, 52–53.

167. *FRUS, 1964–1998*, vol. XIII, document 207, 26 September 1966.

168. *FRUS, 1964–1968*, vol. XIII, document 229, 16 December 1966.

169. *Der Spiegel*, 1967, no. 10.

170. Quoted in James Reston, "United Nations: U Thant's Gloomy Conclusion," *New York Times*, 21 September 1966, 46. ProQuest Historical Newspapers.

171. *FRUS, 1964–1968*, vol. XI, document 152, 22 September 1966; Andrei Gromyko and Dean Rusk, memorandum of conversation, "Non-proliferation of Nuclear Weapons, 21st UNGA Session," 28 October 1966, CWIHP, translated by Angela Greenfield.

172. *FRUS, 1964–1968*, vol. XI, document 153, 24 September 1966.

173. *FRUS, 1964–1968*, vol. XI, document 153, 24 September 1966, footnote 3; Gromyko and Rusk, memorandum of conversation, 28 October 1966.

174. Bunn, *Arms Control by Committee*, 78; Hayes Redmon to Bill Moyers, memorandum, "ACDA Morale," 4 October 1966, box 12, Bill Moyers files, LBJL.

175. Gromyko and Rusk, memorandum of conversation, 28 October 1966.

176. *FRUS, 1964–1968*, vol. XI, document 154, 3 October 1966; "Eisenhower Would Not Bar Atom War in Vietnam," *New York Times*, 4 October 1966. ProQuest Historical Newspapers.

177. "President's Speech on Improving Relations with Eastern Europe to the National Conference of Editorial Writers," transcript, *New York Times*, 8 October 1966, 12.

178. "The Polish-Soviet Talks in Moscow Between Brezhnev and Gomulka, 10–15 October 1966," trans. Malgorzata K. Gnoinska, Sino-Soviet Relations Document Collection, CWIHP, in Andrzej Paczkowski, ed., *Tajne Dokumenty Biura Politycznego PRL-ZSRR, 1956–1970* (London: Aneks, 1996).

179. "The Polish-Soviet Talks in Moscow Between Brezhnev and Gomulka, 10–15 October 1966."

180. *FRUS, 1964–1968*, vol. XI, document 157, 10 October 1966.

181. *FRUS, 1964–1968*, vol. XI, document 158, 10 October 1966.

182. Hayes Redmon to Bill Moyers, memorandum, "*Washington Post* Headline 'Impasse on A-Weapon Spread Broken,'" 11 October 1966, box 12, Bill Moyers files, LBJL.

183. "U.N. Told of Gain on Nuclear Pact," *New York Times*, 21 October 1966, 1. ProQuest Historical Newspapers.

184. Plenum of the Presidium of the Central Committee of the CPSU, 12–13 December 1966, roll 137, delo 49–1, Russian State Archive of Contemporary History, Harvard Library microfilm, 2.

185. Plenum of the Presidium of the CCP of the CPSU, 12–13 December 1966, 12–14, 17, 22–24; Jeremy Friedman, *Shadow Cold War: The Sino-Soviet Competition for the Third World* (Chapel Hill: University of North Carolina Press, 2018), 148–150; James Hershberg, *Marigold: The Lost Chance for Peace in Vietnam* (Stanford, CA: Stanford University Press, 2014).

186. Plenum of the Presidium of the CCP of the CPSU, 12–13 December 1966, 16–17.

187. Plenum of the Presidium of the CCP of the CPSU, 12–13 December 1966, 39.

188. Glenn Seaborg, *Stemming the Tide: Arms Control in the Johnson Years* (Lexington, MA: Lexington Books, 1987), 195.

189. In Küntzel's estimation, "the heart of the agreement lay in the absence of precision." *Bonn and the Bomb*, 59–60.

190. ENDC/PV.265, 16 June 1966, 9.

191. "U.S. and Russia Alter Atom Plea: Accept Neutrals' Draft of Resolution in U.N.," *New York Times*, 26 October 1966, 3. ProQuest Historical Newspapers.

CHAPTER 7

Portions of this chapter were published previously. These portions are copyright © 2017 from "Mexican Nuclear Diplomacy, the Latin American Nuclear-Weapon-Free Zone, & the NPT Grand Bargain, 1962–1968" by Jonathan Hunt, in *Negotiating the Nuclear Non-Proliferation*

Treaty: The Making of a Nuclear Order, edited by Andreas Wenger, Roland Popp, and Liviu Horovitz (New York: Routledge, 2017). Reproduced by permission of Taylor and Francis Group, LLC, a division of Informa PLC.

1. ENDC/PV.287, 21 February 1967, 19.

2. The literature on the Treaty of Tlatelolco is small but growing: Ryan A. Musto, "'A Desire So Close to the Hearts of All Latin Americans': Utopian Ideals and Imperfections Behind Latin America's Nuclear Weapon Free Zone: Latin America's Nuclear Weapon Free Zone," *Bulletin of Latin American Research* 37, no. 2 (April 2018): 160–74; Mónica Serrano, *Common Security in Latin America: The 1967 Treaty of Tlatelolco* (London: Institute of Latin American Studies, 1992); John R. Redick, "Nuclear Illusions: Argentina and Brazil," Occasional Paper (Washington, DC: Henry L. Stimson Center, December 1995), based on "The Politics of Denuclearization: A Study of the Treaty for the Prohibition of Nuclear Weapons in Latin America," dissertation, University of Virginia, 1970; David S. Robinson, "The Treaty of Tlatelolco and the United States: A Latin American Nuclear Free Zone," *American Journal of International Law* 64, no. 2 (1970): 282–309; Elias David Morales Martínez, "La Experiéncia de Tlatelolco: Um Estudo do Regime Latino-Americano e Caribenho de Proscrição de Armas Nucleares, 1963–2008," dissertation, Universidade de São Paulo, 2008). For Spanish- and English-language collections of contemporaneous speeches and draft treaties, respectively, see Alfonso García Robles, *El Tratado de Tlatelolco: Génesis, Alcance Y Propósition de la Proscripción de Las Armas Nucleares en la América Latina* (México: El Colegio de México, 1967), and *The Denuclearization of Latin America*, trans. Marjorie Urquidi (Carnegie Endowment for International Peace, 1967).

3. Stephen G. Rabe, *The Killing Zone: The United States Wages Cold War in Latin America* (New York: Oxford University Press, 2012); Lars Schoultz, *Beneath the United States: A History of U.S. Policy Toward Latin America* (Cambridge, MA: Harvard University Press, 1998).

4. Hal Brands, *Latin America's Cold War* (Cambridge, MA: Harvard University Press, 2010).

5. James G. Hershberg, "The United States, Brazil, and the Cuban Missile Crisis, 1962 (Part 1)," *Journal of Cold War Studies* 6, no. 2 (April 2004): 3–20, and "The United States, Brazil, and the Cuban Missile Crisis, 1962 (Part 2)," *Journal of Cold War Studies* 6, no. 3 (July 2004): 5–67.

6. Renata Keller, "The Latin American Missile Crisis," *Diplomatic History*, 17 March 2015: 195–222.

7. Roland Popp, Liviu Horovitz, and Andreas Wenger, eds., *Negotiating the Nuclear Non-Proliferation Treaty: Origins of the Nuclear Order* (New York: Routledge, 2017); Tony Smith, "New Bottles for New Wine: A Pericentric Framework for the Study of the Cold War," *Diplomatic History* 24, no. 4 (Fall 2000): 567–551; Max Paul Friedman, "Retiring the Puppets, Bringing Latin America Back In: Recent Scholarship on United States-Latin American Relations," *Diplomatic History* 27, no. 5 (November 2003): 621–636.

8. Sergio Duarte, UN High Representative for Disarmament Affairs, statement, "Commemoration of the 45th Anniversary of the Signing of the Treaty of Tlatelolco," Mexico City, Mexico, 14 February 2012, http://www.un.org/disarmament/HomePage/HR/docs/2012/2012-02-14-Opanal-Mexico.pdf.

9. Graham Allison, *Essence of Decision: Explaining the Cuban Missile Crisis* (New York: HarperCollins, 1971). For international sources, see James G. Hershberg and Christian F. Ostermann, eds., "The Global Cuban Missile Crisis: New Evidence from Behind the Iron, Bamboo, and Sugarcane Curtains, and Beyond," *CWIHP Bulletin* 17/18 (Fall 2012): 135–298.

10. Serrano, *Common Security in Latin America*, 11–18; John R. Redick, "The Politics of Denuclearization: A Study of the Treaty for the Prohibition of Nuclear Weapons in Latin America," PhD dissertation, University of Virginia, 92–93.

11. Keller, "The Latin American Missile Crisis," 195.

12. Keller, "The Latin American Missile Crisis," 196–199.

13. Hershberg, "The United States, Brazil, and the Cuban Missile Crisis, 1962," parts 1 and 2. For summaries of the evolving source base for the crisis, see James G. Hershberg, "Anatomy of a Controversy: Anatoly F. Dobrynin's Meeting with Robert F. Kennedy," *CWIHP Bulletin* 5 (Spring 1995): 75, 77–80; "More on Bobby and the Cuban Missile Crisis," *CWIHP Bulletin* 8/9 (Winter 1996/1997): 274, 344–347; James G. Blight and David A. Welch, *On the Brink: Americans and Soviets Reexamine the Cuban Missile Crisis*, 2nd ed. (New York: Noonday, 1990), 83–84.

14. "Telegram from Brazilian Embassy in Washington (Campos), 1 p.m., Tuesday," 23 October 1962, History and Public Policy Program Digital Archive, MD—Washington—Telgr.-Cartas—Receb.-Exped.—1962 (7 á XII), (Cx 324), Ministry of External Relations Archives, Brasília, Brazil, translated from Portuguese by James G. Hershberg, http://digitalarchive.wilsoncenter.org/document/115292.

15. "Telegram from Mexican Foreign Ministry to Mexican Embassy, Rio de Janeiro," 23 October 1962, History and Public Policy Program Digital Archive, Archivo Histórico Diplomático Genaro Estrada, Secretaría de Relaciones Exteriores, Mexico City, obtained by James G. Hershberg, translated by Eduardo Baudet and Tanya Harmer, http://digitalarchive.wilsoncenter.org/document/115199.

16. Adam Rapacki, "The Polish Plan for a Nuclear-Free Zone Today," *International Affairs* 39, no. 1 (January 1963): 1–12.

17. Harlan Cleveland, cable, "Operation Raincoat," 26 October 1962; US Department of State, memorandum, "Evaluation of Brazilian Denuclearization Proposal," 26 October 1962, The Cuban Missile Crisis Revisited, Digital National Security Archive [DNSA].

18. ACDA, "Latin American Nuclear-Free Zone," report, DDRS, CK3100019048, 2–3.

19. Roger Hilsman, memorandum, "Probable Soviet Attitude Toward Regional Denuclearization Proposals"; and U.S. Joint Chiefs of Staff [US JCS], memorandum, "Nuclear-Free or Missile-Free Zones," 26 October 1962, Cuban Missile Crisis Revisited, DNSA.

20. Quoted in Hershberg, "The United States, Brazil, and the Cuban Missile Crisis, 1962 (Part 2)," 49.

21. "Telegram from Yugoslav Embassy in Rio de Janeiro (Barišić) to Yugoslav Foreign Ministry," 26 October 1962, History and Public Policy Program Digital Archive, Archive of the Ministry of Foreign Affairs [AMIP], Belgrade, Serbia, PA (Confidential Archive) 1962, Kuba, folder F-67. obtained by Svetozar Rajak and Ljubomir Dimić and translated by Radina Vučetić-Mladenović, http://digitalarchive.wilsoncenter.org/document/115461.

22. "Telegram from Yugoslav Embassy in Rio de Janeiro (Barišić) to Yugoslav Foreign Ministry," 24 October 1962, History and Public Policy Program Digital Archive, AMIP, Belgrade, Serbia, PA (Confidential Archive) 1962, Kuba, folder F-67, obtained by Svetozar Rajak and Ljubomir Dimić and translated by Radina Vučetić-Mladenović, http://digitalarchive.wilsoncenter.org/document/115455; "Telegram from the Brazilian Embassy in Havana (Bastian Pinto), 6 p.m., Friday," 26 October 1962, History and Public Policy Program Digital Archive, "ANEXO Secreto—600.(24h)—SITUAÇÃO POLITICA—OUTUBRO DE 1962//," Ministry of External Relations Archives, Brasília, Brazil, translated from Portuguese by James G. Hershberg, http://digitalarchive.wilsoncenter.org/document/115303.

23. A. A. Fursenko, *One Hell of a Gamble: Khrushchev, Castro, and Kennedy, 1958–1964* (New York: Norton, 1997), 272–273.

24. "Telegram from the Brazilian Embassy in Washington (Campos), 5 p.m., Wednesday," 24 October 1962, History and Public Policy Program Digital Archive, MD—Washington—Telgr.-Cartas—Receb.-Exped.—1962 (7 á XII), (Cx 324), Ministry of External Relations Archives, Brasília, Brazil, translated from Portuguese by James G. Hershberg, http://digitalarchive.wilsoncenter.org/document/115294.

25. "Telegram from the Brazilian Delegation at the UN General Assembly, New York, 2:30 p.m., Friday," 9 November 1962, History and Public Policy Program Digital Archive, "600. (24h)—SITUAÇÃO POLITICA—CUBA de novembro a dezembre de 1.962//6223," Ministry of External Relations Archives, Brasília, Brazil, translated from Portuguese by James G. Hershberg, http://digitalarchive.wilsoncenter.org/document/115374.

26. "Brazilian Embassy in Washington, Analysis of the Cuban Missile Crisis," 1 November 1962, History and Public Policy Program Digital Archive, Maço, "600.(24h)—SITUAÇÃO POLITICA—CUBA de novembro a dezembro de 1,962//6223," Ministry of External Relations Archives, Brasília, Brazil, translated from Portuguese by James G. Hershberg, http:// digitalarchive.wilsoncenter.org/document/115316.

27. "Telegram from Yugoslav Embassy in Rio (Barišić) to Yugoslav Foreign Ministry," 30 October 1962, History and Public Policy Program Digital Archive, AMIP, Belgrade, Serbia, PA (Confidential Archive) 1962, Kuba, folder F-67, obtained by Svetozar Rajak and Ljubomir Dimić and translated by Radina Vučetić-Mladenović, http://digitalarchive.wilsoncenter.org/ document/115479.

28. "Telegram from Yugoslav Foreign Ministry to Yugoslav Embassies in Havana and Washington and Yugoslav Mission to the United Nations," 29 October 1962, History and Public Policy Program Digital Archive, AMIP, Belgrade, Serbia, PA (Confidential Archive) 1962, Kuba, folder F-67, obtained by Svetozar Rajak and Ljubomir Dimić and translated by Radina Vučetić-Mladenović, http://digitalarchive.wilsoncenter.org/document/115472.

29. "Telegram from Yugoslav Embassy in Rio de Janeiro (Barišić) to Yugoslav Foreign Ministry," 31 October 1962, History and Public Policy Program Digital Archive, AMIP, Belgrade, Serbia, PA (Confidential Archive) 1962, Kuba, folder F-67, obtained by Svetozar Rajak and Ljubomir Dimić and translated by Radina Vučetić-Mladenović, http://digitalarchive.wilson center.org/document/115484.

30. ACDA, "Latin American Nuclear-Free Zone," 4–5.

31. Vincente Sáncez Gavito to Manuel Tello, letter, "White House Meeting re Cuba," 14 November 1962, Secretaría de Relaciones Exteriores [SRE], Mexico, in Hershberg and Ostermann, eds., "The Global Cuban Missile Crisis," pp. 210–212.

32. "Cables from Cuban Foreign Minister Raúl Roa to Cuban Mission to the United Nations (Lechuga), New York," 11 November 1962, History and Public Policy Program Digital Archive, Provided by the Cuban Government for the October 2002 Havana conference ("La Crisis de Octubre: Una vision politica 40 años despues") organized by the National Security Archive, translated from Spanish for CWIHP by Chris Dunlap, http://digitalarchive.wilson center.org/document/115165.

33. ACDA, "Latin American Nuclear-Free Zone," 12.

34. Hershberg, "The United States, Brazil, and the Cuban Missile Crisis, 1962 (Part 2)," 57–58.

35. "Cable from Cuban Foreign Minister Raúl Roa to Cuban Mission to the United Nations (Lechuga), New York," 20 November 1962, History and Public Policy Program Digital Archive, Provided by the Cuban Government for the October 2002 Havana conference ("La Crisis de Octubre: Una vision politica 40 años despues") organized by the National Security Archive, translated from Spanish for CWIHP by Chris Dunlap, http://digitalarchive.wilsoncenter.org/document/115166.

36. Memorandum of conversation, "LA Atom Free Zone" (Secret), 30 November 1962, 1:00–3:40 p.m., in NA, RG 59, Secretary and Under Secretary's Memoranda of Conversations, 1953–1964, box 25, "Oct. 1–5 1962 to January 1963," Lot 65D330, Entry 1566, quoted in Hershberg, "The United States, Brazil, and the Cuban Missile Crisis, 1962 (Part 2)," 58.

37. "Telegram from the Brazilian Embassy in Washington (Campos), 9 p.m., Friday," 16 November 1962, History and Public Policy Program Digital Archive, "600.(24h)—SITUAÇÃO

POLITICA—CUBA de novembro a dezembre de 1.962//6223," Ministry of External Relations Archives, Brasília, Brazil, translated from Portuguese by James G. Hershberg, http://digitalarchive.wilsoncenter.org/document/115388.

38. UN General Assembly, transcript, 1335th Meeting, 13 November 1963, 122.

39. Redick, "Nuclear Illusions."

40. "Telegram from the Brazilian Delegation at the United Nations, New York, 8 p.m., Friday," 2 November 1962, History and Public Policy Program Digital Archive, "600.(24h)—SITUAÇÃO POLITICA—CUBA de novembro a dezembre de 1.962//6223," Ministry of External Relations Archives, Brasília, Brazil, translated from Portuguese by James G. Hershberg, http://digitalarchive.wilsoncenter.org/document/115358.

41. Carlo Patti, *Brazil in the Global Nuclear Order, 1945–2018* (Baltimore: Johns Hopkins University Press, 2022).

42. Miguel Marín Bosch, "Alfonso García Robles: Una Entrevista," in Alfonso García Robles and Miguel Marín Bosch, *Armas Nucleares, Desarme y Carrera Armamentista* (México: Ediciones Gernika, 1985), 25. Translations from Spanish by Jonathan Hunt. Key works that discuss Latin America's outsized influence on international institutions, law, and norms in the decades after the Second World War include Kathryn Sikkink, "Latin America's Protagonist Role in Human Rights," *Sur International Journal of Human Rights* 12, no. 22 (December 2015): 207–219; Steven L. B. Jensen, *The Making of International Human Rights: The 1960s, Decolonization, and the Reconstruction of Global Values* (Cambridge, UK: Cambridge University Press, 2017); and Christopher R. W. Dietrich, *Oil Revolution: Sovereign Rights and the Economic Culture of Decolonization, 1945 to 1979* (New York: Cambridge University Press, 2017); Rogério de Souza Farias, *O Brasil e as Origens das Negociações Comerciais Multilaterais (1946–1967)* (Campina Grande, Brazil: EDUEPB, 2017); Patrick William Kelly, *Sovereign Emergencies: Latin America and the Making of Global Human Rights Politics* (New York: Cambridge University Press, 2018); and Christy Thornton, *Revolution in Development: Mexico and the Governance of the Global Economy* (Berkeley: University of California Press, 2021).

43. Bosch, "Alfonso García Robles: Una Entrevista," 15–32.

44. Biographical information about García Robles from García Robles and Bosch, *Armas Nucleares, Desarme y Carrera Armamentista: Homenaje a Alfonso García Robles*, 15–32; Fernando Solana, *Alfonso García Robles, Diplomático Ejemplar* (México: Secretaría de Relaciones Exteriores, 1990).

45. Alfonso García Robles, *Le panaméricanisme et la politique de bon voisinage* (Paris: Les Éditions Internationales, 1938). For an intellectual and political history of anticolonial appeals for sovereign states to own and control territorial natural resources, see Dietrich, *Oil Revolution*.

46. Alfonso García Robles, *La Question du Pétrole au Mexique et le Droit International* (Paris: Les Éditions Internationales, 1939).

47. Simon Collier, "Simón Bolivar as Political Thinker," in David Bushnell and Lester D. Langley, eds., *Simón Bolivar: Essays on the Life and Legacy of the Liberator* (Lanham, MD: Rowman and Littlefield, 2008), 13–35. The second chapter of John Lynch's biography is illuminating: *Simón Bolivar: A Life* (New Haven, CT: Yale University Press, 2006), 22–39. Also see Michael Zeuske, *Simón Bolivar: History and Myth* (Princeton, NJ: Markus Wiener, 2013).

48. "Benito Juárez," Encyclopaedia of World Biography, http://www.notablebiographies.com/Jo-Ki/Ju-rez-Benito.html.

49. García Robles, *The Denuclearization of Latin America*, xx–xxi.

50. García Robles, *The Denuclearization of Latin America*, xxi.

51. Bosch, "Alfonso García Robles: Una Entrevista," 28.

52. Albert Camus, "Speech of Acceptance upon the Award of the Nobel Prize for Literature, Delivered in Stockholm on the Tenth of December, 1957," in Clifton Fadiman, ed., *Fifty Years* (New York: Knopf, 1965), 723; Solana, *Alfonso García Robles*, 3.

53. Serrano, *Common Security in Latin America*, 23.

54. "Speech Delivered at the 1333rd Meeting of the First Committee of the UNGA on 11 November 1963," in García Robles, *The Denuclearization of Latin America*, 4.

55. "Speech Delivered at the 1333rd Meeting of the First Committee of the UNGA on 11 November 1963," in García Robles, *The Denuclearization of Latin America*, 4.

56. Serrano, *Common Security in Latin America*, 26.

57. US JCS, memorandum 849–63, "Latin American Nuclear Free Zone," 1 November 1963, cited in ACDA, "Latin American Nuclear-Free Zone," 5–6.

58. Circular airgram CA-5253, 17 November 1963, confidential, quoted in ACDA, "Latin American Nuclear-Free Zone," 7.

59. Circular airgram CA-5253, 17 November 1963; ACDA, circular airgram to Mexico City, "Meeting Proposed by Mexico to Discuss Denuclearization of Latin America," 17 November 1964, box 58, Cables, CF—Mexico, NSF, LBJL.

60. Bosch, "Alfonso García Robles: Una Entrevista," 24–25; Fulton Freeman to Dean Rusk, telegram, "Embassy Comments and Recommendations," 21 May 1964, box 58, CF—Mexico, NSF, LBJL.

61. ACDA, circular airgram to Mexico City, "Meeting Proposed by Mexico to Discuss Denuclearization of Latin America," 17 November 1964.

62. Renata Keller, *Mexico's Cold War: Cuba, the United States, and the Legacy of the Mexican Revolution* (New York: Cambridge University Press, 2015); *FRUS, 1964–1968*, vol. XI, 12 August 1964, document 42.

63. ACDA, *Documents on Disarmament, 1963* (Washington, DC: U.S. Government Printing Office, 1964), 582–583.

64. "Speech Delivered at the 1265th Plenary Meeting of the General Assembly of the United Nations on 27 November 1963," in García Robles, *The Denuclearization of Latin America*, 18–20.

65. Memorandum of conversation, February 21, 1964, CF—LA-Honduras, NSC, LBJL.

66. Adrian Fisher to Principals Committee, memorandum, "Position Paper on Nuclear Free Zones, (U)," 30 July 1965, quoted in ACDA, "Latin American Nuclear-Free Zone," 11–13, 22–23.

67. Serrano, *Common Security in Latin America*, 27.

68. Stephen G. Rabe, *Eisenhower and Latin America: The Foreign Policy of Anticommunism* (Chapel Hill: University of North Carolina Press, 1988); Greg Grandin, *The Last Colonial Massacre: Latin America in the Cold War* (Chicago: University of Chicago Press), 2011.

69. Brands, *Latin America's Cold War*.

70. Stephen Rabe, *The Most Dangerous Area in the World: John F. Kennedy Confronts Communist Revolution in Latin America* (Chapel Hill: University of North Carolina Press, 1999); Edwin M. Martin, *Kennedy and Latin America* (Lanham, MD: University Press of America, 1994); Serrano, *Common Security in Latin America*, 28–29.

71. Thompson Committee, draft statement, "U.S. Policy on the Denuclearization of Latin America, Africa, the Arab States and Israel," 4 February 1965, box 3, Spurgeon Keeny papers, NSF, LBJL.

72. "Speech Delivered at the Closing Meeting of the First Session of the Preparatory Commission for the Denuclearization of Latin America on 22 March 1965," in García Robles, *The Denuclearization of Latin America*, 38.

73. Francis J. Gavin, "Blasts from the Past: Proliferation Lessons from the 1960s," *International Security* 29, no. 3 (Winter 2004): 100–135.

74. ACDA, circular airgram to Mexico City, "Meeting Proposed by Mexico to Discuss Denuclearization of Latin America."

75. *FRUS, 1964–1968*, vol. XI, document 64, 21 January 1965.

76. García Robles, *The Denuclearization of Latin America*, 38.

77. Cited from Adolfo López Mateos's 21 March 1963 letter proposing a joint declaration in "Speech Delivered at the Opening Meeting of the Preliminary Meeting on the Denuclearization of Latin American on 23 November 1964," in García Robles, *The Denuclearization of Latin America*, 21.

78. "General Assembly: 16th Session, 1013rd Plenary Meeting," in García Robles, *The Denuclearization of Latin America*, 22.

79. García Robles, *The Denuclearization of Latin America*, 26.

80. Redick, "The Politics of Denuclearization," 32, 98, 106, 111–121, 193–196, 204–207, 219.

81. Fulton Freeman to Dean Rusk, cable, "Preparatory Commission on Latin American Denuclearization," 23 March 1965, box 58, CF—Mexico, NSF, LBJL, 1–2.

82. Freeman to Rusk, cable, 23 March 1965, 1–2.

83. Freeman to Rusk, cable, 23 March 1965, 1–3.

84. U.S. State Department, telegram, "IAEA Safeguards, Non-Proliferation, and Mexico," 22 September 1965, 3: "Draft LA nuclear-free zone treaty submitted 23 July 1965 to Preparatory Commission, calls for IAEA safeguards on all nuclear facilities. This draft unanimously approved by six-state working group, in which Mexican officials played leading role."

85. "Resolution 8," cited by García Robles in "Speech Delivered at the Closing Meeting of the Second Session of the Preparatory Commission, 2 September 1965," in Alfonso García Robles, *The Denuclearization of Latin America*, 43.

86. Quoted in Dean Rusk to Lyndon Johnson, memorandum, "U.S. Adherence to Protocol to Treaty Creating Latin American Nuclear Free Zone," 12 February 1968, DDRS, Doc #CK3100146716, 1–2.

87. US Mission to the United Nations, telegram 5166, 29 June 1965, in ACDA, "Latin American Nuclear-Free Zone," 16.

88. This was not unprecedented. García Robles had sent a telegram to the Cuban foreign minister before the first COPREDAL the year before. Redick, "The Politics of Denuclearization," 135–136.

89. Dean Rusk and Antonio Carrillo Flores, memorandum of conversation, 7 October 1965, box 58, CF—Mexico, NSF, LBJL, 1.

90. US JCS, memorandum 263–65, "Possible US Public Statements on Denuclearization of Certain Areas," 9 April 1965, quoted in ACDA, "Latin American Nuclear-Free Zone," 21.

91. Adrian Fisher, Position Paper to Committee of Principals, "Nuclear Free Zones, (U)," 30 July 1965, quoted in ACDA, "Latin American Nuclear-Free Zone," 21–25.

92. ACDA, *Documents on Disarmament, 1965* (Washington, DC: U.S. Government Printing Office, 1966), 535–536, quoted in ACDA, "Latin American Nuclear-Free Zone," 27.

93. Rusk and Carrillo Flores, memorandum of conversation, 1.

94. Fulton Freeman to Dean Rusk, cable, "Brazilian and Argentinian Reluctance to Move Forward with LANFZ," 9 December 1965, box 59, CF—Mexico, NSF, LBJL.

95. Robert Smith to Spurgeon Keeny Jr., draft telegram to Mexico City, Rio de Janeiro, Buenos Aires, and New York, "LA NFZ," 17 December 1965, box 3, Spurgeon Keeny papers, NSF, LBJL, 1.

96. ACDA, "Latin American Nuclear-Free Zone," 24; ACDA, circular airgram to Mexico City, "Meeting Proposed by Mexico to Discuss Denuclearization of Latin America."

97. Memorandum of conversation, "LA NWFZ," 25–28 April 1966, box 4, Spurgeon Keeny papers, NSF, LBJL, 1–2.

98. Willard F. Barber, Spurgeon Keeny Jr., and William G. Bowdler, memorandum of conversations, "LA NFZ," 25–28 April 1966, box 4, Spurgeon Keeny papers, NSF, LBJL, 1–2.

99. Redick, "Nuclear Illusions."

100. Redick, "Nuclear Illusions."

101. William Foster and Sérgio Corrêa da Costa, memorandum of conversation, 12 December 1966, cited in ACDA, "Latin American Nuclear-Free Zone," 33–34.

102. ACDA, "Latin American Nuclear-Free Zone," 34–38.

103. Leonard Meeker to Dean Rusk, memorandum, 10 February 1967, quoted in ACDA, "Latin American Nuclear-Free Zone," 37.

104. Fulton Freeman to Dean Rusk, cable, telegram 4484 (1), 13 February 1967, quoted in ACDA, "Latin American Nuclear-Free Zone," 38.

105. Dean Rusk, cable 127754, "Non-Proliferation Treaty Safeguards Article," 30 January 1967, National Archives, Record Group 59, DEF 18-6, 2-6, National Security Archive, http://www.gwu.edu/~nsarchiv/nukevault/ebb253/doc03.pdf.

106. ACDA, *Documents on Disarmament, 1967* (Washington, DC: U.S. Government Printing Office, 1968), 65.

107. Scott Kaufman, *Project Plowshare: The Peaceful Use of Nuclear Explosives in Cold War America* (Ithaca, NY: Cornell University Press, 2013).

108. Glenn T. Seaborg, report, "Trip to Australia, Thailand, India, and Pakistan," 3–14 January 1967, box 14, Harold Saunders papers, NSF, LBJL.

109. Fulton Freeman to Dean Rusk et al., cable, "US Government Comment on LA NFZ Draft Proposals for García Robles," 28 August 1966, box 58, CF—Mexico, NSF, LBJL, 2; Trevor Findlay, *Nuclear Dynamite: The Peaceful Nuclear Explosions Fiasco* (Sydney: Pergamon Press Australia, 1990).

110. ACDA, *Documents on Disarmament, 1967*, 126–128, 140–143.

111. Adrian Fisher to Dean Rusk, memorandum, "Adherence of the US to the Protocols of the Treaty of Tlatelolco," 1 June 1967, in ACDA, "Latin American Nuclear-Free Zone," 43.

112. Mexican Secretariat of Foreign Affairs to William Foster, letter, 11 September 1967. Quoted in ACDA, "Latin American Nuclear-Free Zone," 44.

113. Dean Rusk to Lyndon Johnson, memorandum, "Latin American Nuclear Free Zone Treaty," 26 October 1967, confidential, quoted in ACDA, "Latin American Nuclear-Free Zone," 47.

114. Quoted in ACDA, "Latin American Nuclear-Free Zone," 50.

115. George H. Quester, *The Politics of Nuclear Proliferation* (Baltimore: Johns Hopkins University Press, 1973), 44.

116. George Bunn, *Arms Control by Committee: Managing Negotiations with the Russians* (Stanford, CA: Stanford University Press, 1992), 92.

117. *FRUS, 1964–1968*, vol. XI, 10 August 1967, document 201; "Les non alignés de Genève et la non proliferation," note, 20 October 1967, box 769, cote 517INVA, CADLC, 6–7.

118. ACDA, memorandum of conversation, Edward E. Tomkins, Adrian S. Fisher, et al., "NPT," 23 August 1967, Nuclear Nonproliferation Treaty [NPT], DNSA, http://www2.gwu.edu/~nsarchiv/nukevault/ebb253/doc05a.pdf.

119. U.S. Department of State, circular, "Aide-Memoire on the NPT," 24 August 1967, NPT, DNSA, 6–7, http://www2.gwu.edu/~nsarchiv/nukevault/ebb253/doc05b.pdf; "The Treaty of Tlatelolco," https://www.iaea.org/publications/documents/treaties/treaty-prohibition-nuclear-weapons-latin-america-tlatelolco-treaty (accessed 3 August 2018).

120. "Aide-Memoire on the NPT," 24 August 1967, 6–7.

121. ENDC/PV.331, 19 September 1967, 4–11.

122. ENDC/PV.331, 19 September 1967, 9–10; ACDA, *Documents on Disarmament, 1967*, 394–395.

123. Spurgeon Keeny to Dean Rusk, memorandum, "Report on the ENDC," 1 April 1969, box 5, Spurgeon Keeny files, NSF, LBJL.

124. "Les non alignés de Genève et la non proliferation," note, 20 October 1967, 2–3.

125. ACDA, *Documents on Disarmament, 1967*, 413–415.

126. Tom Johnson, notes, "Cabinet Meeting on 2 August 1967, 12:09 p.m. to 1:50 p.m.," 2 August 1967, box 1, Tom Johnson's notes of meetings, LBJL, 7–8.

127. Christopher R. W. Dietrich, "'Arab Oil Belongs to the Arabs': Raw Material Sovereignty, Cold War Boundaries, and the Nationalisation of the Iraq Petroleum Company, 1967–1973," *Diplomacy and Statecraft* 22, no. 3 (September 2011): 450–479.

128. Dean Rusk to Lyndon Johnson, memorandum, "Background on Treaty of Tlatelolco," 27 October 1967, DDRS, CK3100170489.

129. "Mexican Proposal on Creation of Nuclear-Free Zone in LA," 15 May 1967, opis 27, papka 55a, delo 12, listy 2–3, fond 110, Mexico, Foreign Policy Archive of the Russian Federation [AVPRF], translated by Michelle Paranzino.

130. Mexican ambassador and Adrian Fisher, memorandum of conversation, "US Adherence to Protocol II," 10 February 1968, DDRS, CK3100079612, 1–2.

131. Jonathan Hunt, "Mexican Nuclear Diplomacy and the NPT Grand Bargain, 1962–1968," in Popp, Horovitz, and Wenger, *Negotiating the Nuclear Non-Proliferation Treaty*, 178–202.

132. For the NPT regime as a product of superpower collusion, see Andrew J. Coe and Jane Vaynman, "Collusion and the Nuclear Nonproliferation Regime," *Journal of Politics* 77, no. 4 (October 2015): 983–997. Dane Swango downplays peaceful nuclear assistance in "The United States and the Role of Nuclear Co-Operation and Assistance in the Design of the Non-Proliferation Treaty," *International History Review* 36, no. 2 (March 2014): 210–229.

CHAPTER 8

1. Adrian Fisher, oral history, part 2, 7 November 1968, LBJL, 16.

2. Grégoire Mallard, *Fallout: Nuclear Diplomacy in an Age of Global Fracture* (Chicago: University of Chicago Press, 2014), 213–246.

3. Fulton Freeman to Dean Rusk et al., cable, "Latin American Nuclear-Free Zone," box 58, CF—Mexico, NSF, LBJL, 5.

4. Russell Fessenden to Dean Rusk, cable, "Non-Proliferation Treaty and EURATOM," 8 February 1967, box 1729, DEF 18–6, RG 59, NARA II, 2.

5. *FRUS, 1964–1968*, vol. XIV, document 196; Jenny Thompson and Sherry Thompson, *The Kremlinologist: Llewellyn E. Thompson, America's Man in Cold War Moscow* (Baltimore: Johns Hopkins University Press, 2018).

6. *FRUS, 1964–1968*, vol. XIV, document 197, 27 January 1967.

7. *FRUS, 1964–1968*, vol. XI, document 195, 15 April 1967.

8. Adrian S. Fisher, "Issues Involved in a Non-Proliferation Agreement," in Stephen Denis Kertesz, ed., *Nuclear Non-Proliferation in a World of Nuclear Powers* (Notre Dame, IN: University of Notre Dame Press, 1967).

9. Darryl A. Howlett, *EURATOM and Nuclear Safeguards* (Basingstoke, UK: Macmillan, 1990); Mallard, *Fallout*.

10. State Department to U.S. embassy in Bonn, cable 121338, "Non-Proliferation Treaty," 18 January 1967, National Archives, DEF 18–6, RG59, 1, made available by document 2, NPT, NSA, http://www.gwu.edu/~nsarchiv/nukevault/ebb253/doc02.pdf.

11. "Orders Rose in '66 for Atomic Plants," *New York Times*, 11 July 1967, 8. ProQuest Historical Newspapers.

12. Martin J. Hillebrand, reference telegram from Bonn to Washington, DC, "Non-Proliferation," 3 February 1967, box 10, Bator files, NSF, LBJL.

13. David Holloway, "The Soviet Union and the Creation of the International Atomic Energy Agency," *Cold War History* 16, no. 2 (2 April 2016): 177–193; Jacob Darwin Hamblin, "A Glaring Defect in the System: Nuclear Safeguards and the Invisibility of Technology," in Roland Popp, Liviu Horovitz, and Andreas Wenger, eds., *Negotiating the Nuclear Non-Proliferation Treaty: Origins of the Nuclear Order* (New York: Routledge, 2017).

14. Glenn Seaborg to Dean Rusk, memorandum, "Modifying the United States Approach to Article III of the NPT," in *Journal of Glenn T. Seaborg, Chairman, U.S. Atomic Energy Commission, 1961–1971*, vol. 14 (Lawrence Berkeley Laboratory, University of California, 1989), 272–275.

15. Dean Rusk, Cable 127754, "Non-Proliferation Treaty Safeguards Article," 30 January 1967, National Archives, DEF 18–6, RG 592–6, made available by document 3, NPT, NSA, http://www.gwu.edu/~nsarchiv/nukevault/ebb253/doc03.pdf.

16. Seaborg to Rusk, memorandum, 274; *FRUS, 1964–1968*, vol. XI, document 188, 4 March 1967.

17. European Atomic Forum, *Atom Information: German National Reports* (Florence: FORATOM, 1973); James Allen Cooney, "The Politics of Technological Choices: Business-State Relations and Nuclear Energy Policy-Making in West Germany," dissertation, Massachusetts Institute of Technology, 1982).

18. *FRUS, 1964–1968*, vol. XI, document 180, 8 February 1967; Helmut Alexy and Raymond Garthoff, memorandum of conversation, "Non-Proliferation," 10 February 1967, box 1729, DEF 18–6, RG 59, NARA II.

19. Fisher, oral history, part 2, 7 November 1968, 13; William Foster to Lyndon Johnson, memorandum, "Offer to Put U.S. Peaceful Nuclear Facilities Under IAEA Safeguards," 6 April 1967, 472; Albert Legault, *A Diplomacy of Hope: Canada and Disarmament, 1945–1988* (Montréal: McGill-Queen's University Press, 1992), 263, footnote 82.

20. *FRUS, 1964–1968*, vol. XI, document 194, 8 April 1967.

21. Martin Hillenbrand to Dean Rusk, cable, "Non-Proliferation and German Politics," 21 February 1967, box 1729, DEF 18–6, RG 59, NARA II.

22. Martin Hillenbrand to Dean Rusk, cable, "German Aide Memoire on NPT," 6 February 1967, box 1729, DEF 18–6, RG 59, NARA II, 1.

23. Cable from London to Washington, DC, "British Press on NPT," 21 February 1967, box 1729, DEF 18–6, RG 59, NARA II.

24. *FRUS, 1964–1968*, vol. XIII, document 239, 6 March 1967.

25. Spurgeon M. Keeny Jr. to Francis Bator, letter, "Something Good out of Germany for a Change," 17 February 1967, box 6, Spurgeon Keeny papers, NSF, LBJL, attached telegram.

26. Spurgeon M. Keeny Jr. to Walt Rostow, memorandum, "Lunch with Howard Simons, Chalmers Roberts, and Murrey Marder of the *Washington Post*," 19 April 1967, box 5, Spurgeon Keeny papers, NSF, LBJL.

27. *FRUS, 1964–1968*, vol. XIII, document 24, 11 March 1967.

28. *FRUS, 1964–1968*, vol. XI, document 198, 23 June 1967.

29. Jacques de Beaumarchais, telegram from Paris to Ottawa, "Canadian Request for Paris to Rejoin the 4 Western Powers in Consultations," 13 February 1967, box 769, cote 517INVA, CADLC.

30. *FRUS, 1964–1968*, vol. XI, document 199, 24 June 1967; N. Piers Ludlow, *The European Community and the Crises of the 1960s: Negotiating the Gaullist Challenge* (New York: Routledge, 2006).

31. Grégoire Mallard, "Can the Euratom Treaty Inspire the Middle East?: The Political Promises of Regional Nuclear Communities," *Nonproliferation Review* 15, no. 3 (November 2008): 470.

32. Howlett, *EURATOM and Nuclear Safeguards*.

33. Charles de Gaulle and Maurice Couve de Murville, memorandum of conversation, "Une traité de non-prolifération," 5 November 1966, CM8.1967, Maurice Couve de Murville papers [CM], Centre d'histoire contemporaine [CHC], Sciences Po.

34. Francis Perrin, "La politique étrangère française en matière d'armament atomique, particulièrement en ce qui concerne la prolifération de ces armements," 27 February 1967, CM8.1967, CHC, Sciences Po.

35. *FRUS, 1964–1968*, vol. XI, document 183, 25 February 1967.

36. Cable from London to Washington, DC, "German Anxieties re NPT," 17 February 1967, box 1729, DEF 18–6, RG 59, NARA II.

37. *FRUS, 1964–1968*, vol. XI, document 184, 26 February 1967.

38. ENDC/PV.288, 23 February 1967, 5.

39. ENDC/PV.289, 28 February 1967, 7–8.

40. ENDC/PV.289, 28 February 1967, 16.

41. George von Lilienfeld, Adrian Fisher, et al., memorandum of conversation, "Non-Proliferation Treaty," 22 February 1967, box 1729, DEF 18–6, RG 59, NARA II, 7.

42. *FRUS, 1964–1968*, vol. XI, document 195, 15 April 1967.

43. Howard Wriggins to Nicholas Katzenbach, memorandum, "Record of Action of SIG Meeting, February 14, 1967," 21 February 1967, box 14, Harold Saunders files, NSF, LBJL.

44. Robert B. Rakove, *Kennedy, Johnson, and the Nonaligned World* (Cambridge, UK: Cambridge University Press, 2013), 205.

45. This interpretation builds on Guy Laron's *The Six-Day War: The Breaking of the Middle East* (New Haven, CT: Yale University Press, 2017).

46. Howard Wriggins to Walt Rostow, memorandum, "India and the NPT," 15 March 1967, box 14, Harold Saunders files, NSF, LBJL.

47. Wriggins to Rostow, memorandum, "India and the NPT," 15 March 1967.

48. Howard Wriggins to Walt Rostow, memorandum, "Notes on Meetings in India, June 3–6, 1966," 12 July 1966, box 14, Harold Saunders files, NSF, LBJL.

49. Howard Wriggins to Walt Rostow, memorandum, "SIG recommendation regarding military policy toward India and Pakistan," 15 March 1967, box 14, Harold Saunders files, NSF, LBJL.

50. Walt Rostow to Lyndon Johnson, memorandum, "India and the Non-proliferation treaty—Prime Minister Gandhi's Special Envoy L. K. Jha," 28 March 1967, box 14, Harold Saunders files, NSF, LBJL.

51. Howard Wriggins to Walt Rostow, memorandum, "NPT and India," 23 March 1967, box 14, Harold Saunders files, NSF, LBJL.

52. Direction des Affaires Politiques, note, "Garanties des non nucléaires. Projet de resolution du Conseil de Sécurité," 29 March 1968, box 769, cote 517INVA, CADLC, 2.

53. Howard Wriggins to Walt Rostow, memorandum, "Your Meeting with L. K. Jha Saturday, April 15, at Noon," 15 April 1967, box 132 [1 of 2], CF—India, NSF, LBJL, 1.

54. Walt Rostow to the president, memorandum, "Indian Translation into English of Russian Text of Proposed Soviet NPT Security Declaration," with attachment, "Rough Translation of the Revised Russian Draft," 19 April 1967, box 128 [1 of 2], CF—India, NSF, LBJL. Underlining in the original.

55. Wriggins, "Your Meeting with L. K. Jha," 15 April 1967, 2–3.

56. L. K. Jha, "Nuclear Security," 2 May 1967, Indian National Archives, provided by Yogesh Joshi.

57. Rostow to the president, memorandum, "Indian Translation," 19 April 1967.

58. Roger Seydoux, telegram from New York to Paris, "Non Proliferation," 30 March 1967, box 768 (U.N. Comité des Dix-Huit), cote 517INVA, CADLC, 3.

59. U.S. Congress, *Congressional Record*, vol. CXIII (Washington, DC: U.S. Government Printing Office, 1967), 5895.

60. *FRUS, 1964–1968*, vol. XI, document 196.

61. Thomas J. Hamilton, "Pact Still Snagged as Atom Talks Near," *New York Times*, 13 May 1967, 4. ProQuest Historical Newspapers.

62. ENDC/PV.293, 14 March 1967, 11.

63. ENDC/PV.297, 18 May 1967, 15.

64. "Minutes of the Fortieth Session of the Brazilian National Security Council," 4 October 1967, History and Public Policy Program Digital Archive, National Archive (Brasília), 5, Obtained and translated by Fundação Getúlio Vargas, http://digitalarchive.wilsoncenter.org/document/116914.

65. ENDC/PV.298, 23 May 1967, 10. For a comprehensive treatment of Brazil's nuclear history, read Carlo Patti, *Brazil in the Global Nuclear Order, 1945–2018* (Baltimore: Johns Hopkins University Press, 2022).

66. Laron, *The Six-Day War*; Michael B. Oren, *Six Days of War: June 1967 and the Making of the Modern Middle East* (Oxford, UK: Oxford University Press, 2002).

67. Lyndon Johnson and William Fulbright, telephone conversation, 22:57 19 June 1967, WH6706.01 #11908, RTCM, LBJL.

68. Anatoly Dobrynin, *In Confidence: Moscow's Ambassador to America's Six Cold War Presidents* (New York: Random House, 1995); James Cameron, *The Double Game: The Demise of America's First Missile Defense System and the Rise of Strategic Arms Limitation* (New York: Oxford University Press, 2018), 85–93, 124–127.

69. *FRUS, 1964–1968*, vol. XI, document 198, 23 June 1967.

70. *FRUS, 1964–1968*, vol. XI, document 180, 8 February 1967,

71. Howard Wriggins to Walt Rostow, "India-Pakistan Arms Supply Policy and the Press," 15 April 1967, box 14, Harold Saunders files, NSF, LBJL.

72. UN Charter, Chapter VII, Article 51.

73. Jha, "Nuclear Security," 2 May 1967, 4–5.

74. Jha, "Nuclear Security," 2 May 1967, 6–7.

75. L. K. Jha, "Nuclear Security," 3 May 1967, Indian National Archives, 1–3, provided by Yogesh Joshi.

76. Jha, "Nuclear Security," 3 May 1967, 3–4.

77. Embassy of Hungary in the Soviet Union to Hungarian Foreign Ministry, report, "Indian Foreign Policy," 2 June 1967, History and Public Policy Program Digital Archive, Hungarian National Archives (Magyar Országos Levéltár, MOL), XIX-J-1-j India, 1967, 44, doboz, 60–10, 001059/2/1967, obtained and translated by Balazs Szalontai, http://digitalarchive.wilsoncenter.org/document/112883.

78. Douglas Little, "Nasser Delenda Est: Lyndon Johnson, The Arabs, and the 1967 Six-Day War," in H. W. Brands, ed., *The Foreign Policies of Lyndon Johnson: Beyond Vietnam* (College Station: Texas A&M University Press, 1999); Olivia Sohns, "The Future Foretold: Lyndon Baines Johnson's Congressional Support for Israel," *Diplomacy and Statecraft* 28, no. 1 (January 2, 2017): 57–84.

79. Zach Levey, "The United States, Israel, and Nuclear Desalination: 1964–1968," *Diplomatic History* 39, no. 5 (November 2015): 904–925.

80. Howard Wriggins to Ellsworth Bunker, memorandum, "Desalting Project: The Egyptian Quarter of the Problem," 18 August 1966; Walt Rostow to the president, memorandum, "Bunker Announcement," 13 October 1966, box 20, Harold Saunders papers, NSF, LBJL.

81. Lyndon Johnson to Levi Eshkol, letter, "The Dimona Reactor," 21 May 1965, 1–2; Dean Rusk to the president, memorandum, "Appointment of Coordinator on Desalting Projects in Israel and the United Arab Republic," 21 May 1966, box 20, Harold Saunders papers, NSF, LBJL, 1.

82. Walt Rostow to the president, memorandum, "Appointment of Coordinator on Desalting Projects to Israel and the United Arab Republic," 30 May 1966, box 20, 2; and memorandum, "Your Talk with Herzog," 20 November 1967, box 21, Harold Saunders papers, NSF, LBJL, 2–3.

83. Laron, *The Six-Day War*, 212; Avner Cohen, *Israel and the Bomb* (New York: Columbia University Press, 1998), 1. Whether Soviet plans to destroy Dimona precipitated or were revisited during the crisis was less clear: Isabella Ginor and Gideon Remez, *Foxbats over Dimona: The Soviets' Nuclear Gamble in the Six-Day War* (New Haven, CT: Yale University Press, 2007).

84. *FRUS, 1964–1968*, vol. XIII, document 258, 17 June 1967.

85. Zach Levey, "The United States' Skyhawk Sale to Israel, 1966: Strategic Exigencies of an Arms Deal," *Diplomatic History* 28, no. 2 (April 2004): 255–276.

86. Harold H. Saunders, memorandum for the president, "Israeli and UAR Desalting Projects," 6 June 1966, Harold Saunders papers, NSF, LBJL, 1.

87. Memorandum of discussion with Professor and Mrs. Wohlstetter, "Nuclear Proliferation, the Desalting Plant," 29 April 1966, Harold Saunders papers, NSF, LBJL, 1.

88. Harold H. Saunders, memorandum, "Al Wohlstetter's Comments on the Israeli Nuclear Desalting Project," 26 May 1966, box 20, Harold Saunders papers, NSF, LBJL, 1; Paul Wolfowitz, "Nuclear Proliferation in the Middle East: The Politics and Economics of Proposals for Nuclear Desalting," dissertation, University of Chicago, 1972.

89. Walt Rostow to Lyndon Johnson, letter, "Impact of Chinese Communist Nuclear Weapons Program on United States National Security," 1 August 1967, box 20, Subject files, NSF, LBJL.

90. Dean Rusk and Antonio Carrillo Flores, memorandum of conversation, "20th UNGA Session, New York, September–October 1965," 7 October 1965, box 58, CF—Mexico, NSF, LBJ, 1; Michael Lumbers, *Piercing the Bamboo Curtain: Tentative Bridge-Building to China During the Johnson Years* (New York: Manchester University Press, 2008).

91. Embassy of Hungary in North Korea to the Hungarian Foreign Ministry, report, 13 March 1967, History and Public Policy Program Digital Archive, MOL, XIX-J-1-j Korea, 1967, 61, doboz, 5, 002126/1967, obtained and translated for NKIDP by Balazs Szalontai, http://digitalarchive.wilsoncenter.org/document/110621.

92. South African Department of Foreign Affairs, "Nuclear Proliferation Problem," 18 March 1967, History and Public Policy Program Digital Archive, South African Foreign Affairs Archives, Brand Fourie, Nuclear Proliferation Problems, F194, 18 May 1967, obtained and contributed by Anna-Mart van Wyk, Monash South Africa, http://digitalarchive.wilsoncenter.org/document/114139.

93. Hamilton, "Pact Still Snagged as Atom Talks Near," 4.

94. Susan Pedersen, *The Guardians: The League of Nations and the Crisis of Empire* (Oxford, UK: Oxford University Press, 2015).

95. Memorandum, "Your Interview with Dan McAuliff, ABC," folder 8, box 17, William Foster papers, GCML, 2. Underlining in the original.

96. "Remarks by Mr. Foster at Lunch Given by UN Society of Schlosshotel Gehrhus, 12 Noon Sun., July 3—Berlin," transcript, folder 18, box 17, William Foster papers, GCML, 1–2.

97. Ira Katznelson, *Fear Itself: The New Deal and the Origins of Our Time* (New York: Liveright, 2013), 59, 71–83, 92, 95.

98. George Bunn, interview, "Have and Have-Nots," in *War and Peace in the Nuclear Age*, Episode 108, Betacam, 30 November 1986, http://openvault.wgbh.org/catalog/wpna-ffebbo-interview-with-george-bunn-1986.

99. Roland Timerbaev, interview, Rich Hooper and Jenni Rissanen, 14 June 2007, Vienna, Austria, 7.

100. Bunn, interview, 30 November 1986.

101. Roland Timerbaev, "In Memoriam: George Bunn (1925–2013)," *Arms Control Today*, June 2012.

102. George H. Quester, *The Politics of Nuclear Proliferation* (Baltimore: Johns Hopkins University Press, 1973), 173.

103. Legault, *A Diplomacy of Hope*, 246.

104. George Bunn, interview, Thomas Shea and Danielle Peterson, 17 February 2006, Stanford University, Palo Alto, CA.

105. Timerbaev, interview, 14 June 2007. 7.

106. Bunn, interview, 30 November 1986; George Bunn, "Brief History of NPT Safeguards Article," *NPT Negotiating History*, February 2006, 6.

107. Bunn, interview, 17 February 2006, 7–8; Bunn, interview, 30 November 1986. While Bunn remembers a walk in the mountains, Timerbaev claims that they were yachting. Timerbaev, interview, 14 June 2007, 7.

108. *FRUS, 1964–1968*, vol. XI, document 199, 24 June 1967.

109. Bunn, interview, 30 November 1986.

110. *FRUS, 1964–1968*, vol. XI, document 201, 10 August 1967.

111. ACDA, memorandum of conversation, Edward E. Tomkins, Adrian S. Fisher, et al., "Non-Proliferation Treaty," 23 August 1967, document 5a, NPT, NSA, http://nsarchive.gwu.edu/nukevault/ebb253/doc5a.pdf.

112. U.S. Department of State, Bureau of Intelligence and Research, Intelligence Note 88, "Does De Gaulle Want to Torpedo the NPT?," 1 February 1968, document 12, NPT, NSA, http://nsarchive.gwu.edu/nukevault/ebb253/doc12.pdf; ACDA, "Chronology of Principal Events Relating to the Non-Proliferation Treaty," 13 February 1968, box 1, NPT, DOF, RG 383, NARA II, 15.

113. Jonathan Hunt, "The Birth of an International Community: Negotiating the Treaty on the Non-Proliferation of Nuclear Weapons," in Robert L. Hutchings and Jeremi Suri, eds., *Foreign Policy Breakthroughs: Cases in Successful Diplomacy* (New York: Oxford University Press, 2015).

114. Odd Arne Westad, *The Global Cold War: Third World Interventions and the Making of Our Times* (New York: Cambridge University Press, 2005), 158–206.

115. Dimitris Bourantonis, *The United Nations and the Quest for Nuclear Disarmament* (Brookfield, VT: Dartmouth University Press, 1993), reproduced in Mohamed Ibrahim Shaker, *The Nuclear Non-Proliferation Treaty: Origin and Implementation, 1959–1979* (London: Oceana, 1980), 934–936.

116. For previous nonaligned mediation efforts, see Robert B. Rakove, "The Rise and Fall of Non-Aligned Mediation, 1961–6," *International History Review* (24 August 2015): 1–23; ACDA, NSC Status Report, "NPT," March 23, 1968, box 1, DOF, NPT, RG 383, NARA II, 3.

117. ENDC/PV.331, 19 September 1967, 4–11.

118. Roger Tubby, cable, "Proposed Mexican Changes to NPT—Part I of V," 28 September 1967, box 1, NPT, DOF, RG 383, NARA II, 1.

119. ENDC/PV.309, 29 June 1967, 4.

120. ENDC/PV.309, 29 June 1967, 6; Charles Johnson to Walt Rostow, memorandum, "Foster's Proposed Draft Response to Mrs. Myrdal's Statement," box 6, ACDA, NSF, LBJL.

121. *FRUS, 1964–1968*, vol. XI, document 200, 4 August 1967; W. E. Gathright to Howard Wriggins, note, "Paper on Indian Security," 21 December 1966, box 14, Harold Saunders papers, NSF, LBJL.

122. Chester Bowles, telegram from New Delhi to Washington, DC, "Canadians Warn GOI on NPT," 1 December 1967, document 7, NPT, NNSA, http://www2.gwu.edu/~nsarchiv/nukevault/ebb253/doc07.pdf

123. *FRUS, 1964–1968*, vol. XI, document 211, 2 October 1967, and document 216, 11 November 1967. The conditions: (1) application to "source and special fissionable material and not to facilities"; (2) direct Euratom-IAEA talks; (3) continued fissile-material supplies; (4) self-administration; (5) no "guillotine" clause with a date after which IAEA safeguards would be imposed.

124. *FRUS, 1964–1968*, vol. XI, document 215, 7 November 1967.

125. *FRUS, 1964–1968*, vol. XI, document 218, footnote 2, and document 221, 5 December 1967; "President's Tuesday Lunch group," notes, 5 December 1967, Tom Johnson's Notes of Meetings, LBJL.

126. *FRUS, 1964–1968*, vol. XI, document 221, 5 December 1967.

127. *FRUS, 1964–1968*, vol. XI, document 214, 2 November 1967.

128. Alphand Berard, telegram from New York to Paris, "Non-Prolifération," 14 December 1967, box 769, cote 517INVA, CADLC, 2.

129. ACDA, memorandum of conversation, Yuly M. Vorontsov and Lawrence Weiler, "Article III NPT Impasse," 16 December 1967, document 8a, NPT, NSA, http://www2.gwu.edu/~nsarchiv/nukevault/ebb253/doc08a.pdf.

130. R. H. Kranich and Adrian Fisher, cable to Bonn, "Soviet Motivation on NPT," 30 January 1968, document 11, NPT, NSA, http://www2.gwu.edu/~nsarchiv/nukevault/ebb253/doc11.pdf.

131. U.S. Department of State, Bureau of Intelligence and Research, Intelligence Note 88, "Does de Gaulle Want to Torpedo the NPT?," 1 February 1968, document 12, NPT, NSA, 2, http://nsarchive.gwu.edu/nukevault/ebb253/doc12.pdf.

132. U.S. State Department, memorandum of conversation, George Bunn and Yuli Vorontsov, "NPT," 15 February 1968, document 12, NPT, NSA, 1–2.

133. Bernard de Chalvron, telegram from Geneva to Paris, "U.S.-Soviet Joint Nonproliferation Treaty Draft," 18 January 1968, box 768, cote 517INVA, CADLC.

134. William Foster to Goldthwaite H. Dorr, letter, "Your Good Letter of January 26," 2 February 1968, folder 1, box 13, William Foster papers, GCML, 1.

CHAPTER 9

1. Jeremi Suri, *Power and Protest: Global Revolution and the Rise of Detente* (Cambridge, MA: Harvard University Press, 2005); Jeremy Friedman, *Shadow Cold War: The Sino-Soviet Competition for the Third World* (Chapel Hill: University of North Carolina Press, 2018).

2. U.S. Mission to NATO to U.S. State Department, Cable 1393, "NAC January 18—Draft NPT, 18 January 1968, Document 9c, NPT, NSA, 8, http://www.gwu.edu/~nsarchiv/nukevault/ebb253/doc09c.pdf.

3. Plenum of the Presidium of the Central Committee of the CPSU, 9–10 April 1968, roll 142, delo 100–2, Russian State Archive of Contemporary History, Harvard Library microfilm, 23.

4. Grégoire Mallard, *Fallout: Nuclear Diplomacy in an Age of Global Fracture* (Chicago: University of Chicago Press, 2014). For Japan, see John McCloy to William Foster, letter, "GAC Views on NPT Advancement," 10 January 1968, folder 19, box 15, William Foster papers, GCML, 2.

5. ACDA, *Documents on Disarmament, 1967* (Washington, DC: U.S. Government Printing Office, 1968), 413–415; William Foster to Dean Rusk, memorandum, "NPT Status," 23 April 1968, box 8, NPT, DOF, RG 383, NARA II, 1; telegram from Brussels to Paris, "Italian Proposals re NPT at NATO," 17 January 1968, box 768, cote 517INVA, CADLC.

6. Memorandum for the record, 584th NSC meeting, 27 March 1968, box 2, NSC Meetings, NSF, LBJL. Shane Maddock attributes this quotation to Dean Rusk in *Nuclear Apartheid: The Quest for American Atomic Supremacy from World War II to the Present* (Chapel Hill: University of North Carolina Press, 2010), 202.

7. M. E. Sarotte, *Dealing with the Devil: East Germany, Détente, and Ostpolitik, 1969–1973* (Chapel Hill: University of North Carolina Press, 2001), 16, 27.

8. *FRUS, 1964–1968*, vol. XV, document 227, 15 August 1967; Andrew Priest, "From Hardware to Software: The End of the MLF/ANF Debate and the Rise of the NATO Nuclear Planning Group," in Andreas Wenger, Christian Nünlist, and Anna Locher, eds., *Transforming NATO in the Cold War: Challenges Beyond Deterrence in the 1960s* (London: Routledge, 2012).

9. Tom Johnson, note, "President's Meeting," 3 October 1967, Tom Johnson's Notes of Meetings, LBJL, 3; *FRUS, 1964–1968*, vol. XI, document 195, 15 April 1967.

10. *FRUS, 1964–1968*, vol. XV, document 248, 23 February 1968; Alexander Lanoszka, *Atomic Assurance: The Alliance Politics of Nuclear Proliferation* (Ithaca, NY: Cornell University Press, 2018); Gene Gerzhoy, "Alliance Coercion and Nuclear Restraint: How the United States Thwarted West Germany's Nuclear Ambitions," *International Security* 39, no. 4 (April 2015): 108–110.

11. U.S. embassy in Bonn, Cable 7557, "FRG Defense Council Meeting on NPT," 23 January 1968, document 10a, NPT, NSA, http://www2.gwu.edu/~nsarchiv/nukevault/ebb253/doc10a.pdf.

12. Kurt M. Campbell and Tsuyoshi Sunohara, "Japan: Thinking the Unthinkable," in Kurt Campbell, Robert Einhorn, and Mitchell Reiss, eds., *The Nuclear Tipping Point: Why States Reconsider Their Nuclear Choices* (Washington, DC: Brookings Institution Press, 2004), 222–225; *FRUS, 1964–1968*, vol. XXIX, 12 January 1965, document 41.

13. Shingo Yoshida, "In the Shadow of China's Bomb: Defense Commitment, Nuclear Consultation, and Missile Defense in the U.S.-Japan Alliance, 1962–68," in John Baylis and Yōko Iwama, eds., *Joining the Non-Proliferation Treaty: Deterrence, Non-Proliferation and the American Alliance* (New York: Routledge, 2018); *FRUS, 1964–1968*, vol. XI, 28 August 1967, document 202.

14. James Cameron, *The Double Game: The Demise of America's First Missile Defense System and the Rise of Strategic Arms Limitation* (New York: Oxford University Press, 2018), 94–97.

15. *FRUS, 1964–1968*, vol. XXIX, part 2, document 82, footnote 5, January 11, 1967.

16. Tsuneo Akaha, "Japan's Nonnuclear Policy," *Asian Survey* 24, no. 8 (August 1984): 852–877; Fintan Hoey, "Japan and Extended Nuclear Deterrence: Security and Non-Proliferation," *Journal of Strategic Studies* 39, no. 4 (6 June 2016): 488, and Fintan Hoey, *Sato, America and the Cold War: US-Japanese Relations 1964–72* (New York: Palgrave Macmillan, 2017).

17. *FRUS, 1964–1968*, vol. XXIX, part 2, document 113, 24 January 1968, and document 140, 11 January 1969, footnote 2.

18. ENDC/PV.364, 13 February 1968, 14.

19. William Foster to Colleagues, letter, "Joint NPT Draft Tabling," 22 January 1968; William Foster to Samuel De Palma, letter, "Your Good Letter of the 19th," 22 January 1968; William Foster to Adrian Fisher, letter, 1 March 1968; folder 1, box 13, William Foster papers, GCML.

20. Eliza Gheorghe, "Building *Détente* in Europe? East–West Trade and the Beginnings of Romania's Nuclear Programme, 1964–70," *European Review of History* 21, no. 2 (4 March 2014): 235–253.

21. Eliza Gheorghe, "Atomic Maverick: Romania's Negotiations for Nuclear Technology, 1964–1970," *Cold War History* 13, no. 3 (August 2013): 381.

22. Final Verbatim Record of the 376th Meeting of the Conference of the ENDC, 11 March 1968, Geneva, Switzerland, ENDC/PV.376, 4–11.

23. Final Verbatim Record of the 363rd Meeting of the Conference of the ENDC, 8 February 1968, Geneva, Switzerland, ENDC/PV.363, 4–12.

24. Bernard de Chalvron, telegram from Geneva to Paris, "Italian Address and the Non-Aligned Bloc Meeting," 20 February 1968, box 768, cote 517INVA, CADLC, 2.

25. Bernard de Chalvron, telegram from Geneva to Paris, "Disarmament," 29 February 1968, box 768, cote 517INVA, CADLC.

26. George H. Quester, *The Politics of Nuclear Proliferation* (Baltimore: Johns Hopkins University Press, 1973), 75; John Tuthill, cable, "Brazilian Attitude Toward NPT," box 1, NPT, DOF, RG 383, NARA II.

27. Quester, *The Politics of Nuclear Proliferation*, 71–72.

28. Final Verbatim Report of the 370th Meeting of the Conference of the ENDC, 27 February 1968, Geneva, Switzerland, ENDC/PV.370, 4–14.

29. Benjamin H. Read to Dean Rusk, memorandum, "Your Luncheon Meeting with the President," 23 April 1968, document 22, NPT, NSA, http://www2.gwu.edu/~nsarchiv/nuke-vault/ebb253/doc22.pdf.

30. Ambassador Dr. Péter Kós, Embassy of Hungary in India to the Hungarian Foreign Ministry, report, 1968, Hungarian National Archives, XIX-J-1-j Multilateral international treaties, 1968, 107, doboz, 00617/18/1968, obtained and translated by Balazs Szalontai, Cold War International History Project, Wilson Center, https://digitalarchive.wilsoncenter.org/document/112872.

31. Final Verbatim Record of the 376th Meeting of the Conference of the ENDC, 11 February 1968, Geneva, Switzerland, ENDC/PV.376, 11–16.

32. Friedman, *Shadow Cold War*, 148–179.

33. Olivier Wormser, telegram to Paris, "Soviet Newspapers React to End of ENDC Session," 16 March 1968.

34. Plenum of the Presidium of the Central Committee of the CPSU, 9–10 April 1968, roll 142, delo 100–2, Russian State Archive of Contemporary History, Harvard Library microfilm, 23.

35. William Foster, transcript, "Press Conference after the 375th Meeting," 7 March 1968, folder 9, box 18, William Foster papers, GCML, 3.

36. Charles Lucet, telegram from Washington to Paris, "Project de Résolution de Garantie des Puissances Non-Nucléaires," 9 March 1968, box 768, cote 517INVA, CADLC.

37. "Traité de Non-proliferation, Projet de resolution relative à la garantie des Pays non nucléaires," note, 18 March 1968, box 769, cote 517INVA, CADLC, 1–2, 7–8.

38. "Traité de Non-proliferation," note, 18 March 1968, 3–6; note, "Le traité de non proliferation des armes nucléaire—etat de la negotiation," note, 19 March 1968, box 768, cote 517INVA, CADLC, 5–7.

39. Paul M. Kennedy, *The Parliament of Man: The Past, Present, and Future of the United Nations* (New York: Random House, 2006); Mark Mazower, *No Enchanted Palace: The End of Empire and the Ideological Origins of the United Nations* (Princeton, NJ: Princeton University Press, 2009).

40. Ryan M. Irwin, *Gordian Knot: Apartheid and the Unmaking of the Liberal World Order* (New York: Oxford University Press, 2012), 180.

41. "Le traité de non proliferation des armes nucléaire," note, 19 March 1968, 5.

42. U.S. Department of State to U.S. Mission to the UN, Cable 142418, "NPT and Resumed GA," 5 April 1968, document 15, NPT, NSA, 1–8.

43. Robert Jervis, "Cooperation Under the Security Dilemma," *World Politics* 30, no. 2 (January 1978): 167–214.

44. ACDA, report, "The Non-Proliferation Treaty: Prospects and Country Attitudes," March 1968, box 1, NPT, DOF, RG 383, NARA II, 1.

45. Joseph J. Sisco to Dean Rusk, memorandum, "Review of NPT Debate in UN," 10 May 1968, box 1, NPT, DOF, RG 383, NARA II, 1.

46. For more discussion of the ignominious colonial legacy, see Gabrielle Hecht, *Being Nuclear: Africans and the Global Uranium Trade* (Cambridge, MA: MIT Press, 2012).

47. Foster to Rusk, memorandum, "NPT Status," 23 April 1968, 1.

48. William Foster and Anatoly Dobrynin, memorandum of conversation, "Resumed session UNGA; NPT," 4 April 1968, box 9, NPT, DOF, RG 383, NARA II, 1; William Foster and Anatoly Dobrynin, memorandum of conversation, 20 February 1968, box 9, NPT, DOF, RG 383, NARA II, 2.

49. "Checklist of NPT Actions Required," undated, box 9, NPT, DOF, RG 383, NARA II, 2.

50. ACDA, memorandum for the U.S. House and U.S. Senate, "Advantages Soviets Expect to Gain from NPT," 21 February 1968, box 1, NPT, DOF, RG 383, NARA II, 3.

51. ACDA, "Chronology of Principal Events Relating to the Non-Proliferation Treaty," 13 February 1968, box 1, NPT, DOF, RG 383, NARA II, 29.

52. Memorandum, "Romanian Talking Points," 24 May 1968, box 8, RG 383, NARA II; Permanent Mission of Hungary to the UN to the Hungarian Foreign Ministry, memorandum, 12 April 1968, Hungarian National Archives, XIX-J-1-j Multilateral international treaties, 1968, 107, Wilson Center Digital Archive, https://digitalarchive.wilsoncenter.org/document/112873. Italics removed.

53. U.S. Department of State to U.S. embassy in New Delhi, Cable 12775, "NPT," 15 April 1968, box 1739, DEF 18–6, RG 59, box 1739, 2.

54. Michael R. Beschloss, *Presidents of War* (New York: Crown, 2018); Read to Rusk, memorandum, "Your Luncheon Meeting with the President Today," 23 April 1968, 2, 9.

55. John J. McCloy to Kurt Birrenbach, letter, "FRG re NPT," 8 March 1968, box 1, RG 383, NARA II.

56. Georg von Lilienfeld, letter, "Comments on Problems Arising for Germany from the Relations Between NPT and NATO," 2 May 1968, box 1, RG 383, NARA II; Francis J. Gavin, *Gold, Dollars, and Power: The Politics of International Monetary Relations, 1958–1971* (Chapel Hill: University of North Carolina Press, 2003).

57. Eugene V. Rostow to Georg Ferdinand Duckwitz, letter, "The Non-Proliferation Treaty," 30 March 1968, box 1740, DEF 18–6, RG 59, NARA II, 2.

58. Lyndon B. Johnson's Daily Diary, 22 May 1968, 3–4, http://www.lbjlibrary.net/collections/daily-diary.html.

59. *FRUS, 1964–1968*, vol. XXIX, part 2, document 113.

60. Cable, "Aide-memoire re NPT and Security Assurances," 2 July 1968, box 1, RG 383, NARA II.

61. *FRUS, 1964–1968*, vol. XXIX, part 2, document 104, 14 November 1967, document 118, 23 March 1968, and document 120, 26 April 1968.

62. Justin Wilson, "Conflicting Interests: Australia and the Nuclear Non-Proliferation Treaty, 1968," *War and Society* 20, no. 2 (October 2002): 112–113.

63. U.S. embassy in Canberra to Washington, Cable 4842, 6 April 1968, document 16a, NPT, NSA, 1.

64. Wilson, "Conflicting Interests," 118–120.

65. ACDA, memorandum of conversation, "Consultations with Australians on NPT and Status of Interpretations on Articles I and II," 24 April 1968, document 16d, NPT, NSA, 1.

66. U.S. embassy in New Delhi, Cable A-1037, "NPT: Canadians Continue Efforts to Enlist Indian Adherence," 30 April 1968, box 1739, DEF 18-6, RG 59, NARA II.

67. Copy, aide-mémoire, 5 April 1968, box 1, NPT, DOF, RG 383, NARA II; "Instructions to India's Representative to UN on NPT," 20 April 1968, *Prime Minister's Secretariat*, PN Haksar Papers (I & II Installment), file 35 (Top Secret), Nehru Memorial Museum and Library, cited in Yogesh Joshi, "Many Shades of a Nuclear Threat: Exploring India's Response to Chinese Nuclear Capability, 1964–1974," unpublished paper.

68. Telegram from Lima to Paris, "Peruvian and Brazilian Views on NPT After American Pressure Applied," 19 April 1968, box 769, cote 517INVA, CADLC, 1–2.

69. John Tuthill, cable, "NPT," 17 April 1968, box 1, NPT, DOF, RG 383, NARA II.

70. U.S. State Department, Bureau of Intelligence and Research, Intelligence Note 290, "Brazilian Opposition to NPT Draft Likely to Continue," 19 April 1968, document 20a, NPT, NSA, 1–2, http://www2.gwu.edu/~nsarchiv/nukevault/ebb253/doc20a.pdf.

71. Cable from Geneva to New York, "UAR Views on NPT," 9 February 1968, box 1, NPT, DOF, RG 383, NARA II.

72. Avner Cohen, *Israel and the Bomb* (New York, Columbia University Press, 1998), 297–299.

73. Handwritten notes, "We See All of Israel's Atomic Energy Establishment," undated, box 20, Harold Saunders papers, NSF, LBJL.

74. Walt Rostow to the president, memorandum, "Inspecting Israel's Nuclear Reactor," 30 April 1068, box 20, Harold Saunders papers, NSF, LBJL.

75. Memorandum, "Discussions on the Draft Non-Proliferation Treaty held in Cape Town on 27–28 May 1968," 30 May 1968, box 1, RG 383, NARA II.

76. William Rountree, cable, "NPT and South Africa," 21 May 1968, box 1, RG 383, NARA II.

77. ACDA, memorandum, "Euratom Fuel Supply & the NPT," 4 April 1968, box 1, RG 383, NARA II.

78. U.S. Department of State, Cable 152731, "New York Times NPT Article," 24 April 1968, box 1739, DEF 18–6, RG 59, NARA II.

79. Dean Rusk, cable to Brussels, "Euratom Fuel Supply," 30 March 1968, box 1, NPT, DOF, RG 383, NARA II.

80. William Foster, memorandum for Nicholas Katzenbach, "US and USSR Approaches to India on the NPT," 12 June 1968, box 8, NPT, DOF, RG 383, 1, 3–4; U.S. embassy in New Delhi, to Dean Rusk, cable 13839, "Conversation with Senior G[overnment] O[f] I[ndia] Official," 7 May 1968, box 1740, DEF 18–6, RG 59, NARA II.

81. CPSU Decree, "Concerning Our Steps in Promoting the Treaty on the Non-Proliferation of Nuclear Weapons," 29 March 1968, attachment 1, translated by Angela Greenfield, CWIHP.

82. CPSU Decree, 29 March 1968, attachment 4.

83. Boris Ponomarev to the CPSU Central Committee, memorandum, "The Communist Party of India and the NPT," 7 May 1968, CWIHP, translated by Angela Greenfield.

84. William Foster to Dean Rusk, memorandum, "Presidential Letter to Prime Minister Eshkol on NPT," 18 April 1968, and Dean Rusk to the president, memorandum, "Letter to Prime Minister Eshkol on NPT," 19 April 1968, box 1739, DEF 18–6, RG 59, NARA II.

85. William Foster and Anatoly Dobrynin, memorandum of conversation, "Resumed Session UNGA; NPT," 4 April 1968, box 9, DOF, NPT, RG 383, NARA II, 1.

86. U.S. Department of State, Cable 148644, "Dealing with Brazilians on NPT," 17 April 1968, box 1739, DEF 18–6, RG 59; memorandum of conversation, "Brazil's Attitude on NPT," 6 May 1968, document 20b, NPT, NSA, http://www.gwu.edu/~nsarchiv/nukevault/ebb253/doc20b.pdf.

87. Armand Bérard, telegram from New York to Paris, "Non Proliferation," 3 June 1968; telegram from New York to Paris, "Attitude de la R.A.U.," 6 May 1968, box 769, cote 517INVA, CADLC.

88. Foster to Rusk, "NPT Status," 23 April 1968, 2.

89. Armand Bérard, telegram from New York to Paris, "M. Manescu of Romania," 7 May 1968, box 769, cote 517INVA, CADLC.

90. "Appeals by U.S. and Soviet Open U.N. Atom Debate: Approval of a Treaty to Ban Spread of Nuclear Weapons Linked to Survival of World," *New York Times*, 27 April 1968, 1.

91. ACDA, *Documents on Disarmament, 1968* (Washington, DC: U.S. Government Printing Office, 1969), 230–231.

92. George Bunn, Roland M. Timerbaev, and James F. Leonard, *Nuclear Disarmament: How Much Have the Five Nuclear Powers Promised in the Non-Proliferation Treaty?* (Washington, DC: Lawyers Alliance for World Security, Committee for National Security, and Washington Council on Non-Proliferation, 1994), 20. For an exceptional roundtable discussion of contemporary debates about the original intent of the NPT, see Steven E. Miller, *Nuclear Collisions: Discord, Reform and the Nuclear Nonproliferation Regime* (Cambridge, MA: American Academy of Arts and Sciences, 2012).

93. U.S. embassy in Mexico City to U.S. State Department, Cable 04824, "Mexican Attitude Toward NPT," 10 May 1968, box 1740, DEF 18–6, RG 59, NARA II.

94. *FRUS, 1964–1968*, vol. XI, document 239, 17 May 1968; William Foster and Dean Rusk, transcript, "Telephone Call to Mexican Foreign Minister," 17 May 1968, box 9, DOF, NPT, RG 383, NARA II.

95. UNGA 22nd session, First Committee, Verbatim Record, 1569th Meeting, 16 May 1968, A/C.1/PV.1569, Official Record, 11, UN Audio-visual Library of International Law, http://legal.un.org/avl/ha/tnpt/tnpt.html.

96. U.S. Department of State to U.S. Mission to the UN, cable 161473, "NPT: Mexican Amendments," 10 May 1968, document 23a, NSA, NPT, 1–2.

97. Quoted in Christopher Hubbard, "From Ambivalence to Influence: Australia and the Negotiation of the 1968 Nuclear Non-Proliferation Treaty," *Australian Journal of Politics and History* 50, no. 4 (December 2004): 527.

98. Memorandum of conversation, "Meetings with Australians," 8 May 1968, box 1, NPT, DOF, RG 383, NARA II.

99. Hubbard, "From Ambivalence to Influence," 542; Ian Smart and Culver Gleysteen, memorandum of conversation, "NPT Amendments," 21 May 1968, box 1740, DEF 18–6, RG 59, NARA II.

100. U.S. Mission to the UN, Cable 05025, "NPT: Mexican Working Paper," 9 May 1968, box 1740, DEF 18–6, RG 59, NARA II, 1–2.

101. U.S. Mission to the UN, Cable 05127, "NPT at GA," 14 May 1968, box 1740, DEF 18–6, RG 59, NARA II, 2.

102. *FRUS, 1964–1968*, vol. XI, document 239.

103. U.S. Department of State to U.S. Mission to the UN, Cable 05085, "Mexican Amendments," 11 May 1968, box 1740, DEF 18–6, RG 59, NARA II.

104. Armand Bérard to Maurice Couve de Murville, cable, "Non-Prolifération," 9 May 1968, box 769, cote 517INVA, CADLC, 1.

105. U.S. embassy in Mexico City to U.S. Department of State, Cable 04812, "Freeman-Fisher Telecon," 9 May 1968, box 1740, DEF 18–6, RG 59, NARA II.

106. U.S. Department of State to U.S. Mission to the UN, Cable 162528, "Mexican Amendments to NPT," 11 May 1968, confidential, document 23a, NSA, NPT, 1–2.

107. Armand Bérard, French Mission to the UN, telegram to Paris, "Non-Prolifération," 29 May 1968, box 769, cote 517INVA, CADLC, 3.

108. Adrian Fisher to the president, memorandum, "Opening of Resumed UN General Assembly on Draft Non-Proliferation Treaty," 15 April 1968, box 9; Dean Rusk, cable, "Rabin's Call on State," 4 June 1968, box 1, NPT, DOF, RG 383, NARA II.

109. Armand Bérard, French Mission to the UN, telegram to Paris, "Non Prolifération," 3 June 1968, box 769, cote 517INVA, CADLC, 2.

110. U.S. Department of State, memorandum of conversation, Dean Rusk and Nobuhiko Ushiba, NSAEEB 253, NPT, document 26.

111. UNGA, 22nd session, 1672nd plenary, "Non-proliferation of Nuclear Weapons," 12 June 1968, UN Audio-visual Library of International Law, http://legal.un.org/avl/ha/tnpt/tnpt.html, 1–2.

112. Jean Binoche, French embassy in Brazil, telegram to Paris, "Speech by Brazilian Chancellor," 11 June 1968, box 769, cote 517INVA, CADLC, 1.

113. Juan de Onis, "Johnson, at U.N., Asks New Action on Disarmament," *New York Times*, 13 June 1968, 1. ProQuest Historical Newspapers.

114. U.S. Department of State, Bureau of Intelligence and Research, Thomas L. Hughes, memorandum for the Secretary, "Kuznetsov Drops a Hint About Strategic Delivery Systems as an Arms Control Topic," 30 April 1968, box 1739, DEF 18–6, RG 59, NARA II.

115. Cameron, *The Double Game*, 99–106.

116. Lyndon Johnson, "Remarks on Signing the Nuclear Nonproliferation Treaty," 1 July 1968, Miller Center of Public Affairs, University of Virginia, https://millercenter.org/the-presidency/presidential-speeches/july-1-1968-remarks-signing-nuclear-nonproliferation-treaty.

117. Kyle Longley, *LBJ's 1968: Power, Politics, and the Presidency in America's Year of Upheaval* (New York: Cambridge University Press, 2017), 206–231.

118. U.S. Department of State, Cable 179447, "NPT: Security Assurances in SC," 8 June 1968, box 1740, DEF 18–6, RG 59, NARA II.

119. Charles de Gaulle to Maurice Couve de Murville, letter, "NATO," 8 November 1963, CM8.1963, CM, CHC, Sciences Po.

120. Charles de Gaulle to Maurice Couve de Murville, letter, "Non prolifération," 5 November 1966, CM8.1966, CM, CHC, Sciences Po.

121. Francis Perrin, "La politique étrangère française en matière d'armament atomique, particulièrement en ce qui concerne la prolifération de ces armements," 28 February 1967, CM8.1967, CM, CHC, Sciences Po.

122. Perrin, 28 February 1967, 6–7.

123. Jacques de Beaumarchais, French Ministry of Foreign Affairs, telegram from Paris to New York, "Le texte de l'intervention que vous devrez prononcer devant le Conseil de Securité," 15 June 1968, box 769, cote 517INVA, CADLC, 2.

124. Armand Bérard, French Mission to the UN, telegram to Paris, "Entretien avec M. Muznetsov," 17 June 1968, box 769, cote 517INVA, CADLC, 1.

125. Armand Bérard, French Mission to the UN, telegram to Paris, "Conseil de Securité Non-Prolifération," 18 June 1968, box 769, cote 517INVA, CADLC, 1–2.

126. Armand Bérard, French Mission to the UN, telegram to Paris, "La resolution sur les guaranties," 19 June 1968, box 769, cote 517INVA, CADLC, 1–2.

127. Armand Bérard, French Mission to the UN, telegram to Paris, "Debat sur les guaranties de securité," 19 June 1968, box 769, cote 517INVA, CADLC, 1–3, quoted in H. R. Vohra, "India and Nuclear Security: The West Perplexed," *Times of India*, 12 July 1968, 8. ProQuest Historical Newspapers.

128. Direction des Affaires Politiques, note, "Le problem de la sécurité des Etats non nucléaires," 9 July 1968, box 769, cote 517INVA, CADLC.

129. G. M. Telang, "Chou Flays U.S., Russia: 'nuclear colonialism,'" *Times of India*, 20 June 1968. ProQuest Historical Newspapers.

130. "Checklist of NPT Actions Required," undated, 2.

131. Eugene Rostow to Georg von Lilienfeld, "Comments on Problems Arising for Germany from the Relation Between NPT and NATO," 2 May 1968, box 1, DOF, NPT, RG 383, NARA II; Dean Rusk to Lyndon Johnson, memorandum, "Reaffirmation of NATO at Time of Non-Proliferation Treaty Signing," 11 June 1968, document 28, Electronic Briefing Book 253, NPT Collection, NSA, http://www2.gwu.edu/~nsarchiv/nukevault/ebb253/doc28.pdf.

132. NATO Ministerial Meeting Background Paper, "Non-Proliferation Treaty," 19 June 1968, box 1, DOF, NPT, RG 383, NARA II, 4.

133. Harlan Cleveland and William Foster, memorandum, "NATO's Going to Want a Role in Arms Control Talks," 14 July 1968, box 8, NPT, DOF, RG 383, NARA II.

134. *FRUS, 1964–1968*, vol. XXIX, part 2, document 123, 5 June 1968.

135. *FRUS, 1964–1968*, vol. XXIX, part 2, document 130, 21 August 1968.

136. José Gorostiza to Alfonso García Robles, memorandum, "NPT," 22 July 1968, folder B-278–12, Departamento de Concentraciones [DOC], Secretaría de Relaciones Exteriores [SRE], Mexico, 1–2.

137. Alfonso García Robles, memorandum para informacion del Senor Presidente, "NPT," 28 July 1968, folder B-278–12, DOC, SRE, Mexico.

138. José Gorostiza to Alfonso García Robles, memorandum, "NPT," 22 July 1968, 2.

139. Walt Rostow to the president, memorandum, "Eshkol," 10 November 1968, and Lyndon Johnson to Levi Eshkol, letter, 8 November 1968, box 21, Harold Saunders papers, NSF, LBJL.

140. Walt Rostow to the president, memorandum, "Eshkol on the NPT," 12 December 1968, box 21, Harold Saunders papers, NSF, LBJL.

141. Memorandum for the record, 584th NSC meeting, 27 March 1968.

142. *FRUS, 1964–1968*, vol. XIV, document 282, 29 July 1968.

143. Longley, *LBJ's 1968*, 185–204.

144. Harold C. Saunders Jr., draft statement, "Nixon's statements," 13 September 1966, box 44, Harrold McPherson files, NSF, LBJL, 5.

145. Office of the White House Press Secretary, statement by the president, "NPT Ratification," 11 October 1968, box 43, Harold McPherson files, NSF, LBJL, 1–2.

146. Draft statement for the president, "A Non-Proliferation Treaty," with cover note by Charles Maguire, 9 October 1968, box 43, Harold McPherson files, NSF, LBJL.

147. Harry C. McPherson Jr. to the president, memorandum, "NPT," 11 October 1968, box 43, Harold McPherson files, NSF, LBJL.

148. Harry C. McPherson Jr. to the president, memorandum, "Draft on an NPT Statement," 10 October 1968, box 43, Harold McPherson files, NSF, LBJL; Arnold A. Offner, *Hubert Humphrey: The Conscience of the Country* (New Haven, CT: Yale University Press, 2018).

149. Harry C. McPherson Jr. to the president, memorandum, "Possible Television Appearance the Sunday Before Election," 23 October 1968, box 43, Harold McPherson files, NSF, LBJL.

150. Office of the White House Press Secretary, radio address of the president, "Humphrey-Muskie," 27 October 1968, box 43, Harold McPherson files, NSF, LBJL, 5.

151. Barbara J. Keys, *Reclaiming American Virtue: The Human Rights Revolution of the 1970s* (Cambridge, MA: Harvard University Press, 2014).

152. Lyndon Johnson, "Remarks on the Cessation of Bombing of North Vietnam," 31 October 1968, Miller Center of Public Affairs, University of Virginia, https://millercenter.org/the-presidency/presidential-speeches/october-31-1968-remarks-cessation-bombing-north-vietnam.

153. Niall Ferguson et al., eds., *The Shock of the Global: The 1970s in Perspective* (Cambridge, MA: Belknap Press, 2010); Stuart Schrader, *Badges Without Borders: How Global Counterinsurgency Transformed American Policing* (Oakland: University of California Press, 2019).

154. James Cameron and Or Rabinowitz, "Eight Lost Years? Nixon, Ford, Kissinger and the Non-Proliferation Regime, 1969–1977," *Journal of Strategic Studies*, 5 January 2016, 848.

155. *FRUS, 1969–1972*, vol. E-2, document 58, 13 June 1972.

156. Chapin to Henry Kissinger, memorandum, "NPT Deposit Ceremony," 25 February 1970, box 366, Subject files, NSC files, RNPL, 2; issue paper, "The Non-Proliferation Treaty," box H-034, Senior Review Group Meetings, NSC Institutional files, Meeting files, RNPL, 4; Henry Kissinger to Spiro Agnew, memorandum, "NSC Meeting," 28 January 1969, and Minutes of NSC Meeting, 29 January 1969; *FRUS, 1969–1972*, vol. E-2, documents 4 and 5.

157. "Study Requested by NSSM 13 with Individual Country Case Studies," 1 March 1969, box 366, Subject files, NSC files, RNPL.

158. Francis J. Gavin, "Nuclear Nixon: Ironies, Puzzles, and the Triumph of Realpolitik," in Fredrik Logevall and Andrew Preston, eds., *Nixon in the World: American Foreign Relations, 1969–1977* (New York: Oxford University Press, 2008), 139–140.

159. Logevall and Preston, *Nixon in the World*, 1–22.

160. Lanoszka, *Atomic Assurance*, chaps. 4 and 5.

161. Richard McGregor, *Asia's Reckoning: China, Japan, and the Fate of U.S. Power in the Pacific Century* (New York: Penguin Books, 2018), 50–54; *FRUS, 1969–1972*, vol. E-2, document 58.

162. Or Rabinowitz, *Bargaining on Nuclear Tests: Washington and Its Cold War Deals* (New York: Oxford University Press, 2014), 80.

163. Henry Kissinger to Richard Nixon, memorandum, "Israeli Nuclear Program," 19 July 1969, box 0612, National Security Central Files, RNPL.

164. Avner Cohen, *Worst-Kept Secret: Israel's Bargain with the Bomb* (New York: Columbia University Press, 2010), 1–33; "Israel Crosses the Threshold," NSA Electronic Briefing Book 189, https://nsarchive2.gwu.edu/NSAEBB/NSAEBB189/; Avner Cohen with William Burr, "Israeli Crosses the Threshold II," NSA Electronic Briefing Book 485, https://nsarchive2.gwu.edu/nukevault/ebb485/.

165. "Treaty on the Non-Proliferation of Nuclear Weapons," UN library, https://www.un.org/disarmament/wmd/nuclear/npt/text/. Emphasis added.

166. Much of this analysis recapitulates Rabinowitz, *Bargaining on Nuclear Tests*, 70–98. Quotation is on p. 89.

167. Spurgeon M. Keeny Jr., "Non-Proliferation Treaty," 20 January 1969, box 366, Subject files, NSC files, RNPL.

168. Richard M. Moose to Ben Read, letter, "Message to Senate on the NPT," 3 February 1969, box 366, Subject files, NSC files, RNPL.

169. Henry Kissinger, marginalia, Helmut Sonnenfeld to Henry Kissinger, memorandum, "Ceremony for Deposit of NPT Ratifications," 17 January 1970; Memorandum for Henry Kissinger, "NPT Ratification Deposit Ceremony," 24 February 1970; Dwight Chapin to Henry Kissinger, memorandum, 27 February 1970, and Al Haig, "State Is Gushing over Kosygin's Remarks," 5 March 1970, box 366, Subject files, NSC files, RNPL.

170. *Pace* Gerzhoy, "Alliance Coercion and Nuclear Restraint." Walt Rostow's statement that if West Germany did "not sign . . . [it] would . . . tear apart the Alliance" intimated French and British hostility rather than U.S. abandonment. *FRUS, 1964–1968*, vol. XV, document 637, 23 February 1968.

171. *FRUS, 1969–1972*, vol. E-2, document 58.

CONCLUSION

1. Including the People's Republic of China, the population of states that either abstained, were absent, or voted against Resolution 2373 (XXII) commending the NPT equaled 1.627 billion out of an estimated global population of 3.533 billion, amounting to 46 percent of humanity.

2. Daniel J. Sargent, *A Superpower Transformed: The Remaking of American Foreign Relations in the 1970s* (Oxford, UK: Oxford University Press, 2015); Niall Ferguson, Charles S. Maier, Daniel J. Sargent, and Erez Manela, eds., *The Shock of the Global: The 1970s in Perspective* (Cambridge, MA: Belknap Press of Harvard University Press, 2010).

3. "Zangger Committee," http://zanggercommittee.org (accessed 4 October 2021).

4. The members of the committee were the United States, United Kingdom, Switzerland, Sweden, Norway, the Netherlands, Japan, Italy, West Germany, France, Denmark, Canada, Belgium and Austria. France did not attend the meeting but was briefed on the content by the British government. Isabelle Anstey, "Negotiating Nuclear Control: The Zangger Committee and the Nuclear Suppliers' Group in the 1970s," *International History Review* 40, no. 5 (20 October 2018): 975–95.

5. William Burr, "The Making of the Nuclear Suppliers Group, 1974–1976," NPIHP, https://www.wilsoncenter.org/publication/the-making-the-nuclear-suppliers-group-1974-1976 (accessed 3 October 2021).

6. M. V. Kamath, "Secret Cartel Forcing up Uranium Prices," *Times of India*, 31 August 1976. Quoted in Isabelle Anstey, "Negotiating Nuclear Control: The Zangger Committee and the Nuclear Suppliers' Group in the 1970s," *International History Review* 40, no. 5 (October 20, 2018): 975–95.

7. James W. Friedman, *Oligopoly Theory*, reprint (Cambridge, UK: Cambridge University Press, 1993), 1.

8. Glenn Seaborg, testimony, 1 March 1966, JCAE, Hearings on Senate Resolution 179, "Nonproliferation of Nuclear Weapons," Eighty-Ninth Congress, Second Session (Washington, DC: U.S. Government Printing Office, 1966), 53.

9. George Orwell, "You and the Atomic Bomb," *The [London] Tribune*, 19 October 1945.

10. Mariana Budjeryn, "The Power of the NPT: International Norms and Ukraine's Nuclear Disarmament," *Nonproliferation Review* 22, no. 2 (3 April 2015): 203–237; Alexander Lanoszka, *Atomic Assurance: The Alliance Politics of Nuclear Proliferation* (Ithaca, NY: Cornell University Press, 2018); Nicholas Miller, *Stopping the Bomb: The Sources and Effectiveness of US Nonproliferation Policy* (Ithaca, NY: Cornell University Press, 2018).

11. Målfrid Braut-Hegghammer, "Revisiting Osirak: Preventive Attacks and Nuclear Proliferation Risks," *International Security* 36, no. 1 (Summer 2001): 101–132.

12. Orwell, "You and the Atomic Bomb."

13. Andrew Hurrell, *On Global Order: Power, Values, and the Constitution of International Society* (New York: Oxford University Press, 2007), 287.

14. Ferguson et al., *The Shock of the Global*; Christopher R. W. Dietrich, *Oil Revolution: Sovereign Rights and the Economic Culture of Decolonization, 1945 to 1979* (New York: Cambridge University Press, 2017).

15. J. Adam Tooze, *The Deluge: The Great War, America and the Remaking of the Global Order, 1916–1931* (New York: Penguin, 2015).

16. ENDC/PV.99, 18 February 1963, 34.

17. U.S. Public Law 95–242, 10 March 1978, https://www.govinfo.gov/content/pkg/STATUTE-92/pdf/STATUTE-92-Pg120.pdf.

18. *FRUS, 1961–1963*, vol. XVIII, document 247, 14 May 1963.

19. Robert Komer to McGeorge Bundy, memorandum, "A Rounded Foreign Policy Stance," 7 July 1965, box 6, Robert Komer papers, NSF, LBJL.

20. Hayes Redmon to Bill Moyers, memorandum, "Committee of Principals Meetings and Arms Control Agenda," 31 May 1966, box 12, Bill Moyers files, LBJL.

21. John Kennedy and Antonio Segni, memorandum of conversation, "Morning Discussions," 1 July 1963, *FRUS, 1961–1963*, vol. XIII, document 318.

22. David E. Boster to Georgy Korniyenko, letter, "An Agreement on Non-proliferation," November 22, 1966, CWIHP.

23. Andrei Gromyko and Dean Rusk, memorandum of conversation, "Non-proliferation of Nuclear Weapons, 21st UNGA Session," October 28, 1966, CWIHP, translated by Angela Greenfield.

24. Leopoldo Nuti et al., eds., *The Euromissile Crisis and the End of the Cold War* (Washington, DC: Woodrow Wilson Center Press, 2015); Susan Colbourn, *Euromissiles: The Nuclear Weapons That Nearly Destroyed NATO* (Ithaca, NY: Cornell University Press, 2022).

25. Robert McNamara to William Foster, letter, "Implications of an Agreement with the USSR on Non-diffusion," 4 October 1962, box 376, Carl Kaysen files, NSF, JFKL.

26. Introduction to NSAM 239 Review, "Can the Genie Be Put Back in the Bottle?," undated, box 369, Carl Kaysen files, NSF, JFKL, 1–4.

27. "Treaty on the Non-Proliferation of Nuclear Weapons," UN Office for Disarmament Affairs, 1 July 1968, https://www.un.org/disarmament/wmd/nuclear/npt/text.

28. George H. Quester, *The Politics of Nuclear Proliferation* (Baltimore: Johns Hopkins University Press, 1973), 44.

29. "The Evolution of IAEA Safeguards," International Nuclear Verification Series no. 2 (Vienna: International Atomic Energy Agency, 1998), 13–14; "The Structure and Content of Agreement Between the Agency and States Required in Connection with the Treaty on the Non-Proliferation of Nuclear Weapons," INFCIRC/153 (Vienna: International Atomic Energy Agency, June 1972).

30. Dietrich, *Oil Revolution*.

31. Alfonso García Robles, *The Denuclearization of Latin America*, trans. Marjorie Urquidi (Washington, DC: Carnegie Endowment for International Peace, 1967), 26.

32. Alfonso García Robles, "Speech Delivered at the Opening Meeting of the Second Session of the Preparatory Commission for the Denuclearization of Latin America on 23 August 1965," reproduced in *The Denuclearization of Latin America*.

33. U.S. embassy in Mexico City to U.S. State Department, Cable 04824, "Mexican Attitude Toward NPT," 10 May 1968, box 1740, DEF 18–6, RG 59, NARA II.

34. Jonathan Hunt, "Mexican Nuclear Diplomacy, the Latin American Nuclear-Weapon-Free Zone, and the NPT Grand Bargain, 1962–1968," in Roland Popp, Liviu Horovitz, and Andreas Wenger, eds., *Negotiating the Nuclear Non-Proliferation Treaty: Origins of the Nuclear Order* (New York: Routledge, 2017), 179–202.

35. Treaty on the Non-Proliferation of Nuclear Weapons, 1 July 1968, UN Office for Disarmament Affairs, https://www.un.org/disarmament/wmd/nuclear/npt/text; "Treaty for the Prohibition of Nuclear Weapons in Latin America and the Caribbean, 14 February 1967, https://treaties.unoda.org/t/tlatelolco, quoted in Dietrich, *Oil Revolution*, 151–152.

36. Quoted in David Holloway, "The Soviet Union and the Creation of the International Atomic Energy Agency," *Cold War History* 16, no. 2 (2 April 2016): 182–184.

37. Dwight D. Eisenhower, "Speech to the 470th Plenary Meeting of the United Nations General Assembly," 8 December 1953, https://www.iaea.org/about/history/atoms-for-peace-speech.

38. ENDC/PV.297, 18 May 1967, 15.

39. ENDC/PV.331, 19 September 1967, 4–11.

40. ENDC/PV.289, 28 February 1967, 7–8.

41. Alva Myrdal, *The Game of Disarmament: How the United States & Russia Run the Arms Race*, 2nd ed. (New York: Pantheon Books, 1982).

42. "Arme atomique et armes aveugles" (Atomic weapons and non-directed missiles), *Revue Internationale de la Croix-Rouge* 3, no. 4 (English suppl., April 1950): 70–73.

43. Quoted in Sara Z. Kutchesfahani, *Global Nuclear Order* (New York: Routledge, 2019).

44. David Alan Rosenberg, "The Origins of Overkill: Nuclear Weapons and American Strategy," *International Security* 7, no. 4 (April 1983): 37–38.

45. Jeremi Suri, *Power and Protest: Global Revolution and the Rise of Detente* (Cambridge, MA: Harvard University Press, 2005).

46. John F. Kennedy, commencement address, American University, 10 June 1963, https://www.jfklibrary.org/archives/other-resources/john-f-kennedy-speeches/american-university-19630610.

47. James Cameron, "From the Grass Roots to the Summit: The Impact of US Suburban Protest on US Missile-Defence Policy, 1968–72," *International History Review* 36, no. 2 (15 March 2014): 342–362.

48. Boris Ponomarev to the Soviet ambassador in New Delhi, letter, "The Indian Communist Party and the NPT," undated, CWIHP, translated by Angela Greenfield.

49. Walt Rostow to the president, memorandum, "Non-Proliferation and Arms Control," 12 August 1966, box 11, Walt W. Rostow files, NSF, LBJL, 1.

50. Walt Rostow, "Remarks at the National War College: The United States and the Changing World: Problems and Opportunities Arising from the Diffusion of Power," Washington, DC, 8 May 1968, box 7, Name file, NSF, LBJL, 15–17.

51. Robert Bowie to Walt Rostow, note, "This Is Well Worth Your and the President's Reading—Note Conclusion," 12 May 1968, with attachment, Irving Kristol, "We Can't Resign as 'Policeman of the World,'" *New York Times Magazine*, box 54, Agency files, Policy Planning Staff, U.S. Department of State, NSF, LBJL.

52. Frank Aiken, speech at Rotary Club Luncheon, Chicago, "Ireland at the United Nations," 31 October 1960, document 6231, FA, UCD, 1.

53. Paul Thomas Chamberlin, *The Cold War's Killing Fields: Rethinking the Long Peace* (New York: Harper, 2018).

Index

CPSIA information can be obtained
at www.ICGtesting.com
Printed in the USA
JSHW052101220722
28412JS00001B/1